Hockey Scouting Report
1993–1994

SHERRY ROSS

GREYSTONE
BOOKS
Douglas & McIntyre
Vancouver/Toronto

For my brother, Randall

Greystone Books
A division of Douglas & McIntyre Ltd.
1615 Venables Street
Vancouver, British Columbia V5L 2H1

Editing by Maja Grip
Cover design by Eric Ansley & Associates Ltd.
Cover photograph of Eric Lindros by Michael Digirolamo/Bruce
  Bennett Studios
Typesetting by ProPhase Systems Inc.
Printed and bound in Canada
Printed on acid-free paper ∞

SHERRY ROSS was one of the first women sportswriters to cover a major professional sports beat. In her rookie season—1978—she followed the New York Rangers to the Stanley Cup final. Ross became the first female broadcaster in the history of the National Hockey League when she began working as the radio colour analyst for the New Jersey Devils in 1991. She lives in New Jersey with her cat, Jolie, and Cody the Wonder Horse.

Acknowledgements

This is the first year that I've tackled the *Hockey Scouting Report* solo, but there is no way I could have done this book alone.

Massive bouquets to the anonymous gentlemen—general managers, coaches, assistant coaches, scouts and players—whose input provided much of the "inside stuff" for this book. Graciously sharing their time and insight, they did so for little more than the promise of a free lunch sometime during the season and a gratis copy of the book—and some wouldn't even accept these small tokens. They simply love to talk hockey, and one of the great pleasures of doing the *HSR* is that I get to talk with them. I wish Stanley Cup rings for every one.

Team public relations directors and their staff responded promptly to my requests for stats and clips. As ever, the NHL's "Year in Review" was a lifesaver. NHL staff had only about 48 hours between the end of the season and the draft to complete the *Review*, which makes its timely publication an especially towering accomplishment.

Thanks also to the staff at Douglas & McIntyre, especially Rob Sanders and Terri Wershler, for making this a team effort. Editor Maja Grip gets high marks in intangibles; now that she's read through that Milan Tichy copy she can get back to her garden.

This year we tried to incorporate a few ideas suggested by readers, with increased emphasis on newcomers with potential. I hope you will keep reading and writing as the *HSR* keeps changing. Dinosaurs may be "in" in 1993, but we're all for evolution.

Thanks to my family, friends and neglected pets, for accepting that I couldn't make the camping trip/trail ride/christening/movie/party/golf game because of THE BOOK. And to you, Bubelah, let's start the frolic.

Sherry Ross
West Orange, New Jersey
July 1993

CONTENTS

BOSTON BRUINS

RAY BOURQUE

Yrs. of NHL service: 14
Born: Montreal, Que.; Dec. 28, 1960
Position: right defense
Height: 5-11
Weight: 210
Uniform no.: 77
Shoots: left

Career statistics:

GP	G	A	TP	PIM
1028	291	806	1097	799

1991-92 statistics:

GP	G	A	TP	+/-	PIM	PP	SH	GW	GT	S	PCT
80	21	60	81	+11	56	7	1	2	0	334	6.3

1992-93 statistics:

GP	G	A	TP	+/-	PIM	PP	SH	GW	GT	S	PCT
78	19	63	82	+38	40	8	0	7	0	330	5.8

LAST SEASON

Reached 1000-game milestone. Tied for fourth among NHL defensemen in scoring. Third in NHL in plus/minus. Fifth in NHL in shots. Led team in plus/minus and shots. Finalist for Norris Trophy. Missed six games with ankle, back and eye injuries.

THE FINESSE GAME

Bourque has tremendous defensive instincts, although his offensive skills usually get the headlines. His defensive reads are almost unmatched in the league, and he is an excellent transition player.

As a passer, Bourque can go tape-to-tape as well as anybody in the league. He makes it so easy for his teammates to break out of the zone on the small ice surface of Boston Garden because he's not afraid to pass the puck through the middle of the ice, and that's where the openings are.

Bourque is second only to Pittsburgh's Larry Murphy in his uncanny ability to keep the puck in the zone at the point. He is a key player on special teams units. On the point, he has a low, heavy shot with a crisp release. He is an excellent skater who will also shoot from mid-range with a handy snap shot, or deep with a wrist shot. He does not squander his scoring chances and is a precise shooter down low. Bourque is able to go top shelf to either corner, which few other defensemen, let alone forwards, can match.

Bourque will lead a rush or jump up into the play. He is a balanced skater, with speed, agility, and awesome balance. It takes a bulldozer to knock Bourque off the puck.

THE PHYSICAL GAME

Bourque plays a physical game when he has to. It's amazing what kind of punishment Bourque has been able to absorb over the years without missing time with a serious injury since he is such a marked man. Most other teams try to eliminate him physically, and he has paid a big price because of it.

Bourque devotes much of his off-season to conditioning, and it pays off because of all of the ice time he logs. He's tough to beat one on one in open ice or in the trenches. Only once in his 14 seasons has he failed to play more than 60 games, and he is no perimeter player.

Bourque is a team leader who demands the same effort from his teammates. No one is more deserving of a captain's "C."

THE INTANGIBLES

Bourque has been the highest impact defenseman in the NHL for the last 10 years. He may be approaching the beginning of his downturn, only because the seasons and hits are beginning to take their toll. He is still one of the top five defensemen in the league. It's a surprise the Bruins have not won the Stanley Cup with Bourque there. The only way he may win it is to be traded to a team that has a chance — like Quebec.

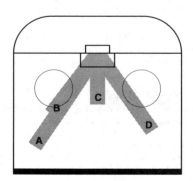

JON CASEY

Yrs. of NHL service: 6
Born: Grand Rapids, Minn.; Mar. 29, 1962
Position: goaltender
Height: 5-10
Weight: 155
Uniform no.: 30
Catches: left

Career statistics:

GP	MINS	GA	SO	GAA	A	PIM
325	18,089	988	12	3.28	11	112

1991-92 statistics:

GP	MINS	GAA	W	L	T	SO	GA	S	SAPCT	PIM
52	2911	3.40	19	23	5	2	165	1401	.882	26

1992-93 statistics:

GP	MINS	GAA	W	L	T	SO	GA	S	SAPCT	PIM
60	3476	3.33	26	26	5	3	193	1683	.885	28

LAST SEASON

Wins three-season high. Traded from the Stars to Boston for Andy Moog.

THE PHYSICAL GAME

Casey's style is a trifle bizarre, but it's not going to change. Coaches have to live with what he does well and try to maximize it, and play him at the right times.

He is very athletic. He seems to get into a groove where it doesn't matter where the pucks are coming from, because he'll find them, make the stop, make the key saves. How he does it, no one knows.

On his game, Casey will be on his feet and at the top of his crease to challenge shooters. He has a quick glove hand and walks the fine line between boldness and patience, not overcommitting.

But when he loses it a bit, he really struggles. He's either very hot or very cold; seldom is there any lukewarm. He isn't very good in any of the technical areas. He is an average skater and poor stickhandler.

THE MENTAL GAME

The Stars were a fragile team, confidence-wise, and the last thing a team with a delicate psyche needs is a goalie who lets in soft ones. Casey did that too many times last season. Casey had a merely above-average year at a time when the Stars needed top-flight, consistent goaltending.

Casey is a competitor and very proud, and he will sometimes carry negative games with him, getting snappish with the press. His mental toughness remains a question mark.

THE INTANGIBLES

Casey has not been seriously challenged for the role of No. 1 goalie for several seasons, and he has found a comfort zone. Although he has a good work ethic (much better than in his past), it's interesting to speculate how much sharper Casey might get if there were a young goalie trying to battle his way into Casey's crease. Unfortunately for the Stars, there doesn't appear to be anyone in their system who fits that description.

TED DONATO

Yrs. of NHL service: 1
Born: Dedham, Mass.; Apr. 28, 1969
Position: centre
Height: 5-10
Weight: 170
Uniform no.: 21
Shoots: left

Career statistics:

GP	G	A	TP	PIM
92	16	22	38	69

1991-92 statistics:

GP	G	A	TP	+/-	PIM	PP	SH	GW	GT	S	PCT
10	1	2	3	-1	8	0	0	0	0	13	7.7

1992-93 statistics:

GP	G	A	TP	+/-	PIM	PP	SH	GW	GT	S	PCT
82	15	20	35	+2	61	3	2	5	0	118	12.7

LAST SEASON
First full NHL season.

THE FINESSE GAME
Donato is a small man who is able to survive in a big man's game in a small building because of his hockey sense. He is an excellent power play man, handling the point duties with Ray Bourque. Donato has always had the knack for scoring big goals at every level he has played. He scored the winning goal in the NCAA Championship game when Harvard beat Minnesota, and he scored the winning goal for his high school to win the championships in Massachusetts.

Donato is also a strong penalty killer. He can thrive as a forward on the shorthanded team because the opponents are more concerned about getting the puck than hitting, and he is usually in the middle part of the ice.

Donato is like a quarterback, very aware of what is going on around him and always communicating with his teammates so they know what is going on, too.

THE PHYSICAL GAME
Donato is cunning and doesn't allow himself to get into situations where he's close to the boards and could get taken out. He is a very elusive, slippery skater, and coach Brian Sutter is careful to use him in spots where he won't get hammered — such as at the point on the power play. Donato can be overpowered by bigger skaters, but he won't be intimidated.

THE INTANGIBLES
There is a recent trend among teams like Boston, Montreal, Quebec and now Toronto to emphasize hometown boys — not to sell tickets, but because playing in your hometown can bring out the best in players who can stand the pressure. Donato is one who seems to thrive on it. Probably the team's biggest surprise of last season.

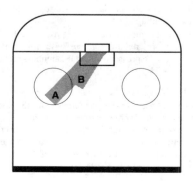

STEVE HEINZE

Yrs. of NHL service: 1
Born: Lawrence, Mass.; Jan. 30, 1970
Position: right wing
Height: 5-11
Weight: 190
Uniform no.: 23
Shoots: right

Career statistics:

GP	G	A	TP	PIM
87	21	17	38	30

1991-92 statistics:

GP	G	A	TP	+/-	PIM	PP	SH	GW	GT	S	PCT
14	3	4	7	-1	6	0	0	2	0	29	10.3

1992-93 statistics:

GP	G	A	TP	+/-	PIM	PP	SH	GW	GT	S	PCT
73	18	13	31	+20	24	0	2	4	0	146	12.3

LAST SEASON

First full NHL season. Missed games with shoulder injury.

THE FINESSE GAME

Heinze is a traditional grinding Bruins forward who skates up and down his wing. He has surprisingly good hands for a grinder, with a quick snap shot. He seems to get goals that go in off his legs, arms and elbows from his work in front of the net.

Heinze usually plays on a checking line alongside Dave Poulin — a great checker to learn the game from. He is a good penalty killer because he has some speed, and he's very efficient.

Heinze was a big scorer at Boston College with David Emma and Marty McInnis (the HEM Line), but he succeeded at that level mainly because he was able to overpower people in college; he doesn't have that same edge in the pros. He plays an intelligent game and is a good playmaker with passing skills on his forehand and backhand.

THE PHYSICAL GAME

Heinze is a smaller forward who plays bigger, especially at home. He has been bothered by a problem shoulder that has slowed him through college and seems to be a recurring ailment in the NHL. It could damage his development if it continues.

THE INTANGIBLES

Heinze is another one of those proud-to-be-a-Bruin Boston kids who plays quicker and tougher for being on his home turf. He is a grinding winger, with extra dimensions and skills, and has a solid future as a checker who can get 20 to 25 goals a season. He is very well liked by his teammates.

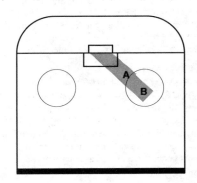

JOE JUNEAU

Yrs. of NHL service: 1
Born: Pont-Rouge, Que.; Jan. 5, 1968
Position: centre/left wing
Height: 6-0
Weight: 175
Uniform no.: 49
Shoots: right

Career statistics:

GP	G	A	TP	PIM
98	37	84	121	37

1991-92 statistics:

GP	G	A	TP	+/-	PIM	PP	SH	GW	GT	S	PCT
14	5	14	19	+6	4	2	0	0	0	38	13.2

1992-93 statistics:

GP	G	A	TP	+/-	PIM	PP	SH	GW	GT	S	PCT
84	32	70	102	+23	33	9	0	3	3	229	14.0

LAST SEASON

First full NHL season. Second on team in goals, assists and points. Led NHL rookies in assists. Second among NHL rookies in points. Third among rookies in goals. Third among rookies in plus/minus. Named to NHL All-Rookie Team. Finalist for Calder Trophy.

THE FINESSE GAME

Juneau is tremendously skilled. Although he played the left wing most of the season with Adam Oates, Juneau played centre in college and with the 1992 Canadian Olympic Team, and will probably succeed in that role in the NHL, too, although it is doubtful he can be a No. 1 centre because he is not strong enough to fight through the checking attention.

Juneau has an extra speed that allows him to pull away from people. He does not have breakaway speed, but he has great anticipation and gets the jump on a defender with his first few steps.

Juneau's greatest gift is his creative playmaking ability, and that will only get better as he spends more time in the league. He has become an impact player in his first season.

He doesn't shoot the puck enough and gets a little bit intimidated when there is a scramble for a loose puck in front of the net. He is not always willing to sacrifice his body that way. He shoots a little prematurely. When he could wait and have the goalie down and out, he unloads quickly, because he hears footsteps. His best shot is a one-timer from the left circle.

THE PHYSICAL GAME

Juneau has improved his toughness and willingness to take a hit to make a play, especially in the last part of the season. He has a reputation of being a soft player, and frequently does not have to fight through traffic because Oates opens up so much ice for him. Juneau did show under fire that he was able to play a tougher game, and that is a tribute to the rookie.

THE INTANGIBLES

The Bruins will probably want to break up the Oates-Juneau combination and move Juneau to centre on a second line to take the checking attention off of their one and only scoring trio. A sophomore slump is always a concern, especially since Juneau will be coming back to his natural position and will have to cope with defensive duties, but he is a very mature 25-year-old, not a raw 19-year-old, and should be able to repeat his rookie success.

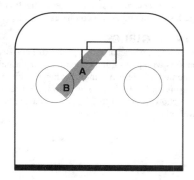

DMITRI KVARTALNOV

Yrs. of NHL service: 1
Born: Voskresensk, Russia; Mar. 25, 1966
Position: left wing
Height: 5-11
Weight: 180
Uniform no.: 10
Shoots: left

Career statistics:

GP	G	A	TP	PIM
73	30	42	72	16

1992-93 statistics:

GP	G	A	TP	+/-	PIM	PP	SH	GW	GT	S	PCT
73	30	42	72	+9	16	11	0	4	2	226	13.3

LAST SEASON
First NHL season. Second on team in power play goals.

THE FINESSE GAME
Kvartalnov scored 12 goals in his first 14 games, and 18 over the next 59. Does the word inconsistency ring a bell?

He has to learn that scoring goals is hard work. It was easy in the beginning, when he was a surprise to everyone in the league, but shock wears off quickly in this era of electronic scouting via satellite and videotape. Kvartalnov succeeds when he drives to the net and competes for loose pucks, but he doesn't always do it.

In his own end, his nickname is Dmitri "Take-a-day-off." Unless he wants to improve his backchecking, he may not be a Bruin for very long. The Bruins have some promising players coming on the right side, and he may be worth more to the team in the trade market.

THE PHYSICAL GAME
Kvartalnov picks his spots. He does not battle through checking and is not very courageous against tougher opponents. He can get hammered early and taken out of a game. He was targeted in the playoffs and wasn't even noticeable — he had no points and registered only five shots on goal.

THE INTANGIBLES
The Bruins took a big gamble when they drafted Kvartalnov at 26 from San Diego (IHL) in 1992. They hoped they would be getting a finished player who could give them immediate scoring help, and for a time, Kvartalnov fit that bill. He's not going to get much better. He's already gone through his development stage, and the ceiling is lower for him than it is for a younger player.

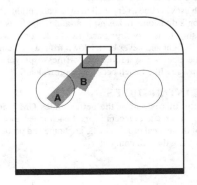

STEPHEN LEACH

Yrs. of NHL service: 8
Born: Cambridge, Mass.; Jan. 16, 1966
Position: right wing
Height: 5-11
Weight: 180
Uniform no.: 27
Shoots: right

Career statistics:

GP	G	A	TP	PIM
403	100	108	208	595

1991-92 statistics:

GP	G	A	TP	+/-	PIM	PP	SH	GW	GT	S	PCT
78	31	29	60	-8	147	12	0	4	0	243	12.8

1992-93 statistics:

GP	G	A	TP	+/-	PIM	PP	SH	GW	GT	S	PCT
79	26	25	51	-6	126	9	0	4	1	256	10.2

LAST SEASON

Missed five games with rib injury. Fifth on team in points. Second on team in shots.

THE FINESSE GAME

Leach has been consistent ever since coming to Boston. He is a tremendous forechecker and an effective player in a physical game.

Leach has a very heavy, deceptive shot. It has an ability to find its way through traffic and not many of his shots are blocked. In a small building, where Leach plays at least half his games, that is the sign of a good release. He doesn't have a great touch or soft hands, but he is always going to the net amd making things happen with his hard work.

Leach uses the boards like a partner: he bangs the puck off the wall, intimidates the defender as he barrels along, and then picks up the pass to himself and keeps on going. He is not a fast skater, but he keeps his legs churning constantly.

Defensively, you have to be concerned with that -6. Leach does not read or react well to defensive plays, and gets caught out of position. It is the overwhelming weakness in his otherwise strong game.

THE PHYSICAL GAME

Leach uses his body very well in the small buildings in Boston's division. He has no fear, and while he is not imposing, he is very strong and uses his leg drive well. He will fight and never backs down from a challenge. As the Bruins are adding more finesse players, a scrappy guy like Leach becomes more valuable.

THE INTANGIBLES

Quietly, this is one of the better trades GM Harry Sinden has made in recent years. Leach is yet another one of those local products who are home and proud to be wearing the hub emblem.

CAM NEELY

Yrs. of NHL service: 10
Born: Comox, B.C.; June 6, 1965
Position: right wing
Height: 6-1
Weight: 210
Uniform no.: 8
Shoots: right

Career statistics:

GP	G	A	TP	PIM
586	292	241	533	1084

1991-92 statistics:

GP	G	A	TP	+/-	PIM	PP	SH	GW	GT	S	PCT
9	9	3	12	+9	16	1	0	2	0	30	30.0

1992-93 statistics:

GP	G	A	TP	+/-	PIM	PP	SH	GW	GT	S	PCT
13	11	7	18	+4	25	6	0	1	0	45	24.4

LAST SEASON
Missed 71 games recovering from thigh/knee injury.

THE FINESSE GAME
Before his injury in the 1991 playoffs, Neely was the premier power forward in the NHL. His scoring touch is still with him, but his physical status makes everything about his game a huge question mark.

Neely has a big-time goal-scoring release, and at his peak was perhaps second only to Brett Hull in his ability to get a shot away on net. He has excellent scoring instincts and is a particular terror down low on the power play. His point totals for his limited ice time at the end of last season are nothing short of amazing.

Neely never was a gifted skater, but once in motion he is like a tank. Defensemen have to get all of him, otherwise they will simply bounce off as Neely bulls past them.

THE PHYSICAL GAME
Neely played on a lot of adrenaline and with reckless abandon last season, but over an 84-game season he can't endure that pace. He is still given a lot of room because he is so respected as a tough player and a fighter. His physical play will hinge on his hinge, so to speak — the continued rehab of his damaged leg.

THE INTANGIBLES
Over the short period of time last season, Neely was very effective, but anyone who thinks he can predict what this upcoming season will be like for Neely is kidding himself. He played every shift of his 17 games (counting playoffs) as if each one might be his last — and that is the telling story. He has battled hard over the past two years to fight his way back from injury, and he deserves tremendous respect for his dedication.

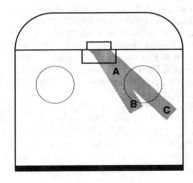

ADAM OATES

Yrs. of NHL service: 8
Born: Weston, Ont.; Aug. 27, 1962
Position: centre
Height: 5-11
Weight: 189
Uniform no.: 12
Shoots: right

Career statistics:

GP	G	A	TP	PIM
551	167	490	657	178

1991-92 statistics:

GP	G	A	TP	+/-	PIM	PP	SH	GW	GT	S	PCT
80	20	79	99	-9	22	6	0	4	2	191	10.5

1992-93 statistics:

GP	G	A	TP	+/-	PIM	PP	SH	GW	GT	S	PCT
84	45	97	142	+15	32	24	1	11	0	254	17.7

LAST SEASON

Led NHL in assists. Third in NHL in points. Tied for NHL lead in game-winning goals. Tied for fifth in NHL in power play goals. One of four Bruins to appear in all 84 games. Led team in goals, assists, points, power play goals and game-winning goals. Career highs in all scoring categories.

THE FINESSE GAME

What's amazing about Oates is how strong he is on the puck. He is as good a backhand passer as he is on the forehand; that is why, as a right-handed shooter, his right wingers have so much success.

Oates loves to attack down the left-wing side of the ice and use his backhand, which makes a difficult task for the defenseman. If the puck is on a player's forehand coming down the off wing, it's an easier shot on the goalie, so the defenseman tries to stay between the puck and the net. All Oates has to do is bump it past the defenseman on his forehand, take it past him on his backhand, and drive to the net, with his linemates driving with him. If Oates gets dragged down by the defenseman, he usually earns his team a power play.

Oates still doesn't shoot enough, even though he had 60 more shots than a season ago. His decision to shoot more made him a less predictable player, since the defense could no longer back off and anticipate the pass. Oates is one of the best playmakers in the league because of his passing ability and creativity. He is often used to play the point on the power play but is more effective down low where he can open up more ice. His contribution as a point man is more restricted. He is patient with the puck.

Oates is among the top five players in the league on face-offs, which makes him a natural on penalty-killing because a successful draw eats up seconds on the clock. He is not a great skater, but he is quick and agile enough, especially in his small home rink.

THE PHYSICAL GAME

He is not a physical player, but he doesn't avoid contact. He's smart enough at this stage of career to avoid the garbage, he plays in traffic, and he'll take a hit to make the play. Oates is a very intense player and has a wiry strength. He is durable and can play a lot of minutes.

THE INTANGIBLES

Oates needs to play with a finisher, and a healthy Cam Neely would be the perfect partner. Oates exceeded all expectations in Boston with his goal-scoring and was worthy of Hart Trophy consideration. A repeat of last season's numbers should be in order.

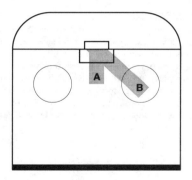

GREGORI PANTALEYEV

Yrs. of NHL service: 1
Born: Riga, Latvia; Nov. 13, 1972
Position: left wing
Height: 5-9
Weight: 194
Uniform no.: 13
Shoots: left

Career statistics:

GP	G	A	TP	PIM
39	8	6	14	12

1992-93 statistics:

GP	G	A	TP	+/-	PIM	PP	SH	GW	GT	S	PCT
39	8	6	14	-6	12	2	0	1	0	45	17.8

LAST SEASON
First NHL season.

THE FINESSE GAME
First impression: Pantaleyev's speed. He has tremendous acceleration and can carry the puck with speed. He chips in some key goals and has a powerful shot for a small player.

When Pantaleyev is effective, he will drive to the net with his quickness and generate scoring opportunities that way. But on too many nights, Pantaleyev is a passenger when he could be the conductor.

Pantaleyev was a defensive liability. He has a lot to learn about life in the NHL.

THE PHYSICAL GAME
Pantaleyev is small and his lack of size is a factor. Pantaleyev won't be pushed off the puck when he has it, but he won't battle to get control, and his play away from the puck is uninspired.

THE INTANGIBLES
Pantaleyev is not the most disciplined player and enjoyed his first brush with capitalism. His youth is in his favour, since it is far too early to give up on him, but a sluggish training camp will find him starting the season in the minors.

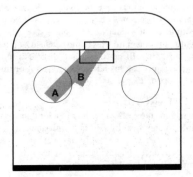

DAVE POULIN

Yrs. of NHL service: 10
Born: Timmins, Ont.; Dec. 17, 1958
Position: centre
Height: 5-11
Weight: 190
Uniform no.: 19
Shoots: left

Career statistics:

GP	G	A	TP	PIM
632	195	301	509	420

1991-92 statistics:

GP	G	A	TP	+/-	PIM	PP	SH	GW	GT	S	PCT
18	4	4	8	-2	18	0	1	1	0	31	12.9

1992-93 statistics:

GP	G	A	TP	+/-	PIM	PP	SH	GW	GT	S	PCT
84	16	33	49	+29	62	0	5	0	0	112	14.3

LAST SEASON

One of four Bruins to appear in all 84 games. First time playing more than 60 games in a season since 1989-90. Goals four-season high. Assists six-season high. Tied for team lead in shorthanded goals. Finalist for Selke Trophy.

THE FINESSE GAME

Poulin is one of the top checking forwards in the NHL. At 35 he still has the legs, the speed, and the desire to be a high-calibre NHL player.

He is easily in the top 10 in the league among penalty-killing forwards. He is an excellent face-off man (giving the Bruins two, along with Adam Oates) who will tie up the opposing centre if he does not win the draw outright.

Poulin will chip in his fair share of points, but not many. His goals will come from digging hard around the net and his assists from forechecking and forcing turnovers. He has a good wrist shot and strong arms for winning control of the puck in scrums. Poulin is not a fast skater, but he is a digger. Poulin is an intelligent, almost cerebral, player.

THE PHYSICAL GAME

Poulin has to play hard to be effective, and he is playing in the most vicious division in the NHL. He could probably add a season or two to his career if he went to a team in the new Pacific Division.

Poulin's frequent injuries come because he refuses to play soft. He will get down and dirty if it means winning a game, use his stick without guilt or throw his body at people or shots.

THE INTANGIBLES

Poulin had his most effective year in a long time as he was able to stay healthy. He is a well-spoken, well-respected leader who probably has a future in team management once his playing days are over. He has at least one solid season left in him if he can stay intact.

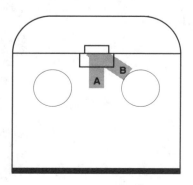

DAVE REID

Yrs. of NHL service: 7
Born: Toronto, Ont.; May 15, 1964
Position: left wing
Height: 6-1
Weight: 205
Uniform no.: 17
Shoots: left

Career statistics:

GP	G	A	TP	PIM
419	88	102	190	125

1991-92 statistics:

GP	G	A	TP	+/-	PIM	PP	SH	GW	GT	S	PCT
43	7	7	14	+5	27	2	1	0	0	70	10.0

1992-93 statistics:

GP	G	A	TP	+/-	PIM	PP	SH	GW	GT	S	PCT
65	20	16	36	+12	10	1	5	2	0	116	17.2

LAST SEASON

Tied for team lead in shorthanded goals. Games played two-season high. Goals career high. Missed games with knee injury.

THE FINESSE GAME

Reid was a major reclamation project in his second stint with the Bruins, and he paid huge dividends as a defensive forward, especially when teamed with Dave Poulin. Reid is a shorthanded specialist. Power plays getting ready to face the Bruins always have to be aware of taking away Reid's space if they lose the puck, because he has the ability to blow the puck by the goalie from a lot of places on the ice.

Reid has an underrated, accurate shot with a quick release. He can freeze a lot of goalies with his unexpected shot.

He is a good skater with mobility, especially for a big player. He has proven he can play regularly in the league and contribute.

THE PHYSICAL GAME

Reid can create a little maelstrom on the ice. He is a big guy who can get his skating revved up, and he causes problems once he is in motion. He isn't a big hitter, though, and there is no nasty side to him. He is just an honest checker.

THE INTANGIBLES

Reid is an ideal checking winger who has the offensive skills to contribute 20 goals a season. His knee injury at the end of the season was a concern, and it kept him from participating in the playoffs.

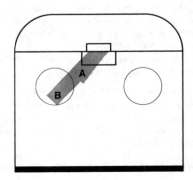

GORDIE ROBERTS

Yrs. of NHL service: 14
Born: Detroit, Mich.; Oct. 2, 1957
Position: left defense
Height: 6-0
Weight: 190
Uniform no.: 14
Shoots: left

Career statistics:

GP	G	A	TP	PIM
1038	60	353	413	1542

1991-92 statistics:

GP	G	A	TP	+/-	PIM	PP	SH	GW	GT	S	PCT
73	2	22	24	+19	87	1	0	1	0	29	6.9

1992-93 statistics:

GP	G	A	TP	+/-	PIM	PP	SH	GW	GT	S	PCT
65	5	12	17	+23	105	0	0	1	0	40	12.5

LAST SEASON

Goals seven-season high. Missed games with viral infection in arm. Signed as free agent from Pittsburgh.

THE FINESSE GAME

Roberts has a calming influence whenever he is on the ice. He's a stay-at-home, rocking-chair style defenseman. He will clear rebounds and work the boards, and he always seems to be in the way of anyone trying to get to the net or make a pass.

Roberts makes it tough for forwards to get around him. He will step up and deny the blue line, creating turnovers and quick counterattacks. In Boston Garden, a quick counter-game is how you win.

He does not have a great shot, nor is he a great passer. He will use the left-wing glass a lot for conservative clearing attempts, and he does not like to carry the puck.

Roberts doesn't get involved in the play offensively, which makes him the ideal partner for the more freewheeling Bourque. Roberts is steady and reliable, unruffled under pressure, and is always in the right position.

THE PHYSICAL GAME

Roberts is very solid on his feet. He is well respected around the league and gets generous licence from the officials, so he gets away with more than his share of holding and hooking, which helps make him effective in smaller buildings.

Roberts plays bigger than his size. He is a willing checker but not a huge, glass-rattling hitter.

THE INTANGIBLES

Roberts is a very effective partner to Ray Bourque. He is a consummate old pro who shows up every game and is a battler. The move to Boston may have added some years to his career.

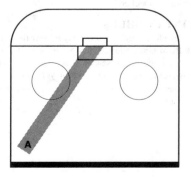

BRYAN SMOLINSKI

Yrs. of NHL service: 0
Born: Toledo, Ohio; Dec. 27, 1971
Position: centre
Height: 6-1
Weight: 195
Uniform no.: 20
Shoots: right

Career statistics:

GP	G	A	TP	PIM
9	1	3	4	4

1992-93 statistics:

GP	G	A	TP	+/-	PIM	PP	SH	GW	GT	S	PCT
9	1	3	4	+3	4	0	0	0	0	10	10.0

LAST SEASON
Joined Bruins after finishing career at Michigan State. First-round pick, 21st overall, in 1990.

THE FINESSE GAME
Smolinski is a very crafty player who is reminiscent of a young Jean Ratelle. He has great hockey sense. He has a quick release and gets his shot away quickly in traffic. He has good, soft hands and makes smart, heady plays.

Smolinski's skating is adequate, but it could improve with some lower body work. He has good balance and lateral movement but is not very quick.

He has the smarts to be an asset on both special teams once he gains more experience. He has good defensive awareness, and his play away from the puck is sound.

THE PHYSICAL GAME
Smolinski's limitation is that he's not very strong, but the Bruins have an excellent strength and conditioning program, and if he dedicates himself during the off-season, he could develop what he needs to survive in the NHL. He will take a hit to make a play.

THE INTANGIBLES
Smolinski is in the perfect atmosphere for a kid coming out of a somewhat cushy college situation. He can have his attitude adjusted by the likes of Ray Bourque and Cam Neely, who will demonstrate that a lazy, selfish player will not last very long in Boston. Although his stint with the Bruins was brief, Smolinski worked like a dog. Two years ago, some scouts were saying Smolinski was looking like a bust. Now it looks like he'll be a player.

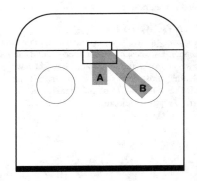

15

DON SWEENEY

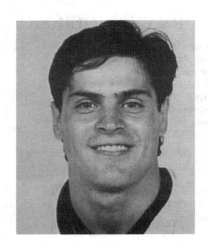

Yrs. of NHL service: 5
Born: St. Stephen, N.B.; Aug. 17, 1966
Position: defense
Height: 5-11
Weight: 170
Uniform no.: 32
Shoots: left

Career statistics:

GP	G	A	TP	PIM
330	24	61	85	287

1991-92 statistics:

GP	G	A	TP	+/-	PIM	PP	SH	GW	GT	S	PCT
75	3	11	14	-9	74	0	0	1	0	92	3.3

1992-93 statistics:

GP	G	A	TP	+/-	PIM	PP	SH	GW	GT	S	PCT
84	7	27	34	+34	68	0	1	0	0	107	6.5

LAST SEASON

One of four Bruins to appear in all 84 games. Second on team in plus/minus. Assists career high.

THE FINESSE GAME

Sweeney has found a niche for himself in the NHL. He's mobile, physical and greatly improved in the area of defensive reads. He has good hockey sense for recognizing offensive situations as well.

Sweeney mostly stays at home and out of trouble, but he is a good enough skater to get involved in the attack. He is a good passer and good shooter, and has developed more and more confidence in his skills. He skates his way out of trouble and moves the puck well, and the puck travels faster than a skater.

Sweeney is also an intelligent player who knows his strengths and weaknesses. He didn't get much playing time in his first two seasons in Boston, and, despite being a low draft pick (166th overall), he wouldn't let anyone overlook him.

THE PHYSICAL GAME

Sweeney is built like a little human Coke machine. He is tough to play against, and while wear and tear is a factor, he never hides. He is always in the middle of physical play. He utilizes his lower body drive and has tremendous leg power.

THE INTANGIBLES

Sweeney might have been the most unheralded player in the NHL last season. He has speed, smarts and tons of heart, and over the long haul he might have been the Bruins' most consistent defenseman. If he were three inches taller and 15 pounds heavier, he would be a Norris Trophy candidate.

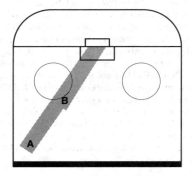

GLEN WESLEY

Yrs. of NHL service: 6
Born: Red Deer, Alta.; Oct. 2, 1968
Position: defense
Height: 6-1
Weight: 195
Uniform no.: 26
Shoots: left

Career statistics:

GP	G	A	TP	PIM
456	63	186	249	357

1991-92 statistics:

GP	G	A	TP	+/-	PIM	PP	SH	GW	GT	S	PCT
78	9	37	46	-9	54	4	0	1	0	211	4.3

1992-93 statistics:

GP	G	A	TP	+/-	PIM	PP	SH	GW	GT	S	PCT
64	8	25	33	-2	47	4	1	0	0	183	4.4

LAST SEASON

Games played career low. Goals lowest since rookie season. Missed 14 games with foot injury.

THE FINESSE GAME

Wesley is a capable defenseman of whom a great deal has been expected. He isn't to be blamed for the expectations, but should get credit his solid play.

He is very good with the puck. He works well on the power play because he knows when to jump into the holes. He has outstanding offensive instincts, gauging when to pinch, when to rush, when to pass the puck and when to back off. Wesley is a good skater who is not afraid to veer into the play deep, and he seldom gets trapped there. He has a good slap shot from the point and a snap shot from the circle.

You could count on two hands the number of times Wesley has been beaten one on one throughout his career, and there are very few defensemen you can say that about. He makes the defensive plays with confidence and is poised even when outnumbered in the rush.

THE PHYSICAL GAME

Wesley is not a bone-crunching defenseman, but neither was Jacques Laperriere, and he's in the Hall of Fame. We're not suggesting that Wesley is in that class, but just that you don't have to shatter glass to be a solid checker, which he is. He's not a mean hitter, but he will make a take-out check and not let his man get back into the play.

THE INTANGIBLES

Get this much straight: Wesley will never be Ray Bourque Jr. With that out of that way, we can tell you that the oft-maligned Wesley is a very solid, reliable, talented No. 3 or 4 defenseman (and with the right partner, maybe even a No. 2). If the Bruins don't want him, there are 25 other NHL teams who would say, "Call us first."

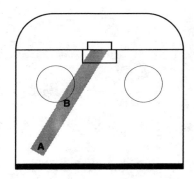

BUFFALO SABRES

DONALD AUDETTE

Yrs. of NHL service: 2
Born: Laval, Que.; Sept. 23, 1969
Position: right wing
Height: 5-8
Weight: 175
Uniform no.: 28
Shoots: right

Career statistics:

GP	G	A	TP	PIM
115	47	27	74	130

1991-92 statistics:

GP	G	A	TP	+/-	PIM	PP	SH	GW	GT	S	PCT
63	31	17	48	-1	75	5	0	6	1	153	20.3

1992-93 statistics:

GP	G	A	TP	+/-	PIM	PP	SH	GW	GT	S	PCT
44	12	7	19	-8	51	2	0	0	0	92	13.0

LAST SEASON

Missed first two months of season after reconstructive surgery at the end of 1991-92.

THE FINESSE GAME

Injury woes have plagued Audette for two seasons, and last season his comeback from knee surgery caused him to do too much offensively to make up for lost time. Battling for a new contract added more pressure and made for a very inconsistent year.

Audette is a bustling forward who barrels to the net at every opportunity. He is eager and feisty down low, and has very good hand skills. He has good scoring instincts, along with the quickness to make good things happen. His feet move so fast, with a choppy stride, that he doesn't look graceful, but he can really get moving, and he has good balance.

Audette is a scorer first. He has a great top-shelf move that he gets away quickly and with accuracy. He can also make a play, but he will do this at the start of a rush. Once he is inside the offensive zone and low, he wants the puck. His selfishness can be forgiven, given his scoring ability.

Audette has to improve his defensive play.

THE PHYSICAL GAME

Audette's lax defensive play led to benchings by coach John Muckler. He will forecheck and scrap for the puck but isn't as diligent coming back. He's not very big, but around the net he plays like he's at least a 6-footer. He keeps jabbing and working away until he is bowled over by an angry defender.

THE INTANGIBLES

Audette was eligible to become a Group I free agent after the season, meaning that the Sabres would have to match the highest contract offer he gets to keep him. He will be attractive to a lot of teams, provided they aren't scared off by his lack of durability.

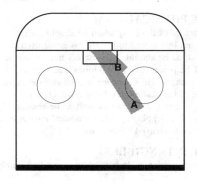

DOUG BODGER

Yrs. of NHL service: 9
Born: Chemainus, B.C.; June 18, 1966
Position: left defense
Height: 6-2
Weight: 210
Uniform no.: 8
Shoots: left

Career statistics:
GP	G	A	TP	PIM
643	79	311	390	657

1991-92 statistics:
GP	G	A	TP	+/-	PIM	PP	SH	GW	GT	S	PCT
73	11	35	46	+1	108	4	0	1	0	180	6.1

1992-93 statistics:
GP	G	A	TP	+/-	PIM	PP	SH	GW	GT	S	PCT
81	9	45	54	+14	87	6	0	0	1	154	5.8

LAST SEASON
Led team in plus/minus. Assists career high. Led team defensemen and was fourth on team in points.

THE FINESSE GAME
Bodger is a smooth skater with good quickness, and he can make tight pivots while carrying the puck. He's among the better-skating defensemen in the league, although he lacks the dynamite speed of the more charismatic defensemen. He is the major puck-carrier for the Sabres. It is Bodger who will collect the puck from the goalie behind the net, let his teammates wheel back and get ready to attack, then move out with the puck. He can either carry up or, if Pat LaFontaine and Alexander Mogilny are on duty, feed one of those two stars with a smooth pass and then jump into the play. Bodger sees his passing options well and is very smart with the puck.

Bodger is a natural on the point on the power play. He works the left point on the first unit with the crafty Dale Hawerchuk working the right. Bodger has a big slap that he keeps down for tips and scrambles in front. His best shot is a one-timer off a feed from Hawerchuk.

Bodger has great poise with the puck. He gives his team a sense of control when he is quarterbacking.

THE PHYSICAL GAME
Bodger takes the body when he absolutely must, but he is not by nature a hitter. He has never used his size as well as he should. Because his hand skills are so good, he prefers to position himself and try to poke or sweep check. He's a strong one-on-one defender because of his skating, but he will not clear people out from in front of his net as well as he should. He is aggressive stepping up into the neutral zone and challenges on penalty-killing as well.

THE INTANGIBLES
The acquisition of Petr Svoboda signalled content-ment for Bodger, who is not cut out mentally to bear the role of being a No. 1 defenseman, but Svoboda's injury early in the season put the pressure back on Bodger. He responded well and had one of his best seasons. If Svoboda comes back healthy this season, Bodger should have another quietly effective season.

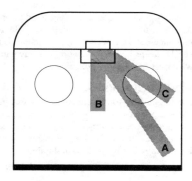

BOB ERREY

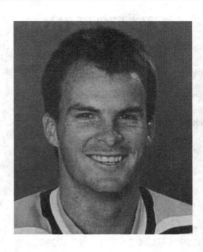

Yrs. of NHL service: 10
Born: Montreal, Que.; Sept. 21, 1964
Position: left wing
Height: 5-10
Weight: 183
Uniform no.: 12
Shoots: left

Career statistics:

GP	G	A	TP	PIM
580	133	143	276	655

1991-92 statistics:

GP	G	A	TP	+/-	PIM	PP	SH	GW	GT	S	PCT
78	19	16	35	+1	119	0	3	1	0	122	15.6

1992-93 statistics:

GP	G	A	TP	+/-	PIM	PP	SH	GW	GT	S	PCT
62	9	9	18	0	80	0	0	2	0	88	10.2

LAST SEASON

Acquired from Pittsburgh for Mike Ramsey. Goals six-season low. Missed 14 games with ankle injury. Missed two games with bruised tailbone.

THE FINESSE GAME

Errey has such good skating ability that he did not look out of place when the Sabres tried him as a left wing with the explosive Pat LaFontaine/Alexander Mogilny duo. Because Errey does not rack up the points or the dramatic scoring chances — he lacks the hand skills and offensive instincts to push his game up to that level — his skating is the strongest part of his game.

Couple that with Errey's work ethic and you get a forward who is always in position and rarely takes a night off. He is a safety valve, a heady winger who will always be the third man high or the forward dropping back to cover for a defenseman who has pinched in. He is a solid checker who can play against the league's top lines and help shut it down.

Errey's few scoring chances will come from his hard work around the net, but it's unlikely he'll score more than 20 goals in a season. His priority is defense.

THE PHYSICAL GAME

Errey is an abrasive forward. He is a small player but plays much larger, using every ounce of his body in his checks. He is built very solidly and plays with game-in, game-out intensity. He's a leader by example. It's easy for a bigger man to underestimate him on looks alone, but his size is deceptive.

THE INTANGIBLES

Errey is a winner. The Penguins missed his sandpaper play after trading him to the Sabres, and he will help bring a championship aura to a team in Buffalo that has long been noted for its underachieving. Errey will do what it takes to win. He is a free agent this summer and would make a nice acquisition for a team that is looking for some attitude adjustment in its dressing room, provided the Sabres don't recognize his worth.

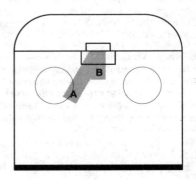

GRANT FUHR

Yrs. of NHL service: 12
Born: Spruce Grove, Alta.; Sept. 28, 1962
Position: goaltender
Height: 5-10
Weight: 186
Uniform no.: 31
Catches: right

Career statistics:

GP	MINS	GA	SO	GAA	A	PIM
546	31,043	1885	12	3.64	37	68

1991-92 statistics:

GP	MINS	GAA	W	L	T	SO	GA	S	SAPCT	PIM
65	3774	3.66	25	33	5	2	230	1933	.881	4

1992-93 statistics:

GP	MINS	GAA	W	L	T	SO	GA	S	SAPCT	PIM
58	3359	3.30	24	24	6	1	185	1729	.893	10

LAST SEASON

Reached 20-win mark for ninth time in career. Acquired from Toronto for Dave Andreychuk, Daren Puppa and a first-round draft choice in 1993. Missed 10 games with arthroscopic knee surgery. Missed three games with bruised collarbone.

THE PHYSICAL GAME

Injuries are starting to chip away at some of the attributes that make Fuhr so special. The knee injury is a special concern. Although he was able to bounce back off the original surgery early in the season, he seemed slowed by ailments late in the playoffs.

When healthy, Fuhr is among the most spectacularly quick goalies in the league. He is a great skater with outstanding balance. He can dart in and out of his net to play pucks and never appears to be scrambling. NHL shooters have just about given up trying to beat him on his glove side — and since he is a southpaw goalie, his glove side is most other goalies' stick side.

Fuhr recovers well for rebounds. His recovery time is so short that he can make second-shot saves that most other goalies cannot. His sole weakness remains low between the pads.

He has logged a lot of ice time over the years, with the Oilers going deep into the playoffs every spring back in their glory days, and he may be starting to wear down physically.

THE MENTAL GAME

Fuhr has such an unruffled playing style that his relaxed and calm carriage on the ice has a soothing effect on his teammates. He is very focussed and keeps his attention through screens and scrambles. He doesn't allow many soft goals because his attention doesn't waver.

Fuhr is as good in the first minute of the game as in the last minute of overtime. He has five Stanley Cup rings but remains as competitive as ever. He's smart, too. He reads plays coming at him as well as the top defensemen. Fuhr is a master of "read and react."

THE INTANGIBLES

Fuhr has become increasingly fragile over the last few seasons. He has problems with both knees now, and after the Sabres paid a stiff price for him, it seemed that nothing less than a Stanley Cup would do. The Sabres got past the first round of the playoffs (for the first time since 1983), with much of the credit going to Fuhr, but the goalie was singled out for his poor play in the Adams Division Final, in which the Sabres were swept by Montreal. He will be 31 this season, hardly old in goalie years, but the big question mark is his physical status.

DALE HAWERCHUK

Yrs. of NHL service: 12
Born: Toronto, Ont.; Apr. 4, 1963
Position: centre
Height: 5-11
Weight: 185
Uniform no.: 10
Shoots: left

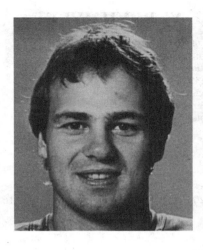

Career statistics:

GP	G	A	TP	PIM
951	449	763	1212	579

1991-92 statistics:

GP	G	A	TP	+/-	PIM	PP	SH	GW	GT	S	PCT
77	23	75	98	-22	27	13	0	4	0	242	9.5

1992-93 statistics:

GP	G	A	TP	+/-	PIM	PP	SH	GW	GT	S	PCT
81	16	80	96	-17	52	8	0	2	0	259	6.2

LAST SEASON

Third on team in points. Second on team in assists. Goals career low. Assists career high.

THE FINESSE GAME

Hawerchuk needs less space to turn than just about any NHL player, and he can do it quickly and with control of the puck. Shifty and smart, he lacks the breakaway speed to be a dynamic skater who can intimidate through his power skating, but he can outwit most defenders because he's downright sneaky.

Hawerchuk is a terrific passer. He sees all of his passing options, and if the lanes are closed down he'll dance down the ice with the puck himself. He has such a fine touch and is so confident that he will make bold feeds through a defender's legs and stick or feather a fine backhander. Anyone playing with Hawerchuk has to be alert, because he will make a creative play out of what looks like a closed-off situation. Hawerchuk is excellent on draws, using his hand-eye co-ordination and quick stick to win most face-offs outright.

He runs the Sabres' power play from the point, and keys one of the most mobile power plays in the league. No one stands around on a static pattern with the Sabres: everything is in motion, and Hawerchuk's timing and control keep it from being chaotic.

THE PHYSICAL GAME

Hawerchuk doesn't go around slamming people or wasting his energy on futile battles in the corners. He doles himself out like a parent does an allowance, making the big hit when he's sure his team will control the puck, or else using his stick to whack at ankles for possession. He does not use his body well on draws, though. If he does not win it cleanly, he will not always tie up the opposing centre as well as he should.

THE INTANGIBLES

Hawerchuk is durable (he's missed only 16 games in 12 seasons) and gritty. He's an intelligent player who will not make the mistake that costs a game, but he may well make the big play that wins it. His work on the power play could make for another 95- to 100-point season for him.

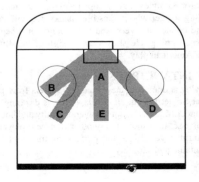

YURI KHMYLEV

Yrs. of NHL service: 1
Born: Moscow, Russia; Aug. 9, 1964
Position: left wing
Height: 6-1
Weight: 196
Uniform no.: 13
Shoots: right

Career statistics:

GP	G	A	TP	PIM
68	20	19	39	28

1992-93 statistics:

GP	G	A	TP	+/-	PIM	PP	SH	GW	GT	S	PCT
68	20	19	39	+6	28	0	3	3	0	122	16.4

LAST SEASON
First NHL season.

THE FINESSE GAME
After trading Dave Andreychuk to Toronto in the Grant Fuhr deal, the Sabres needed a left wing to go with scooters Pat LaFontaine and Alexander Mogilny. The Yuri Khmylev experiment may pay dividends.

The line needs a safety valve, and Khmylev was very cognizant of his duty as the defensive winger on the line. When a defenseman would get overexcited and caught down on the rush, Khmylev would be the player dropping back to help out.

Khmylev is a strong skater with outstanding balance. If his stick is tied up, he'll keep the puck going with his feet, and makes smart "soccer" passes. He doesn't worry much about the offensive zone, but he has a nice wrist shot and will work through traffic with the puck.

Khmylev was used to kill penalties and was very effective and aggressive.

THE PHYSICAL GAME
The adjustment from European ice to the smaller standard NHL rink was one thing. Adapting to the even smaller ice in Buffalo was yet another stumbling block for Khmylev, but he coped well. He is a tough, grinding winger who makes big checks. He will step up and create turnovers, and will bounce off checks and keep going. He shows every sign of handling North American play.

THE INTANGIBLES
Khmylev is one of the new breed of players from the former Soviet Union. His skills aren't as dazzling as Alexander Mogilny's, but his overall ability and hockey sense set him above many other first-year players. He could develop into the perfect complement for LaFontaine and Mogilny.

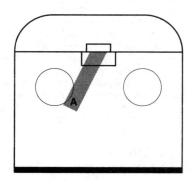

PAT LAFONTAINE

Yrs. of NHL service: 10
Born: St. Louis, Mo.; Feb. 22, 1963
Position: centre
Height: 5-10
Weight: 175
Uniform no.: 16
Shoots: right

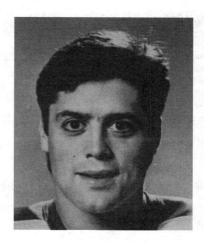

Career statistics:

GP	G	A	TP	PIM
671	386	421	807	470

1991-92 statistics:

GP	G	A	TP	+/-	PIM	PP	SH	GW	GT	S	PCT
57	46	47	93	+10	98	23	0	5	1	203	22.7

1992-93 statistics:

GP	G	A	TP	+/-	PIM	PP	SH	GW	GT	S	PCT
84	53	95	148	+11	63	20	2	7	1	306	17.3

LAST SEASON

Runner-up in Art Ross Trophy scoring race. Third in NHL in assists. Led team in assists and points. Only Sabre to appear in all 84 games. Goals, assists and points at career highs. Second season with 100 or more points. Finalist for Hart and Lady Byng trophies.

THE FINESSE GAME

If LaFontaine were a baseball player, he would be like the midget Bill Veeck once sent up to the plate. With LaFontaine's skating crouch, there is no strike zone. He's a ball of fire on the ice, low to the ground and almost impossible to catch or knock off stride. He gears up in the defensive zone and simply explodes.

LaFontaine is inexhaustible. He is double-shifted almost every night and doesn't miss a call. Nor does he float: he's like a shark, always circling and in motion. He has great quickness and acceleration, with deep edges for turns. Few players can get as many dekes into a short stretch of ice at high speed as LaFontaine does when he is bearing down on a goalie. His favourite move is "Patended" but still almost unstoppable. LaFontaine streaks in, moves the puck to his backhand, then strides right with the puck on his forehand. A goalie's only hope is for LaFontaine to lose control. Slim chance.

LaFontaine takes almost all of the Sabres' offensive zone draws. He has quick hands and after winning will burst past the opposing centre for the front of the net.

On the power play, LaFontaine likes to lurk behind the net, then burst out into the open ice at either side of the net for a pass and a scoring chance.

Opposing teams have to make the percentage play in their defensive zone against LaFontaine because of his anticipation and alertness in picking off passes.

THE PHYSICAL GAME

LaFontaine's strength and toughness are underrated. He came back early from a broken jaw in 1991-92,

playing with a modified helmet that made him look like a space cadet. Last season, he stayed in the line-up through nagging injuries, and it wasn't until Game 4 of the Adams Division Final that he was forced to the sidelines.

LaFontaine gets tremendous power from his legs and is very strong on his stick. He won't get into corner battles, but he'll go through traffic in front of the net with the puck. He is strong enough to push off a defender with one arm and get a shot away one-handed.

THE INTANGIBLES

LaFontaine has stamped himself as a player who can carry the team. He has a special chemistry with Mogilny, erasing the stigma LaFontaine had early in his career as a player who wanted to do it himself and didn't use his teammates well. LaFontaine can play it either way. He is clearly among the NHL's elite forwards, and he assumed the captaincy and the leadership of this team as well.

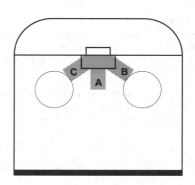

GRANT LEDYARD

Yrs. of NHL service: 9
Born: Winnipeg, Man.; Nov. 19, 1961
Position: left defense
Height: 6-2
Weight: 200
Uniform no.: 3
Shoots: left

Career statistics:

GP	G	A	TP	PIM
533	57	154	211	534

1991-92 statistics:

GP	G	A	TP	+/-	PIM	PP	SH	GW	GT	S	PCT
50	5	16	21	-4	45	0	0	0	0	87	5.7

1992-93 statistics:

GP	G	A	TP	+/-	PIM	PP	SH	GW	GT	S	PCT
50	2	14	16	-2	45	1	0	0	0	79	2.5

LAST SEASON

Missed 25 games with broken finger. Missed three games with eye injury.

THE FINESSE GAME

Ledyard is a good skater with range, mobility and balance. He is ideal paired with a more physical defenseman, since he'll gladly patrol the defensive zone and handles the puck with confidence.

Ledyard can kill penalties and contribute on the power play (he worked on the second units of both for the Sabres last season). Though not flashy, he will jump into the play nicely and has a decent point shot. Once in a while he will make a deep foray.

Ledyard can carry the puck or make a smart outlet pass.

THE PHYSICAL GAME

Ledyard does not use his body well. He prefers to angle an attacker wide, then gently push him rather than make a solid take-out. He will rely first on a poke check rather than a hit. He will block shots, but he has to do a better job of clearing out the front of his crease to stay in the coaches' good graces, or they will always be looking for a younger defenseman to take his place.

THE INTANGIBLES

Ledyard returned from a mangled finger to become one of the Sabres' most reliable defensemen, a contributor who was needed after the injury to Petr Svoboda.

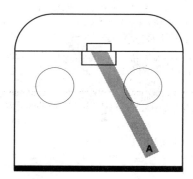

BRAD MAY

Yrs. of NHL service: 2
Born: Toronto, Ont.; Nov. 29, 1971
Position: left wing
Height: 6-0
Weight: 209
Uniform no.: 27
Shoots: left

Career statistics:

GP	G	A	TP	PIM
151	24	19	43	551

1991-92 statistics:

GP	G	A	TP	+/-	PIM	PP	SH	GW	GT	S	PCT
69	11	6	17	-12	309	1	0	3	0	82	13.4

1992-93 statistics:

GP	G	A	TP	+/-	PIM	PP	SH	GW	GT	S	PCT
82	13	13	26	+3	242	0	0	1	0	114	11.4

LAST SEASON

Goals, assists, points and games played all higher than rookie season. Led team in PIM.

THE FINESSE GAME

May is a quick learner. In his second season, he decided that he was better off trying to make the safe play instead of the big play — and discovered that more often than not, the safe play led to the big play. He is a power forward in the making, with more than brute strength on his side. He has very nice passing skills and good hockey sense.

May is not much of a finisher, although as he becomes more relaxed and confident this may develop. He is certainly not a natural scorer, and his goals will come off his hard work around the net.

May has sound defensive instincts. He is not a very fast or agile skater, so he has to be conscious of keeping his position because he will not be able to race back to cover for an error in judgement.

THE PHYSICAL GAME

May is tough and rugged, and he uses his size well. He is strong along the boards and in front of the net. A well-conditioned athlete, he's very sturdy and durable. He has very good balance and leg drive and is difficult to knock off his feet. He'll take a hit to make a play and protects the puck well.

THE INTANGIBLES

May is going to be a late bloomer. Certainly the Sabres will be thrilled if he follows a Rick Tocchet blueprint. He has completed the first part by establishing himself physically. Now he has to continue with his work ethic to make himself a more valuable player on the ice.

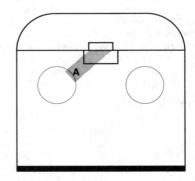

ALEXANDER MOGILNY

Yrs. of NHL service: 4
Born: Khabarovsk, Russia; Feb. 18, 1969
Position: right wing
Height: 5-11
Weight: 195
Uniform no.: 89
Shoots: left

Career statistics:

GP	G	A	TP	PIM
271	160	158	318	145

1991-92 statistics:

GP	G	A	TP	+/-	PIM	PP	SH	GW	GT	S	PCT
67	39	45	84	+7	73	15	0	2	0	235	16.5

1992-93 statistics:

GP	G	A	TP	+/-	PIM	PP	SH	GW	GT	S	PCT
77	76	51	127	+7	40	27	0	11	0	360	21.1

LAST SEASON

Tied for NHL lead in goals with Winnipeg's Teemu Selanne, but played in seven fewer games than the Jet rookie. Tied for seventh in NHL in scoring. Third in NHL in power play goals. Tied for NHL lead in game-winning goals. Fourth in NHL in shots. Led team in goals, power play goals, game-winning goals, shots and shooting percentage. Goals, assists and points at career highs. Underwent off-season surgery for broken leg suffered in playoffs.

THE FINESSE GAME

Marvel at Mogilny's skating: the ease with which he accelerates...the accuracy with which he can fire a shot through traffic...his burst of speed from a standstill. He hits his top speed in just a few strides. When he streaks down the ice, there is a good chance you'll see something new, something you didn't expect. He is unbelievably quick. Mogilny may hate to fly in a plane but he loves to fly over the ice.

Mogilny's anticipation sets him apart from other players who are merely fast. He won't skate deeply into his own defensive zone, but awaits a turnover and a chance to get a jump on the defenseman, with a preferred move to the outside — but he is not afraid to go inside either, so a defenseman intent in angling him to the boards could just as easily get burned inside.

Mogilny can beat you in so many ways. He has a powerful and accurate wrist shot from the tops of the circles in. He shoots without breaking stride. He and linemate Pat LaFontaine work a give-and-go that is a thing of beauty. He one-times with the best of them. And everything is done at racehorse speed.

THE PHYSICAL GAME

The major knock on Mogilny is that, as good as he is, there always seems to be something left in the tank, that Mogilny doesn't push himself to the limit. He takes very long shifts and has tremendous endurance. He plays much better at home, where he scored two-thirds of his goals, leading some critics to claim he gets "road flu."

Mogilny intimidates with his speed but will also add a physical element. He has great upper body strength and will drive through a defender to the net.

THE INTANGIBLES

The financial reward for Mogilny's scoring success is staggering: 60 goals meant a bonus of $140,000, and each subsequent goal earned another $4,000. This season might prove a little too much for him. Even before the last season was over, he was worrying about the impact it would have on this year, likening it to Brett Hull scoring 50 goals and being raked for having a bad season.

Mogilny was the first young Russian to leave the former USSR, and he has had great difficulty adjusting to North American life. He is still afraid of flying and makes an erratic bet to repeat his stunning season. He is just starting to realize what the responsibility of being a team's game-breaker is, and he has to be up to that pressure every night. His comeback from leg surgery will make it a difficult start this season.

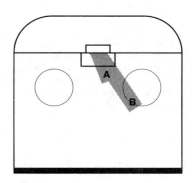

WAYNE PRESLEY

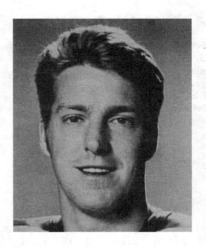

Yrs. of NHL service: 8
Born: Detroit, Mich.; Mar. 23, 1965
Position: right wing
Height: 5-11
Weight: 180
Uniform no.: 18
Shoots: right

Career statistics:

GP	G	A	TP	PIM
493	118	126	244	724

1991-92 statistics:

GP	G	A	TP	+/-	PIM	PP	SH	GW	GT	S	PCT
59	10	16	26	-27	133	3	0	1	0	135	7.4

1992-93 statistics:

GP	G	A	TP	+/-	PIM	PP	SH	GW	GT	S	PCT
79	15	17	32	+5	96	0	1	2	0	97	15.5

LAST SEASON
Goals and games played two-season highs.

THE FINESSE GAME
Presley has adequate shooting skills in tight, when everything is reaction. When he has too much time to think, he'll overhandle the puck and get tight. He has nice hands for doing something with deflections and rebounds, and he is willing to work to get himself in position for those chances.

Presley has become more and more of a defensive specialist. He keyed the Sabres' top penalty-killing unit. He's a good skater who will always hustle in all zones, and he's a determined forechecker.

THE PHYSICAL GAME
Presley crashes the crease and is very good at getting to the goalie — even right on top of the goalie. Presley can make it look as if the defender has knocked him into the crease when it is actually Presley who is dragging the defender in and getting away with interference.

Presley takes the body consistently, and he is highly annoying to play against — he's just about obnoxious at times. He can goad rivals into taking bad penalties, whereas he usually keeps his cool and knows just what he's doing.

THE INTANGIBLES
We predicted Presley might be a sleeper last season with 20 to 25 goals, but even though he was healthy for much of the season, he did not threaten that total. He has been defined as a checker, and we would be surprised if he hit 25 this season.

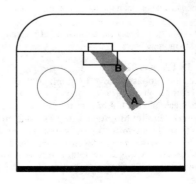

ROB RAY

Yrs. of NHL service: 4
Born: Stirling, Ont.; June 8, 1968
Position: left wing
Height: 6-0
Weight: 203
Uniform no.: 32
Shoots: left

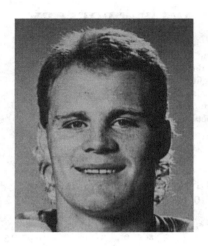

Career statistics:

GP	G	A	TP	PIM
224	18	14	32	1014

1991-92 statistics:

GP	G	A	TP	+/-	PIM	PP	SH	GW	GT	S	PCT
63	5	3	8	-9	354	0	0	0	0	29	17.2

1992-93 statistics:

GP	G	A	TP	+/-	PIM	PP	SH	GW	GT	S	PCT
68	3	2	5	-3	211	1	0	0	0	28	10.7

LAST SEASON

PIM three-season low. Missed two games with knee injury.

THE FINESSE GAME

Ray continued to develop as a checking winger. He is a good skater for a big guy, very mobile and surprisingly quick. He is a solid forechecker and is learning to keep his gloves and stick down (note his lowered PIM totals). There is nothing wrong with taking aggressive penalties, but Ray is big enough to check cleanly and effectively.

Ray has to work hard for his points. He has a nice wrist shot from in deep and a hard slapshot. He doesn't do much creatively, but patrols up and down his wing. He has good balance and can plant himself in front of the net, but doesn't have really quick hands for picking up loose pucks.

THE PHYSICAL GAME

Ray is one of those hitters who can galvanize a bench and a building. A defender with the puck knows Ray is coming and either has to be willing to stand up to the check or bail out — either way, Ray has a good shot at loosening a puck on the turnover. The problem is that he can't do much with the puck once he gets it and needs a clever linemate to trail in and pick up the pieces.

Ray is a good fighter and doesn't get challenged much anymore.

THE INTANGIBLES

Despite the supposed move to eliminate fighting, there is still a place for a Rob Ray, especially on a team that has valuable players like Pat LaFontaine and Alexander Mogilny to protect. Ray has sufficient skills to earn a jersey, and just having him on the bench is a deterrent to other teams' headhunters. A question mark for Ray is his return from torn knee ligaments suffered late in the season.

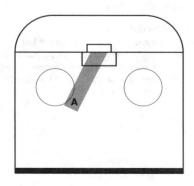

RICHARD SMEHLIK

Yrs. of NHL service: 1
Born: Ostrava, Czechoslovakia; Jan. 23, 1970
Position: right defense
Height: 6-3
Weight: 208
Uniform no.: 42
Shoots: left

Career statistics:

GP	G	A	TP	PIM
80	4	27	31	59

1992-93 statistics:

GP	G	A	TP	+/-	PIM	PP	SH	GW	GT	S	PCT
80	4	27	31	+9	59	0	0	0	0	82	4.9

LAST SEASON
First NHL season.

THE FINESSE GAME
Smehlik skates well with a strong stride. He is not fast, but he's agile with good lateral movement and is very solid on his skates. His balance is very good, and he is tough to knock down.

Smehlik doesn't handle the puck much. Being paired with the mobile Doug Bodger, he is more than willing to let the senior defenseman control the puck. But Smehlik does have good passing skills and fair hockey vision, and can spot and hit the breaking forward. Most of his assists will be traced back to a headman feed out of the defensive zone.

Smehlik is vulnerable to a strong forecheck. Teams were aware of his experience and tried to work his corner to keep the puck away from Bodger, and Smehlik was prone to turnovers.

THE PHYSICAL GAME
Smehlik is still adapting to the North American game. He will use his body well but has to be more consistent and authoritative. He gained confidence through the season and was willing to step up aggressively, especially when killing penalties. He has to clean up his crease better, but he's not a very mean hitter.

THE INTANGIBLES
By the end of the season, this rookie defenseman was on the top Buffalo defense pairing with Bodger. He will never be a headline-grabbing defenseman, but he is well on his way to being a solid NHL contributor and has a great deal of sense for a 22-year-old defenseman.

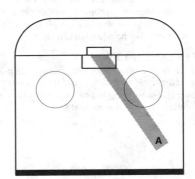

KEN SUTTON

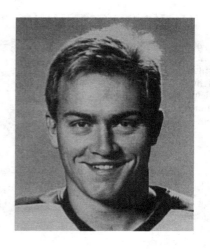

Yrs. of NHL service: 2
Born: Edmonton, Alta.; May 11, 1969
Position: left defense
Height: 6-0
Weight: 190
Uniform no.: 41
Shoots: left

Career statistics:

GP	G	A	TP	PIM
142	13	38	51	114

1991-92 statistics:

GP	G	A	TP	+/-	PIM	PP	SH	GW	GT	S	PCT
64	2	18	20	+5	71	0	0	0	0	81	2.5

1992-93 statistics:

GP	G	A	TP	+/-	PIM	PP	SH	GW	GT	S	PCT
63	8	14	22	-3	30	1	0	2	1	77	10.4

LAST SEASON

Goals and points improved over rookie season. Missed 19 games with broken ankle.

THE FINESSE GAME

Sutton is a smooth skater, although he does not have very quick feet. He seems to just glide into position, and he can make a tight pivot with the puck, but you won't see any bursts of quickness. He usually looks like he's chasing people all over his corner because most of them have a quick-step advantage over him.

Sutton has average-to-good skills in puckhandling and shots. When he ventures in deep, he can utilize a decent snap shot. He is smart and effective from the point with a low slap shot. He concerns himself more with keeping the shot low and on net rather than enjoying the sound of a booming shot clunking off the boards or glass.

He shows signs of getting more involved offensively. He has good hockey sense and will pinch aggressively. A healthy season would help him along that route.

THE PHYSICAL GAME

Sutton guards the front of his net but doesn't do much to keep it clean. He is not very strong on his skates and ends up simply bumping people instead of preventing them from getting involved in the play. Give him points for trying, but he's just not effective.

THE INTANGIBLES

A sleeper. Sutton was injured in training camp last season and got off to a slow start. He is coming to hand slowly, but we wouldn't be a bit surprised to see his offensive numbers double next season.

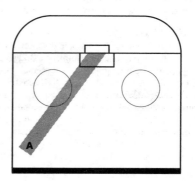

PETR SVOBODA

Yrs. of NHL service: 9
Born: Most, Czechoslovakia; Feb. 14, 1966
Position: right defense
Height: 6-1
Weight: 170
Uniform no.: 7
Shoots: left

Career statistics:

GP	G	A	TP	PIM
587	42	220	262	872

1991-92 statistics:

GP	G	A	TP	+/-	PIM	PP	SH	GW	GT	S	PCT
71	6	22	28	+1	146	1	0	3	0	111	5.4

1992-93 statistics:

GP	G	A	TP	+/-	PIM	PP	SH	GW	GT	S	PCT
40	2	24	26	+3	59	1	0	1	0	61	3.3

LAST SEASON

Despite missing more than half the season with a knee injury and subsequent surgery, assists were higher than previous season and total points were just two fewer than previous season, in which Svoboda played 71 games.

THE FINESSE GAME

One of Svoboda's greatest gifts is his skating, and since he did not come back late in the season off his knee surgery, we just have to surmise those skills will still be with him. Svoboda was never strong on his skates, but he had great quickness, balance and agility — and you can't hit what you can't catch.

Svoboda has (had?) a long stride. Not a very solid player, he is lean and wiry, and his skating is economical.

Svoboda has excellent instincts. He can carry the puck well and join the rush. He has a quick release on his wrist and snap shots, and also a good one-timer that he uses on the power play. He reads plays well offensively and defensively.

THE PHYSICAL GAME

Svoboda isn't one for physical play, but he is a feisty foe who will take the body and then use his stick to rap a player in the choppers or pull his skates out from under him. He ticks off a lot of people.

Svoboda is very lean and can't do much one-on-one in a close battle. He will ride an opponent out of the play well when he can use his skating to generate some power.

THE INTANGIBLES

A healthy Svoboda will make the Sabres' attack even more potent. Last season he appeared to be on the verge of a breakout career year before the injury. But even if he comes off the surgery well, don't expect him to crank it up until the second half of the season.

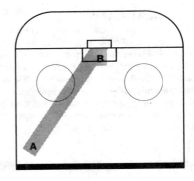

BOB SWEENEY

Yrs. of NHL service: 7
Born: Concord, Mass.; Jan. 25, 1964
Position: centre
Height: 6-3
Weight: 200
Uniform no.: 20
Shoots: left

Career statistics:

GP	G	A	TP	PIM
462	102	138	240	622

1991-92 statistics:

GP	G	A	TP	+/-	PIM	PP	SH	GW	GT	S	PCT
63	6	14	20	-9	103	0	1	1	0	70	8.6

1992-93 statistics:

GP	G	A	TP	+/-	PIM	PP	SH	GW	GT	S	PCT
80	21	26	47	+2	118	4	3	3	0	120	17.5

LAST SEASON

Acquired on waivers from Boston. Tied for team lead in shorthanded goals. Goals three-season high. Missed two games with a bruised shoulder.

THE FINESSE GAME

Sweeney is a tenacious forechecker who is at his best in traffic. He will wade in to try to get the puck bouncing around loose in front. Then he will send it out to a teammate while he himself works to set a screen for the shot. He doesn't have the best hand skills, but he can make a tip or bat in a rebound; he earned some power play time for his willingness to work in front of the net. He has a long reach for wraparound tries and occasionally ventures a Denis Savard Memorial spin-a-rama.

Sweeney isn't the quickest decision maker when it comes to handling the puck. His hockey vision is somewhat short-sighted. His skating isn't quite up to par, either, which doesn't hurt him too much in small buildings like his home rink.

Sweeney works on the first penalty-killing unit for the Sabres and has improved on his face-offs to the point where he took most of the key defensive zone draws. He is not a very good skater and has to be positionally alert.

THE PHYSICAL GAME

Sweeney can play with some toughness, but his past history has been to take too many off-nights. He had spells of this last season as well, but to his credit he is getting more consistent. He may have been motivated just because of the Bruins cutting him loose. He can't lose that competitive drive because he needs the desire and effort to be a solid contributor. He has a bit of a nasty streak when provoked, which will earn him a little room and time around the net.

THE INTANGIBLES

The equivalent of a flea-market find, Sweeney was a reliable performer for the Sabres in the regular season and in the playoffs. The change in scenery may have been just what he needed, because he has developed into a checking forward with a knack for scoring timely goals.

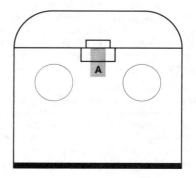

RANDY WOOD

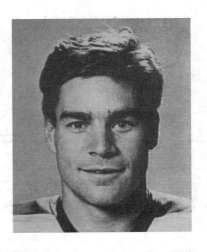

Yrs. of NHL service: 6
Born: Princeton, N.J.; Oct. 12, 1963
Position: left wing
Height: 6-0
Weight: 195
Uniform no.: 19
Shoots: left

Career statistics:

GP	G	A	TP	PIM
418	126	114	240	375

1991-92 statistics:

GP	G	A	TP	+/-	PIM	PP	SH	GW	GT	S	PCT
78	22	18	40	-12	86	7	1	3	0	215	10.2

1992-93 statistics:

GP	G	A	TP	+/-	PIM	PP	SH	GW	GT	S	PCT
82	18	25	43	+6	77	3	2	2	0	176	10.2

LAST SEASON

Assists career high. Points three-season high.

THE FINESSE GAME

The story of Wood's career has always been hard work, speed, intelligence and hands of...well, wood. Wood is always around the net, usually barrelling in at top speed, but his trouble is that he can't handle the puck while he is tearing along. He doesn't have great balance either, so he usually ends up plowing into the goalie (which drives opposing teams nuts) or sliding past the net into the boards with nothing to show for all of his hard work.

And Wood does work. He is constantly jumping the holes on the attack or coming back to help out defensively. He is a strong penalty killer who checks aggressively and can pick off passes and start shorthanded rushes. He's a constant threat on the ice because of his straightaway speed.

Wood wants to be better offensively. He tried creative plays down low but is better off just ramming and jamming. He is a dedicated, durable player who is always in top condition and can take every shift at top speed.

THE PHYSICAL GAME

Wood will do the dirty work along the boards. He is a good size and he uses it well, bumping and scrapping for the puck. He gets other teams made at him because he's always in their face, and he should take this as a compliment. He's that annoying.

THE INTANGIBLES

If Wood ever had the hands to go with his speed, he would score 40 goals. Do not expect to see this in our lifetime. He will be a consistent 20-goal scorer whose speed always creates the illusion of more promise than he can deliver.

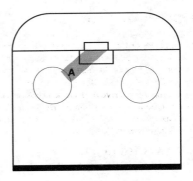

CALGARY FLAMES

KEVIN DAHL

Yrs. of NHL service: 1
Born: Regina, Sask.; Dec. 30, 1968
Position: right defense
Height: 5-11
Weight: 190
Uniform no.: 4
Shoots: right

Career statistics:

GP	G	A	TP	PIM
61	2	9	11	56

1992-93 statistics:

GP	G	A	TP	+/-	PIM	PP	SH	GW	GT	S	PCT
61	2	9	11	+9	56	1	0	0	0	40	5.0

LAST SEASON
First NHL season. Missed 18 games with knee injury.

THE FINESSE GAME
Dahl is a stay-at-home defenseman who has the skills to get more involved in the attack than he did in his rookie season. His points will come from his play-making. He is a smooth skater and is poised with the puck in his own end. He will only occasionally jump into the play. When he does, he will trail the play and has a nice one-timer from the right point. However, he seems reluctant to shoot.

Dahl is mobile but not fast. With Gary Suter, his usual defense partner, he can cover a lot of ice. Since Suter likes to roam and get into things in the offensive zone, Dahl concentrates on guarding his defensive zone. He is a smart player and solid penalty killer. He was quietly one of Calgary's most effective players last season.

THE PHYSICAL GAME
Dahl is not very big, but he is solidly built. He is tough and plays hurt, but he does not make loud hits. He plays a positional game.

THE INTANGIBLES
Dahl played for Calgary coach Dave King on the 1992 Canadian Olympic Team, which won a silver medal. More experienced than a lot of other rookie defensemen, he came out of the Montreal minor league system and by season's end was a reliable defenseman for the Flames. He has a solid future as an NHL regular, but he won't be heating up the defensemen's scoring race.

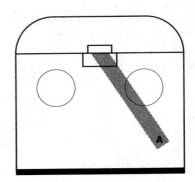

CHRIS DAHLQUIST

Yrs. of NHL service: 7
Born: Fridley, Minn.; Dec. 14, 1962
Position: right defense
Height: 6-1
Weight: 196
Uniform no.: 5
Shoots: left

Career statistics:

GP	G	A	TP	PIM
385	16	52	68	386

1991-92 statistics:

GP	G	A	TP	+/-	PIM	PP	SH	GW	GT	S	PCT
74	1	13	14	-10	68	0	0	0	0	63	1.6

1992-93 statistics:

GP	G	A	TP	+/-	PIM	PP	SH	GW	GT	S	PCT
74	3	7	10	0	66	0	0	1	0	64	4.7

LAST SEASON

Acquired from Minnesota on waivers. Missed two games with charleyhorse. Missed five games with rib injury.

THE FINESSE GAME

Dahlquist uses all of his skills in the defensive zone. He is a little slow with his passes but conscious of protecting the puck with his body. He is a good skater who is better taking a stride or two and just guiding the puck to centre ice rather than trying to make a play. That process simply seems to take too long.

Dahlquist seldom gets involved at the other end of the ice. He has a decent shot off the fly, but does not venture down deep. He is positionally sound.

THE PHYSICAL GAME

Dahlquist uses his size well and will bring his stick or elbow up when play gets chippy. He is a stalwart along the boards, in the corners and in front of the net. He can be beaten one-on-one in open ice, so he plays a containment game. Like his defensive brethren on the Flames, Dahlquist is a good shot-blocker.

THE INTANGIBLES

Dahlquist is a defensive defenseman who will not score more than 10 to 15 points a season. He is a complementary player who works well with a more offense-minded partner, like Trent Yawney.

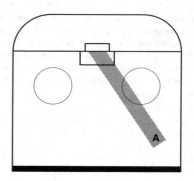

THEOREN FLEURY

Yrs. of NHL service: 4
Born: Oxbow, Sask.; June 29, 1968
Position: right wing/centre
Height: 5-6
Weight: 160
Uniform no.: 14
Shoots: right

Career statistics:

GP	G	A	TP	PIM
358	163	214	377	693

1991-92 statistics:

GP	G	A	TP	+/-	PIM	PP	SH	GW	GT	S	PCT
80	33	40	73	0	133	11	1	6	0	225	14.7

1992-93 statistics:

GP	G	A	TP	+/-	PIM	PP	SH	GW	GT	S	PCT
83	34	66	100	+14	88	12	2	4	0	250	13.6

LAST SEASON

Led Flames in assists and points. Reached 100-point mark for second time in career. Set an NHL record by earning a +9 ranking in a game against San Jose on Feb. 10, 1993, in Flames' 13-1 win.

THE FINESSE GAME

Fleury has great speed and quickness, and he often seems to be dancing over the ice with his blades barely touching the frozen surface. He is always on the move, which is as much a tactic as an instinct for survival. You can't catch what you can't hit. He uses his outside speed to burn slower, bigger defensemen, or he can burst up the middle and split two defenders.

Fleury is a better finisher than playmaker. He is not at his best handling the puck, but is much better receiving the pass late and then making things happen. He always has his legs churning, and he draws penalties by driving to the net. He has a strong wrist shot that he can get away from almost anywhere. He can score even if he is pulled to his knees.

Fleury is a strong penalty killer, blocking shots and getting the puck out by using the boards as a teammate.

His hand quickness makes him very effective on draws, and he will take offensive-zone draws.

THE PHYSICAL GAME

Fleury did not report to camp last season in good shape, and for a player whose game relies on hustle and effort, he started out at a disadvantage. The Flames staff had him skating in a weighted vest at practice to get into condition, and by midseason he was close to his old self.

Moving from centre to wing takes Fleury out of the high confrontation areas on a nightly basis. He goes fearlessly to the front of the net and takes a beating. He has a huge heart, but his feisty nature sometimes leads to bad penalties. Fleury is weak defensively down low.

THE INTANGIBLES

Only his size prohibits Fleury from being among the NHL's elite forwards. He had a sluggish start to the season but finished strong, with a solid playoff despite Calgary's disappointing ouster. He played most of the season on the wing, which is his best position, and the results showed as he hit the 100-point mark again.

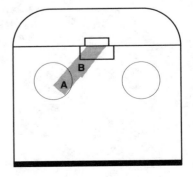

CHRIS LINDBERG

Yrs. of NHL service: 1
Born: Fort Frances, Ont.; Apr. 16, 1967
Position: left wing
Height: 6-1
Weight: 190
Uniform no.: 11
Shoots: left

Career statistics:

GP	G	A	TP	PIM
79	11	17	28	35

1991-92 statistics:

GP	G	A	TP	+/-	PIM	PP	SH	GW	GT	S	PCT
17	2	5	7	+3	17	0	0	0	0	19	10.5

1992-93 statistics:

GP	G	A	TP	+/-	PIM	PP	SH	GW	GT	S	PCT
62	9	12	21	-3	18	1	0	1	0	74	12.2

LAST SEASON

First full NHL season. Missed two games with knee injury.

THE FINESSE GAME

Lindberg is a fast skater who would be far more dangerous if he had a scoring touch, but he has not been much of a finisher at any level of hockey.

A good penalty-killer, he has the quickness and the anticipation to key shorthanded breaks by picking off passes and sending one of his teammates in on a break.

THE PHYSICAL GAME

Lindberg does not have a physical presence. Since he plays on a checking line with two bigger forces (Joel Otto and Paul Ranheim), Lindberg can do his job quietly. He is a sound player defensively.

THE INTANGIBLES

Lindberg played for Calgary coach Dave King on the silver medal-winning Team Canada at the 1992 Olympics. He adds speed to the checking line, but does not have many other dimensions.

AL MACINNIS

Yrs. of NHL service: 9
Born: Inverness, N.S.; July 11, 1963
Position: right defense
Height: 6-2
Weight: 195
Uniform no.: 2
Shoots: right

Career statistics:

GP	G	A	TP	PIM
728	185	555	740	855

1991-92 statistics:

GP	G	A	TP	+/-	PIM	PP	SH	GW	GT	S	PCT
72	20	57	77	+13	83	11	0	0	1	304	6.6

1992-93 statistics:

GP	G	A	TP	+/-	PIM	PP	SH	GW	GT	S	PCT
50	11	43	54	+15	61	7	0	4	0	201	5.5

LAST SEASON

Games played career low due to missing 34 games with a dislocated hip. Goals matches career low.

THE FINESSE GAME

MacInnis has one of the hardest shots in the NHL, but he also knows when to take something off it. It doesn't hurt his game a bit that he plays on a team that has major appliances masquerading as hulking forwards, obscuring the goaltender's view and making facing a MacInnis shot even more of a health hazard. Al is among the best in the league at keeping his shot low, and he can overpower a goalie with his vicious slap from the blue line.

MacInnis knows when to jump into the play and when to back off. He can start a rush with a rink-wide pass, then be quick enough to burst up-ice and be in position for a return pass. Because his shot is such a formidable weapon, he can freeze the opposition by faking a big wind-up, then quickly dish a pass in low to an open teammate. Even when he merely rings the puck off the boards, he's a threat, since there is so much on the shot the goalie has to be careful to stop it.

MacInnis skates well with the puck. He is not very mobile, but he gets up to speed in a few strides and can hit his outside speed to beat a defender one on one. He will gamble and is best paired with a defensively alert partner.

He has improved his defensive play. He is very smart against a two-on-one.

THE PHYSICAL GAME

MacInnis is a fairly big defenseman but does not play to his size. He plays his position and will tie up attackers rather than try to knock them down. In his own way, he is a tough competitor who will pay the price to win.

THE INTANGIBLES

MacInnis is not a favourite of coach Dave King, and

trade rumours should abound this season. MacInnis came back well off his hip injury and looks in perfect shape to hit the 20-goal, 70-point mark again. His defense always suffers in comparison to his offense, but he is a complete defenseman.

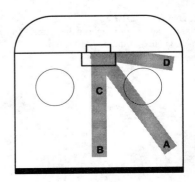

FRANK MUSIL

Yrs. of NHL service: 6
Born: Vysoké Mýto, Czechoslovakia; Dec. 17, 1964
Position: left defense
Height: 6-3
Weight: 215
Uniform no.: 3
Shoots: left

Career statistics:

GP	G	A	TP	PIM
496	31	78	109	941

1991-92 statistics:

GP	G	A	TP	+/-	PIM	PP	SH	GW	GT	S	PCT
78	4	8	12	+12	103	1	1	0	0	71	5.6

1992-93 statistics:

GP	G	A	TP	+/-	PIM	PP	SH	GW	GT	S	PCT
80	6	10	16	+28	131	0	0	0	0	87	6.9

LAST SEASON
Best plus/minus among team defensemen. Missed one game with back injury.

THE FINESSE GAME
Musil is a strong skater with good lateral movement. He is tough to beat one on one because he surrenders nothing, and he won't be fooled by head fakes. Poised and confident, he has a relaxed look even when he is working hard.

Musil skates well with the puck and can even turn with it on his backhand, but he employs this skill only to skate the puck out of danger in the defensive zone and does not get involved in the attack. He is not very fast and does not overcommit in the offensive zone.

In the neutral zone, he will often step up and challenge. He can start a transition play when he takes the puck away, as he is a smooth passer. His offensive contributions are limited.

THE PHYSICAL GAME
Musil is strong but doesn't play the type of physical game he should on a consistent basis. If anything is lacking, it is his intensity. He can be a presence when he steps up his play. He finishes his checks and is not above adding a little spice with a jab with his stick.

THE INTANGIBLES
Musil is a steadying influence on the Flames' blue line and makes a nice partner for Al MacInnis.

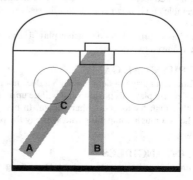

JOE NIEUWENDYK

Yrs. of NHL service: 6
Born: Oshawa, Ont.; Sept. 10, 1966
Position: centre
Height: 6-1
Weight: 195
Uniform no.: 25
Shoots: left

Career statistics:

GP	G	A	TP	PIM
467	257	234	491	232

1991-92 statistics:

GP	G	A	TP	+/-	PIM	PP	SH	GW	GT	S	PCT
69	22	34	56	-1	55	7	0	2	1	137	16.1

1992-93 statistics:

GP	G	A	TP	+/-	PIM	PP	SH	GW	GT	S	PCT
79	38	37	75	+9	52	14	0	6	0	208	18.3

LAST SEASON

Led team in power play goals and game-winning goals. Goal production improved by 16 after worst production in 1991-92. Missed one game with flu.

THE FINESSE GAME

If a "puck tipping" contest is ever added to the NHL All-Star Game skills competition, Nieuwendyk would be one of the favourites. He has fantastic hand-eye coordination and not only gets his blade on the puck but acts as if he knows where he's directing it. Consider the fact that most of those shots he tips come off the stick of Al MacInnis, and the respect for his skill rises even more.

He is aggressive, tough and aware around the net. Nieuwendyk can finish or make a play down low. He has the good vision, poise and hand skills to make neat little passes through traffic. He is a better playmaker than finisher, but never doubt that he will convert his chances.

Those same hand skill serve him well on draws. The Flames may have the NHL's best contingent of face-off men with Joel Otto, Theo Fleury and Nieuwendyk. He is also defensively sound.

Unfortunately for Nieuwendyk, major knee surgery a few seasons ago robbed him of most of his speed. He is still sneaky-fast, but without that added quickness he won't be a 50-goal scorer again.

THE PHYSICAL GAME

Nieuwendyk does not initiate, but he will take the punishment around the front of the net and stand his ground. He won't be intimidated, but he won't scare anyone else, either.

THE INTANGIBLES

Nieuwendyk's name has cropped up in numerous trade rumours, and he is a likely candidate to be in a new uniform next season.

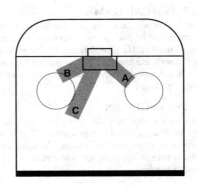

JOEL OTTO

Yrs. of NHL service: 8
Born: Elk River, Minn.; Oct. 29. 1961
Position: centre
Height: 6-4
Weight: 220
Uniform no.: 29
Shoots: right

Career statistics:

GP	G	A	TP	PIM
602	148	236	384	1424

1991-92 statistics:

GP	G	A	TP	+/-	PIM	PP	SH	GW	GT	S	PCT
78	13	21	34	-10	163	5	1	3	0	105	12.4

1992-93 statistics:

GP	G	A	TP	+/-	PIM	PP	SH	GW	GT	S	PCT
75	19	33	52	+2	150	6	1	4	1	115	16.5

LAST SEASON

Assists five-season high. Finalist for Selke Trophy. Missed eight games with rib injury.

THE FINESSE GAME

Otto was recognized for his checking work when he was named a finalist for the trophy for the NHL's best defensive forward. For years Wayne Gretzky's worst nightmare in the now-defunct Smythe Division, Otto is a powerful presence on the ice.

On draws, Otto doubles over his huge frame so that his head and shoulders prevent the opposing centre from seeing the puck drop. Helmets clash on Otto's face-offs. He has lost a little hand speed on the draws but is still among the best in the league.

Otto is not effective offensively. Although he has the build to be a power centre, his production has always been a disappointment, especially as he is given considerable power play time, but he doesn't have the quick hands in deep for tips and rebounds.

Otto is not very fast, but he is quite agile for a player of his size, and he is so strong and balanced on his skates that he has to be dynamited out of place. Even players close to his size bounce off him when they try to check him.

THE PHYSICAL GAME

Otto is big, strong and involved. He knows he is a brute force, and he likes to make people scatter as he drives to the net. He also delivers bruising checks along the wall. He loves the hitting part of the game, and he has the work ethic to perform consistently to his own high level.

THE INTANGIBLES

While Otto was sidelined for eight games with his rib injury, the Flames failed to win a game. That is how valuable he is to the team. He is a fierce competitor, an intelligent veteran and a checker who can also provide 20 goals a season.

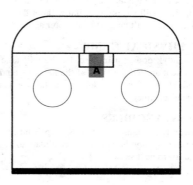

PAUL RANHEIM

Yrs. of NHL service: 3
Born: St. Louis, Mo.; Jan. 25, 1966
Position: left wing
Height: 6-0
Weight: 195
Uniform no.: 28
Shoots: right

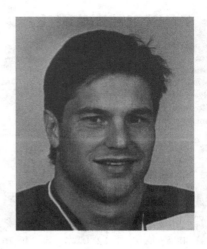

Career statistics:

GP	G	A	TP	PIM
287	84	86	170	85

1991-92 statistics:

GP	G	A	TP	+/-	PIM	PP	SH	GW	GT	S	PCT
80	23	20	43	+16	32	1	3	3	0	159	14.5

1992-93 statistics:

GP	G	A	TP	+/-	PIM	PP	SH	GW	GT	S	PCT
83	21	22	43	-4	26	3	4	1	0	179	11.7

LAST SEASON
Led team in shorthanded goals.

THE FINESSE GAME
Ranheim is one of the fastest skaters in the NHL, as he proved by finishing second (to San Jose's Mike Sullivan) in the Campbell Conference preliminaries for the NHL All-Star Game skills competition.

Ranheim has outstanding outside speed and a quick shot — all the weapons that should make him a constant offensive threat — yet he is the left wing on the Flames' top checking line with Joel Otto. There is nothing pretty, nothing fancy about Ranheim. Just shoot and skate. He is not the least bit creative, which is why he is limited as an offensive threat and does not get power play time on the top unit.

Ranheim uses his speed to keep himself in position defensively. This part of the game does not come naturally to him, and he works hard at it, which has made him a better all-around hockey player.

THE PHYSICAL GAME
Ranheim plays a solid physical game, although with his leg drive and power he could deliver more impressive hits. He does not initiate hits as well as he should.

THE INTANGIBLES
Ranheim looked on his way to becoming a 40-goal scorer when he first broke into the league, but those expectations have been dropped. He lacks the key ingredient — hockey sense — to be a more dangerous offensive player. His role as a checking winger and a 20- to 25-goal scorer is his present and future.

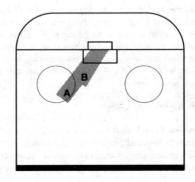

ROBERT REICHEL

Yrs. of NHL service: 3
Born: Litvinov, Czechoslovakia; June 25, 1971
Position: centre
Height: 5-10
Weight: 170
Uniform no.: 26
Shoots: left

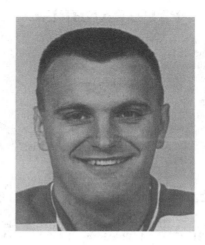

Career statistics:

GP	G	A	TP	PIM
223	79	104	183	110

1991-92 statistics:

GP	G	A	TP	+/-	PIM	PP	SH	GW	GT	S	PCT
77	20	34	54	+1	34	8	0	3	0	181	11.0

1992-93 statistics:

GP	G	A	TP	+/-	PIM	PP	SH	GW	GT	S	PCT
80	40	48	88	+25	54	12	0	5	0	238	16.8

LAST SEASON

Games played and all totals career highs. Goal output doubled over previous season. Led team in goals.

THE FINESSE GAME

Reichel's pursuit of loose pucks has improved. He wants and needs the puck, especially down low where he is extremely dangerous. He is a threat off the rush, but he is more effective in working out turn-backs from behind the net. He is not very fast, but he's quick in small spaces.

He has an explosive shot. For a smallish player, he puts a lot of velocity on the shot, and he is quick and accurate in its release. He does not shoot enough, but he is so creative with the puck that his playmaking can be as effective as his shot.

Reichel played with Jaromir Jagr and Bobby Holik in Czechoslovakia — talk about a dream line — and showed good chemistry with Theo Fleury last season. Since neither player is big or physical, the Flames are hunting for a big dude to handle the left side. If they do, this will be a devastating trio.

Reichel needs consistency and has to pay more attention to his defense.

THE PHYSICAL GAME

Reichel did not come to training camp in top physical condition, and before this season was never one to stay late on the ice for extra practice. When he was playing in Czechoslovakia, he was one of the stars and averaged 35 minutes per game. In breaking into the NHL, he worked on the third or fourth line, and that took some adjustment.

Reichel will take a hit to make the play, but he tries to stay out of high-contact zones.

THE INTANGIBLES

Reichel was benched around Game 20 and responded the way the coaches hoped, by playing strong two-way hockey. He has the potential to improve even more, although it is doubtful he will be a franchise player. He lacks the size and the dedication.

Success shouldn't make Reichel relax, but instead spur him to accomplish even more. He cannot step back. If he continues to show the same drive he did last season, the results will come. He could be a 100-point scorer.

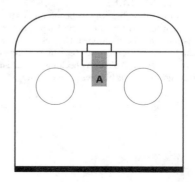

GARY ROBERTS

Yrs. of NHL service: 6
Born: North York, Ont.; May 23, 1966
Position: left wing
Height: 6-1
Weight: 190
Uniform no.: 10
Shoots: left

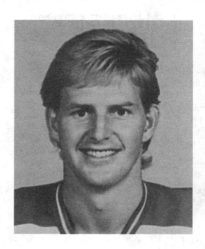

Career statistics:

GP	G	A	TP	PIM
469	192	183	375	1482

1991-92 statistics:

GP	G	A	TP	+/-	PIM	PP	SH	GW	GT	S	PCT
76	53	37	90	+32	219	15	0	2	3	196	27.0

1992-93 statistics:

GP	G	A	TP	+/-	PIM	PP	SH	GW	GT	S	PCT
58	38	41	79	+32	172	8	3	4	2	166	22.9

LAST SEASON

Led team in plus/minus and shooting percentage. Missed 26 games with quadricep injury. Games played career low since rookie season in 1986-87.

THE FINESSE GAME

Roberts has excellent hands and instincts around the net. He works hard for loose pucks, and when he gets control, he wastes little time trying to do anything fancy. As soon as the puck is on his blade, it's launched toward the net. He is not very creative with the puck as a playmaker, either. His theory is throw it in front and see what happens. Frequently, he creates something good.

Roberts is not a very agile skater, and his thigh injury did nothing to help him in this area. He can beat the defender one on one on the occasional rush, powered by his strong stride and his ability to handle the puck at a fair pace.

Roberts sees the ice well and will spot an open teammate for a smart pass. He forechecks well and creates turnovers with his persistent work. A scary sight when he's bearing down on a defenseman, Roberts will force many a hurried pass.

THE PHYSICAL GAME

Roberts has worked hard for his NHL success. In addition to the thigh injury that jeopardized his career, he has battled asthma. For Roberts, hockey is a job that lasts 12 months. He works on conditioning and nutrition, and the results have paid off on the ice.

He is strong and determined around the net. He creates a lot of room with his physical play and is respected around the league for his toughness. He works the boards and corners, and wins most of his battles.

THE INTANGIBLES

Roberts is the best on-ice leader on the Flames. He reformed himself from a pure goon into one of the

NHL's premier power forwards. A healthy Roberts should flirt with the 100-point mark this season.

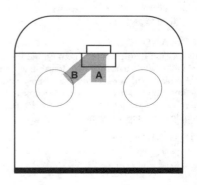

RONNIE STERN

Yrs. of NHL service: 4
Born: Ste-Agathe, Que.; Jan. 11, 1967
Position: right wing
Height: 6-0
Weight: 195
Uniform no.: 22
Shoots: right

Career statistics:

GP	G	A	TP	PIM
252	29	33	62	1094

1991-92 statistics:

GP	G	A	TP	+/-	PIM	PP	SH	GW	GT	S	PCT
72	13	9	22	0	338	0	1	1	0	96	13.5

1992-93 statistics:

GP	G	A	TP	+/-	PIM	PP	SH	GW	GT	S	PCT
70	10	15	25	+4	207	0	0	1	0	82	12.2

LAST SEASON

PIM three-season low. Assists career high. Missed 11 games with injuries.

THE FINESSE GAME

Stern is a rugged, seek-and-destroy missile with modest skills. He is not a pretty skater or a good shooter, but he has the offensive instincts to make some smart plays in the attacking zone. He has some quickness to the puck to get a jump on the defender, and looks for help from his linemates. He will drive to the net and create his scoring chances off his physical involvement in front of the net.

Stern doesn't become mesmerized with the puck. He doesn't make many pretty plays, but instead looks to get rid of the puck quickly with a pass or a shot.

Stern would be ideally suited as a checking winger but for his lack of skating ability. He also isn't as alert defensively as offensively, but he works hard at whatever task he is given.

THE PHYSICAL GAME

Stern has no fear of anyone or any situation. He never bails out of a corner no matter what's coming. He's willing and able to go toe to toe with anybody. Playing on a checking line with Joel Otto, Stern is defensively aware and finishes every check. He will be on the ice at crunch time to protect a lead.

THE INTANGIBLES

Stern's mission is to get momentum on the Flames' side. He may be the most effective fourth-liner in the game. He plays with a sense of purpose now, and by cutting down on bad penalties he has become a more effective player. He just doesn't have the finishing skills to do much more than net 10 to 15 goals a season.

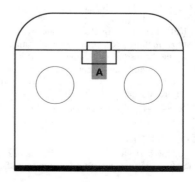

GARY SUTER

Yrs. of NHL service: 8
Born: Madison, Wisc.; June 24, 1964
Position: left defense
Height: 6-0
Weight: 190
Uniform no.: 20
Shoots: left

Career statistics:

GP	G	A	TP	PIM
592	124	428	552	850

1991-92 statistics:

GP	G	A	TP	+/-	PIM	PP	SH	GW	GT	S	PCT
70	12	43	55	+1	126	4	0	0	0	189	6.3

1992-93 statistics:

GP	G	A	TP	+/-	PIM	PP	SH	GW	GT	S	PCT
81	23	58	81	-1	112	10	1	2	1	263	8.7

LAST SEASON

Third on team in points. Led team defensemen in scoring. Led team in shots. Second on team in assists. Goals at career high.

THE FINESSE GAME

Suter has great natural skills, starting with his skating. He is secure on his skates with a wide stance for balance. He has all of the components that make a great skater: acceleration, flat-out speed, quickness and mobility. He skates well backwards and can't be bested one on one except by the slickest skaters. He loves to jump into the attack, and he will key a rush with a smooth outlet pass or carry the puck and lead the parade.

Suter has a superb shot. It's not as vicious as that of his power play partner, Al MacInnis, but Suter will keep his shot low. His first priority is to feed the puck to MacInnis, and Suter is a better quarterback. He will shoot or set up a MacInnis one-timer.

Suter is not a great playmaker. His creativity comes from his speed and his dangerous shot. He saw some penalty-killing time, although it is not his strong suit.

THE PHYSICAL GAME

Suter averaged around 30 minutes per game and held up under the grind. He is a mean hitter (it was his check in the 1991 Canada Cup that was the source of Wayne Gretzky's back troubles). He can get too carried away with the hitting game and will take himself out of position, even when penalty-killing. He doesn't like to be hit, and he'll bring his stick up at the last second before contact to protect himself. His defensive reads are average to fair, and he doesn't play hard consistently, although he did a better job last season than he has in years.

THE INTANGIBLES

Under new coach Dave King, Suter bloomed again, and those annual trade whispers were silenced. With Al MacInnis sidelined for almost half of the season by injury, Suter took on the added offensive responsibility and was a top-level defenseman.

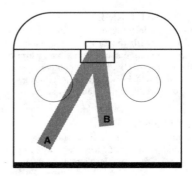

MIKE VERNON

Yrs. of NHL service: 8
Born: Calgary, Alta.; Feb. 24, 1963
Position: goaltender
Height: 5-9
Weight: 170
Uniform no.: 30
Catches: left

Career statistics:

GP	MINS	GA	SO	GAA	A	PIM
419	23,780	1323	6	3.34	30	162

1991-92 statistics:

GP	MINS	GAA	W	L	T	SO	GA	S	SAPCT	PIM
63	3640	3.58	24	30	9	0	217	1853	.883	8

1992-93 statistics:

GP	MINS	GAA	W	L	T	SO	GA	S	SAPCT	PIM
64	3732	3.26	29	26	9	2	203	1804	.887	42

LAST SEASON

Seventh consecutive season with 20 or more wins. Missed five games with hand injury.

THE PHYSICAL GAME

As Vernon gets older, he has to rely more on his angle play than his reflexes, and technique was never the best part of his game. He has a very quick glove hand, and he does a good job of setting himself to tempt the shooter to try for the top right corner. Now they are beating him there more often than they did in the past.

Vernon is aggressive, and at the top of his game he is on the top of his crease, trying to make his small body look bigger. He forces the shooter to make a quick decision. He is a good skater from post to post. He doesn't venture out of his net much to handle the puck. Fortunately for him, Calgary has traditionally had good skaters and puckhandlers in its defense corps.

Vernon does use his stick well to break up plays around the net, cutting off low passes and sweeping his stick at a forward trying to come out from behind the net.

He recovers fairly well for a second shot. His reflexes just seem a tad slower than they were two years ago.

THE MENTAL GAME

A contract battle hung over Vernon this season, which, along with the fatigue of a team record 27-game consecutive starts streak, wore him down mentally and physically. His competitive edge seems to be dulling, and he will have to come back off damage to his right ankle ligaments, suffered during the playoffs.

THE INTANGIBLES

Vernon missed the deciding game of the playoffs with an ankle injury, and he had a subpar season, suffering through an 11-game winless streak (0-9-2) in mid-season. He is likely in his last season as a No. 1 goalie and will either be dealt or will work backup to one of two hotshot prospects, Trevor Kidd or Alexei Trefilov.

TRENT YAWNEY

Yrs. of NHL service: 5
Born: Hudson Bay, Sask.; Sept. 29, 1965
Position: left defense
Height: 6-3
Weight: 192
Uniform no.: 18
Shoots: left

Career statistics:

GP	G	A	TP	PIM
325	20	80	100	402

1991-92 statistics:

GP	G	A	TP	+/-	PIM	PP	SH	GW	GT	S	PCT
47	4	9	13	-5	45	1	0	0	0	33	12.1

1992-93 statistics:

GP	G	A	TP	+/-	PIM	PP	SH	GW	GT	S	PCT
63	1	16	17	+9	67	0	0	0	0	61	1.6

LAST SEASON

Goals career low. Assists most since rookie season in 1988-89. Missed 20 games with injury to clavicle.

THE FINESSE GAME

Yawney does a nice job when he has time with the puck, like on the power play, but under pressure he is just as likely to throw a blind pass or just get rid of the puck.

　　When he works the point, he is clever enough to make a shot/pass wide of the net to where a teammate is standing for a redirect. It may look like he's misfiring, but it's an intentional play, and an effective one.

　　Yawney is a heady player defensively and is conscious of playing his position, but he still gets beaten because he plays soft. He is a good skater, but none of his finesse skills are outstanding.

THE PHYSICAL GAME

Yawney plays much, much smaller than his size. He gets in the way of people in the defensive zone, but doesn't hit or tie up the attackers efficiently. As a result, forwards — even smaller ones — skate through his zone with impunity, and his defensive partner will often come over to support him physically, leaving an outnumbered situation in an area of the attacking zone.

THE INTANGIBLES

Yawney played his best hockey for Dave King on the Canadian Olympic team, and he performed fairly well when his coach came to Calgary last season. However, the same problem plagues Yawney now as it has throughout his career: he doesn't have sufficient offensive skill to compensate for his lack of physical play. He will never be more than a fifth or sixth defenseman.

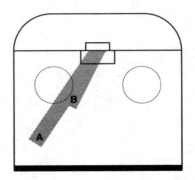

CHICAGO BLACKHAWKS

ED BELFOUR

Yrs. of NHL service: 3
Born: Carman, Man.; Apr. 21, 1965
Position: goaltender
Height: 5-11
Weight: 182
Uniform no.: 30
Catches: left

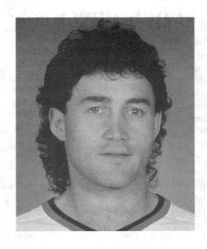

Career statistics:

GP	MINS	GA	SO	GAA	A	PIM
220	12,312	553	16	2.69	6	108

1991-92 statistics:

GP	MINS	GAA	W	L	T	SO	GA	S	SAPCT	PIM
52	2928	2.70	21	18	10	5	132	1241	.894	40

1992-93 statistics:

GP	MINS	GAA	W	L	T	SO	GA	S	SAPCT	PIM
71	4106	2.59	41	18	11	7	177	1880	.906	28

LAST SEASON

Second-lowest GAA in NHL. Second-most wins in NHL. Save percentage third in NHL. Career-high shutouts led league. Finalist for Vezina Trophy.

THE PHYSICAL GAME

There seem to be a lot of goalies who are succeeding with playing styles not to be found in any how-to manual, and Belfour is at the head of their class.

Belfour has great instincts and reads the play well in front of him. He plays with an inverted V, giving the five-hole but then taking it away from the shooter with his quick reflexes. He is very aggressive and frequently comes so far out of his crease that he gets into tangles with his own defenders — as well as running interference on the opponents. He knows he is well-padded and is not afraid to use his body.

Even though Belfour is not very big, he seems to take away a lot of the net from the shooter, even when he drops down quickly, as he has a penchant for doing. He will give away the top corners and dare the shooter to be pinpoint-accurate, since it's the toughest spot to hit. Belfour drops to his knees often but is seldom on his side and out of play.

He sometimes gives up bad rebounds, but his defense is so good and so quick that they will swoop in on the puck before the offense gets a second or third whack. When play is developing around his net, Belfour uses the odd-looking tactic of dropping his stick low along the ice to take away low shots and lunges at the puck. It's weird, but it works.

Belfour has a lot of confidence and an impressive ability to handle the puck, although he sometimes overdoes it. He will usually go for short passes but can go for the home-run play as well. He uses his body to screen as he is handling the puck for a 15-foot pass.

THE MENTAL GAME

Belfour is a fierce competitor and keeps himself in good condition so that he can play often. He is the undisputed No. 1 goalie in Chicago, which has had two promising young goalies in its system (Dominik Hasek and Jimmy Waite), neither of whom had a prayer of challenging Belfour for the job.

Belfour has few quiet games. He is so involved physically that it has a visible effect on his teammates. He also has a temper, as he displayed when he began an early demolition of the Blues' arena after the Hawks were stunned in four straight by St. Louis.

THE INTANGIBLES

Belfour doesn't get the credit he feels he deserves, but let's face it, Tom Barrasso doesn't either, and he has two Cup rings. Belfour has the no-win situation of playing behind a strong defense, so everyone says the credit belongs to the team instead of the goalie. The two obviously go hand in hand. He wouldn't be as good without them, and the Hawks wouldn't be the team they are without Belfour.

CHRIS CHELIOS

Yrs. of NHL service: 9
Born: Chicago, Ill.; Jan. 25, 1962
Position: right defense
Height: 6-1
Weight: 186
Uniform no.: 7
Shoots: right

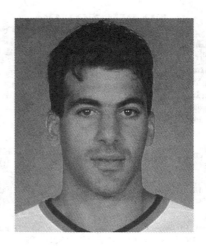

Career statistics:

GP	G	A	TP	PIM
643	108	394	502	1502

1991-92 statistics:

GP	G	A	TP	+/-	PIM	PP	SH	GW	GT	S	PCT
80	9	47	56	+24	245	2	2	2	1	239	3.8

1992-93 statistics:

GP	G	A	TP	+/-	PIM	PP	SH	GW	GT	S	PCT
84	15	58	73	+14	282	8	0	2	0	290	5.2

LAST SEASON

One of five Blackhawks to appear in all 84 games. Did not miss a game for second consecutive season. Second on team in scoring. Led team in assists, matching career high. Led team in shots. Second on team in PIM with career high. Norris Trophy finalist.

THE FINESSE GAME

Chelios is an instinctive player. When he is on his game, he reacts and makes plays few other defensemen can. When he struggles, which is seldom, he is back on his heels. He tries to do other people's jobs and becomes undisciplined.

Chelios is among the top two-way defensemen in the league. Whatever the team needs, they will get from Chelios. He can become a top offensive defenseman, pinching boldly at every opportunity. He can create offense off the rush, make a play through the neutral zone or quarterback the power play from the point. He has a good, low, hard slapshot (it was clocked as the fastest in the Campbell Conference in the preliminaries for the All-Star Game skills competition). Chelios is not afraid to skate in deep, where he can handle the puck well and use a snap shot or wrist shot with a quick release.

If defense is needed, Chelios will rule in his own zone. He is extremely confident and poised with the puck and doesn't overhandle it. He wants to get the puck away from his net by the most expedient means possible. He is aggressive in forcing the puck carrier to make a decision by stepping up.

Chelios has excellent anticipation and is a strong penalty killer when he's not doing time in the box himself. He's a mobile, smooth skater with good lateral movement. He is seldom beaten one on one, and he's even tough facing a two on one. In his mind, he can do anything. He usually does.

THE PHYSICAL GAME

Chelios doesn't seem to tire, no matter how much ice time he gets, and he gets plenty. He is tough and physical, strong and solid on his skates, and has a mean streak the size of Lake Michigan. He plays very strong in front of the net for someone who is considered primarily an offensive defenseman.

It's small wonder Chicago was the most penalized team in the league last season when their team leader was the brash and chippy Chelios. A little more restraint in this area would better serve Chelios and his teammates, but hey, look at all the practice time the penalty killers get.

THE INTANGIBLES

Chelios knows how much the Hawks rely on him, and he relishes his leadership role. He is among the league's elite defensemen and has been for a number of years. Now his only goal is to lead the Hawks to the Stanley Cup, as he helped do in Montreal. But the Canadiens weren't Chelios's team. The Blackhawks are.

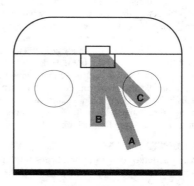

GREG GILBERT

Yrs. of NHL service: 11
Born: Mississauga, Ont.; Jan. 22, 1962
Position: left wing
Height: 6-1
Weight: 190
Uniform no.: 14
Shoots: left

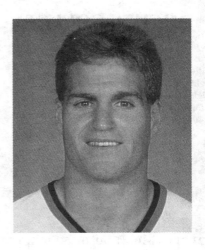

Career statistics:

GP	G	A	TP	PIM
698	135	202	337	528

1991-92 statistics:

GP	G	A	TP	+/-	PIM	PP	SH	GW	GT	S	PCT
50	7	5	12	+4	35	0	0	1	0	45	15.6

1992-93 statistics:

GP	G	A	TP	+/-	PIM	PP	SH	GW	GT	S	PCT
77	13	19	32	+5	57	0	1	2	0	72	18.1

LAST SEASON

Games played highest since 1983-84. Points three-season high.

THE FINESSE GAME

Gilbert complements almost any kind of line, although the offensive part of his game has withered. That is either from atrophy as he has concentrated more and more on his defensive role in recent seasons, or from loss of hand quickness, as Gilbert is now 31.

Gilbert is reliable in all three zones. He is a diligent forechecker, making the dump-and-chase play work because he is pursuing with all due speed and hunger. He will be back in the defensive zone, and has good hands and anticipation to break up plays, and sufficient quickness to sprint the puck out of danger. He does not have end-to-end speed, but he's agile.

Gilbert's goals come from close range. He is poised with the puck in deep and has quick enough hands to do something useful with the puck in traffic, whether he uses a wrist shot or makes a goal-mouth pass.

THE PHYSICAL GAME

Gilbert plays a very physical game, earning his living by throwing his body around in the corners, along the boards and in front of the net. He will not be intimidated, and he protects the puck at all costs. He takes great pride in his defensive game and pays the price.

THE INTANGIBLES

Gilbert is an honest third-line, checking winger. His work ethic is unquestioned, and he is a great character player to have on a team or in a dressing room.

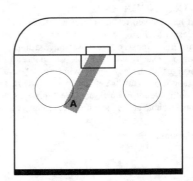

MICHEL GOULET

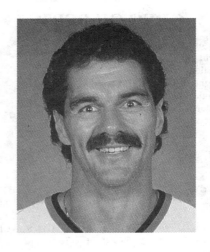

Yrs. of NHL service: 14
Born: Péribonka, Que.; Apr. 21, 1960
Position: left wing
Height: 6-1
Weight: 195
Uniform no.: 16
Shoots: left

Career statistics:

GP	G	A	TP	PIM
1033	532	610	1122	797

1991-92 statistics:

GP	G	A	TP	+/-	PIM	PP	SH	GW	GT	S	PCT
75	22	41	63	+20	69	9	0	4	0	176	12.5

1992-93 statistics:

GP	G	A	TP	+/-	PIM	PP	SH	GW	GT	S	PCT
63	23	21	44	+10	41	10	0	5	0	125	18.4

LAST SEASON

Reached 1000-game milestone. Scored 20 or more goals in his 14th consecutive season.

THE FINESSE GAME

Goulet has lost some quickness, some of his scoring touch and some durability. He no longer has the jump to get to the right spot for a scoring opportunity, and he is no longer effective as an offensive threat.

Goulet works hard on his defense, and since he was once a one-way offensive player, it doesn't come very naturally to him. He could be an average two-way player, but he would have to produce more to be a good one, and we think he's very near the end of the line.

He can still function as a power play specialist. He likes to stand off to the side of the net, and move in at the right moment for a tip or reach in with his stick.

THE PHYSICAL GAME

The years have taken their toll on Goulet. He has always gone into congested areas and bumped and scraped for the loose pucks or to get into position in front of the goalie. He is not very strong and doesn't dominate anyone physically.

THE INTANGIBLES

Goulet has adapted to the role of a defensive player but doesn't seem to be a real defensive specialist. Without his offensive threat, we have a hard time figuring out exactly what his role is supposed to be. He survives as the No. 1 left wing by default, but when (and if) the Hawks get someone to play that position with Jeremy Roenick and Joe Murphy, Goulet may have trouble getting ice time. He remains a classy individual.

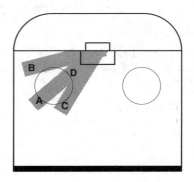

DIRK GRAHAM

Yrs. of NHL service: 9
Born: Regina, Sask.; July 29, 1959
Position: right wing
Height: 5-11
Weight: 198
Uniform no.: 33
Shoots: right

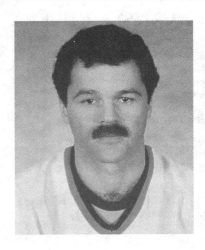

Career statistics:

GP	G	A	TP	PIM
665	200	242	442	827

1991-92 statistics:

GP	G	A	TP	+/-	PIM	PP	SH	GW	GT	S	PCT
80	17	30	47	-5	89	6	1	1	0	222	7.7

1992-93 statistics:

GP	G	A	TP	+/-	PIM	PP	SH	GW	GT	S	PCT
84	20	17	37	0	141	1	2	5	1	187	10.7

LAST SEASON

Reached 20-goal mark for seventh season. One of five Blackhawks to appear in all 84 games. Has not missed a game in the past three seasons.

THE FINESSE GAME

Graham is the ideal two-way, checking forward. No matter who the opponent is, you can throw Graham's line at them and get a top-level performance.

Offensively, Graham is a blue collar Tony Granato, although his hands aren't quite as deft. He is always on the move, poking and jabbing for the puck. He creates scoring chances from this pressure, and he has the hands, head and poise to make the smart play once he does win the battle for the puck.

Graham's end-to-end speed is good, and he can take charge of a shift. He is a powerful skater with good balance, and it suits his penalty-killing work. He is a threat to score on shorthanded breakaways.

He is a very honest player who plays with physical prowess and intensity. He has the knack for big goals. Perimeter players get the softer goals, but when the going gets tough, it is the battlers like Graham who net the important ones.

THE PHYSICAL GAME

Graham plays with guts and grit. He does the dirty work in the trenches and doesn't think twice before making a play that he knows is going to hurt either him or the player on the receiving end. He doesn't take bad penalties, but he draws time in the box because he always keeps his legs driving to the net and forces defenders to haul him down.

THE INTANGIBLES

Graham is a team leader who stands up to or for his teammates and even confronts his coaches if he believes in the cause. He has made his way through the NHL the hard way and is very well respected by coaches and players around the league. It's why he retains the captaincy even with leaders like Chris Chelios and Brent Sutter on the team. Graham deserves it.

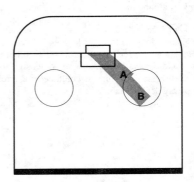

FRANTISEK KUCERA

Yrs. of NHL service: 3
Born: Prague, Czechoslovakia; Feb. 3, 1968
Position: left defense
Height: 6-2
Weight: 205
Uniform no.: 6
Shoots: left

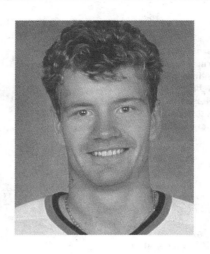

Career statistics:

GP	G	A	TP	PIM
172	10	36	46	127

1991-92 statistics:

GP	G	A	TP	+/-	PIM	PP	SH	GW	GT	S	PCT
61	3	10	13	+3	36	1	0	1	0	82	3.7

1992-93 statistics:

GP	G	A	TP	+/-	PIM	PP	SH	GW	GT	S	PCT
71	5	14	19	+7	59	1	0	1	0	117	4.3

LAST SEASON
Games played, goals, assists and points at career highs.

THE FINESSE GAME
Kucera seems to be a *nouvelle cuisine* skater on a meat-and-potatoes team. Offensively, he's always looking to make a fancy play at the blue line, when the Blackhawks' style is to make the basic play. He doesn't want to play dump and chase, and Chicago thrives on it. There are times when he doesn't seem used to the pinching game Chicago plays.

Kucera is a very good skater for a big player. He can handle the puck well on the move and can carry it deep and make a nice backhand pass for the trailing player.

Defensively, his skating makes it very difficult for the opposition to outmanoeuvre him one on one or anywhere in open ice. He sends a nice breakout pass out of the defensive zone, which he prefers to trying to carry the puck out.

THE PHYSICAL GAME
Kucera has to develop more consistency in his physical game. He is a good-sized defenseman who plays smaller, and he loses many of the one-on-one confrontations around the net.

THE INTANGIBLES
Since Kucera does not have the high skill level to be a defenseman whose forte is offense, he has to become stronger and cement his game in the defensive zone. He is worth watching, since he could become a reliable two-way defenseman.

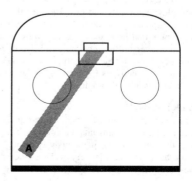

STEVE LARMER

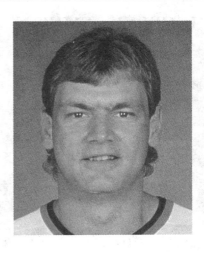

Yrs. of NHL service: 11
Born: Peterborough, Ont.; June 16, 1961
Position: right wing
Height: 5-11
Weight: 189
Uniform no.: 28
Shoots: left

Career statistics:

GP	G	A	TP	PIM
891	406	517	923	475

1991-92 statistics:

GP	G	A	TP	+/-	PIM	PP	SH	GW	GT	S	PCT
80	29	45	74	+10	65	11	2	3	0	292	9.9

1992-93 statistics:

GP	G	A	TP	+/-	PIM	PP	SH	GW	GT	S	PCT
84	35	35	70	+23	48	14	4	6	1	228	15.4

LAST SEASON

Consecutive games played streak reached 884 (and counting). One of five Blackhawks to appear in all 84 games. Led team in plus/minus, shorthanded goals and game-winning goals. Marked 11th consecutive season with 20 or more goals.

THE FINESSE GAME

Larmer struggled a bit at times during the season, when his play around the net seemed just out of synch. He wasn't hitting the holes at the right time: he seemed to be either two feet ahead of the play or two feet behind it.

For most of his career, Larmer has been among the most reliable and, of course, durable players in the league. He has great one-step quickness, which he can turn into a rink-long rush, then stop and start and tie a defenseman into a knot. And he can do it all with the puck.

Larmer is honest offensively and reliable defensively. He is an intelligent player in all zones. His hand-eye co-ordination is excellent. Not only is he quick enough to tip pucks, but he tips them as if he controls where they're going, which very few players can do. He has a good shot and plays the power play well, working down low, although he lost his spot on the No. 1 unit with the arrival of Joe Murphy. Larmer is a challenging threat for any defender, as he is a good-skating right wing with a left-handed shot. His slap and snap shots are threatening. He will look low and fire high to deceive the goalie.

THE PHYSICAL GAME

Larmer can get feisty and has earned himself some room through his career. He plays every game hard, checking in the corners and making take-out checks. It's amazing that someone who plays as energetically as Larmer does, shift after shift, has played so long without missing a game due to injury. It's a mystery to us and a credit to him.

THE INTANGIBLES

Larmer was nearly benched twice during the season, which would have put an end to the Iron Man streak. That might not be such a bad idea, since the stress of the streak might be grating on his nerves a bit. He will probably lose his spot on the top line this season, and his production could slip dramatically.

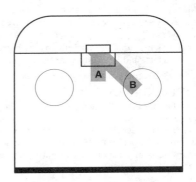

JOCELYN LEMIEUX

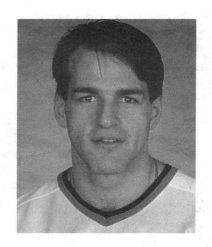

Yrs. of NHL service: 6
Born: Mont-Laurier, Que.; Nov. 18, 1967
Position: right wing
Height: 5-10
Weight: 200
Uniform no.: 26
Shoots: left

Career statistics:

GP	G	A	TP	PIM
376	47	60	107	554

1991-92 statistics:

GP	G	A	TP	+/-	PIM	PP	SH	GW	GT	S	PCT
78	6	10	16	-2	80	0	0	1	0	103	5.8

1992-93 statistics:

GP	G	A	TP	+/-	PIM	PP	SH	GW	GT	S	PCT
81	10	21	31	+5	111	1	0	2	1	117	8.5

LAST SEASON

Assists and points at career highs. Goals matched career high.

THE FINESSE GAME

Lemieux starts things with his body and finishes with his hands. Power forwards are all the rage in the NHL these days, and though Lemieux lacks the instincts to be among the best of them, he can do a pretty credible job around the net. He thrashes and bashes, and when he gets the puck he can turn into a finesse player, feathering passes to teammates or making a quick shot. Lemieux is not coy. His theory is that the shortest distance between two points means eliminating one of the points, which he usually does with a flattening check.

Lemieux skates with short, powerful strides. He is very well balanced and does not get knocked off the puck easily. He has good end-to-end speed but is not real fancy and doesn't have a very clever head.

His quick little strides serve him well along the boards and in the corners, and he keeps driving through traffic. He has a good wrist and snap shot.

THE PHYSICAL GAME

Lemieux is a bulldog with the puck or without it. He has little regard for his physical safety or, it seems, his lifespan, as he fearlessly throws himself in the face of bigger players with even meaner reputations than his.

Lemieux knows that physical play is the biggest part of his game, and he brings it to the ice almost every night.

THE INTANGIBLES

While he has not made the name his brother Claude has, this Lemieux is more consistently feisty and physical than his older sibling. He is a power forward who is improving, but 20 to 25 goals would be a career year. He is much more fun to play with than against.

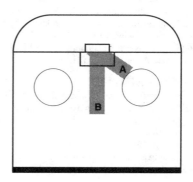

BRYAN MARCHMENT

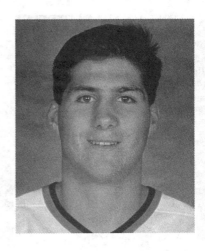

Yrs. of NHL service: 3
Born: Toronto, Ont.; May 1, 1969
Position: left defense
Height: 6-1
Weight: 200
Uniform no.: 2
Shoots: left

Career statistics:

GP	G	A	TP	PIM
173	12	29	41	602

1991-92 statistics:

GP	G	A	TP	+/-	PIM	PP	SH	GW	GT	S	PCT
58	5	10	15	-4	168	2	0	0	0	55	9.1

1992-93 statistics:

GP	G	A	TP	+/-	PIM	PP	SH	GW	GT	S	PCT
78	5	15	20	+15	313	1	0	1	0	75	6.7

LAST SEASON

Led team in PIM. Games played, PIM, assists and points at career highs.

THE FINESSE GAME

Marchment was counted on a lot by Chicago last season, and he responded. He is fearless in the sense that he will try anything, and will keep trying until he eventually gets it right and the skill becomes second nature to him. He plays as if nothing he does comes easily for him, but at least you get the sense of a player who is making an effort and trying to improve.

Marchment has fair skating ability and sometimes tries to do too much. He will step up aggressively into the neutral zone, which the Hawks like their defensemen to do. He is also a competent enough skater to join in the rush. He has a quick release on his snap shot and can drill a one-timer.

There is one more level for Marchment to attain, and that is where the question of his head for the game comes in. He is not always consistent.

Marchment will do a few dumb things. He gets tunnel vision with the puck in his own zone, and sees only the first receiver, not the second. He will use a hard pass when a soft one would do, and vice versa. But he can skate and handle the puck on the blue line, and can work himself into a pretty good defenseman.

THE PHYSICAL GAME

Marchment is a big open-ice hitter. He eagerly plays the physical game and loves to hear the boards rattle. He is not a well-balanced skater and sometimes loses one-on-one battles that he should be winning. He seems strong through the upper body, so some lower body work might help.

THE INTANGIBLES

Marchment has stepped up his game to the point where he might be the best defenseman on the team behind the top pairing of Chris Chelios and Steve Smith. It has taken him some time to develop, as it often does with defensemen (especially large ones, of whom so much is expected), and Marchment has gotten better every season.

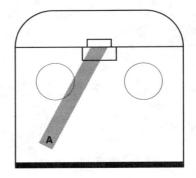

STEPHANE MATTEAU

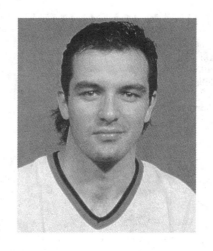

Yrs. of NHL service: 3
Born: Rouyn-Noranda, Que.; Sept. 2, 1969
Position: left wing
Height: 6-3
Weight: 195
Uniform no.: 32
Shoots: left

Career statistics:

GP	G	A	TP	PIM
181	36	45	81	255

1991-92 statistics:

GP	G	A	TP	+/-	PIM	PP	SH	GW	GT	S	PCT
24	6	8	14	+5	64	1	0	0	0	38	15.8

1992-93 statistics:

GP	G	A	TP	+/-	PIM	PP	SH	GW	GT	S	PCT
79	15	18	33	+6	98	2	0	4	0	95	15.8

LAST SEASON

Games played and assists at career highs.

THE FINESSE GAME

Matteau is a power forward without hands and without intensity on a nightly basis. He shows good hustle and always works hard to get into scoring position in front of the net, but he doesn't have the touch to finish off the play.

Matteau can play either wing, but neither side very well. It's his effort that keeps him in the line-up. Coaches keep looking at Matteau and thinking Kevin Stevens, but all they get is...Matteau. He's not a very threatening offensive force.

Not a very pretty skater, he's coming off an injury from the 1991-92 season involving a calcification in his left thigh that sidelined him for most of that year.

THE PHYSICAL GAME

Matteau is big and strong, but nowhere near as physical as he has to be. His size almost demands that he be more involved, but he seldom is.

THE INTANGIBLES

He hasn't established a specialty that makes him unique. He plays a conservative game, but when other teams prepare to play Chicago, no one spends much time worrying about how to play against him. At this stage, he is a nonentity.

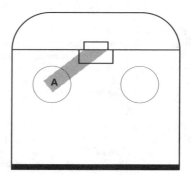

JOE MURPHY

Yrs. of NHL service: 6
Born: London, Ont.; Oct. 16, 1967
Position: right wing
Height: 6-1
Weight: 190
Uniform no.: 17
Shoots: left

Career statistics:

GP	G	A	TP	PIM
331	90	92	182	232

1991-92 statistics:

GP	G	A	TP	+/-	PIM	PP	SH	GW	GT	S	PCT
80	35	47	82	+17	52	10	2	2	2	193	18.1

1992-93 statistics:

GP	G	A	TP	+/-	PIM	PP	SH	GW	GT	S	PCT
19	7	10	17	-3	18	5	0	1	0	43	16.3

LAST SEASON

Games played four-season low. Held out most of season until trade from Edmonton to Chicago for Igor Kravchuk and Dean McAmmond.

THE FINESSE GAME

Murphy has tremendous speed and great hands. His timing was obviously off in his brief stint at the end of the season, but judging from his performance of a season ago with the Oilers, he is a bona fide NHL scorer.

Murphy creates off the forecheck and has confidence with the puck. He is sometimes too selfish, single-minded when he has made the decision to shoot even when a better option to pass suddenly presents itself.

Murphy has a lot of zip on his slap and wrist shots. He gets both away quickly and through a crowd, and he's been a high-percentage shooter through much of his career.

Murphy is fairly keen defensively and can kill penalties and take defensive zone draws. The knock on him in the past has been his inconsistency.

THE PHYSICAL GAME

Murphy makes the pre-emptive hits when going for the puck in the corners — which is a nice way of saying he takes a lot of interference calls. He will use his size and strength in front of the net to establish position, and he'll fight along the wall and in the corners. He's not a big banger or crasher, but he does have a nasty streak.

THE INTANGIBLES

The Hawks paid a steep price to get Murphy, as Kravchuk is a player of some promise and McAmmond was a first-round draft pick. If Murphy can add the depth the Hawks so desperately need up front, he will be worth it. He was a non-factor in the playoffs, but that had more to do with him missing three-quarters of the season than any defect in his game. A 35- to 40-goal season should be his payoff this year once he is back in condition.

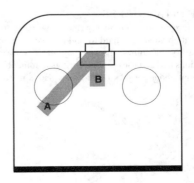

BRIAN NOONAN

Yrs. of NHL service: 4
Born: Boston, Mass.; May 29, 1965
Position: right wing
Height: 6-1
Weight: 192
Uniform no.: 10
Shoots: right

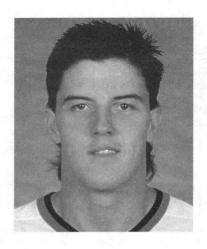

Career statistics:

GP	G	A	TP	PIM
265	49	64	113	243

1991-92 statistics:

GP	G	A	TP	+/-	PIM	PP	SH	GW	GT	S	PCT
65	19	12	31	+9	81	4	0	0	2	154	12.3

1992-93 statistics:

GP	G	A	TP	+/-	PIM	PP	SH	GW	GT	S	PCT
63	16	14	30	+3	82	5	0	3	0	129	12.4

LAST SEASON

Missed games with right shoulder injury.

THE FINESSE GAME

Noonan has some slick moves in front of the net and a quick release, but he often rushes his shots and misses the net more than he should for someone who is usually shooting from close range. He is a very streaky scorer, but there are long droughts between his goal-scoring outbursts.

He has lot of finesse skills. He is very creative and sneaky, and is a very shifty skater who can come at a defenseman at a snail's pace, then suddenly hop around and drive to the net. Once he gets there, though, he doesn't do much damage.

Noonan doesn't have very good vision of the ice, missing obvious passing options, and he doesn't know when to zip a pass hard or feather it.

THE PHYSICAL GAME

Noonan is not very strong and doesn't have much zest for a physical game. There will be the odd night when he competes, but he doesn't do it on a consistent basis. It's rare to find a player on the Blackhawks with as little interest in the hitting game as Noonan. He finishes checks but finishes them lightly.

THE INTANGIBLES

Nothing about Noonan's game is worth getting worked up about. It's hard to find a player with more versatility than him — he can play all three forward positions and defense — which brings to mind the old chestnut about the jack of all trades. He is master of none.

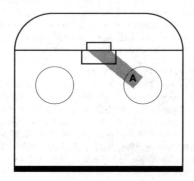

JEREMY ROENICK

Yrs. of NHL service: 5
Born: Boston, Mass.; Jan. 17, 1970
Position: centre
Height: 6-0
Weight: 200
Uniform no.: 27
Shoots: right

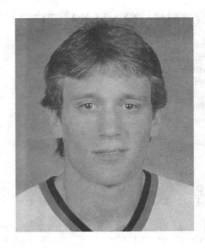

Career statistics:

GP	G	A	TP	PIM
341	179	209	388	322

1991-92 statistics:

GP	G	A	TP	+/-	PIM	PP	SH	GW	GT	S	PCT
80	53	50	103	+23	98	22	3	13	0	234	22.6

1992-93 statistics:

GP	G	A	TP	+/-	PIM	PP	SH	GW	GT	S	PCT
84	50	57	107	+15	86	22	3	3	3	255	19.6

LAST SEASON

Led team in goals, assists, points, power play goals and shooting percentage. Second consecutive season with 50 or more goals and 100 or more points. One of five Blackhawks to appear in all 84 games.

THE FINESSE GAME

Roenick is driven by an overwhelming desire to succeed. He has a palpable fear of not being respected or considered a winner. That fear pushes him to the max, every shift, every night.

Roenick has great quickness and is tough to handle one on one. He won't make the same move or take the same shot twice in a row. He has a variety of shots and can score from almost anywhere on the ice. He is strong and can rifle a wrist shot from 30 feet away, or else wait until the goalie is down and lift in a backhand from in tight.

Roenick commands a lot of attention when he is on the ice. He has great acceleration. He can turn quickly, change directions, or burn a defender with outside speed. A defenseman who plays aggressively against him will be left staring at the back of Roenick's jersey as he skips by en route to the net. Roenick has to be forced into the high traffic areas, where his lack of size and strength are the only things that derail him.

Roenick does have some defensive shortcomings once he leaves the forechecking mode, and he needs to play with at least one defensively alert winger.

THE PHYSICAL GAME

Roenick plays hockey as if he were in a demolition derby, and you wonder how much his relatively small body can take. He ends each season about 10 pounds lighter than opening night, then each off-season he works hard at bulking up again.

Roenick takes aggressive penalties — smashing people into the boards, getting his elbows up — and he never backs down. He plays through pain, not missing a game last season despite suffering a broken toe.

THE INTANGIBLES

Roenick represents everything that is right about a professional athlete. In an era of high-priced stars who think the world owes them a living, Roenick's first resonsibility is to his teammates. He would never demand more from them than he himself would deliver.

In addition to that, he respects his fans and understands the role a hockey hero has to play in a sport that needs stars, especially in the U.S.

We just have to wonder how long Roenick will last playing his headlong style.

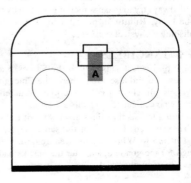

CHRISTIAN RUUTTU

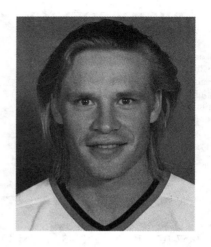

Yrs. of NHL service: 6
Born: Lappeenranta, Finland; Feb. 20, 1964
Position: centre
Height: 5-11
Weight: 194
Uniform no.: 22
Shoots: left

Career statistics:

GP	G	A	TP	PIM
522	118	267	385	617

1991-92 statistics:

GP	G	A	TP	+/-	PIM	PP	SH	GW	GT	S	PCT
70	4	21	25	-7	76	0	2	1	0	108	3.7

1992-93 statistics:

GP	G	A	TP	+/-	PIM	PP	SH	GW	GT	S	PCT
84	17	37	54	+14	134	3	1	6	0	187	9.1

LAST SEASON

One of five Blackhawks to appear in all 84 games. Tied for team lead with six game-winning goals. Goals, assists and points at three-season highs. Acquired from Winnipeg for Stephane Beauregard.

THE FINESSE GAME

Ruuttu is a crunch-time player. When a lead needs to be protected, a key draw won or a penalty killed, Ruuttu merits the call. He skates very well, with light feet, good speed and quickness and stamina. He works hardest defensively, is a conscientious forechecker and anticipates well.

Ruuttu is skilled enough offensively that he can take an odd-numbered situation and make something happen or finish the play. He does not have a big shot from the blue line to the top of the circle, but can work the puck well down low. He is better at the bang-bang play than when he has time to think too much. He doesn't have a great deal of patience with the puck.

THE PHYSICAL GAME

Ruuttu is very strong along the boards and in the corners. In his first few seasons in the NHL, he let his defensive responsibilities lapse at odd times. He is much more consistent now and is a tenacious checker. He will always try to make something happen by playing the body. Ruuttu surprised a lot of people by establishing a physical presence.

THE INTANGIBLES

A fringe player last season with the Sabres, Ruuttu found new life and a secure niche in the Chicago defensive system. He is a good role-playing defensive forward who can get 15-20 goals a season.

Ruuttu's transaction lines always merit a double take. He was traded twice for the same player, first from Buffalo to Winnipeg for Beauregard, then to Chicago for the goalie again after the Hawks had acquired him in another deal.

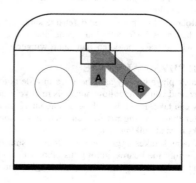

STEVE SMITH

Yrs. of NHL service: 8
Born: Glasgow, Scotland; Apr. 30, 1963
Position: left defense
Height: 6-4
Weight: 215
Uniform no.: 5
Shoots: left

Career statistics:

GP	G	A	TP	PIM
539	65	240	305	1598

1991-92 statistics:

GP	G	A	TP	+/-	PIM	PP	SH	GW	GT	S	PCT
76	9	21	30	+23	304	3	0	1	0	153	5.9

1992-93 statistics:

GP	G	A	TP	+/-	PIM	PP	SH	GW	GT	S	PCT
78	10	47	57	+12	214	7	1	2	0	212	4.7

LAST SEASON

Fourth on team in points. Points and assists at career highs.

THE FINESSE GAME

Smith is a tower of strength on the blue line, an aggressive, smart and confident defenseman who probably doesn't get the credit he deserves because of his partner, Chris Chelios, who has the decided edge in offensive play.

But don't sell Smith short. For one thing, he's huge. For another, he's mobile. And he's developed more confidence to get involved in the attack, which makes him scary in all three zones now.

Smith is not a clever passer, but he's effective at getting the puck from point A to point B. He makes a great outlet pass from his defensive zone and can see the second option. He can carry the puck if he has to.

Smith does not have an overwhelming shot, but it is accurate and low from the point, and he can work on the power play. Defensively, Smith is tough to beat one on one. He has great balance, which allows him to drop to one knee, drag his back skate, and place his stick flat along the ice while in motion. That shuts off a tremendous stretch of any passing lane from the sideboards to the middle. He steps up in the neutral zone and plays aggressively to kill penalties.

THE PHYSICAL GAME

Smith is a powerful and punishing hitter whose only problem is that he's too tall. When he works along the boards, smaller players are sometimes able to wriggle free underneath him, if they're tenacious enough.

He's a force in front of the net and is an intimidating presence. He doesn't get in many fights, but he will keep 90 percent of the players wondering and worrying.

THE INTANGIBLES

Smith has become the kind of reliable defenseman that his skills promised he would someday be. His head has caught up to the rest of him, and he should have several more seasons of being among the league's best. One thing he does not do is dominate the game. Despite his size, he is more effective in a quiet way.

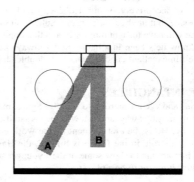

BRENT SUTTER

Yrs. of NHL service: 12
Born: Viking, Alta.; June 10, 1962
Position: centre
Height: 5-11
Weight: 180
Uniform no.: 12
Shoots: left

Career statistics:

GP	G	A	TP	PIM
820	325	389	714	858

1991-92 statistics:

GP	G	A	TP	+/-	PIM	PP	SH	GW	GT	S	PCT
69	22	38	60	-10	36	8	1	3	1	206	10.7

1992-93 statistics:

GP	G	A	TP	+/-	PIM	PP	SH	GW	GT	S	PCT
65	20	34	54	+10	67	8	2	3	0	151	13.2

LAST SEASON

Scored 20 or more goals for 12th consecutive season. Missed 14 games with a broken foot.

THE FINESSE GAME

The offensive part of Sutter's game has trailed off as he has concentrated more and more on his defensive role, but he always has to be respected for his shot and his playmaking capacity.

He has great arm strength and can hold off a defender with one arm while shooting or passing with the other. He has a strong wrist shot and will pay the price in front of the net, plowing through traffic with the puck with good control. He will pounce on loose pucks and create scoring chances off the turnovers forced by his forechecking.

Sutter is among the best in the league on draws and is a solid penalty killer. He is also still a threat on the power play and will work for tips and screens in front of the net.

Sutter is not a good skater. He is a labourer and gets where he has to go by sheer force of will. But when his skating starts to drag, he gets hit a little more and is more open to injury.

THE PHYSICAL GAME

Sutter is deceptively strong. He's wiry and on the small side, but anybody who wants Sutter's piece of the ice will have to fight him for it, and that opponent will know he's been in a battle. Sutter always keeps himself in excellent condition and can double-shift if needed.

THE INTANGIBLES

Injuries and age are starting to wear on Sutter, but he can only play one way, and that way means sacrificing his body. He is the embodiment of the work ethic. Even if his role in the future is limited, the Hawks need him around to show some of their younger skaters what it means to be a player.

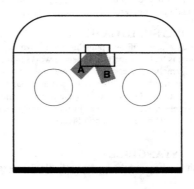

NEIL WILKINSON

Yrs. of NHL service: 4
Born: Selkirk, Man.; Aug. 16, 1967
Position: left defense
Height: 6-3
Weight: 180
Uniform no.: 5
Shoots: right

Career statistics:

GP	G	A	TP	PIM
205	7	36	43	410

1991-92 statistics:

GP	G	A	TP	+/-	PIM	PP	SH	GW	GT	S	PCT
60	4	15	19	-11	97	1	0	0	0	95	4.2

1992-93 statistics:

GP	G	A	TP	+/-	PIM	PP	SH	GW	GT	S	PCT
59	1	7	8	-50	96	0	1	0	0	51	2.0

LAST SEASON

Tied with two teammates for worst plus/minus on team and in NHL. Missed 25 games because of injuries, including back strain.

THE FINESSE GAME

Wilkinson is solid in most areas of the game, although nothing really stands out. He carries the puck, although he wouldn't be categorized as a rushing defenseman. He will play back, but his defensive reads are in serious need of improvement. Wilkinson does not move the puck quickly.

Wilkinson is a good skater, although he has some difficulty with his foot speed when backskating and is vulnerable to outside speed. He has to learn to angle his man to the boards.

Wilkinson has a good attitude and will try anything the coaching staff asks.

THE PHYSICAL GAME

Wilkinson is tall and gives the impression that he will be more of a bruiser, but his checks aren't that jarring. He will play tough and help his teammates. He is not a great fighter, but he will give it a go if provoked.

THE INTANGIBLES

Wilkinson should flourish in the Blackhawks' defensive system.

DALLAS STARS

NEAL BROTEN

Yrs. of NHL service: 12
Born: Roseau, Minn.; Nov. 29, 1959
Position: centre
Height: 5-9
Weight: 170
Uniform no.: 7
Shoots: left

Career statistics:

GP	G	A	TP	PIM
930	249	547	796	457

1991-92 statistics:

GP	G	A	TP	+/-	PIM	PP	SH	GW	GT	S	PCT
76	8	26	34	-15	16	4	1	1	0	119	6.7

1992-93 statistics:

GP	G	A	TP	+/-	PIM	PP	SH	GW	GT	S	PCT
82	12	21	33	+7	22	0	3	3	0	123	9.8

LAST SEASON

Led team in shorthanded goals. Led team forwards in plus/minus.

THE FINESSE GAME

Broten has not lost much of his skating ability in terms of straight-ahead speed, but he has lost a bit of his quickness. In addition, he's lost a little quickness in his hands. He was never a prolific goal-scorer at any point in his career, but he was always consistent with what were pretty good chances. He seems to be getting to the point where he can't find the net anymore.

Whether that is a result of his age or of his changing role as a defensive specialist is open to debate. Maybe Broten just doesn't think about offense anymore, so it's hard to judge whether his decreased production stems from his hands or his head.

He still plays with competitive fire and knows his way around the ice with good anticipation. He has become a good penalty killer and is still creative offensively if given the right people to play with. He is solid on draws.

THE PHYSICAL GAME

Broten is a small player who has to use his skating and smarts to compensate for his lack of size and strength. He has always been able to do that and get away with it, which is easier to do as an offensive player. As a defensive player, he is sometimes overmatched.

THE INTANGIBLES

Broten is a quiet team leader, and apparently the Stars are content to live with him as a one-way defensive forward. Like a lot of older athletes, Broten is paying better attention to conditioning and will prolong his career several seasons because of it. He still loves to play the game.

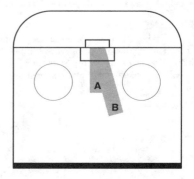

SHANE CHURLA

Yrs. of NHL service: 5
Born: Fernie, B.C.; June 24, 1965
Position: right wing
Height: 6-1
Weight: 200
Uniform no.: 27
Shoots: right

Career statistics:

GP	G	A	TP	PIM
292	15	28	43	1443

1991-92 statistics:

GP	G	A	TP	+/-	PIM	PP	SH	GW	GT	S	PCT
57	4	1	5	-12	278	0	0	0	0	42	9.5

1992-93 statistics:

GP	G	A	TP	+/-	PIM	PP	SH	GW	GT	S	PCT
73	5	16	21	-8	286	1	0	1	0	61	8.2

LAST SEASON

Led team in PIM for third consecutive season. Goals, assists and points at career highs. Missed one game with shoulder injury.

THE FINESSE GAME

Churla is among the new breed of protectors, in that he has better hands and better skating ability than the average goon.

He can be effective with his checking and play without being a heavyweight fighter, and he has made himself more valuable. He doesn't have sharp scoring instincts but will go to the net and get his goals by thrashing around for loose pucks.

Churla has to try to believe a little more in himself, because he can do more. He was moved around to a lot of different lines, even playing with Mike Modano on the top line, and the more he played, the better he played.

THE PHYSICAL GAME

Churla hits hard and loves it. He's a tenacious checker and isn't afraid of anyone. He moves to the front of the net with authority and power, and stays there. He can still use his mitts when he has to, but he has already earned a fair amount of respect around the league and has learned more discipline.

THE INTANGIBLES

Churla is evolving into the prototypical tough player. He stepped into the role of top cop when Basil McRae left, and can protect some of the Stars' more skilled players without looking out of place on their line.

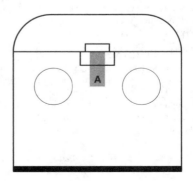

RUSS COURTNALL

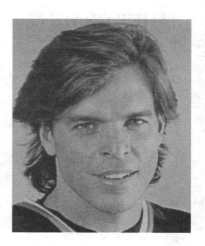

Yrs. of NHL service: 9
Born: Duncan, B.C.; June 2, 1965
Position: right wing
Height: 5-11
Weight: 183
Uniform no.: 26
Shoots: right

Career statistics:

GP	G	A	TP	PIM
643	208	284	492	369

1991-92 statistics:

GP	G	A	TP	+/-	PIM	PP	SH	GW	GT	S	PCT
27	7	14	21	+6	6	0	1	1	1	63	11.1

1992-93 statistics:

GP	G	A	TP	+/-	PIM	PP	SH	GW	GT	S	PCT
84	36	43	79	+1	49	14	2	3	2	294	12.2

LAST SEASON

Acquired from Montreal for Brian Bellows. One of four Stars to play in all 84 games. Led team in goals with career high. Tied for second on team in assists. Second on team in points with career high. Second on team in power play goals. Second on team in shots.

THE FINESSE GAME

Courtnall has dragster speed. He goes straight down the runway, creating fear in the opposition and opening up a lot of room for his teammates, because he pushes people back with sheer velocity.

Courtnall got off to a tremendous start, using his speed very intelligently and putting a lot of pucks in the net despite playing on the Stars' top checking line. He has to have a more consistent year, however, as he cooled off considerably in the second half, despite getting increased power play time.

Courtnall does not use his teammates well. He likes to take the puck and go, and when he finally runs out of room, that's when he'll start looking for help. It takes quite a lot of effort to keep up with him, too. At times, he's too fast for his own good. If he could start using the neutral zone better, looking for the give and go and planning a better overall attack, he would be deadlier.

Courtnall uses his speed well defensively and is a shorthanded threat.

THE PHYSICAL GAME

Courtnall is tough for his size. While he tends to stick to the open ice where he can flash and dash, he will make a hit to drive to the net. For the most part, though, he avoids scrums and corner work.

THE INTANGIBLES

After Courtnall demanded a trade from Montreal to Los Angeles in 1992, we took a shot at Courtnall by suggesting Kings owner Bruce McNall wouldn't want another overpaid forward. Maybe the Kings didn't,

but the Stars did, and Courtnall proved worth the price with a big season. And while he begged to get out of Montreal, he has to thank the Canadiens for helping him to develop a defensive game that has made him a solid two-way forward.

Courtnall wasn't the same player last season after he injured then-teammate Todd Elik by accidentally drilling him in the head with a shot. The incident might have affected Courtnall mentally.

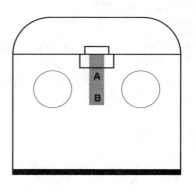

MIKE CRAIG

Yrs. of NHL service: 3
Born: London, Ont.; June 6, 1971
Position: right wing
Height: 6-0
Weight: 180
Uniform no.: 20
Shoots: right

Career statistics:

GP	G	A	TP	PIM
176	38	43	81	293

1991-92 statistics:

GP	G	A	TP	+/-	PIM	PP	SH	GW	GT	S	PCT
67	15	16	31	-12	155	4	0	4	0	136	11.0

1992-93 statistics:

GP	G	A	TP	+/-	PIM	PP	SH	GW	GT	S	PCT
70	15	23	38	-11	106	7	0	0	0	131	11.5

LAST SEASON

Career highs in assists and points. Matched career high in goals.

THE FINESSE GAME

Craig is a choppy skater, but he chops with enthusiasm. Almost everything Craig does he does with great intensity, Tony Granato style.

Craig has good hands and is very tenacious. He can play well with top offensive people because he will do the grunt work for them in the corners and along the boards. With his nice touch, he will produce goals when he goes to the front of the net. His wrist shot is especially effective, accurate and quickly unleashed.

Craig's short game is his best. He is smart and poised through traffic. He can play the power play down low.

THE PHYSICAL GAME

Craig likes to play bigger than he is. He has to continue gaining more strength so he can hold that game through an 84-game schedule — either that or learn to pace himself better, because he tends to wear down in the second half.

THE INTANGIBLES

Craig is continuing to develop slowly. He will be a support player, not a star, and we would be surprised at every point he gets over 50 this season. He is a bit of a free spirit, but very coachable.

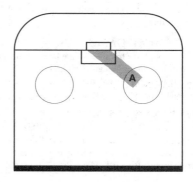

ULF DAHLEN

Yrs. of NHL service: 6
Born: Östersund, Sweden; Jan. 12, 1967
Position: right wing
Height: 6-2
Weight: 195
Uniform no.: 22
Shoots: left

Career statistics:

GP	G	A	TP	PIM
430	165	151	316	128

1991-92 statistics:

GP	G	A	TP	+/-	PIM	PP	SH	GW	GT	S	PCT
79	36	30	66	-5	10	16	1	5	0	216	16.7

1992-93 statistics:

GP	G	A	TP	+/-	PIM	PP	SH	GW	GT	S	PCT
83	35	39	74	-20	6	13	0	6	0	223	15.7

LAST SEASON

Led team in shooting percentage. Second on team in game-winning goals. Third on team in power play goals. Fourth on team in points with career high. Assists career high. Goals one short of career high. Second on team in goals.

THE FINESSE GAME

Dahlen is a funny skater, slow but with some deceptive moves. He has good balance and strength, and always protects the puck with his body. Along the boards, it's almost impossible to beat him to the puck. It doesn't matter what the size or speed of the opponent is, Dahlen won't surrender the puck. He is one of the best board and corner men in the league as long as the puck is on his blade.

Dahlen is a very intelligent hockey player who sees the ice well and has good vision. He has great puck skill, although he does not move the puck quickly. He is very effective down low on the power play.

Dahlen has good hands and scores all of his goals from 10 inches to 10 feet away from the net. He slides out once in a while, but he is usually willing to pay the price to stay in the high traffic area.

THE PHYSICAL GAME

Dahlen doesn't scare anyone with his physical play. While he is willing to do just about anything to protect the puck when he has control, he will not win many one-on-one fights to strip the puck away from an opponent. He lacks the aggressiveness to bump his game up a notch.

THE INTANGIBLES

Dahlen is a solid player who is well liked by his teammates and coaches. When healthy, he should produce a consistent 30 to 35 goals and 65 to 70 points.

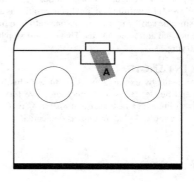

DEAN EVASON

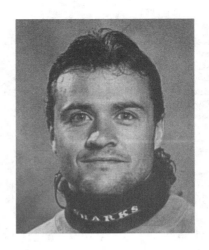

Yrs. of NHL service: 9
Born: Flin Flon, Man.; Aug. 22, 1964
Position: centre
Height: 5-10
Weight: 180
Uniform no.: 12
Shoots: right

Career statistics:

GP	G	A	TP	PIM
609	113	186	299	845

1991-92 statistics:

GP	G	A	TP	+/-	PIM	PP	SH	GW	GT	S	PCT
74	11	15	26	-22	94	1	0	1	0	88	12.5

1992-93 statistics:

GP	G	A	TP	+/-	PIM	PP	SH	GW	GT	S	PCT
84	12	19	31	-35	132	3	0	1	1	107	11.2

LAST SEASON

One of two Sharks to play in all 84 games. Goals and points at three-season high. Fourth on team in points. Acquired by Dallas for sixth-round draft choice in 1993.

THE FINESSE GAME

Evason is constantly in motion. Since he has lost a step over recent season, he is determined to keep up through sheer energy. He forechecks hard, and smart. There is little wasted motion.

Evason doesn't generate much offense despite always being on the puck carrier and forcing turnovers. He creates scoring chances but is incapable of finishing most plays. He is unselfish to a fault because he lacks confidence in the scoring touch. Even on a two on one, he will pass across to a teammate who is covered rather than take the open shot himself.

Evason kills penalties well. He is agile and doesn't give up in his pursuit. He is built low to the ground and took most of San Jose's defensive draws last season, winning his share.

THE PHYSICAL GAME

Evason's game is limited by his small size, but he has a sturdy build and can take a lot of bumps. He is durable and won't be intimidated, but his frustration is evident, since he can't win the one-on-one battles in front of the net and along the boards. That doesn't stop him from trying.

THE INTANGIBLES

Evason leads by example every night with his hard work and hustle. He is a reliable defensive forward who is still in the game because of his intensity. Other players are more skilled, but not as dedicated.

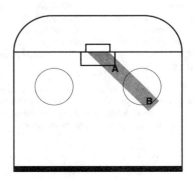

DAVE GAGNER

Yrs. of NHL service: 7
Born: Chatham, Ont.; Dec. 11, 1964
Position: centre
Height: 5-10
Weight: 180
Uniform no.: 15
Shoots: left

Career statistics:

GP	G	A	TP	PIM
520	198	233	431	622

1991-92 statistics:

GP	G	A	TP	+/-	PIM	PP	SH	GW	GT	S	PCT
78	31	40	71	-4	107	17	0	3	0	229	13.5

1992-93 statistics:

GP	G	A	TP	+/-	PIM	PP	SH	GW	GT	S	PCT
84	33	43	76	-13	141	17	0	5	1	230	14.3

LAST SEASON

One of four Stars to play in all 84 games. Led team in power play goals. Third on team in points. Fifth consecutive season with 30 or more goals and 70 or more points.

THE FINESSE GAME

Gagner can score from just about anywhere except way out by the blue line. He can score off the rush or set other people up. He will pick up garbage goals, scoop up clean ones, finish off an outnumbered attack or score off a drive down the wing with just his shot. Gagner doesn't overpower goalies with his shot, but he has a quick and cunning release. Defensemen will sometimes back off him on a rush, because he does have some moves to slip past them.

On the power play he can work down low, although he works better coming off the half-wall.

Gagner's speed isn't as noticeable as his quickness. In a 20-foot radius, he's pretty quick, and he can throw in several dekes low as he drives to the net.

He is not a good defensive player, although he has worked to improve this. He is only average on face-offs.

THE PHYSICAL GAME

Gagner plays a tenacious, in-your-face offensive style. For a smaller player, he is pretty resilient. He stays in the traffic and doesn't get bounced out too easily. He can get overmatched one-on-one, but he tries to avoid battles where he can't use his quickness.

THE INTANGIBLES

The reliable Gagner can be counted upon to deliver another 30/70 season. He can get the bench fired up with some inspirational hard work.

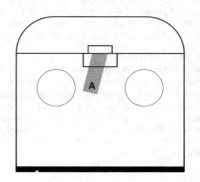

BRENT GILCHRIST

Yrs. of NHL service: 5
Born: Moose Jaw, Sask.; Apr. 3, 1967
Position: centre
Height: 5-11
Weight: 181
Uniform no.: 41
Shoots: left

Career statistics:

GP	G	A	TP	PIM
304	56	78	134	160

1991-92 statistics:

GP	G	A	TP	+/-	PIM	PP	SH	GW	GT	S	PCT
79	23	27	50	+29	57	2	0	3	2	146	15.8

1992-93 statistics:

GP	G	A	TP	+/-	PIM	PP	SH	GW	GT	S	PCT
68	10	11	21	-12	49	2	0	0	0	106	9.4

LAST SEASON

Acquired from Edmonton for Todd Elik. Missed 16 games with collarbone injury.

THE FINESSE GAME

Gilchrist is a versatile forward who can play all three positions up front. It would probably help him if he could find a niche (he has played centre throughout most of his career), because he is a good defensive player with some offensive flair. He was a scorer at the junior and AHL levels, but so far the best season he has been able to manage in the NHL is his 57 points two seasons ago in Montreal. None of his scoring touch showed up in his brief stint (eight games) with the Stars after the trade.

Gilchrist has good knowledge of the ice. He is an intelligent player, alert to his defensive role, and is best suited to centre ice, perhaps as the heir to Neal Broten.

Gilchrist will work hard around the net and generates most of his scoring chances there. He has good balance and quickness in small areas.

THE PHYSICAL GAME

Gilchrist is a strong player, although he doesn't take command of the ice. His good skating helps him move around and create a little more havoc, and he's not afraid to stand in and take some drubbing around the net. He won't back down from a challenge.

THE INTANGIBLES

Before being slowed by injuries, Gilchrist was a solid all-around player in Montreal. Two quick stops in Edmonton and now Minnesota/Dallas have probably done little for his confidence, but if he can stay intact and get his ice time, a 20-goal season is a reasonable expectation. The Stars might look for a little more offense, though, and play him with Mike Modano, and Gilchrist could surprise.

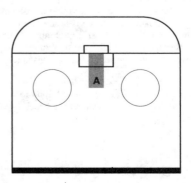

DERIAN HATCHER

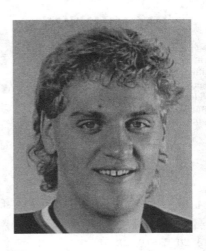

Yrs. of NHL service: 2
Born: Sterling Heights, Mich.; June 4, 1972
Position: left defense
Height: 6-5
Weight: 205
Uniform no.: 2
Shoots: left

Career statistics:

GP	G	A	TP	PIM
110	11	20	31	266

1991-92 statistics:

GP	G	A	TP	+/-	PIM	PP	SH	GW	GT	S	PCT
43	7	5	12	+7	88	0	0	2	0	51	13.7

1992-93 statistics:

GP	G	A	TP	+/-	PIM	PP	SH	GW	GT	S	PCT
67	4	15	19	-27	178	0	0	1	1	73	5.5

LAST SEASON

Missed six weeks with knee injury. Second on team in PIM. Worst plus/minus on team.

THE FINESSE GAME

Hatcher's skating looks like he's labouring, but for the most part he gets where he has to go. He is sturdy and well balanced, and he plays well enough positionally that he can be economical in his skating. The fewer strides he has to take, the better.

He has very good hands for a big man, and he has a good head for the game. He sees the game and understands it, especially offensively. Hatcher is effective from the point — not because he has a big booming slapshot, but because he has a good wrist shot and will get the puck on net quickly. He will join the rush eagerly, and he handles the puck nicely.

Hatcher is usually paired with Mark Tinordi, which gives the Stars great size and smarts on the blue line.

THE PHYSICAL GAME

Hatcher is a big force, but he has too long a fuse now and has to learn to bring more energy and impact to every shift. He does have a mean streak when provoked and can be a punishing hitter. It shouldn't be long before he solidly establishes his physical presence.

Hatcher came back well off his knee injury and should develop into the type of defenseman who can play 30 to 35 minutes a game. The more work he gets, the better.

THE INTANGIBLES

Hatcher was given a lot of responsibility for a young defenseman, getting thrown into a No. 2 role where he was expected to play poised, experienced, no-mistake hockey, and he is not at that level. He has a top end that nobody has seen yet, and we probably won't see it for a few seasons yet.

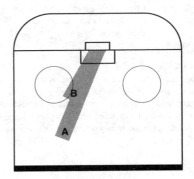

JIM JOHNSON

Yrs. of NHL service: 8
Born: New Hope, Minn.; Aug. 9, 1962
Position: right defense
Height: 6-1
Weight: 190
Uniform no.: 6
Shoots: left

Career statistics:

GP	G	A	TP	PIM
584	22	134	156	965

1991-92 statistics:

GP	G	A	TP	+/-	PIM	PP	SH	GW	GT	S	PCT
71	4	10	14	+11	102	0	0	1	0	86	4.7

1992-93 statistics:

GP	G	A	TP	+/-	PIM	PP	SH	GW	GT	S	PCT
79	3	20	23	+9	105	1	0	0	0	67	4.5

LAST SEASON

Led team in plus/minus. Points five-season high. Missed two games with face laceration.

THE FINESSE GAME

Johnson plays a strong role as a defensive defenseman, killing penalties and getting the job of being on ice against the other team's top scoring lines night after night. He does his job with very quiet success.

Johnson uses his skating more in a defensive role now, positioning himself, getting in and out. He was a bit more offensively inclined in his first few years in the league, and he can still get involved in the attack. If a good play is to be made down deep, Johnson will take the chance, but he won't pinch or pressure unwisely. He has a good wrist shot and makes sure to play the safe play. If he does get caught, he can usually scramble back quickly to return to the play defensively.

He blocks shots well and understands the game. He plays an aggressive game in terms of stepping up and forcing the attacker.

THE PHYSICAL GAME

Johnson is an average-sized defenseman who picks his spots. He uses most of his weight and strength for conditioning and to control people, and for the most part he can control. He can make the occasional hard thump, but he doesn't go out of his way to try to knock opponents into the 12th row.

THE INTANGIBLES

Johnson has become one of the Stars' top penalty killers and a reliable defenseman who gives you few highs but almost no lows. For the second consecutive season, he led the team defensemen in plus/minus, and on a team with so many minuses, that's an accomplishment.

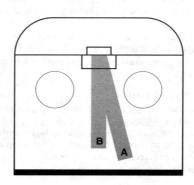

CRAIG LUDWIG

Yrs. of NHL service: 11
Born: Rhinelander, Wisc.; Mar. 15, 1961
Position: left defense
Height: 6-3
Weight: 215
Uniform no.: 3
Shoots: left

Career statistics:

GP	G	A	TP	PIM
823	30	138	167	903

1991-92 statistics:

GP	G	A	TP	+/-	PIM	PP	SH	GW	GT	S	PCT
73	2	9	11	0	54	0	0	0	0	51	3.9

1992-93 statistics:

GP	G	A	TP	+/-	PIM	PP	SH	GW	GT	S	PCT
78	1	10	11	+1	153	0	0	0	0	66	1.5

LAST SEASON

Missed games with knee and neck injuries.

THE FINESSE GAME

Ludwig is a classic defensive defenseman. He exists in his stay-by-the-fireplace mode, using his defensive reads, rangy reach and strength to deny space inside his blue line.

Ludwig still wears the oldest, widest shinpads in the league, and he's one of the best shot-blockers in the game.

He didn't build his game on an offensive foundation, and that is not about to change now. He does not get involved in the rush and has little interest in being part of the attack. He plays an ultra-conservative game. He's a very good penalty killer.

THE PHYSICAL GAME

Ludwig is very strong, but is not a hard checker. He prefers to keep people under wraps, and he is one of those veteran defenseman who gets away with holds and hooks that a more inexperienced defenseman gets called for. When provoked, he will strike back, but he is not an instigator or a fighter (although he did receive one instigation penalty last season).

Ludwig is also strong mentally. Not much gets him down or bothers him, and he is still a competitor who wants to win.

THE INTANGIBLES

Because of injuries, Ludwig was elevated by necessity to the role of No. 2 defenseman. Once he steps out of the role of a No. 3 or 4, the cracks in his armour are wider, but Ludwig tried to do his utmost. He still has several years left because he knows how to play the game. As his skating slows down, his brain speeds up.

Ludwig suffered one of the most bizarre sports injuries last season when he ducked to avoid getting hit in the face by a cream pie at a party and hurt his neck.

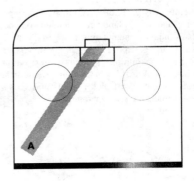

RICHARD MATVICHUK

Yrs. of NHL service: 1
Born: Edmonton, Alta.; Feb. 5, 1973
Position: defense
Height: 6-2
Weight: 190
Uniform no.: 4
Shoots: left

Career statistics:

GP	G	A	TP	PIM
53	2	3	5	26

1992-93 statistics:

GP	G	A	TP	+/-	PIM	PP	SH	GW	GT	S	PCT
53	2	3	5	-8	26	1	0	0	0	51	3.9

LAST SEASON
First NHL season.

THE FINESSE GAME
Matvichuk is a good skater with a long stride, and he skates well backwards and pivots in either direction. He likes to come up-ice and get involved in the attack. He has the hand skills and instincts to develop into a good two-way defenseman.

Matvichuk has a low, hard shot with an accurate release. He makes smart, crisp passes and uses other players well. He can play either side on defense.

Matvichuk has good instincts and reads plays well. He is very competitive. A leader at the junior level, he shows signs of developing along the same lines as an NHLer.

THE PHYSICAL GAME
Matvichuk is an avid weight lifter and he's going to have to keep at it, because in order to compete at the NHL level he has to get stronger. He is tough and aggressive. He sometimes abandons his physical play and pokechecks too much. Playing the body consistently well (once he adds strength) will open up an extra dimension.

THE INTANGIBLES
Matvichuk was probably rushed, because he was caught in a no-man's-land between being too good to play back in junior and not quite ready for the NHL — but was restricted from playing in the minors. He is learning and making mistakes, but by next season he should be one of the team's top four defensemen. He was a first-round draft pick in 1991 and shows no signs of proving the scouts wrong.

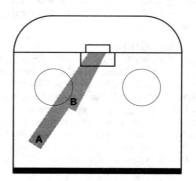

MIKE MCPHEE

Yrs. of NHL service: 9
Born: Sydney, N.S.; July 14, 1960
Position: left wing
Height: 6-1
Weight: 203
Uniform no.: 17
Shoots: left

Career statistics:

GP	G	A	TP	PIM
665	180	184	364	625

1991-92 statistics:

GP	G	A	TP	+/-	PIM	PP	SH	GW	GT	S	PCT
78	16	15	31	+6	63	0	0	1	0	146	11.0

1992-93 statistics:

GP	G	A	TP	+/-	PIM	PP	SH	GW	GT	S	PCT
84	18	22	40	-2	44	1	2	2	0	161	11.2

LAST SEASON

Acquired from Montreal for fifth-round draft pick in 1993. One of four Stars to play in all 84 games. Assists matched career high.

THE FINESSE GAME

McPhee spent most of his career in Montreal as a checker, but the Stars asked him to play left wing on their top line with Mike Modano because they simply didn't have anyone else who could do it. He balanced the line with defense and even played a little power play, which he had done very little of so far in his career.

McPhee kills penalties and is very responsible defensively. He understands the game well, especially from the defensive side.

McPhee has deceptive speed. He lacks dazzling moves, but he has some surprising quickness, which is one of the reasons why he excels at killing penalties. He was able to keep up with the fleet Modano.

McPhee will score most of his goals from work in front of the net. He has a very long reach and is strong on his stick. His interest seemed to be flagging in his last season in Montreal, but he perked up with the trade to the Stars.

THE PHYSICAL GAME

McPhee is strong and solid. He picks his spots a little better, but can be ferocious along the boards and in the corners. He won't back down and is very strong on the puck.

THE INTANGIBLES

McPhee is a great team man. He brought his experience to the Stars and did whatever was asked. Playing for his ex-Habs teammate Bob Gainey proved no problem. His dedication to the game was a great example for his younger teammates to follow. He's the strong, silent type, which should play well in Texas.

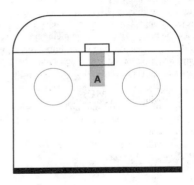

MIKE MODANO

Yrs. of NHL service: 4
Born: Livonia, Mich.; June 7, 1970
Position: centre
Height: 6-3
Weight: 190
Uniform no.: 9
Shoots: left

Career statistics:

GP	G	A	TP	PIM
317	123	186	279	257

1991-92 statistics:

GP	G	A	TP	+/-	PIM	PP	SH	GW	GT	S	PCT
76	33	44	77	-9	46	5	0	8	2	256	12.9

1992-93 statistics:

GP	G	A	TP	+/-	PIM	PP	SH	GW	GT	S	PCT
82	33	60	93	-7	83	9	0	7	0	307	10.7

LAST SEASON

Led team in assists and points with career highs. Matched career high in goals. Led team in game-winning goals and shots.

THE FINESSE GAME

Modano was inconsistent last season, but his game overall has continued to grow and improve. As it does, more is quickly expected of him, so Modano must feel at times as if he is on a treadmill.

Modano can be a thrilling player to watch on nights when he decides the game is his to toy with. He has outstanding offensive instincts and great hands, and is a smooth passer and a remarkable skater in all facets.

The question is, do the the Stars have to get Modano better players to play with, or does Modano have to get better at playing with the partners he has, to elevate their game and become more knowledgeable in how to play with them? The latter is the mark of a great player. Right now he is like a home-run hitter who has to learn to hit the doubles and singles and maybe even bunt once in a while. He has to learn to be a better goal-scorer by picking up the third rebound in front of the net as well as scoring off his blazing solo efforts. He must better utilize players coming through the neutral zone and pick off an open lane to the top of the circle, as opposed to carrying it. His game is offense, and he has to develop a complete repertoire.

Modano's defensive game has improved a great deal, and his anticipation and quick hands help him intercept passes. He needs work on his face-offs.

THE PHYSICAL GAME

Modano is getting stronger and can lean on people. He doesn't play a very physical game, because he has the size to earn some respect for himself. He can already create room with his speed. If he does it with his size as well, the ice will be his.

THE INTANGIBLES

Modano probably has more sheer talent than anyone else in his age group, with the exception of Teemu Selanne (both were drafted in 1988, along with Trevor Linden, Jeremy Roenick, and Rod Brind'Amour). Modano can be an elite player but has yet to show his desire to get to that next level. He just had his best year statistically, but he has only scratched the surface. Instead of growing by leaps and bounds, he is growing by inches and feet.

Modano is quiet and will not be one of the team leaders off the ice. He can't demand anything from others until he demands more of himself.

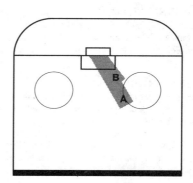

ANDY MOOG

Yrs. of NHL service: 12
Born: Penticton, B.C.; Feb. 18, 1960
Position: goaltender
Height: 5-8
Weight: 170
Uniform no.: 35
Catches: left

Career statistics:

GP	MINS	GA	SO	GAA	A	PIM
496	27,963	1549	17	3.32	21	156

1991-92 statistics:

GP	MINS	GAA	W	L	T	SO	GA	S	SAPCT	PIM
62	3640	3.23	28	22	9	1	196	1727	.887	52

1992-93 statistics:

GP	MINS	GAA	W	L	T	SO	GA	S	SAPCT	PIM
55	3194	3.16	37	14	3	3	168	1357	.876	14

LAST SEASON

Third among NHL goalies in wins. Missed games with back and kidney injuries, and also due to personal reasons.

THE PHYSICAL GAME

Moog is a fairly good technical goalie who has relied on his reflexes, but he is getting to the stage in his career where those reflexes might not be enough.

He is aggressive and comes so far out of his net that most teams know enough to come down the wing, fake a shot, go around him and pass to an open man for a lot of gimme chip-ins. His five-hole is not as good as it should be for a technically good goalie, and he is now more vulnerable high than he was earlier in his career when he had such a good glove hand.

Moog scrambles back to his feet quickly when he is down, but he keeps to his feet rather well and plays his angles.

He does not handle the puck well and has always left that chore to his defense.

THE MENTAL GAME

Few goalies have more chances to break down mentally than Moog. First he became the scapegoat for Boston's more open offensive style as his GAA rose in the first half of the season. Off the ice, he had to deal with family concerns because of the illness of his father. And everything was complicated by his injuries and by trade rumours. Yet Moog finished the regular season on a positive note, winning his last seven decisions.

The unexpected competition from John Blue (who really doesn't figure in Boston's plans) proved the theory that Moog is always better when he is challenged for his job.

THE INTANGIBLES

The years are starting to catch up to Moog. He is a tough competitor and a consummate pro, but at 34 he's at the point in his career when he has to start sharing the starting role rather than being the No. 1 goalie.

TOMMY SJODIN

Yrs. of NHL service: 1
Born: Sundsvall, Sweden; Aug. 13, 1965
Position: right defense
Height: 5-11
Weight: 190
Uniform no.: 33
Shoots: right

Career statistics:

GP	G	A	TP	PIM
77	7	29	36	30

1992-93 statistics:

GP	G	A	TP	+/-	PIM	PP	SH	GW	GT	S	PCT
77	7	29	36	-25	30	5	0	1	0	175	4.0

LAST SEASON
First NHL season. Missed games with hand injury.

THE FINESSE GAME
An excellent point man and power play specialist, Sjodin played the right point on the Stars' top power play unit. He has a powerful slap shot and can fire it as he glides along the blue line.

Sjodin has great patience with the puck and holds it until a teammate is open, taking the hit if he must to make the well-timed play. He has the ability to find the open man and get the puck to him.

He doesn't have the real dynamic speed that is usually associated with European players, nor is he very fluid or graceful. Though he doesn't fly up the ice, he has good agility and lateral movement. He skates very well with the puck and moves it up well under pressure. He comes up-ice slowly but sees his options without being very flashy.

THE PHYSICAL GAME
Not a young player despite his sophomore status, the 28-year-old Sjodin has to learn to play a more physical game. Not very tall, but solidly built, he can still learn to play the man instead of reaching for the puck. He plays with some spunk and with the proper tutelage can become a more effective player on defense.

THE INTANGIBLES
Sjodin arrived in Minnesota labelled as a one-way defenseman and was pigeonholed as such. There was a false impression that he couldn't play sound defense, but after adjusting to the NHL, Sjodin will probably make a better all-around defenseman than a lot of people gave him credit for. If he gets the ice time, he could produce 15 goals.

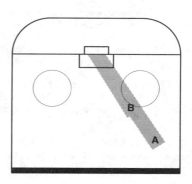

MARK TINORDI

Yrs. of NHL service: 5
Born: Deer River, Alta.; May 9, 1966
Position: left defense
Height: 6-4
Weight: 205
Uniform no.: 24
Shoots: left

Career statistics:

GP	G	A	TP	PIM
338	30	90	120	922

1991-92 statistics:

GP	G	A	TP	+/-	PIM	PP	SH	GW	GT	S	PCT
63	4	24	28	-13	177	4	0	0	0	93	4.3

1992-93 statistics:

GP	G	A	TP	+/-	PIM	PP	SH	GW	GT	S	PCT
69	15	27	42	-1	157	7	0	2	0	122	12.3

LAST SEASON

Missed four weeks with broken collarbone. Led team defensemen in scoring. Career highs in goals and points. Tied career high in assists.

THE FINESSE GAME

Tinordi doesn't have much in the way of finesse skills, but oh, how he loves to go to the net. He starts out at the point on the power play but doesn't hesitate to crash down low. He is an impact player and a big force on the ice.

Tinordi is becoming more and more effective offensively. He has a big-time point shot, low, hard and accurate, and he also sees the play well and moves his passes crisply. He intimidates when he moves low and bulls his way to the net. He is poised with the puck and will use a wrist shot in deep.

Tinordi is an above-average skater, very good for his large size. He lacks one-step quickness but once in gear he has a long stride with good balance and mobility. He can use his long reach well around the net or to take the puck away from a defender. He is a strong penalty killer with good hockey sense.

THE PHYSICAL GAME

Tinordi plays with the throttle wide open and doesn't recognize any other playing style. One of the reasons why he is so susceptible to getting hurt is that he is more concerned with making the play than with protecting himself, and he ends up in vulnerable situations. A little less reckless abandon would help keep him in one piece, but we're not sure if Tinordi knows how to play that way.

As honest and tough as they come, Tinordi commands respect on the ice. He has too short a fuse, although in recent years he has done a better job of curbing his temper as he realizes he is more important to his team on the ice than in the penalty box. He is competitive and fearless.

THE INTANGIBLES

Tinordi hasn't been the same since his 1991 injury (foot palsy as the result of getting hit in the foot while blocking an Al MacInnis shot). It was frustrating for him because he used to be confident on every shift that he could go out and do just what he wanted to do, regardless of the opposition, but the injury checked that. Two seasons ago we predicted a Norris Trophy for Tinordi, but he will probably never reach that elite status.

Tinordi is one of the more remarkable NHL stories, as he reformed himself from a goon into one of the league's top defensemen and most respected team leaders. Health is now his major concern, as he has missed considerable playing time over the past two seasons due to injuries. There are bigger names among NHL defensemen, but few with a bigger heart than Tinordi.

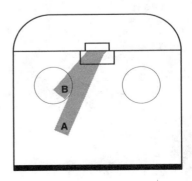

DETROIT
RED WINGS

SHAWN BURR

Yrs. of NHL service: 8
Born: Sarnia, Ont.; July 1, 1966
Position: left wing
Height: 6-1
Weight: 200
Uniform no.: 11
Shoots: left

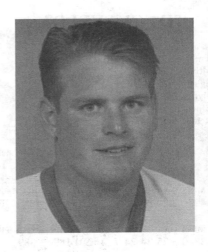

Career statistics:

GP	G	A	TP	PIM
566	132	194	326	674

1991-92 statistics:

GP	G	A	TP	+/-	PIM	PP	SH	GW	GT	S	PCT
79	19	32	51	+26	118	2	0	3	1	140	13.6

1992-93 statistics:

GP	G	A	TP	+/-	PIM	PP	SH	GW	GT	S	PCT
80	10	25	35	+18	74	1	1	2	0	99	10.1

LAST SEASON

Goal and point production lowest for full season. Missed three games with back injury.

THE FINESSE GAME

Burr is an aggressive forechecker who has earned a place on Detroit's top checking line alongside 1992 Selke Trophy runner-up Sergei Fedorov. Burr was a scorer in junior, but his skating skills didn't translate well enough to the NHL level to allow him to continue in that role. Still, he goes hard to the nets and along the boards, trying to make up with energy what he lacks in acceleration.

Burr is a smart hockey player, which makes him a natural against other teams' top lines and on the penalty-killing unit. He has the instincts to produce more offense off his checking role, since he and Fedorov can create so many turnovers with their combined anticipation, but Burr doesn't seem to have the finishing touch — odd, given his junior reputation. Most of Burr's chances will come in scrums right around the net. If he has a decent array of shots, we haven't seen them.

THE PHYSICAL GAME

Burr is on the lean side but uses his body well. He will always be banging along the boards or in front of the net, and he makes puck-carriers rush their passes because he sticks to them tenaciously. Because he is not a very good skater, with limited range, he is less of a threat as an open-ice hitter. He is scrappy and can be very annoying to play against.

THE INTANGIBLES

Burr is well respected for his honest defensive work despite his lack of production, but he has the skills and the brains to be much more than a 10-goal scorer. Perhaps he is so intimidated by the scoring talent surrounding him on the Red Wings that he has settled into his role as a mere checker.

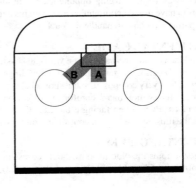

TIM CHEVELDAE

Yrs. of NHL service: 4
Born: Melville, Sask.; Feb. 15, 1968
Position: goaltender
Height: 5-11
Weight: 180
Uniform no.: 32
Catches: left

Career statistics:

GP	MINS	GA	SO	GAA	A	PIM
234	13,453	760	8	3.39	14	14

1991-92 statistics:

GP	MINS	GAA	W	L	T	SO	GA	S	SAPCT	PIM
72	4236	3.20	38	23	9	2	226	1978	.886	6

1992-93 statistics:

GP	MINS	GAA	W	L	T	SO	GA	S	SAPCT	PIM
67	3880	3.25	34	24	7	4	210	1897	.889	4

LAST SEASON

Fourth in NHL in wins. Tied for third in NHL in shutouts.

THE PHYSICAL GAME

Cheveldae doesn't rely on his reflexes — a darned good thing, because he's a pretty slow mover, with the exception of his fairly sharp glove hand. He is a strict angle player who is out at the top of his crease and very aggressive. He doesn't like any wasted motion, which is why he's been able to be one of the league's real workhorses without showing any stress and strain physically.

Cheveldae is an average skater at best with limited lateral movement. The key to beating him is to go east-west from dot-to-dot in front of him to get him moving from side to side. He allows few soft goals, so the trick is to get him in motion. When he is able to keep his feet, he is so good technically that he takes away a huge portion of the net.

Cheveldae is an average to below-average puck-handler, an area where he needs to show improvement, as that skill has become more important to modern goalies.

He skates boldly out of his net to stickhandle pucks away from charging opponents, but he often seems to have missed communications with his defensive partners on how to handle the puck.

THE MENTAL GAME

Cheveldae is a bounce-back goalie who can shake off a bad goal, period or game and suffer few lingering effects. He is very composed, and it shows in his physical carriage, which has a comforting effect on his teammates. Even when facing a barrage, Cheveldae gives the illusion that he is in control, not under siege.

THE INTANGIBLES

No goalie joins the elite ranks without success in the playoffs, and Cheveldae has yet to achieve that. He has such sound fundamentals and such a good mental approach to the game...and yet there are rumours that the Red Wings are in the market for a goalie. It may be that Cheveldae is good, but not good enough to take that next step to join the top flight of NHL netminders.

STEVE CHIASSON

Yrs. of NHL service: 6
Born: Barrie, Ont.; Apr. 14, 1967
Position: left defense
Height: 6-0
Weight: 205
Uniform no.: 3
Shoots: left

Career statistics:

GP	G	A	TP	PIM
389	54	167	221	764

1991-92 statistics:

GP	G	A	TP	+/-	PIM	PP	SH	GW	GT	S	PCT
62	10	24	34	+22	136	5	0	2	1	143	7.0

1992-93 statistics:

GP	G	A	TP	+/-	PIM	PP	SH	GW	GT	S	PCT
79	12	50	62	+14	155	6	0	1	0	227	5.3

LAST SEASON

Games played, PIM, goals, assists and points at career highs. Missed two games with leg injury and one game with hamstring injury.

THE FINESSE GAME

Chiasson's finesse game has improved along with his skating. The two go hand in hand (or foot in skate), and Chiasson has dedicated himself to improving in this critical area. He still has a bit of a choppy stride, but he's quick and better at getting himself into position offensively. He has a cannon shot. Working in tandem with the gifted Paul Coffey on the point on the power play (which ranked first overall during the regular season), Chiasson moved to the right point to open up his forehand for his booming one-timer.

Chiasson is not afraid to gamble in deep, either, and has good instincts about when to pinch in. He handles the puck well down low and uses a snap or wrist shot. He is poised with the puck on the attack.

Defensively, he plays a solid positional game and reads rushes well. While not great in any one area (save, perhaps, his shot), he has quite a nice overall package of skills.

THE PHYSICAL GAME

Chiasson is a competitor. He will play hurt, he will defend his teammates, and he comes to play every night. He lacked conditioning early in his career and it hurt him, but he has matured in his approach to his livelihood and it's paying off.

Chiasson still has to use his body more consistently to establish a physical presence. The book on the Red Wings is to bang their defense, and Chiasson is their most physical regular.

THE INTANGIBLES

Chiasson has become more and more of a team leader and is just starting to come into his prime. He is on the verge of becoming a complete two-way defenseman, maybe one of the most underrated blueliners in the NHL.

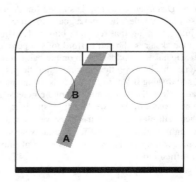

DINO CICCARELLI

Yrs. of NHL service: 13
Born: Sarnia, Ont.; Feb. 18, 1960
Position: right wing
Height: 5-10
Weight: 175
Uniform no.: 22
Shoots: right

Career statistics:

GP	G	A	TP	PIM
907	485	472	957	1001

1991-92 statistics:

GP	G	A	TP	+/-	PIM	PP	SH	GW	GT	S	PCT
78	38	38	76	-10	78	13	0	7	0	279	13.6

1992-93 statistics:

GP	G	A	TP	+/-	PIM	PP	SH	GW	GT	S	PCT
82	41	56	97	+12	81	21	0	8	0	200	20.5

LAST SEASON

Led team in power play goals and shooting percentage. Tied for team lead in game-winning goals. Second on team in goals and points. Assists at career high. Goals three-season high. Missed two games with flu. Set team record with 21 power play goals.

THE FINESSE GAME

Yapping and jabbing, Ciccarelli plays few invisible games. His attitude and aggressive style enhance his skills, which are highlighted by his quickness and his scoring knack.

Ciccarelli has great hands for finishing plays. Though he has a big slapshot, he is more frequently found in front of the net digging for loose pucks and screening the goaltender. His offensive game is straightforward. He's not a very creative playmaker, so he shoots first and asks questions later.

Ciccarelli is a strong forechecker, taking the body well despite his small size, and he can do something with the puck when it does squirt free. He doesn't have breakaway speed and dazzling moves, but he is a strong and well-balanced skater who is very quick in small spaces.

THE PHYSICAL GAME

Dino the Disturber. Ciccarelli is starved for attention and isn't happy unless he's got a goalie in a tizzy or a goal judge pushing that red-light button. He isn't a very good skater, so he can't afford to be a perimeter player. He has to be parked right on the paint in front of the net, his heels on the crease, taking the punishment and dishing it out. Intimidation is a huge part of his game. He will check goalies out of their crease and try to get a piece of them while they're still in it.

Ciccarelli plays as if he has to prove his courage every night, and he's pound for pound as strong as most bigger players. He has a low centre of gravity and is difficult to move.

THE INTANGIBLES

What a steal of a deal for the Red Wings, who acquired Ciccarelli from Washington for Kevin Miller. Ciccarelli was a brash young kid when he first broke into the league. Now he's a brash old kid. He is always willing to pay any price to win.

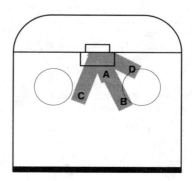

PAUL COFFEY

Yrs. of NHL service: 13
Born: Weston, Ont.; June 1, 1961
Position: left defense
Height: 6-0
Weight: 200
Uniform no.: 77
Shoots: left

Career statistics:

GP	G	A	TP	PIM
953	330	871	1201	1368

1991-92 statistics:

GP	G	A	TP	+/-	PIM	PP	SH	GW	GT	S	PCT
64	11	58	69	+1	87	5	0	1	0	232	4.7

1992-93 statistics:

GP	G	A	TP	+/-	PIM	PP	SH	GW	GT	S	PCT
80	12	75	87	+16	77	5	0	0	0	254	4.7

LAST SEASON

Acquired from Los Angeles with Jim Hiller and Sylvain Couturier for Jimmy Carson, Marc Potvin, and Gary Shuchuk. Led team defensemen in scoring. Second on team in assists. Second among NHL defensemen in scoring.

THE FINESSE GAME

Coffey may be the best-skating defenseman of all time. He doctors his skates so there is minimal hollow in the blades, and he just glides over the ice.

He handles the puck while he is skating and whirling at top speed or changing directions and tempo. Few players are better at the long home-run pass, and Coffey has all the finesse skills of a forward when he works down low. He has tremendous vision to make a play, feather a pass, work a give-and-go. He understands the concept of time and space.

Coffey has a whole menu of shots, from wristers to slaps. He is a world-class point man on the power play, faking slaps and sending passes low, sliding the puck over to his point partner for a one-timer, or drilling the shot himself.

He has enough speed and skill to split the defense or beat a defender one on one. He is almost impossible to hit because he is so shifty and strong on his skates. He creates a lot of open ice for his teammates because he is intimidating as a skater.

THE PHYSICAL GAME

Coffey has the size to hit and clear the slot, but he doesn't, and at this stage in his distinguished career, that is not about to change. There will be occasions when he gets beaten coming out of the corner because he doesn't hit the opponent or make more than a half-hearted attempt to slow him down with his stick. Anyone who gets Coffey for his offensive gifts has to be willing to put up with his defensive shortcomings.

Coffey will block shots when it counts (like in the playoffs), but most of his defense is based on his anticipation in picking off passes.

THE INTANGIBLES

Coffey can make good players better and very good players great. But even though he's an ideal fit with the talented forwards in Detroit, he could be on the move again now that Scotty Bowman is coach there, since the two didn't get along well in Coffey's final season in Pittsburgh.

Coffey is still afraid of losing and wants to be a winner. He needs to play on a team with a strong supporting cast, or his minuses could be mind-boggling.

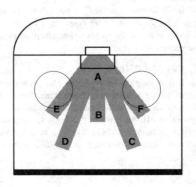

DALLAS DRAKE

Yrs. of NHL service: 1
Born: Trail, B.C.; Feb. 4, 1969
Position: centre
Height: 6-0
Weight: 170
Uniform no.: 28
Shoots: left

Career statistics:

GP	G	A	TP	PIM
72	18	26	44	93

1992-93 statistics:

GP	G	A	TP	+/-	PIM	PP	SH	GW	GT	S	PCT
72	18	26	44	+15	93	3	2	5	0	89	20.2

LAST SEASON

First NHL season. Second among NHL rookies in shooting percentage. Tied for third among NHL rookies in game-winning goals. Missed seven games with injuries: charleyhorse (three), back (one), kneecap (three).

THE FINESSE GAME

Drake has the makings of a solid two-way centre. He is an aggressive forechecker who is strong along the boards and in front of the net. He's on the small side, so he doesn't stand in and take a bashing, but he'll jump in and out of traffic to fight for the puck or bounce on rebounds.

Drake is very aware defensively and was named the WCHA's Defensive Player of the Year at Northern Michigan in 1991-92, after leading the WCHA in goals. But one of his weaknesses appears to be draws; the Red Wings usually send out one of their other top centres (Steve Yzerman or Sergei Fedorov) for key draws when Drake's line is on.

Drake has good shots and good sense in close, and is poised with the puck. He is a good skater, although not overly fast.

THE PHYSICAL GAME

Drake is limited by his size, but he will give a team whatever he's got. He's feisty enough to get other team's attention, and he works to keep himself in scoring position.

THE INTANGIBLES

Drake is in a tough position given Detroit's strength up the middle, but his grit and determination set him apart from some finesse players who might take too many nights off. Definitely the biggest surprise of Detroit's season, and worthy of a regular shift. Capable of 30 goals once he gets regular ice time.

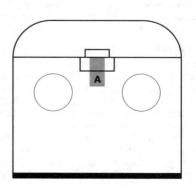

SERGEI FEDOROV

Yrs. of NHL service: 3
Born: Pskov, Russia; Dec. 13, 1969
Position: centre
Height: 6-1
Weight: 191
Uniform no.: 91
Shoots: left

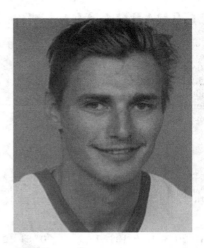

Career statistics:

GP	G	A	TP	PIM
230	97	155	252	210

1991-92 statistics:

GP	G	A	TP	+/-	PIM	PP	SH	GW	GT	S	PCT
80	32	54	86	+26	72	7	2	5	0	249	12.9

1992-93 statistics:

GP	G	A	TP	+/-	PIM	PP	SH	GW	GT	S	PCT
73	34	53	87	+33	72	13	4	3	0	217	15.7

LAST SEASON

Third on team in points. Tied for team lead in plus/minus. Tied for second in power play goals. Points at career high. Missed seven games with shoulder injury. Missed two games with flu.

THE FINESSE GAME

Fedorov is a tremendous package of offensive and defensive skills. He can go from checking the opponent's top centre to powering the power play from shift to shift. His skating is nothing short of phenomenal, and he can handle the puck while he is dazzling everyone with his blades.

Fedorov likes to gear up from his own defensive zone on the rush, using his acceleration and balance to drive wide to his right, carrying the puck on his backhand and protecting the puck with his body. If the defenseman lets up at all, then Fedorov is by him, pulling the puck quickly to his forehand. Nor is he by any means selfish. He has 360-degree vision of the ice and makes rock-solid, confident passes right under opponents' sticks and smack onto the tape of his teammates.

Fedorov also has the strength and acceleration to drive right between two defenders, keep control of the puck and wrist a strong shot on goal. He does all of these scary things while playing some of the best defense in the league.

THE PHYSICAL GAME

Fedorov is wiry, and though he would prefer to stay in open ice, he will go to the trenches when he has to. Much of his power is generated from his strong skating. For the most part, his defense is dominated by his reads, anticipation and quickness in knocking down passes and breaking up plays. He is not much of a bodychecker, and he gets most of his penalties from stick and restraining fouls.

THE INTANGIBLES

Because of his skating and finesse skills, sub-100- point seasons seem to disappoint Fedorov watchers. As long as he continues in his current role as a two-way centre, though, 85 to 90 points seems about right for Fedorov.

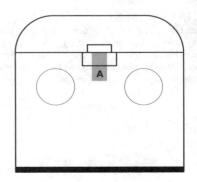

GERARD GALLANT

Yrs. of NHL service: 9
Born: Summerside, P.E.I.; Sept. 2, 1963
Position: left wing
Height: 5-10
Weight: 185
Uniform no.: 17
Shoots: left

Career statistics:

GP	G	A	TP	PIM
563	207	260	467	1600

1991-92 statistics:

GP	G	A	TP	+/-	PIM	PP	SH	GW	GT	S	PCT
69	14	22	36	+16	187	4	0	1	1	116	12.1

1992-93 statistics:

GP	G	A	TP	+/-	PIM	PP	SH	GW	GT	S	PCT
67	10	20	30	+20	188	0	0	0	0	81	12.3

LAST SEASON

Points two-season low. Missed five games with illness/injury: back (one), hip (three), flu (one).

THE FINESSE GAME

Gallant is a very basic player, an up-and-down winger who acts as a safety valve when playing with some of Detroit's more skilled forwards. He isn't a plodder, but he doesn't have game-breaking speed, either. Gallant's poise and overall hockey smarts keep him in the line-up — and on the ice in key situations — despite the fact that some of his skills have been dulled by time and injuries.

Gallant is a strong forechecker, still very effective as a penalty killer. On the attack, he will drive to the net for rebounds and tip-ins. He doesn't have much of a shot anymore and scores mostly from close range.

But his goal totals keep shrinking, and his roster spot may easily be up for grabs. Gallant no longer gets ice time on the power play.

THE PHYSICAL GAME

Gallant is a chippy, aggressive player who needs to get in the game early with a few hits. He carries his stick high, hits well after the whistle and acts as a bodyguard for his team's finesse players.

THE INTANGIBLES

Gallant fell in and out of favour with coach Bryan Murray during the season, but by year's end had regained his familiar spot on the left side of Steve Yzerman. His flaws are outweighed by his character, but he is no longer a No. 1 left winger.

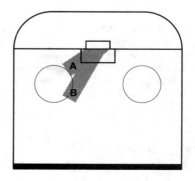

SHELDON KENNEDY

Yrs. of NHL service: 2
Born: Brandon, Man.; June 15, 1969
Position: right wing
Height: 5-11
Weight: 175
Uniform no.: 15
Shoots: right

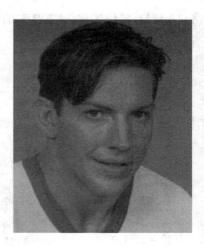

Career statistics:

GP	G	A	TP	PIM
122	25	26	51	92

1991-92 statistics:

GP	G	A	TP	+/-	PIM	PP	SH	GW	GT	S	PCT
27	3	8	11	-2	24	0	0	1	1	33	9.1

1992-93 statistics:

GP	G	A	TP	+/-	PIM	PP	SH	GW	GT	S	PCT
68	19	11	30	-1	46	1	0	2	1	110	17.3

LAST SEASON

Games played, goals, assists and points at career highs. Missed one game with shoulder injury.

THE FINESSE GAME

With the depth of talent up front on the Red Wings, a player has to have something exceptional to earn any playing time. Kennedy is close. He has outstanding breakaway speed and could well be one of the team's fastest skaters up front.

Kennedy is like Randy Wood in that he has the speed to make coaches dream of a 40-goal season, but Kennedy can't do much with the puck at high tempo. His playmaking is average, and his play of choice is to drive wide left and drive to the net.

Unlike Wood, however, Kennedy hasn't shown he can be valuable in other ways, like penalty-killing.

THE PHYSICAL GAME

Kennedy is not a very big player and prefers open ice to traffic. He does not play the body and goes into traffic only for the puck.

THE INTANGIBLES

He has spent parts of four seasons trying to earn a regular role with the Red Wings, but he seems to lack the finishing touch to be more than a fourth-line winger.

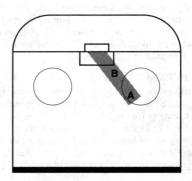

VLADIMIR KONSTANTINOV

Yrs. of NHL service: 2
Born: Murmansk, Russia; Mar. 19, 1967
Position: right defense
Height: 5-11
Weight: 176
Uniform no.: 16
Shoots: right

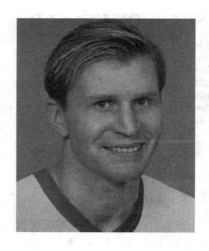

Career statistics:

GP	G	A	TP	PIM
161	13	42	55	309

1991-92 statistics:

GP	G	A	TP	+/-	PIM	PP	SH	GW	GT	S	PCT
79	8	25	33	+25	172	1	0	2	0	102	7.4

1992-93 statistics:

GP	G	A	TP	+/-	PIM	PP	SH	GW	GT	S	PCT
82	5	17	22	+22	137	0	0	0	0	85	5.9

LAST SEASON

Games played career high in second NHL season. Point production decreased by 11. Missed two games with groin injury.

THE FINESSE GAME

Dynamic skating buoys Konstantinov's game. He is all over the ice, to the extent that he has to be calmed down or else he is too aggressive in the neutral zone and gets caught. He does not get overly involved in the attack, but when he does he'll make a good passing play rather than waste a shot when he is in deep, because he doesn't want to chance the shot being blocked before he has a chance to turn back up ice.

Konstantinov is a fine skater with speed, agility, lateral movement, balance and strength. He is used on the first penalty-killing unit and will be on the ice to protect a lead late. He has good hand skills but sometimes is guilty of overhandling the puck in the defensive zone.

There were some mix-ups between Konstantinov and goalie Tim Cheveldae, which means his thought process in English might still be a little slow.

THE PHYSICAL GAME

We are hard-pressed to think of a small defenseman who plays tougher and meaner than Konstantinov. If he gets the chance, he will put the hurt on an attacker. He will ride a skater into the boards, and he might use his stick high, too. People are always trying to swat him, but he's not afraid of retaliation.

THE INTANGIBLES

Konstantinov is still learning the game, and he made some glaring blunders in the playoffs, but along with Steve Chiasson (his regular partner), Konstantinov formed part of Detroit's top defensive tandem. He's only going to get better and more annoying to play against. He was the captain of his Central Red Army team in Russia, and wants to be a leader.

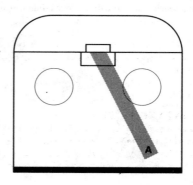

MARTIN LAPOINTE

Yrs. of NHL service: 0
Born: Lachine, Que.; Sept. 12, 1973
Position: right wing
Height: 5-11
Weight: 200
Uniform no.: 22
Shoots: right

Career statistics:

GP	G	A	TP	PIM
7	0	1	1	5

1991-92 statistics:

GP	G	A	TP	+/-	PIM	PP	SH	GW	GT	S	PCT
4	0	1	1	+2	5	0	0	0	0	2	0.0

1992-93 statistics:

GP	G	A	TP	+/-	PIM	PP	SH	GW	GT	S	PCT
3	0	0	0	-2	0	0	0	0	0	2	0.0

LAST SEASON

Played for Laval (QMJHL) and was second on team in scoring despite missing half of season; scored 38-51-89 in 35 games with 41 PIM. Played for gold medal-winning Team Canada in World Junior Championships. Also played conditioning stint with Adirondack (AHL), scoring 1-2-3 in eight games.

THE FINESSE GAME

Yet another sparkler from the blueblooded 1991 draft (taken 10th overall by Detroit), Lapointe appears ready to make the jump to the NHL this season. He is a strong, powerful, quick skater, with a work ethic that enhances all of his natural skills.

Lapointe is as much a finisher as a playmaker. He has a good short game, working passes low between the face-off dots. He doesn't have breakaway speed, but his acceleration helps him create odd-man situations deep in the zone, and he is adept at getting open for the return pass on a give-and-go.

His defensive play is advanced for a player out of the Quebec league. He is an intelligent player who should blossom under new coach Scotty Bowman.

THE PHYSICAL GAME

Lapointe is an opportunist around the net, jumping on loose pucks like a miner finding gold nuggets. He finishes his checks and, with his sturdy build and dynamic skating, can hit hard. He has improved his upper body strength and cardiovascular conditioning over the past two season (after showing up last fall in disappointing shape), which may indicate a mature approach to the game that is about to become his livelihood.

THE INTANGIBLES

Lapointe was the captain of his Laval team and the Canadian World Junior Team (where he led his team with 5-4-9 in seven games). He is said to be as much a budding leader as a budding star. The Red Wings could use some shoring up on the right side behind Dino Ciccarelli, and Lapointe should move right in. If he gets the ice time, he is easily capable of a 25-goal rookie season.

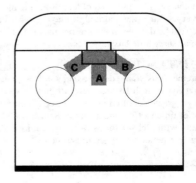

NICKLAS LIDSTROM

Yrs. of NHL service: 2
Born: Västerås, Sweden; Apr. 28, 1970
Position: right defense
Height: 6-1
Weight: 176
Uniform no.: 5
Shoots: left

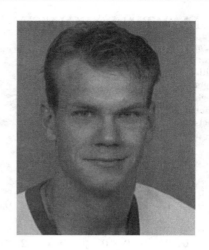

Career statistics:

GP	G	A	TP	PIM
164	18	83	101	50

1991-92 statistics:

GP	G	A	TP	+/-	PIM	PP	SH	GW	GT	S	PCT
80	11	49	60	+36	22	5	0	1	1	168	6.5

1992-93 statistics:

GP	G	A	TP	+/-	PIM	PP	SH	GW	GT	S	PCT
84	7	34	41	+7	28	3	0	2	0	156	4.5

LAST SEASON

One of two Red Wings to appear in all 84 games. Has not missed a game in his two seasons in NHL. Point production dropped by 19.

THE FINESSE GAME

After a strong first half in his rookie season (1991-92), Lidstrom has come back to earth a little, but he will be better for the struggle as he continues to adjust to life in the NHL.

Lidstrom is an excellent skater and has good vision of the ice. He prefers to look for the breakout pass, rather than carry the puck, and he has a very good point shot. He is not as effective moving the puck in the attacking zone, although he sees point duty on the second power play unit. He does not like to venture in much beyond his point, and he has yet to develop a glide across the blue line that would help his point shot.

Lidstrom seems to have a little trouble handling the puck in his feet, which is unusual for European skaters, who traditionally have some soccer training.

THE PHYSICAL GAME

Lidstrom does not take the body well, but he does take great pains to protect the puck with his body. He won't cough up the puck out of fear of getting hit. He is a very solid skater, although playing with Paul Coffey (as he did late in the season) means Lidstrom has to be sharper defensively.

THE INTANGIBLES

The tremendous young defense corps in Los Angeles (Darryl Sydor, Rob Blake, Alexei Zhitnik) give Paul Coffey a great deal of credit for their development in the brief time Coffey was with the Kings. If Coffey remains with Detroit this season, he could have a similarly beneficial effect on Lidstrom.

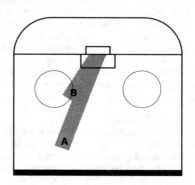

KEITH PRIMEAU

Yrs. of NHL service: 3
Born: Toronto, Ont.; Nov. 24, 1971
Position: left wing/centre
Height: 6-4
Weight: 220
Uniform no.: 55
Shoots: left

Career statistics:

GP	G	A	TP	PIM
166	24	39	63	341

1991-92 statistics:

GP	G	A	TP	+/-	PIM	PP	SH	GW	GT	S	PCT
35	6	10	16	+9	83	0	0	0	0	27	22.2

1992-93 statistics:

GP	G	A	TP	+/-	PIM	PP	SH	GW	GT	S	PCT
73	15	17	32	-6	152	4	1	2	1	75	20.0

LAST SEASON

Games played, goals, assists, points and PIM at career highs. Missed two games with flu, seven games with shoulder and knee injuries.

THE FINESSE GAME

Watching Primeau skate really makes one appreciate Eric Lindros. The two behemoths are about the same size (Lindros is listed as an inch taller and seven pounds heavier), yet Lindros could skate rings around the slow-footed Primeau. Primeau is actually a fairly good skater once he gets moving, but it just...takes...so...long, especially when Primeau is turning out of a corner with the puck.

With Jimmy Carson dealt to L.A. for Paul Coffey, ice time opened up for Primeau at centre. Primeau has been shifted from centre to left wing, and we actually like him better on the left side because of Detroit's depth at centre and the reduced defensive responsibility.

Primeau has very nice hands for a big guy and can control the puck in traffic. Most of his scoring chances come from a snap shot from the left circle or work in front of the net. He has all the makings and instincts of a power forward.

THE PHYSICAL GAME

Primeau is massive and loves to hit. Nonetheless, he loses some battles to smaller players because he is not as good a skater as he should be and his balance is below average. He looks far less clumsy and coltish than he did a season ago, as if he's gotten accustomed to a new body. Patience will pay off, because Primeau is a hard worker who needs ice time and confidence to improve.

THE INTANGIBLES

Primeau is the subject of many trade rumours — because who wouldn't want a forward this huge? Forget it, he's staying in Detroit, and is due for a breakout season soon. We predicted in last year's *HSR* that a 30-goal season would be coming "this season or next." This is "next" for Primeau, and with a regular role he should hit the mark.

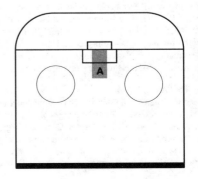

BOB PROBERT

Yrs. of NHL service: 6
Born: Windsor, Ont.; June 5, 1965
Position: right wing
Height: 6-3
Weight: 215
Uniform no.: 24
Shoots: left

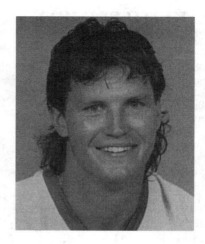

Career statistics:

GP	G	A	TP	PIM
408	107	135	242	1815

1991-92 statistics:

GP	G	A	TP	+/-	PIM	PP	SH	GW	GT	S	PCT
63	20	24	44	+16	276	8	0	1	0	96	20.8

1992-93 statistics:

GP	G	A	TP	+/-	PIM	PP	SH	GW	GT	S	PCT
80	14	29	43	-9	292	6	0	3	0	128	10.9

LAST SEASON

Restrictions on Probert's travel out of the U.S. were lifted by the Immigration Department in mid-season, allowing him to play in a career-high 80 games. Led team in PIM.

THE FINESSE GAME

Probert is a slugger with a nice touch. He needs a little time to get away his shot, but let's face it, not too many brave souls play him that tight. In traffic, he can stickhandle and even slide a backhand pass down low. His shots aren't very heavy, but he is accurate and shoots mostly from close range.

Probert doesn't have open-ice speed, but in tight he has one-step quickness and can even pivot surprisingly well with the puck. He can be used up front on the power play because he parks himself right in front of the net, and the goaltender looks like a bobble-head doll as he tries to peer around his frame for a view of the puck. Probert just has to be careful not to take a penalty while his team is a man up.

Probert has to play with linemates who get him the puck since he can't help out in pursuing the disc.

THE PHYSICAL GAME

Probert is the best fighter in the NHL, no matter what Tie Domi says. He is strong, quick-fisted and mean, but he is slow to rile on some nights when other teams decide it is best to let a sleeping dog lie. When he falls asleep on the ice, he is a non-factor.

The clamp-down on goalie interference rules has taken away one of the Probert's favourite tactics.

THE INTANGIBLES

Probert benefited from the arrival of defenseman Paul Coffey, who seemed to regard the big winger as a personal reclamation project. Under Coffey's urging, Probert intensified his off-ice workouts and, after almost two seasons of being out of shape, his conditioning improved, and he is a stronger player with better stamina. However, rumours abounded that the Red Wings have given up on Probert because of his inconsistency, and he might be shopped around during the off-season.

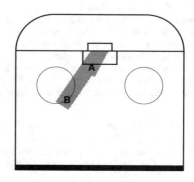

YVES RACINE

Yrs. of NHL service: 4
Born: Matane, Que.; Feb. 7, 1969
Position: right defense
Height: 6-0
Weight: 185
Uniform no.: 33
Shoots: left

Career statistics:

GP	G	A	TP	PIM
231	22	102	124	230

1991-92 statistics:

GP	G	A	TP	+/-	PIM	PP	SH	GW	GT	S	PCT
61	2	22	24	-6	94	1	0	0	0	103	1.9

1992-93 statistics:

GP	G	A	TP	+/-	PIM	PP	SH	GW	GT	S	PCT
80	9	31	40	+10	80	5	0	0	0	163	5.5

LAST SEASON

Games played and goals career highs. Missed four games with shoulder injury.

THE FINESSE GAME

Racine is a good skater with agility and quickness. He can carry the puck on a rush, but he is also capable of finding the open man for a long up-ice pass.

He likes to get involved in the attack and will make the occasional foray deep into the offensive zone. He controls the puck well and protects it with his body. Breaking out of his defensive zone, Racine's long passes may be second only to Paul Coffey's on the team, when he has the time.

Racine was moved from left to right defense last season. On the point, that opens up his left shot for the one-timer.

He is a good skater with speed and agility.

THE PHYSICAL GAME

Racine tends to play soft. He is not a big defenseman, but since he lacks overwhelming finesse skills, he has to play a more physical style to earn an NHL job on a nightly basis. Currently he is fifth on the Detroit depth chart, but would move up if he would hit more consistently.

Racine is susceptible to a strong forecheck, and he tends to hurry his passes or overhandle the puck under pressure.

THE INTANGIBLES

Racine continued to show steady development until last season, when his overall play levelled off, although his offensive totals improved. We're willing to give him the benefit of the doubt for another year, but this could be his make-or-break season.

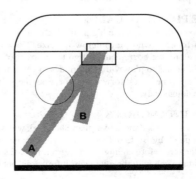

RAY SHEPPARD

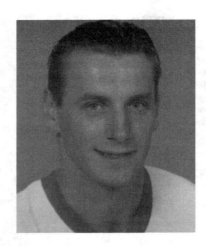

Yrs. of NHL service: 6
Born: Pembroke, Ont.; May 27, 1966
Position: right wing
Height: 6-1
Weight: 182
Uniform no.: 26
Shoots: right

Career statistics:

GP	G	A	TP	PIM
362	156	133	289	106

1991-92 statistics:

GP	G	A	TP	+/-	PIM	PP	SH	GW	GT	S	PCT
74	36	26	62	+7	27	11	1	4	1	178	20.2

1992-93 statistics:

GP	G	A	TP	+/-	PIM	PP	SH	GW	GT	S	PCT
70	32	34	66	+7	29	10	0	1	0	183	17.5

LAST SEASON

Assists and points at career highs. Missed eight games with knee injury.

THE FINESSE GAME

Sheppard is a finisher. He is not a very good skater. He looks excruciatingly slow, but this is deceptive because he is almost always in a good scoring position. He doesn't turn quickly and doesn't have great balance, but he can curl out of the right circle on his backhand and get off a wrist or snap shot. He is also strong enough to ward off a defender with one hand and shovel a pass or push a shot toward the net with his other hand.

There are times when Sheppard looks like a puck magnet. He is always eager to move to the puck and has good hockey sense and vision. Although he is a winger, he has a centre's view of the ice. Sheppard is not selfish, and though he loves to shoot he will dish off if he spies a teammate with a better percentage shot. He has good hands with a quick release and doesn't waste any time with a big backswing. He prefers efficiency and accuracy.

Because of his sluggish skating, Sheppard is a defensive liability. He is usually the last player back when play breaks back out of the offensive zone.

THE PHYSICAL GAME

Sheppard does not play a big game. He's an average-sized forward who plays below his size. He won't work along the boards but will go to the front of the net, so he has to play with one grinder to get him the puck and one quick forward to serve as the safety valve defensively.

THE INTANGIBLES

Few cats have had more lives than Sheppard, who was given up on by Buffalo, then let go as a free agent by the Rangers before ending up in Detroit. He lacks the skills to match with the elite Detroit forwards, but his work on the power play and his willingness to pay a physical price in front of the net establish him right at the top of the second flight.

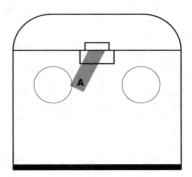

STEVE YZERMAN

Yrs. of NHL service: 10
Born: Cranbrook, B.C.; May 9, 1965
Position: centre
Height: 5-11
Weight: 183
Uniform no.: 19
Shoots: right

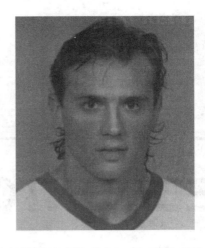

Career statistics:

GP	G	A	TP	PIM
757	445	595	1040	476

1991-92 statistics:

GP	G	A	TP	+/-	PIM	PP	SH	GW	GT	S	PCT
79	45	58	103	+26	64	9	8	9	0	295	15.3

1992-93 statistics:

GP	G	A	TP	+/-	PIM	PP	SH	GW	GT	S	PCT
84	58	79	137	+33	44	13	7	6	0	307	18.9

LAST SEASON

Reached 1000-point milestone. One of two Red Wings to appear in all 84 games. Scored 50 or more goals for fifth time in last six seasons; scored 100 or more points for sixth consecutive season. Led team in goals, assists, points, shorthanded goals and shots. Tied for team lead in plus/minus. Fourth in NHL in scoring. Tied for league lead in shorthanded goals.

THE FINESSE GAME

Yzerman is the very model of consistency. His lapses during the season are few, and he seldom goes through a prolonged scoring slump. Considering how much ice time he gets, and how active a skater he is, this is a great tribute to his devotion to conditioning and preparing himself for a game. Yzerman has always seemed mature beyond his years, even when he broke into the league at age 18, and he is hitting his peak now at 28.

He is a sensational skater. He zigs and zags all over the ice, spending very little time in the centre. He can turn on a dime and give a nickel change. He has great balance and quick feet, and is adroit at kicking the puck up onto his blade for a shot, in seamless motion. Yzerman is also strong for an average-sized forward. He protects the puck well with his body and has the arm strength for wraparound shots and off-balance shots through traffic.

Yzerman prefers to stickhandle down the right side of the ice. In addition to using his body to shield the ice, he uses the boards to protect the puck, and if a defender starts reaching in with his stick he usually ends up pulling Yzerman down for a penalty.

Yzerman uses his stop-and-start skating to great effect on the power play. He works down low from the left wing, creating havoc as he lures defenders into chasing him while Dino Ciccarelli or Bob Probert is camped in front of the net, Sergei Fedorov is wheeling, and Paul Coffey is loading up his shot from the point. Small wonder the Red Wings led the NHL in power play efficiency last season.

One of Yzerman's weaknesses is on face-offs. He is only average for a centre of his overall skill and reputation. Defensively, he still has a few flaws, but he is an outstanding penalty killer because of his speed and anticipation.

THE PHYSICAL GAME

Yzerman sacrifices his body willingly in the right circumstances. Detroit certainly doesn't want to see him going haywire and checking bigger players all over the ice. He will pay the price along the boards and around the net, and he's deceptively strong and durable. Yzerman has missed only two of 404 games over the past five seasons.

THE INTANGIBLES

The only knock on Yzerman's imminent greatness is his failure to achieve any playoff success in Detroit. With the team's first-round failure last season, the sounds of dissatisfaction are even louder in the Motor City, but don't look for Yzerman to be changing addresses, no matter what trade rumours are whispered. He is the heart of this team and isn't the one to blame for the Wings' playoff failures.

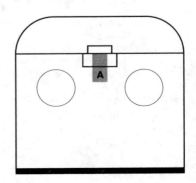

EDMONTON OILERS

BRIAN BENNING

Yrs. of NHL service: 7
Born: Edmonton, Alta.; June 10, 1966
Position: right defense
Height: 6-1
Weight: 195
Uniform no.: 19
Shoots: left

Career statistics:

GP	G	A	TP	PIM
471	56	202	258	834

1991-92 statistics:

GP	G	A	TP	+/-	PIM	PP	SH	GW	GT	S	PCT
75	4	42	46	-5	134	2	0	0	0	152	2.6

1992-93 statistics:

GP	G	A	TP	+/-	PIM	PP	SH	GW	GT	S	PCT
55	10	24	34	-1	152	6	0	0	0	115	8.7

LAST SEASON

Acquired from Philadelphia for Greg Hawgood and Josef Beranek. Due to injuries, games played matches career low. Goals most since rookie season in 1986-87.

THE FINESSE GAME

Benning is a smooth skater, all offense, but his skills don't quite make up for his deficiencies in other areas. He is a lefthanded shot playing the right shot, and he covers a lot of ground.

Not a great puck carrier, Benning is better at making the pass and then moving up into the play and getting into open ice for a return pass, and he does so eagerly. He's an asset on the power play. He reads offensive situations well, and his forehand is always open for one-timers.

Benning can be a liability defensively, and he loses ice time because he sits when the bench gets shortened.

THE PHYSICAL GAME

Benning has trouble with anyone grinding against him. He is fine in open ice, because he can read plays and intercept passes, but he is not very strong in the close one-on-one confrontations. He can be beaten along the boards and sometimes carelessly tries to fish for the puck instead of play the body. He has a little bit of a mean streak and will bring his stick up now and again.

THE INTANGIBLES

The points will come for Benning, who should be in the 15 to 20 goals range. But the Oilers are his fourth team in four seasons, which indicates that he wears out his welcome (and a coach's patience) rather quickly.

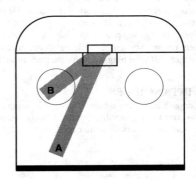

KELLY BUCHBERGER

Yrs. of NHL service: 5
Born: Langenburg, Sask.; Dec. 2, 1966
Position: left wing
Height: 6-2
Weight: 210
Uniform no.: 16
Shoots: right

Career statistics:

GP	G	A	TP	PIM
366	43	58	91	933

1991-92 statistics:

GP	G	A	TP	+/-	PIM	PP	SH	GW	GT	S	PCT
79	20	24	44	+9	157	0	4	3	1	90	7.3

1992-93 statistics:

GP	G	A	TP	+/-	PIM	PP	SH	GW	GT	S	PCT
83	12	18	30	-27	133	1	2	3	0	92	13.0

LAST SEASON

Point production slipped 14 points from career high last season. PIM declined for fifth consecutive season.

THE FINESSE GAME

Buchberger is an ideal third-line player. Night in and night out, he faces other teams' top forwards and does a terrific shadow job, harassing without taking bad penalties.

He works hard and provides a consistent effort. He will grind, go to the net, kill penalties — all of the grunt work. He can finish off some plays now and then, but that is not his objective. The biggest change in Buchberger is that he has developed some degree of confidence in his finesse moves and is now willing to try something that looks too difficult for a "defensive" player. Sometimes it works, sometimes it doesn't.

Buchberger has some straight-ahead speed and will go to the net and muck, but this kind of player needs some luck to get goals. He has earned a great deal of respect for his work ethic.

THE PHYSICAL GAME

Buchberger is a legitimately tough customer. Honest and gritty, he won't get knocked around and is a solid hitter who likes the physical part of the game. He is a very disciplined player. He's also very determined. He keeps his legs moving constantly, and a player who lets up on this winger will be sorry, because Buchberger will keep plugging with the puck or to the net.

THE INTANGIBLES

Buchberger's points are a bonus. His job is being aggressive and killing penalties, and 20 goals (scored two seasons ago) is his absolute ceiling.

ZDENO CIGER

Yrs. of NHL service: 3
Born: Martin, Czechoslovakia; Oct. 19, 1969
Position: left wing
Height: 6-1
Weight: 190
Uniform no.: 8
Shoots: left

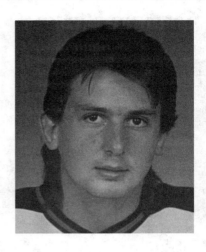

Career statistics:

GP	G	A	TP	PIM
129	27	45	72	26

1991-92 statistics:

GP	G	A	TP	+/-	PIM	PP	SH	GW	GT	S	PCT
20	6	5	11	-2	10	1	0	0	0	33	18.2

1992-93 statistics:

GP	G	A	TP	+/-	PIM	PP	SH	GW	GT	S	PCT
64	13	23	36	-13	8	2	0	2	0	106	12.3

LAST SEASON

Games played, goals, assists and points at career highs. Acquired from New Jersey with Kevin Todd for Bernie Nicholls.

THE FINESSE GAME

Ciger has an excellent variety of shots, and the problem that plagues many shooters out of European systems is that they don't tee it up as often as they should. Ciger will look to make a play first, hesitating just long enough that the goalie moves or the defenseman blocks the shot.

Ciger has a slapshot with great velocity, and better snap and wrist shots from in tight. He is a very accurate shooter and doesn't waste shots from low-risk scoring areas.

He does not skate well with the puck, which slows him down. He is a quick skater, and strong and light on his feet, but he shouldn't spend much time with the puck on his blade.

Though still a pretty anonymous player, he has the ability to be more of a presence.

THE PHYSICAL GAME

Ciger is wiry and strong, but he doesn't use his body well in traffic areas. If he were just a little more willing to go to the front of the net and use his wrist shot, he would be much more of an offensive force. We've seen little indication that Ciger will develop along those lines.

Defensively, he has good awareness, but he doesn't work hard in the defensive zone.

THE INTANGIBLES

The change of scenery did wonders for Ciger, who had trouble getting into the New Jersey line-up and was frustrated by his lack of ice time. In his 37 games with the Oilers, he collected 9 goals and 15 assists, double the points he had in 27 games with the Devils. Injuries have been an excuse in the past, and now he has a fresh start. This could be the last season for Ciger to establish himself as an NHLer.

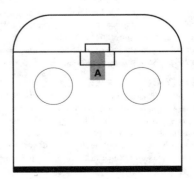

SHAYNE CORSON

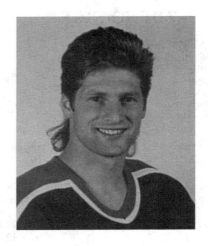

Yrs. of NHL service: 7
Born: Barrie, Ont.; Aug. 13, 1966
Position: centre
Height: 6-0
Weight: 175
Uniform no.: 9
Shoots: left

Career statistics:

GP	G	A	TP	PIM
500	137	197	334	1100

1991-92 statistics:

GP	G	A	TP	+/-	PIM	PP	SH	GW	GT	S	PCT
64	17	36	53	+15	118	3	0	2	0	165	10.3

1992-93 statistics:

GP	G	A	TP	+/-	PIM	PP	SH	GW	GT	S	PCT
80	16	31	47	-19	209	9	2	1	0	164	9.8

LAST SEASON

Acquired from Montreal with Brent Gilchrist and Vladimir Vujtek for Vincent Damphousse and a 1993 fourth-round draft choice. Games played matched career high. Tied for team lead in assists. Goals at five-season low. PIM at career high.

THE FINESSE GAME

Corson gets his goals mucking around the front of the net, and he's an above-average mucker in that he has hands around the cage.

He can play wing or centre. Corson can pick up a lot of rebound goals if he gets on a line with people who throw the puck to the net, because he will go barrelling in for it. He's freed up to play that style more on the left wing than on centre, but he also has some nice playmaking abilities when put in the middle. He won't do anything too fancy but is intelligent enough to play a basic short game.

Corson is a powerful skater but not very fast or agile. He has good balance for his work along the boards. He has all the attributes of a power forward, but hasn't yet put the ingredients together to play that style of game consistently.

He works on both special teams. He does his dirty work in front of the net for screens and deflections, and has the hands to guide hard point shots. (Although most of his shots are made from close range, he can be a wildly inaccurate shooter.)

Corson can be used on draws and uses his strength to neutralize the opposing forwards.

THE PHYSICAL GAME

His longest suit is his play along the boards, but because he was played at centre most of the season, that effectiveness was neutralized. He can lose it once in a while and take some bad penalties. Corson doesn't give up on his checks, but he needs to develop more consistent focus and concentration in all areas of the ice.

THE INTANGIBLES

Fans tend to think of players' worlds being limited to a 200' x 85' sheet of ice, but reality beyond the boards intruded on Corson last season. His father's illness with cancer and eventual death drained all possible reserves of energy from the fine power forward, and anyone analyzing his stats should be careful to take his personal concerns into account. Corson is capable of scoring 35 to 40 goals if he gets some help on this dreadful Edmonton squad.

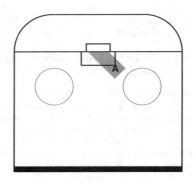

TODD ELIK

Yrs. of NHL service: 4
Born: Brampton, Ont.; Apr. 15, 1966
Position: centre
Height: 6-2
Weight: 190
Uniform no.: 34
Shoots: left

Career statistics:

GP	G	A	TP	PIM
244	60	118	178	243

1991-92 statistics:

GP	G	A	TP	+/-	PIM	PP	SH	GW	GT	S	PCT
62	15	31	46	0	125	4	3	1	0	118	12.7

1992-93 statistics:

GP	G	A	TP	+/-	PIM	PP	SH	GW	GT	S	PCT
60	14	27	41	-4	56	4	0	1	1	104	13.5

LAST SEASON

Acquired from Minnesota for Brent Gilchrist. Underwent surgery on left shoulder. Games played and points lowest since rookie season.

THE FINESSE GAME

Elik's hand skills aren't up to his high speed, so he can't carry the puck or make many moves at high tempo. He often looks off-balance when he starts a rush because he is having trouble moving the puck.

He has to work hard for his goals by going to the net. He doesn't shoot well in stride, because he has to slow down to get the shot off. He has a decent wrist shot that he uses at close range.

Elik will have an occasional night when everything is going his way offensively, and he can dazzle, but when his offensive contributions aren't forthcoming, he gets down mentally and does little to help his team in any other way.

He needs to improve his defensive game if he wants a regular job in the NHL, since it's clear his future is as a checking forward.

THE PHYSICAL GAME

Elik has the size and speed to be more of an impact player physically. He will use his body fairly consistently in the offensive zone, and he has the agility to be a good forechecker. But he isn't very strong, and he loses many of the one-on-one battles in traffic.

THE INTANGIBLES

Injuries have bothered Elik in recent seasons, and he has played for three different teams in three years. It's tough to find a niche that way; now 27, he may not have too many more chances to prove himself. He has found a groove as a journeyman spare winger. It would take 25 goals to change that opinion.

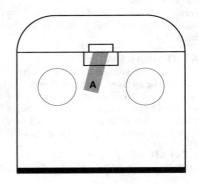

IGOR KRAVCHUK

Yrs. of NHL service: 2
Born: Ufa, Russia; Sept. 13, 1966
Position: right defense
Height: 6-1
Weight: 200
Uniform no.: 21
Shoots: left

Career statistics:

GP	G	A	TP	PIM
73	11	25	36	36

1992-93 statistics:

GP	G	A	TP	+/-	PIM	PP	SH	GW	GT	S	PCT
55	10	17	27	+3	32	4	0	0	0	143	7.0

LAST SEASON

Acquired from Chicago with Dean McAmmond for Joe Murphy. First full NHL season. Missed games with a sprained left ankle.

THE FINESSE GAME

Kravchuk is a big defenseman who does a lot of little things very well. There is no one facet of his game that stands out from the rest, but there are no serious flaws, either. Kravchuk's skills are subtle. He has very good offensive instincts, with a sound defensive game as the basis for his world class skills. Kravchuk was a member of the CIS team that won the gold medal at the 1992 Olympics.

Kravchuk is an exceptionally mobile skater. He can pivot like a figure skater with the puck and accelerate quickly. Kravchuk likes to jump into the play and keeps the puck moving. He sees the ice well.

Kravchuk plays the point on the power play, and will freeze a defenseman with a fake slap shot before sliding a pass down low. Kravchuk can also fire, and he has the moves to beat a defender in open ice.

Kravchuk will also play dump and chase hockey, and is seldom guilty of trying to force a play at the attacking blue line, thus minimizing the risk of turnovers and counterattacks.

Kravchuk is also an intelligent penalty killer, and utilizes his skating well, and he is strong in four-on-four team play.

THE PHYSICAL GAME

Kravchuk has some strength but he is a pusher, not a hitter. He will tie up his man in front of the net, or lean with his stick on top of an opponent's to keep that player from doing something with the puck, but Kravchuk won't wipe anyone out. It won't hurt to keep him paired with the physical Dave Manson.

THE INTANGIBLES

Kravchuk became the Oilers' No. 1 defenseman the day he was traded. Kravchuk gets a lot of ice on the first power play and when the bench is shortened. He is a reliable player who will produce 15-20 goals a season when healthy, a very good two-way defenseman.

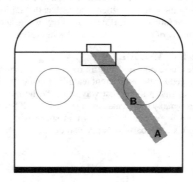

CRAIG MACTAVISH

Yrs. of NHL service: 12
Born: London, Ont.; Aug. 15, 1958
Position: centre
Height: 6-1
Weight: 195
Uniform no.: 14
Shoots: left

Career statistics:

GP	G	A	TP	PIM
852	183	232	415	674

1992-93 statistics:

GP	G	A	TP	+/-	PIM	PP	SH	GW	GT	S	PCT
82	10	20	30	-16	110	0	3	3	0	101	9.9

LAST SEASON

Missed two games with back injury to end a consecutive games played streak of 518. Led team in short-handed goals.

THE FINESSE GAME

MacTavish's game is all defense. He could once be counted on for a steady 20-25 goals a season, but that has been cut in half. Yet MacTavish remains a valuable role player.

He is among the best in the league at face-offs. He is among the best in the league at cheating on face-offs. MacTavish always seems to have his body turned a little more than he should, or doesn't have his stick on the ice the way he supposed to. Subtle enough to not get caught, effective enough to give him an edge.

MacTavish plays a basic offensive game, just getting the puck and moving it quickly. He can hang on and rag the puck when he's killing penalties, but he seldom overhandles.

MacTavish keeps himself fit and his effort is non-stop.

THE PHYSICAL GAME

MacTavish's competitive fire still burns, even though he is one of the dinosaurs left to remind the Oilers of their old glory days. He gives his all, and his durability is amazing given the way he sacrifices every night. Think of how tough it must have been mentally for MacTavish to watch his team's ownership strip the once-proud franchise over the past few seasons. It hasn't stopped MacTavish from being a gamer.

MacTavish forechecks tenaciously, and will drive to the net dragging a defender with him.

THE INTANGIBLES

Although he is very near the end of his career, MacTavish remains a terrific penalty killer and clutch player. Note that 3 of his 10 goals were game-winners,

and 3 were shorthanders. MacTavish doesn't score often, but it seems that when he does, they really count. MacTavish is an on-ice leader.

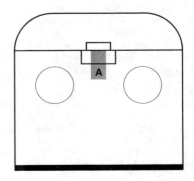

DAVE MANSON

Yrs. of NHL service: 7
Born: Prince Albert, Sask.; Jan. 27, 1967
Position: left defense
Height: 6-2
Weight: 202
Uniform no.: 24
Shoots: left

Career statistics:

GP	G	A	TP	PIM
492	69	150	219	1607

1991-92 statistics:

GP	G	A	TP	+/-	PIM	PP	SH	GW	GT	S	PCT
79	15	32	47	+9	220	7	0	2	0	206	7.3

1992-93 statistics:

GP	G	A	TP	+/-	PIM	PP	SH	GW	GT	S	PCT
83	15	30	45	-28	210	9	1	1	1	244	6.1

LAST SEASON

Led team in PIM and shots on goal. Led team defensemen in scoring. Worst plus/minus on team.

THE FINESSE GAME

Defensively Manson could be ranked among the top defensemen in the league. He has all of the physical tools to be there, but he's his own worst enemy. He needs more maturity and patience. He will often leave his position to support his defense partner, even when his partner has things under control and doesn't need the help. This simply results in a hole on the left side of the ice.

Manson's best scoring weapon is a one-timer from the point. He is smart and effective on the power play, because he will mix up his shot with a big fake and freeze. But there isn't much that's subtle about Manson. His game is power.

Manson is a very good skater for a big player. He jumps into the play eagerly (sometimes too eagerly — he will get caught out of position up-ice) and can make a 360 in a small space with the puck. He will gamble down deep and is canny enough to use an accurate wrist shot when he is in close.

THE PHYSICAL GAME

Manson can throw himself off his game. He will lose control, run after people and take bad penalties. He patrols the front of his net well, can hit to hurt, and intimidates players into getting rid of the puck faster than they want to. They flinch from even the threat of a Manson bodycheck.

THE INTANGIBLES

Manson is not yet a true No. 1 defenseman. He looked that way playing alongside Chris Chelios in Chicago, but he hasn't been the player in Edmonton that he was with the Blackhawks. He works hard and wants to do well, but being No. 1 is too hot for him to handle. Playing with Igor Kravchuk should help Manson.

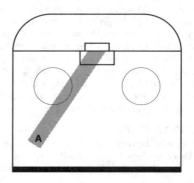

SHJON PODEIN

Yrs. of NHL service: 1
Born: Rochester, Minn.; Mar. 5, 1968
Position: centre
Height: 6-2
Weight: 200
Uniform no.: 26
Shoots: left

Career statistics:

GP	G	A	TP	PIM
40	13	6	19	25

1992-93 statistics:

GP	G	A	TP	+/-	PIM	PP	SH	GW	GT	S	PCT
40	13	6	19	-2	25	2	1	1	0	64	20.3

LAST SEASON
First NHL season.

THE FINESSE GAME
Podein is a labourer. He works hard, has nice size and uses it around the net well.

He has had a long trek to the NHL. Drafted 166th overall in 1988, he played three years at Minnesota-Duluth, had two years in the minors and graduated last season to the NHL.

Podein developed as a centre, but he is better suited to play wing. He is a mucker, not a fancy scorer. He gets most of his goals from digging around the net for rebounds. He doesn't have many finesse skills, and he isn't a good stickhandler, so he must remain intent on scoring.

Podein is not a smooth skater. He seems to run on the ice, but he gets to where he has to go by effort.

THE PHYSICAL GAME
Podein has to use his size consistently. He needs to establish himself around the net and in the corners. Kind of a happy-go-lucky guy, right now he's a follower instead of a leader. That's okay, as long as he follows the right person.

THE INTANGIBLES
A young player, Podein has to put his career ahead of other things. He had the option of going back to play for Cape Breton (AHL) in the Calder Cup playoffs after participating with Team USA in the World Championships, and he went, which shows a commitment on his part. It would have been easy to say no, but he took that step to make himself a better player. He must continue his commitment to off-ice conditioning as well.

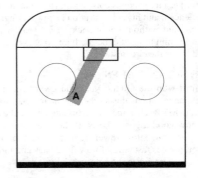

BILL RANFORD

Yrs. of NHL service: 7
Born: Brandon, Man.; Dec. 14, 1966
Position: goaltender
Height: 5-10
Weight: 170
Uniform no.: 30
Catches: left

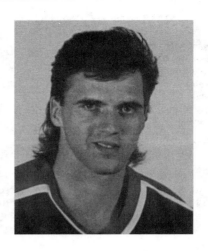

Career statistics:

GP	MINS	GA	SO	GAA	A	PIM
330	18,405	1053	7	3.43	15	48

1991-92 statistics:

GP	MINS	GAA	W	L	T	SO	GA	S	SAPCT	PIM
67	3822	3.58	27	26	10	1	228	1971	.884	4

1992-93 statistics:

GP	MINS	GAA	W	L	T	SO	GA	S	SAPCT	PIM
67	3753	3.84	17	38	6	1	240	2065	.885	10

LAST SEASON

Fewest wins since 1988-89. Highest GAA of career.

THE PHYSICAL GAME

Ranford is notable for his great first-save capability. He is probably among the top five goalies in the league in that regard, but Edmonton was such a poor team defensively last season that he was frequently called upon to make the third, fourth and fifth saves. That would be too much for even Georges Vezina.

Ranford is a shining example of a goalie who made it to the NHL on his reflexes and continues there because he added elements of angle play and focus. He comes out of his net and, when he is on his game, he doesn't leave a lot of rebounds.

Very patient, Ranford hardly ever commits before the shooter does. He has good lateral movement and great confidence in his skating. He moves with the shooter well, keeping the five-hole closed. He doesn't drop down unless he has to, and when he does, he bounces back up quickly.

Ranford uses his stick aggressively around the net to break up passes. He also stops hard-arounds and whips passes out to his teammates.

THE MENTAL GAME

Ranford is a tremendous competitor. He is mature and experienced, and his concentration is unwavering. He is confident without being cocky. Last season was tough for him to handle, but he bore up as well as he could under the circumstances.

THE INTANGIBLES

Ranford won the Oilers' year-end award for most three-star selections during the season and was voted the team MVP. That, more than his numbers, indicates just how good a goalie he is. If the Oilers improve defensively to allow fewer quality shots and clear away rebounds faster, Ranford will be back among the league leaders, where he belongs.

LUKE RICHARDSON

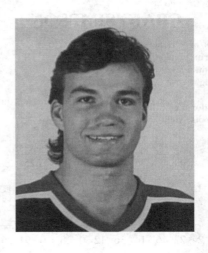

Yrs. of NHL service: 6
Born: Ottawa, Ont.; Mar. 26, 1969
Position: right defense
Height: 6-3
Weight: 215
Uniform no.: 22
Shoots: left

Career statistics:

GP	G	A	TP	PIM
435	16	65	81	816

1991-92 statistics:

GP	G	A	TP	+/-	PIM	PP	SH	GW	GT	S	PCT
75	2	19	21	-9	118	0	0	0	0	85	2.4

1992-93 statistics:

GP	G	A	TP	+/-	PIM	PP	SH	GW	GT	S	PCT
82	3	10	13	-18	142	0	2	0	0	78	3.8

LAST SEASON

Assists and points at two-season lows.

THE FINESSE GAME

You've heard of two-way defensemen. Richardson is a no-way defenseman.

There isn't enough hitting to designate him as a take-charge guy, insufficient positioning and smarts to mark him as a steady stay-at-home type, and he lends minimal offensive input.

Richardson is a good skater with lateral mobility and balance but not much speed. He can't carry the puck and doesn't jump up into the rush well. He seldom uses his point shot, which is adequate.

Defensively, Richardson doesn't know when to stay in front of his net and when to challenge in the corners. It's his sixth year in the league now, and the necessary improvement hasn't shown.

THE PHYSICAL GAME

Richardson takes the body well and has a healthy interest in hitting. He will take that too far, though, and start running around getting caught out of position. He needs to improve his patience and reads. He doesn't have as imposing a presence on the ice as someone of his size should.

THE INTANGIBLES

Hockey sense is slow in coming to Richardson. He has good size and strength, but his lack of effectiveness on special teams limits his usefulness.

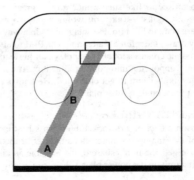

CRAIG SIMPSON

Yrs. of NHL service: 8
Born: London, Ont.; Feb. 15, 1967
Position: left wing
Height: 6-2
Weight: 195
Uniform no.: 18
Shoots: right

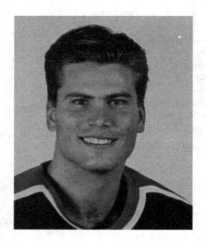

Career statistics:

GP	G	A	TP	PIM
588	235	235	470	625

1991-92 statistics:

GP	G	A	TP	+/-	PIM	PP	SH	GW	GT	S	PCT
79	24	37	61	+8	80	6	0	2	0	128	18.8

1992-93 statistics:

GP	G	A	TP	+/-	PIM	PP	SH	GW	GT	S	PCT
60	24	22	46	-14	36	12	0	3	0	91	26.4

LAST SEASON

Led NHL in shooting percentage. Second on team in power play goals. Games played at career low. Points lowest since rookie season. Missed 24 games with back injury.

THE FINESSE GAME

Simpson is a righthanded shot on the left wing, but he handles it well and takes advantage of being on the off-side. He has very soft hands that allow him to take a pass on his backhand without breaking stride. He then goes to the net, cuts to his right and pulls the puck to his forehand in one smooth movement. He can also pass well off his backhand and lift the puck over a defender's stick.

Simpson does not travel with much speed. His scoring chances come from in tight; he doesn't drive there, but rather slithers to the front. He is effective on the power play because he has such a good touch in tight and he's willing to accept a hit for making the play. Half of his goals came with the extra attacker.

Simpson is a liability one on one. He is not very mobile and doesn't pay much attention to defensive detail.

THE PHYSICAL GAME

Simpson seems like such a nice guy — great smile, clean-cut looks — that you wonder why so many players want to kill him. He antagonizes in a way that rarely draws the referee's attention. His PIM totals are low, but he creates a lot of power plays for his team by goading opponents into coming after him. It doesn't seem to bother him to get clobbered. He knows he'll be out there on the power play.

THE INTANGIBLES

Simpson's back injury took Edmonton's best centre out of the line-up for more than a quarter of the season. He gets the lion's share of the ice time and is on the first unit on the power play. If he receives any sort of help from his teammates, he should be up around 35 goals again this season.

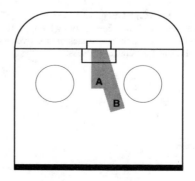

GEOFF SMITH

Yrs. of NHL service: 4
Born: Edmonton, Alta.; Mar. 7, 1969
Position: left defense
Height: 6-3
Weight: 200
Uniform no.: 25
Shoots: left

Career statistics:

GP	G	A	TP	PIM
285	11	53	64	180

1991-92 statistics:

GP	G	A	TP	+/-	PIM	PP	SH	GW	GT	S	PCT
74	2	16	18	-5	43	0	0	0	0	61	3.3

1992-93 statistics:

GP	G	A	TP	+/-	PIM	PP	SH	GW	GT	S	PCT
78	4	14	18	-11	30	0	1	0	0	67	6.0

LAST SEASON

Goals matched career high. Games played at career high.

THE FINESSE GAME

Smith is a good skater with light feet, good lateral movement and ample range, yet he plays a very conservative game. His style entails getting back into position, moving the puck and providing steady play in the defensive zone. He is not very fancy.

Always alert positionally, he reads defensive-zone plays well. He knows when to stay near the front of the net and when to go into the corner for the puck. He can move the puck well when he gets it. He is an intelligent passer and isn't afraid to go for a home run play up the middle. He will also use either wing.

Smith rarely gets any power play time. He does a good job of getting the puck through a crowd to the net, but he puts very little juice on the shot and doesn't shoot frequently enough.

Smith kills penalties on the second unit, and plays a conservative style.

THE PHYSICAL GAME

Smith doesn't have much offensively, so he has to take guys out a little more strongly. He has good size and should use it better, but that doesn't come naturally to him. He wasn't a physical player in college.

He uses his stick more than his body. He doesn't chop, but he keeps his stick leaning on an opponent to make his presence felt. When he checks, he is more of a pusher than a banger.

THE INTANGIBLES

Smith has been an inconsistent defenseman. Last season was a big step backwards for a player who had seemed to be steadily improving over the previous seasons. This year should tell if that slide was more a reflection of the team's decline or Smith's.

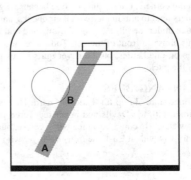

KEVIN TODD

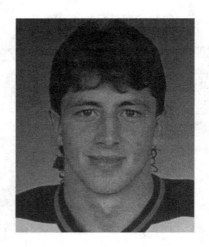

Yrs. of NHL service: 2
Born: Winnipeg, Man.; May 4, 1968
Position: centre
Height: 5-10
Weight: 175
Uniform no.: 15
Shoots: left

Career statistics:

GP	G	A	TP	PIM
137	30	56	86	95

1991-92 statistics:

GP	G	A	TP	+/-	PIM	PP	SH	GW	GT	S	PCT
80	21	42	63	+8	69	2	0	2	1	131	16.0

1992-93 statistics:

GP	G	A	TP	+/-	PIM	PP	SH	GW	GT	S	PCT
55	9	14	23	-9	26	0	0	3	0	87	10.3

LAST SEASON

Games played, goals, assists and points below rookie season production in 1991-92. Acquired from New Jersey with Zdeno Ciger for Bernie Nicholls. Missed games with separated right shoulder.

THE FINESSE GAME

Some players get their shot in the NHL because of their coach. That was the case for Todd two seasons ago when Tom McVie, who had coached the feisty centre in the minors, took over as coach of the Devils and promoted Todd with him.

The reverse happened for Todd when Herb Brooks took over the following season. Todd didn't fit into the new system, and when he got off to a slow start, his days in New Jersey were numbered. The trade gave Todd a short-lived boost before he was sidelined by injury.

Not a very good skater, Todd gets his goals in tight because his wide-based stance allows him to dig in. He is wiry and tough, and he scraps for rebounds. He isn't overly creative, but he keeps goalies guessing since he is just as likely to shoot as pass.

THE PHYSICAL GAME

Todd is small but works tirelessly along the boards and in the corners, often squirting free because bigger defenders tend to aim higher with their checks, and he can duck under the hit. He is not intimidated and will take his abuse in front of the net. Todd loses most of the one-on-one battles, but he never quits in his pursuit of the puck.

THE INTANGIBLES

The sophomore slump hit Todd but hard. He was a part-timer with the Devils and never recovered from the slow start. He could be a nice No. 2 centre, but he needs to play with at least one rugged winger who can finish.

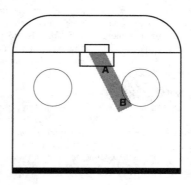

DOUG WEIGHT

Yrs. of NHL service: 2
Born: Mt. Clemens, Mich.; Jan. 21, 1971
Position: centre
Height: 5-11
Weight: 195
Uniform no.: 39
Shoots: left

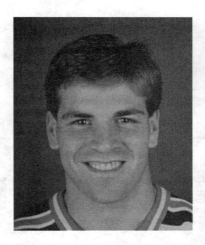

Career statistics:

GP	G	A	TP	PIM
131	25	53	78	88

1991-92 statistics:

GP	G	A	TP	+/-	PIM	PP	SH	GW	GT	S	PCT
53	8	22	30	-3	23	0	0	2	0	72	11.1

1992-93 statistics:

GP	G	A	TP	+/-	PIM	PP	SH	GW	GT	S	PCT
78	17	31	48	+2	65	3	0	1	0	125	13.6

LAST SEASON

Acquired from New York Rangers for Esa Tikkanen. Led Oilers in assists.

THE FINESSE GAME

Weight made his NHL debut out of Lake Superior State in a 1991 playoff game for the Rangers, and he probably planned on competing for a No. 1 or 2 role the next season. Instead, the Rangers acquired Mark Messier, Sergei Nemchinov arrived with a strong two-way game, and Weight found himself battling for ice time.

Weight will get his chance in Edmonton. Depending on what the Oilers do with Shayne Corson, Weight could be the team's No. 1 centre. He will get a lot of offensive ice time and prime shifts on the power play. He has to provide offense — and that is his strong suit.

His hands are good. He uses wrist and snap shots. He can pass equally well to either side. He plays a good game in tight, and he'll battle in the corners and in front of the net. He can handle the puck in traffic and will spot an open man if he is double-teamed.

Weight is not a speed demon, but he has decent quickness, good balance and a fair change of direction.

THE PHYSICAL GAME

Weight is on the short side but built like a fire hydrant. He hits with enthusiasm, finishing every check. He will initiate and annoy.

When he isn't getting an opponent's attention physically, he'll do it verbally. Weight yaps and plays with a great deal of spirit — and now he is on a team where energy has been in short supply. He can be counted on to provide a spark to the darkest of nights.

THE INTANGIBLES

Weight is at a crossroads, and where he determines this trade will take him will make the difference between him being a top level NHL player and a journeyman. He worked during the off-season with a personal trainer to improve his strength and conditioning, so he seems prepared to make the most of the opportunity.

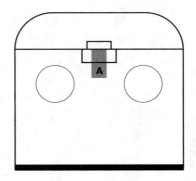

FLORIDA PANTHERS

JESSE BELANGER

Yrs. of NHL service: 0
Born: St-Georges-de-Beauce, Que.; June 15, 1969
Position: centre
Height: 6-0
Weight: 170
Uniform no.: 29
Shoots: right

Career statistics:

GP	G	A	TP	PIM
0	0	0	0	0

1991-92 statistics:

GP	G	A	TP	+/-	PIM	PP	SH	GW	GT	S	PCT
4	0	0	0	-1	0	0	0	0	0	4	0.0

1992-93 statistics:

GP	G	A	TP	+/-	PIM	PP	SH	GW	GT	S	PCT
19	4	2	6	+1	4	0	0	0	0	24	16.7

LAST SEASON

Acquired from Montreal in expansion draft. Played 39 games with Fredericton (AHL), scoring 19-32-51.

THE FINESSE GAME

Belanger was a dynamic scorer at the junior and minor league levels, but like so many flashy players who come into the Montreal system, he was taught to play defense. Now many scouts liken him to a young Guy Carbonneau.

His defensive work habits aren't yet as honed as Carbonneau's, but he has decent speed and anticipation, and all the makings of a successful two-way forward.

He has a good short game. He sees his options well and uses a wrist shot from close range.

THE PHYSICAL GAME

Belanger does not have a physical presence, but he uses his wiry strength and good balance well around the net.

THE INTANGIBLES

Probably the team's No. 1 centre in terms of skill, and after having won a Cup in Montreal last season, Belanger will bring confidence and enthusiasm to his new job. It could have taken him years to get as much ice time if he had stayed in Montreal. We can foresee Bob Clarke stepping out of the front office for a few on-ice sessions to help Belanger along.

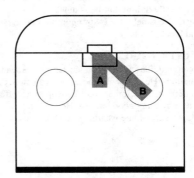

JOE CIRELLA

Yrs. of NHL service: 10
Born: Hamilton, Ont.; May 9, 1963
Position: right defense
Height: 6-3
Weight: 210
Uniform no.: 6
Shoots: right

Career statistics:

GP	G	A	TP	PIM
739	63	204	267	1322

1991-92 statistics:

GP	G	A	TP	+/-	PIM	PP	SH	GW	GT	S	PCT
67	3	12	15	+11	121	1	0	0	0	58	5.2

1992-93 statistics:

GP	G	A	TP	+/-	PIM	PP	SH	GW	GT	S	PCT
55	3	6	9	+1	85	0	1	0	0	37	8.1

LAST SEASON
Acquired from New York Rangers in expansion draft.

THE FINESSE GAME
Cirella can play the right or left side equally well, something few defensemen can do, and it has marked him as an ideal fill-in defenseman through much of his later career.

He likes to get to the puck, move it and follow the play. He gets into trouble when he tries to do too much, like beat a man coming out of the zone, so he doesn't try unless he has absolutely no other choice. He's an average skater at best. He doesn't get up to speed quickly and is not very agile, so he must guard against being beaten to the outside by angling the attacker to the corner. If Cirella hesitates, the skater is past him and he is forced to hook or hold.

Cirella is intelligent enough with the puck to work the point on the power play. He doesn't have a great shot, and his slapshot release is so slow that the shot is frequently blocked. He will more often use a strong wrist shot just to throw the puck on target and see what transpires.

THE PHYSICAL GAME
Cirella stands up for his teammates. Fighting doesn't come naturally to him, but he is quick to jump in if a teammate needs help. He is strong in one-on-one battles and blocks shots.

THE INTANGIBLES
The veteran defenseman was acquired for his leadership qualities. He'll probably be asked to do more than he can deliver, but Cirella won't give up in his efforts to make something good happen. He gets an "A" for attitude, and should be wearing one on his sweater as well.

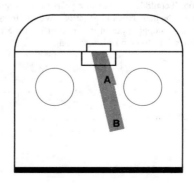

TOM FITZGERALD

Yrs. of NHL service: 3
Born: Melrose, Mass.; Aug. 28, 1968
Position: right wing/centre
Height: 6-1
Weight: 195
Uniform no.: 14
Shoots: right

Career statistics:

GP	G	A	TP	PIM
205	25	44	69	100

1991-92 statistics:

GP	G	A	TP	+/-	PIM	PP	SH	GW	GT	S	PCT
45	6	11	17	-3	28	0	2	2	0	71	8.5

1992-93 statistics:

GP	G	A	TP	+/-	PIM	PP	SH	GW	GT	S	PCT
77	9	18	27	-2	34	0	3	1	0	83	10.8

LAST SEASON

Tied for team lead in shorthanded goals. Games played, goals, assists and points at career highs. Missed four games with rib injury, one game with flu. Acquired by Florida from N.Y. Islanders in expansion draft.

THE FINESSE GAME

After four years of trying to find a niche in the organization, Fitzgerald finally came into his own with the Islanders last season. He just didn't bring as much to the table as they had hoped.

Fitzgerald is a good penalty killer and by the end of the season he was playing smart and in control, showing a new maturity. He has developed into a crunch-time player.

He has a good shot but barely used it at the NHL level. With more confidence, and maybe with a change of scenery, another dimension of his game will surface. Otherwise, Fitzgerald will remain a journeyman defensive forward.

THE PHYSICAL GAME

Fitzgerald is gritty and strong. He has fairly good size and uses it along the boards and in front of the net, and he's a pesky checker who gets people teed off, although his own discipline keeps him from taking many cheap penalties. He gives his team some bang and pop and finishes his checks.

THE INTANGIBLES

Fitzgerald has never lived up to the role expected from first-round draft choices (he was 17th overall in 1986), but he is a solid checking forward. Unfortunately for him, he seems to have lost the scoring touch he had in college and in the minors. He has a knack for timely goals, but 15 a season would probably be his max.

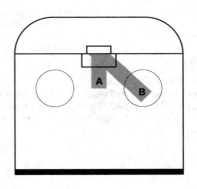

MIKE HOUGH

Yrs. of NHL service: 6
Born: Montreal, Que.; Feb. 6, 1963
Position: right wing
Height: 6-1
Weight: 190
Uniform no.: 18
Shoots: left

Career statistics:

GP	G	A	TP	PIM
363	68	97	165	461

1991-92 statistics:

GP	G	A	TP	+/-	PIM	PP	SH	GW	GT	S	PCT
61	16	22	38	-1	77	6	2	1	0	92	17.4

1992-93 statistics:

GP	G	A	TP	+/-	PIM	PP	SH	GW	GT	S	PCT
77	8	22	30	-11	69	2	1	2	0	98	8.2

LAST SEASON

Worst plus/minus on team. Goals lowest since rookie season. Assists matched career high. Acquired from Quebec for Paul MacDermid and Reggie Savage. Acquired by Florida from Washington in expansion draft.

THE FINESSE GAME

The offensive part of Hough's game — never his strong suit — has become less of an issue now that he has been relegated to the role of checking winger and penalty killer.

Hough takes to his tasks with enthusiasm. He is willing and able to do the work in the trenches, and he's strong and feisty along the boards. He can't do a whole lot with the puck when he gets it, but if he plays with alert linemates, they will pounce on the loose pucks that his hard work turns over. His shots are limited, but he can get away a quick shot off the face-off that will earn him a few surprise goals.

Hough is a strong skater but not very fast. He will be outgunned on open ice but skates quickly in tight areas. He is a smart defensive player.

THE PHYSICAL GAME

Hough is a physical player, uses his body well and is a clean checker. He is very solid on his skates and gets the maximum oomph out of his body-slamming hits.

He will use his strength down low to establish position in front of the goalie for screens and to pick up some garbage goals.

THE INTANGIBLES

Hough was one of a precious few grinding forwards on the Nordiques. They kept him around just for demonstration purposes — and to emphasize that skill alone doesn't win Stanley Cups.

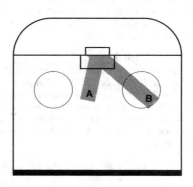

PAUL LAUS

Yrs. of NHL service: 0
Born: Beamsville, Ont.; Sept. 26, 1970
Position: right defense
Height: 6-1
Weight: 212
Uniform no.: na
Shoots: right

1992-93 minor statistics:

GP	G	A	TP	PIM
76	8	18	26	427

LAST SEASON

Selected from Pittsburgh in expansion draft. Played
for Cleveland (IHL) and led league in PIM.

THE FINESSE GAME

Finesse? Take a second look at those PIM totals.

Laus has borderline NHL skating speed. He is
powerful and well balanced for battles along the
boards and in the corners, and he seems to know his
limitations. He won't get involved in the offense, but
he'll be happy to move the puck and stay back. He
needs to be paired with a mobile partner.

He uses his size and strength effectively at all
times. He has to control both his temper and his playing style, since his success at the NHL game will result from playing his angles and not running around.

THE PHYSICAL GAME

Laus hits. Anyone. At any opportunity. And he hits to
hurt. He's big but not scary-sized like some of today's
NHL forwards; he is, however, mean. He'll make that
panther on his jersey look like Garfield.

THE INTANGIBLES

He was a surprise pick, but the Panther obviously feel
they won't get pushed around with Laus in the line-up.
And they won't, if they can keep him on the ice.

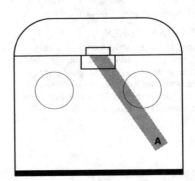

SCOTT LEVINS

Yrs. of NHL service: 0
Born: Spokane, Wash.; Jan. 30, 1970
Position: centre/right wing
Height: 6-4
Weight: 210
Uniform no.: na
Shoots: right

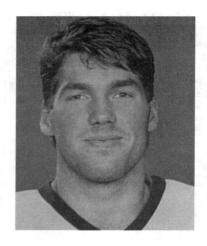

Career statistics:

GP	G	A	TP	PIM
9	0	1	1	18

1992-93 statistics:

GP	G	A	TP	+/-	PIM	PP	SH	GW	GT	S	PCT
9	0	1	1	-2	18	0	0	0	0	8	0.0

LAST SEASON

Acquired from Winnipeg in expansion draft. Played with Moncton (AHL) and was fifth on team in scoring with 22-26-48 in 54 games with 158 PIM.

THE FINESSE GAME

Levins is far too big to be considered a playmaker. By rights, this guy should be banging and finishing in front of the net, and that's why he has spent the last three seasons in the minors. The Jets moved him from centre (his position in junior) to wing, hoping to bring out the power forward in him, but he hasn't developed along those lines.

Levins has a reputation as an unselfish team player. His skating is borderline NHL level for quickness and agility, but he is strong on his feet. He brings a centre's touch and passing ability to the wing. He can make things happen with his work off the boards.

No doubt the Panthers will experiment with using him up front on the power play, where his bulk will be an effective screen.

THE PHYSICAL GAME

Levins throws his weight around and works along the boards and in the corners. He will have to establish himself physically in the NHL; with his size, he should be able to handle the challenge.

THE INTANGIBLES

Perhaps the European influence around the Jets kept him from getting his shot, but the Jets were in desperate need of size and toughness (the reason for the Tie Domi and Kris King acquisition) and if Levins were the genuine article, he would have played more than a handful of games.

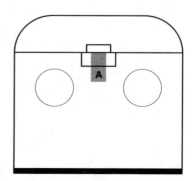

ANDREI LOMAKIN

Yrs. of NHL service: 2
Born: Voskresensk, Russia; Apr. 3, 1964
Position: left wing
Height: 5-10
Weight: 175
Uniform no.: 23
Shoots: left

Career statistics:

GP	G	A	TP	PIM
108	22	28	50	60

1991-92 statistics:

GP	G	A	TP	+/-	PIM	PP	SH	GW	GT	S	PCT
57	14	16	30	-6	26	2	0	0	0	82	17.1

1992-93 statistics:

GP	G	A	TP	+/-	PIM	PP	SH	GW	GT	S	PCT
51	8	12	20	+15	34	0	0	0	0	64	12.5

LAST SEASON

Goals, assists and points declined from rookie season. Missed games with shoulder separation. Acquired by Florida from Philadelphia in expansion draft.

THE FINESSE GAME

Lomakin likes to be all over the ice instead of skating up and down his wing. That's fine if your teammates have a sense of what you are doing, but he seemed to run into more fellow Flyers than opponents.

Lomakin is an open-ice player with good finesse skills. He has a beauty of a shot from the top of the left circle on the fly, but he doesn't shoot nearly enough. Even partnering him with fellow players from the Soviet system, such as Viacheslav Butsayev, did nothing to help.

Lomakin has sneaky speed, but he doesn't use it to get in the right position. He is defensively solid, but that is small consolation given the extra dimension his skills promise.

THE PHYSICAL GAME

Two seasons in the NHL, two injuries that took away a quarter of the season. That doesn't bode well for Lomakin's durability. He has to improve his physical conditioning or learn to avoid the danger zones. He is a pretty soft player.

THE INTANGIBLES

In his second NHL season, Lomakin looked lost and uncomfortable on the ice. He has yet to play a full season, due to injuries, which has stalled his adjustment. This could be a critical season for him as he struggles to find a niche. He is on the bubble.

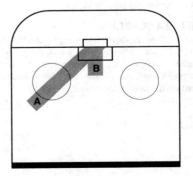

DAVE LOWRY

Yrs. of NHL service: 8
Born: Sudbury, Ont.; Feb. 14, 1965
Position: left wing
Height: 6-1
Weight: 195
Uniform no.: 10
Shoots: left

Career statistics:

GP	G	A	TP	PIM
476	72	72	144	789

1991-92 statistics:

GP	G	A	TP	+/-	PIM	PP	SH	GW	GT	S	PCT
75	7	13	20	-11	77	0	0	1	0	85	8.2

1992-93 statistics:

GP	G	A	TP	+/-	PIM	PP	SH	GW	GT	S	PCT
58	5	8	13	-18	101	0	0	0	0	59	8.5

LAST SEASON

Games played, goals and points four-season lows. Missed two months with sprained knee. Acquired by Florida from St. Louis in expansion draft.

THE FINESSE GAME

Lowry is a strong forechecker and defensive forward. That isn't what the Blues projected for him, since he showed a good scoring touch in junior and the minors; however, Lowry has never been able to take his offensive game up to NHL tempo.

Skating stands out among Lowry's skills. He is fast and powerful, although he lacks any subtleties. All Lowry knows is straight ahead, whether it's to smack into an opponent or to crash the net for a scoring chance. He does little in the way of shooting from anywhere other than dead in front of the net.

Lowry is not a creative playmaker, and is most content in the role of an up-and-down checking winger.

THE PHYSICAL GAME

Lowry has decent size, and when he combines it with his speed he becomes an effective hitter. He will harry the puck carrier on a forechecking mission, and will use his stick and body to slow a skater down. Lowry plays on the second penalty-killing unit.

THE INTANGIBLES

Lowry is a third- or fourth-line role player who should be giving his team 15 to 20 goals a season. That he has slumped to below double figures for two seasons (even projecting goals for the time lost to injury last season) makes him expendable.

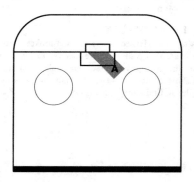

SCOTT MELLANBY

Yrs. of NHL service: 7
Born: Montreal, Que,; June 11, 1966
Position: right wing
Height: 6-1
Weight: 205
Uniform no.: 27
Shoots: right

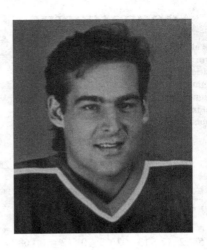

Career statistics:

GP	G	A	TP	PIM
504	121	158	279	1038

1991-92 statistics:

GP	G	A	TP	+/-	PIM	PP	SH	GW	GT	S	PCT
80	23	27	50	+5	197	7	0	5	0	159	14.5

1992-93 statistics:

GP	G	A	TP	+/-	PIM	PP	SH	GW	GT	S	PCT
69	15	17	32	-4	147	6	0	3	1	114	13.2

LAST SEASON

Games played, goals and points at three-season lows. Acquired by Florida from Edmonton in expansion draft.

THE FINESSE GAME

Mellanby does not have a great deal of speed or agility, so most of his effectiveness comes in tight spaces where he can use his size. He is good on the power play, working down low for screens to tips. He doesn't have many moves, but he can capitalize on a loose puck.

Mellanby seems to score goals that count. Fourteen out of his 58 goals over the past three seasons were game-winners (24 percent).

Mellanby has become very responsible defensively and can kill penalties, although he is never a short-handed scoring threat. He lacks the speed bursts or scoring instincts to convert turnovers into dangerous scoring chances.

THE PHYSICAL GAME

Mellanby forechecks aggressively, using his body well to hit and force mistakes in the attacking zone. He participates in one-on-one battles in tight areas and tries to win his share. He is also willing to mix it up and takes penalties of aggression.

THE INTANGIBLES

Mellanby has to maintain his work ethic to keep an NHL job. He is a third- or fourth-line player, a two-way forward who can score the odd key goal. He missed playing time with nerve damage in his right shoulder, a difficult injury to assess.

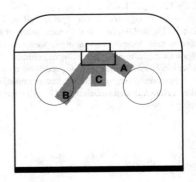

GORD MURPHY

Yrs. of NHL service: 5
Born: Willowdale, Ont.; Mar. 23, 1967
Position: right defense
Height: 6-2
Weight: 195
Uniform no.: 28
Shoots: right

Career statistics:

GP	G	A	TP	PIM
352	39	115	154	367

1991-92 statistics:

GP	G	A	TP	+/-	PIM	PP	SH	GW	GT	S	PCT
73	5	14	19	-2	84	0	0	0	0	132	3.8

1992-93 statistics:

GP	G	A	TP	+/-	PIM	PP	SH	GW	GT	S	PCT
49	5	12	17	-13	62	3	0	2	0	68	7.4

LAST SEASON

Acquired from Dallas in expansion draft.

THE FINESSE GAME

Murphy does a lot of little things nicely, but never consistently or forcefully enough to be much of a presence as an NHL defenseman.

He is a strong and agile skater, and he executes tight turns and accelerates in a stride or two, which makes him an ideal player in smaller buildings. He moves the puck well and then joins the play eagerly.

He also carries the puck well, although he gets into trouble when he overhandles in his own zone. Murphy usually makes a safe pass, holding on until he is just about decked and then making a nice play. He plays the point on the power play, using a slap or strong snap from the blue line, and will occasionally cheat to the top of the circle.

THE PHYSICAL GAME

Murphy uses his finesse skills to defend. His long reach makes him an effective poke-checker, and he would rather wrap his arms around an attacker than move him out of the crease with a solid hit. He's more of a pusher than a hitter.

THE INTANGIBLES

He was never a tough sort to begin with, and an ugly incident during the 1990-91 season took much of the heart out of him. Murphy was racing to touch down a puck for an icing, when he was hit from behind with a high check by Dale Hunter. Hunter received a four-game suspension. Murphy was knocked unconscious and taken off the ice on a stretcher, and hasn't been the same player after.

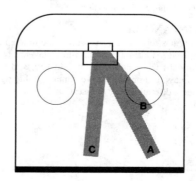

ROB NIEDERMAYER

Yrs. of NHL service: 0
Born: Cassiar, B.C.; Dec. 28, 1974
Position: centre
Height: 6-2
Weight: 200
Uniform no.: na
Shoots: left

Career junior statistics:

GP	G	A	TP	PIM
194	99	106	205	152

1992-93 junior statistics:

GP	G	A	TP	PIM
52	43	34	77	67

LAST SEASON
Played for Medicine Hat (WHL). Named top prospect from WHL. Played for 1993 Canadian World Junior team. Drafted fifth overall by Florida in 1992.

THE FINESSE GAME
When the San Jose Sharks invited Niedermayer in for a look-see, they timed the young centre in skating drills. He posted numbers close to Mike Gartner — who was merely named the fastest skater at the NHL All-Star Game. Niedermayer is a gamebreaker.

To complement his speed, the younger brother of New Jersey defenseman Scott can play a power game. He is a strong passer and an unselfish player, probably too unselfish. The only knock against Niedermayer is that he might not be able to produce goals at the NHL level. He controls the puck well at tempo and can beat a defender one-on-one.

Niedermayer concentrates on two-way play. His speed allows him to recover from play in deep to whisk back and help out defensively.

He underwent arthroscopic knee surgery late in the season.

THE PHYSICAL GAME
While not overly physical, Niedermayer has good size and is still growing. He has a bit of a temper, but he is an intelligent player and doesn't hurt his team by taking bad penalties. His attitude is outstanding. A coachable kid and good team man.

THE INTANGIBLES
Not only is Niedermayer a smart hockey player, but he's also shown off-ice intelligence and dedication. He's an honour-roll student who may become a doctor when his hockey career is over. Hockey excellence seems to run in families, and you have to look no further than his brother's rave reviews in New Jersey to see what Rob might accomplish. Different players, different positions, but similar promise.

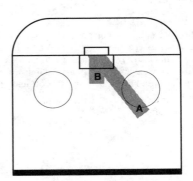

BRIAN SKRUDLAND

Yrs. of NHL service: 8
Born: Peace River, Alta.; July 31, 1963
Position: centre
Height: 6-0
Weight: 185
Uniform no.: 39
Shoots: left

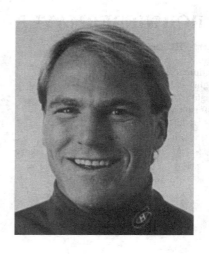

Career statistics:

GP	G	A	TP	PIM
491	80	143	223	602

1991-92 statistics:

GP	G	A	TP	+/-	PIM	PP	SH	GW	GT	S	PCT
42	3	3	6	-4	36	0	0	1	0	51	5.9

1992-93 statistics:

GP	G	A	TP	+/-	PIM	PP	SH	GW	GT	S	PCT
39	7	7	14	+4	65	0	2	1	0	51	13.7

LAST SEASON

Acquired from Calgary in expansion draft. Missed games with broken thumb, broken ankle and shoulder injuries.

THE FINESSE GAME

Skrudland is among the top face-off men in the league, and that, along with his strong skating and tenacious forechecking, helps make him one of the NHL's more reliable defensive forwards.

Don't look to Skrudland for scoring. His role is to keep the other team's top lines off the board, although he has the ability to chip in the odd goal here and there from turnovers. He has a good short game and will look to make a creative play with the puck once he gains control. If he ever stays healthy through a full season, he could score 20 goals — but that's a mighty big "if" given the way the past few seasons have gone for him.

THE PHYSICAL GAME

Skrudland is tough to knock off balance. He has a wide skating stance, which also gives him a strong power base for checking. He seldom fails to get a piece of his opponent. He has a compact build and makes his presence felt.

THE INTANGIBLES

Skrudland never takes a night off. He is a team leader who deserves to wear the first "C" in Panther history. Injuries continue to be a concern, since he has failed to play 60 or more games in each of the last four seasons, but you can't ask him to take any edge off his game. He doesn't know how.

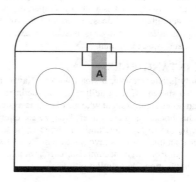

MILAN TICHY

Yrs. of NHL service: 0
Born: Helsinki, Finland; Jan. 25, 1965
Position: left defense
Height: 6-3
Weight: 198
Uniform no.: 43
Shoots: left

Career statistics:

GP	G	A	TP	PIM
13	0	1	1	30

1992-93 statistics:

GP	G	A	TP	+/-	PIM	PP	SH	GW	GT	S	PCT
13	0	1	1	+7	30	0	0	0	0	12	0.0

LAST SEASON

Acquired from Chicago in expansion draft. Also played 49 games for Indianapolis (IHL), scoring 7-32-39 in 49 games with 62 PIM.

THE FINESSE GAME

A slick two-way defenseman, Tichy is a tall, somewhat gangly skater who has spent the better part of the last two seasons in the minors. He was a low draft pick (159th overall in 1989) who has been allowed to develop slowly.

Tichy isn't a flashy skater, but he does a lot of little things well. He moves the puck and follows the play, either for gap control or to get involved in the attack. He sees the ice well and makes smart plays.

He makes things look easy because he sticks to basic plays and executes well. The Panthers may want him to push the envelope a bit, since they will need a puck-carrying defenseman.

THE PHYSICAL GAME

Tichy once piled up 72 PIM in 39 games in the Czechoslovakian league, which means either a tantrum or someone hit the wrong key on the computer. We're a little suspicious that an organization like Chicago would let Tichy get free if he's really that promising, especially after giving up Igor Kravchuk in the Joe Murphy deal.

Tichy plays a physical game without running around. He's been compared to current Hawks defenseman Frank Kucera.

THE INTANGIBLES

Tichy was the first defenseman selected by the Panthers. Some scouts see the pick as a gamble, but knowing Roger Neilson, his eyes must have lit up at Tichy's +7 in just 13 games. Even on a defense-minded team like Chicago, that's a nifty stat. We just like the way his last name is pronounced: Tee-hee.

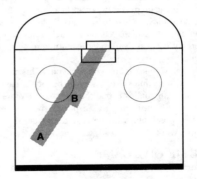

JOHN VANBIESBROUCK

Yrs. of NHL service: 9
Born: Detroit, Mich.; Sept. 4, 1963
Position: goaltender
Height: 5-9
Weight: 175
Uniform no.: 34
Catches: left

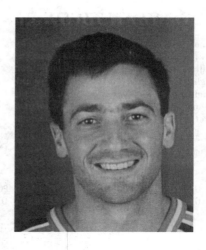

Career statistics:

GP	MINS	GA	SO	GAA	A	PIM
449	25,380	1458	16	3.45	25	212

1991-92 statistics:

GP	MINS	GAA	W	L	T	SO	GA	S	SAPCT	PIM
45	2526	2.85	27	13	3	2	120	1331	.910	23

1992-93 statistics:

GP	MINS	GAA	W	L	T	SO	GA	S	SAPCT	PIM
48	2757	3.31	20	18	7	4	152	1525	.900	18

LAST SEASON

Traded to Vancouver by New York Rangers for future considerations (Doug Lidster). Acquired from Vancouver in expansion draft. Tied for third in the NHL in shutouts. Fifth in NHL in save percentage.

THE PHYSICAL GAME

Vanbiesbrouck blends a strong technical game with good reflexes, anticipation and confidence. Although he has not enjoyed much team success in recent seasons, he's near the top of the list of goalies we would want on the ice in a big game.

He isn't very big, so he plays his angles and squares himself to the shooter to take away as much of the net as possible. He is very aggressive, forcing the shooter to make the first move. He plays breakaways very well and is patient against even such one-on-one stars as Pavel Bure.

Vanbiesbrouck plays an inverted-V style but does not put too much pressure on his inside edges, so he is able to move quickly to either side. He takes away much of the low net and has a good glove hand as well, so most shooters hope to take advantage of him on the stick side.

This is possible because Vanbiesbrouck is very active with his stick, using it to poke-check, guide rebounds, break up passes or whack at any ankles camping out too close to his crease. Billy Smith has a reputation as a stick man. Vanbiesbrouck's not quite as mean, but he won't surrender a centimetre of his ice, either.

Vanbiesbrouck is also confident out of his net with the puck, sometimes overly so. The history of past expansion team goalies is that they have to be more active out of their net to help out the defense. Vanbiesbrouck helps his defense tremendously with his stick work.

THE MENTAL GAME

The one-time Vezina Trophy winner is tops in his approach to the game. Vanbiesbrouck is a fighter. If a game starts off badly, he digs in, and bad goals don't seem to bother him. He also says what he thinks, so some of his teammates had better brace themselves. The important thing about him is that he will make his teammates believe in front of him.

Vanbiesbrouck can steal games, and there will be many nights this season when he will have to.

THE INTANGIBLES

Drafting Vanbiesbrouck gave the Panthers instant credibility (along with the veteran, the Panthers drafted Mark Fitzpatrick from the Islanders). After seasons of battling for the No. 1 role in New York, Vanbiesbrouck is the undisputed top dog — er, cat — in south Florida. He will be 30 at the start of the season and certainly has a few good seasons of hockey left. The pressure will be on, though, John. We expect a very cool mask.

HARTFORD
WHALERS

SEAN BURKE

Yrs. of NHL service: 4
Born: Windsor, Ont.; Jan. 29, 1967
Position: goaltender
Height: 6-4
Weight: 210
Uniform no.: 1
Catches: left

Career statistics:

GP	MINS	GA	SO	GAA	A	PIM
212	11,719	736	4	3.77	6	141

1991-92 statistics:
Did not play in NHL

1992-93 statistics:

GP	MINS	GAA	W	L	T	SO	GA	S	SAPCT	PIM
50	2656	4.16	16	27	3	0	184	1485	.876	25

LAST SEASON

Acquired from New Jersey with Eric Weinrich for Bobby Holik, a second-round draft choice in 1993, and future considerations. Sidelined with back and ankle injuries.

THE PHYSICAL GAME

Burke is so big and so tough and so quick that he is just about as hard to beat in a scramble as a small, reflex goalie. His problem is that he does not use his size well enough to eliminate bad goals that should be harmless shots. He has refined his angle play but must continue to improve his fundamentals or his size will go to waste. He gives up a lot of five-hole goals because he is not confident in his angle play. Working with a goalie coach (Steve Weeks) won't be of any help unless Burke cooperates.

Burke's stickhandling improved as the season progressed, but he could work harder in this area as well to help out his defense.

He spent the 1991-92 season with the Canadian Olympic team and helped lead Canada to a silver medal. International play helped his lateral movement but also produced a tendency to stay back too deep in his net.

Burke has a quick glove hand, but he will often drop it and give the shooter the top corner over his left shoulder. He also holds his blocker hand too low on his stick, which makes him lean over too far and throws him off balance. All of these defects are correctable. It's up to Burke.

THE MENTAL GAME

When Burke is competing with another goalie for the job, as he was two seasons ago in New Jersey with Chris Terreri, he loses track of what he should be doing on the ice. It's important for him to know he's the man right from the start, and when he does, he's very effective.

He has matured and regained much of the focus and unflappable calm that were his leading traits as a young goalie. He has the big-save mentality.

THE INTANGIBLES

Burke has to be secure in his No. 1 role or he is just about useless. In Hartford he has that position, and now he must prove he can handle the job. He may not ever repeat his amazing 1988 playoff run with the New Jersey Devils, but a healthy Burke can come back in a big way behind an improving Whalers team.

ADAM BURT

Yrs. of NHL service: 4
Born: Detroit, Mich.; Jan. 15, 1969
Position: left defense
Height: 6-0
Weight: 195
Uniform no.: 6
Shoots: left

Career statistics:

GP	G	A	TP	PIM
241	21	44	65	383

1991-92 statistics:

GP	G	A	TP	+/-	PIM	PP	SH	GW	GT	S	PCT
66	9	15	24	-16	93	4	0	1	0	89	10.1

1992-93 statistics:

GP	G	A	TP	+/-	PIM	PP	SH	GW	GT	S	PCT
65	6	14	20	-11	116	0	0	0	0	81	7.4

LAST SEASON

Missed 19 games with broken toe. Goals, assists and points declined after previous season's career highs.

THE FINESSE GAME

Burt has evolved into a pretty smart defenseman. He makes much better decisions with the puck and has limited his mental mistakes. He moves the puck smartly without creating opportunities for the opposing team — once one of his grave weaknesses — and has cut down on his turnovers.

Burt used to play the power play strictly by default. Now he works on the second unit. He has a powerful shot and is developing the confidence to use it more often, although he will not get involved gambling deep on the attack.

He comes prepared to play every night. His attitude is upbeat, and he was quick to learn and improve.

THE PHYSICAL GAME

Burt has established himself physically. If he has to fight, he will fight, and compete. He is a stiff bodychecker and displays more of a willingness to hit and an understanding that his physical presence is needed. Hitting also gives him more room to execute; since he doesn't have the greatest foot or hand skills, he can buy himself valuable time, which makes his decision-making process look quicker.

THE INTANGIBLES

Burt enjoyed his best professional season, quality-wise. Any offense from him is a bonus. He will never be a 50-point player, but he is one of the prototypical defensemen of the '90s. He is mobile, tough and moves the puck well, but doesn't do any one thing outstandingly well.

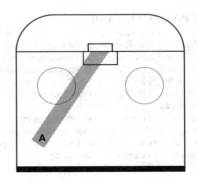

ANDREW CASSELS

Yrs. of NHL service: 3
Born: Bramalea, Ont.; July 23, 1969
Position: centre
Height: 6-0
Weight: 192
Uniform no.: 21
Shoots: left

Career statistics:

GP	G	A	TP	PIM
211	40	113	153	102

1991-92 statistics:

GP	G	A	TP	+/-	PIM	PP	SH	GW	GT	S	PCT
67	11	30	41	+3	18	2	2	3	0	99	11.1

1992-93 statistics:

GP	G	A	TP	+/-	PIM	PP	SH	GW	GT	S	PCT
84	21	64	85	-11	62	8	3	6	2	235	16.6

LAST SEASON

One of two Whalers to appear in all 84 games. Goals, assists and points at career highs. Second on team in points. Led team in assists.

THE FINESSE GAME

Cassels is the smartest player on the Whalers, and a very underrated talent. He has tremendous hockey instinct and knows when to recognize passing situations, when to move the puck and who to move it to. He has a good backhand pass in traffic and is almost as good on his backhand as his forehand.

Cassels was never a great shooter, but he's worked to improve it. He spends a lot of time after practice working on his shot and release. He has very quick hands and can swipe a shot off a bouncing puck in mid-air. He is shooting much more because of the confidence in his shot (he averaged twice as many shots per game over 1991-92).

He is a mainstay on both specialty teams. But he has to get better at face-offs to be a legitimate No. 1 or No. 2 NHL centre.

Cassels has good speed but lacks one-step quickness. He has improved his puckhandling at a high tempo. He is sometimes a little careless in the defensive zone.

THE PHYSICAL GAME

Cassels needs to add some muscle. As the centre for Hartford's top line, Cassels, as the biggest of the trio (with Geoff Sanderson and Pat Verbeek), has to help out physically when his line is the focus of checking attention by opposing teams. The trick is to add weight without bulking up too much so that his quickness is affected. He is a willing hitter.

Cassels used to pay precious little attention to conditioning and off-ice preparation, but he has settled down into a serious new regime under Paul Holmgren and the results are right there on the ice.

THE INTANGIBLES

Cassels is a cautionary tale about giving up on a young player too soon. He started in the Montreal system as a number-one draft pick, but was dealt (for a second-round pick) in his second NHL season. A trade can be a wake-up call, and Cassels didn't hit the snooze button. He enjoyed his best year ever, and is going to be even better. An Adam Oates-type, 100-point season is looming either this season or next for Cassels.

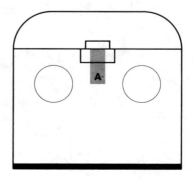

YVON CORRIVEAU

Yrs. of NHL service: 6
Born: Welland, Ont.; Feb. 8, 1967
Position: left wing
Height: 6-1
Weight: 202
Uniform no.: 11
Shoots: left

Career statistics:

GP	G	A	TP	PIM
277	48	40	88	310

1991-92 statistics:

GP	G	A	TP	+/-	PIM	PP	SH	GW	GT	S	PCT
38	12	8	20	+5	36	3	0	0	0	69	17.4

1992-93 statistics:

GP	G	A	TP	+/-	PIM	PP	SH	GW	GT	S	PCT
57	8	12	20	-20	14	2	0	1	0	77	10.4

LAST SEASON

Games played career high. Acquired from San Jose as future considerations for Michel Picard trade. Points matched career high.

THE FINESSE GAME

Corriveau is a good skater, with good size and strength. He has marginal hands and is a marginal shooter, and he has to compete harder to be successful. He was on that track a season ago, but derailed last year.

When he does establish himself physically, Corriveau earns more room and time, and his skills are magnified. He will bore his way to the net for rebounds, or gain position to use his nice wrist shot.

Corriveau was one of the surprises for the Whalers in the 1992 playoffs, but he was upset when he was moved to Washington during the off-season to complete a previous deal. He didn't fit into the Caps' plans, either, and they let him go in the waiver draft to San Jose. No doubt all of that rejection eroded Corriveau's newfound confidence.

THE PHYSICAL GAME

Corriveau has far too many quiet nights for a player of his size and strength. He needs to bang some bodies on his first few shifts, but instead, he waits for the action to come to him, and if it doesn't, he dozes off. He has to pay attention to detail and not lose track of his check.

He's a lazy player by nature and has to work harder to maintain a conditioning edge. He came to the Whalers out of shape after starting the season in San Jose.

THE INTANGIBLES

Corriveau became a Whaler for the third time last season, but it could be the last if he does not perform consistently enough. Not a self-starter, he needs the coaches to be on him constantly.

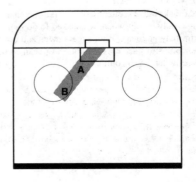

DOUG HOUDA

Yrs. of NHL service: 5
Born: Blairmore, Alta.; June 3, 1966
Position: right defense
Height: 6-2
Weight: 190
Uniform no.: 27
Shoots: right

Career statistics:

GP	G	A	TP	PIM
304	11	39	50	584

1991-92 statistics:

GP	G	A	TP	+/-	PIM	PP	SH	GW	GT	S	PCT
56	3	6	9	-2	125	1	0	1	0	40	7.5

1992-93 statistics:

GP	G	A	TP	+/-	PIM	PP	SH	GW	GT	S	PCT
60	2	6	8	-19	167	0	0	0	0	43	4.7

LAST SEASON

Games played second highest of career.

THE FINESSE GAME

Houda makes the most of his minimal skills. When he plays within his limitations, he is very effective; when he tries to do more than he's capable of, he gets into trouble.

Houda is a very underrated passer and an under-rated shooter. Since he is not terribly flashy, neither of those skills garners much attention, but Houda's intelligence produces the correct play, rather than the showy one.

He is not a very quick player and doesn't have great lateral mobility. He can lug the puck out of trouble if need be, but don't expect any Phil Housley dashes.

THE PHYSICAL GAME

Houda is a throwback to the old-style defensemen. He plays a physical game every night, and he's game. He'll go with anybody. Houda also willingly blocks shots, but his reaction time is sometimes slow, and he does little more than allow a screen shot to slip under his falling body.

THE INTANGIBLES

Houda makes an excellent fifth or sixth defenseman. Trouble only sets in when he is asked to do more. He is extremely popular with his teammates and coaches alike, comes to play every night and doesn't grouse publicly when he sits out.

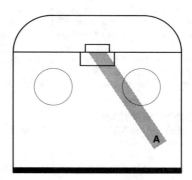

MARK JANSSENS

Yrs. of NHL service: 3
Born: Surrey, B.C.; May 19, 1968
Position: centre
Height: 6-3
Weight: 216
Uniform no.: 22
Shoots: left

Career statistics:

GP	G	A	TP	PIM
236	26	32	58	575

1991-92 statistics:

GP	G	A	TP	+/-	PIM	PP	SH	GW	GT	S	PCT
7	0	0	0	-2	5	0	0	0	0	1	0.0

1992-93 statistics:

GP	G	A	TP	+/-	PIM	PP	SH	GW	GT	S	PCT
76	12	17	29	-15	237	0	0	1	0	63	19.0

LAST SEASON

Acquired from Minnesota for James Black. Goals, assists and points at career highs. Games played second highest of career. Second on team in PIM. Missed five games with shoulder injury.

THE FINESSE GAME

Janssens, a regular with the Rangers in 1989-90, saw his career spiral downward until he was spending more time in the minor leagues than the NHL by 1991-92. Since coming to Hartford, he has worked hard at making himself better. He is very slow afoot — the major reason why he was in the minors — but with hustle can camouflage that flaw. The gone-but-not-forgotten Adams Division was probably the quickest division in the NHL last season, and Janssens was able to compete at that level.

Janssens is excellent on face-offs and takes the key defensive draws. He is part of the No. 1 penalty-killing unit and is a tenacious hitter and forechecker.

THE PHYSICAL GAME

Janssens will hit, harass and battle anyone in the league and not be embarrased. He has excellent size and balance in tight quarters and along the boards. He is out of his element in open ice, but he is aware enough of his limitations to play a conservative defensive game.

THE INTANGIBLES

Janssens was rescued from the minors by the Whalers, and he responded the way an abandoned puppy does to someone who gives him a good home. His eagerness to please and improve himself meant the difference between a marginal forward and a reliable third-line checking centre. He made the most of an excellent opportunity, but he can't afford to lose that edge of desperation.

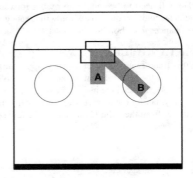

ROBERT KRON

Yrs. of NHL service: 3
Born: Brno, Czechoslovakia; Feb. 27, 1967
Position: centre
Height: 5-10
Weight: 174
Uniform no.: 38
Shoots: left

Career statistics:

GP	G	A	TP	PIM
157	28	35	63	41

1991-92 statistics:

GP	G	A	TP	+/-	PIM	PP	SH	GW	GT	S	PCT
36	2	2	4	-9	2	0	0	0	0	49	4.1

1992-93 statistics:

GP	G	A	TP	+/-	PIM	PP	SH	GW	GT	S	PCT
45	14	13	27	+5	18	4	2	2	1	97	14.4

LAST SEASON

Acquired from Vancouver with Jim Sandlak for Murray Craven.

THE FINESSE GAME

Kron is very quick and is able to handle the puck well at top speed. In Vancouver, Kron was overshadowed by the wealth of size and talent up front, but he emerged in Hartford and impressed in his brief stint at the end of the season.

One of the best things to happen to his career was the reinstatement of four-on-four play in the case of coincidental minor penalties. Kron thrives on the extra open ice. There are so many game situations where four-on-four comes into play, and he'll fit in well with some of the more skilled forwards that the Whalers are quietly accumulating.

Kron is aware in all three zones. He can kill penalties and work on the power play as well.

He is a very creative player, more of a playmaker than a shooter. He likes to use a snap shot more than a slapper, and will get a quick release away from 15 to 20 feet out.

THE PHYSICAL GAME

Kron is a small player and doesn't play a physical style. He will need to be shored up by big forwards, but linemates with hands, since Kron will create good scoring chances that shouldn't go to waste.

THE INTANGIBLES

When this trade is analyzed in a few years, it might become one of the best of Brian Burke's tenure as GM of the Whalers. The change in scenery will help Kron, and his playmaking could give Hartford what it had hoped to get from the John Cullen deal of a few seasons back.

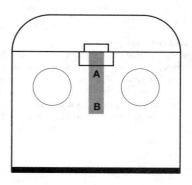

NICK KYPREOS

Yrs. of NHL service: 4
Born: Toronto, Ont.; June 4, 1966
Position: left wing
Height: 6-0
Weight: 195
Uniform no.: 20
Shoots: left

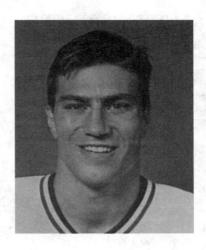

Career statistics:

GP	G	A	TP	PIM
250	35	29	64	809

1991-92 statistics:

GP	G	A	TP	+/-	PIM	PP	SH	GW	GT	S	PCT
65	4	6	10	-3	206	0	0	0	0	28	14.3

1992-93 statistics:

GP	G	A	TP	+/-	PIM	PP	SH	GW	GT	S	PCT
75	17	10	27	-5	325	0	0	2	1	81	21.0

LAST SEASON

Served two-game suspension. Missed seven games with stomach muscle injury. Goals, assists, points and PIM at career highs. Led team and fourth in NHL in PIM.

THE FINESSE GAME

Kypreos is a prime example of how a change in scenery can rejuvenate a player. Under coach Paul Holmgren, who appreciates Kypreos's pugnacious style, the belligerent left wing became the anchor of the checking line.

While his PIM totals are duly noted, it should also be pointed out that Kypreos scored 62 goals one season in junior and has some offensive knack. He has a very powerful and accurate shot, and with his reputation gets all the room in the world to take advantage of it. He will also do the dirty work in front of the net digging for loose pucks.

Kypreos was given more ice time with the Whalers than he ever earned with the Capitals, and responded to the responsibility of playing against the other team's top lines. Against Buffalo's Alexander Mogilny, one of the league's best skaters, Kypreos at least held his own. He is not a great skater, but he has above average mobility and agility. He is not in the least bit creative — strictly an up-and-down-the-wing man.

THE PHYSICAL GAME

Kypreos delivered two of the most vicious hits of the season. One was a check on Greg Adams that put the Vancouver centre out for 31 games. Another was a flying elbow on Philadelphia defenseman Garry Galley that resulted in a concussion and a major brawl. He is a major physical presence and makes everyone else on his team stand a little taller.

THE INTANGIBLES

Kypreos has to bring down his PIM total. He can keep the tough penalties, but the lazy ones, from interference and hooking, he needs to eliminate. He has developed into too valuable a player for the Whalers and has to make his penalty minutes count. Another 20-goal season should be a given, and a 200 PIM total would be ideal.

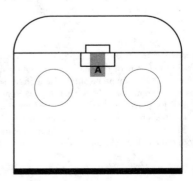

RANDY LADOUCEUR

Yrs. of NHL service: 11
Born: Brockville, Ont.; June 30, 1960
Position: left defense
Height: 6-2
Weight: 220
Uniform no.: 29
Shoots: left

Career statistics:

GP	G	A	TP	PIM
742	26	110	136	1165

1991-92 statistics:

GP	G	A	TP	+/-	PIM	PP	SH	GW	GT	S	PCT
74	1	9	10	-1	127	0	0	0	0	59	1.7

1992-93 statistics:

GP	G	A	TP	+/-	PIM	PP	SH	GW	GT	S	PCT
62	2	4	6	-18	109	0	0	0	0	37	5.4

LAST SEASON

Missed four games with elbow infection. Missed one game with bruised knee. Games played at six-season low. Acquired by Anaheim from Hartford in expansion draft.

THE FINESSE GAME

Ladouceur is limited in his stick and skating skills, but not in his heart and smarts. He has a championship attitude and plays about as sound a stay-at-home style as you can find in the NHL.

He will ice the puck when he has to, or shoot it off the glass near the end of a game when he doesn't want to risk a turnover in his own end. He is always very aware of the game situation and the appropriate play, and he's a crunch time player when protecting a lead (those precious few leads that the Whalers had to protect last season, anyway).

Ladouceur's offensive involvement is limited to a slapshot from the point. One or two will sneak through every season, but he generates little on the attack.

THE PHYSICAL GAME

Ladouceur is a clean, solid hitter. His skating limits his range, but he will win one-on-one battles along the boards or in front of the net by sheer force of will. He is very strong and competes every single shift. He does what it takes to win.

THE INTANGIBLES

Ladouceur had to give up his captain's "C" (to Pat Verbeek) at the start of the season, a demotion that could have had a profound negative effect on his season. Instead, he remained a leader in his quiet way and is still a major player in the Hartford dressing room, where he retains his teammates' respect. He serves in a reduced capacity, and his ice time is becoming more and more limited, but he is an important role player.

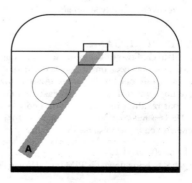

MICHAEL NYLANDER

Yrs. of NHL service: 1
Born: Stockholm, Sweden; Oct. 3, 1972
Position: centre
Height: 5-11
Weight: 184
Uniform no.: 36
Shoots: left

Career statistics:

GP	G	A	TP	PIM
59	11	22	33	36

1992-93 statistics:

GP	G	A	TP	+/-	PIM	PP	SH	GW	GT	S	PCT
59	11	22	33	-7	36	3	0	1	0	85	12.9

LAST SEASON

First NHL season. Missed 15 games with a broken jaw.

THE FINESSE GAME

Nylander is an excellent skater who had absolutely no problem adjusting to NHL speed. For a 20-year-old rookie, his composure with the puck is awesome. Nylander hangs on to the disc and looks at all the options to make a play. This is a gift, and not a skill that any coach can teach. In a few seasons, Nylander will rank among the best forwards in holding the puck until the last split second before making the pass (right now, the best in the game at this skill is Quebec's Joe Sakic).

Nylander has great poise and composure, as well as a tremendous awareness with the puck and vision of the ice. His shot was measured by its hang time at the start of the season, but Nylander worked at improving it and keeping the shot down. He is primarily a passer, but he has good hands for shooting as well.

He has excellent work habits and loves to play.

THE PHYSICAL GAME

Nylander came into a man's league with a boy's body. His injury may have actually helped him. While he was sidelined, the Whalers put him on an intensive weight program and a 5,000-calorie (mostly liquid) diet — and he gained eight pounds despite the broken jaw.

He returned from the injury without any signs of being headshy. He needs to continue to improve his strength to play at the NHL level, but he has good hockey courage.

THE INTANGIBLES

Nylander has the potential, and the apparent drive, to be a future star. He finished the season strong, with 14 points in his last eight games. Then he reported to play for Team Sweden (runner-up to Russia) and tied for the team lead in scoring. He wasn't done yet, but came back to the U.S. to play for Springfield in the AHL's Calder Cup playoffs. His only challenge is to get stronger.

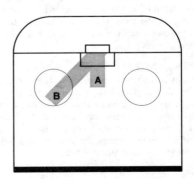

ROBERT PETROVICKY

Yrs. of NHL service: 1
Born: Kosice, Czechoslovakia; Oct. 26, 1973
Position: centre
Height: 5-11
Weight: 172
Uniform no.: 39
Shoots: left

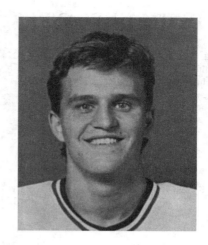

Career statistics:

GP	G	A	TP	PIM
42	3	6	9	45

1992-93 statistics:

GP	G	A	TP	+/-	PIM	PP	SH	GW	GT	S	PCT
42	3	6	9	-10	45	0	0	0	0	41	7.3

LAST SEASON
First NHL season.

THE FINESSE GAME
Petrovicky is a good skater with quick bursts of acceleration. He can't carry the puck well, because he slows down when he has the puck on his stick and doesn't maintain his speed, and that eliminates his greatest talent.

He has a big-time shot and excellent hands with a quick release. He was a leading goal-scorer in Czechoslovakia, so he is accustomed to shouldering the offensive responsibilities.

Still, Petrovicky didn't see the ice time he was used to. He has to understand the rigours of North American hockey. He was bounced down to the minors, was often not dressed, and saw time as a fourth-line centre for much of the season when he did play.

THE PHYSICAL GAME
Petrovicky is a lightweight who needs to develop more strength, or he will continue to be bowled over. He has shown little aptitude for the North American style of play and has to play with big wingers who will get him the puck. He also needs wingers who will take a pass from him and hold and shoot it. Petrovicky likes to carry the puck and shoot it himself, or else dish it to a linemate for a shot. He does not work the give-and-go well.

THE INTANGIBLES
Petrovicky came to training camp without a contract and played well enough to earn rave reviews and a regular salary. But the adjustment to the NHL did not progress smoothly. Petrovicky is remarkably mature for an 18-year-old, but he needs to fine-tune many parts of his game. Perhaps the addition of a fellow countryman (Robert Kron) will help.

PATRICK POULIN

Yrs. of NHL service: 1
Born: Vanier, Que.; Apr. 23, 1973
Position: left wing
Height: 6-1
Weight: 208
Uniform no.: 24
Shoots: left

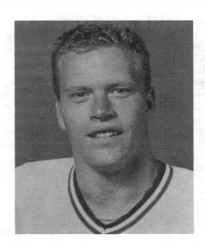

Career statistics:

GP	G	A	TP	PIM
82	20	31	51	39

1991-92 statistics:

GP	G	A	TP	+/-	PIM	PP	SH	GW	GT	S	PCT
1	0	0	0	-1	2	0	0	0	0	0.0	0

1992-93 statistics:

GP	G	A	TP	+/-	PIM	PP	SH	GW	GT	S	PCT
81	20	31	51	-19	37	4	0	2	0	160	12.5

LAST SEASON

First NHL season. Tied for ninth among NHL rookies in points.

THE FINESSE GAME

High marks all around for Poulin, who has just about every attribute for NHL stardom. A first-round draft choice in 1991, he has the size, strength, speed, shot and smarts to really make his mark in the league. But he's not dominating games yet, and that is where he has to take his next stride.

On the one hand, Poulin is a dream to coach, since he is intelligent and attentive, but on the other hand, he's a nightmare, because he needs to be carped at constantly to keep his intensity up. As he matures, he has to take more of the burden upon himself to motivate his game. It's not an uncommon tendency for a player who starred at the junior level with little effort, as Poulin did, to try to cruise on talent alone his first season or two in the NHL.

Poulin has an excellent shot with a quick release, and his wrist shot is very strong; however, he does not skate well with the puck.

Poulin needs work on his defensive game, but he has good hockey instincts and a grasp of positional play.

THE PHYSICAL GAME

When Poulin does not establish himself in a physical sense by finishing his checks, he isn't effective. He is not a great transition player. He won't score a lot of goals off the rush. The patented Poulin move is to create openings and build scoring opportunities by coming off the wall, knocking down the puck-carrier off the forecheck and angle in off the boards for a shot, using his explosive speed.

In terms of conditioning, Poulin is a peak performer who has excellent cardiovascular endurance and can skate all day.

THE INTANGIBLES

The Whalers are very high on Poulin, whom they project as being one of the top three left wingers in the NHL in three seasons. That's a lot of hype, and hope, to pin on this 20-year-old. He does seem to have all the tools to deliver on that prediction, but he will have to show up more nights on a more consistent basis to evolve from the ranks of the merely good and move up to the elite class.

We have to admit we were among the first to jump on the Poulin bandwagon in last year's *HSR,* and we thank him for coming through. This is an exciting player to track.

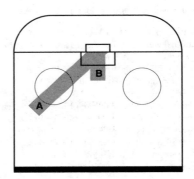

CHRIS PRONGER

Yrs. of NHL service: 0
Born: Dryden, Ont.; Oct. 10, 1974
Position: defense
Height: 6-6
Weight: 190
Uniform no.: na
Shoots: left

Career junior statistics:

GP	G	A	TP	PIM
124	32	107	139	198

1992-93 junior statistics:

GP	G	A	TP	PIM
61	15	62	77	77

LAST SEASON

Played for Peterborough (OHL). Won Max Kaminsky Trophy as Outstanding OHL Defenseman. Played on World Junior Team. First Team OHL All-Star. Drafted second overall by Hartford in 1993.

THE FINESSE GAME

Pronger is not a great skater, but he is powerful in tight quarters and can squish people into the boards with his nice lateral movement and strength. He can make tight pivots, even with the puck, but won't be flying down the ice.

Pronger has very nice hands and is an accurate forehand and backhand passer. He's the guy who skates the puck up on the power play, but he doesn't go for the fancy, one-on-one moves. Pronger is very decisive with the puck, knows what he wants to do with it and gets it to his intended receiver, but he'll also dump and chase if that's the right play. He works the point on the power play. Like a lot of tall defensemen, he doesn't get his slapshot away quickly, but he compensates with a snap shot that he uses liberally, just to get the puck away fast, low, on net and tippable.

Pronger is disciplined away from the puck and alert defensively. He shows good anticipation, going where the puck is headed before it's shot there.

THE PHYSICAL GAME

Pronger lost weight during the season from getting so much ice time, and he'll need to concentrate on nutrition and conditioning to maintain a healthy weight once he gets into the NHL grind.

He finishes his checks and gets a piece of everybody, and also makes use of his stick for chopping, but he is not an overly physical defenseman. He makes his stand between the blue line and the top of the circle, forcing the forward to react. His long reach has a lot to do with making that style effective. He also uses his stick and reach killing penalties.

THE INTANGIBLES

Pronger is an alternate captain on a junior team that has a long history of producing polished, balanced, disciplined performers. He fits the profile perfectly with the same quiet excellence. He doesn't need to show how effective he is or how important he is to his team. You know all that, because he is *always* on the ice. Pronger plays so much that he would be worn down to nothing if he went around crunching people and rushing the puck end-to-end. He needs time to mature and fill out, but he looks like a player.

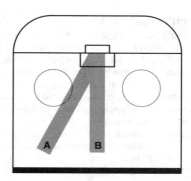

GEOFF SANDERSON

Yrs. of NHL service: 2
Born: Hay River, Northwest Territories; Feb. 1, 1972
Position: left wing
Height: 6-0
Weight: 185
Uniform no.: 8
Shoots: left

Career statistics:

GP	G	A	TP	PIM
148	60	61	121	46

1991-92 statistics:

GP	G	A	TP	+/-	PIM	PP	SH	GW	GT	S	PCT
64	13	18	31	+5	18	2	0	1	0	98	13.3

1992-93 statistics:

GP	G	A	TP	+/-	PIM	PP	SH	GW	GT	S	PCT
82	46	43	89	-21	28	21	2	4	0	271	17.0

LAST SEASON

Led team in goals, points, power play goals and shots. Tied for third on team in assists. Career highs in all categories. Missed one game with the flu.

THE FINESSE GAME

Speed, speed, speed. Then more speed. Great speed. This is Sanderson's outstanding weapon, the one that gives him the edge. Not only can he skate like the wind, but he is agile and mobile and can carry the puck while he's motoring. He can also use his quickness as an intimidating factor.

Confidence restored Sanderson's shot, which once netted him 62 goals in junior. In his rookie season, he was often afraid to shoot and looked instead to make a play. But he has an excellent release and put it to optimum use. He has a superb one-timer on the power play. He also uses his skating to beat defenders wide and bear down on the goalie from the right circle. He has an excellent, Mark Recchi-type release on his shot. Sanderson saw his share of feeds from centre Andrew Cassels, who is a lefthanded shooter but is just as good a backhand passer as a forehand playmaker.

Sanderson also benefited from a move from centre to left wing. He lacks the defensive awareness down low to be an NHL centre, and while his new position carries some defensive responsibilities, he has more freedom as a winger.

Sanderson became a very effective penalty killer at the end of the season, adding another line to his impressive résumé.

THE PHYSICAL GAME

Sanderson has to develop more upper body strength. He is wiry but gets outmuscled, and he'll be tested even more now that he's posted some gaudy numbers. He is very competitive and won't be intimidated, but the Whalers don't want to see him getting tossed around on a nightly basis, either.

THE INTANGIBLES

Sanderson is no longer Hartford's secret weapon. He has the tools to maintain his burgeoning superstardom, but performing under pressure will be a new role.

In last year's *HSR,* we called Sanderson one of the game's sleepers, one capable of becoming a great player. He's well on his way. If he can handle the physical play that will be thrown at his line, he will score consistently in the 90-point range.

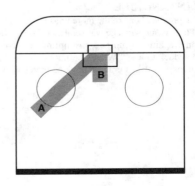

JIM SANDLAK

Yrs. of NHL service: 7
Born: Kitchener, Ont.; Dec. 12, 1966
Position: right wing
Height: 6-4
Weight: 220
Uniform no.: 25
Shoots: right

Career statistics:

GP	G	A	TP	PIM
476	100	115	225	783

1991-92 statistics:

GP	G	A	TP	+/-	PIM	PP	SH	GW	GT	S	PCT
66	16	24	40	+22	176	3	0	2	1	122	13.1

1992-93 statistics:

GP	G	A	TP	+/-	PIM	PP	SH	GW	GT	S	PCT
59	10	18	28	+2	122	1	0	1	0	104	9.6

LAST SEASON

Missed 25 games with injuries. Goals, assists and points at two-season lows. Acquired by Hartford as future considerations with Robert Kron for Murray Craven and fifth-round draft pick.

THE FINESSE GAME

Sandlak isn't much of a skater, and the move to Hartford and the smaller rinks of the new Northwest Division (Boston, Buffalo) may be a boon to his career. Sandlak takes big, big strides, and he'll only need one or two to get from the corners to the front of the net, where he does his best work.

Sandlak doesn't have great hands for picking up loose pucks or deflecting in point shots, but the nice thing about being this big and sturdy is that he can afford to take two or three whacks at the puck.

More has always been expected of Sandlak than he could deliver (he was a former first-round draft pick of Vancouver).

THE PHYSICAL GAME

Sandlak hits big and has to do it consistently. Injuries slowed him last season, but he can be a force and open up a lot of ice for himself and his teammates.

THE INTANGIBLES

Sandlak provoked one of the more unusual controversies of last season when he was scratched from a playoff game against Winnipeg, prompting Jets coach John Paddock to ask, "What's he got? Road flu?... I don't think Sandlak is brave. I think he pretends to be brave."

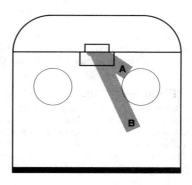

PAT VERBEEK

Yrs. of NHL service: 10
Born: Sarnia, Ont.; May 24, 1964
Position: right wing
Height: 5-9
Weight: 195
Uniform no.: 16
Shoots: right

Career statistics:

GP	G	A	TP	PIM
783	318	313	631	1857

1991-92 statistics:

GP	G	A	TP	+/-	PIM	PP	SH	GW	GT	S	PCT
76	22	35	57	-16	243	10	0	3	0	163	13.5

1992-93 statistics:

GP	G	A	TP	+/-	PIM	PP	SH	GW	GT	S	PCT
84	39	43	82	-7	197	16	0	6	2	235	16.6

LAST SEASON

One of two Whalers to appear in all 84 games. Has missed only four games over past four seasons. Second on team in goals, shots and power play goals. Third on team in points. Tied for third in assists. Led team in game-winning goals. PIM at four-season low.

THE FINESSE GAME

Verbeek loves to shoot, and last season he got back to what he does best. In better shape than he was at the start of the 1991-92 season, which was one of the worst of his NHL career, Verbeek has regained his zip and energy. The not-so-vicious circle is that more energy nets him more goals, and scoring more goals gives him renewed energy. Verbeek was up 72 shots over the previous season, and his scoring totals reflect the effort.

Verbeek is a human square. Stocky and barrel-chested, he is powerful through his upper and lower body, and he wins battles against larger opponents because he has a low centre of gravity and is tough to knock off the puck. He scores most of his goals from in front of the net, where his hands are soft and quick enough to surprise with a backhand shot.

Verbeek is most effective coming in late and drilling the shot. He had the right chemistry on the Whalers' top line with centre Andrew Cassels. Verbeek went through a spell in midseason when the coaching staff worried that he might have lost his scoring touch, but with his new confidence and responsibilities it was regained. He plays the way a team leader is supposed to.

THE PHYSICAL GAME

Verbeek pared down his PIM total and, more importantly, cut down on stupid penalties. In fact, it seemed that he spent his time in the penalty box wisely, because he is now among the best in the league at drawing penalties. He can cleverly hold the opponent's stick and fling himself to the ice as if he were the injured party, and it is an effective tactic. He also draws calls honestly with his hard work by driving to the net and forcing the defender to slow him down by any means possible.

Verbeek is tough, rugged and strong, with a nasty disposition that he is learning to tame without losing his ferocious edge.

THE INTANGIBLES

Verbeek got a clean slate when a new management team took over the Whalers prior to last season, and they immediately indicated his value by naming him captain. He responded with one of his finest seasons, returning to the hard-nosed game that got him to the NHL in the first place. He will never hit the 100-point mark, but 80 to 90 a season should be the norm.

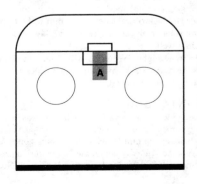

ERIC WEINRICH

Yrs. of NHL service: 3
Born: Roanoke, Va.; Dec. 19, 1966
Position: right defense
Height: 6-1
Weight: 210
Uniform no.: 4
Shoots: left

Career statistics:

GP	G	A	TP	PIM
252	20	95	115	190

1991-92 statistics:

GP	G	A	TP	+/-	PIM	PP	SH	GW	GT	S	PCT
76	7	25	32	+10	55	5	0	0	0	97	7.2

1992-93 statistics:

GP	G	A	TP	+/-	PIM	PP	SH	GW	GT	S	PCT
79	7	29	36	-11	76	0	2	2	0	104	6.7

LAST SEASON

Acquired from New Jersey with Sean Burke for Bobby Holik and a second-round draft pick. Missed two games with concussion.

THE FINESSE GAME

Weinrich is a package of nice finesse skills, and he is reaching the stage in his career when he has to take the next step forward in his development and become a leader.

Weinrich's skating is above average. He accelerates quickly and has good straightaway speed, but he doesn't have great balance for pivots or superior leg drive for power. He's worked to improve his skating but needs to get even better.

He is strong on the puck, shooting and passing hard. Weinrich works on the point on the first power play unit and has a low, accurate shot that he gets away quickly. He joins the rush very well. He will not gamble down low but will sometimes sneak into the top of the circle for a one-timer. His offensive reads are much better than his defensive reads.

THE PHYSICAL GAME

Weinrich has always played smaller than his size. It might be a case of too much Mr. Nice Guy, since he has a very easy-going nature and little desire to crunch people. His lack of balance allows him to be tipped over by smaller players. More lower-body work will serve him well.

On some nights, Weinrich will come out and do just as the coaches ask physically, but he does not perform on a consistent level.

THE INTANGIBLES

A message was sent to Weinrich when he was benched for a game after scoring a goal. The message is that the Whalers need him to shine in all three zones and not just in the offensive end of the ice. Weinrich needs more mental toughness to become a legitimate No. 1 or 2 defenseman, but he seems to be thriving on the challenge and improved steadily over the second half of last season.

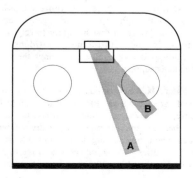

ZARLEY ZALAPSKI

Yrs. of NHL service: 5
Born: Edmonton, Alta.; Apr. 22, 1968
Position: right defense
Height: 6-1
Weight: 210
Uniform no.: 3
Shoots: left

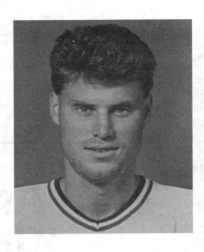

Career statistics:

GP	G	A	TP	PIM
363	70	193	263	376

1991-92 statistics:

GP	G	A	TP	+/-	PIM	PP	SH	GW	GT	S	PCT
79	20	37	57	-7	116	4	0	3	1	230	8.7

1992-93 statistics:

GP	G	A	TP	+/-	PIM	PP	SH	GW	GT	S	PCT
83	14	51	65	-34	94	8	1	0	0	192	7.3

LAST SEASON

Worst plus/minus on team. Led team defensemen in scoring with career high in points. Second on team in assists with career high.

THE FINESSE GAME

Zalapski has all-world offensive skills. He is a tremendous skater with speed and agility. He has great acceleration and scoring instincts to join or lead a rush, although his passing skills are overrated. The problem is that his vision of the ice is so weak that he might as well be hockey blind. Zalapski does not see any of his playmaking options, nor is he an intellgent shooter. He simply blasts away from the point, and he has a good enough shot to get by. But he could do so much more, and that is where frustration sets in. He could take something off his shot to make it more tippable. He could fake a slap and slide a pass into an open area of the ice. But he does not keep anyone guessing.

He is not a very good back skater, either. He doesn't read plays coming at him well, which makes him just a mess in the defensive zone. Zalapski was mentioned in a torrent of trade rumours last season, but there are plenty of reasons why none of them came true.

Once or twice a season, Zalapski will piece together a brilliant game, where he will concentrate and dominate. All he does is illustrate what a waste the other 80 or so nights are.

THE PHYSICAL GAME

Zalapski is probably the strongest player on the Whalers. He has tremendous power from his upper legs and is very well conditioned. But Zalapski has never established himself physically. He has the potential to be an absolutely dominating defenseman, but until he plays the body instead of the stick, he will never be thought of as more than an offensive defenseman.

THE INTANGIBLES

Zalapski has had six coaches in his five (and a fraction) NHL seasons. That either marks him as one of the great coach-killers, or means he deserves some slack because he hasn't been able to develop good rapport and confidence with a coach who has any kind of tenure.

Zalapski is only 25 years old, and it is too soon to give up. But he has to mature, and he has to have his breakthrough season soon.

LOS ANGELES KINGS

ROB BLAKE

Yrs. of NHL service: 3
Born: Simcoe, Ont.; Dec. 10, 1969
Position: right defense
Height: 6-3
Weight: 215
Uniform no.: 4
Shoots: right

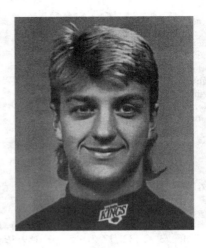

Career statistics:

GP	G	A	TP	PIM
212	35	90	125	383

1991-92 statistics:

GP	G	A	TP	+/-	PIM	PP	SH	GW	GT	S	PCT
57	7	13	20	-5	102	5	0	0	0	131	5.3

1992-93 statistics:

GP	G	A	TP	+/-	PIM	PP	SH	GW	GT	S	PCT
76	16	43	59	+18	152	10	0	4	1	243	6.6

LAST SEASON

Led team defensemen in scoring. Tied for team lead in plus/minus. Career highs in games played, goals, assists and points. Missed three games with broken rib. Missed four games with lower back contusion.

THE FINESSE GAME

Blake is a prototypical defenseman for the '90s. He hits, he plays defense, and he possesses sufficient finesse skills to make an impact in any zone of the ice.

Blake is a powerful skater, quick and agile, with good balance, and skates very well backwards. Most of the Los Angeles defense corps like to step up and challenge at the blue line, and Blake is their leader in this department. He has great anticipation and is very bold, forcing turnovers at the blue line with his body positioning and quick stickwork. On occasion, he will rely too much on his poke-checks and will get caught flat-footed. He has to play a physical game to be at his best.

Blake works the point on the power play, though he doesn't have the vision to be as creative as he could be (but note that 10 of his 16 goals came on the power play). He does have a good, low shot, and he can rifle it off the pass. He has very good hand skills and is not afraid to skip in deep and try to make something happen low. Blake became much more confident about attempting to force the play deep in the offensive zone last season. He has good enough passing skills to use a backhand pass across the goalmouth.

Blake will never post Paul Coffey-type numbers, but playing with Coffey during that defenseman's brief stay in L.A. has added another facet to Blake's improving game.

THE PHYSICAL GAME

Blake has become one of the hardest hitters in the league, along with Scott Stevens, a defenseman his style closely resembles. Blake has a nasty streak and will bring up his gloves and stick into the face of an opponent when he thinks the referee isn't watching. He can dominate with his physical play, and when he does he opens up a lot of ice for himself and his teammates.

THE INTANGIBLES

A few seasons ago, people snickered when Wayne Gretzky proclaimed Blake as one of the best young defensemen he had ever seen. Now coach Barry Melrose and others are labelling Blake as a potential Norris Trophy candidate in the near future. After Blake's excellent playoffs, people should listen more closely when Wayne speaks.

Blake was as much the Kings' leader in the drive to the Stanley Cup Finals as Gretzky was. He will be captain of the team in no time, and a Norris Trophy candidate soon — perhaps even this season.

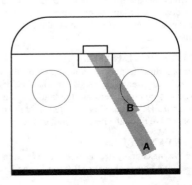

JIMMY CARSON

Yrs. of NHL service: 7
Born: Southfield, Mich.; July 20, 1968
Position: centre
Height: 6-1
Weight: 200
Uniform no.: 12
Shoots: right

Career statistics:

GP	G	A	TP	PIM
518	254	259	513	201

1991-92 statistics:

GP	G	A	TP	+/-	PIM	PP	SH	GW	GT	S	PCT
80	34	35	69	+17	30	11	0	3	0	150	22.7

1992-93 statistics:

GP	G	A	TP	+/-	PIM	PP	SH	GW	GT	S	PCT
86	37	36	73	-2	32	17	0	5	0	189	19.6

LAST SEASON

Acquired from Detroit with Gary Shuchuk and Marc Potvin for Paul Coffey, Sylvain Coutourier and Jim Hiller. Tied for second on team in goals. Second on team in power play goals. Goals four-season high. Has not missed a game in two seasons (and played an extra two last season due to trade). Appeared in NHL record 86 games.

THE FINESSE GAME

Carson is a nifty skater with good acceleration and direction changes — all with firm control of the puck. He can make a lot of dekes and move in a short space, and excels from between the circles. He's more of a finisher than a playmaker, but he has one tricky move where he curls out from behind the goal cage from the goalie's right to the goalie's left, then moves a pass back against the grain to an open teammate.

Carson is a short-game player, strictly nine-irons and pitching wedges. He is not a well-balanced skater and gets tipped over on some hits by smaller players, but he can maintain his edges fairly well when he dances through traffic in front of the net.

He won't pay the price in other areas of the ice, though, and quickly incurs the wrath of his coaches for his lack of attention to defense. On face-offs, Carson does not tie up the opposing centre, for example. He also tends to overhandle the puck at the blue line.

THE PHYSICAL GAME

Carson is a durable player, as indicated by the few games he has missed in recent seasons, but he doesn't get involved much, either, and tends to stay out of contact areas. He will use his body to shield the puck but won't drive through checks. A soft centre.

THE INTANGIBLES

Should Wayne Gretzky decide to retire this season (he made serious noises about it after the Kings lost to Montreal in the Stanley Cup Final), Carson would inherit the role of No. 1 centre, a job he hasn't held in some time. There are doubts that he's up to it.

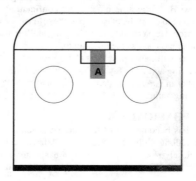

PAT CONACHER

Yrs. of NHL service: 5
Born: Edmonton, Alta.; May 1, 1959
Position: centre/left wing
Height: 5-8
Weight: 190
Uniform no.: 15
Shoots: left

Career statistics:

GP	G	A	TP	PIM
341	35	51	86	134

1991-92 statistics:

GP	G	A	TP	+/-	PIM	PP	SH	GW	GT	S	PCT
32	7	3	10	+16	16	0	1	1	0	38	18.4

1992-93 statistics:

GP	G	A	TP	+/-	PIM	PP	SH	GW	GT	S	PCT
81	9	8	17	-16	20	0	2	1	0	65	13.8

LAST SEASON

Acquired from New Jersey for future considerations. Games played 26 more than any previous NHL season.

THE FINESSE GAME

Conacher's intangibles rate much higher than his skills, which are average at best. Whatever scoring touch he had has virtually vanished. His role is as a checker, but he can't create much when his hard work results in a turnover. He concentrates mostly on shutting down the other team's scoring lines, and he will hurl his body at anyone.

Conacher is smart and has good anticipation and quickness. He is a good penalty killer and a shorthanded scoring threat. He scores by driving to the net, but he will surprise a goalie with a long shot from the wing when he has a screen.

THE PHYSICAL GAME

Conacher is solidly built and so low to the ground that he is difficult to handle on face-offs. He is also hard to bowl over because of his low centre of gravity. He isn't afraid of anyone or any situation, but he is too small to intimidate anyone.

THE INTANGIBLES

According to conventional wisdom, Conacher should have been out of the game years ago. He is too small, too old, too slow, too...well, too tough to take out of the line-up. He loves the game and was voted the team's unsung hero by his teammates last season, especially for the work he did during Wayne Gretzky's absence. He is a veteran who won't give you points but will give you heart. He may have one season left as a penalty-killing specialist.

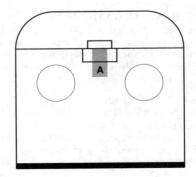

MIKE DONNELLY

Yrs. of NHL service: 6
Born: Detroit, Mich.; Oct. 10, 1963
Position: left wing
Height: 5-11
Weight: 185
Uniform no.: 11
Shoots: left

Career statistics:

GP	G	A	TP	PIM
313	79	80	159	176

1991-92 statistics:

GP	G	A	TP	+/-	PIM	PP	SH	GW	GT	S	PCT
80	29	16	45	+5	20	0	1	4	0	197	14.7

1992-93 statistics:

GP	G	A	TP	+/-	PIM	PP	SH	GW	GT	S	PCT
84	29	40	69	+17	45	8	1	2	0	244	11.9

LAST SEASON

One of three Kings to appear in all 84 games. Second consecutive season without missing a game. Assists career high — more than double any previous season. Has played in 182 consecutive games.

THE FINESSE GAME

Donnelly played with the Kings' "Little Princes" (Corey Millen and Tony Granato) on what was L.A.'s most dynamic line in the playoffs. Donnelly is a digger and gets his goals from in close. He is tenacious around the net, using his quickness to dart in and out of holes. He has a good nose for the net and good hands for his shots. He was more eager to shoot last season and was a more effective player because of it.

Donnelly can also work passes is tight areas. He has good open-ice speed to drive to the outside on a defenseman. Many of his scoring chances develop from two-on-one breaks that are created quickly and just inside the blue line.

Despite not scoring a power play goal in 1991-92, Donnelly saw some power play duty last season and actually scored with the man advantage. He is a savvy player who can work both special teams. He has worked hard to make himself into a reliable two-way winger.

THE PHYSICAL GAME

Donnelly plays bigger than his size. He is tenacious and uses his body as well as he can to get in people's way, but he is too small to do any damage. It's pretty remarkable, given the way he plays, that he hasn't done much damage to himself.

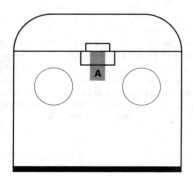

THE INTANGIBLES

Donnelly's small size is the only thing that limits him from being more of an impact player. Still, 30 goals from a solid two-way winger is nothing to complain about. Donnelly proved that his breakthrough season in 1991-92 was no fluke.

TONY GRANATO

Yrs. of NHL service: 5
Born: Downers Grove, Ill.; July 25, 1964
Position: left wing
Height: 5-10
Weight: 185
Uniform no.: 21
Shoots: right

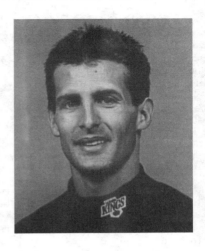

Career statistics:

GP	G	A	TP	PIM
363	154	159	313	774

1991-92 statistics:

GP	G	A	TP	+/-	PIM	PP	SH	GW	GT	S	PCT
80	39	29	68	+4	187	7	2	8	1	223	17.5

1992-93 statistics:

GP	G	A	TP	+/-	PIM	PP	SH	GW	GT	S	PCT
81	37	45	82	-1	171	14	2	6	0	247	15.0

LAST SEASON

Third on team in scoring and tied for third in goals. Second in game-winning goals. Assists and points career highs. Missed three games with back strain.

THE FINESSE GAME

Granato has a wide scoring stance, which makes it tough to knock him off balance, and he's fast and quick, which makes it hard for anyone to catch him and even try.

Granato can play any forward position and with any other forwards. This versatility has probably hurt him in the long run, because a coach doesn't hesitate to shift him around, knowing he will fit in anywhere and complement the players he is teamed with. Other skaters might complain that all the shifting around hurts their game because they don't get to become familiar with their linemates, but if that's what the coach wants, it's good enough for Tony.

Granato uses his quickness to good effect down low. When he was playing on the Kings' "Little Princes" line with Mike Donnelly and Corey Millen, the three of them looked like Keystone Kops jumping in and out of holes and driving defensemen batty.

Granato has very strong wrists, a quick release and an accurate shot. Most of his goals come from within 10 feet of the net. He has an infuriating knack of lifting an opponent's stick to steal the puck with his quick hands.

THE PHYSICAL GAME

Few small players loom larger than this buzzsaw. He is fierce and intense, sometimes overly so, in that he gets frustrated and will take bad penalties. But Granato also draws calls. He has the quickness to get his body between the puck and the defender, and he keeps his legs pumping to attract holding and hooking calls. He still lacks defensive awareness, but is always outworking his rivals, so it doesn't hurt him too much.

THE INTANGIBLES

Granato looks too slight to stand up to the abuse of a long NHL grind, but even with his kamikaze play, he nets his 35 or 40 goals a season. He is gritty and inspirational, and if the Kings ever want to deal him, teams will be lining up. You don't get many opportunities at a player who combines this much talent and character.

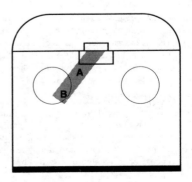

WAYNE GRETZKY

Yrs. of NHL service: 14
Born: Brantford, Ont.; Jan. 26, 1961
Position: centre
Height: 6-0
Weight: 170
Uniform no.: 99
Shoots: left

Career statistics:

GP	G	A	TP	PIM
1044	765	1563	2328	447

1991-92 statistics:

GP	G	A	TP	+/-	PIM	PP	SH	GW	GT	S	PCT
74	31	90	121	-12	34	12	2	2	1	215	14.4

1992-93 statistics:

GP	G	A	TP	+/-	PIM	PP	SH	GW	GT	S	PCT
45	16	49	65	+6	6	0	2	1	0	141	11.3

LAST SEASON

Missed 39 games with career-threatening back injury. First season without scoring a power play goal. Games played, goals, assists and points at career lows. Failed to reach 100-point mark for first time in career.

THE FINESSE GAME

Gretzky's game has changed; if anything, he has perhaps become an even better all-around forward. He now manages his ice time better. His shifts last a minute instead of two and a half, and he stays fresher with those shorter stints. This also allows his team to keep its line rotation rolling over.

It is so difficult for a player to come back in mid-season as Gretzky did, and while he came back with a lot of jump, he also struggled. At one point, the Great One went 16 games without a goal. Gretzky concentrated more on his defense, and told his linemates not to worry, that he would be the forward staying back.

Yet Gretzy is more eager to shoot than in the past, when he was known primarily as a passer. Playmaking is still his forte, but defenders can no longer just look to shut off his passing lanes, because Gretzky will rifle one of his deceptive shots if they play off him. He doesn't overpower goalies, but he masks his shot well and gets it off quickly.

Gretzky has lost half a step in his skating, but he has such great anticipation that this is barely noticeable. As ever, he has patience, patience, patience with the puck, waiting until the last split-second to dish off a pass. Only Joe Sakic is close to him in this special talent.

THE PHYSICAL GAME

When new coach Barry Melrose met Gretzky for the first time, he was shocked at how slightly built the Great One is. His image and aura are so imposing that you expect Gretzky to be built more along the lines of Mario Lemieux, or the Statue of Liberty, but he re-mains whippet lean — and that makes his career all the more remarkable.

Since the hit from Gary Suter in the 1991 Canada Cup (the source of his subsequent back ailment), Gretzky has become even more leery of contact along the boards. Who can blame him?

THE INTANGIBLES

Gretzky ended the 1991-92 season needing just one game to reach the 1000-game milestone. The hockey world wondered during training season if he would ever attain it. The forced layoff brought a fresh and fit Gretzky to the second half of the season and the playoffs, in which the Kings reached the final four for the first time in their history — and make no mistake about it, they were carried there on Gretzky's fragile spine. Gretzky was also relieved by his father Walter's rapid recovery from a brain aneurysm in 1991.

Personal and physical problems resolved, Gretzky was professionally redeemed by his awesome playoff performance of 1993. He was talking retirement at the end of the season (although we think he'll hang in long enough to beat Gordie Howe's last record of 801 career goals). If you haven't had a chance to see Gretzky in person, get a ticket the next time he's in town. It could be your last chance.

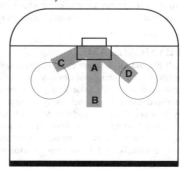

KELLY HRUDEY

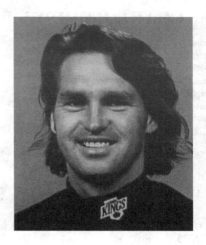

Yrs. of NHL service: 10
Born: Edmonton, Alta.; Jan. 13, 1961
Position: goaltender
Height: 5-10
Weight: 180
Uniform no.: 32
Catches: left

Career statistics:

GP	MINS	G	SO	AVG	A	PIM
466	26,409	1532	15	3.48	15	161

1991-92 statistics:

GP	MINS	GAA	W	L	T	SO	GA	S	SAPCT	PIM
60	3509	3.37	26	17	13	1	197	1916	.897	12

1992-93 statistics:

GP	MINS	GAA	W	L	T	SO	GA	S	SAPCT	PIM
50	2718	3.86	18	21	6	2	175	1552	.887	10

LAST SEASON

Minutes played fewest since 1986-87. Goals-against at three-season high. Fewest wins of career. Missed two games with the flu.

THE PHYSICAL GAME

Hrudey's technique has improved, but he is still prone to lapses in discipline. He lives by his reflexes, and on his worst nights he's a lunging, sprawling mess. At his best, Hrudey uses his glove hand to take away the high shots and positions his stick shaft low and parallel to the ice to take away the low shots.

Hrudey loves to challenge the shooter, and one of his biggest flaws is that he is overly aggressive. He also likes to handle the puck and has worked hard to improve in this important area over the past few seasons. He is a good skater and moves confidently in and out of his net.

He is very quick and recovers well for the second shot. He doesn't always control his rebounds well, and this leads to mad scrambles around his cage. He hangs tough through the pressure.

He has excellent concentration through screens and can't be taken off his game with goalie-bumping tactics. In fact, he will often strike the first blow with his blocker.

THE MENTAL GAME

Hrudey has developed a big-save capacity. In the past, he would play in many games where he was the heroic loser; now, he's winning those games. He plays on emotion, and he gained a tremendous amount of respect from his teammate with his playoff showing, where he put together the most consistent hockey of his career, especially as the team got deeper and deeper into the playoffs.

THE INTANGIBLES

Hrudey had to fend off challenges from Robb Stauber and Rick Knickle, and he didn't always handle the pressure well. At one stage, the usually cooperative Hrudey refused to talk to the media. The likeable goalie had a strong playoffs season as he regained his No. 1 role, but we wouldn't be surprised if the Kings went after a young goalie during the off-season.

CHARLIE HUDDY

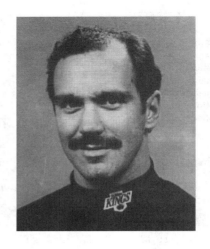

Yrs. of NHL service: 13
Born: Oshawa, Ont.; June 2, 1959
Position: right defense
Height: 6-0
Weight: 210
Uniform no.: 22
Shoots: left

Career statistics:

GP	G	A	TP	PIM
832	87	331	418	607

1991-92 statistics:

GP	G	A	TP	+/-	PIM	PP	SH	GW	GT	S	PCT
56	4	19	23	-10	43	2	1	0	0	109	3.7

1992-93 statistics:

GP	G	A	TP	+/-	PIM	PP	SH	GW	GT	S	PCT
82	2	25	27	+16	64	0	0	1	0	106	1.9

LAST SEASON

Assists four-season high. Missed one game with flu.

THE FINESSE GAME

Huddy is an intelligent, stay-at-home defenseman. He can still get involved in the rush, but with teammates on the blue line like Rob Blake and Alexei Zhitnik, he worries less about his contribution to the attack and concentrates on defense first.

Huddy is a confident positional player. He angles attackers to the wall and rubs them out with sturdy but not bone-jarring checks. His anticipation for picking off passes is excellent, and he can quickly turn the play back up-ice with a smart pass.

Huddy's finesse skills are above average. He keeps his point shot low and on target. His skating is average, but he doesn't push the envelope.

THE PHYSICAL GAME

Huddy is not a big checker — never was — but he is still valuable for his experience and composure. He will tie attackers up in front of the net but won't move many people out, especially now that many forwards look like extras from *Jurassic Park*.

THE INTANGIBLES

Huddy can still contribute in a limited role as a fifth or sixth defenseman. The Kings' young defense corps has developed so quickly that Huddy has been out-distanced.

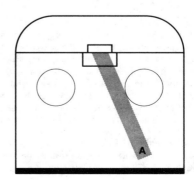

JARI KURRI

Yrs. of NHL service: 11
Born: Helsinki, Finland; May 18, 1960
Position: right wing
Height: 6-1
Weight: 195
Uniform no.: 17
Shoots: right

Career statistics:

GP	G	A	TP	PIM
909	524	666	1190	410

1991-92 statistics:

GP	G	A	TP	+/-	PIM	PP	SH	GW	GT	S	PCT
73	23	37	60	-24	24	10	1	3	0	167	13.8

1992-93 statistics:

GP	G	A	TP	+/-	PIM	PP	SH	GW	GT	S	PCT
82	27	60	87	+19	38	12	2	3	0	210	12.9

LAST SEASON

Led team in plus/minus. Second on team in assists and points. Missed one game with the flu. Reached 500-goal milestone.

THE FINESSE GAME

When Wayne Gretzky missed the first half of the season with a back injury, Kurri moved into the No. 1 centre's role and proceeded to play his best hockey of the season. When he was finally reunited with his former Oilers teammate — the main reason Kurri returned to the NHL after a year's absence in Italy — he went into the barn. His first-half stats: 17-41 for 58. His second half: 10-19 for 29.

Kurri made his name and fame in the NHL as Gretzky's right wing, so his rapid demise was puzzling. It may just be that he doesn't have much gas left in the tank.

Certainly the shot that Kurri made famous, the one-timer off the pass down the right wing, was no longer in evidence on a regular basis. He is no longer the impact player he used to be on the power play, either. Kurri can be used to kill penalties and work on the power play, but he saw little special teams time in the playoffs.

THE PHYSICAL GAME

Kurri has become more and more of a perimeter player. Maybe he has soured on the physical part of the game, because he used to be willing to pay the price along the wall to fight for the puck. Though he never used to be a physical force, he wasn't intimidated, either, but now it appears that he is.

THE INTANGIBLES

Perhaps Kurri's shift to centre should remain permanent. He is more involved in that position, and he plays well enough defensively to make a go of it. Still, there is no reason to expect more than 30 goals and 80 points from him.

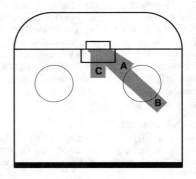

MARTY MCSORLEY

Yrs. of NHL service: 10
Born: Hamilton, Ont.; May 18, 1963
Position: right defense
Height: 6-1
Weight: 235
Uniform no.: 33
Shoots: right

Career statistics:

GP	G	A	TP	PIM
601	78	158	236	2448

1991-92 statistics:

GP	G	A	TP	+/-	PIM	PP	SH	GW	GT	S	PCT
71	7	22	29	-13	268	2	1	0	0	119	5.9

1992-93 statistics:

GP	G	A	TP	+/-	PIM	PP	SH	GW	GT	S	PCT
81	15	26	41	+1	401	3	3	0	0	197	7.6

LAST SEASON

Led NHL in PIM. Third season with 300 or more PIM. PIM career high. Led team in shorthanded goals. Points career high.

THE FINESSE GAME

One of the first things you notice about McSorley is his feet. His skates are big and heavy (he has specially made skates that are more cumbersome than the average player's). Add to that his sluggish skating and you get a player whose rushes can be timed with a calendar.

To compensate for his lack of speed, McSorley works hard and plays a pretty smart game. He was used almost exclusively on the backline by the Kings last season, although in the past he has been used up front and he will be posted in front of the net on the power play at times.

McSorley's finesse skills are average at best. He does not have good vision of the ice for creative playmaking. Unfortunately, every so often he tries to make the fancy play instead of the safe shot, and he gets burned because he can't recover quickly defensively. He has to be paired with a mobile defense partner.

THE PHYSICAL GAME

McSorley is a conditioned athlete who can take all the ice time a coach wants to give him. He also probably ranks among the top five fighters in the league. He does annoying things after the whistle — well after the whistle — like shoot the puck at the goalie on an offside call or give an attacker a shove after a save.

McSorley is intense and does start running around sometimes, but this is a sin of commission, since he is always trying so hard.

THE INTANGIBLES

McSorley is a Group III free agent and could be ending his long-running job as Wayne Gretzky's protector. He is a pretty complete player for a tough guy, and could help more than a few teams in the bravery department.

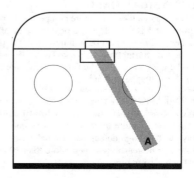

LUC ROBITAILLE

Yrs. of NHL service: 7
Born: Montreal, Que.; Feb. 17, 1966
Position: left wing
Height: 6-1
Weight: 190
Uniform no.: 20
Shoots: left

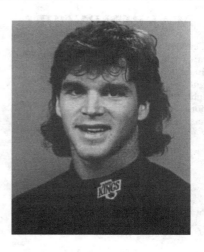

Career statistics:

GP	G	A	TP	PIM
557	348	369	717	476

1991-92 statistics:

GP	G	A	TP	+/-	PIM	PP	SH	GW	GT	S	PCT
80	44	63	107	-4	95	26	0	6	1	240	18.3

1992-93 statistics:

GP	G	A	TP	+/-	PIM	PP	SH	GW	GT	S	PCT
84	63	62	125	+18	100	24	2	8	1	265	23.8

LAST SEASON

Set NHL record for goals and points in a season by a left winger with career-highs. Tied for fifth in NHL in power play goals. Led team in goals, assists, points, power play goals, game-winning goals, shots and shooting percentage. Fifth in NHL in shooting percentage. Second consecutive season without missing a game. One of three Kings to appear in all 84 games. Points career high. Fourth season with 100 or more points. Seventh consecutive season with 40 or more goals. PIM career high.

THE FINESSE GAME

Robitaille is a pure shooter, and he's one of the best in the league at roofing a shot. Most of his goals come from in tight. He is so strong with his arms and stick that a defender will think he has him wrapped up, only to see the puck end up in the net after Robitaille has somehow gotten his hands free for a shot on net.

Robitaille is always among the NHL leaders in shooting percentage. He works to get himself in the high percentage areas, and doesn't waste any time with his shots. He unloads quickly, before a goalie has time to move, and his shots are not easily blocked because of his short release. He simply buries his passes.

He will fake goalies when he has time, looking high and shooting low, or vice versa. He has great hands for work in front of the net on the power play, tipping shots.

His skating is only average, but he has improved and it doesn't hurt his game.

THE PHYSICAL GAME

Robitaille wins a lot of one-on-one battles in the attacking zone through determination and will. He loves to score so much that he will pay almost any price to do it. He is a frequent target of other team's hitters, yet is not easily intimidated. He doesn't do nearly as good a job away from the puck, although his defensive awareness has improved.

THE INTANGIBLES

He has regained his status as the league's premier left wing. His biggest asset is his consistency. Few players have produced as much for as many seasons as Robitaille has, and he is reaching his prime. When Wayne Gretzky was sidelined, Robitaille wore the "C" and carried the team's offense for the first half of the season. He may be the most underappreciated 100-point player in the game.

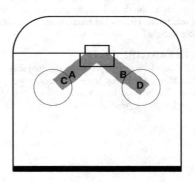

WARREN RYCHEL

Yrs. of NHL service: 1
Born: Tecumseh, Ont.; May 12, 1967
Position: left wing
Height: 6-0
Weight: 190
Uniform no.: 10
Shoots: left

Career statistics:

GP	G	A	TP	PIM
72	6	7	13	331

1991-92 statistics:
Did not play in NHL

1992-93 statistics:

GP	G	A	TP	+/-	PIM	PP	SH	GW	GT	S	PCT
70	6	7	13	-15	314	0	0	1	0	67	9.0

LAST SEASON

First full NHL season. Second on team in PIM. Missed 13 games with ankle contusion.

THE FINESSE GAME

Rychel is a classic overachiever. With minimal finesse skills but a wicked reputation, he finally earned an NHL job last season. He gets his goals from effort and not instinct. He works hard around the net and in the high slot, and has a fairly accurate shot although he needs to hurry his release.

Rychel is a go-getter, and will retrieve the puck along the boards. The problem is that he doesn't have much of a clue about what to do once he gets it. More ice time and more confidence should improve that part of his game.

Rychel is a fair skater and uses his feet well to keep the puck moving along the boards.

THE PHYSICAL GAME

In Indianapolis (IHL) in 1990-91, Rychel scored 33 goals and accumulated 338 PIM. Splitting his time between Moncton (AHL) and Kalamazoo (IHL) in 1991-92, he notched 29 goals and 376 PIM. You don't need to know much more about him, except that he's working to add other elements to his game besides goonery. He is tough and strong and will step in to help a teammate. He is a big hitter, more than willing and able to fight.

THE INTANGIBLES

Rychel's development is probably the major reason why the Marty McSorley trade rumours cropped up last year. Rychel has to develop a more complete game, and he has a good head start on the process.

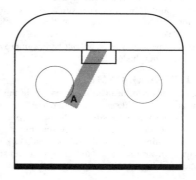

TOMAS SANDSTROM

Yrs. of NHL service: 9
Born: Jakobstad, Finland; Sept. 4, 1964
Position: right wing
Height: 6-2
Weight: 200
Uniform no.: 7
Shoots: left

Career statistics:

GP	G	A	TP	PIM
591	273	320	593	824

1991-92 statistics:

GP	G	A	TP	+/-	PIM	PP	SH	GW	GT	S	PCT
49	17	22	39	-2	70	5	0	4	0	147	11.6

1992-93 statistics:

GP	G	A	TP	+/-	PIM	PP	SH	GW	GT	S	PCT
39	25	27	52	+12	57	8	0	3	1	134	18.7

LAST SEASON

Second consecutive season playing fewer than 50 games. Missed 45 games with injuries: concussion (one), fractured right radius (12), right arm (11), and fractured jaw (21).

THE FINESSE GAME

Sandstrom is one of the few players in the league who can release a shot when the puck is in his feet. He uses a short backswing and surprises goalies with the shot's velocity and accuracy. He can beat a goalie in a number of ways, but this shot is unique.

Sandstrom combines size, speed, strength and skill. He doesn't react well to change. He wants a regular role and lots of ice time, but injuries (his own and his team's) have made a set line-up almost impossible in recent seasons. One thing is certain: Sandstrom needs to play to keep his legs going.

His skating is impressive for a skater of his dimensions. Quick and agile, he intimidates with his skating. He has a superb passing touch and shoots well on the fly or off the one-timer. He has all the weapons to be a 100-point scorer but has never been able to attain that mark.

THE PHYSICAL GAME

Sandstrom is wildly abrasive. He will give facials with his gloves, make late hits, get his stick up and take the body. Usually Sandstrom hits and runs, resulting in angry opponents chasing him around the ice.

Sandstrom will also pay an honest physical price along the boards and in front of the net. He wants the puck and will scrap to control it.

THE INTANGIBLES

Sandstrom's health is a major concern as he has become increasingly fragile in recent years. Some of his injuries are flukes (his jaw was broken by a shot by then-teammate Paul Coffey), some result from his play in the more dangerous areas of the ice. If he stays healthy this season, it could be his last shot at a 50/100 season.

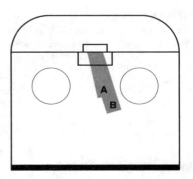

DARRYL SYDOR

Yrs. of NHL service: 1
Born: Edmonton, Alta.; May 13, 1972
Position: right defense
Height: 6-0
Weight: 205
Uniform no.: 25
Shoots: left

Career statistics:

GP	G	A	TP	PIM
98	7	28	35	85

1991-92 statistics:

GP	G	A	TP	+/-	PIM	PP	SH	GW	GT	S	PCT
18	1	5	6	-3	22	0	0	0	0	18	5.6

1992-93 statistics:

GP	G	A	TP	+/-	PIM	PP	SH	GW	GT	S	PCT
80	6	23	29	-2	63	0	0	1	0	112	5.4

LAST SEASON

First full NHL season. Missed two games with hip injury, two with abdominal strain.

THE FINESSE GAME

Sydor is a very good skater with balance and agility and excellent lateral movement. He can accelerate well for a big skater and changes directions easily.

He has a good shot from the point and played on the second power play unit. He had good sense for jumping into the attack, and controls the puck ably when carrying it, although he doesn't always protect the puck well with his body. Sydor makes nice outlet passes and has good vision of the ice.

Sydor will develop into a reliable player on both special teams. He is smart and showed a great deal of poise for a freshman who was thrown into some pressure situations.

THE PHYSICAL GAME

Sydor needs to establish more of a physical presence. It was much easier for him in junior, where he was bigger than many of his peers, but now he is a boy among men and he has to learn to pay the price on a nightly basis. He is a good size and appears to be willing to get down and dirty when he has to.

THE INTANGIBLES

Sydor has leader written all over him. He loves the game and is a fast learner. He had a strong rookie season and is part of a strong defensive nucleus (with Rob Blake and Alexei Zhitnik). Sydor should move forward off this season.

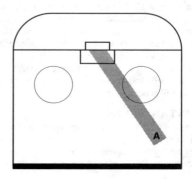

DAVE TAYLOR

Yrs. of NHL service: 15
Born: Levack, Ont.; Dec. 4, 1955
Position: right wing
Height: 6-0
Weight: 190
Uniform no.: 18
Shoots: right

Career statistics:

GP	G	A	TP	PIM
1078	427	635	1062	1561

1991-92 statistics:

GP	G	A	TP	+/-	PIM	PP	SH	GW	GT	S	PCT
77	10	19	29	+10	63	0	0	2	0	81	12.3

1992-93 statistics:

GP	G	A	TP	+/-	PIM	PP	SH	GW	GT	S	PCT
48	6	9	15	+1	49	1	0	1	0	53	11.3

LAST SEASON

Games played, goals, assists and points at career lows. Missed 18 games with a concussion. Missed 16 games with vertigo.

THE FINESSE GAME

The effort is never lacking in Taylor's game. One of the most telling incidents of his career was a short-handed breakaway goal he scored: he chugged down the ice, just about down to the last drop in the tank, before scoring. It was one of his finest moments.

Taylor is smart and plays a strong defensive game, and is a good penalty killer not because of his feet but because of his head.

He is a slow skater and doesn't have much of a shot. He is relegated to a checking role.

THE PHYSICAL GAME

Taylor plays an honest checking game. He takes the body well, takes punishment to make the play, and establishes a physical presence without being a major force anymore.

THE INTANGIBLES

The consummate old pro, Taylor is close to retirement. He finished last season as the oldest player in the NHL, and after the Kings reached the final for the first time in their history, Taylor may want to exit on a high note.

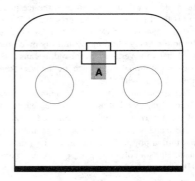

ALEXEI ZHITNIK

Yrs. of NHL service: 1
Born: Kiev, Ukraine; Oct. 10, 1972
Position: left defense
Height: 5-10
Weight: 178
Uniform no.: 2
Shoots: left

Career statistics:
GP	G	A	TP	PIM
78	12	36	48	80

1992-93 statistics:
GP	G	A	TP	+/-	PIM	PP	SH	GW	GT	S	PCT
78	12	36	48	-3	80	5	0	2	0	136	8.8

LAST SEASON
First NHL season. Second among NHL rookie defensemen in scoring. Missed four games with the flu.

THE FINESSE GAME
Zhitnik's skating style reminds his coach, Barry Melrose, of Bobby Orr. Certainly the physical comparisons are there. Both players are about the same size, and the Ukrainian rookie has the same bowlegged stance as the Canadian Hall of Famer. Zhitnik was born with skates on. He has speed, acceleration and lateral mobility.

He plays the point on the power play with Rob Blake, a pairing that gave the Kings the confidence to deal Paul Coffey away. Zhitnik likes to rush the puck and shoots well off the fly. He uses all of the blue line well on the power play. He has a good, hard shot but needs to work on keeping it low for tips and deflections in front.

Zhitnik sees the ice well and is a good playmaker. He can snap a long, strong headman pass or feather a short pass on a give-and-go. He can also grab the puck and skate it out of danger.

THE PHYSICAL GAME
Zhitnik progressed so rapidly that by the playoffs it was the rookie who was sent out onto the ice to contend with the likes of Vancouver's Pavel Bure (a former teammate on the Soviet World Junior Team) and Toronto's Doug Gilmour. Zhitnik is much more advanced than the average 20-year-old, because of his extensive international experience, but he has taken to the physical game with elan.

In fact, he has a wacky side to his game. He makes wild, leaping checks that are borderline charges, but for the most part he plays a disciplined game and doesn't take bad penalties. He was a target in the playoffs and took a physical pounding, wearing down by the finals. He is a solid competitor who has taken to the NHL style.

THE INTANGIBLES
Zhitnik is a prototypical '90s defenseman: mobile, strong, a big shooter and adept at both ends of the ice. He is the heart of what could be a very strong young defense corps in L.A. with Darryl Sydor, Rob Blake and Brent Thompson.

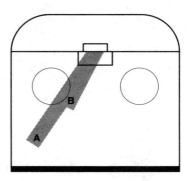

MIGHTY DUCKS
OF ANAHEIM

BOB CORKUM

Yrs. of NHL service: 1
Born: Salisbury, Mass.; Dec. 18, 1967
Position: centre
Height: 6-2
Weight: 212
Uniform no.: 29
Shoots: right

Career statistics:

GP	G	A	TP	PIM
96	10	8	18	61

1991-92 statistics:

GP	G	A	TP	+/-	PIM	PP	SH	GW	GT	S	PCT
20	2	4	6	-9	21	0	0	0	0	23	8.7

1992-93 statistics:

GP	G	A	TP	+/-	PIM	PP	SH	GW	GT	S	PCT
68	6	4	10	-3	38	0	1	1	0	69	8.7

LAST SEASON

First full NHL season. Acquired by Anaheim from Chicago in expansion draft.

THE FINESSE GAME

Corkum has good overall speed, balance and acceleration. He drives to the net for short-range shots and likes to use a strong wrist shot, although he does not get it away quickly.

Corkum likes to use a short, sure pass. He will pass off rather than carry the puck. He anticipates well and will hit the open man. He is not terribly clever with the puck, but he'll make the bread-and-butter play with confidence.

Most of Corkum's skills are average. Anything he achieves will be the result of his hard work and desire.

THE PHYSICAL GAME

He stands tough in front of the net and works hard along the boards. He is a strong forechecker who likes to take the body. He relishes the physical game and makes big hits — anyone hit by Corkum knows it.

THE INTANGIBLES

At this stage in his career, Corkum is a fourth-liner with undistinguished skills. He is a hard worker, though, and won't hurt his team through lack of effort. He has the reputation of being a coachable, team player with a good attitude.

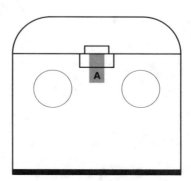

STU GRIMSON

Yrs. of NHL service: 3
Born: Kamloops, B.C.; May 20, 1965
Position: left wing
Height: 6-5
Weight: 220
Uniform no.: 23
Shoots: left

Career statistics:

GP	G	A	TP	PIM
171	3	4	6	632

1991-92 statistics:

GP	G	A	TP	+/-	PIM	PP	SH	GW	GT	S	PCT
54	2	2	4	-2	234	0	0	0	0	23	8.7

1992-93 statistics:

GP	G	A	TP	+/-	PIM	PP	SH	GW	GT	S	PCT
78	1	1	2	+2	193	1	0	0	0	14	7.1

LAST SEASON

Games played career high. Acquired by Anaheim from Chicago in expansion draft.

THE FINESSE GAME

Grimson is a limited role player. He is smart enough to know that this kind of player is starting to vanish from the NHL scene, and he has been working at improving his skills. Right now the Catch-22 (or Catch-23) is that Grimson can't get much ice because he's not good enough, and he doesn't have any chance of getting better until he gets the ice.

With only two or three shifts a game, it was hard to judge much of Grimson's skills. He has little confidence to do much more than what is expected of him, which, for the moment, is to fight.

THE PHYSICAL GAME

Grimson doesn't have much of a physical presence for someone who has the reputation of being a good fighter. The problem is obvious: he can't be a factor unless he is on the ice more often.

THE INTANGIBLES

Grimson may be a dinosaur, one of the nuclear warhead players who are being legislated out of the league. He will find it harder and harder to get any ice time unless he is able to expand his role.

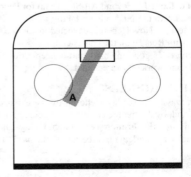

GUY HEBERT

Yrs. of NHL service: 1
Born: Troy, N.Y.; Jan. 7, 1967
Position: goaltender
Height: 5-11
Weight: 180
Uniform no.: 29
Catches: left

Career statistics:

GP	MINS	GA	SO	GAA	A	PIM
37	1948	110	1	3.39	1	2

1991-92 statistics:

GP	MINS	GAA	W	L	T	SO	GA	S	SAPCT	PIM
13	738	2.93	5	5	1	0	36	393	.908	0

1992-93 statistics:

GP	MINS	GAA	W	L	T	SO	GA	S	SAPCT	PIM
24	1210	3.67	8	8	2	1	74	630	.883	2

LAST SEASON

First full NHL season. Recorded first career shutout. Acquired from St. Louis in expansion draft.

THE PHYSICAL GAME

Hebert combines good angle play with quick reflexes. He keeps his feet well, although that technique will be challenged playing behind an expansion team, where he will be expected to make not only the first save but also the second, third and fourth.

Hebert uses his stick well around the net to control rebounds and deflect passes, but he doesn't handle the puck aggressively outside his net. He will probably be asked to do more stickhandling to help out his defense. He doesn't have to whip the puck up ice like Ron Hextall, but he should be secure enough to make little passes to avoid forecheckers.

He needs to improve his lateral movement. He takes away a lot of the net low and forces shooters to go high. Since he is a small goalie, shooters expect him to go down and scramble, but he stands his ground effectively.

THE MENTAL GAME

Hebert proved himself at the minor league level, where he toiled for three seasons (and in 1990-91 was named to the IHL's second All-Star Team for Peoria). Moving up to the NHL meant taking a back seat to Curtis Joseph. Now Hebert is expected to win the No. 1 role, with Ron Tugnutt as his backup.

Hebert has good intensity and concentration. His attitude and work ethic are sound.

THE INTANGIBLES

Hebert was the first player chosen by the expansion team. And, by the by, the correct pronunciation of his name is not the French version, but Guy (as in Lombardo, not Lafleur) Hee-bert, with the hard "t."

SEAN HILL

Yrs. of NHL service: 1
Born: Duluth, Minn.; Feb. 14, 1970
Position: right defense
Height: 6-0
Weight: 195
Uniform no.: 38
Shoots: right

Career statistics:

GP	G	A	TP	PIM
31	2	6	8	54

1992-93 statistics:

GP	G	A	TP	+/-	PIM	PP	SH	GW	GT	S	PCT
31	2	6	8	-5	54	1	0	1	0	37	5.4

LAST SEASON

First NHL season. Acquired from Montreal in expansion draft.

THE FINESSE GAME

Hill has some fine potential as a two-way defenseman and is projected as a No. 1 or 2 defenseman for the Mighty Ducks.

A very good skater, Hill is agile, strong and balanced, if not overly fast. He can skate the puck out of danger or make a smart first pass. His play with Montreal has mostly focussed on defense, but he can be expected to get a lot of power play time with the Mighty Ducks. He has a good point shot and good offensive sense.

His defensive reads still need work. All he really lacks at this stage is seasoning, but he has experience at the collegiate, minor and international levels, and he appears ready to take the next step.

THE PHYSICAL GAME

Hill is a solidly built player who needs to add a consistent physical element to his game to become a more complete defenseman. Anaheim will need him to work along the boards and in the corners.

THE INTANGIBLES

Adding a player with a Cup ring never hurts. Although Hill played sparingly in Montreal and saw action in only three playoff games, he played parts of two seasons in the Canadiens' minor league system, in which defensive play is also stressed. He is also a product of the U.S. Olympic program, which has no success at the Games and yet for the last 12 years has turned out excellent pro players. The Mighty Ducks' philosophy was to build more on promise than past performance, and Hill is a gamble who can pay off.

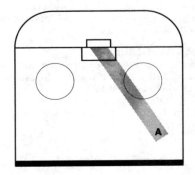

BILL HOULDER

Yrs. of NHL service: 3
Born: Thunder Bay, Ont.; Mar. 11, 1967
Position: left defense
Height: 6-3
Weight: 218
Uniform no.: 23
Shoots: left

Career statistics:

GP	G	A	TP	PIM
111	6	23	29	60

1991-92 statistics:

GP	G	A	TP	+/-	PIM	PP	SH	GW	GT	S	PCT
10	1	0	1	-2	8	0	0	0	0	18	5.6

1992-93 statistics:

GP	G	A	TP	+/-	PIM	PP	SH	GW	GT	S	PCT
15	3	5	8	+5	6	0	0	0	1	29	10.3

LAST SEASON

Acquired from Buffalo in expansion draft.

THE FINESSE GAME

Houlder's skills are all average at best. He struggles as a skater, especially in his turns, but he has a decent first step to the puck and he is strong on his skates.

He makes smart options with his passes. He does not like to carry the puck but is a stay-at-home type who is aware he is limited by his range; he will make a pass to a teammate or chip the puck out along the wall rather than try to carry it past a checker.

His offensive input is minimal and mostly limited to point shots, although he will get brave once in a while and gamble to the top of the circle.

THE PHYSICAL GAME

Houlder is a gentle giant. There is always the expectation of bigger players that they will make monster hits, but we have the feeling that a lot of them were big as youngsters and were told by their parents not to go around picking on smaller kids. Houlder is definitely among the big guys who don't hit to hurt — one of the reasons he has spent six seasons trying to land an NHL regular's role.

He will take out his man with quiet efficiency. He has to angle the attacker to the boards because of his lack of agility. He is vulnerable to outside speed when he doesn't close off the lane.

THE INTANGIBLES

Houlder has failed in two previous organizations to become an NHL regular. If it weren't for expansion, he would not be in the NHL.

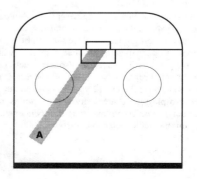

PAUL KARIYA

Yrs. of NHL service: 0
Born: North Vancouver, B.C.; Oct. 16, 1974
Position: left wing
Height: 5-10
Weight: 157
Uniform no.: na
Shoots: left

Career college statistics:

GP	G	A	TP	PIM
39	25	75	100	12

1992-93 college statistics:

GP	G	A	TP	PIM
39	25	75	100	12

LAST SEASON
Played at University of Maine. Won Hobey Baker Award as top player at U.S. college, the first freshman ever to do so. Drafted fourth overall by Anaheim in 1993.

THE FINESSE GAME
Kariya is a silky skater, so smooth and fluid that his movement is effortless. He is explosive, with a good change of direction, and he can turn a defender inside-out on a one-on-one rush. His speed is a weapon, since he forces defenders to play off him for fear of being toasted, and that opens the ice for his playmaking options. He combines his skating with no-look passes that are uncanny. Anyone playing on a line with this gifted winger has to be ever vigilant, because a pass could come at any time.

Kariya is smart, some say cerebral. He is a consummate playmaker who takes control when the game is on the line, as he did for Maine in the NCAA Championship. He is very focussed and poised.

Kariya's overall positional play is well advanced for a youngster.

THE PHYSICAL GAME
Okay, so he's small. To hear some people talk, you would think he had been one of Snow White's pals. No doubt his size is a question mark because he cannot get into any physical confrontations at the NHL level, but his skill levels are so astronomical that it's worth the trade-off.

THE INTANGIBLES
Everyone is willing is excuse Europeans of small stature because of their skill level, but few seem as willing to grant North Americans some licence for the same qualities. Well, Kariya deserves that much. Obviously, he will need some bigger forwards to complement his finesse style, but in the right spot he has the chance to become a franchise player.

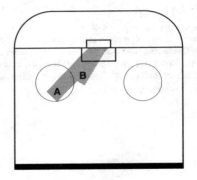

ALEXEI KASATONOV

Yrs. of NHL service: 4
Born: St. Petersburg, Russia; Oct. 14, 1959
Position: right defense
Height: 6-1
Weight: 210
Uniform no.: 7
Shoots: left

Career statistics:

GP	G	A	TP	PIM
257	31	88	119	219

1991-92 statistics:

GP	G	A	TP	+/-	PIM	PP	SH	GW	GT	S	PCT
76	12	28	40	+14	70	3	2	1	0	107	11.2

1992-93 statistics:

GP	G	A	TP	+/-	PIM	PP	SH	GW	GT	S	PCT
64	3	14	17	+4	57	0	0	0	0	63	4.8

LAST SEASON
Acquired from New Jersey in expansion draft.

THE FINESSE GAME
Kasatonov is a powerful skater, strong in his lower body with balance from his "railroad tracks" stance. He never had much open ice speed, and he's lost a step off of his best, but he still possesses a good first step to the puck.

His offensive game has dropped off considerably. Never a great offensive force, the power play duty he used to see was all but eliminated last season as he struggled at both ends of the ice. He will not lead a rush, but he's savvy enough to jump into the play and, when he is hit with a pass as the trailer, will use a strong wrist shot.

Kasatonov is an excellent penalty killer. He is expert at breaking up passes, plays well positionally and has a great knack for clearing the zone by lifting the puck out on his backhand. It's a rare skill.

THE PHYSICAL GAME
He was one of the first Russian players who showed a real liking for the physical part of the game, but last season he seemed more reluctant to bang, as if the hits hurt more.

THE INTANGIBLES
Kasatonov has logged a lot of miles, first in all of his international and Olympic competitions for the former Soviet Union, and then with the Devils. He is worn out and worn down. He hasn't been the same player since the middle of the 1991-92 season, and the decline will probably continue.

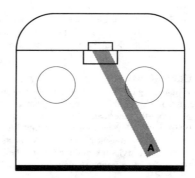

STEVEN KING

Yrs. of NHL service: 1
Born: Greenwich, R.I.; July 22, 1969
Position: right wing
Height: 6-0
Weight: 190
Uniform no.: 25
Shoots: right

Career statistics:

GP	G	A	TP	PIM
24	7	5	12	16

1992-93 statistics:

GP	G	A	TP	+/-	PIM	PP	SH	GW	GT	S	PCT
24	7	5	12	+4	16	5	0	2	0	42	16.7

LAST SEASON

First NHL season. Acquired from New York Rangers in expansion draft. Played 53 games with Binghamton (AHL), scoring 35-33-68.

THE FINESSE GAME

King doesn't play a glamorous game. He is an average skater whose game consists of the grunt work. King pays the price in high traffic areas in the fight for the puck, and he drives to the net for his scoring chances.

He has an adequate scoring touch, but his future will be as a plumber on a line with a finesse player or two, since he is willing to do the work others won't.

He plays up front on the power play and does the dirty work in front of the net for screens, tips and rebounds. He won't overpower a goalie with his long-range shot. His goals will be of the slam-dunk variety, and he will get his shots. If his numbers from his short stint with the Rangers are any indication, he could average anywhere from 160 to 200 shots a season, and he'll get most of those on the power play.

THE PHYSICAL GAME

King will bang and scrape along the boards and in the corners, but he isn't classified as a physical player because he doesn't establish a presence on the ice. He has to bring some bump and grind to his game every night to be effective. He gets involved, but at a mild and moderate level.

THE INTANGIBLES

King played for Brown University, and he spent the better part of the past two seasons in the AHL with Binghamton. There are a lot of things King is not: not fast, not huge, not scrappy, not timid. And we're not sure he's much more than a third-line winger at the NHL level, although he has potential as a power specialist.

The problem with his call-up by the Rangers last season is that he often played the first two or three games with a great deal of energy, then quickly fizzled out, leaving some doubt as to what he would do over the long haul.

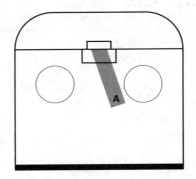

181

TROY LONEY

Yrs. of NHL service: 8
Born: Bow Island, Alta.; Sept. 21, 1963
Position: left wing
Height: 6-3
Weight: 209
Uniform no.: 24
Shoots: left

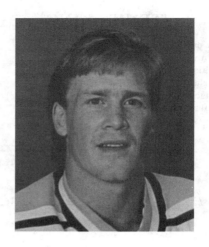

Career statistics:

GP	G	A	TP	PIM
532	69	100	169	980

1991-92 statistics:

GP	G	A	TP	+/-	PIM	PP	SH	GW	GT	S	PCT
76	10	16	26	-5	127	0	0	1	0	94	10.6

1992-93 statistics:

GP	G	A	TP	+/-	PIM	PP	SH	GW	GT	S	PCT
82	5	16	21	+1	99	0	0	1	0	83	6.0

LAST SEASON

Goals four-season low. Missed two games with neck injury. Acquired by Anaheim from Pittsburgh in expansion draft.

THE FINESSE GAME

Loney's chief attraction is his checking game. His skills are average. He is an up-and-down winger who is a fair skater in a straight line, although he has little lateral mobility or change-of-direction quickness. He can't do much with the puck when he has it and is better moving without it.

Loney will go to the net and gets in front for scrambles, tips and screens. He doesn't have much of a shot and doesn't shoot frequently.

Loney's ice time is limited, but he can be used to kill penalties, and he minds his checking duty. He won't make costly errors for lack of effort or smarts.

THE PHYSICAL GAME

Loney likes to hit, but since he isn't much of a skater he is less effective than he could be. He isn't very nasty either, but he will stick up for his teammates, and with so many finesse players on the Penguins, there is considerable value to that virtue.

THE INTANGIBLES

Loney saw limited ice time last season with Pittsburgh, but should provide character and leadership for his new team.

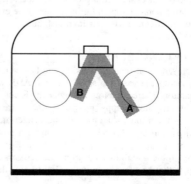

ANATOLI SEMENOV

Yrs. of NHL service: 3
Born: Moscow, Russia; Mar. 5, 1962
Position: centre
Height: 6-2
Weight: 190
Uniform no.: 20
Shoots: left

Career statistics:

GP	G	A	TP	PIM
191	47	75	122	74

1991-92 statistics:

GP	G	A	TP	+/-	PIM	PP	SH	GW	GT	S	PCT
59	20	22	42	+12	16	3	0	3	0	105	19.0

1992-93 statistics:

GP	G	A	TP	+/-	PIM	PP	SH	GW	GT	S	PCT
75	12	37	49	+16	32	3	2	1	0	102	11.8

LAST SEASON

Acquired by Vancouver from Tampa Bay for Dave Capuano and a draft pick. Acquired from Vancouver in expansion draft. Games played and points at career highs, goals at career low.

THE FINESSE GAME

Semonov is a skilled playmaker. He has good speed and marvellous hands. He will lift a cup-and-saucer pass over a defender's stick and the puck will lie flat for the recipient. Semenov's sense of timing allows him to lead his man at just the right tempo with either a hard or soft pass.

He can finish, too, although he is unselfish and his first option is to set up a teammate. He will work himself into a high-quality shooting area before he pulls the trigger. Semenov seldom wastes a shot. He would rather hold on to the puck, curl back and start the attacking rush all over again than dump a shot in. He needs to play with wingers who finish.

His smart play pays off on both special teams. He is a shorthanded threat because of his speed and anticipation.

THE PHYSICAL GAME

Semenov goes through traffic with the puck, and he has the hand skills to control the puck through sticks and skates. He will take a hit to make a play and is strong, but he doesn't particularly relish play along the boards. Killing penalties, he will use his stick to lift an opponent's stick and strip the puck.

THE INTANGIBLES

Semenov was wasted in Tampa Bay at the start of last season, since there was no talented winger there whose style complemented his. He meshed well with Pavel Bure's all-over-the-ice style in Vancouver, since Bure could always relax knowing Semenov would either get him the puck or get back defensively. Semenov might have been too good to play for the Lightning, and could run into the same problem with the Mighty Ducks.

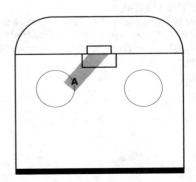

JARROD SKALDE

Yrs. of NHL service: 0
Born: Niagara Falls, Ont; Feb. 26, 1971
Position: centre
Height: 6-0
Weight: 170
Uniform no.: 10
Shoots: left

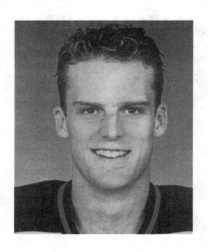

Career statistics:

GP	G	A	TP	PIM
27	2	7	9	8

1991-92 statistics:

GP	G	A	TP	+/-	PIM	PP	SH	GW	GT	S	PCT
15	2	4	6	-1	4	0	0	2	0	25	8.0

1992-93 statistics:

GP	G	A	TP	+/-	PIM	PP	SH	GW	GT	S	PCT
11	0	2	2	-3	4	0	0	0	0	11	0.0

LAST SEASON

Played most of season with Utica (AHL), scoring 21-39-60 in 59 games. Acquired from New Jersey in expansion draft.

THE FINESSE GAME

Skalde skates well, with good acceleration, although not much open-ice speed. He is a good give-and-go player, making the first play and then finding open ice for the return pass. He's unselfish with the puck, probably to a fault, but he has a good passing touch.

He can snap a shot coming in off the wing, but since he doesn't have a great deal of speed this is not a particularly scary shot for a goalie to handle. Skalde is more effective working down low and using his wrist shot.

He is a good penalty killer with anticipation and handy bursts of speed.

THE PHYSICAL GAME

Skalde is slightly built and loses any of the one-on-one battles he engages in. He can be pushed off the puck easily and outmuscled on draws. He can make plays in traffic because he has nice hand skills, but he could really use more bulk.

THE INTANGIBLES

Skalde has not yet been able to move his game to the NHL level. He has the potential to be a solid third-line centre, at best, but probably won't make much of an impact.

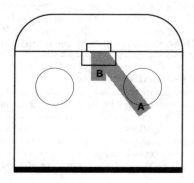

TIM SWEENEY

Yrs. of NHL service: 1
Born: Boston, Mass.; Apr. 12, 1967
Position: left wing
Height: 5-11
Weight: 180
Uniform no.: 41
Shoots: left

Career statistics:

GP	G	A	TP	PIM
67	9	18	27	18

1991-92 statistics:

GP	G	A	TP	+/-	PIM	PP	SH	GW	GT	S	PCT
11	1	2	3	0	4	0	0	1	0	16	6.3

1992-93 statistics:

GP	G	A	TP	+/-	PIM	PP	SH	GW	GT	S	PCT
14	1	7	8	+1	6	0	0	0	0	15	6.7

LAST SEASON

Played most of season with Providence (AHL) and led the Baby Bruins in scoring with 41-55-96. Acquired from Boston in expansion draft.

THE FINESSE GAME

Sweeney is a quick, shifty skater who moves well with the puck. He loves to shoot, and he'll get himself into scoring position by always being on the move and jumping in and out of holes. Sweeney wants the puck.

His best weapon is a wrist shot, and he can shoot off of either foot. He can also one-time a puck and should see a lot of power play time with the new expansion team.

He kills penalties as well, although his overall defensive play still needs a great deal of work.

THE PHYSICAL GAME

Sweeney is on the small side and doesn't even play up to his measurements. His finesse skills aren't good enough to compensate for his lack of involvement. He definitely has to get more sand in his game.

THE INTANGIBLES

Three seasons ago, Sweeney looked like the second coming of Joe Mullen in Calgary. The players are about the same size, play the same position and attended the same college (Boston College) — and even took the same route to the NHL, via Salt Lake City. The Flames even gave Sweeney Mullen's No. 7, but the comparisons ended there. Sweeney is coming off a strong year in the minors and should have a good first half thanks to an adrenaline rush.

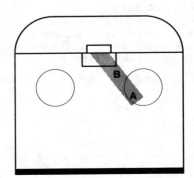

DAVID WILLIAMS

Yrs. of NHL service: 2
Born: Plainfield, N.J.; Aug. 25, 1967
Position: right defense
Height: 6-2
Weight: 195
Uniform no.: 3
Shoots: right

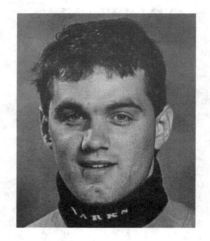

Career statistics:

GP	G	A	TP	PIM
96	4	36	40	89

1991-92 statistics:

GP	G	A	TP	+/-	PIM	PP	SH	GW	GT	S	PCT
56	3	25	28	-13	40	2	0	1	0	91	3.3

1992-93 statistics:

GP	G	A	TP	+/-	PIM	PP	SH	GW	GT	S	PCT
40	1	11	12	-27	49	1	0	0	0	60	1.7

LAST SEASON

Acquired from San Jose in expansion draft.

THE FINESSE GAME

Williams has some good finesse skills but also one key flaw: he is not a very good skater, and that limits his ability to use his other weapons.

He gets some power play time and has a nice point shot. It's not a blast, but he keeps it low and to the front of the net for deflections. He will also gamble deep in the zone (although he really shouldn't).

Williams does not carry the puck out of the zone well, an area that was a real problem for the Sharks last season. He is not poised under a strong forecheck and tends to throw the puck away rather than chip a safe pass out or protect the puck with his body until a teammate can help him out.

He does not read defensive situations well.

THE PHYSICAL GAME

Williams needs to play a more physical game. He has fairly good size but must play smarter and avoid running around to make the hit. He is an intelligent player who doesn't seem to have much confidence. The right coach could do wonders.

THE INTANGIBLES

We told you last year that Williams wouldn't have a job except with an expansion team. He's now gone from the Sharks to an even newer expansion franchise, and this is probably his last stop.

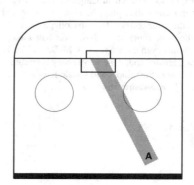

TERRY YAKE

Yrs. of NHL service: 1
Born: New Westminster, B.C.; Oct. 22, 1968
Position: centre
Height: 5-11
Weight: 185
Uniform no.: 25
Shoots: right

Career statistics:

GP	G	A	TP	PIM
104	24	37	61	60

1991-92 statistics:

GP	G	A	TP	+/-	PIM	PP	SH	GW	GT	S	PCT
15	1	1	2	-2	4	0	0	0	0	12	8.3

1992-93 statistics:

GP	G	A	TP	+/-	PIM	PP	SH	GW	GT	S	PCT
66	22	31	53	+3	46	4	1	2	0	98	22.4

LAST SEASON
First full NHL season. Acquired from Hartford in expansion draft.

THE FINESSE GAME
Yake's skill levels are very high — high enough to
suggest his point totals aren't commensurate with
those skills. He is a very streaky scorer, but his slumps
are longer than his streaks.

He moves with good speed and acceleration. He
stickhandles and controls the puck well while skating
and can pass equally well off his forehand or backhand. Yake has a real knack around the net. He is intelligent, clever and creative. He can play both special
teams.

But there are just as many nights when that Terry
Yake doesn't show up. It's most frustrating when you
get a glimpse of his impressive talent one night, then
don't see it again for a week.

THE PHYSICAL GAME
Yake can play a feisty style, *à la* Tony Granato, when
the mood strikes him. He would be a much more effective player if he were willing to pay the price. He
can be a tenacious forechecker.

THE INTANGIBLES
Yake might have been the biggest enigma on the
Whalers last season. He could be a consistent 30-goal
scorer, but if he doesn't compete every night, then
he's of no use at all to his team.

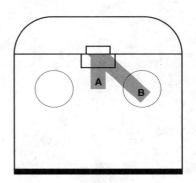

MONTREAL
CANADIENS

BRIAN BELLOWS

Yrs. of NHL service: 11
Born: St. Catharines, Ont.; Sept. 1, 1964
Position: left wing
Height: 5-11
Weight: 195
Uniform no.: 23
Shoots: left

Career statistics:

GP	G	A	TP	PIM
835	382	428	810	581

1991-92 statistics:

GP	G	A	TP	+/-	PIM	PP	SH	GW	GT	S	PCT
80	30	45	75	-20	41	12	1	4	0	255	11.8

1992-93 statistics:

GP	G	A	TP	+/-	PIM	PP	SH	GW	GT	S	PCT
82	40	48	88	+4	44	16	0	5	0	260	15.5

LAST SEASON

Acquired from Minnesota for Russ Courtnall. Led team in goals and power play goals. Fourth season with 40 or more goals. Missed games (two) for first time in four seasons.

THE FINESSE GAME

While you won't notice him much in open ice, Bellows is scary around the net. A power play specialist, he has great hands and instincts in deep. He is not as big as the prototypal power forward, but he plays that style in driving to the crease. He is nimble in traffic and can handle the puck in a scrum. He has good balance for scrapping in front. Bellows works down low on the first power play unit.

Bellows moves and shoot the puck quickly. He doesn't like to fool around with the puck. He has a strong one-timer and powerful wrist shot. Once in a while he'll score from a drive off the wing, but most of his goals come from in tight.

Bellows' five-on-five play improved because he was teamed with just the right kind of centre, Kirk Muller. Muller grinds and gets Bellows the puck, and is also defensively alert, which covers up for Bellows's shortcomings. You couldn't ask for a happier combo.

THE PHYSICAL GAME

Bellows plays bigger than his size. He will bump and crash and work the boards in the offensive zone, but he is better as a finisher in front of the net, and when he has the right linemate (like Muller), he can concentrate on scoring.

He has hockey courage, heart and hunger. He played with fractured ribs through the playoffs but kept plunging into the trenches.

THE INTANGIBLES

Montreal coach Jacques Demers not only opened up his team's offense, but used his veterans like Bellows and Denis Savard well. Bellows will be 29 at the start of the season and has quite a few productive seasons left. Another 35 to 40 goals can be expected from him.

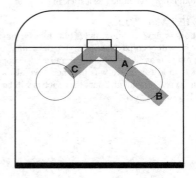

PATRICE BRISEBOIS

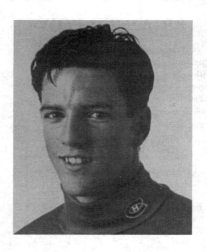

Yrs. of NHL service: 2
Born: Montreal, Que.; Jan. 27, 1971
Position: right defense
Height: 6-2
Weight: 175
Uniform no.: 43
Shoots: right

Career statistics:

GP	G	A	TP	PIM
106	12	31	43	103

1991-92 statistics:

GP	G	A	TP	+/-	PIM	PP	SH	GW	GT	S	PCT
26	2	8	10	+9	20	0	0	1	0	37	5.4

1992-93 statistics:

GP	G	A	TP	+/-	PIM	PP	SH	GW	GT	S	PCT
70	10	21	31	+6	79	4	0	2	0	123	8.1

LAST SEASON

Games played, goals, assists, points, PIM at career highs in second full NHL season.

THE FINESSE GAME

Brisebois has a nice first step to the puck. He has a good stride with some quickness, although he won't rush end-to-end. He carries the puck with authority but will usually take one or two strides and look for a pass, or else make the safe dump out of the zone.

Brisebois has some finesse skills he can use on the attack. He plays the point well enough to merit more power play time in the future. He has a great point shot, with a sharp release, and he keeps it low and on target. He doesn't often venture to the circles on offense, but when he does he has the passing skills and the shot to make something happen.

Brisebois improved on his positional play but often starts running around as if he is looking for someone to end, and he winds up hitting no one.

THE PHYSICAL GAME

Brisebois does not take the body much and will play the puck instead of the man. He'll have to work on his conditioning since he does not appear to be a very strong player — at least, he doesn't use his body well. He's tough only when he has a stick in his hands.

THE INTANGIBLES

Brisebois is developing slowly, but thus far hasn't shown he will become a take-charge defenseman. His likely future is as a solid No. 3 or 4, more of a support player than a leader. He was benched several times during the season, and no doubt the coaches will be on his tail again this year.

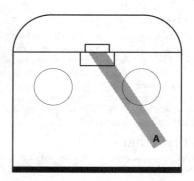

GUY CARBONNEAU

Yrs. of NHL service: 11
Born: Sept-Îles, Que.; Mar. 18, 1960
Position: centre
Height: 5-11
Weight: 180
Uniform no.: 21
Shoots: right

Career statistics:

GP	G	A	TP	PIM
833	207	302	509	575

1991-92 statistics:

GP	G	A	TP	+/-	PIM	PP	SH	GW	GT	S	PCT
72	18	11	39	+2	39	1	1	4	0	120	15.0

1992-93 statistics:

GP	G	A	TP	+/-	PIM	PP	SH	GW	GT	S	PCT
61	4	13	17	-9	20	0	1	0	0	73	5.5

LAST SEASON

Games played, goals, assists and points at career lows. Only minus player among Canadiens regulars. Missed games with tendonitis in right knee.

THE FINESSE GAME

The offensive part of Carbonneau's game is just about gone (although he did come through with a key overtime winner in the playoffs). He is no longer a solid two-way centre who could shut down the opposition centre and score 20 goals a season. He now plays defense. Period.

He remains among the league's best centres on face-offs, especially when the draw in the defensive zone. He has quick hand-eye coordination and gets low to the ice. If he loses the draw, he will make sure his opponent is tied up and doesn't get into the play.

Last year's *HSR* referred to him as a singles hitter when it came to his scoring touch around the net. We'll amend that now to make him a bunter. Carbonneau has a nice wrist shot and will also make little passes in tight.

THE PHYSICAL GAME

Carbonneau has always played bigger than his size and continues to do so. He works hard every game and stays in his opponent's face. He isn't very powerful, but he is deceptively strong. He has good skating balance and gets strong leg-drive for checking.

THE INTANGIBLES

Carbonneau has tremendous pride and just about demanded that Jacques Demers play him against Wayne Gretzky in the Stanley Cup final. All Carbonneau did was completely stifle Gretzky.

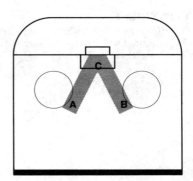

J.J. DAIGNEAULT

Yrs. of NHL service: 8
Born: Montreal, Que.; Oct. 12, 1965
Position: left defense
Height: 5-11
Weight: 185
Uniform no.: 48
Shoots: left

Career statistics:

GP	G	A	TP	PIM
468	34	122	148	320

1991-92 statistics:

GP	G	A	TP	+/-	PIM	PP	SH	GW	GT	S	PCT
79	4	14	18	+16	36	2	0	0	1	108	3.7

1992-93 statistics:

GP	G	A	TP	+/-	PIM	PP	SH	GW	GT	S	PCT
66	8	10	18	+25	57	0	0	1	0	68	11.8

LAST SEASON

Goals career high. Missed 11 games with sprained ankle.

THE FINESSE GAME

Daigneault uses his considerable finesse skills on defense. While he can join in a rush, he's concerned with defense first. He will move the puck out of the zone to get the forwards moving with a pass. He is a very good skater but does not handle the puck well at top speed and won't stickhandle his way through the neutral zone.

Daigneault has a good slap shot from the point, but he is also smart enough to use his long wrist shot for more accuracy.

He angles his attackers to the wall. He does not read plays well defensively and can sometimes be duped by crisscrossing forwards. Overall his positional play has improved.

THE PHYSICAL GAME

Daigneault does not use his body well. He lacks the size and strength to be a powerful force in front of the net, so he must concentrate on his angles and on taking away the passing lane. He will do what he can to keep his man tied up. He is limited by his size.

THE INTANGIBLES

A solid NHL defenseman with two-way skills, Daigneault responded well when given more responsibility by coach Jacques Demers last season.

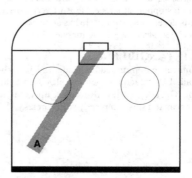

VINCENT DAMPHOUSSE

Yrs. of NHL service: 7
Born: Montreal, Que.; Dec. 17, 1967
Position: left wing
Height: 6-1
Weight: 185
Uniform no.: 25
Shoots: left

Career statistics:

GP	G	A	TP	PIM
558	195	320	515	413

1991-92 statistics:

GP	G	A	TP	+/-	PIM	PP	SH	GW	GT	S	PCT
80	38	51	89	+10	53	12	1	8	1	247	15.4

1992-93 statistics:

GP	G	A	TP	+/-	PIM	PP	SH	GW	GT	S	PCT
84	39	58	97	+5	98	9	3	8	1	287	13.6

LAST SEASON

Acquired from Edmonton with a fourth-round draft choice for Shayne Corson, Brent Gilchrist and Vladimir Vujtek. Led team in assists, points, short-handed goals, game-winning goals and shots. Only Canadien to play in all 84 games. Goals, assists and points at career highs. Has played in 558 of 564 games in his seven NHL seasons.

THE FINESSE GAME

Damphousse won't leave any vapour trails with his skating, but he is very quick around the net, especially with the puck. He has exceptional balance to hop through sticks and checks. In open ice, he will use his weight shift and change of direction to make it appear as if he's going faster than he is — and he can juke without losing the puck and while looking for his passing and shooting options.

Damphousse is cool in tight. He has a marvellous backhand shot that he can roof, and he will set up out-numbered situations low by shaking and faking checkers with his skating.

Damphousse, who can also play centre, has good poise with the puck. While he is primarily a finisher, he will also make the play to a teammate if that is a better option. He's superb player in the four-on-four situations. He has good offensive instincts, although his defensive game is woefully lacking.

THE PHYSICAL GAME

Damphousse will use his body to protect the puck, but he is not much of a grinder and loses most of his one-on-one battles. He has to be supported with physical linemates who will get him the puck. He will expend a great deal of energy in the attacking zone, but little in his own end of the ice. He is a well-conditioned athlete who can handle long shifts and lots of ice time.

THE INTANGIBLES

Last season we predicted a 100-point season for Damphousse. We missed by just three points. He plays on Montreal's top line and gets prime power play time, and this season he'll hit that century mark.

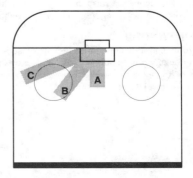

ERIC DESJARDINS

Yrs. of NHL service: 5
Born: Rouyn, Que.; June 14, 1969
Position: right defense
Height: 6-1
Weight: 200
Uniform no.: 28
Shoots: right

Career statistics:

GP	G	A	TP	PIM
312	31	108	139	252

1991-92 statistics:

GP	G	A	TP	+/-	PIM	PP	SH	GW	GT	S	PCT
77	6	32	38	+17	50	4	0	2	0	141	4.3

1992-93 statistics:

GP	G	A	TP	+/-	PIM	PP	SH	GW	GT	S	PCT
82	13	32	45	+20	98	7	0	1	0	163	8.0

LAST SEASON

Goals and points at career highs. Assists match career high.

THE FINESSE GAME

Desjardins is an all-around defenseman who is solid in all areas without being exceptional in any single facet of the game.

Defensively, he's stalwart. He has good defensive instincts and plays well positionally. He seldom loses his cool and doesn't run around getting caught up-ice.

Offensively, he moved his game up a notch last season. He is a very good skater with speed, balance and agility, and is more willing to join the attack. He can work the point on the power play and has an excellent one-timer, probably his best shot. He also moves the puck well, either breaking out of his own zone or sliding along the blue line and looking to move the puck in deep.

Desjardins is also an excellent penalty killer because of his skating and his anticipation.

THE PHYSICAL GAME

Desjardins has worked hard to become stronger. He is very strong and patrols the front of his net like a doberman. He makes take-out checks, and if his team needs a booming hit as a wake-up call, he will deliver the collision. He has a long fuse and does not fight.

THE INTANGIBLES

Desjardins had a disappointing regular season but came through when it really counted, and he was the team's best defenseman in the playoffs. He's one of the team's quiet leaders.

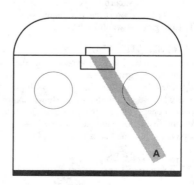

GILBERT DIONNE

Yrs. of NHL service: 2
Born: Drummondville, Que.; Sept. 19, 1970
Position: left wing
Height: 6-0
Weight: 194
Uniform no.: 45
Shoots: left

Career statistics:

GP	G	A	TP	PIM
116	41	41	82	73

1991-92 statistics:

GP	G	A	TP	+/-	PIM	PP	SH	GW	GT	S	PCT
39	21	13	34	+7	10	7	0	2	0	90	23.3

1992-93 statistics:

GP	G	A	TP	+/-	PIM	PP	SH	GW	GT	S	PCT
75	20	28	48	+5	63	6	1	2	0	145	13.8

LAST SEASON

Games played, assists and points at career highs in second full NHL season.

THE FINESSE GAME

Dionne has great anticipation and scoring instincts. He is a finisher but also has good playmaking ability. He doesn't have a big shot, but uses wrist and snap shots from the left face-off dot in. He has nice hands for a pass but usually looks to shoot first.

Dionne's skating is his major weakness. He is slow in open ice, but he can handle himself in the high traffic areas of the ice. He is strong and well balanced.

Dionne was demoted to the minors during the season, and he had his mind more on a new contract than the work at hand. He ended up scoring fewer goals over a full season than he did during half a season in his rookie year.

THE PHYSICAL GAME

Dionne is pesky but isn't yet smart enough to get people chasing him and taking bad penalties. It's usually Dionne who takes the dumb calls. He has size and strength and uses it well, especially around the net. He likes to go into the corners and come up with the puck, and he will keep battling through checks. At least that's what we see when Dionne is playing well, but last season he was inconsistent.

THE INTANGIBLES

Dionne is immature and irritates not only his opponents but also his teammates, coaches, the media and almost anyone who comes into contact with him. He spent too much time after his rookie season reading his press clippings. He needs to come back to earth, because he has too much talent to squander. He reported to training camp in 1992 overweight and out of shape, and never did recover his form during the season.

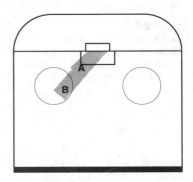

PAUL DIPIETRO

Yrs. of NHL service: 2
Born: Sault Ste. Marie, Ont.; Sept. 8, 1970
Position: centre
Height: 5-9
Weight: 181
Uniform no.: 15
Shoots: left

Career statistics:

GP	G	A	TP	PIM
62	8	19	27	39

1991-92 statistics:

GP	G	A	TP	+/-	PIM	PP	SH	GW	GT	S	PCT
33	4	6	10	+5	25	0	0	0	0	27	14.8

1992-93 statistics:

GP	G	A	TP	+/-	PIM	PP	SH	GW	GT	S	PCT
29	4	13	17	+11	14	0	0	0	0	43	9.3

LAST SEASON

Spent part of season with Fredericton (AHL).

THE FINESSE GAME

For a centre, DiPietro doesn't spend much time in the middle of the ice. He is all over the place, including both wings, in both ends of the ice. This isn't to say that he's undisciplined. Far from it. DiPietro is a very conscientious two-way centre. He can be used to check a high-flying opponent (e.g., Joe Sakic in the playoffs) or to provide offensive spark.

DiPietro is a grinder with quickness and hands. He gets most of his goals from being aggressive around the net, but he also has the speed to create up-tempo plays off of breakaways or by peeling off the wall. He drives to the net but also has the finesse to skate across the grain and lift a backhander.

DiPietro has been a scorer at the junior and minor league level, but his defensive awareness makes him a player with more than one dimension.

THE PHYSICAL GAME

DiPietro is listed at 5 foot 9 inches. Very generous. All that is holding him back is his size, but he plays a very feisty game. He got his chance when the Canadiens moved Brian Skrudland and then Stephan Lebeau was injured. DiPietro capitalized on his opportunity.

THE INTANGIBLES

DiPietro was Montreal's unlikely hero of the Cup triumph. The problem with some unlikely playoff heroes is that they can't always sustain their effort over an entire season. Is DiPietro the 1993 version of John Druce?

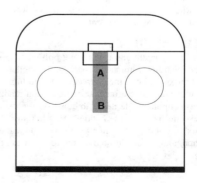

KEVIN HALLER

Yrs. of NHL service: 2
Born: Trocho, Alta.; Dec. 5, 1970
Position: left defense
Height: 6-3
Weight: 182
Uniform no.: 14
Shoots: left

Career statistics:

GP	G	A	TP	PIM
162	20	39	59	229

1991-92 statistics:

GP	G	A	TP	+/-	PIM	PP	SH	GW	GT	S	PCT
66	8	17	25	-9	92	3	0	1	0	85	9.4

1992-93 statistics:

GP	G	A	TP	+/-	PIM	PP	SH	GW	GT	S	PCT
73	11	14	25	+7	117	6	0	1	0	126	8.7

LAST SEASON

Games played, goals, points and PIM at career highs in second full NHL season.

THE FINESSE GAME

Haller has fine finesse skills, but he addressed himself more to playing defense last season. The offensive part of his game should start to shine through in another season.

An excellent skater with an easy stride, he makes skating look effortless, and he likes to carry the puck. He will join the attack or even lead a rush. Haller can make a play. He is a good passer who spots the open receiver and can find a second option quickly.

He has a hard, low, shot from the point that seems to get through traffic.

Defensively, he works hard but has to improve his defensive reads.

THE PHYSICAL GAME

Haller is still a little light and needs to add more muscle. The Canadiens need his physical presence around the net, but he has a difficult time keeping weight on during the season.

Haller has the inclination to play tough but doesn't yet have the power.

THE INTANGIBLES

We predicted Haller would get 15 goals and 30 points last season, and if he hadn't missed 11 games, he probably would have come very close. He still has to improve his all-around game to get more ice time, and 15/30 should be his target again this season. Haller is still green.

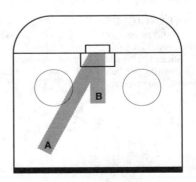

MIKE KEANE

Yrs. of NHL service: 5
Born: Winnipeg, Man.; May 28, 1967
Position: right wing
Height: 5-11
Weight: 175
Uniform no.: 12
Shoots: right

Career statistics:

GP	G	A	TP	PIM
360	64	132	196	356

1991-92 statistics:

GP	G	A	TP	+/-	PIM	PP	SH	GW	GT	S	PCT
67	11	30	41	+16	64	2	0	2	1	116	9.5

1992-93 statistics:

GP	G	A	TP	+/-	PIM	PP	SH	GW	GT	S	PCT
77	15	45	60	+29	95	0	0	1	0	120	12.5

LAST SEASON

Second on team in plus/minus. Assists and points at career highs.

THE FINESSE GAME

Keane is one of the NHL's most underrated forwards, even though he is now a member of a Stanley Cup champion. There are few forwards better on the boards and in the corners than Keane, who is the perfect linemate for a finisher. If you want the puck, he'll get it. Not only will he win the battle for the puck, but he will make a pass and then set a pick or screen.

Keane is a good skater and will use his speed to forecheck or create shorthanded threats when killing penalties. He is not much of a finisher, although he will contribute the odd goal from his work in front of the net.

Keane can play either wing but is better on the right side. He is a smart player who can be thrust into almost any playing situation.

THE PHYSICAL GAME

Keane is a physical catalyst. He is constantly getting in someone's way. He always finishes his checks in all three zones. He is aggressive and will stand up for his teammates, although he is not a fighter.

THE INTANGIBLES

Keane has taken over for Guy Carbonneau as the checking forward capable of scoring 15 to 20 goals a season. But he has the added element of being able to play on a scoring line because of how well he sets up the more skilled players.

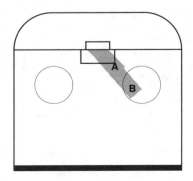

STEPHAN LEBEAU

Yrs. of NHL service: 4
Born: St-Jérôme, Que.; Feb. 28, 1968
Position: centre
Height: 5-10
Weight: 180
Uniform no.: 47
Shoots: right

Career statistics:

GP	G	A	TP	PIM
279	95	132	227	71

1991-92 statistics:

GP	G	A	TP	+/-	PIM	PP	SH	GW	GT	S	PCT
77	27	31	58	+18	14	13	0	5	0	178	15.2

1992-93 statistics:

GP	G	A	TP	+/-	PIM	PP	SH	GW	GT	S	PCT
71	31	49	80	+23	20	8	0	7	0	150	20.7

LAST SEASON

Led team in shooting percentage. Goals, assists and points at career highs. Missed nine games with sprained ankle.

THE FINESSE GAME

Under the traditional Montreal system, Lebeau's offensive game was throttled as he was taught to play defense. New coach Jacques Demers shook the reins loose, and Lebeau broke free.

Despite his small size, Lebeau has 40-goal potential. He is a sniper with quickness and has a great touch around the net. His shooting is uncanny in its accuracy.

Lebeau stays in the middle of the ice and needs to work with players who will get him the puck. He doesn't have outstanding breakaway speed, but he can key odd-man rushes with a well-timed pass, then jump into the play as the trailer. He doesn't have a lot on his shot, but he gets it away quickly and finds openings.

He gets ice time on the second power play unit and thrives on the extra open ice.

THE PHYSICAL GAME

Lebeau can't win one-on-one battles. He is at his best in front of the net and working for the puck. He generally stays out of corners. He has to use his quickness to avoid confrontations. Fortunately for him, he is very good at finding open ice and has the quickness to jump into the holes.

THE INTANGIBLES

Lebeau is an excellent two-way centre (behind Muller). With the other teams focussing their checking attention on Montreal's top line, Lebeau and his linemates should have another productive season.

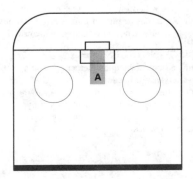

JOHN LECLAIR

Yrs. of NHL service: 2
Born: St. Albans, Vt.; July 5, 1969
Position: left wing
Height: 6-2
Weight: 215
Uniform no.: 17
Shoots: left

Career statistics:

GP	G	A	TP	PIM
141	29	41	70	49

1991-92 statistics:

GP	G	A	TP	+/-	PIM	PP	SH	GW	GT	S	PCT
59	8	11	19	+5	14	3	0	0	0	73	11.0

1992-93 statistics:

GP	G	A	TP	+/-	PIM	PP	SH	GW	GT	S	PCT
72	19	25	44	+11	33	2	0	2	0	139	13.7

LAST SEASON

Games played, assists, points and PIM at career highs in second full NHL season.

THE FINESSE GAME

LeClair has the hardest shot on the Canadiens and can dominate with speed, size and hands. He is a strong skater who can drive the defense back when they see this big dude barrelling at them in overdrive with the puck. LeClair sees the ice well and makes creative plays. He is not an instinctive scorer, but has to work hard for what he achieves.

LeClair, who can also play centre, can pass to either side and makes good use of the extra ice he gets, getting the puck free to a linemate if he attracts too much defensive attention.

He needs to shoot more. Like Kevin Stevens, he will have to work himself into a zone where he shoots the moment the puck gets on his stick, even if he's not sure where it's going.

LeClair's defensive awareness is adequate.

THE PHYSICAL GAME

On nights when he is on, LeClair wins the one-on-one battles and beats everyone to the loose pucks. His problem has been that he does not play that way consistently. He relied on his finesse to get him to the NHL. To be a star, he must use his size and dominate games physically. Does he want to pay the price?

THE INTANGIBLES

LeClair and coach Jacques Demers had their battles during the season, because Demers rightly believes that where there's a will there's a way — to the net — and LeClair has to find that way consistently. LeClair could be a Kevin Stevens in the making. At least that's what Demers hopes.

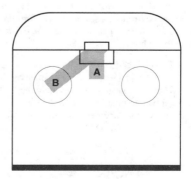

KIRK MULLER

Yrs. of NHL service: 9
Born: Kingston, Ont.; Feb. 8, 1966
Position: centre
Height: 6-0
Weight: 200
Uniform no.: 11
Shoots: left

Career statistics:

GP	G	A	TP	PIM
714	258	433	691	735

1991-92 statistics:

GP	G	A	TP	+/-	PIM	PP	SH	GW	GT	S	PCT
78	36	41	77	+15	86	15	1	7	1	191	18.8

1992-93 statistics:

GP	G	A	TP	+/-	PIM	PP	SH	GW	GT	S	PCT
80	37	57	94	+8	77	12	0	4	0	231	16.0

LAST SEASON

Second on team in assists and points, third in goals. Second on team in power play goals. Goals career high. Assists and points matched career high. Missed four games with wrist and knee injuries; has missed only 10 games out of 724 during NHL career.

THE FINESSE GAME

When you pay to see Muller play, you are never cheated. His effort is intense and consistent. His leadership comes from example. Muller is a gritty player who makes the most of his skills — which are above average, but shy of world class — by exerting himself to the utmost. He has become a more heady and intelligent player; where he once ran around making noisy but ineffective plays, it now looks as though there is a purpose to everything he does.

He plays at his best with linemates who have good enough hockey sense to pounce on the pucks he works free with his efforts along the wall. He is a sturdy player through traffic and has some speed, but he won't dazzle. He doesn't give up until the buzzer sounds, and he takes nothing for granted.

Muller is not an especially gifted playmaker or shooter. None of his plays will make highlight films. Their *ooh* and *ahh* factor is low, but the result is in the net one way or another.

Muller is defensively strong and can shut down the opposing team's top centres. He can work both special teams.

THE PHYSICAL GAME

Remarkably durable, Muller plays with great intensity on every shift and always pays the price in all three zones. His motto is: Whatever it takes.

Muller blocks shots. He ties up players along the boards and uses his feet to kick the puck to a teammate. Ditto for his work on face-offs. Strong on his skates, he uses his skate blades almost as well as his stick blade.

THE INTANGIBLES

No offense to Patrick Roy, but we thought Muller was Montreal's playoff MVP. He will never be a 100-point scorer, but he will produce 85 to 90 points and provide invaluable leadership. Once Guy Carbonneau gives up his "C," it will go to Captain Kirk.

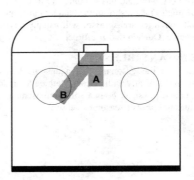

LYLE ODELEIN

Yrs. of NHL service: 3
Born: Quill Lake, Sask.; July 21, 1968
Position: right defense
Height: 5-10
Weight: 205
Uniform no.: 24
Shoots: left

Career statistics:

GP	G	A	TP	PIM
214	3	25	28	709

1991-92 statistics:

GP	G	A	TP	+/-	PIM	PP	SH	GW	GT	S	PCT
71	1	7	8	+15	212	0	0	0	0	43	2.3

1992-93 statistics:

GP	G	A	TP	+/-	PIM	PP	SH	GW	GT	S	PCT
83	2	14	16	+35	205	0	0	0	0	79	2.5

LAST SEASON

Led team in plus/minus and PIM. Tied for fifth in NHL in plus/minus.

THE FINESSE GAME

Odelein is very calm with the puck. He can hold on until a player is on top of him and then carries the puck or finds an open man. He does not move up ice into the play, but is a classic stay-at-home defender.

His skating is average at best, but he keeps himself out of trouble by playing a conservative game and not getting caught out of position. An attacker who comes through Odelein's piece of the ice will have to pay the price by getting through him.

Odelein does not get involved in the attack. He is intent on getting the puck out of the zone, and he doesn't worry about the other half of the ice.

THE PHYSICAL GAME

Odelein is a banger, a limited player who knows what those limits are, stays within them and plays effectively as a result. He's rugged and doesn't take chances, he takes the man at all times in front of the net, and he plays tough. Heavy but not tall, he gives the impression of being a much bigger man. Odelein will fight, but not very well. He has become more disciplined and willing to take a shot in the chops to get a power play, although the transgressor will usually pay later in the game. Odelein doesn't forget.

THE INTANGIBLES

Odelein spent the season matched against the league's top forwards, usually with partner Mathieu Schneider. Reliable and physical, he is a solid defenseman who continues to improve season by season.

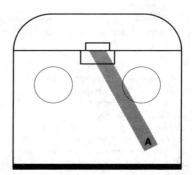

PATRICK ROY

Yrs. of NHL service: 8
Born: Quebec City, Que.; Oct. 5, 1965
Position: goaltender
Height: 6-0
Weight: 175
Uniform no.: 33
Catches: left

Career statistics:

GP	MINS	GA	SO	GAA	A	PIM
418	24,225	1126	20	2.79	26	54

1991-92 statistics:

GP	MINS	GAA	W	L	T	SO	GA	S	SAPCT	PIM
67	3935	2.36	36	22	8	5	155	1806	.914	4

1992-93 statistics:

GP	MINS	GAA	W	L	T	SO	GA	S	SAPCT	PIM
62	3595	3.20	31	25	5	2	192	1814	.894	16

LAST SEASON

First time in seven seasons with a GAA above 3.00. Second-highest GAA of career. Fourth season with 30 or more wins.

THE PHYSICAL GAME

Roy's technique might not be textbook perfect — he flops too much for purists — but he has perfected what he does. He is tall but not broad, yet he uses his body very well. He plays his angles, stays at the top of his crease and squares his body to to shooter. Roy is able to absorb the shot and deaden it, so there are few juicy rebounds left on his doorstep.

Roy is a butterfly goalie, but he goes down much sooner than he did earlier in his career. The book on Roy is to try to beat him high, but there isn't much net there and it's a small spot for a shooter to hit. He is most vulnerable five-hole, and when he is in a slump that is where he gives up the goals.

Roy comes back to the rest of the pack in his puck-handling, where he is merely average, and his skating. He seldoms moves out of his net. When he gets in trouble, he will move back and forth on his knees rather than try to regain his feet. His glove hand isn't great, either. It's good, but he prefers to use his body.

THE MENTAL GAME

Roy is aggressive but doesn't always force the action. He's a very patient goalie, holding his ground and making the shooter commit first.

Among the best in the league at maintaining his concentration and focus in traffic, he always looks in control. His defense did an excellent job last season letting him see the puck. Roy can't be intimidated by crease-crashing.

Roy was exasperated by Montreal's more wide-open style, since he was the one paying the price. But after some midseason chats with coach Jacques Demers, he relaxed through the second half.

THE INTANGIBLES

Roy won his second Conn Smythe Trophy as playoff MVP. Perhaps he didn't steal any games, but he didn't lose any. He rebounded off his poor playoff performance of 1992 and has reestablished himself among the league's best.

DENIS SAVARD

Yrs. of NHL service: 13
Born: Pointe Gatineau, Que.; Feb. 4, 1961
Position: centre
Height: 5-10
Weight: 175
Uniform no.: 18
Shoots: right

Career statistics:

GP	G	A	TP	PIM
946	423	769	1192	1043

1991-92 statistics:

GP	G	A	TP	+/-	PIM	PP	SH	GW	GT	S	PCT
77	28	42	70	+12	73	12	1	5	0	174	16.1

1992-93 statistics:

GP	G	A	TP	+/-	PIM	PP	SH	GW	GT	S	PCT
63	16	34	50	+1	90	4	1	2	1	99	16.2

LAST SEASON

Goals and points career lows. Failed to reach 20 goals for first time in career. Served one-game suspension. Missed games with shoulder, knee and back injuries.

THE FINESSE GAME

The spin-o-rama is semi-retired, but Savard can still weave his magic when he is behind the net and is given a little time to set up a play. He has learned to rely more on his teammates and less on his diminishing skills. Instead of trying to stickhandle through three defenders, Savard might beat one man and make a play, beat one man and send the puck deep. Few players work a give-and-go as skillfully as he does.

Great players hang on because they retain their skating ability, and Savard hasn't lost his legs. He is very agile and is very dangerous from the top of the ice between the circles down to the left and right slots. A better playmaker than shooter, he is using his linemates better than he did earlier in his career. He can't beat defenders one-on-one on a consistent basis anymore, so he needs the support.

He still has his very effective wrist shot as his major weapon. It is heavy, quick and accurate.

THE PHYSICAL GAME

Savard does not push along the walls or in the corners. He is strong with the puck only because few people can catch up to him to try to take it away when he is dancing through the crowd.

THE INTANGIBLES

Savard's ice time is much more limited than it used to be, but he has adjusted to that fact of life and remains a valuable contributor. It wasn't an easy adjustment — it required one momentous benching from new coach Jacques Demers to get the message across — but the quality player that Savard is accepted the new challenge. He is now a fourth-line centre, but he still loves the game and will probably play another season.

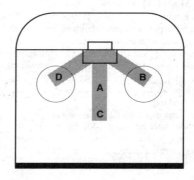

MATT SCHNEIDER

Yrs. of NHL service: 4
Born: New York, N.Y.; June 12, 1969
Position: left defense
Height: 5-11
Weight: 180
Uniform no.: 8
Shoots: left

Career statistics:

GP	G	A	TP	PIM
255	38	89	127	253

1991-92 statistics:

GP	G	A	TP	+/-	PIM	PP	SH	GW	GT	S	PCT
78	8	24	32	+10	72	2	0	1	0	194	4.1

1992-93 statistics:

GP	G	A	TP	+/-	PIM	PP	SH	GW	GT	S	PCT
60	13	31	44	+8	91	3	0	2	0	169	7.7

LAST SEASON

Goals, assists and points at career highs. Games played at three-season low due to shoulder injury.

THE FINESSE GAME

Schneider has developed into a good two-way defenseman. He has the offensive skills to get involved in the attack and work the point on the power play, while his major concern is his solid positional play.

Schneider is a very good skater. Strong, balanced and agile, he lacks breakaway speed but is quick with his first step and changes directions smoothly. He can carry the puck but does not lead many rushes.

We have a feeling we haven't seen the best of Schneider yet. He has improved his point play, doing more with the puck than just drilling shots. He handles the puck well and looks for the passes down low. Given the green light, he is likely to get involved down low more often. He has the skating ability to recover quickly when he takes the chance.

THE PHYSICAL GAME

Schneider plays with determination, but he lacks the size and strength to be an impact defenseman physically. His goal is to play a containment game and be able to move the puck quickly and intelligently out of the zone, and this he does well. Along with his usual defense partner, the hard-hitting Lyle Odelein, Schneider is matched against other teams' top scoring lines.

THE INTANGIBLES

Schneider gave up his old uniform number (18) to Denis Savard and last season changed his number again, from 27 to 8, because of injury problems. Those woes have slowed his development, because Schneider was on his way to a career year last season. We see 20 goals and 60 points in his future if he stays intact.

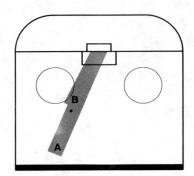

NEW JERSEY DEVILS

DAVE BARR

Yrs. of NHL service: 9
Born: Toronto, Ont.; Nov. 30, 1960
Position: centre
Height: 6-1
Weight: 195
Uniform no.: 11
Shoots: right

Career statistics:

GP	G	A	TP	PIM
594	126	199	325	499

1991-92 statistics:

GP	G	A	TP	+/-	PIM	PP	SH	GW	GT	S	PCT
41	6	12	18	+9	32	0	1	0	0	49	12.2

1992-93 statistics:

GP	G	A	TP	+/-	PIM	PP	SH	GW	GT	S	PCT
62	6	8	14	+1	61	0	1	1	0	41	14.6

LAST SEASON

Missed two games with foot injury; missed three games with flu.

THE FINESSE GAME

That Barr played at all last season was something of a miracle, given the ghastly injury he suffered during the 1991-92 season, when tendons in his right wrist were severed by the skate of Winnipeg's Tomas Steen. Barr still lacks some feeling and strength in his hand. The accident has understandably limited his already subpar scoring skills, which is a shame given his greatest asset: his hockey sense.

Barr is an excellent forechecker and routinely draws the toughest checking assignments against the other league's top centres. That hard work frequently puts Barr in a position to nab a loose puck on a turnover and get his team a countering goal, but the finishing flourishes are all but gone.

Barr is a slow skater, but his smart play saves him strides here and there, making him a more efficient player than one with better skating ability but duller reactions. He is good on draws. His best work comes on penalty-killing, and he headed the Devils' top unit.

THE PHYSICAL GAME

Barr heads willingly into the down and dirty areas of the ice. His boards and corner work is very solid, and he will sacrifice his body. Even when he faces a player with superior talent, such as Super Mario, Barr will not be outgamed. Sic him on anyone, and he'll do what he can to get the job done. Only his physical limitations keep him from accomplishing more.

THE INTANGIBLES

A quiet leader whose efforts very often go unnoticed, Barr is tough to keep out of the line-up. He was a frequent scratch in the first half of the season but proved too valuable a contributor to keep out for very long.

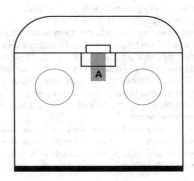

KEN DANEYKO

Yrs. of NHL service: 9
Born: Windsor, Ont.; Apr. 17, 1964
Position: right defense
Height: 6-0
Weight: 210
Uniform no.: 3
Shoots: left

Career statistics:

GP	G	A	TP	PIM
613	26	87	113	1703

1991-92 statistics:

GP	G	A	TP	+/-	PIM	PP	SH	GW	GT	S	PCT
80	1	7	8	+7	170	0	0	0	0	57	1.8

1992-93 statistics:

GP	G	A	TP	+/-	PIM	PP	SH	GW	GT	S	PCT
84	2	11	13	+4	236	0	0	0	0	71	2.8

LAST SEASON

Only Devil to appear in all 84 games; has streak of 311 consecutive games played. Led team in PIM. Fifth season with 200 or more PIM.

THE FINESSE GAME

Average skater, average passer, below-average shooter. How does that all add up to a defenseman who enjoyed his best season ever and may be on the upswing? Put it down to Daneyko's improving hockey sense and his willingness to do whatever it takes to complete a play.

Daneyko has evolved into one of the team's top penalty-killers. He is a good shot-blocker, although he could still use some improvement. When Daneyko goes down and fails to block a shot, he does little more than screen his goalie with his burly body.

A Daneyko rush is a rare thing. He's smart enough to recognize his limitations and seldom joins the play or gets involved deep in the attacking zone. His offensive involvement is usually limited to a smart, safe breakout pass.

Though not a fast skater, he is fairly agile for his size in tight quarters.

THE PHYSICAL GAME

Daneyko is very powerful, with great upper and lower body strength. His legs give him drive when he's moving opposing forwards out from around the net. He is a punishing hitter, and when he makes a take-out hit, the opponent stays out of the play. Daneyko is smart enough not to get beaten by superior skaters and will force an attacker to the perimeter. He has cut down on his bad penalties; emotions still sometimes get the better of him, but he will usually get his two or five minutes' worth.

He is a very good fighter, a player few are willing to tangle with. Now that his reputation is well established, and he is proving himself to be more and more valuable on the ice, Daneyko can maintain his toughness while avoiding nuisance penalties. If somebody wants a scrap, though, he's willing and extremely able.

THE INTANGIBLES

Daneyko seems to have rededicated himself to hockey, with an improved work ethic and better off-ice habits. He was one of the Devils' most consistent defensemen, and his leadership on and off the ice has become even more apparent. He will speak up in the dressing room to quell teammates' arguments, and a coach never has to worry about Daneyko being "up" for a game. He had few bad nights last season, and when other teams came calling with trade talk, Daneyko was one of the first names mentioned. It's unlikely the Devils will part with him any time soon.

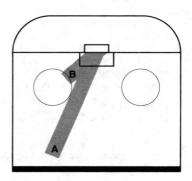

BRUCE DRIVER

Yrs. of NHL service: 9
Born: Toronto, Ont.; Apr. 29, 1962
Position: left defense
Height: 6-0
Weight: 185
Uniform no.: 23
Shoots: left

Career statistics:

GP	G	A	TP	PIM
595	71	280	351	453

1991-92 statistics:

GP	G	A	TP	+/-	PIM	PP	SH	GW	GT	S	PCT
78	7	35	42	+5	66	3	1	1	0	205	3.4

1992-93 statistics:

GP	G	A	TP	+/-	PIM	PP	SH	GW	GT	S	PCT
83	14	40	54	-10	66	6	0	0	0	177	7.9

LAST SEASON

Second among team defensemen in scoring. Goals one short of career high; points at career high; assists match career high.

THE FINESSE GAME

Driver's game is based in his skates and in his helmet. He's a fluid skater, with secure strides and quick acceleration. Driver is hardly greased lightning, but he can get the jump on flat-out faster skaters with his mobility and is very good moving laterally and backwards.

He sees the ice well offensively and defensively and can kill penalties or work on the power play. He has a nice wrist shot, which he uses when he cheats into the right circle, but his point shot is a waste. Despite his skills, Driver is a poor choice to use high on the power play. He would be much better posted low, using his one-timer, but the Devils play a static, stand-around style on their power play. If they ever got into moving and weaving, Driver would excel. He knows when to time a rush or pinch and seldom makes poor choices on the attack.

He has very good hand skills for passing, receiving a pass or carrying the puck, and he is an above-average playmaker.

THE PHYSICAL GAME

Driver does not play a hitting game. He lacks the size, strength and temperament for it. He plays defense by containment, trying to occupy as much good ice space as possible by his positioning against the rush, and then using his pokecheck to try to knock the puck free. With his good finesse kills, he can easily mount a countering rush.

He fails in the one-on-one battles in the trenches, simply outmuscled along the boards and in front of the net. With the NHL trend toward power forwards like Eric Lindros and Trevor Linden, this makes the weak link in Driver's game more and more of a detriment, since he does not have the high scoring numbers to offset it.

THE INTANGIBLES

Losing the team captaincy to Scott Stevens may have contributed to a horrendous start by Driver, who is a proud individual oddly lacking in confidence. Driver never quite recovered from his opening season stumble. Though his offensive numbers were solid, his overall play slumped for the second straight year. This smart, skilled player needs to right himself quickly.

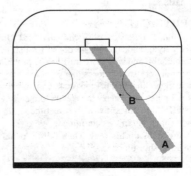

VIACHESLAV FETISOV

Yrs. of NHL service: 3
Born: Moscow, Russia; May 20, 1958
Position: left defense
Height: 6-1
Weight: 205
Uniform no.: 2
Shoots: left

Career statistics:

GP	G	A	TP	PIM
285	18	96	111	380

1991-92 statistics:

GP	G	A	TP	+/-	PIM	PP	SH	GW	GT	S	PCT
70	3	23	23	+11	108	0	0	1	0	70	4.3

1992-93 statistics:

GP	G	A	TP	+/-	PIM	PP	SH	GW	GT	S	PCT
76	4	23	27	+7	158	1	1	0	0	63	6.3

LAST SEASON

Career-high PIM. Games played career high.

THE FINESSE GAME

Fetisov is a highly skilled, intelligent and creative defenseman who is coming to the end of one of the most distinguished careers in hockey history. Toughest for him has been coming to grips with the realization that he now has the reactions of a 35-year-old, not a 25-year-old. He still tries to do too much, although he has cut back on the frightening passes across the front of his own goal. He will still overhandle the puck in his zone.

Fetisov no longer rushes up ice, but uses his terrific reads to start rushes with his passes. He is an outstanding skater with balance and agility but lacks rink-length speed. Without young legs, Fetisov compensates with a wise, old head. He is smart in all zones, probably at his best in neutral ice play because of his anticipation.

Fetisov has very good hand skills, and if the Devils can pair him with a younger defenseman (long-time defensive partner Alexei Kasatonov, two years younger, has deteriorated faster than Fetisov), a successful partnership might emerge. A young player could do far worse than learn the game alongside one of the masters.

THE PHYSICAL GAME

Fetisov has learned to play the physical North American style, and, though he doesn't relish it, he will willingly hit and wade into traffic. The problem is that he is not very strong, loses many one-on-one battles and can get knocked off the puck. Opponents will still work on Fetisov and try to take him out early with rough stuff. Sometimes it works; sometimes it makes Fetisov meaner and more determined.

Fetisov steps up his play when killing penalties and is a good shot-blocker.

THE INTANGIBLES

Once regarded as one of the greatest defensemen in the world and a certain future Hall of Famer, Fetisov has worn down physically, but the glimmers of greatness are still there. He has learned to pace himself through the grind of an NHL season, but this season he will have to be rested even more to remain effective. He remains one of the true aristocrats of the sport.

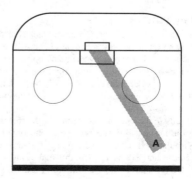

BILL GUERIN

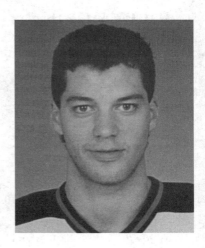

Yrs. of NHL service: 1
Born: Wilbraham, Mass.; Nov. 9, 1970
Position: right wing
Height: 6-2
Weight: 190
Uniform no.: 12
Shoots: right

Career statistics:

GP	G	A	TP	PIM
70	14	21	35	72

1991-92 statistics:

GP	G	A	TP	+/-	PIM	PP	SH	GW	GT	S	PCT
5	0	1	1	0	9	0	0	0	0	8	0.00

1992-93 statistics:

GP	G	A	TP	+/-	PIM	PP	SH	GW	GT	S	PCT
65	14	20	34	+14	63	0	0	2	0	123	11.4

LAST SEASON

First full NHL season. Third on team in plus/minus.

THE FINESSE GAME

Guerin's shot is a thing of beauty — and terror. He unleashes his drive off the pass or a rush coming off the right wing, and sometimes the goalie never moves. It's that fast, that hard and that accurate. Woe to the defenseman brave enough to try to block it.

Combined with Guerin's powerful skating, his shot becomes even more of a potent weapon. He puts on a strong burst of speed and has good balance and agility. He is an excellent passer who leads the man well. He does not telegraph his passes, but frankly, with his shot, he should be more selfish and skip the passes.

Hockey sense and creativity are lagging a tad behind his other attributes, but Guerin is a smart and conscientious player, and those qualities will develop. He is aware defensively and has worked hard at learning that part of the game.

THE PHYSICAL GAME

Guerin is big, strong and tough in every sense of the word. He can play it clean or mean, with big body checks or the drop of a glove. He will move to the puck carrier and battle for control until he gets it, and he's hard to knock off his skates.

In front of the net, Guerin is at his best. He works to establish position and has the good hand skills to make something happen with the puck when it gets to his stick.

Experience is the only thing lacking in his game. He already plays hard; now he has to play smart. Willing and coachable, Guerin is a blue-chip prospect.

THE INTANGIBLES

Guerin first showed his grit in the 1992 playoffs, when, with only five games of NHL experience, he skated into the white-hot rivalry against the New York Rangers and was one of the Devils' top forwards. He is an intense competitor with all the right stuff to become a consistent 30-goal man.

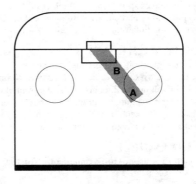

BOBBY HOLIK

Yrs. of NHL service: 3
Born: Jihlava, Czechoslovakia; Jan. 1, 1971
Position: left wing
Height: 6-3
Weight: 210
Uniform no.: 16
Shoots: right

Career statistics:

GP	G	A	TP	PIM
215	62	65	127	233

1991-92 statistics:

GP	G	A	TP	+/-	PIM	PP	SH	GW	GT	S	PCT
76	21	24	45	+4	44	1	0	2	1	207	10.1

1992-93 statistics:

GP	G	A	TP	+/-	PIM	PP	SH	GW	GT	S	PCT
61	20	19	39	-6	76	7	0	4	0	180	11.1

LAST SEASON

Acquired from Hartford with a second-round draft pick and future considerations for Sean Burke and Eric Weinrich. Missed 22 games with fractured thumb. Games played at career low. Reached 20-goal mark for third consecutive season.

THE FINESSE GAME

Holik has a terrific shot, a bullet drive that he gets away quickly from a rush down the left wing. He also has the great hands to work in tight, in traffic and off the backhand. On the backhand (which Europeans are so much more adept at than North Americans), Holik uses his great bulk to obscure the vision of his defenders, protecting the puck and masking his intentions. He has a fair wrist shot.

As a playmaker, Holik is a great shooter. He needs someone to give him the puck and get out of the way.

Although he's a powerful skater with good balance, he lacks jump and agility. Once he starts churning, he can get up a good head of steam, but he can be caught out of position if his team loses the puck and the opposition breaks back the other way. He often loses his man defensively and leaves the defensive zone too quickly.

The Devils experimented with Holik at centre, a position he played in Europe, but he lacks the defensive responsibility and creativity to play centre. Now it's time to stop tinkering and leave him at left wing.

THE PHYSICAL GAME

Holik is just plain big. On the nights when he is on, he's a human wrecking ball, bowling over skaters along the boards and bulling his way to the front of the net. He will not be bullied or intimidated, but his game is still too much reaction and not enough initiative. Involvement is the key to his future development.

THE INTANGIBLES

For the third season, Holik remained a frustrating package. He has all the makings of a power forward, and once every eight games or so will play like one. But there are too many nights when he is simply invisible, and that's criminal given his skill level. He is a 20-goal player masquerading in a 40-goal body. Since Holik was playing well before the hand injury but did not come back well after the surgery, we'll give him the benefit of the doubt for another year.

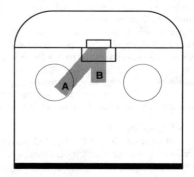

CLAUDE LEMIEUX

Yrs. of NHL service: 7
Born: Buckingham, Que.; July 16, 1965
Position: right wing
Height: 6-1
Weight: 215
Uniform no.: 22
Shoots: right

Career statistics:

GP	G	A	TP	PIM
512	198	187	385	945

1991-92 statistics:

GP	G	A	TP	+/-	PIM	PP	SH	GW	GT	S	PCT
74	41	27	68	+9	109	13	1	8	3	296	13.9

1992-93 statistics:

GP	G	A	TP	+/-	PIM	PP	SH	GW	GT	S	PCT
77	30	51	81	+2	155	13	0	3	2	311	9.6

LAST SEASON

Led team in assists, points, power play goals and shots. Assists and points at career highs.

THE FINESSE GAME

Although Lemieux led the Devils in scoring, only three teams had team scoring leaders with fewer points: Edmonton (Petr Klima, with 48 points), Ottawa (Norm Maciver, 63), and San Jose (Kelly Kisio, 78), all of them non-playoff teams. Lemieux loves the puck, wants the puck, needs the puck, and is sometimes so obsessed with the puck that his tunnel vision costs him creatively. He won't seek out the best-percentage play, especially when he is carrying the puck at high tempo, and when everybody knows what's coming, he is easy to defend against.

When Lemieux is on, he can rock the joint. He has a great slapshot and shoots well off the fly. He isn't afraid to go to the front of the net for tips and screens and will battle for loose pucks. He has great hands for close-in shots.

He's a fast, strong skater with good balance, but isn't particularly nifty and frequently causes offsides. Lemieux is so anxious to go on the attack that he will exit the zone too early and leave his team scrambling defensively.

THE PHYSICAL GAME

Lemieux is strong, with good skating balance and great upper body and arm strength. He is very tough along the boards and in traffic in front of the net, out-duelling many bigger opponents because of his fierce desire. Because Lemieux is always whining and yapping, the abuse he takes is often ignored, but it's not unusual to find him with welts across his arms and cuts on his face. The satisfaction for Lemieux is knowing that his opponent usually looks even worse.

THE INTANGIBLES

Affected by Coach Brooks's public criticism,

Lemieux's play faltered badly over the last quarter of the season. He led the team in power play goals, yet did not score on a single power play from mid-February through the end of the season. Lemieux's emotions still get the better of him. In a game in Buffalo, he was more intent on screaming at referee Denis Morel for a non-penalty call than on picking up his man, Pat LaFontaine, who promptly scored a goal in a Devils loss. Instead of being upset with himself, Lemieux continued his tirade against the ref.

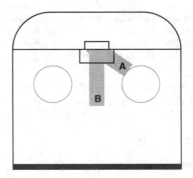

JOHN MACLEAN

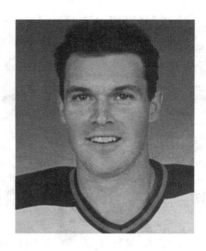

Yrs. of NHL service: 9
Born: Oshawa, Ont.; Nov. 20, 1964
Position: right wing
Height: 6-0
Weight: 200
Uniform no.: 15
Shoots: right

Career statistics

GP	G	A	TP	PIM
626	241	248	489	887

1991-92 statistics
Did not play in NHL

1992-93 statistics:

GP	G	A	TP	+/-	PIM	PP	SH	GW	GT	S	PCT
80	24	24	48	-6	102	7	1	3	0	195	12.3

LAST SEASON

First season back after major reconstructive knee surgery in 1991. Goals, assists and points four-season lows. Fourth on team in goals.

THE FINESSE GAME

MacLean has always been a goal scorer, pure and simple, and his top qualities always consisted of getting himself into position and firing away. As simple as it sounds, that game has been compromised by his year off from the game to rehab his knee. For most of the first half of the season, he was just not getting shots on net, wildly misfiring (the fallacy of a player's shooting percentage is that it does not take into account shots *at* the net, just shots *on* the net). MacLean had only 8 goals in the first 42 games of the season, then popped in 16 over the second half, which may have given the Devils organization some hope that MacLean will regain his old touch.

MacLean's skating, never the strongest part of his game, has been crippled by his knee surgery. He used to be able to get from point A or point B somehow in his ungainly style, but now watching him is torture. Yet his intense competitiveness made it impossible to bench him. He was not an instant success out of junior and had to work hard to earn an NHL spot, so hard work and overcoming others' doubts is nothing new.

The Devils even used MacLean killing penalties — more to help him get in game shape than for any special knack. Yet he developed into a fair penalty killer and his work there has helped his overall defensive awareness.

THE PHYSICAL GAME

MacLean is a solid player but doesn't get the same leg drive he used to because of his injury. He uses a wide-based skating stance and is tough to budge from the front of the net. He will take a lot of abuse to get the job done in traffic, and will not be intimidated. He has cut down on his retaliatory penalties.

THE INTANGIBLES

Coming back from surgery as serious as MacLean's requires time — and few players are ever the same. No one with as much proven ability and promise as his has ever rebounded successfully in the NHL. Once projected as a 50-goal scorer, MacLean will be a stunning success if he ever nets more than 30 again. His outgoing personality and drive still make him an asset.

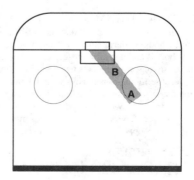

RANDY MCKAY

Yrs. of NHL service: 4
Born: Montreal, Que.; Jan. 25, 1967
Position: right wing
Height: 6-1
Weight: 185
Uniform no.: 21
Shoots: right

Career statistics

GP	G	A	TP	PIM
236	32	40	72	686

1991-92 statistics

GP	G	A	TP	+/-	PIM	PP	SH	GW	GT	S	PCT
80	17	16	33	+6	246	2	0	1	0	111	15.3

1992-93 statistics:

GP	G	A	TP	+/-	PIM	PP	SH	GW	GT	S	PCT
73	11	11	22	0	206	1	0	2	0	94	11.7

LAST SEASON

Missed nine games with sprained knee. Missed one game with eye injury. Second on team in PIM.

THE FINESSE GAME

McKay is an average skater, a policeman with adequate skills to merit a regular spot in the line-up for more than his fistic ability. He has a shot that he needs a long time to get away — his physical play frequently yields him the room — and fools goalies with its velocity and accuracy. The problem is that McKay is such a slow skater that he has to concentrate on staying back in a defensive mode. Thus, he is seldom in a good scoring position in the offensive zone.

McKay does not create much offense with a pass, and can't carry the puck well. Shoot and retreat is his basic tenet.

McKay finished the season poorly, never coming back from the knee injury, and will probably benefit from the time off in the summer.

THE PHYSICAL GAME

McKay is an absolutely ferocious fighter. He is a legitimate heavyweight who is among the first to step in to protect a teammate. He won't initiate with cheap nonsense. He does everything with intensity, whether it's a body check or bulling his way to the front of the net.

THE INTANGIBLES

While McKay is lacking in a lot of areas, he is impossible to keep out of the line-up because of his competitive nature. When healthy, he can contribute a steady 15 to 20 goals to the attack.

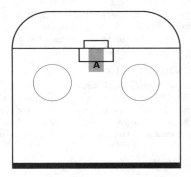

COREY MILLEN

Yrs. of NHL service: 2
Born: Cloquet, Minn.; Apr. 29, 1964
Position: centre
Height: 5-7
Weight: 168
Uniform no.: 23
Shoots: right

Career statistics:

GP	G	A	TP	PIM
107	47	42	89	110

1991-92 statistics:

GP	G	A	TP	+/-	PIM	PP	SH	GW	GT	S	PCT
57	21	25	46	+2	66	8	1	3	0	109	19.3

1992-93 statistics:

GP	G	A	TP	+/-	PIM	PP	SH	GW	GT	S	PCT
42	23	16	39	+16	42	9	2	1	1	100	23.0

LAST SEASON

Missed 38 games with groin injury. Missed four games with back strain. Career high in goals. Acquired from Los Angeles for a fifth-round draft pick in 1993.

THE FINESSE GAME

Millen is always on the move. He has great jump and quickness, and always uses his skating to intimidate, even if he is just driving down-ice and cutting inside a defender to negate an icing call.

Millen is a veteran of international and minor league play who has paid his dues to get to the NHL. He is smart and savvy, and he has great hand skills for passing or shooting the puck in tight. His weapon is his quickness, with either his feet or his hands. He uses open ice well and can get things jumping in the attacking zone, especially when he and quick linemates are whirling and swirling all over the place, enticing defenders out of position.

THE PHYSICAL GAME

Those height and weight statistics are pretty generous, because this is one little guy. Millen is smart enough to try to avoid situations where he will get pasted, but his first concern is the team, not his own personal safety. If he were just a few inches taller and a few pounds heavier, we wouldn't worry so much about his strength and stamina, but he finishes every check and drives through traffic to the net, and he is just bound to erode over an entire season.

THE INTANGIBLES

The spunky Millen did so much in so little ice time last season. But injuries may always be a part of what holds him back. A small player who nevers back down, Millen will always be vulnerable to big hits. He would be most effective playing with a burly finisher or two.

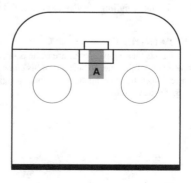

BERNIE NICHOLLS

Yrs. of NHL service: 12
Born: Haliburton, Ont.; June 24, 1961
Position: centre
Height: 6-0
Weight: 185
Uniform no.: 19
Shoots: right

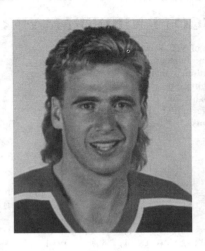

Career statistics:

GP	G	A	TP	PIM
824	397	580	977	1001

1991-92 statistics:

GP	G	A	TP	+/-	PIM	PP	SH	GW	GT	S	PCT
50	20	29	49	+4	40	7	0	2	0	117	17.1

1992-93 statistics:

GP	G	A	TP	+/-	PIM	PP	SH	GW	GT	S	PCT
69	13	47	60	-13	80	5	0	1	0	132	9.8

LAST SEASON

Acquired from Edmonton for Zdeno Ciger and Kevin Todd. Missed 13 games with fractured foot. Missed six games due to personal reasons.

THE FINESSE GAME

A loose and loopy personality off the ice, Nicholls exhibits some of those same tendencies on the ice. Sometimes this is a plus, as Nicholls can be wonderfully inventive with the puck, especially when creating plays from behind the net. The down side comes on nights when it looks like Bernie's mind is elsewhere. Bad penalties and baffling defensive work then follow.

Nicholls is an excellent passer, equally deft on the forehand to his left wing or the backhand to his right wing. The Devils employed Nicholls on the point on the power play not for his slapshot, which is ordinary, but for his vision and ability to hit the open man with a pass.

Nicholls is good down low. He will not plant himself in front of the net, being a bit too frail for that, but will hang on the fringes and then move through the goalie's line of sight, either screening or picking a puck out of the air for a re-direct. He has quick reactions for picking caroms off the goalie's pads.

Skating is a weakness. Nicholls is slow but has some nice moves in cramped quarters.

THE PHYSICAL GAME

Nicholls is strong for his size and has a real nasty streak. When playing with the right bodyguard, he can become an outrageous opponent. He will needle, nettle and intimidate with his words and his stick. He generally avoids traffic areas along the boards and in front of the net.

Nicholls is erratic on face-offs. He is fairly quick, but has trouble against big, physical centres who can simply overpower him.

THE INTANGIBLES

The last season was a nightmare for Nicholls in many respects, one he would like to erase on and off the ice. The serious illness of an infant son superseded anything else, and Nicholls deserves to have his hockey slate wiped clean. Although he is now 32, he still has a lot of crafty hockey left in him and would be an ideal No. 2 centre. The problem is that the Devils will be asking him to be a No. 1, and we're not sure Nicholls is up to it, unless he is flanked by more skilled individuals.

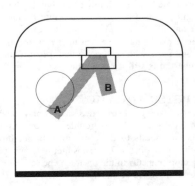

SCOTT NIEDERMAYER

Yrs. of NHL service: 1
Born: Edmonton, Alta.; Aug. 31, 1973
Position: right defense
Height: 6-0
Weight: 200
Uniform no.: 27
Shoots: left

Career statistics:

GP	G	A	TP	PIM
84	11	30	41	49

1991-92 statistics:

GP	G	A	TP	+/-	PIM	PP	SH	GW	GT	S	PCT
4	0	1	1	+1	2	0	0	0	0	4	0.0

1992-93 statistics:

GP	G	A	TP	+/-	PIM	PP	SH	GW	GT	S	PCT
80	11	29	40	+8	47	5	0	0	1	131	8.4

LAST SEASON
First full NHL season. Finished third among rookie defensemen in scoring.

THE FINESSE GAME
There hasn't been this much excitement about a Devils prospect since...well, there's simply never been a prospect as promising as Niedermayer. The 20-year-old is an exceptional skater, one of the best-skating defensemen in the NHL. Niedermayer has it all: speed, balance, agility, mobility, lateral movement and strength. He has unbelievable edge for turns and eluding pursuers. Even when he makes a commitment mistake in the offensive zone, Niedermayer can get back so quickly that his defense partner is seldom outnumbered.

Once the Devils dropped the reins on his neck and let Niedermayer loose (after having him concentrate on defense in the first half of the season), the rookie was a marvel. He had only 3 goals in the first 42 games, 8 over the last half.

Niedermayer has great confidence in his puck-carrying ability, and can lead a rush or join the attack and come in for a late one-timer. He can make a soft lead pass or a firm, crisp one, and always sees his options well. He has a good, low point shot that he gets away quickly, and he will develop into a first-rate point man.

Niedermayer has excellent hockey sense in all zones and plays with such poise that it is difficult to remember he is still a kid whose favourite meal is cereal.

THE PHYSICAL GAME
Not blessed with great size, Niedermayer plays a willing physical game. He has trouble with one-on-one battles and needs to develop more upper-body strength. His skating ability helps him tremendously, giving more impetus to his open-ice checks. He will sacrifice his body to block shots.

THE INTANGIBLES
Niedermayer has been frequently compared to Paul Coffey, but his veteran defense partner, Scott Stevens, likes to liken Niedermayer to Ray Bourque. He can't be judged too quickly, because defensemen need time to mature. He is already ahead of the game, and he should take another giant step forward this season.

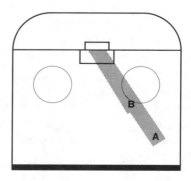

MIKE PELUSO

Yrs. of NHL service: 3
Born: Pengilly, Minn.; Nov. 8, 1965
Position: left wing
Height: 6-4
Weight: 200
Uniform no.: 44
Shoots: left

Career statistics:

GP	G	A	TP	PIM
199	27	14	41	1046

1991-92 statistics:

GP	G	A	TP	+/-	PIM	PP	SH	GW	GT	S	PCT
63	6	3	9	+1	408	2	0	0	0	32	18.8

1992-93 statistics:

GP	G	A	TP	+/-	PIM	PP	SH	GW	GT	S	PCT
81	15	10	25	-35	318	2	0	1	0	93	16.1

LAST SEASON

Led team in PIM. Goals, assists and points at career highs. PIM at three-season low. Acquired by New Jersey as future considerations with Peter Sidorkiewicz for Craig Billington, Troy Malletee and a fourth-round draft pick in 1993.

THE FINESSE GAME

Peluso has enough speed to get in on top of a defenseman, and seeing a player of his size rocketing in can force many a panic pass. He played a much more restrained game last season and actually turned into a reliable forward. He gets so much room in front that he will get two or three swats at the puck where most forwards would get only one.

Peluso's balance isn't very good, though, and this prevents him from standing in front of the goal as well as he should. He can be tipped over by smaller players. If he learns better technique, he could add five to 10 goals a season just by screening in front and letting pucks plunk in off his massive body, especially on the power play.

His offensive skills are below average. He doesn't have very good hands for shooting or passing, and he doesn't know when to move the puck hard or soft.

THE PHYSICAL GAME

Peluso slashed 90 minutes off his PIM total without losing any of his toughness. He may have soured on his role as an enforcer since he was really the only Senator with any interest in the rough stuff, but most of his discipline seemed deliberate. Since he could go off at any time, other people are always wary of him. He is a very good fighter.

THE INTANGIBLES

Peluso is an enforcer who got the ice time to develop other parts of his game. While he'll never be a good power forward, what's wrong with a role player who can get 20 goals or so a season? Peluso can.

He will get more physical support in New Jersey from players like Ken Daneyko and Scott Stevens. His leadership and intensity will be a major bonus.

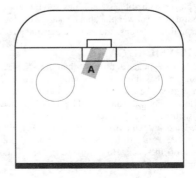

STEPHANE RICHER

Yrs. of NHL service: 8
Born: Ripon, Que.; June 7, 1966
Position: right wing
Height: 6-2
Weight: 200
Uniform no.: 44
Shoots: right

Career statistics:

GP	G	A	TP	PIM
565	265	238	503	431

1991-92 statistics

GP	G	A	TP	+/-	PIM	PP	SH	GW	GT	S	PCT
74	29	35	64	-1	25	5	1	6	1	240	12.1

1992-93 statistics:

GP	G	A	TP	+/-	PIM	PP	SH	GW	GT	S	PCT
78	38	35	73	-1	44	7	1	7	1	286	13.3

LAST SEASON

Led team in goals and game-winning goals. Goals and points at three-season highs. Reached 30-goal mark for fourth time. Missed three games with knee injury. Missed two games with back injury.

THE FINESSE GAME

Wonderful hands, a blistering shot and excellent skating all add up to a player who should be among the NHL's elite. Attitude and confidence keep Richer from being a complete package, since he has the skills and the size to dominate, but does so too infrequently.

Richer gets great drive from his legs. He has powerful acceleration and true rink-length speed. He can intimidate with his rush, opening up the ice for himself and his linemates. He can also be crafty, slipping in and out of the open ice. He has very good vision offensively, and good hockey sense.

His slapshot is a wonder. It's the hardest on the team and in the top five of the league. A Richer rocket ticketed for a top corner is simply unstoppable, and he loves to fire in from the tops of the circles. He has even improved on it. Teeing up a shot used to be a laborious process for Richer, but now he has a hair-trigger release. When the shot isn't there, he will wisely opt for a pass.

A player with Richer's abilities should be more successful on the power play, but he has not hit double figures in three seasons, and that is a genuine puzzle.

THE PHYSICAL GAME

Richer is much better in open ice than in traffic areas. Although he has the size, strength and balance for trench warfare, he doesn't always show the inclination. He will go to the net with the puck, though, and has a wonderful long reach that allows him to be checked and still whip off a strong shot on net. When Richer is determined, it is just about impossible to peel him off the puck. He is slow to rile and seldom takes bad penalties.

THE INTANGIBLES

Richer was often lauded by coach Herb Brooks, but the team's failure to come up with a new contract for the right wing led to wild mood swings for the talented but erratic winger. He is deserving of the $1 million a year he is seeking (easy for us to say, since it's not our chequebook). But Richer led the team in goals, played centre and both wings, and did everything else asked of him. He also has the capability to do much more. Soothing his ego and his bank account might assure the Devils of that, since another 50-goal season is very likely.

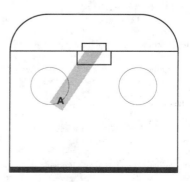

ALEXANDER SEMAK

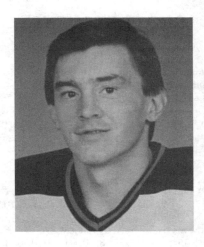

Yrs. of NHL service: 2
Born: Ufa, Russia; Feb. 11, 1966
Position: centre
Height: 5-10
Weight: 185
Uniform no.: 20
Shoots: right

Career statistics:

GP	G	A	TP	PIM
107	42	48	90	70

1991-92 statistics:

GP	G	A	TP	+/-	PIM	PP	SH	GW	GT	S	PCT
25	5	6	11	+5	0	0	0	1	0	45	11.1

1992-93 statistics:

GP	G	A	TP	+/-	PIM	PP	SH	GW	GT	S	PCT
82	37	42	79	+24	70	4	1	6	1	217	17.1

LAST SEASON

Led team in plus/minus and shooting percentage. Second on team in goals, assists and points.

THE FINESSE GAME

Semak drives goalies crazy with his disguises. No, we don't mean a funny nose and glasses, but the way the Russian centre hides his intentions. Shoot or pass? Forehand or backhand? Semak has a nice variety and runs through his options very quickly and in a few quick strides in from the blue line to the hash marks, always keeping the opposition guessing. He will open, close, and re-open his stickface, and has an excellent wrist shot off either foot.

Semak is not a fast skater with a rink-long rush, but he is very shifty, with one-step quickness that can leave a checker in the embarrassing position of checking himself into the boards while Semak continues on his merry way to the net.

Semak is very creative, seeing or sensing the attackers coming in behind him late on the play for a drop pass. He works well criss-crossing, especially with frequent linemate and fellow Russian Valeri Zelepukin.

Semak is so-so on face-offs. He is a very good penalty-killer because of his anticipation.

THE PHYSICAL GAME

Semak lacks the speed to intimidate opponents on the rush, and he is not strong enough to win one-on-one battles in traffic, so he must always work hard at the weaving game with his teammates to stay in open ice. He is less effective on the road than at home, where the Devils have last change and can juggle him away from the other team's top checkers.

THE INTANGIBLES

After a brief glimpse of Semak in the old up-and-down mould of the 1991-92 Devils, no one was prepared for the new and improved 1992-93 model. In addition to the confidence in his skills, which improved as he was given more and more ice time and responsibility, he has shown some fire and had referees complaining about his yapping. (Funny — we didn't know Semak knew that much English.)

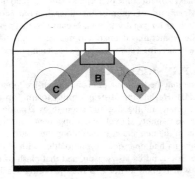

SCOTT STEVENS

Yrs. of NHL service: 11
Born: Kitchener, Ont.; Apr. 11, 1964
Position: left defense
Height: 6-2
Weight: 215
Uniform no.: 4
Shoots: left

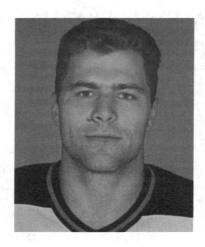

Career statistics:

GP	G	A	TP	PIM
828	132	462	594	2022

1991-92 statistics:

GP	G	A	TP	+/-	PIM	PP	SH	GW	GT	S	PCT
68	17	42	59	+24	124	7	1	2	0	156	10.9

1992-93 statistics:

GP	G	A	TP	+/-	PIM	PP	SH	GW	GT	S	PCT
81	12	45	57	+14	120	8	0	1	0	146	8.2

LAST SEASON

Led team defensemen in scoring. Second on team in power play goals. Missed three games with concussion.

THE FINESSE GAME

Stevens gets a lot of ice time on the power play (8 of his 12 goals came with the man advantage), but don't go thinking he is very offensively blessed. He has a nice pair of hands for work in close to the net, which is where he is posted on the power play, doing yeoman work to establish himself in front of the goalie. But he doesn't have a great shot. Most of his scoring chances from the point are wild slapshots, untippable and not on target.

Stevens does not read plays well consistently, either offensively or defensively. He makes some dreadfully timed pinches and was bailed out more than one by his quick defensive partner, Scott Niedermayer.

Stevens is a very good skater, secure and strong. He is good forward and backward, and has good lateral mobility. He will overhandle the puck in the defensive zone, when a simpler play would do.

Stevens has a tremendous work ethic that more than makes up for some of his shortcomings (and most of those are sins of commission rather than omission). He is a bear on penalty-killing, because he just won't quit, but sometimes is unable to make a simple bank off the boards for a clear and keeps his team pinned in.

THE PHYSICAL GAME

Stevens may be the most punishing open-ice hitter in the NHL. He has the skating ability to line up the puck-carrier, and the size and strength to explode on impact. He simply shovels most opponents out from in front of the net, and crunches along the boards.

Stevens had epic one-on-one battles with Flyers rookie Eric Lindros last season, and that clash of the titans will be one to track in the upcoming season.

Stevens fights well when provoked, and other teams make a point of trying to goad Stevens into bad penalties. He has matured and is able to keep a better lid on his temper, but he'll still blow every now and again.

THE INTANGIBLES

Though the Devils paired the veteran Stevens with the rookie Scott Niedermayer to help the youngster, it reaped unusual benefits. Stevens no longer felt compelled to be a do-it-all defenseman (which he's not; his offensive skills aren't up to it) and settled into a more limited role, at which he can excel. The Great Scotts should be together again on the New Jersey blue line this season, and Niedermayer should assume more of the scoring and rushing duties while Stevens concentrates on a defensive role.

Stevens was given the captain's "C" last season, an overdue move. He is a leader who takes his role seriously on and off the ice.

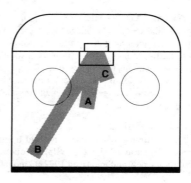

CHRIS TERRERI

Yrs. of NHL service: 6
Born: Providence, R.I.; Nov. 15, 1964
Position: goaltender
Height: 5-9
Weight: 160
Uniform no.: 31
Catches: left

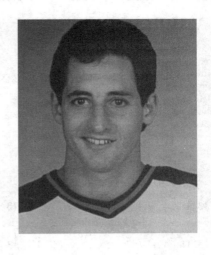

Career statistics:

GP	MINS	GA	SO	AVG	A	PIM
205	11,432	613	4	3.22	4	21

1991-92 statistics:

GP	MINS	GAA	W	L	T	SO	GA	SA	SAPCT	PIM
54	3169	3.20	24	22	10	1	169	1511	.888	13

1992-93 statistics:

GP	MINS	GAA	W	L	T	SO	GA	SA	SAPCT	PIM
48	2672	3.39	19	21	3	2	151	1324	.886	6

LAST SEASON

Games and minutes played three-season lows.

THE MENTAL GAME

The more shots he gets, the more Terreri fights. He plays off emotion and adrenaline, and used to wear down mentally and physically over the course of a long season because his small frame couldn't take the wear and tear. Using Craig Billington more has allowed Terreri to stay stronger throughout the entire season.

An upbeat (some might even say hyper) personality, Terreri doesn't dwell on bad games or bad goals within a game. He is a battler who doesn't collapse under pressure, and he's a steady man in the nets on breakaways.

THE INTANGIBLES

Terreri had a lower GAA than goal mate Billington (3.39 to 3.67) yet ended up two games under .500 while Billington was five over. The Devils just seemed to win for Billington, much as they won for Terreri when he shared the goaltending duties with Sean Burke for two seasons. It might be that his teammates relied too much on Terreri to win games for them, or that he got little offensive support. Either way, his play slumped slightly.

VALERI ZELEPUKIN

Yrs. of NHL service: 2
Born: Voskresensk, Russia; Sept. 17, 1968
Position: left wing
Height: 5-11
Weight: 180
Uniform no.: 25
Shoots: left

Career statistics:

GP	G	A	TP	PIM
122	36	59	95	98

1991-92 statistics:

GP	G	A	TP	+/-	PIM	PP	SH	GW	GT	S	PCT
44	13	18	31	+11	28	3	0	3	0	94	13.8

1992-93 statistics:

GP	G	A	TP	+/-	PIM	PP	SH	GW	GT	S	PCT
78	23	41	64	+19	70	5	1	2	0	174	13.2

LAST SEASON

Second on team in plus/minus. Fourth on team in points.

THE FINESSE GAME

In his rookie season, Zelepukin showed a flair and a willingness to fight to the front of the net, but in his sophomore year much of that desire seemed to have burned out of his game. There were still occasional nights when he (and linemate Alexander Semak) were flying, but not on a consistent enough basis to match Zelepukin's skill level.

Zelepukin is a very discriminating shooter, but he has become too unselfish. He will pass up a less than ideal shot and dish off to a teammate who is in an even worse position. Zelepukin has a shot worth using. He has very strong wrists and with his constant motion is almost always in a high percentage position. He has a very good one-timer.

Zelepukin is not straightaway fast, but he has good one-step quickness. He is strong and balanced on his skates, and he thinks creatively in getting involved in the rush. He reads plays well and is a sound defensive player.

THE PHYSICAL GAME

Zelepukin cannot win one-on-one battles in front of the net, but he does have a wiry strength and that skating ability to play more of a grinding style. There are too many nights when he is merely a perimeter player, and an added element of physical play would open up a lot of ice.

THE INTANGIBLES

Zelepukin is among the third wave of players from the former Soviet Union. The first were the exceptional players whose better days were behind them, like Viacheslav Fetisov and Igor Larionov. Then came the brilliant stars like Pavel Bure and Alexander Mogilny. And now it's the mixed bag, the Russians who are not the cream of their generation, but who have to work to establish themselves in the NHL. Zelepukin must be more productive to prove he belongs, since his skills are not dazzling.

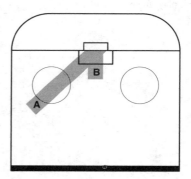

NEW YORK ISLANDERS

BRAD DALGARNO

Yrs. of NHL service: 4
Born: Vancouver, B.C.; Aug. 11, 1967
Position: right wing
Height: 6-3
Weight: 215
Uniform no.: 15
Shoots: right

Career statistics:

GP	G	A	TP	PIM
208	34	48	82	242

1991-92 statistics:

GP	G	A	TP	+/-	PIM	PP	SH	GW	GT	S	PCT
15	2	1	3	-8	12	1	0	0	0	17	11.8

1992-93 statistics:

GP	G	A	TP	+/-	PIM	PP	SH	GW	GT	S	PCT
57	15	17	32	+17	62	2	0	2	0	62	24.2

LAST SEASON

Led team in plus/minus and shooting percentage. Games played, goals, assists and points at career highs. Missed one game with back injury and one with shoulder injury.

THE FINESSE GAME

Dalgarno is a solid forechecker and has a good future (and present) as a checking winger.

His offensive skills are limited. He was never a flashy scorer at any level, and he gets his scoring chances from around the net. He will get some power play time on the second unit because he is willing to go into the traffic areas in front of the goal for screens and rebounds.

His skating is average. He is not very quick, but he has a long stride. Once he gets going, he is a force. He has a long reach that he puts to good use around the net and in breaking up plays by reaching around an opponent. He has good balance and gets the leg drive he needs in the tussles in the trenches.

THE PHYSICAL GAME

Dalgarno is very strong along the boards and in the corners. He finishes every check and can be used against other teams' top power forwards. In the Islanders' playoff upset over the Pittsburgh Penguins, Dalgarno was matched against Kevin Stevens and nullified him.

Dalgarno used to be a pretty fair scrapper, but during the 1988-89 season he was seriously injured in a fight with Joe Kocur (then with Detroit) and required surgery to repair the damage to his face. He went into retirement the following season, and when he did come back he had to wear a face shield. He was tested (by opponents and teammates both) and has passed.

THE INTANGIBLES

Dalgarno may have been the Islanders' most consistent forward last season. Whatever doubts he may have had about commitment to his career seem to have been replaced by a new resolve to succeed in the NHL. Several years ago, before Dalgarno was injured, coach Al Arbour compared him to a young Bob Nystrom. Dalgarno is back on that track.

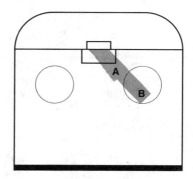

RAY FERRARO

Yrs. of NHL service: 9
Born: Trail, B.C.; Aug. 23, 1964
Position: centre
Height: 5-10
Weight: 185
Uniform no.: 20
Shoots: left

Career statistics:

GP	G	A	TP	PIM
629	230	263	493	617

1991-92 statistics:

GP	G	A	TP	+/-	PIM	PP	SH	GW	GT	S	PCT
80	40	40	80	+25	92	7	0	4	2	154	26.0

1992-93 statistics:

GP	G	A	TP	+/-	PIM	PP	SH	GW	GT	S	PCT
46	14	13	27	0	40	3	0	1	0	72	19.4

LAST SEASON

Missed 36 games with broken leg. Missed one game with flu. Games played, goals, assists and points lowest since rookie season.

THE FINESSE GAME

Ferraro excels at the short game, no pun intended. From the bottoms of the circle in, Ferraro uses his quickness and hand skills to work little give-and-go plays through traffic.

Ferraro is a streaky player, and when he is in the groove he plays with great concentration and hunger around the net. He is alert to not only his first but also his second and third options, and he makes a rapid play selection. His best shot is his wrist shot from just off to the side of the net, which is where he likes to work on the power play. He has good coordination and timing for deflections.

Ferraro's skating won't win medals. He has a choppy stride and lacks rink-long speed, but he shakes loose in a few quick steps and maintains his balance well. Handling the puck does not slow him down.

Defensively, Ferraro has improved tremendously and is no longer a liability. In fact, he's a pretty decent two-way centre, although the scales still tip in favour of his offensive ability. He has particularly improved in his defensive work down low. He's good on face-offs.

THE PHYSICAL GAME

Ferraro is on the small side but is deceptively strong. Many players aren't willing to wade into the areas where they will get crunched, and Ferraro will try to avoid those situations when he can. But if it's the right play, he will take the abuse and whack a few ankles himself.

THE INTANGIBLES

Ferraro caught fire in the playoffs with a remarkable performance (he led the Islanders with 13-7-20, including two overtime goals).

There are few players this size with hearts as big.

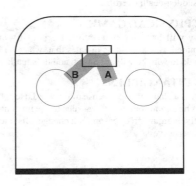

PATRICK FLATLEY

Yrs. of NHL service: 10
Born: Toronto, Ont.; Oct. 3, 1963
Position: right wing
Height: 6-2
Weight: 195
Uniform no.: 26
Shoots: right

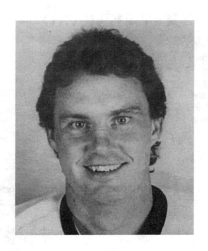

Career statistics:

GP	G	A	TP	PIM
556	133	269	402	587

1991-92 statistics:

GP	G	A	TP	+/-	PIM	PP	SH	GW	GT	S	PCT
38	8	28	36	+14	31	4	1	0	0	76	10.5

1992-93 statistics:

GP	G	A	TP	+/-	PIM	PP	SH	GW	GT	S	PCT
80	13	47	60	+4	63	1	2	1	0	139	9.4

LAST SEASON

First time playing more than 63 games in seven seasons. Assists and points at career highs. Fourth on team in assists. Missed four games with rib injury.

THE FINESSE GAME

The sum of Flatley's game is much greater than its parts. Broken down into components, we have a slow skater with average hand skills and a tendency to get damaged. But all assembled, the package is a solid, two-way forward with tremendous heart. Flatley's desire to get the job done helps him find a way from Point A to Point B, even if that means going through a bigger player. He isn't fast in open ice, but he's sneaky-quick in tight.

Flatley is superb along the boards and in the corners. He fights for the puck, and when he gets it, he protects it with his body until a teammate is in position for a pass. That is one of the reasons why Flatley has been seriously hurt in the pass. He will leave himself physically vulnerable in order to make the right play.

His scoring touch is minimal. He does seem to score timely goals, and he works with great poise in front of the net whether the game is in the first minute or in sudden-death overtime.

THE PHYSICAL GAME

Flatley will bang on every shift. He is gritty and determined. His work ethic dictates that, whatever he has to do to win, he will attempt it, and he's fearless.

THE INTANGIBLES

Flatley is a leader in every sense of the word. He is the team's heart and soul, and it was nice to see him enjoy a relatively injury-free season for a change. His intensity never wavers.

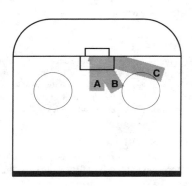

TRAVIS GREEN

Yrs. of NHL service: 1
Born: Creston, B.C.; Dec. 20, 1970
Position: centre
Height: 6-0
Weight: 195
Uniform no.: 39
Shoots: right

Career statistics:

GP	G	A	TP	PIM
61	7	18	25	43

1992-93 statistics:

GP	G	A	TP	+/-	PIM	PP	SH	GW	GT	S	PCT
61	7	18	25	+4	43	1	0	0	0	115	6.1

LAST SEASON
First NHL season.

THE FINESSE GAME
Green hasn't made the adjustment that players must when they step up to the NHL level, in getting a quicker release on his shot. He still needs an extra half-second to get it unleashed, and that sliver of time means the difference between scoring and having his shot blocked or stopped by the goaltender. He has a hard, booming shot when he gets it off.

Green has taken some time to develop. He has had to work on his skating and now has better balance and agility, with some quickness, although he lacks straight-ahead speed.

Green controls the puck well. He plays more of a finesse game than a power game, and he has to learn to charge the net with more authority. He is an unselfish player and passes equally well to either side. He sees the ice well.

Green is the Islanders' top man on draws.

THE PHYSICAL GAME
Green has learned to be involved in the play. He's not a huge guy, but he will use his body to get in the way. He is not by nature an intense competitor, but now that he has had his taste of NHL life, he may want to work hard enough to stick.

THE INTANGIBLES
Green has been a scorer throughout his career, but worked hard at the junior and minor league levels to improve his defense. He was so successful at it that the Islanders used him primarily in a checking role. If his scoring touch comes around as well, he could score 20 to 25 goals as a two-way forward.

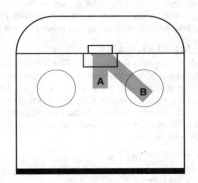

RON HEXTALL

Yrs. of NHL service: 7
Born: Brandon, Man.; May 3, 1964
Position: goaltender
Height: 6-3
Weight: 192
Uniform no.: 27
Catches: left

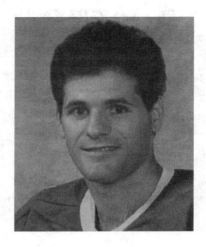

Career statistics:

GP	MINS	GA	SO	GAA	A	PIM
335	19,225	1058	4	3.30	17	436

1991-92 statistics:

GP	MINS	GAA	W	L	T	SO	GA	S	SAPCT	PIM
45	2668	3.40	16	21	6	3	151	1294	.883	35

1992-93 statistics:

GP	MINS	GAA	W	L	T	SO	GA	S	SAPCT	PIM
54	2988	3.45	29	16	5	0	172	1529	.888	56

LAST SEASON

Led NHL goalies in PIM. Wins at four-season high. Missed 14 games with thigh/groin injury. Acquired from New York Islanders with first-round draft pick in 1993 for Mark Fitzpatrick and a first-round draft pick in 1993.

THE PHYSICAL GAME

Injuries have plagued Hextall through the past few seasons, in particular a problem with groin injuries. Despite his work with ballet teachers on stretching techniques, the injury physically inhibits Hextall's playing.

Hextall is one of the most aggressive goalies in the league. He loves to come out to the top of his crease to challenge, but sometimes he is overenthusiastic in this department. This was the case in the playoffs, when he permitted some bad angle goals because he was too far out of his net.

Hextall is very quick down low and especially tough on his stick side. He had more trouble with his glove hand last season, even on low shots. He keeps his feet well and is tough to beat five-hole.

Hextall doesn't handle the puck as much as he used to. He is playing with some very highly skilled defensemen, and that is probably part of the team's strategy. But he can still help out with a quick pass and is very good at blocking passes around the net.

THE MENTAL GAME

Hextall is extremely fiery, and his PIM total attests to the fact that he will do anything to get an edge: chop at ankles, or retaliate with his blocker if someone dares enter the crease. Hextall could take a little off his temper, but it's just part of his hockey nature (who can forget his memorable playoff confrontation with Chris Chelios several seasons ago?).

THE INTANGIBLES

Hextall was one of the sulkers when he was traded to Quebec, but he adjusted quickly and actually wound up enjoying himself. He got a fresh start, and he made the most of it. He could be on the move again, though, as another expansion draft looms this year.

BENOIT HOGUE

Yrs. of NHL service: 5
Born: Repentigny, Que.; Oct. 28, 1966
Position: centre/right wing
Height: 5-10
Weight: 190
Uniform no.: 33
Shoots: left

Career statistics:

GP	G	A	TP	PIM
338	108	154	262	450

1991-92 statistics:

GP	G	A	TP	+/-	PIM	PP	SH	GW	GT	S	PCT
75	30	46	76	+30	67	8	0	5	0	149	20.1

1992-93 statistics:

GP	G	A	TP	+/-	PIM	PP	SH	GW	GT	S	PCT
70	33	42	75	+13	108	5	3	5	0	147	22.4

LAST SEASON

Tied for team lead in shorthanded goals. Fourth on team in scoring. Goals career high. Missed 14 games with injuries: neck (five), foot (three), knee (six).

THE FINESSE GAME

Hogue plays all three forward positions, and he brings to each of them the intensity and confidence he never displayed in Buffalo prior to the 1991 trade. Hogue became a new player with the Islanders, and one of their best.

His chief asset is his speed. He is explosive, leaving defenders flat-footed with his acceleration. Add to that his anticipation and ability to handle the puck at a high tempo, and the result is an ever-lurking breakaway threat. Hogue is not a great puckhandler or shooter, but he capitalizes on each situation with his quickness and agility.

Hogue plays primarily on the left side and even when playing centre will cut to the left wing boards as he drives down the ice. He is not a great playmaker, but he creates scoring chances off his rushes.

Hogue is an excellent, aggressive penalty killer who is a shorthanded threat, and he can also be used on the power play, although he lacks the patience to be as effective as he could be. He is very good on draws.

THE PHYSICAL GAME

Hogue is a strong one-on-one player who will use his body to lean on an opponent. He is not a big checker, but he gets involved and uses his speed as a weapon to intimidate. He is a crunch-time player, whether a team needs to protect a lead or create one.

THE INTANGIBLES

Hogue can get down on himself, but for the most part he has attained a level of consistency that coaches can rely on. Next to Pierre Turgeon, he is the Islanders' best game-breaker.

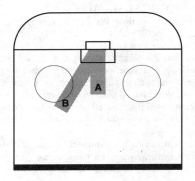

DARIUS KASPARAITIS

Yrs. of NHL service: 1
Born: Elektrenai, Lithuania; Oct. 16, 1972
Position: right defense
Height: 5-11
Weight: 187
Uniform no.: na
Shoots: left

Career statistics:
GP	G	A	TP	PIM
79	4	17	21	166

1992-93 statistics:
GP	G	A	TP	+/-	PIM	PP	SH	GW	GT	S	PCT
79	4	17	21	+15	166	0	0	0	0	92	4.3

LAST SEASON
First NHL season. Led team defensemen in plus/minus. Second on team in PIM. Missed three games with back injuries.

THE FINESSE GAME
Kasparaitis is a strong, powerful skater who can accelerate in all directions. You can run, but you can't hide from this defenseman, who accepts all challenges. He is aggressive in the neutral zone, sometimes overly so, stepping up to break up a team's attack.

Kasparaitis concentrated mainly on his defensive role last season, but it wouldn't be a surprise to see him get more involved in the offense. He will make a good outlet pass and then follow up into the play. This season, he may see more time on the point on the power play. He has good offensive instincts, moves the puck well and, if he plays on his off side, will open up his forehand for the one-timer.

Kasparaitis has infectious enthusiasm that is an inspiration to the rest of his team. There is a purpose to whatever he does, and he's highly competitive. When he develops more consistency, he may become the team's No. 1 defenseman. His skills are world class.

THE PHYSICAL GAME
Kasparaitis is well on his way to succeeding Ulf Samuelsson as the player most of the NHL would like to see run over by a bus. It's always borderline interference with Kasparaitis, who uses his stick liberally and waits three or four seconds after a victim has gotten rid of the puck to apply the lumber. Crosscheck, butt-end, high stick — through the course of a season Kasparaitis will illustrate all of the stick infractions, and he served a one-game suspension for incurring two stick majors.

But Kasparaitis is legitimately tough. It doesn't matter whose name is on back of the jersey — Lemieux, Tocchet, McKay, Messier — he will goad the stars and the heavyweights equally. He will often take bad penalties, but he can just as often drive the opposition into taking bad calls. He yaps, too, and as his English improves will become as irritating as jock itch.

THE INTANGIBLES
Kasparaitis brings to mind Lou Grant's line from the old "Mary Tyler Moore Show": "Ya got spunk. I *HATE* spunk!"

He has to keep his head on straight, though. Too much thumbing through his press clippings may have resulted in some undisciplined, uneven nights.

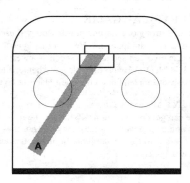

DEREK KING

Yrs. of NHL service: 6
Born: Hamilton, Ont.; Feb. 11, 1967
Position: left wing
Height: 6-1
Weight: 200
Uniform no.: 27
Shoots: left

Career statistics:

GP	G	A	TP	PIM
386	136	182	318	201

1991-92 statistics:

GP	G	A	TP	+/-	PIM	PP	SH	GW	GT	S	PCT
80	40	38	78	-10	46	21	0	6	2	189	21.2

1992-93 statistics:

GP	G	A	TP	+/-	PIM	PP	SH	GW	GT	S	PCT
77	38	38	76	-3	47	21	0	7	0	201	18.9

LAST SEASON

Assists match career high. Goals and points two short of career highs. Second on team in power play goals. Tied for second on team in game-winning goals. Second on team in goals. Third on team in points. Missed six games with hip injuries and one game with finger injury.

THE FINESSE GAME

Some players just click when they are teamed up on the ice, and such was the case with King and Pierre Turgeon, who was acquired in a 1991 trade. Turgeon opens up so much of the ice and is such a gifted play-maker that the role of finishing left wing can be filled by King.

King is at his best from the face-off dot of the left circle to the front of the net. He has great concentration through traffic and soft, soft hands for cradling passes and then snapping off the shot as soon as the puck hits his blade. He has to play with someone who will get him the puck at the right time, and that ideal someone is Turgeon. King knows that if he heads to the net, Turgeon will find a way to thread the puck through. All he has to worry about is getting to the front and keeping his stick on the ice.

He's among the best in the league on the power play. He has good anticipation and reads the offensive plays well.

King is not a great skater, and his defensive play remains his weakness.

THE PHYSICAL GAME

King is a solid and durable player who takes a pounding in front of the net. He doesn't use his body well in other areas of the ice, though, which is one of the reasons for his defensive problems.

King has improved his off-ice habits and his conditioning, a problem in the past. Sometimes it takes time for a young player to realize that playing in the NHL is a job, not just a game.

THE INTANGIBLES

King had a poor playoffs (three goals in 18 games) to follow up what had been his second strong season. He will probably be looking to redeem himself this year, and 40 goals is easily within his grasp if he stays on the top line with Pierre Turgeon. King played out his option, and his contract hassles may have weighed on him mentally.

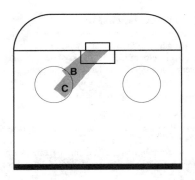

UWE KRUPP

Yrs. of NHL service: 7
Born: Cologne, West Germany; June 24, 1965
Position: right defense
Height: 6-6
Weight: 235
Uniform no.: 4
Shoots: right

Career statistics:

GP	G	A	TP	PIM
466	40	136	176	496

1991-92 statistics:

GP	G	A	TP	+/-	PIM	PP	SH	GW	GT	S	PCT
67	8	29	37	+13	49	2	0	0	0	128	6.3

1992-93 statistics:

GP	G	A	TP	+/-	PIM	PP	SH	GW	GT	S	PCT
80	9	29	38	+7	67	2	0	2	0	116	7.8

LAST SEASON

Games played career high. Missed one game with flu and three games with shoulder injury.

THE FINESSE GAME

Krupp has a hard shot, and in fact was clocked among the best in the Wales Conference in the preliminaries for the All-Star skills competition. But standing at the blue line and facing only a radar gun is vastly different from trying to get the shot away under pressure from an attacker, and it takes Krupp far too long to get his big shot under way during competition. He doesn't one-time the puck well, but instead must stop it and tee it up. He has a good wrist shot that he can use to better purpose, because he can get it away cleanly and with some velocity.

He reads plays well both offensively and defensively. He is a good skater for his size, but makes sure to position himself well so he needs only a stride to cut off the attacker. He is very steady and has been moved more and more into a defensive role, although he has good offensive instincts.

Krupp moves the puck well out of the zone. He is a smart passer and creates a lot of odd-man rushes by spotting the developing play and making the solid first pass.

THE PHYSICAL GAME

Krupp could use his body a lot more, but it's not his style. He gets in the way, and with his big body and reach covers a lot of ice. He blocks shots willingly and is a very good penalty killer. He plays with restraint and takes few bad penalties. Checkers seem to bounce off him.

THE INTANGIBLES

Krupp is the man on the ice when the Islanders need to protect the lead. He has been used with a lot of partners and complements all of them well, especially younger defenseman. He is a steadying influence.

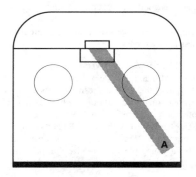

SCOTT LACHANCE

Yrs. of NHL service: 1
Born: Charlottesville, Va.; Oct. 22, 1972
Position: left defense
Height: 6-1
Weight: 197
Uniform no.: 7
Shoots: left

Career statistics:

GP	G	A	TP	PIM
92	8	21	29	76

1991-92 statistics:

GP	G	A	TP	+/-	PIM	PP	SH	GW	GT	S	PCT
17	1	4	5	+13	9	0	0	0	1	20	5.0

1992-93 statistics:

GP	G	A	TP	+/-	PIM	PP	SH	GW	GT	S	PCT
75	7	17	24	-1	67	0	1	2	0	62	11.3

LAST SEASON

First full NHL season. Missed one game with wrist injury.

THE FINESSE GAME

After an up-and-down season, Lachance started playing well at the end of the year before he was sidelined with a wrist injury that forced him to miss out on the playoffs and an important part of his maturation.

He can't start his rookie season over again, but he would probably like to. His approach at the start of the year was that he could get by on his talent alone, but after occasional benchings he began to apply himself more.

Lachance has great hockey sense. He is very smart with the puck, and it wouldn't be a surprise to see him get more power play time this season. He moves the puck smartly and is poised under pressure. He doesn't take many chances down low, but uses a strong shot from the point.

Lachance is not an exceptional skater. He has to work on his quickness because his feet look a little heavy at times, but he is balanced and strong on his skates.

THE PHYSICAL GAME

This is the area where Lachance has to apply himself most. Though not a very big defenseman, he is built solidly enough to be an effective if not devastating checker, but there were nights when he just let his attacker skate through without paying the price. Lachance kills penalties well and blocks shots.

THE INTANGIBLES

Lachance was very impressive in his short stint with the Islanders after the 1992 Olympics at season's end, and he may have thought it was going to be just that easy. He had to learn, as so many young players do, that once you reach the NHL, hockey becomes more than a game. It's also a job. The edge was off Lachance's effort last season, and he has to regain that fear of not succeeding, instead of easing into training camp. He should have a strong rebound.

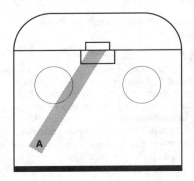

VLADIMIR MALAKHOV

Yrs. of NHL service: 1
Born: Sverdlovsk, Russia; Aug. 30, 1968
Position: right defense
Height: 6-2
Weight: 207
Uniform no.: 23
Shoots: left

Career statistics:

GP	G	A	TP	PIM
64	14	38	52	59

1992-93 statistics:

GP	G	A	TP	+/-	PIM	PP	SH	GW	GT	S	PCT
64	14	38	52	+14	59	7	0	0	0	178	7.9

LAST SEASON

First NHL season. Led NHL rookie defensemen in scoring. Missed 16 games with injuries: groin (two), knee (one), right shoulder (eight), left shoulder (five).

THE FINESSE GAME

Malakhov has the hardest shot on the team, an absolute bullet that he rifles off the one-timer or on the fly. He has outstanding offensive instincts for both shooting and playmaking. He is a lot like Brian Leetch in his ability to move the puck and jump into the play, but he has a better shot than Leetch does. Malakhov has to be urged to shoot more. He usually looks for the pass first.

Malakhov learned on the job, and as he doesn't speak very good English, he struggled through some of the learning process. He seemed discouraged at times when things weren't going well, but overall he delivered the goods.

Malakhov is also very strong defensively and can be used on both special teams. He is a mobile skater, with good agility and balance.

THE PHYSICAL GAME

Malakhov relies on his positioning and anticipation for his defensive plays more than his hitting. He could be a major physical force because of his size and strength, but injuries may have made him leery of getting hurt.

THE INTANGIBLES

Malakhov had three or four seasons within a season, because of injuries and inconsistencies. There was a stretch of about 10 games in December when he was dominating, but other times when he struggled because of injury and lack of confidence. He is a complete defenseman, but his adjustment to the NHL is not quite complete.

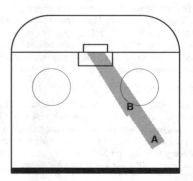

BRIAN MULLEN

Yrs. of NHL service: 11
Born: New York, N.Y.; Mar. 16, 1962
Position: left wing
Height: 5-10
Weight: 180
Uniform no.: 16
Shoots: left

Career statistics:

GP	G	A	TP	PIM
832	260	362	622	414

1991-92 statistics:

GP	G	A	TP	+/-	PIM	PP	SH	GW	GT	S	PCT
72	18	28	46	-14	66	5	3	1	0	168	10.7

1992-93 statistics:

GP	G	A	TP	+/-	PIM	PP	SH	GW	GT	S	PCT
81	18	14	32	+5	28	1	0	1	0	126	14.3

LAST SEASON

Acquired from San Jose for rights to Markus Thuresson. Sixth consecutive season playing at least 72 games. Missed one game with neck injury.

THE FINESSE GAME

Mullen was off to a slow start with the Islanders, but once he found a role on the checking line he became a useful performer. The key to his game has always been his speed, and while he has lost a half-step in breakaway speed, he is still very agile and quick in small areas of the ice.

He plays all three forward positions and does a reliable job at each. His scoring approach is to throw the puck at the net and see what happens, and he will score goals from the most unlikely positions because to him there is no such thing as an impossible angle.

Mullen has excellent hockey sense, which serves him well as a checker and penalty killer. When the offensive play develops, he has the hand skills to jump into the attack.

THE PHYSICAL GAME

Mullen is not very strong, but he is wiry and gritty and gets in the way. He is durable and works hard every night. A coach knows just what he is getting from Mullen when he sends him over the boards.

THE INTANGIBLES

Returning to the New York area was a boost for Manhattan-born Mullen. Some players can't handle the pressure of playing near their hometown, but Mullen (an ex-Ranger and former Rangers stickboy) enjoys it tremendously. This versatile forward could find a home anywhere.

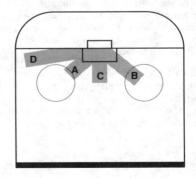

RICH PILON

Yrs. of NHL service: 5
Born: Saskatoon, Sask.; Apr. 30, 1968
Position: left defense
Height: 6-0
Weight: 200
Uniform no.: 47
Shoots: left

Career statistics:

GP	G	A	TP	PIM
245	3	29	32	746

1991-92 statistics:

GP	G	A	TP	+/-	PIM	PP	SH	GW	GT	S	PCT
65	1	6	7	-1	183	0	0	0	0	27	3.7

1992-93 statistics:

GP	G	A	TP	+/-	PIM	PP	SH	GW	GT	S	PCT
44	1	3	4	-4	164	0	0	0	0	20	5.0

LAST SEASON

Missed 25 games with injuries: back (11), hand (six), knee (eight).

THE FINESSE GAME

Pilon is power. He takes charge of his own end of the ice and is a very steady defensive defenseman. He doesn't get involved in the offense at all (note his career scoring totals, which amount to about a week's work for Larry Murphy).

Pilon's main concern is keeping the puck out of his zone. He will make the safe pass rather than hold on to the puck too long to look to make a play, although he is a capable passer. He can also move the puck out of the zone, but he will not venture beyond the red line with it. His offensive input is reduced to a so-so slapshot from the point.

Pilon is not a speedball, but he is above average in mobility and balance. He is a very determined penalty killer and blocks shots well.

THE PHYSICAL GAME

Pilon keeps the other team honest. He is a hard hitter, very competitive and gritty. Typical of his powerful checking is the hit he put on Kevin Stevens in the playoffs, a clean collision that Stevens got the worst of, as he was knocked cold and suffered facial injuries. Pilon will also fight, but he wears a face shield (for insurance purposes) to protect an eye damaged by a shot several seasons ago. He will lose his composure and take poor penalties.

THE INTANGIBLES

While we have seen many players who are the prototypal defensemen of the '90s, Pilon is a prototype of the '60s. He is a young man in an old-timer's role, and he plays it to the hilt.

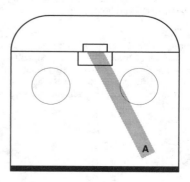

STEVE THOMAS

Yrs. of NHL service: 9
Born: Stockport, England; July 15, 1963
Position: left wing
Height: 5-11
Weight: 185
Uniform no.: 32
Shoots: left

Career statistics:

GP	G	A	TP	PIM
542	216	260	476	689

1991-92 statistics:

GP	G	A	TP	+/-	PIM	PP	SH	GW	GT	S	PCT
82	30	48	78	+8	97	3	0	3	1	245	12.2

1992-93 statistics:

GP	G	A	TP	+/-	PIM	PP	SH	GW	GT	S	PCT
79	37	50	87	+3	111	12	0	7	0	264	14.0

LAST SEASON

Second on team in assists and points. Third on team in goals. Third on team in power play goals. Second on team in shots. Assists and points at career high. Missed five games with rib injuries.

THE FINESSE GAME

Thomas complements his centreman, Pierre Turgeon, as well as Derek King does on the other side of the ice. Thomas has a great shot, and he loves to fire away. Thomas will look to shoot first instead of pass, sometimes to his detriment, but subtlety is not his forte. Speed and power are.

He has a strong wrist shot and an excellent one-timer. He likes to win the battle for the puck in deep, feed the playmaking Turgeon, then head for the right circle for the return pass.

Thomas is a wildly intense player. His speed is straight-ahead, without much deking or trying to put a move on a defender. He works along the boards and in the corners, willing to do the dirty work to keep Turgeon out of the danger zone.

Defense remains a problem. Thomas often has a tendency to leave the zone too early in his eagerness to get on the attack.

THE PHYSICAL GAME

Thomas is hard-nosed and finishes his checks. He is a very good forechecker because he comes at the puck carrier like a human train. He is not a very big player, but he is wide, and he is tough. He is great along the boards and among the best in the league (with Kirk Muller and Peter Zezel) at keeping the puck alive by using his feet.

Thomas is a feisty and fierce competitor and will throw the odd punch.

THE INTANGIBLES

Thomas is a finisher, and he remains a streaky scorer. Mentally, he gets down on himself, and it shows in his game when things aren't going well. He will try to get too cute and make the perfect play instead of relying on his instincts.

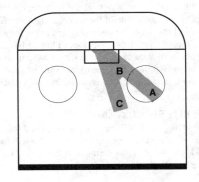

PIERRE TURGEON

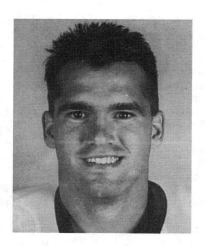

Yrs. of NHL service: 6
Born: Rouyn, Que.; Aug. 29, 1969
Position: centre
Height: 6-1
Weight: 203
Uniform no.: 77
Shoots: left

Career statistics:

GP	G	A	TP	PIM
474	218	324	542	161

1991-92 statistics:

GP	G	A	TP	+/-	PIM	PP	SH	GW	GT	S	PCT
77	40	55	95	+7	20	13	0	6	0	207	19.3

1992-93 statistics:

GP	G	A	TP	+/-	PIM	PP	SH	GW	GT	S	PCT
83	58	74	132	-1	26	24	0	10	2	301	19.3

LAST SEASON

Winner of the 1993 Lady Byng Trophy. Led team in goals, assists, points, power play goals, game-winning goals and shots. Goals, assists and points at career highs. Second season with 100 or more points. Tied for fifth in NHL in scoring. Tied for fifth in NHL in power play goals. Tied for fourth in NHL in game-winning goals.

THE FINESSE GAME

Turgeon is a marvel. He never seems to be looking at the puck, yet he is always in perfect control of it.

He has a style unlike just about anyone else in the NHL. He's not a fast skater, but he can deke a defender or make a sneaky surprise pass. He is tough to defend, because if you aren't aware of where he is on the ice and don't deny him the pass, he can kill a team with several moves.

He can slow or speed up the tempo of a game. He lacks the breakout speed of, say, Pat LaFontaine — the player he was dealt for — but because he is slippery and can change speeds so smoothly, he is deceptive. His control with the puck down low is remarkable. He protects the puck well with the body.

While best known for his playmaking, Turgeon has an excellent shot. He will curl out from behind the net with a wrist shot, shoot off the fly from the right wing (his preferred side of the ice) or stand just off to the side of the net on a power play and reach for a tip or redirect of a point shot. He doesn't have a bazooka shot, but he uses quick, accurate wrist and snap shots.

The only thing that keeps him from joining the elite centres is his defensive play, but he's getting closer.

THE PHYSICAL GAME

Turgeon has to decide if he wants to be a good statistical player or a winner, and to be the latter he will have to add a more physical element to his game. He is strong but clearly does not like the contact part of the game, and he can be taken out of a game by a team that hounds him. Turgeon must play through it.

THE INTANGIBLES

Turgeon was, outside of Mario Lemieux, the top performer in the Patrick Division last season, and he excelled with a less talented cast than Lemieux had in Pittsburgh. Turgeon elevates the play of those around him. The only question about him concerned his ability to lead a team in the playoffs. He performed well in the first round against Washington but was sidelined through the Pittsburgh upset (thanks to Dale Hunter's cheap shot), so the question remains only half answered. He is an immense talent, a franchise player, and he's only getting better. He hasn't peaked yet.

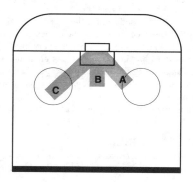

MICK VUKOTA

Yrs. of NHL service: 6
Born: Saskatoon, Sask.; Sept. 14, 1966
Position: right wing
Height: 6-2
Weight: 195
Uniform no.: 12
Shoots: right

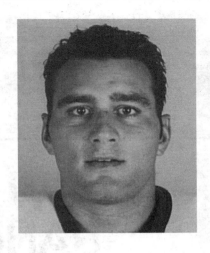

Career statistics:

GP	G	A	TP	PIM
349	11	25	36	1302

1991-92 statistics:

GP	G	A	TP	+/-	PIM	PP	SH	GW	GT	S	PCT
74	0	6	6	-6	293	0	0	0	0	34	0.0

1992-93 statistics:

GP	G	A	TP	+/-	PIM	PP	SH	GW	GT	S	PCT
74	2	5	7	+3	216	0	0	0	0	37	5.4

LAST SEASON

Led team in PIM. Went 99 games without a goal until scoring Jan. 17, 1993, at Ottawa. Missed two games with shoulder injury.

THE FINESSE GAME

Vukota has average skills but has always worked hard, and that is what keeps him in the league — that, and his toughness.

Vukota is strong on his skates, and balanced, but has very limited range. He has some straight-ahead quickness but no mobility. The game appears too fast for him.

His few scoring chances come from banging in close. We actually saw him score a hat trick once, which made us think the end of the world was nigh; now we would be shocked to see him score three times in a season.

THE PHYSICAL GAME

Vukota may be one of a vanishing breed in the NHL, but his toughness and nuclear warhead factor still make it necessary to keep him on the bench. He is a good fighter and an intimidating presence, a legitimate tough guy who will stand up for his teammates. Vukota is a decent size, but he seems even bigger on the ice.

THE INTANGIBLES

In addition to his toughness, Vukota is one of the most respected leaders in the Islanders' dressing room. He is upbeat and bright (surprisingly, many of the game's so-called goons are among the most thoughtful people on the team) and will do anything for his team. He knows his ice time is limited, but he accepts his role.

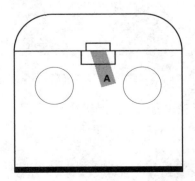

NEW YORK
RANGERS

TONY AMONTE

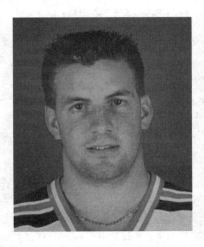

Yrs. of NHL service: 2
Born: Hingham, Mass.; Aug. 2, 1970
Position: right wing
Height: 6-0
Weight: 185
Uniform no.: 33
Shoots: left

Career statistics:

GP	G	A	TP	PIM
162	68	77	145	104

1991-92 statistics:

GP	G	A	TP	+/-	PIM	PP	SH	GW	GT	S	PCT
79	35	34	69	+12	55	9	0	4	0	234	15.0

1992-93 statistics:

GP	G	A	TP	+/-	PIM	PP	SH	GW	GT	S	PCT
83	33	43	76	0	49	13	0	4	0	270	12.2

LAST SEASON

Second on team in assists and points. Tied for team lead in power play goals.

THE FINESSE GAME

Amonte is blessed with exceptional speed and acceleration. His timing is accurate (it hasn't hurt that for most of his two NHL seasons he has played alongside future Hall of Fame centre Mark Messier). Amonte has good balance and can carry the puck at a pretty good clip, although he is more effective when streaking down the right wing and getting the puck late.

He has a quick release on his wrist shot, and he also one-times the puck well. He likes to go top-shelf, just under the crossbar, and can also go to the backhand shot or a wrist shot off his back foot, like a fadeaway jumper. Amonte is a top power play man, since he is always working himself into open ice. He is an accurate shooter, but is also creative in his playmaking. He passes very well for a left-handed shot playing the right wing. He is conscious of where his teammates are and usually makes the best percentage play.

Offensively, Amonte is a smart player away from the puck. He sets picks and creates openings for his teammates. Defensively, he still needs to improve his checking and his awareness down low.

THE PHYSICAL GAME

Amonte's speed and movement keep him out of a lot of trouble zones, but he will also drive to the front of the net and take the punishment there if that's the correct play. He loves to score, he loves to help his linemates score, and though he is outweighed by a lot of NHL defensemen, he is seldom outworked.

He takes a lot of abuse and plays through the checks. He seldom takes bad retaliatory penalties. He just keeps his legs driving and draws calls with his nonstop skating.

THE INTANGIBLES

Amonte was one of the few bright lights in a dismal Rangers season. Instead of having a sophomore slump, he improved off a rookie season in which he was a Calder Trophy finalist. A little more attention to defense, and he will be one of the Rangers' most consistent and reliable forwards.

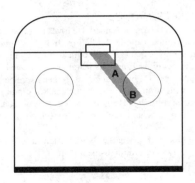

JEFF BEUKEBOOM

Yrs. of NHL service: 7
Born: Ajax, Ont.; Mar. 28, 1965
Position: right defense
Height: 6-4
Weight: 215
Uniform no.: 23
Shoots: right

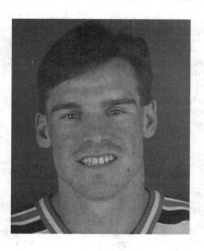

Career statistics:

GP	G	A	TP	PIM
422	15	84	99	1008

1991-92 statistics:

GP	G	A	TP	+/-	PIM	PP	SH	GW	GT	S	PCT
74	1	15	16	+23	200	0	0	0	0	48	2.1

1992-93 statistics:

GP	G	A	TP	+/-	PIM	PP	SH	GW	GT	S	PCT
82	2	17	19	+9	153	0	0	0	0	54	3.7

LAST SEASON

Third on team in PIM. Points highest since 1987-88.

THE FINESSE GAME

Beukeboom is not a very agile skater, but he takes up a lot of room on the ice and he has learned to take away even more of the ice by using his long reach. He has a quick stick. On penalty-killing shifts, he is able to get the stick down on the left or right side of his body into the passing lanes. He will also use his stick to reach around a puck carrier and knock the puck loose, or for a sweep check at the blue line.

Beukeboom suffered when regular partner Brian Leetch was out of the line-up, since Leetch's mobility balanced Beukeboom's somewhat clumsy style, and Beukeboom was forced to do more than he is capable of. He is at his most effective when he angles the attacker to the corners, then uses his superior size and strength to eliminate the player physically.

Beukeboom moves the puck fairly well. He certainly has no fear of anyone bearing down on him, but he needs support because he can't carry the puck out himself. That's what Leetch is there for. When Beukeboom was paired with Kevin Lowe, the veteran pair knew what they wanted to do with the puck but just didn't have the skills to execute it.

THE PHYSICAL GAME

Beukeboom is so aptly named. He loves to hit, and the resulting thunder along the boards and glass sounds not unlike his name. He likes to make an early hit in a game, to get himself and his teammates involved. He can make open ice hits, but he has to make sure he has his man lined up or he can be beaten wide and left looking pretty silly. He is more effective crunching along the boards, and he clears the front of his net efficiently.

He blocks shots fearlessly and often limps to the bench, only to return on his next shift.

THE INTANGIBLES

Beukeboom keeps it simple. The fancy Dan accolades can go to more polished partners like Leetch, while Beukeboom stays back and does the dirty work. He knows what his role is, and he performs it well. On top of that, his style is one much admired by new coach Mike Keenan.

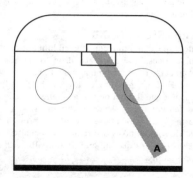

MIKE GARTNER

Yrs. of NHL service: 14
Born: Ottawa, Ont.; Oct. 29, 1959
Position: right wing
Height: 6-0
Weight: 190
Uniform no.: 22
Shoots: right

Career statistics:

GP	G	A	TP	PIM
1089	583	524	1107	977

1991-92 statistics:

GP	G	A	TP	+/-	PIM	PP	SH	GW	GT	S	PCT
76	40	41	81	+11	55	15	0	6	0	286	14.0

1992-93 statistics:

GP	G	A	TP	+/-	PIM	PP	SH	GW	GT	S	PCT
84	45	23	68	-4	59	13	0	3	1	323	13.9

LAST SEASON

Led team in goals and shots. Tied for team lead in power play goals. One of two Rangers to appear in all 84 games. Third on team in points. Reached 40-goal mark for fourth consecutive season. Scored 30 or more goals for 14th consecutive season. Points lowest since initial NHL season (1979-80).

THE FINESSE GAME

Whoever said the legs are the first to go never saw Mike Gartner play hockey. Gartner will probably still be winning All-Star skills skating races when he's 80. Certainly he appears to be as fast as ever, although his drop-off in points last season has to be a concern. Our guess is that he is the Ranger who most missed Brian Leetch's beautiful breakout passes. The goals, the shot, the hands and the quickness still appear to be there.

Gartner is ever alert to his offensive chances. He is sometimes guilty of hanging a little at the red line, looking for the break into the attacking zone. He can accept a pass in full flight and likes to drive outside around a defender. He doesn't have an inside move, but he has a clever little play he uses where he treats the boards as an extra teammate, giving himself a little pass off the wall or setting up a linemate with a smart feed.

Gartner drives his shot off the wing on the fly, or uses a strong wrist shot from closer range. If his lane to the net is blocked, he will curl around behind the net — still at good speed — for a wraparound try. He isn't much of a playmaker. His assists come from teammates smart enough to follow up his play for rebounds.

THE PHYSICAL GAME

Gartner is wiry and strong. When he doesn't beat a checker cleanly to the outside, he will still manage to squeeze through along the boards and keep going forward with the puck, even if dragged to his knees.

Gartner goes to the net and into the corners for the puck. He has very strong arms and wrists to reach into scrums and control the puck. He can flick a puck to the net one-handed. He seldom takes bad penalties, though he attracts a lot of unwanted attention.

THE INTANGIBLES

Few players took the Rangers' fall from grace harder than Gartner, who has yet to win his first Cup ring, or even play in a final. He is one of the classiest and most respected players around for his intelligence, talent and work ethic. This may be his last season at top form.

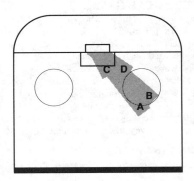

ADAM GRAVES

Yrs. of NHL service: 5
Born: Toronto, Ont.; Apr. 12, 1968
Position: left wing/centre
Height: 6-0
Weight: 185
Uniform no.: 9
Shoots: left

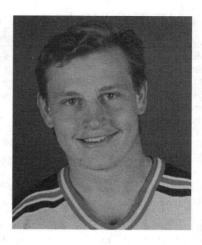

Career statistics:

GP	G	A	TP	PIM
381	85	99	184	949

1991-92 statistics:

GP	G	A	TP	+/-	PIM	PP	SH	GW	GT	S	PCT
80	26	33	59	+19	139	4	4	4	0	228	11.4

1992-93 statistics:

GP	G	A	TP	+/-	PIM	PP	SH	GW	GT	S	PCT
84	36	29	65	-4	148	12	1	6	1	275	13.1

LAST SEASON

One of two Rangers to appear in all 84 games. Led team in game-winning goals. Third on team in power play goals. Second on team in goals. Goals and points at career highs.

THE FINESSE GAME

A tenacious forechecker, he plows into the corners and plunges into his work along the boards with intelligence but no fear. He knows what to do with the puck to set up a teammate, and he can finish the play as well.

Graves is a somewhat awkward skater. His balance and strength are good, and he gets a few quick steps on a rival, but he isn't very fast in open ice. He is smart with the puck. He protects it with his body, and is strong enough to fend off a checker with one arm and shovel the puck to a linemate with the other.

He isn't a pretty playmaker or scorer. Once in a while he will fire a heavy shot on the fly from the left wing, but more of his chances come from buzzing around the net.

Graves is excellent on draws and takes more and more of the face-offs, even when Mark Messier is ostensibly the centre on the line he's out with.

THE PHYSICAL GAME

Graves is a physical player who plays (or at least tries to play) Eric Lindros size. Graves grinds and plays against other teams' top defensemen without fear. He blocks shots and is a force on the ice. Other teams are always aware of when Graves is on, because he doesn't play a quiet game. He finishes every check.

Graves stands up for his teammates and fights when necessary. He's so valuable to his team as a penalty killer that the Rangers hate to see him in the box, but he can't play any other way than tough.

THE INTANGIBLES

The next Rangers captain. Graves has been called Mark Messier Jr. for the way he has consciously moulded his game and his conduct after his teammate, the current Rangers captain. He's a natural leader, and on those nights when the rest of his teammates fail to show up, Graves does. His probable future is at centre, and while he is not likely to hit the 100-point mark, we see him in a consistent 80-point range.

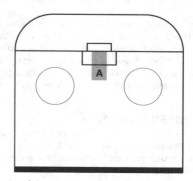

GLENN HEALY

Yrs. of NHL service: 6
Born: Pickering, Ont.; Aug. 23, 1962
Position: goaltender
Height: 5-10
Weight: 175
Uniform no.: 35
Catches: left

Career statistics:

GP	MINS	GA	SO	AVG	A	PIM
259	14,430	897	5	3.73	9	75

1991-92 statistics:

GP	MINS	GAA	W	L	T	SO	GA	S	SAPCT	A	PIM
37	1960	3.80	14	16	4	1	124	1045	.881	1	18

1992-93 statistics:

GP	MINS	GAA	W	L	T	SO	GA	S	SAPCT	A	PIM
47	2655	3.30	22	20	2	1	146	1316	.889	2	2

LAST SEASON

Wins four-season high. Goals-against career low. Missed four games with wrist injury. Drafted by Anaheim from N.Y. Islanders in expansion draft. Drafted by Tampa Bay in second phase of expansion draft. Acquired by N.Y. Rangers for a third-round draft pick.

THE PHYSICAL GAME

Healy was once all reflexes, but in recent years he has become better at playing his angles and keeping his feet, and so has become a more consistent goalie. His soft goals are fewer, and he doesn't become as worn down late in the season as he once did, because he is playing a much more efficient style.

Whatever it takes to stop the puck, Healy will do. If he does get down in a scramble, he battles until the puck is in the net, smothered or cleared. He has a big first-save capacity.

Healy does not handle the puck well. Fortunately for him, the Islanders' defense has become increasingly mobile, and about all he has to do is stop the puck behind the net and leave it. He sometimes has trouble handling hard-arounds, though, and he gets caught out of his net in the ensuing confusion.

He bounces back onto his feet quickly and moves well from post to post.

THE MENTAL GAME

Healy is a battler, a player with a great attitude in the dressing room or on the ice. He bounces back from bad goals, bad games and weird injuries (two seasons ago, part of a finger on his stick hand was severed and had to be surgically reattached). Healy received, and deserved, much of the credit for the Islanders' upset win over the Pittsburgh Penguins. He is gritty and provides a catalyst.

He concentrates well through screens, although he is a small goalie and other teams try to get a lot of bodies in front of him.

THE INTANGIBLES

Healy became a free agent at the end of the season. With the acquisition of Ron Hextall, Healy again becomes relegated to the No. 2 role with the Islanders, but the starter's role was handed to Mark Fitzpatrick several times over the past few seasons, and Healy always won it back. Never count him out.

JOE KOCUR

Yrs. of NHL service: 8
Born: Calgary, Alta.; Dec. 21, 1964
Position: left wing
Height: 6-0
Weight: 210
Uniform no.: 26
Shoots: right

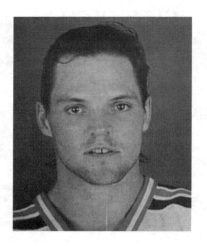

Career statistics:

GP	G	A	TP	PIM
520	66	65	131	2002

1991-92 statistics:

GP	G	A	TP	+/-	PIM	PP	SH	GW	GT	S	PCT
51	7	4	11	-4	121	0	0	2	0	72	9.7

1992-93 statistics:

GP	G	A	TP	+/-	PIM	PP	SH	GW	GT	S	PCT
65	3	6	9	-9	131	2	0	0	0	43	7.0

LAST SEASON

Passed 2000 PIM mark for career. Third on team in PIM.

THE FINESSE GAME

Although the game is changing, teams still need a player like Kocur around as health insurance for their finesse players. Kocur doesn't fight as often as he once did, but he doesn't need to — his fierce reputation precedes him.

He was used up front on the power play in a short-lived experiment, and he produced two goals (his first power play goal since 1989-90, when he scored one for Detroit). Kocur will go to the front of the net, more in the hope of drawing the attention of the defense and opening room for his teammates than with an actual intent to score.

Kocur doesn't do much with the puck. His hand skills are minimal, and his skating is just adequate. He has little speed or agility, but he is very strong and balanced.

THE PHYSICAL GAME

Kocur's hands are swollen and misshapen from the years of punching faces and helmets. Few other players hit to hurt as he does. Anyone who thinks players don't actually get hurt in hockey fights should have a look at some of Kocur's victims over the years.

THE INTANGIBLES

The Rangers protected Kocur in the expansion draft over some younger prospects, a pretty good indication that there is still plenty of value in a tough guy like this.

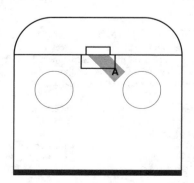

ALEXEI KOVALEV

Yrs. of NHL service: 1
Born: Togliatti, Russia; Feb. 24, 1973
Position: right wing
Height: 6-1
Weight: 189
Uniform no.: 27
Shoots: left

Career statistics:

GP	G	A	TP	PIM
65	20	18	38	79

1992-93 statistics:

GP	G	A	TP	+/-	PIM	PP	SH	GW	GT	S	PCT
65	20	18	38	-10	79	3	0	3	1	134	14.9

LAST SEASON
First NHL season.

THE FINESSE GAME
Kovalev is like a great peewee player on a sad-sack team. He wants to do it all himself, or not do it at all. While he is a brilliant solo performer, he has to learn to move the puck quicker and make better use of his teammates. He has to be dragged off the ice with one of the old vaudeville hooks in order to get him to change up.

Make no mistake, Kovalev's skills are world class. Ranger GM Neil Smith stunned the hockey world when he drafted Kovalev in the first round (15th overall) in 1991, but now some GMs will be kicking themselves (or their scouts) for missing him. (The 1991 draft, absurd in its depth and quality, has already produced NHLers Eric Lindros, Pat Falloon, Scott Niedermayer and Scott Lachance.) Kovalev defies adjectives, because on any given night there is a chance you'll witness something you've never seen him (or any other player) do. He has genius about him, but like many geniuses, he is erratic in the application of his talent, and that's where the coaches get crazy.

Kovalev is an outstanding skater with speed, acceleration and balance. He wants to score goals and is selfish with the puck. Kovalev wants to put the puck through the net, not just across the goal line, and he is gifted from close range with a great touch and uncanny knack for the right shot.

THE PHYSICAL GAME
Kovalev is sneaky dirty. He will run goalies and try to make it look as if he was pushed in by a defender. He's so strong and balanced on his skates that when he goes down odds are it's a dive. He may become one of the league's best divers before the referees cotton on.

Kovalev is a finesse player, but he can take a hit and will whack around in the corners for the puck.

THE INTANGIBLES
Kovalev had the distinction of being benched by three different coaches: by Roger Neilson, before Neilson was fired in midseason; by Ron Smith, who took over for Neilson; and by Colin Campbell, who coached the Rangers' AHL farm team in Binghamton. Does the phrase "discipline problem" sound familiar?

Kovalev is a free-spirited 19-year-old just getting used to the idea of a flashy car, designer clothes and living in New York. Under Mike Keenan, expect the high jinks to cease and Kovalev to get down to the serious business of making a living. The results could be eye-popping. We think he'll net 40 goals. And he will be tremendously entertaining to watch.

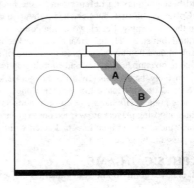

BRIAN LEETCH

Yrs. of NHL service: 6
Born: Corpus Christi, Tex.; Mar. 3, 1968
Position: left defense
Height: 5-11
Weight: 192
Uniform no.: 2
Shoots: left

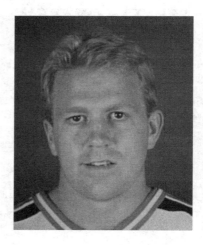

Career statistics:

GP	G	A	TP	PIM
353	80	287	367	170

1991-92 statistics:

GP	G	A	TP	+/-	PIM	PP	SH	GW	GT	S	PCT
80	22	80	102	+25	26	10	1	3	1	245	9.0

1992-93 statistics:

GP	G	A	TP	+/-	PIM	PP	SH	GW	GT	S	PCT
36	6	30	36	+2	26	2	1	1	0	150	4.0

LAST SEASON

Missed 35 games with neck injury. Missed 12 games with ankle injury sustained in off-ice accident. Despite missing more than half the season, led team defensemen in scoring.

THE FINESSE GAME

Leetch suffered two of the more bizarre injuries of last season. He hurt his neck and shoulder when he missed a check on St. Louis left wing Philippe Bozon and put himself into the boards. After returning from that ailment, Leetch broke his ankle jumping out of a cab on a snow-slick Manhattan street.

Of the two injuries, the first may leave the biggest question mark. Even though Leetch returned to play, the nerve damage he suffered did not allow him the full wind-up on his slap shot. He could only use snap or wrist shots.

His puck control, and not his shooting, is the most valuable part of his game. He mesmerizes the opposition as he glides out of the defensive zone, then he makes a shifty move around a forechecker, hits an open teammate at the red line, and scoots into the play. Leetch keeps his head up and sees all of his options. He has tremendous vision of the ice and may be the second-best playmaking defenseman in the league (Paul Coffey is still first, but Leetch is right up there).

On the power play, Leetch works the point, but he is anything but static. He has great hands for keeping the puck in, and he moves across to the centre of the blue line to open up his passing and shooting options.

Defensively, he uses his great speed to get back in position and doesn't leave his partner alone, even when he gambles. His hand-eye co-ordination is so good that opposing players are warned not to go cross-ice inside the attacking blue line, or Leetch will pick off the pass and be gone.

THE PHYSICAL GAME

Leetch is never going to knock anyone into the seats,

and he can be expected to play even more gingerly, at least for the first half of the season, due to the nature of his neck injury. The Rangers don't want him risking his body — that's why they went out and got Jeff Beukeboom. Leetch gets his body in the way, but he plays the stick, and he tries to win his defensive battles with his finesse skills. He can do it, too.

THE INTANGIBLES

Leetch's physical condition is a major question mark. Return to his Norris Trophy-winning form is at least a season away. He is a quiet leader, self-effacing but very proud of his ability, and it could be a long road back.

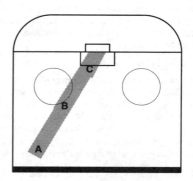

KEVIN LOWE

Yrs. of NHL service: 14
Born: Lachute, Que.; Apr. 15, 1959
Position: left defense
Height: 6-2
Weight: 195
Uniform no.: 4
Shoots: left

Career statistics:

GP	G	A	TP	PIM
1015	76	308	384	1222

1991-92 statistics:

GP	G	A	TP	+/-	PIM	PP	SH	GW	GT	S	PCT
55	2	7	9	-4	107	0	0	0	0	33	6.1

1992-93 statistics:

GP	G	A	TP	+/-	PIM	PP	SH	GW	GT	S	PCT
49	3	12	15	-2	58	0	0	0	0	52	5.8

LAST SEASON

Missed 35 games in holdout in Edmonton before being acquired by Rangers for Roman Oksyuta and a third-round draft pick in 1993. Played 1000th career NHL game.

THE FINESSE GAME

Lowe's experience often compensates for what his body can no longer do. It didn't help that he missed half of the season sitting out, because joining the Rangers at midseason while he wasn't even in training camp form meant Lowe looked woefully out of shape and out of synch.

His contributions are subtle. He is not a big playmaker, but he makes the big defensive plays. He has mastered the quick clutch and grabs, just enough to slow a rival down without getting the attention of the referee.

He stays back, and he needs to be paired with a more mobile partner. It never hurts to pair an inexperienced skater with him, either as a defense partner or even on the forward line, since Lowe has a calming influence and communicates well with his teammates. He doesn't get involved in the attack. He simply moves the puck.

THE PHYSICAL GAME

Lowe plays a strong game. Not a towering specimen, he makes the effective takeouts and keeps the front of his net tidy. He blocks shots well. He keeps his cool and is a crunch-time player.

THE INTANGIBLES

Due to injuries to Brian Leetch and James Patrick, Lowe was pushed to a No. 1 or 2 role. He is, at best, a No. 4 at this stage of his career. When allowed to play his role, he will continue to be an effective contributor. He is a quiet leader, well respected around the league and still valuable for his modest capabilities.

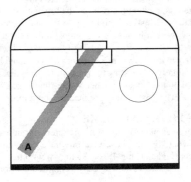

MARK MESSIER

Yrs. of NHL service: 14
Born: Edmonton, Alta.; Jan. 18, 1961
Position: centre
Height: 6-1
Weight: 210
Uniform no.: 11
Shoots: left

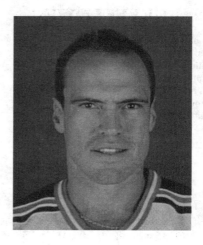

Career statistics:

GP	G	A	TP	PIM
1005	452	780	1232	1270

1991-92 statistics:

GP	G	A	TP	+/-	PIM	PP	SH	GW	GT	S	PCT
79	35	72	107	+31	76	12	4	6	0	212	16.5

1992-93 statistics:

GP	G	A	TP	+/-	PIM	PP	SH	GW	GT	S	PCT
75	25	66	91	-6	72	7	2	2	0	215	11.6

LAST SEASON

Missed nine games with back and wrist injuries. Reached 20-goal mark for 12th time in career. Led team in assists and points.

THE FINESSE GAME

Messier is a power forward with many facets. Tops among his skills are his skating and creative play-making. He accelerates quickly, is strong on his skates, changes directions, pivots, bursts into open ice, and does it all with or without the puck. He is one of the few NHL players who can bend a game to his will. There were just fewer nights last season when he was able to put it all together — likely a consequence of injuries to himself and his teammates.

Messier is smart when he is being shadowed. In the offensive zone, he will go into an area where there is another defensive player, drawing his checker with him. That puts two defenders in a small zone and opens up ice for his teammates.

He is so gifted with the puck that he will try anything. He can lift the puck from behind the net over the lower pipe and netting to the front corner for a teammate (a move he says he learned from former teammate Wayne Gretzky). He will use his speed to drive the defenders back, then stop and quickly check his options, making the most of the time and space he has earned. Messier is unlikely to try many one-on-one moves, but he makes the utmost use of his teammates.

He can overpower a goalie with his goal, and he is just as likely to wrist a strong shot off the wing, bull his way to the front of the net or one-time a pass from the slot. There is nothing predictable about him.

THE PHYSICAL GAME

Messier has played a lot of hockey throughout his career, what with all those Cup runs in Edmonton and various Canada Cups. It is catching up with him. The bumps and aches aren't so easy to ignore, and opponents aren't as intimidated by Messier as they were a few seasons ago. Messier will turn savage once in a while, but too often he is not a physical presence.

THE INTANGIBLES

Messier was probably more banged up than he let on, but he didn't grouse. He took the heat in the ouster of coach Roger Neilson — whose philosophy Messier did not agree with — and never failed to stand up for what he believed in. That character has marked Messier throughout his career. The Rangers know a lot of Messier's best hockey is behind him. The Rangers can't waste this window of opportunity when they have, at most, another top season out of Messier to help bring a Stanly Cup to New York.

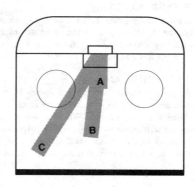

SERGEI NEMCHINOV

Yrs. of NHL service: 2
Born: Moscow, Russia; Jan. 14, 1964
Position: centre
Height: 6-0
Weight: 205
Uniform no.: 13
Shoots: left

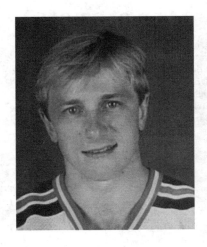

Career statistics:

GP	G	A	TP	PIM
154	53	59	112	49

1991-92 statistics:

GP	G	A	TP	+/-	PIM	PP	SH	GW	GT	S	PCT
73	30	28	58	+19	15	2	0	5	0	124	24.2

1992-93 statistics:

GP	G	A	TP	+/-	PIM	PP	SH	GW	GT	S	PCT
81	23	31	54	+15	34	0	1	3	0	144	16.0

LAST SEASON

Led team in plus/minus. Assists career high in second season. Goals and points lower than first NHL season. Led team in shooting percentage.

THE FINESSE GAME

Defensively, Nemchinov is probably the Rangers' best forward. If there is a five-on-three against, this is the forward who is sent out for the draw.

But there is much more to Nemchinov. In addition to defense, he has good offensive skills and instincts — good enough to be a fairly regular player with 40-goal scorer Mike Gartner. Not many checking centres get to enjoy that kind of dual duty.

Nemchinov is not a pretty skater. He doesn't have the skating ability usually associated with players out of the old Soviet system, but he is strong and balanced and is a dedicated chopper.

Nemchinov passes better to his forehand side than backhand. He has a decent snap shot, but his release is slow and he is quite deliberate about his shot selection.

THE PHYSICAL GAME

Powerfully built, he forechecks with zest, and drives through the boards and the corners. Linemates have to be alert, because Nemchinov will churn up loose pucks. He is very sneaky at holding an opponent's stick when the two players are tied up in a corner and his body shields the infraction from the officials.

Nemchinov blocks shots, hits and takes hits to make plays, and ties up his opposing centre on draws.

THE INTANGIBLES

It's hard to believe this guy was billed as a Jan Erixon type when the Rangers brought him over two seasons ago. Nemchinov provides more offense than Erixon ever dreamed of, while performing like a Selke Trophy candidate (which he soon will be).

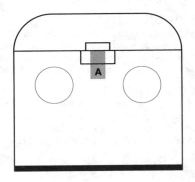

ED OLCZYK

Yrs. of NHL service: 9
Born: Chicago, Ill.; Aug. 16, 1966
Position: left wing/centre
Height: 6-1
Weight: 200
Uniform no.: 12
Shoots: left

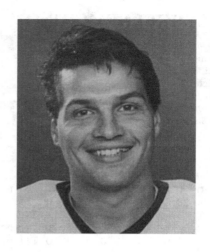

Career statistics:

GP	G	A	TP	PIM
681	260	358	618	642

1991-92 statistics:

GP	G	A	TP	+/-	PIM	PP	SH	GW	GT	S	PCT
64	32	33	65	+11	67	12	0	7	1	245	13.1

1992-93 statistics:

GP	G	A	TP	+/-	PIM	PP	SH	GW	GT	S	PCT
71	21	28	49	-2	52	2	0	1	1	190	11.1

LAST SEASON

Acquired from Winnipeg for Kris King and Tie Domi. Eighth season with 20 or more goals. Points and assists at career lows. Missed games with right knee injury.

THE FINESSE GAME

Olczyk doesn't have great speed, but he is one sneaky player, and so seems much faster than he is, because he works so hard at getting open. When the play is off the draw in the attacking zone, Olczyk (if he doesn't take the face-off) will curl around behind traffic while the defense is focussed on the puck. Suddenly he materializes in the slot and takes the one-timer.

Olczyk is a goal-scorer with a centre's sense of playmaking. He loves to shoot but is unselfish, and if a linemate is in better position, he will give up the shot for a good short pass. He is most effective from short range but will also fire from the top of the left circle. With his long reach, he also has an effective backhand.

He has a favourite "Wayne Gretzky" play where he drives down the off-wing and pulls up at the top of the circle. That means his linemates should drive to the net for a pass or rebound off his shot, because Olczyk will get the puck through.

THE PHYSICAL GAME

Olczyk has never been a physical player. He will take a hit to make a play, but doesn't initiate and generally avoids boards and corners. He will have to show more enthusiasm in that department if he stays on the wing.

THE INTANGIBLES

Olczyk has a better future as a winger than a centre. It took some time for him to find his role with his new team in New York, but he finished well once he felt comfortable and could return to the 30-goal range.

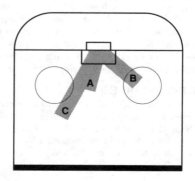

JAMES PATRICK

Yrs. of NHL service: 9
Born: Winnipeg, Man.; June 14, 1963
Position: right defense
Height: 6-2
Weight: 205
Uniform no.: 3
Shoots: right

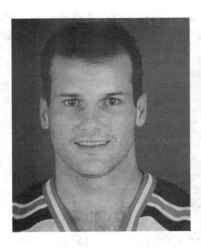

Career statistics:

GP	G	A	TP	PIM
665	104	360	464	539

1991-92 statistics:

GP	G	A	TP	+/-	PIM	PP	SH	GW	GT	S	PCT
80	14	57	71	+34	54	6	0	1	0	148	9.5

1992-93 statistics:

GP	G	A	TP	+/-	PIM	PP	SH	GW	GT	S	PCT
60	5	21	26	+1	61	3	0	0	0	99	5.1

LAST SEASON

Goals, assists and points at career lows as a result of missing 24 games with knee and back injuries.

THE FINESSE GAME

Patrick is a wonderful skater, fluid and effortless, and he skates backwards faster than many NHLers can skate forwards. He carries the puck out of the zone, or makes the smart first pass and follows up on the play. Defensively he is tough to beat one on one, because he can stop on a dime and give a nickel change.

The criticism of Patrick over the years is that he makes everything look so easy that it never appears he is challenging himself, never pushing the envelope to see if there is another level to his game. The flip side of that — the conservative side — is that he is aware of his limitations and plays within them. There will always be two camps as far as Patrick is concerned.

There is doubt that he is a better support player than star. Patrick would rather pass than shoot, and if the pass isn't there he will take a stride over the red line and dump in the puck, always timing it well so that his mates are on the chase.

He plays the point on the power play and uses a strong, accurate wrist shot that he keeps low and on net. He will also cheat to the top of the circle for a one-timer.

THE PHYSICAL GAME

Patrick doesn't play to his size. He gets in the way. He bumps. He ties people up. But he doesn't bulldoze his crease or scrap one on one along the boards. He uses his finesse skills as his defense, and he is too big to play that way all the time.

THE INTANGIBLES

Patrick is mentioned in trade rumours every season. If Brian Leetch comes back well off his injuries, and Sergei Zubov continues the improvement he showed last season, expect Patrick's name to surface again. He is not Mike Keenan's favourite kind of player, since his finesse skills aren't enough to offset his lack of physical involvement.

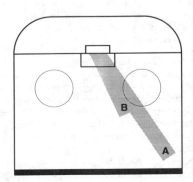

MIKE RICHTER

Yrs. of NHL service: 4
Born: Abingdon, Pa.; Sept. 22, 1966
Position: goaltender
Height: 5-10
Weight: 185
Uniform no.: 35
Catches: left

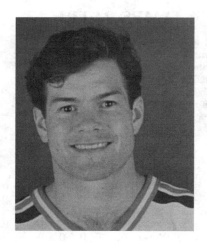

Career statistics:

GP	MINS	GA	SO	GAA	A	PIM
147	8320	454	4	3.27	6	12

1991-92 statistics:

GP	MINS	GAA	W	L	T	SO	GA	S	SAPCT	PIM
41	2298	3.11	23	12	2	3	119	1205	.901	6

1992-93 statistics:

GP	MINS	GAA	W	L	T	SO	GA	S	SAPCT	PIM
38	2105	3.82	13	19	3	1	134	2105	.886	2

LAST SEASON

Wins fewest since rookie season. GAA worst of career.

THE PHYSICAL GAME

Richter stays on his angle without charging out. He is still vulnerable on passes across, but playing for Team USA in the World Championships might have helped, since that is a popular tactic on larger international ice surfaces. He applied himself to drills involving his feet, and during play stoppages late in the season could be seen putting himself through a regimen to improve his footwork.

Richter moves well laterally, yet tends to lose his balance. He sometimes takes too big a stride, so that his motion isn't all of a piece but looks choppy and leaves him vulnerable.

He doesn't use his stick well. He hesitates in coming out to play a puck away from an onrushing attacker. He stops hard-arounds but does not move the puck. That is acceptable when Brian Leetch and James Patrick are in the line-up, but Richter has to be more of a '90s goalie and work on handling the puck.

He stands up well but leaves a lot of rebounds. Not a problem, again, when the likes of Leetch and Patrick are around to scoop up the puck and go. But the Rangers spent far too much time in the defensive zone, and Richter's GAA revealed the price as the opposition took shot after shot.

THE MENTAL GAME

The weight of the long Ron Francis goal in the 1992 playoffs still seems to drag Richter down, because he hasn't been the same goalie in the clutch ever since. Teams like to test him early with shots from outside the blue line, just in case he forgets (how could he? The goal came in Game 4 and turned the series around).

Richter wavered so badly last season that he was briefly demoted to Binghamton (AHL) to straighten out his game. For some reason, he had trouble winning on the road. Of course, the Rangers had trouble winning almost anywhere.

THE INTANGIBLES

The great question of who's No. 1 in the Ranger net seemed answered after the Rangers dealt John Vanbiesbrouck, but within days the team acquired the rights to former Islanders playoff hero and free agent Glenn Healy (prompting Ranger GM Neil Smith to quip, "Now we've got somebody who can win a game in Nassau Coliseum."). Is Healy a threat to Richter? Somebody has got to tell Richter he's their No. 1, if indeed he is, but the Rangers don't seem sure.

ESA TIKKANEN

Yrs. of NHL service: 8
Born: Helsinki, Finland; Jan. 25, 1965
Position: left wing
Height: 6-1
Weight: 200
Uniform no.: 10
Shoots: left

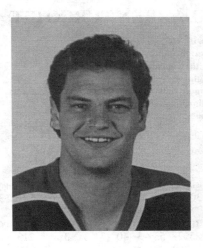

Career statistics:

GP	G	A	TP	PIM
537	170	263	443	777

1991-92 statistics:

GP	G	A	TP	+/-	PIM	PP	SH	GW	GT	S	PCT
40	12	16	28	-8	44	6	2	1	0	117	10.3

1992-93 statistics:

GP	G	A	TP	+/-	PIM	PP	SH	GW	GT	S	PCT
81	16	24	40	-24	94	2	4	3	0	202	7.9

LAST SEASON

Acquired from Edmonton for Doug Weight. Led team in shorthanded goals. Worst plus/minus on team (-11 with Edmonton, -13 in just 15 games with New York).

THE FINESSE GAME

Tikkanen plays all three forward positions and applies his considerable finesse skills all to the defensive aspects of the game. Once a consistent 30-goal scorer, he's unlikely to hit that mark again, although he can provide 20 and some solid two-way play.

Tikkanen has good speed, which he uses most effectively killing penalties. He is an aggressive forechecker, creating offensive chances off his work in the offensive zone. He blocks shots, hooks, holds and bumps, and if assigned to shadow a specific player will hound that mark relentlessly.

Tikkanen has good enough offensive skills to work on the power play as well, from either the point or by working the puck down low. He has confidence in his puckhandling ability and and sees the ice well. Despite taking chances low, he will be the first forward back to help out on defense.

Last season, he made many more major mistakes than anyone expected. His focus wavers, and his activities away from the puck divert his attention from the game itself.

THE PHYSICAL GAME

Tikkanen underwent major shoulder surgery in 1992 but it hasn't changed his style a whit. He is in your face — and also in your armpit or crawling up your back. He is as annoying as a mosquito and almost impossible to swat, since he is a master at the hit and run. One of the funniest sights in hockey is Tikkanen's wounded-victim look after he has goaded an opponent into taking a bad penalty.

THE INTANGIBLES

Tikkanen needs to be annoying to be effective. Before his trade to the Rangers, the only people he succeeded in annoying were his coaches. He never recovered from his slow start (one goal in his first 25 games) and should bloom under the fresh start with yet another new Rangers coach, Mike Keenan.

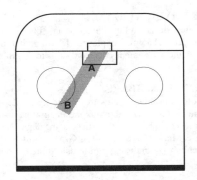

DARREN TURCOTTE

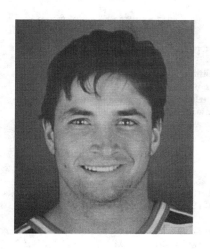

Yrs. of NHL service: 4
Born: Boston, Mass.; Mar. 2, 1968
Position: centre
Height: 6-0
Weight: 180
Uniform no.: 8
Shoots: right

Career statistics:

GP	G	A	TP	PIM
312	120	129	249	170

1991-92 statistics:

GP	G	A	TP	+/-	PIM	PP	SH	GW	GT	S	PCT
71	30	23	53	+11	57	13	1	4	1	216	13.9

1992-93 statistics:

GP	G	A	TP	+/-	PIM	PP	SH	GW	GT	S	PCT
71	25	28	53	-3	40	7	3	3	1	213	11.7

LAST SEASON

Missed 13 games with broken left foot. Fourth consecutive season with 20 or more goals.

THE FINESSE GAME

Turcotte is much better on special teams than at even strength. He seems to need the extra open ice — even when his team is shorthanded — and makes things happen when there is that extra split-second of time and space. A fine skater, he seems to hover above the ice and takes long, fluid strides that cover a lot of territory. He creates with his speed, driving the defenders back and daring them to come up to challenge him.

Turcotte kills penalties aggressively. He forces the point men, and when he gets a turnover he springs down-ice on a break. He makes the points nervous, because when he's gone, only the fastest defender can catch up. Teams who use forwards on the points are especially vulnerable.

On the power play, Turcotte works the point. He doesn't have an overpowering slap, but looks to work the puck down low or set up his fellow point man with a one-timer. His scoring range is low. He has a fine snap shot, as well as a good wrist and one-timer.

He has good hand-eye co-ordination and is good on draws.

THE PHYSICAL GAME

Turcotte will take a hit to make a play, but he could not be deemed a physical player. He will go into traffic with the puck and has the hand skills to control the puck in a crowd.

THE INTANGIBLES

Turcotte's problem seems to be finding a role and sticking with it. The Rangers are deep at centre — Turcotte could be ranked fourth on some depth charts, behind Mark Messier, Adam Graves and Sergei Nemchinov — and using him in that limited role is a waste.

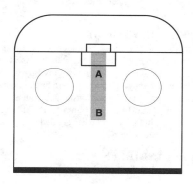

SERGEI ZUBOV

Yrs. of NHL service: 1
Born: Moscow, Russia; July 22, 1970
Position: left defense
Height: 6-0
Weight: 187
Uniform no.: 21
Shoots: right

Career statistics:

GP	G	A	TP	PIM
49	8	23	31	4

1992-93 statistics:

GP	G	A	TP	+/-	PIM	PP	SH	GW	GT	S	PCT
49	8	23	31	-1	4	3	0	0	0	93	8.6

LAST SEASON

First NHL season. Second among team defensemen in scoring.

THE FINESSE GAME

Zubov is a high-risk defenseman. When his gambles pay off, he looks brilliant; other times, he's Mr. Turnover. With Zubov, it's big plays or big giveaways.

He can beat the first man coming out of the zone, but he often tries this as the last defender back, so he has to make the play or he's toast. Other times, he'll carry the puck (he loves to) and try to make a lateral play at the offensive blue line. Too stubborn to simply get the puck deep if there is no other play, Zubov will force a move, then leave his partner hanging out to dry against an odd-man rush.

Either Zubov's skills are advanced compared to those of many of his teammates, or else his teammates need to become smarter at reading off him, because Zubov is ahead of the forwards half the time. He would be happiest if he could pass to himself, but he has to learn to use his support better.

He has some world-class skills. He is an elite skater, with good balance and power from his leg drive. He is agile in his stops and starts, even backwards.

Zubov works the point on the power play. He has good vision of the ice and a quick release on his shot.

THE PHYSICAL GAME

Zubov is not physical, but he is solidly built and will take a hit to make a play. His boyhood idol was Viacheslav Fetisov, and that role model should give you some idea of Zubov's style. He isn't an accomplished penalty killer, nor will he block shots — some things Fetisov has added to his game late in his career.

THE INTANGIBLES

Zubov is Reijo Ruotsalainen in a bigger body. The job he did when he stepped up from the minors to fill in for injured defensemen was nothing short of remarkable, and he is pencilled in as one of the team's top four "D" for this season.

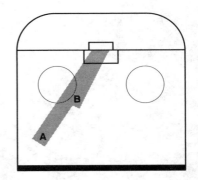

OTTAWA SENATORS

DAVE ARCHIBALD

Yrs. of NHL service: 4
Born: Chilliwack, B.C.; April 14, 1969
Position: centre/left wing
Height: 6-1
Weight: 190
Uniform no.: 15
Shoots: left

Career statistics:

GP	G	A	TP	PIM
225	39	53	92	84

1991-92 statistics:
Did not play in NHL

1992-93 statistics:

GP	G	A	TP	+/-	PIM	PP	SH	GW	GT	S	PCT
44	9	6	15	-16	32	6	0	0	0	93	9.7

LAST SEASON
Acquired from N.Y. Rangers for fifth-round draft choice. First season in NHL since 1989-90. Missed more than a quarter of season with back and rib injuries.

THE FINESSE GAME
Archibald regained his scoring touch and his confidence with the 1992 Canadian Olympic Team, but his touch isn't sizzling. A nice skater with good balance, he handles the puck well through traffic and has the ability to cut in and out with the puck. His best shot is a wrister, and he can shoot in stride off either foot. He should mix up his shots more. He could use his slap shot more often — he has a good one — or fake a slap and cut around a defender after he freezes him.

Archibald can play the point on the power play. He carries the puck up the ice well and has good offensive vision and sense. His good speed is used well on the penalty-killing unit also.

Archibald is a support player, and he'll need more talent around him before he has much impact.

THE PHYSICAL GAME
Archibald will go into the traffic areas for or with the puck, but he is not a physical presence. He can take a hit because his balance is so good, but he does not initiate.

THE INTANGIBLES
Just when it seemed Archibald was putting his game back together again, he suffered a back injury in January and missed more than two months of the season. He broke into the league with Minnesota but never posted the kind of numbers expected from a first-round draft pick (1987). He spent two seasons with the Canadian National team and led the 1992 Olympic silver medallists in goals (seven). If he comes off his back injury in good shape, he could be a useful No. 2 centre, but don't expect more than 20 goals.

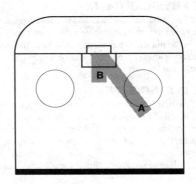

JAMIE BAKER

Yrs. of NHL service: 2
Born: Ottawa, Ont.; Aug. 31, 1966
Position: centre
Height: 6-0
Weight: 190
Uniform no.: 13
Shoots: left

Career statistics:

GP	G	A	TP	PIM
147	28	39	67	94

1991-92 statistics:

GP	G	A	TP	+/-	PIM	PP	SH	GW	GT	S	PCT
52	7	10	17	-5	32	3	0	1	0	77	9.1

1992-93 statistics:

GP	G	A	TP	+/-	PIM	PP	SH	GW	GT	S	PCT
76	19	29	48	-20	54	10	0	2	0	160	11.9

LAST SEASON

Games played career high. Led team forwards in scoring. Second on team in power play goals. Missed six games with sprained ankle.

THE FINESSE GAME

His skills and style have Baker pegged as a checking line centre, but the Senators need more and he was able to deliver last season.

He does his best work in the corners. He hustles and is always quickly onto the puck carrier on the forecheck. Baker reads offensive plays nicely, so if he is able to force a turnover he knows where to make the pass or whether or not to head to the net. He protects the puck well along the boards and while skating. This is his biggest asset.

He's a better playmaker than scorer, but he can finish around the net when given the chance. He passes off his forehand or backhand, and is effective down low. He has a choppy stride but can move quickly for the first step or two. On the power play, Baker is a set-up man, and he likes to lurk behind the goal line.

Baker is average on draws. He is a smart penalty killer and is very aggressive. He is a reliable player to have on the ice at crunch time.

THE PHYSICAL GAME

Baker has good size and has added some strength to make himself a more effective hitter, but continued work in the muscle department would help his career. The effort is always there with Baker: he goes full out, regardless of the score.

THE INTANGIBLES

Being the best player on the worst team in hockey may not be much of a boast, but he can fairly claim consistent effort through the season. Until the arrival of Bob Kudelski, Baker was the most talented forward on the Senators. He is also one of the most coachable and will do whatever is asked. Since some of the scoring pressure will be off him this season, he can produce in a more relaxed role, and his point totals should improve.

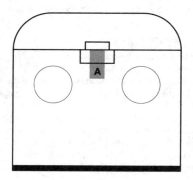

CRAIG BILLINGTON

Yrs. of NHL service: 4
Born: London, Ont.; Sept. 11, 1966
Position: goaltender
Height: 5-10
Weight: 170
Uniform no.: 1
Catches: left

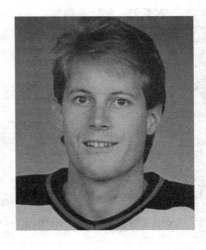

Career statistics:

GP	MINS	G	SO	AVG	A	PIM
111	5907	392	4	3.98	3	12

1991-92 statistics:

GP	MINS	GAA	W	L	T	SO	GA	S	SAPCT	PIM
26	1363	3.04	13	7	1	2	69	637	.892	2

1992-93 statistics:

GP	MINS	GAA	W	L	T	SO	GA	S	SAPCT	PIM
42	2389	3.67	21	16	4	2	146	1178	.876	8

LAST SEASON

Career high in games played, minutes played, wins. Missed one game with sore throat. Acquired from New Jersey with Troy Mallette for Peter Sidorkiewicz and Mike Peluso.

THE PHYSICAL GAME

Season-ending arthroscopic knee surgery in 1991-92 made Billington a question mark for last season, but he showed no ill effects from the procedure. Part of that is due to his conditioning and playing style. He is a smart player and one of the league's better technical goalies in his positioning. His angle play has improved, and he maximizes his size with his technique. When he starts losing his focus, Billington will give up goals stick-side high.

Billington's post-to-post play used to be a problem, but he improved that with a stint with the Canadian National Team in 1991 — and he avoided the trap of staying deep in his net, a problem for so many goalies with international experience on wider ice surfaces.

Billington is a poor stickhandler, although he has worked at overcoming this flaw and there were a few games when he was able to help out his teammates with some work off the boards. Stickhandling is an absolute must for goalies because of the speed of today's game, and Billington has to improve this aspect. He is hesitant about leaving his net to play the puck because he lacks confidence in his stickwork.

THE MENTAL GAME

He came into last season again unsure of his role with regard to No. 1 goalie Chris Terreri, but Billington ended up almost equally dividing the playing time with his more established partner. Billington's selection to play in the midseason NHL All-Star Game was another boost, although he seemed to play better in the first half of the season.

Billington has grown up a great deal, although he is still very uptight before games — just about unapproachable. He did have a few games this season where everything fell apart in front of him, but he's able to scare bad games off.

THE INTANGIBLES

Billington may get the chance to become a No. 1 goalie for the Senators. It will be a new role for Billington, and he will face that pressure for the first time in his NHL career.

NEIL BRADY

Yrs. of NHL service: 1
Born: Montreal, Que.; April 12, 1968
Position: centre/right wing
Height: 6-2
Weight: 200
Uniform no.: 12
Shoots: left

Career statistics:

GP	G	A	TP	PIM
84	9	21	30	74

1991-92 statistics:

GP	G	A	TP	+/-	PIM	PP	SH	GW	GT	S	PCT
7	1	0	1	+1	4	0	0	0	0	3	33.3

1992-93 statistics:

GP	G	A	TP	+/-	PIM	PP	SH	GW	GT	S	PCT
55	7	17	24	-25	57	5	0	0	0	68	10.3

LAST SEASON
First full season in NHL.

THE FINESSE GAME
Brady's biggest problem is his lack of skating speed. He has the size and the hands to be a more productive player, but he doesn't have the jump to get anything done. He should be a power forward who drives to the net; instead, when he has the puck he tends to curl and wait for support. He usually ends up just losing the puck instead of doing much creatively. He can't afford to be a perimeter player.

Brady has soft hands for passing. He developed as a centre in junior but played a lot of right wing for Ottawa last season. He gets his chances in front of the net but never seems to finish (although he scored the first goal in the expansion team's history — the first NHL goal by an Ottawa Senator since Cyclone Taylor).

The talent level of the Senators' forwards will bump up sharply this season with the addition of the rookies Alexandre Daigle and Alexei Yashin, and Brady will be challenged for his ice time.

THE PHYSICAL GAME
Brady does nothing with his size, which is considerable. He is a quiet big man, and there are nights when he is just about invisible on the ice.

THE INTANGIBLES
It was unfortunate for Brady that he was a high first-round draft pick (third overall in 1986, by New Jersey). The expectations were high and he failed to meet them. He is a journeyman forward at best. He was left unprotected in the expansion draft and was not taken.

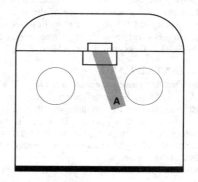

ALEXANDRE DAIGLE

Yrs. of NHL service: 0
Born: Laval, Que.; Feb. 7, 1975
Position: centre
Height: 6-0
Weight: 170
Uniform no.: na
Shoots: left

Career junior statistics:

GP	G	A	TP	PIM
119	80	167	247	148

1992-93 junior statistics:

GP	G	A	TP	PIM
53	45	92	137	85

LAST SEASON

Played for Victoriaville (QMJHL). Played for champion Canada in 1993 World Junior Championships. Named top pro prospect of QMJHL (Mike Bossy Trophy). Named to QMJHL First All-Star Team. Third in league in scoring. Drafted first overall in 1993 by Ottawa.

THE FINESSE GAME

Daigle was being called "Alexandre the Great" from the time he was 16, and not only did he stand up under the scrutiny, but he thrived on the pressure. He wanted to be the No. 1 pick overall when his turn came.

He has the ability to control the tempo of a game, if not his own temper. He is hungry for success, an outstanding playmaker and skater whose competitive edge and feistiness remind some scouts of Jeremy Roenick.

Daigle has a smooth stride with one-step quickness, and he changes directions effortlessly. He handles the puck well at tempo and spies his option quickly. His offensive instincts are flawless. A strong forechecker, he's effective as a penalty killer not because of his defensive awareness because he wants the puck so desperately.

Daigle is aggressive on the power play, using his speed to intimidate.

Like most scorers to come out of the QMJHL, Daigle has shown neither interest in nor instinct for defensive play.

THE PHYSICAL GAME

Daigle received two separate suspensions in the QMJHL for flagrant stick fouls for a total of 10 games, and a game misconduct in the World Junior Championships for a hit from behind on everybody's Mr. All-World, Peter Forsberg.

THE INTANGIBLES

There is a dark side to Daigle's brilliance. He is flashy, cocky and charismatic, but also driven, intense and prone to outbursts of anger. He will have to be handled gently but firmly. He would have threatened Mario Lemieux's QMJHL records if he hadn't been sidelined for 10 games with suspensions. Daigle has the most talent of the class of '93, and he has the potential to be an impact player in the NHL.

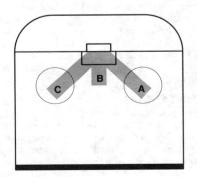

MARK FREER

Yrs. of NHL service: 2
Born: Peterborough, Ont.; July 14, 1968
Position: centre
Height: 5-10
Weight: 185
Uniform no.: 11
Shoots: left

Career statistics:

GP	G	A	TP	PIM
122	16	23	39	57

1991-92 statistics:

GP	G	A	TP	+/-	PIM	PP	SH	GW	GT	S	PCT
50	6	7	13	-1	18	0	0	2	0	41	14.6

1992-93 statistics:

GP	G	A	TP	+/-	PIM	PP	SH	GW	GT	S	PCT
63	10	14	24	-35	39	3	3	0	0	80	12.5

LAST SEASON

Led team in shorthanded goals. Games played and all point totals at career highs in second full NHL season. Missed 11 games with neck injury.

THE FINESSE GAME

Freer has good hockey sense and sees a lot of ice time in all situations. He has a short skating stride with good quickness and agility, but not much open-ice speed.

Freer was a good scorer in junior and in the minors, but he doesn't have the shot or the release to be more than a 15- to 18-goal scorer at the NHL level.

He takes a lot of face-offs but is only average on draws. A good penalty killer because of his intelligence and hustle, he can make things happen with a shorthanded scoring chance. He also sees time on the power play.

Freer has to learn to play a little smarter, dip in and out of the slot and use the backdoor play more often. He developed much more confidence with his increased ice time last season and could take another step forward, but he will always be limited by his size.

THE PHYSICAL GAME

Freer lacks the size and strength to be an effective checking centre, since he can't handle other team's bigger centremen. He is always trying to get in people's way, though, and when he is knocked down (as he consistently is), he gets right back up on his feet again. He always gets a piece of his target. There is no lack of bravery on Freer's part. He's a smaller Doug Jarvis.

THE INTANGIBLES

Freer gives an honest effort on every shift, but it is difficult to find a niche for him. He is too small to be a checking centre and not gifted enough offensively to work on a scoring line. He was left unprotected in the expansion draft and was not taken.

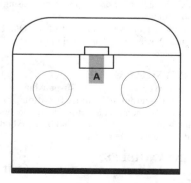

KEN HAMMOND

Yrs. of NHL service: 3
Born: Port Credit, Ont.; Aug. 22, 1963
Position: right defense
Height: 6-1
Weight: 190
Uniform no.: 5
Shoots: left

Career statistics:

GP	G	A	TP	PIM
193	18	29	47	290

1991-92 statistics:

GP	G	A	TP	+/-	PIM	PP	SH	GW	GT	S	PCT
46	5	10	15	-17	82	2	0	0	0	93	5.4

1992-93 statistics:

GP	G	A	TP	+/-	PIM	PP	SH	GW	GT	S	PCT
62	4	4	8	-42	104	0	0	0	0	64	6.3

LAST SEASON
Games played at career high.

THE FINESSE GAME
Hammond is a good skater with some quickness and mobility but not a great deal of speed. He is a stay-at-home defenseman, but occasionally he'll take it into his head to step up and play a little more aggressively. He doesn't do this on a consistent level.

Hammond can skate with the puck but does not join the rush well. He limits his offensive involvement to shots from the point, but there isn't enough to his offensive reads to make him much of a threat. He can kill penalties and does so with a degree of boldness.

He has to stick to the simple things and learn to use his teammates better. He has a good shot, so he could get into the attack and score a few goals, but he can't do things all by himself. He will often overhandle the puck in the defensive zone, and Ottawa doesn't have the players to help bail him out when he gets himself into trouble. Hammond shouldn't try to make a fancy pass through someone when a bang off the glass would do. He is his own worst enemy in that regard.

THE PHYSICAL GAME
Hammond is a solid checker but doesn't have the size, strength or nasty streak to intimidate. The Senators could really use someone to scare people in front of the net, but Hammond is not a likely candidate.

THE INTANGIBLES
This is Hammond's second stint with an expansion team (he played for San Jose in 1991-92). That is enough punishment for any man. He also played for six other NHL organizations without being able to stick consistently at the major league level. He is a fringe defenseman who will have to fight for a job this season. His leadership qualities in the dressing room are a plus.

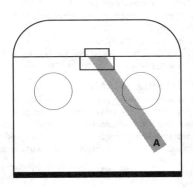

BOB KUDELSKI

Yrs. of NHL service: 5
Born: Springfield, Mass.; Mar. 3, 1964
Position: right wing
Height: 6-1
Weight: 200
Uniform no.: 26
Shoots: right

Career statistics:

GP	G	A	TP	PIM
317	93	68	161	192

1991-92 statistics:

GP	G	A	TP	+/-	PIM	PP	SH	GW	GT	S	PCT
80	22	21	43	-15	42	2	1	2	0	155	14.2

1992-93 statistics:

GP	G	A	TP	+/-	PIM	PP	SH	GW	GT	S	PCT
63	24	17	41	-25	30	12	0	3	0	137	17.5

LAST SEASON

Acquired from Los Angeles with Shawn McCosh for Jim Thomson and Marc Fortier. Led Senators in power play goals, despite playing only 48 games with Ottawa after trade.

THE FINESSE GAME

A versatile two-way forward, Kudelski became the team's most productive player the moment he slipped on a Senators sweater.

All 12 of Kudelski's power play goals came following the December trade to Ottawa, which illustrates how much of an impact he had. Because of the wealth of talent among the Kings' forwards, Kudelski saw very little power play time, but he has the brains to make things happen. On the power play, he one-times a wrist shot, *à la* Tim Kerr, and even though everyone on the opposition knew the Senators were looking to set Kudelski up, he was able to work himself free for the scoring chance.

Not a natural scorer, Kudelski has to work hard around the net for his chances. He has good enough hands to be able to reach forward and lift a backhander over a goalie in tight. He can also drive a shot off a one-timer and beat the netminder from 25 feet. Even when Kudelski doesn't get all of his shot, it seems to dribble toward the target and often into the net. He is a pure goal scorer.

He isn't a very pretty skater, but he has the one-step quickness to beat a defender. He is also very effective killing penalties and can take face-offs.

THE PHYSICAL GAME

Kudelski doesn't use his size well unless he is driving to the net. Defensively, he is more intent on positional play than bodying anyone, but he has a little mean streak that creeps in every now and then. He could use some more upper body strength for his work around the net.

THE INTANGIBLES

Kudelski's career can be revived with the move to Ottawa. As the Senators add more talented forwards, Kudelski will still merit considerable ice time and should hit 30 to 35 goals. His confidence has been restored, and that was a big hindrance in the past.

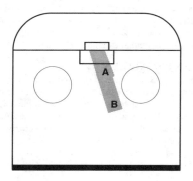

DARCY LOEWEN

Yrs. of NHL service: 1
Born: Calgary, Alta.; Feb. 26, 1969
Position: left wing
Height: 5-10
Weight: 185
Uniform no.: 10
Shoots: left

Career statistics:

GP	G	A	TP	PIM
91	4	5	9	159

1991-92 statistics:

GP	G	A	TP	+/-	PIM	PP	SH	GW	GT	S	PCT
2	0	0	0	0	2	0	0	0	0	1	0.0

1992-93 statistics:

GP	G	A	TP	+/-	PIM	PP	SH	GW	GT	S	PCT
79	4	5	9	-26	145	0	0	0	0	42	9.5

LAST SEASON

First full season in NHL. Second on team in PIM.

THE FINESSE GAME

Loewen plays a very conservative game. His role is to check, and that is all he devotes his skating and thoughts to. He is Ottawa's Tasmanian Devil.

A choppy skater, he works hard to keep up with the play. His leg drive helps his work along the boards and in the corners. Loewen has a low centre of gravity and is tough to push off the puck.

He has never been a scorer at any professional level. He rarely shoots and doesn't do anything creative with the puck. He drives fearlessly to the net but forgets to bring the puck with him.

Loewen is an energetic player who is active on the bench, always giving his linemates pats and encouragements through the game. He wants desperately to play in the NHL, and is a coach's dream in that he will tackle any assignment. Unfortunately for Loewen, his absent scoring touch may doom his career.

THE PHYSICAL GAME

Loewen is a rugged customer. He is not a fighter, but he will bump and agitate and finish every check. For a player who isn't very big, he thumps with enthusiasm. Even though he only comes up to Eric Lindros's Flyers crest, Loewen was in the big guy's face whenever Ottawa played Philadelphia.

THE INTANGIBLES

Loewen is a serviceable third-line checking winger with limited skills, but his desire, effort and work ethic add to his value. How many checking forwards with four goals have their own fan clubs?

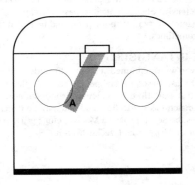

NORM MACIVER

Yrs. of NHL service: 4
Born: Thunder Bay, Ont.; Sept. 8, 1964
Position: right defense
Height: 5-11
Weight: 180
Uniform no.: 22
Shoots: left

Career statistics:

GP	G	A	TP	PIM
262	35	133	168	188

1991-92 statistics:

GP	G	A	TP	+/-	PIM	PP	SH	GW	GT	S	PCT
57	6	34	40	+20	38	2	0	3	0	69	8.7

1992-93 statistics:

GP	G	A	TP	+/-	PIM	PP	SH	GW	GT	S	PCT
80	17	46	63	-46	84	7	1	2	0	184	9.2

LAST SEASON

Only defenseman in NHL to lead his team in scoring. Games played and all point totals at career highs. Acquired from Edmonton in waiver draft.

THE FINESSE GAME

Maciver is on the ice for one reason only: to provide offense. The rest of the ice is pretty much neglected, and any team that has Maciver in its line-up knows the trade-off. Maciver is the Reijo Ruotsalainen of the '90s.

Maciver is a speedy little skater with a lot of wiggly moves and decent hand skills. He loves to rush the puck from his own end and quarterback the action in the attacking zone. He has good vision of the ice and moves the puck well. He doesn't have a very heavy shot, but his release is quick and he keeps his shots low.

Of course, Maciver is a natural on the power play, and he will stay on nearly the full two minutes.

THE PHYSICAL GAME

Maciver is a stick-checker who manages to hold his own in open ice but is a detriment when play comes to the boards or corners. He has to play with a physical partner, because he is weak and can't move anybody. His defensive play is limited to pass interception. He will gamble a try to strip the puck, and he gets it that way sometimes.

THE INTANGIBLES

Maciver was mentioned in about 20 trade rumours prior to last season's deadline. He needs to play for a team that can afford his defensive shortcomings; the right match has yet to be made. He may be expendable, as the Senators have a Maciver clone in 18-year-old Radek Hamr from Czechoslovakia.

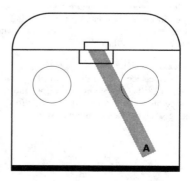

ANDREW MCBAIN

Yrs. of NHL service: 10
Born: Scarborough, Ont.; Jan. 18, 1965
Position: right wing
Height: 6-10
Weight: 205
Uniform no.: 20
Shoots: right

Career statistics:

GP	G	A	TP	PIM
553	118	164	282	569

1991-92 statistics:

GP	G	A	TP	+/-	PIM	PP	SH	GW	GT	S	PCT
6	1	0	1	-1	0	0	0	0	0	11	9.1

1992-93 statistics:

GP	G	A	TP	+/-	PIM	PP	SH	GW	GT	S	PCT
59	7	16	23	-37	43	1	0	0	0	71	9.9

LAST SEASON

Games played and all scoring totals at three-season highs. Missed two weeks with knee injury. Missed games with groin injury.

THE FINESSE GAME

McBain used to be notable for one weapon, his tremendous shot, but even that was nowhere to be seen last season.

Injury problems made him even more of an immobile player than he is when healthy. He has little bursts of speed but doesn't use them to go anywhere productive. He is not a creative player. The only thing he can do is shoot, and he didn't do enough of that to make himself very useful.

Defensively, he always positions himself as though he has an idea of where he should be, but then gives up on his man. Offensively and defensively, McBain always seems about a half-step from getting the job done.

THE PHYSICAL GAME

McBain makes no impact despite his decent size. He will go into traffic once in a while for the puck but is usually more of a disinterested spectator.

THE INTANGIBLES

McBain brings nothing to the table. As the Senators get a little deeper up front, his ice time will become scarcer. He was left exposed in the expansion draft but was not selected.

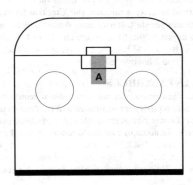

DARREN RUMBLE

Yrs. of NHL service: 1
Born: Barrie, Ont.; Jan. 23, 1969
Position: left defense
Height: 6-1
Weight: 200
Uniform no.: 34
Shoots: left

Career statistics:

GP	G	A	TP	PIM
72	4	13	17	61

1992-93 statistics:

GP	G	A	TP	+/-	PIM	PP	SH	GW	GT	S	PCT
69	3	13	16	-24	61	0	0	0	0	92	3.3

LAST SEASON
First full NHL season.

THE FINESSE GAME
Rumble is a special project of the Ottawa coaching staff, who have obviously spotted some gemlike qualities under the rough exterior.

Rumble can do the little things well, like clearing his zone offensively and joining the rush. What players like him have to learn is how to play with consistent intensity. He must play 65 to 70 good games a season, not 15 or 20, to stay in the NHL. Rumble has average skating ability, decent size and adequate puckhandling skills.

He has to make better decisions in the offensive zone. He will pass instead of shoot, and vice versa. He is vulnerable to outside speed and has to learn to play better positionally and angle off the attacker.

THE PHYSICAL GAME
Rumble likes open-ice hits so much that he will run halfway across the ice to deliver. Since he is not very agile, he misses about half his targets amd leaves his defense partner outnumbered.

For the first half of the season, Rumble seemed intimidated by the mere fact of being on the ice. He was afraid to make a mistake, thinking that he might not see another shift. It took him at least half the season to adjust to the NHL bench and learn by doing. Then, in the second half, he was too unrestrained. He needs to find a happy medium.

THE INTANGIBLES
Rumble will never become a star, but it would be a major accomplishment just for him to become a competent offensive defenseman. He could graduate to the top defensive foursome on the Senators. A No. 1 pick of the Flyers in 1987, he was saddled with the expectations that brings. He is getting a second shot with Ottawa; he'll have no excuses if he fails in this spot.

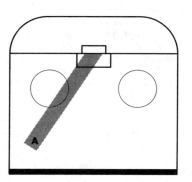

BRAD SHAW

Yrs. of NHL service: 5
Born: Cambridge, Ont.; Apr. 28, 1964
Position: left defense
Height: 6-0
Weight: 190
Uniform no.: 4
Shoots: right

Career statistics:

GP	G	A	TP	PIM
293	18	118	136	141

1991-92 statistics:

GP	G	A	TP	+/-	PIM	PP	SH	GW	GT	S	PCT
62	3	22	25	+1	44	0	0	0	0	101	3.0

1992-93 statistics:

GP	G	A	TP	+/-	PIM	PP	SH	GW	GT	S	PCT
81	7	34	41	-47	34	4	0	0	0	166	4.2

LAST SEASON

Tied for worst plus/minus on team. Games played, goals, assists and points at career highs.

THE FINESSE GAME

Shaw is a No. 3 or 4 defenseman thrust into the role on the top pairing with the expansion Senators. It is asking more of Shaw than he can deliver, but to his credit, he is a gamer. He is a steady all-around defenseman who can play effectively on both special teams.

Shaw is a decent skater with a long stride, but he is not very agile or quick. He is aware of his limitations and won't try any rink-long rushes. He will make an outlet pass and join the play.

Shaw plays the point almost by default. He does not have a very good shot, but he will give his teammates a chance at the tip by keeping it low and on net. He does not risk making plays deep in the offensive zone.

Since he is often paired with Norm Maciver, Shaw has to be very conservative defensively. This guy faced a lot of two-on-ones last season. Being paired with Maciver also meant Shaw was moved to left defense, not his best side, but since Maciver is all over the ice, left or right means little to his partner.

THE PHYSICAL GAME

Shaw is not a strong or willing hitter. He relies on his positional play and his long reach to tie up an attacker. He bumps but won't move anyone from in front of the net and doesn't intimidate. He gets a lot of ice time and keeps himself very fit.

THE INTANGIBLES

Shaw is a character player who produces a steady effort. Unfortunately, he is being asked to do more than his abilities will allow. The addition of Dimitri Filimonov, a 6-4, 207-pound defenseman from Moscow Dynamo, is expected to improve Ottawa's blueline corps.

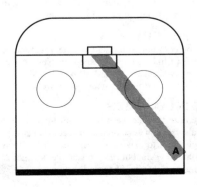

SYLVAIN TURGEON

Yrs. of NHL service: 10
Born: Noranda, Que.; Jan. 17, 1965
Position: left wing
Height: 6-0
Weight: 200
Uniform no.: 61
Shoots: left

Career statistics:

GP	G	A	TP	PIM
589	247	203	450	610

1991-92 statistics:

GP	G	A	TP	+/-	PIM	PP	SH	GW	GT	S	PCT
56	9	11	20	-4	39	6	0	1	0	99	9.1

1992-93 statistics:

GP	G	A	TP	+/-	PIM	PP	SH	GW	GT	S	PCT
72	25	18	43	-29	104	8	0	2	1	249	10.0

LAST SEASON

Games played, goals, assists and points at three-season highs. Led team in shots. Missed 12 games with groin injury.

THE FINESSE GAME

Turgeon still has some speed and quickness to go along with his scoring instincts, and he enjoyed a bit of a resurgence with Ottawa.

He can do one thing well, and that's pull the trigger. He has very good instincts around the net and a wicked release. Turgeon doesn't give up on a shot, but will follow to the net for a rebound. He is not a creative playmaker; he gets his assists from teammates scoring off his shots.

On the power play, Turgeon will stand off to the side and sneak in for a tip or redirect. He has very good hand-eye co-ordination.

Turgeon still has the moves to beat a defender one on one. He would be much more effective if he looked to use his linemates, but that is never an option for him.

He is hopeless on defense. The first-year Senators barely bothered to ask, just telling him to go out and score goals and not worry about his defense, and Turgeon was happy to comply. Ottawa will ask more of him defensively as the team improves.

THE PHYSICAL GAME

Turgeon does not go through anyone to get the puck. He doesn't like contact and keeps his stick up in the face of any checkers to ward off hits. He doesn't perform even the most rudimentary body work.

THE INTANGIBLES

Turgeon has never recovered from his abdominal/hernia surgery of several seasons ago. He can't score enough goals to make up for his liabilities. He will never hit 40 again, but can probably net another 25 to 30 with the Senators if he stays healthy.

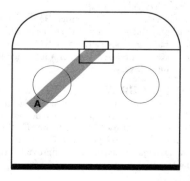

DENNIS VIAL

Yrs. of NHL service: 2
Born: Sault Ste. Marie, Ont.; Apr. 10, 1969
Position: left defense
Height: 6-1
Weight: 215
Uniform no.: na
Shoots: left

Career statistics:

GP	G	A	TP	PIM
63	1	1	2	169

1991-92 statistics:

GP	G	A	TP	+/-	PIM	PP	SH	GW	GT	S	PCT
27	1	0	1	+1	72	0	0	0	0	6	16.7

1992-93 statistics:

GP	G	A	TP	+/-	PIM	PP	SH	GW	GT	S	PCT
9	0	1	1	+1	20	0	0	0	0	5	0.0

LAST SEASON

Acquired by Anaheim from Tampa Bay in first phase of expansion draft. Acquired by Ottawa from Anaheim in second phase of expansion draft.

THE FINESSE GAME

Vial has spent most of his career in the AHL (with Adirondack, in Detroit's system) because the most crucial part of the game, his skating, is only AHL calibre. He is strong on his skates in a contained area, and he lets the attackers come to him and then to pay the price to get through him.

Vial plays a simple system. He is most effective when he isn't flashy. He will move the puck out but not up, and he does not get involved in the attack.

Last season with Adirondack, Vial picked up two goals and 11 assists in 30 games with 177 PIM, so it's clear where his value lies.

THE PHYSICAL GAME

Vial is a legitimate tough guy who will add a much-needed element to the Ottawa defense. With the addition of finesse forwards like Alexandre Daigle and Alexei Yashin, most of the bodyguard role will have to be filled by Vial.

THE INTANGIBLES

Vial will have to be used prudently, paired with a mobile defense partner, but because toughness is in short supply in Ottawa, he is virtually assured a starting role.

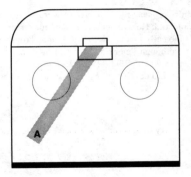

ALEXEI YASHIN

Yrs. of NHL service: 0
Born: Sverdlovsk, Russia; Nov. 5, 1973
Position: centre
Height: 6-2
Weight: 196
Uniform no.: na
Shoots: right

1992-93 statistics: (in Russia)

GP	G	A	TP	PIM
31	9	22	31	18

LAST SEASON

Second player drafted overall in 1992. Expected to join Senators for 1993-94 season after playing with Moscow Dynamo.

THE FINESSE GAME

Yashin has extensive international experience, and most scouts have been impressed by what they have seen so far.

Yashin is a powerful skater and can shoot without breaking stride. He plays a confident finesse game and can beat a defender one on one. He has a variety of shots but will score most often by driving the defense back with his intimidating skating. He has great hands.

Yashin works the puck well down low and will be a staple on the power play. He has terrific hockey sense in the offensive zone. His defense is suspect, but that is not unusual for a young player.

THE PHYSICAL GAME

A question mark. Yashin will take a licking on a poor Ottawa team, and the team no longer has Mike Peluso to serve as bodyguard. He uses his size and strength well to control and protect the puck.

THE INTANGIBLES

Yashin is projected as a power forward with leadership potential. He will get tons of ice time and may be one of the early favourites for the Calder Trophy next season (although Peter Forsberg still ranks as the top rookie prospect of 1993-94). Clearly a franchise player who should develop along Pierre Turgeon lines.

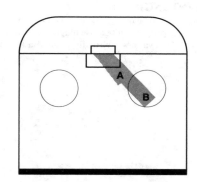

PHILADELPHIA FLYERS

KEITH ACTON

Yrs. of NHL service: 13
Born: Stouffville, Ont.; Apr. 15, 1958
Position: centre
Height: 5-8
Weight: 170
Uniform no.: 25
Shoots: left

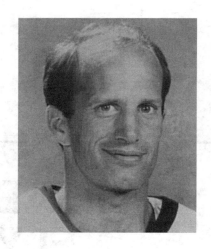

Career statistics:

GP	G	A	TP	PIM
946	224	350	574	1121

1991-92 statistics:

GP	G	A	TP	+/-	PIM	PP	SH	GW	GT	S	PCT
50	7	9	16	-4	98	0	0	3	0	79	8.9

1992-93 statistics:

GP	G	A	TP	+/-	PIM	PP	SH	GW	GT	S	PCT
83	8	15	23	-10	51	0	0	0	0	74	10.8

LAST SEASON

Goals, assists and points improved over previous season. Worst plus/minus on team.

THE FINESSE GAME

Acton just doesn't quit. He is like one of those annoying, yappy little dogs with just enough fur to distinguish it from a rat. Many of Acton's opponents don't make that distinction with him.

That's fine by Acton. His role is to check and annoy, and he does it with flair. He serves on the first penalty-killing unit, taking draws and using his excellent hockey sense to always be well placed positionally. Acton is aggressive and likes to step on and annoy the puck handler.

He is tenacious on draws. He has good hand-eye co-ordination and, most of all, intense focus.

The offensive facet of Acton's game is just about gone, but he has the quickness and will score the odd goal off a turnover. He lacks the speed to be a short-handed threat anymore.

THE PHYSICAL GAME

Acton stays so close to his opposite number that the two could wear the same jersey. He is not a big hitter — he just doesn't have the strength — but he will hurl his body at his opponent. All the while, he keeps his jaw flapping.

THE INTANGIBLES

Acton is nearing the end of his playing days, but there is still enough spark and pluck left for another season or two. He can give the most comatose team a reason for living with his drive.

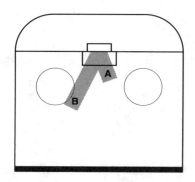

JOSEF BERANEK

Yrs. of NHL service: 2
Born: Litvinov, Czechoslovakia; Oct. 25, 1969
Position: left wing/centre
Height: 6-2
Weight: 185
Uniform no.: 42
Shoots: left

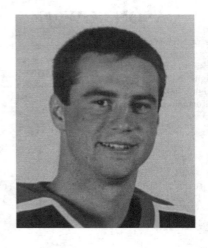

Career statistics:

GP	G	A	TP	PIM
124	27	34	61	96

1991-92 statistics:

GP	G	A	TP	+/-	PIM	PP	SH	GW	GT	S	PCT
58	12	16	28	-2	18	0	0	1	0	79	15.2

1992-93 statistics:

GP	G	A	TP	+/-	PIM	PP	SH	GW	GT	S	PCT
66	15	18	33	-8	78	1	0	0	0	130	11.5

LAST SEASON

Acquired from Edmonton with Greg Hawgood for Brian Benning. Goals, assists and points improved over rookie season.

THE FINESSE GAME

Beranek needs the ice time and the chance to develop confidence in a league that is still new to him, and he may get that chance in Philadelphia.

He doesn't just skate up and down his wing, but uses all of the ice. He is a strong one-on-one player, but he also uses his teammates well.

Beranek has good hockey vision and the skills and size to finish or be a smart playmaker. He has very good hands and a wrist shot from the tops of the circle in. He will also drive to the net for rebounds.

THE PHYSICAL GAME

Beranek is just starting to learn to initiate more in his hitting, which he does very well in his forechecking. He won't be intimidated or pushed around.

THE INTANGIBLES

Beranek was used as a left wing by the Flyers, but he is also a capable centre. He is just starting to flex his muscles as a power forward. If he adds a little more strength (he's tall but on the light side), he could have a breakthrough season and be in the 30-goal range.

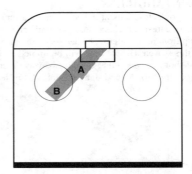

JASON BOWEN

Yrs. of NHL service: 0
Born: Port Alice, B.C.; Nov. 11, 1973
Position: left wing/left defense
Height: 6-4
Weight: 210
Uniform no.: 28
Shoots: left

Career statistics:

GP	G	A	TP	PIM
7	1	0	1	2

1992-93 statistics:

GP	G	A	TP	+/-	PIM	PP	SH	GW	GT	S	PCT
7	1	0	1	+1	2	0	0	0	0	3	33.3

LAST SEASON

Will be entering first NHL season. Played last season for Tri-Cities (WHL).

THE FINESSE GAME

As a defenseman, Bowen uses his big size well and is not afraid to move up into the attack and get involved in the offensive play. He doesn't have a lot of clever moves. As a left wing, his goals come from driving to the net and making something happen in front.

Bowen's skating is very solid. He lacks open-ice speed but he has surprising quickness for such a big skater. He is very strong on his skates. In his brief stay with the Flyers, Bowen did little more than skate up and down his wing, so if he has any dazzling moves, we haven't seen them yet.

The only question about Bowen is his hands. He will force his chances around the net, but will he be able to convert them?

THE PHYSICAL GAME

Bowen is big and tough, and he appears to have the hunger and eagerness to pay the price in the NHL. Once he establishes himself, he will merit a lot of room.

THE INTANGIBLES

Bowen got a close look at the end of the season after his junior career came to a close. Versatile enough to play up front or on defense, he has a shot to make the team this season. His ice time will be limited at first, but he should develop into a solid two-way defenseman (or forward). A good sign: his idol is Cam Neely.

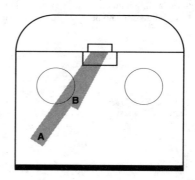

ROD BRIND'AMOUR

Yrs. of NHL service: 4
Born: Ottawa, Ont.; Aug. 9, 1970
Position: centre
Height: 6-1
Weight: 202
Uniform no.: 17
Shoots: left

Career statistics:

GP	G	A	TP	PIM
318	113	160	273	328

1991-92 statistics:

GP	G	A	TP	+/-	PIM	PP	SH	GW	GT	S	PCT
80	33	44	77	-3	100	8	4	5	0	202	16.3

1992-93 statistics:

GP	G	A	TP	+/-	PIM	PP	SH	GW	GT	S	PCT
81	37	49	86	-8	89	13	4	4	1	206	18.0

LAST SEASON

Second on team in assists and points with career highs. Career high in goals. Tied for team lead in shorthanded goals. Second on team in power play goals.

THE FINESSE GAME

Brind'Amour is a solid two-way forward who appears to be settling comfortably into the role as No. 2 centre behind Eric Lindros. If he handles the assignment well mentally, this could parallel the Mario Lemieux-Ron Francis situation in Pittsburgh.

Brind'Amour's biggest asset is that he is a complete player. He is not fancy and won't beat many players one on one in open ice, but he will outwork defenders along the boards and use a quick burst of speed to drive to the net. He's a playmaker in the mucking sense, where scoring chances emerge from his hard work and checking. He has a long, powerful stride with a quick first step to leave a defender behind. He has the hand skills to go along with the hard work. He drives well into a shot on the fly, and he also has a quick-release snap shot and a strong backhand. His passes are crisp to either side.

Brind'Amour is as good without the puck as with it, because he will work ferociously for control.

THE PHYSICAL GAME

Brind'Amour uses his size well and is a strong skater. He can muck with the best of them in the corners and along the boards. He will carry the puck through traffic in front of the net and battle for position for screens and tip-ins.

THE INTANGIBLES

Brind'Amour could be very close to developing into a solid Kirk Muller style forward who provides offense and defense along with strength and grinding. The next step for him will be to develop Muller's intense focus and concentration.

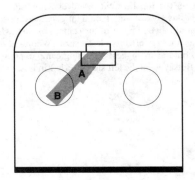

VIACHESLAV BUTSAYEV

Yrs. of NHL service: 1
Born: Togliatti, Russia; June 13, 1970
Position: centre
Height: 6-2
Weight: 200
Uniform no.: 22
Shoots: left

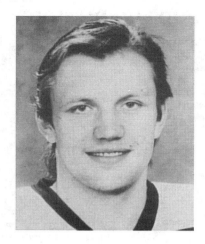

Career statistics:

GP	G	A	TP	PIM
52	2	14	16	61

1992-93 statistics:

GP	G	A	TP	+/-	PIM	PP	SH	GW	GT	S	PCT
52	2	14	16	+3	61	0	0	0	0	58	3.4

LAST SEASON

First NHL season. Missed games with groin injury.

THE FINESSE GAME

Butsayev's skill levels are so high that the "2" in his goals column reads like a misprint. He should have been in the 20-goal range, but he is shy about shooting, as many Russian players traditionally are (or were in the past). He saw almost no power play time as a result.

He has an excellent wrist shot, which he can use from the top of the circles. He doesn't spend much time in the middle of the ice, and he could be more successful using his shot from the off (right) wing.

Butsayev is very effective defensively and could succeed in just that role, but there are untapped resources here.

THE PHYSICAL GAME

Butsayev is big and strong. He hasn't established a physical presence, but he is slow to adjust to the NHL and should develop confidence in his size and physical ability and grinding.

THE INTANGIBLES

Butsayev played in the World Championships as a left wing on the top line with Andrei Khomutov and Viacheslav Bykov, and that might give the Flyers the notion to move him out of his centre position, where he was not very effective last season. We might even be so bold as to suggest a training camp experiment with Butsayev on the left side of Eric Lindros.

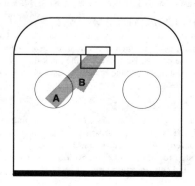

TERRY CARKNER

Yrs. of NHL service: 7
Born: Smiths Falls, Ont.; Mar. 7, 1966
Position: left defense
Height: 6-3
Weight: 205
Uniform no.: 29
Shoots: left

Career statistics:

GP	G	A	TP	PIM
491	34	140	174	1142

1991-92 statistics:

GP	G	A	TP	+/-	PIM	PP	SH	GW	GT	S	PCT
73	4	12	16	-14	195	0	1	0	0	70	5.7

1992-93 statistics:

GP	G	A	TP	+/-	PIM	PP	SH	GW	GT	S	PCT
83	3	16	19	+18	150	0	0	0	0	45	6.7

LAST SEASON

Tied for second on team in plus/minus. Third on team in PIM. Reached 1000-PIM mark for career.

THE FINESSE GAME

When he stays within himself, Carkner can be a useful defenseman. He has limited skills, but if he plays a containment game he can be effective. He has to make the outlet pass and play steady, and not try to over-achieve. When he tries to stretch his game, the chinks show up immediately. He should not, for example, try to carry the puck out of the zone and stickhandle through defenders in the neutral zone. He tries this move every so often, never with happy results.

Carkner is not a very good skater. He has a decent first step to the puck, but often his feet look heavy and he doesn't have great overall quickness or agility.

He sees some time on the second power play. He has a nice point shot, using a low and strong wrist shot that he gets on net for tips and redirections. He will get aggressive and venture in deep.

THE PHYSICAL GAME

Carkner is a banger and gets room for himself — when he plays that way. He dropped off in that respect last season and didn't consistently have the impact a player of his size and strength should. As a result, he gets less room, people take him out, and the fore-checkers are on him faster. He must reestablish himself physically every night.

THE INTANGIBLES

Carkner should study some Brad Marsh tapes and learn how the veteran defenseman turned his career around, first with conditioning and then by learning to let the ice work for him. The patient Marsh let attackers go wide and then cut them off in the corners. That is the style that would look good on Carkner.

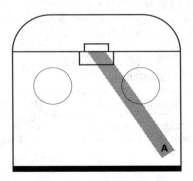

KEVIN DINEEN

Yrs. of NHL service: 9
Born: Quebec City, Que.; Oct. 28, 1963
Position: right wing
Height: 5-11
Weight: 195
Uniform no.: 11
Shoots: right

Career statistics:

GP	G	A	TP	PIM
636	275	290	565	1352

1991-92 statistics:

GP	G	A	TP	+/-	PIM	PP	SH	GW	GT	S	PCT
80	30	32	62	-5	143	6	3	5	0	225	13.3

1992-93 statistics:

GP	G	A	TP	+/-	PIM	PP	SH	GW	GT	S	PCT
83	35	28	63	+14	201	6	3	7	1	241	14.5

LAST SEASON

Led team in game-winning goals. Second on team in shots and PIM. PIM second-highest of career. Fifth season with 30 or more goals. Fourth on team in goals and points.

THE FINESSE GAME

Dineen is a streaky scorer, but his veteran experience shows through when he's not seeing the results on the scoresheet. He never fails to contribute in other ways when he is in a drought, by hitting, killing penalties and keeping up the grinding part of his game.

Dineen never seems to be still. His feet keep moving and pumping, and he does a good job drawing penalties. He is very scrappy in battles for the loose puck. Confident and determined, he has the skating and hand quickness to make things happen when he gains control.

During his slumps, Dineen appears to double-clutch his stick and just about grind it into sawdust. When he's connecting, the game looks easy, but it's all a result of his hard effort. He doesn't waste his shots. He gets into high-quality scoring positions low and uses his wrist shot, although he can also fire from the wing.

THE PHYSICAL GAME

Dineen's skating gives him the momentum to pile into traffic for the loose puck. He has a hard edge to him most nights, and while he is not a very big player, he doles out every last ounce of himself.

THE INTANGIBLES

Dineen came to the Flyers (in a trade) before his father Bill became the team's coach. Now that Dad has been replaced by Terry Simpson, it's unlikely to affect Dineen's status. In fact, Dineen's style should make just about any coach smile, and he's a lock for 30 goals a season.

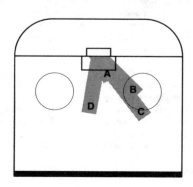

PELLE EKLUND

Yrs. of NHL service: 8
Born: Stockholm, Sweden; Mar. 22, 1963
Position: centre/left wing
Height: 5-10
Weight: 175
Uniform no.: 9
Shoots: left

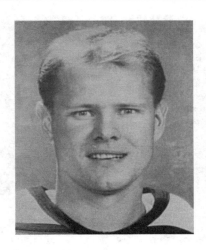

Career statistics:

GP	G	A	TP	PIM
541	117	318	435	99

1991-92 statistics:

GP	G	A	TP	+/-	PIM	PP	SH	GW	GT	S	PCT
51	7	16	23	0	4	1	2	1	0	74	9.5

1992-93 statistics:

GP	G	A	TP	+/-	PIM	PP	SH	GW	GT	S	PCT
55	11	38	49	+12	16	4	0	0	0	82	13.4

LAST SEASON

Missed 22 games with broken foot. Goals, assists and points improved over last season, which was also shortened by injury.

THE FINESSE GAME

Eklund is very alert and has a very quick first few steps to the puck. He doesn't like to hang on to the puck long. He doesn't rush or make forced moves, but his game is one of motion, passing, jumping into holes, getting the puck back and then looking for a receiver in front. Despite all his years in the NHL, he has never adapted to the shooter's mentality, and his first option is to look to make a play.

Eklund has a strong wrist shot, when he uses it. He does not crash in front of the net, but swoops in late to pick up rebounds. He is a two-way player and could be used in a strictly defensive role, but he has too many finesse skills to waste in that exclusive job.

Eklund is a very strong skater and has more of an impact than a player of his size might suggest.

THE PHYSICAL GAME

Eklund needs to play with forwards with some size. He does pay the price in front of the net on occasion, and also to protect the puck, but does not initiate much contact.

The Flyers use Eklund as a second-line power play centre. He is not effective down low because he does not go to the front of the net after setting up one of the points for a shot.

THE INTANGIBLES

Putting the playmaking Eklund with the finisher Eric Lindros was the Flyers' plan last season, but Lindros was hurt during training camp and his injuries resulted in the two playing barely a half-year together. Although he is starting to show some signs of brittleness, Eklund may again be paired with the wunderkind and should complement him well.

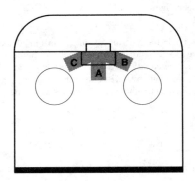

BRENT FEDYK

Yrs. of NHL service: 4
Born: Yorkton, Sask.; Mar. 8, 1967
Position: right wing
Height: 6-0
Weight: 195
Uniform no.: 18
Shoots: right

Career statistics:

GP	G	A	TP	PIM
236	45	70	115	136

1991-92 statistics:

GP	G	A	TP	+/-	PIM	PP	SH	GW	GT	S	PCT
61	5	8	13	-5	42	0	0	1	0	60	8.3

1992-93 statistics:

GP	G	A	TP	+/-	PIM	PP	SH	GW	GT	S	PCT
74	21	38	59	+14	48	4	1	2	2	167	12.6

LAST SEASON

Acquired from Detroit for a fourth-round draft choice. Career highs in goals, assists and points. Missed 10 games with fractured thumb and shoulder injury.

THE FINESSE GAME

While with the Red Wings, Fedyk was relegated to the job of a third-line checking winger. The Flyers don't have nearly as much depth as Detroit, and for much of the season Fedyk enjoyed life as Eric Lindros's left-hand man (well, right-handed but on the left wing) on the "Crazy Eights" line with Mark Recchi (so named for uniform numbers 18, 88 and 8, respectively).

Fedyk regained the scoring touch he had shown in the minors. His willingness to crash to the net for shots was coupled nicely with a strong wrist shot that he can use from the off wing.

Fedyk is strong defensively and can kill penalties. He is a shorthanded threat thanks to his reads in picking off passes.

THE PHYSICAL GAME

Fedyk doesn't use his body as well as he should, but when he does get to play with Lindros the big guy draws a lot of attention and opens up some ice. Hitting doesn't come naturally to Fedyk. He checks, but without much vigour.

THE INTANGIBLES

Fedyk made the most of his chance in Philadelphia. The key to any further development will be his consistency. He could earn a comfortable living as a 20- to 25-goal man and safety valve if the Crazy Eights line stays intact. Otherwise it's back to checking duty for him.

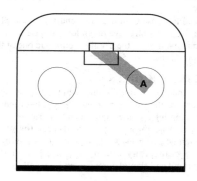

GARRY GALLEY

Yrs. of NHL service: 9
Born: Montreal, Que., Apr. 16, 1963
Position: left defense
Height: 6-0
Weight: 190
Uniform no.: 3
Shoots: left

Career statistics:

GP	G	A	TP	PIM
612	70	233	303	710

1991-92 statistics:

GP	G	A	TP	+/-	PIM	PP	SH	GW	GT	S	PCT
77	5	27	32	-2	117	3	0	1	0	125	4.0

1992-93 statistics:

GP	G	A	TP	+/-	PIM	PP	SH	GW	GT	S	PCT
83	13	49	62	+18	115	4	1	3	1	231	5.6

LAST SEASON

Led team defensemen in scoring with 24 points more than any previous season total. Missed one game with concussion. Played at least 70 games for fifth consecutive season, despite battling chronic fatigue syndrome. Tied for second on team in assists with career high. Goals career high. Tied for second on team in plus/minus. Finalist for Masterton Trophy.

THE FINESSE GAME

Galley has some nice finesse skills and has learned later in his career to add a physical element. The result was Philadelphia's No. 1 defenseman last season.

Galley is a puck mover. He follows the play and jumps into the attack. He has decent speed to keep up with the play, although he won't be rushing the puck himself. He is mobile and has a good shot which he can get away on the fly. He will pinch aggressively, but he's also quick enough to get back if there is a counterattack.

Galley is most vulnerable to outside speed. Last year we attributed that to him playing on his off side, but when the Flyers moved him back to his natural position on the left side he still struggled with his angles.

Galley works well on the power play. His lateral movement allows him to slide away from the point to the middle of the blue line, and he keeps his shots low. He is a smart player, and his experience shows.

THE PHYSICAL GAME

Galley is not that big and strong (especially with the illness that wore away at him during the season), so he has to be cautious in how he apportions his energy. When he does grind, he doesn't stop the play right away, but continues for a little while.

Galley has a quick stick and uses a sweep and poke check well. He will also get a little chippy now and then, just to keep people guessing.

THE INTANGIBLES

Galley is a leader and character person. He learned the physical game well in his years with the Bruins, but since coming to the Flyers he has emerged from the shadow of Ray Bourque and made the most of his added ice time. Galley is a media favourite for his honest and thoughtful interviews. Teammates and coaches like him even more for his intensity and sacrifice.

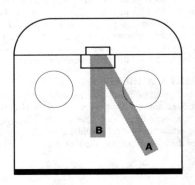

GREG HAWGOOD

Yrs. of NHL service: 3
Born: Edmonton, Alta.; Aug. 10, 1968
Position: left defense
Height: 5-10
Weight: 190
Uniform no.: 20
Shoots: left

Career statistics:

GP	G	A	TP	PIM
229	40	98	138	262

1991-92 statistics:

GP	G	A	TP	+/-	PIM	PP	SH	GW	GT	S	PCT
20	2	11	13	+22	22	0	0	0	0	24	8.3

1992-93 statistics:

GP	G	A	TP	+/-	PIM	PP	SH	GW	GT	S	PCT
69	11	35	46	-8	74	7	0	1	0	138	8.0

LAST SEASON

Acquired from Edmonton with Josef Beranek for Brian Benning. Assists and points at career highs.

THE FINESSE GAME

A mere slip of a lad, Hawgood is a power play specialist in the Norm Maciver mode, but he also does a fair job defensively.

Hawgood is fleet and mobile. He can rush with the puck, gain the blue line with speed, and if he can't make a play there will throw it into the corner and follow the puck in deep. He isn't very big, so he has to rely on his speed to get him there ahead of a crunching defender. He always seems to be alert to who is on the ice against him, and will take his chances against bigger but less agile defensemen.

Hawgood is a natural on the power play. He will glide along the blue line with the puck looking for a man down low or to receive a pass to one-time. He always seems to hit the right person with his pass. He moves the puck quickly and puts life into the power play.

THE PHYSICAL GAME

Hawgood had his best season playing for the Bruins (1988-89), an organization that demands even its lightweight players pay the price defensively. That part of Hawgood's game has vanished. He doesn't have to knock people onto Broad Street to be an effective hitter. His skating ability allows him to take the body, but he doesn't do it consistently enough.

THE INTANGIBLES

Hawgood is a No. 5 or 6 defenseman at this stage, with limited use as a power play point man. He has to add a few more facets to his game to be a complete enough defenseman to get a regular shift. This guy can rack up the points if he gets the ice time.

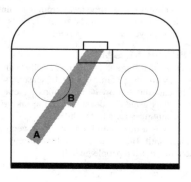

ERIC LINDROS

Yrs. of NHL service: 1
Born: London, Ont.; Feb. 28, 1973
Position: centre
Height: 6-5
Weight: 227
Uniform no.: 88
Shoots: right

Career statistics:

GP	G	A	TP	PIM
61	41	34	75	147

1992-93 statistics:

GP	G	A	TP	+/-	PIM	PP	SH	GW	GT	S	PCT
61	41	34	75	+28	147	8	1	5	1	180	22.8

LAST SEASON

Missed 23 games with knee injuries. Third among NHL rookies in scoring. Second among NHL rookies in goals. Tied for fourth among NHL rookies in power play goals. Led team regulars and all NHL rookies in shooting percentage. Led team and second among NHL rookies in plus/minus.

THE FINESSE GAME

Every night he plays, all eyes are on Lindros, and what an eyeful he gives them. Physically, his game is just about flawless.

Over an 84-game schedule, Lindros's statistics projected to 58-46-104, not close to Teemu Selanne's astonishing rookie numbers but still mighty impressive for a player who carried the burden of expectation on his broad back. More importantly, the Flyers were 7-14-2 with Lindros sidelined, and a healthy Eric might well have meant a playoff berth for the Flyers.

Lindros may be the best big skater the game has ever seen. He isn't the least bit clumsy, gets up to speed in just a few strides and can hurdle a defenseman to avoid a check, keeping his balance and the puck.

Lindros works for his goals. He is not a natural goal-scorer rifling shots from the top of the circles, but drives down low and intimidates the defense and the goalie. He can take a pass with his soft hands and rifle a wrist or snap shot. He has strong arms for his shots and may roof the puck as well as anyone in the league. None of this comes easily — Lindros has worked hard on his shots, and the results show.

He is a better finisher than playmaker, but he can make accurate passes off his forehand or backhand. He does just about everything well except kill penalties, but there are enough teammates to handle that.

Lindros is good on face-offs because he simply overpowers his opposite number.

THE PHYSICAL GAME

Lindros doesn't need to score to be effective. The glamour and glory of opening the paper to read his stats in the box score was a siren call, but on those nights when Lindros is being effectively shadowed, he has to learn to help his team in other ways instead of sulking.

There are very few defensemen and no opposing centres able to match up to Lindros physically. His body slams make other players tentative. Instead of concerning themselves first with what to do with the puck, they are bracing themselves for the Lindros hit, and the puck goes bye-bye.

Lindros put on weight while he was sidelined with the knee injury, had to play his way back into shape, then finished like a freight train.

THE INTANGIBLES

Lindros's off-ice involvement in a fracas at a bar — leading to a criminal complaint and the unforgettable sight of the hulking rookie in handcuffs — underlined just how vulnerable this 20-year-old truly is. This is the future captain of the Flyers, but right now he could benefit from some guidance (think of Mark Messier's influence on a young Brian Leetch in his Norris Trophy year). Lindros needs somebody to give him a shove, and we don't mean a woman in a bar.

A 60-goal, 100-point season is just about guaranteed. One question: how could Lindros not be a finalist for the Calder Trophy, considering what he was able to accomplish in only three-quarters of a season?

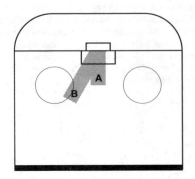

RYAN MCGILL

Yrs. of NHL service: 1
Born: Sherwood, Alta.; Feb. 28, 1969
Position: right defense
Height: 6-2
Weight: 197
Uniform no.: 27
Shoots: right

Career statistics:

GP	G	A	TP	PIM
81	3	12	15	258

1991-92 statistics:

GP	G	A	TP	+/-	PIM	PP	SH	GW	GT	S	PCT
9	0	2	2	+1	20	0	0	0	0	15	0.0

1992-93 statistics:

GP	G	A	TP	+/-	PIM	PP	SH	GW	GT	S	PCT
72	3	10	13	+9	238	0	0	0	0	68	4.4

LAST SEASON
First NHL season. Led team in PIM.

THE FINESSE GAME
McGill, drafted in 1987, finally played his first full season in the NHL, and the flaws in his game were considerable. The fault was not with McGill but with his supporting cast.

McGill is a strong skater with fair mobility. He isn't very fast, but compared to usual defense partner Terry Carkner, he's Seattle Slew.

He seems aware enough of his limitations to play a conservative game, and he can be an effective player in a narrowly defined role.

He has a nasty slapshot. He needs time to get it away, but when he does there are few souls brave enough to want to block it.

THE PHYSICAL GAME
McGill has a strong presence on the ice. He's a mean hitter and makes opponents pay the price in front of the net. He has to have a physical impact to stick in the NHL, and he knows it.

THE INTANGIBLES
If the Flyers weren't hurting so much on defense (having given up Steve Duchesne and Kerry Huffman in the Eric Lindros deal, and losing Mark Howe to free agency), McGill would have been been in Hershey, or at most, a No. 5 or 6 defenseman. Instead, he was pushed to be part of the team's second pairing, and it's too much for McGill to handle. At least he gives it a game try every night.

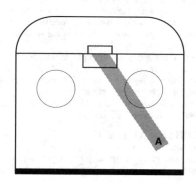

MARK RECCHI

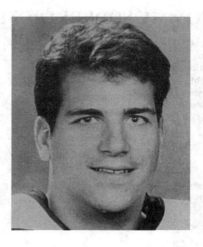

Yrs. of NHL service: 4
Born: Kamloops, B.C.; Feb. 1, 1968
Position: right wing
Height: 5-9
Weight: 185
Uniform no.: 8
Shoots: left

Career statistics:

GP	G	A	TP	PIM
331	167	235	402	283

1991-92 statistics:

GP	G	A	TP	+/-	PIM	PP	SH	GW	GT	S	PCT
80	43	54	97	-21	96	20	1	5	1	210	20.5

1992-93 statistics:

GP	G	A	TP	+/-	PIM	PP	SH	GW	GT	S	PCT
84	53	70	123	+1	95	15	4	6	0	274	19.3

LAST SEASON

Led team in goals and points with career highs. Second season with 100 or more points. First season with 50 or more goals. Led team in assists with second-highest total of career. Led team in shots and power play goals and tied for team lead in shorthanded goals. Second on team in game-winners. Second among team regulars in shooting percentage.

THE FINESSE GAME

Recchi is a small package with a lot of firepower. He may be the best small player in the game (we can think of only Theo Fleury and Ray Ferraro as challengers). Recchi is feisty and is a relentless worker in the offensive zone. He busts into open ice, finding the holes almost before they open. He excels at the give-and-go, and with the extra ice afforded him by playing alongside Eric Lindros, he enjoyed his best season.

He has a dangerous shot from the off wing. While he's not as dynamic as Maurice Richard, he likes to use the Richard cut-back and rifle a wrist shot back across. It's heavy, it's on net, and it requires no backswing. Recchi will follow his shot to the net for a rebound. He can make a play as well. He has excellent hands, vision and anticipation for any scoring opportunity.

Recchi has worked hard to improve his defense and is getting better, although it is still the weakest part of his game. He kills penalties well because he hounds the point men aggressively and knocks the puck out of the zone. Then he heads off on a breakaway or forces the defender to pull him down.

He isn't a pretty skater but always keeps his feet moving. While other players are coasting, Recchi's blades are in motion. He is ready to spring into any play. He seems like a puck magnet because he is always going where the puck is.

THE PHYSICAL GAME

Recchi gets chopped at because he doesn't hang around the perimeter. He accepts the punishment to get the job done, but he gets a lot more freedom with Lindros. He is a solid player, with a low centre of gravity, and is tough to knock off the puck. He is remarkably durable for the style of game he plays.

THE INTANGIBLES

Recchi is a gamer. He had a remarkable season before Lindros arrived, and this looks like the beginning of a beautiful partnership. Now if the Flyers can get a second line to take some of the pressure off the top trio, the sky's the limit.

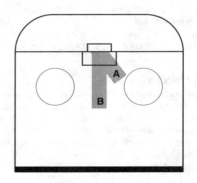

TOMMY SODERSTROM

Yrs. of NHL service: 1
Born: Stockholm, Sweden; July 17, 1969
Position: goaltender
Height: 5-9
Weight: 165
Uniform no.: 30
Catches: left

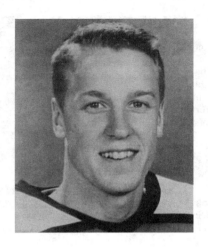

Career statistics:

GP	MINS	GA	SO	GAA	A	PIM
44	2512	143	5	3.42	2	4

1992-93 statistics:

GP	MINS	GAA	W	L	T	SO	GA	S	SAPCT	PIM
44	2512	3.42	20	17	6	5	143	1327	.892	4

LAST SEASON

First NHL season. Missed playing time with surgeries to correct a heart abnormality. Second in NHL in shutouts.

THE PHYSICAL GAME

Soderstrom has a peculiar habit of scrunching himself under the crossbar and deep into his net, a position he assumes during face-offs anywhere from centre ice to deep in his zone. On Soderstrom's bad nights, it seems that he never untucks himself. Very few European goalies have succeeded in the NHL because of their tendency to stay deep in the net. It's a necessary tactic in international play because of the wider ice surfaces, but in the NHL it is a fatal flaw. He is going to have to learn to come out of the net (as did the late Pelle Lindbergh, one of the few European goalies to excel in the NHL).

Soderstrom is very quick. He is a reflex goalie. With experience, he will learn the NHL is a shooter's league, and he has to be more effective with his rebounds. He gets down with his pads low, to take away the low part of the net (where most goals are scored), but then he dives face-first for the puck after the save. If the Flyers' defense improves and helps him out in clearing rebounds, he can continue to play his style. Otherwise he is at the mercy of a team that is willing to go to the net hard.

Soderstrom's style is all or nothing, which explains the five shutouts. He will have nights when he is just spectacular.

THE MENTAL GAME

Soderstrom assumed way too much blame for some of the Flyers' losses. While he did have the occasional bad night that might have cost his team a win, he also played splendidly behind a team defense that was decimated by the trade for Eric Lindros and had been weak to begin with. How did Soderstrom get five shutouts with this crew?

THE INTANGIBLES

Soderstrom is tough. He underwent five medical procedures during the season and was scheduled for more during the off-season. The adjustment that he needs to his game are slight, and with just a little technical tinkering he will be an effective NHL goalie.

DIMITRI YUSHKEVICH

Yrs. of NHL service: 1
Born: Cherepovets, Russia; Nov. 19, 1971
Position: right defense
Height: 5-11
Weight: 187
Uniform no.: 2
Shoots: left

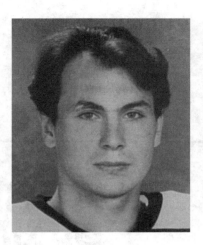

Career statistics:

GP	G	A	TP	PIM
82	5	27	32	71

1992-93 statistics:

GP	G	A	TP	+/-	PIM	PP	SH	GW	GT	S	PCT
82	5	27	32	+12	71	1	0	1	0	155	3.2

LAST SEASON
First NHL season.

THE FINESSE GAME
Yushkevich is a terrific skater in all facets. He is strong and well balanced; he can move laterally, pivot and put on a burst of short speed or sustain a rush the length of the rink; he has the stamina to play all night long. Occasionally he can be beaten with outside speed, but it takes a pretty fast and strong skater to do it.

Positionally, Yushkevich plays a smart game. He is intelligent and poised, and he gets the crunch-time exposure because he is capable of making the big plays, offensively and defensively.

He can work the point on the power play, using his hard, low shot or moving the puck around.

Yushkevich has all the skills but is also willing to play a grinding game. He follows the play up well and gets involved in the attack. He puts so much on his shots that defensemen have been known to limp off the ice after blocking his *wrist* shots from the point.

THE PHYSICAL GAME
Yushkevich has a nasty streak and will step in to protect his teammates. He was the first Flyer to retaliate when partner Garry Galley was levelled by a Nick Kypreos cheap shot in a meaningless game against Hartford. Yushkevich is an enthusiastic hitter and likes to wade in and use his body to win puck battles. His hits are take-outs, because the hittee doesn't get back into the play. He is very annoying to play against. Not quite a Broad Street Bully, but he's at least a Broad Street Brat.

THE INTANGIBLES
Yushkevich had an impressive first season and carried that through to the World Championships, where he was named the best defenseman in the tournament for gold medallist Russia. He will only get better with ex-perience. Now that he has that first year in, he can't be satisfied, but must want to improve.

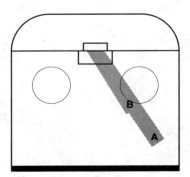

PITTSBURGH
PENGUINS

TOM BARRASSO

Yrs. of NHL service: 10
Born: Boston, Mass.; Mar. 31, 1965
Position: goaltender
Height: 6-3
Weight: 211
Uniform no.: 35
Catches: right

Career statistics:

GP	MINS	GA	SO	GAA	A	PIM
502	28,948	1655	19	3.43	39	333

1991-92 statistics:

GP	MINS	GAA	W	L	T	SO	GA	S	SAPCT	PIM
57	3329	3.53	25	22	9	2	196	1702	.885	30

1992-93 statistics:

GP	MINS	GAA	W	L	T	SO	GA	S	SAPCT	PIM
63	3702	3.01	43	14	5	4	186	1885	.901	24

LAST SEASON

Led NHL goalies in assists. Led NHL in wins with career high. Third in NHL in GAA. Fourth in NHL in save percentage. Career-best GAA. Finalist for Vezina Trophy. Missed nine games with chicken pox.

THE PHYSICAL GAME

One of the most impressive things about Barrasso is that though he is often on his knees, he is almost never on his side. He might be the best in the league at recovering from going down, and will be back on his skates with his glove in position for the next shot.

Barrasso loves to handle the puck, and he's like a third defenseman in both his willingness to leave the crease and his ability to pass. He is a good skater who is able to get to and control a lot of pucks that most goalies wouldn't dare try to reach. Staying on his feet more (a fundamental that he has improved on with experience) allows him to make the most of his skating skills. Most of the time he will use the boards for his passes, rather than make a risky play up the middle, but every so often he is vulnerable to the interception.

Because of Barrasso's range, teams have to adapt their attack. Hard dump-ins won't work, because he will stop them behind the net and wing the puck right back out for an alert counterattack by his teammates. Since he comes out around the post to his right better than his left, teams have to aim soft dumps to his left, making him more hesitant about making the play and giving the forecheckers time to get in on him.

Barrasso's lone weakness appears to be shots low on the glove side — at least that's an area the Islanders successfully exploited in their playoff shocker. He is also prone to five-hole shots.

THE MENTAL GAME

Barrasso's confidence borders on arrogance, and it's visible from the way he carries himself on the ice. He is possibly the best big-save goalie in the NHL. If asked, most scouts would name him as the goalie they would pick to play a Game 7.

The flip side of this is that he doesn't think he gets the credit he deserves (we don't think he does, either), and he gets whiny and petulant if, for example, he thinks he should have been one of the three stars of the game and isn't. This is petty minutiae for a goaltender of his stature.

Barrasso has good anticipation and concentration, almost a sixth sense of what the shooter is going to do. He has to be beaten because he seldom beats himself.

THE INTANGIBLES

Barrasso was on the top of the hockey world after two consecutive Cups. Now that he and his teammates failed in their bid for a threepeat, the pressure will be on to regain their status. Barrasso is still at the top of his game, still the best goaltender in the NHL and, like the Penguins, he'll stay there until he is dethroned.

RON FRANCIS

Yrs. of NHL service: 12
Born: Sault Ste. Marie, Ont.; Mar. 1, 1963
Position: centre
Height: 6-2
Weight: 200
Uniform no.: 10
Shoots: left

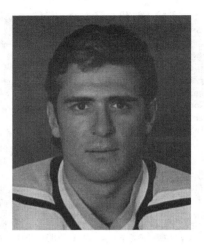

Career statistics:

GP	G	A	TP	PIM
882	311	675	986	657

1991-92 statistics:

GP	G	A	TP	+/-	PIM	PP	SH	GW	GT	S	PCT
70	21	33	54	-7	30	5	1	2	1	121	17.4

1992-93 statistics:

GP	G	A	TP	+/-	PIM	PP	SH	GW	GT	S	PCT
84	24	76	100	+6	68	9	2	4	0	215	11.2

LAST SEASON

One of four 100-point scorers on team. Reached 100-point mark for second time in career. Fourth on team in scoring. Second on team in assists with career high. Marked 12th consecutive season with 20 or more goals. One of two Penguins to play all 84 games.

THE FINESSE GAME

Francis may have had the quietest 100-point season in league history. The best two-way player in the NHL, he played defense first, yet stepped into the No. 1 role when Mario Lemieux was sidelined with his battle with Hodgkin's disease. When Lemieux returned, Francis slipped right back to the No. 2 line.

Francis is excellent on face-offs, allowing goalie Tom Barrasso the freedom to freeze pucks if there is even the slightest chance of a dangerous scramble around the net. Francis wins about 80 percent of his draws and does so cleanly, with quick hands.

Those same hands enable him to turn from checker to playmaker in an instant. He is smart in his defensive role, anticipating passes and blocking shots. Once Francis controls the puck, he can either lead a rush, start a teammate on a breakout and jump up into the play, or transform a turnover into a scoring chance.

Francis doesn't have a screamingly hard shot, nor is he a flashy player. He works from the centre of the ice, between the circles, and has a quick release on a one-timer. He can kill penalties or work the point on the power play with equal effectiveness.

THE PHYSICAL GAME

Francis is not a big, imposing hitter, but he will use his body to get the job done. He will bump and grind and go into the trenches. Back on defense, he can function as a third defenseman; on offense, you will find him going into the corners or heading for the front of the net for tips and rebounds. Francis is a strong and balanced skater with quickness. He doesn't have a pretty stride — in fact, it's pretty choppy — but he gets to where he has to be.

THE INTANGIBLES

Poise and professionalism have always marked Francis's career, and he has only enhanced that reputation with the way he has conducted himself in his three seasons in Pittsburgh. He has never gotten the credit he deserves because he lacks the charisma of so many other Penguins stars, but without his acquisition from the Whalers in 1991, the Penguins probably wouldn't have won a single Cup, let alone two.

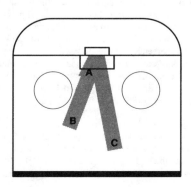

JAROMIR JAGR

Yrs. of NHL service: 3
Born: Kladno, Czechoslovakia; Feb. 15, 1972
Position: right wing
Height: 6-2
Weight: 208
Uniform no.: 68
Shoots: left

Career statistics:

GP	G	A	TP	PIM
231	93	127	220	137

1991-92 statistics:

GP	G	A	TP	+/-	PIM	PP	SH	GW	GT	S	PCT
70	32	37	69	+12	34	4	0	4	0	194	16.5

1992-93 statistics:

GP	G	A	TP	+/-	PIM	PP	SH	GW	GT	S	PCT
81	34	60	94	+30	61	10	1	9	0	242	14.0

LAST SEASON

Fourth on team in scoring with career high in points. Goals and assists career highs. Production has increased in every season. Second on team in game-winning goals. Missed three games with separated shoulder.

THE FINESSE GAME

Brilliant and erratic, Jagr is a hockey player who lives and loves to play the game. He is one of the most dynamic players on a glamorous team. His long hair flowing out from beneath his helmet, Jagr is poetry is motion with his beautifully effortless skating style.

Jagr has Lemieux-like reach, and he can control the puck at high tempo while he's gliding and swooping. He is an almost unstoppable breakaway shooter (although he was thwarted by Washington's Don Beaupre in his lone penalty shot try of the season). Jagr will fake the backhand and go to his forehand in a flash. He a powerful skater as well, and when he is inclined, he will drag a defender with him to the net and push off a strong one-handed shot. He has a big slapshot and can drive it on the fly or off a pass with a one-timer.

One of the reasons for Jagr's wicked shots are his barely legal sticks. He gets them illegally curved on order from the factory, and sharp-eyed opposing coaches (or their equipment managers) should keep a lookout for those he hasn't doctored to NHL specifications. The more severe the curve, though, the less control Jagr has of a backhand shot that could be a more effective weapon with a straighter blade.

THE PHYSICAL GAME

Jagr can be intimidated, and that is one of the worst-kept secrets in the NHL. The Islanders made him a target in their Patrick Division Semifinal upset, and Jagr had a very quiet series as a result of the attention. He plays far too soft for a player of his size.

Jagr gets very selfish with the puck when there is extra attention. Instead of trying to find his teammates — who are getting more open ice because of the focus on Jagr — he develops tunnel vision.

THE INTANGIBLES

Jagr is still only 21 years old and has a lot of growing up to do. Two seasons ago, we predicted a 50-goal year for Jagr in "the next season or two." There was more pressure on Jagr to produce last season because of Lemieux's illness, and he didn't respond as well as he should have. We'll chalk it up to a learning experience and predict he will get even better this season.

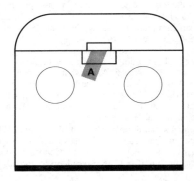

MARIO LEMIEUX

Yrs. of NHL service: 9
Born: Montreal, Que.; Oct. 5, 1965
Position: centre
Height: 6-4
Weight: 210
Uniform no.: 66
Shoots: right

Career statistics:

GP	G	A	TP	PIM
577	477	697	1174	586

1991-92 statistics:

GP	G	A	TP	+/-	PIM	PP	SH	GW	GT	S	PCT
64	44	87	131	+27	94	12	4	5	1	249	17.7

1992-93 statistics:

GP	G	A	TP	+/-	PIM	PP	SH	GW	GT	S	PCT
60	69	91	160	+55	38	16	6	10	0	286	24.1

LAST SEASON

Despite missing 24 games with various ailments — the most serious and lengthy being treatment for Hodgkin's disease — Lemieux won his fourth scoring title in six seasons. Won Hart Trophy for second time in career. Won Masterton Trophy. Third in NHL in goals with third-highest mark of career. Third season with 60 or more goals. Led NHL in plus/minus. Eighth season with 100 or more points. Led team in goals, assists, points, game-winning goals and short-handed goals. Tied for third in NHL in shorthanded goals. Third on team in power play goals.

THE FINESSE GAME

This guy had cancer. Think about that and then consider the kind of season Lemieux had.

As often as we've seen Lemieux play, he always seems to have some new move ready to dazzle and amaze, as if he spends his idle hours reinventing the game. Lemieux is one of those rare athletes who can seize a game by the throat, as if to say, "Enough fooling around. I want to win this thing." Then he goes out and does what has to be done, whether it is breaking a goalie's heart with a shorthanded breakaway or calmly sneaking into the slot to bury a power play rebound.

Lemieux has such tremendous presence on the ice that the defense has to back off him. Step up to challenge Lemieux, and he is by you in a flash, pulling the puck through a defender's legs with his huge reach. Back off him, and he will use the open ice to wheel and send a perfect pass to a breaking teammate.

His shots are accurate, and he never telegraphs where the shot is going, which makes him nearly unbeatable on a breakaway. With his long, strong reach, he can flick off a shot when he looks out of position and off balance. The goalie will position himself for Lemieux's body, but the shot comes from so far away that the netminder is at his mercy.

Lemieux can do everything at high tempo. He is an excellent skater, and his vision of the ice is so acute he seems to be watching from one of those overhead cameras hanging from the centre ice scoreboard. He knows where everyone is and where they're going. This makes him as dangerous killing penalties as he is on the power play.

THE PHYSICAL GAME

Between therapy for Hodgkin's disease and an ailing back, it's a wonder Lemieux had any body left at all. Forgive him for not going into the corners and hanging around the red line for breakout passes, because when the game is on the line Lemieux will do what has to be done to win. He was so battered at playoff time that he couldn't even take face-offs, so we will grant him clemency for not bodying people all over the ice. When he is healthy, he is the dominant player in the NHL.

THE INTANGIBLES

Lemieux's accomplishments of the past season could only have been capped by a third Stanley Cup. He didn't have that in him, and you have to wonder what will be next for the big guy who has been through so much. He is simply the premier athlete of his sport, perhaps the best performer in any pro sport at his peak. Yes, Lemieux whines and dives and maybe loses some sportsmanship points, but when a game is on the line, he is a gifted and gutsy player. If he could have stayed healthy last season, he was on a pace to obliterate Wayne Gretzky's single-season scoring records.

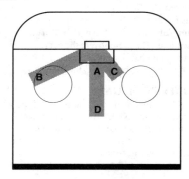

SHAWN MCEACHERN

Yrs. of NHL service: 1
Born: Waltham, Mass.; Feb. 28, 1969
Position: centre/left wing
Height: 6-1
Weight: 180
Uniform no.: 15
Shoots: left

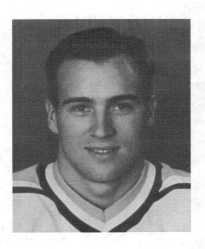

Career statistics:

GP	G	A	TP	PIM
99	28	37	65	46

1991-92 statistics:

GP	G	A	TP	+/-	PIM	PP	SH	GW	GT	S	PCT
15	0	4	4	0	0	0	0	0	0	14	0.0

1992-93 statistics:

GP	G	A	TP	+/-	PIM	PP	SH	GW	GT	S	PCT
84	28	33	61	+21	46	7	0	6	0	196	14.3

LAST SEASON

First NHL season. Tied for fourth among NHL rookies in goals. Second among NHL rookies in game-winning goals. Fourth among NHL rookies in plus/minus. One of two Penguins to play all 84 games.

THE FINESSE GAME

McEachern has dazzling speed that shines even on a Penguins team full of strong skaters. He was a bit of a longshot to make the NHL (selected 110th overall in 1987 out of Boston University), and even after joining the Penguins after the 1992 Olympics there was some doubt whether he would be able to crack the Penguins' line-up. He simply forced his way in.

McEachern can shift speeds and direction smoothly without losing control of the puck. His playmaking instincts are excellent. He played centre in college, although he played mostly left wing last season. He hides the puck while stickhandling and makes quick, short, soft passes.

McEachern is a very accurate shooter with a hard wrist shot. He also has a quick release on his slapshot.

THE PHYSICAL GAME

Generally an open-ice player, he will also pursue the puck with some diligence in the attacking zone. He is light, and though he can sometimes build up momentum with his speed for a solid bump, he loses most of the close-in battles for the puck.

THE INTANGIBLES

McEachern is a diligent worker who has overcome long odds to get to the NHL. With his skating ability as a strong foundation, and good hockey sense to go with it, he should only improve off his solid rookie season.

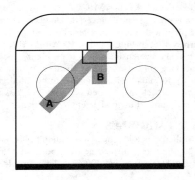

JOE MULLEN

Yrs. of NHL service: 12
Born: New York, N.Y.; Feb. 26, 1957
Position: right wing
Height: 5-9
Weight: 180
Uniform no.: 7
Shoots: right

Career statistics:

GP	G	A	TP	PIM
842	433	486	919	246

1991-92 statistics:

GP	G	A	TP	+/-	PIM	PP	SH	GW	GT	S	PCT
77	42	45	87	+12	30	14	0	4	1	226	18.6

1992-93 statistics:

GP	G	A	TP	+/-	PIM	PP	SH	GW	GT	S	PCT
72	33	37	70	+19	70	9	3	3	2	175	18.9

LAST SEASON

Missed 11 games with knee injury. Recorded at least 30 goals for ninth time in career. Third on team in shooting percentage.

THE FINESSE GAME

Players who last long in the NHL usually do so because of their skating ability, and Mullen has lost little of his edge (or his edges) in this department through the seasons and despite knee problems. He doesn't have straightaway speed and is an unlikely candidate to win a one-on-one rush in open ice. He doesn't have a long reach, but he will get the jump on defenders with his deceptive quickness.

Mullen's shot is sneaky, too. He hides the puck with his body and uses his patience with the puck to create space for his linemates. He is a terrific give-and-go player. He will hit a teammate with a smart pass, giving that player sufficient time to manoeuvre, then head to open ice for a return pass. He has a great head for the power play. He'll dart in and out of openings around the net, and he's tough to knock off his feet because of his balance.

Mullen has quick feet and can kick pucks up onto his stick and get the shot away in an instant.

THE PHYSICAL GAME

Mullen is not a physical player, due to his small size, but he plays with a grit and determination that should embarrass a lot of bigger fellas. He will sacrifice his body to make a defensive play or to pursue the puck in the attacking zone. He is smart about it, though, and won't try to make noise when the more intelligent choice is to back off. Mullen is a very quick skater who keeps himself in good defensive position.

THE INTANGIBLES

First Mullen was told Americans couldn't play hockey. Then he was informed he was too small. Now, more than 800 games and 400 goals later, people are trying to tell him that he's too old (at 36). True, the injuries are getting harder to avoid, but we think that a well-spotted Mullen still has another 30-goal season in him. Personally, we would love to see him join the 500 Club. Few players are as respected for what they've overcome (learning hockey on roller skates in Manhattan's Hell's Kitchen) and what they've achieved (three Stanley Cups) as Mullen.

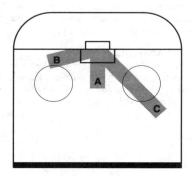

LARRY MURPHY

Yrs. of NHL service: 13
Born: Scarborough, Ont.; Mar. 8, 1961
Position: right defense
Height: 6-2
Weight: 210
Uniform no.: 55
Shoots: right

Career statistics:

GP	G	A	TP	PIM
1020	203	631	834	834

1991-92 statistics:

GP	G	A	TP	+/-	PIM	PP	SH	GW	GT	S	PCT
77	21	56	77	+33	50	7	2	3	0	206	10.2

1992-93 statistics:

GP	G	A	TP	+/-	PIM	PP	SH	GW	GT	S	PCT
83	22	63	85	+45	73	6	2	2	0	230	9.6

LAST SEASON

Third among NHL defensemen in scoring. Second on team and in NHL in plus/minus. Led team defensemen in scoring. Finalist for Norris Trophy. Missed one game with back injury. Played in his 1,000th NHL game.

THE FINESSE GAME

Murphy is big and nimble, and he was an underrated part of the Penguins' success. So strong was his game that other team's game plans usually involved keeping the puck away from his side of the ice, to prevent him from gearing up behind his goal line.

Murphy is not the offensive force he was early in his career, only because he has concentrated on his defense and has become a better all-around player as a result. He can either rush the puck out of his zone or make the nice first pass that gives his team the jump on the opponents. Murphy and goalie Tom Barrasso have excellent communication, and the puck frequently comes out of the Penguin zone as sharply as it came in, thanks to those two.

Murphy is smart and poised. He will not force bad passes up the middle but will use the boards if that's the safest play. His pinches are well timed, and he has the reach to prevent a lot of pucks from getting by him at the point. His shot selection is intelligent. He loves to shoot, but he won't fire blindly. He will use a low wrist shot rather than a big slap to keep the puck on net. Murphy's positional play is where he has shown the most improvement. He reads plays well and seldom seems to be floundering around on the ice.

THE PHYSICAL GAME

Murphy does not play a physical game. He will bump his man in front but doesn't make strong takeouts. He prefers to position his body and force the shooter to make a play while he himself goes for the puck or stick. It is the weakest part of his game, and is just adequate.

THE INTANGIBLES

Murphy finally started getting some of the attention he deserves last season (witness his finish in the top three for the Norris Trophy). At 32, he sees a lot of ice time, and if the Penguins don't secure another top defenseman, he could start wearing down quickly during the season. But he's still one of the best two-way defensemen in the NHL.

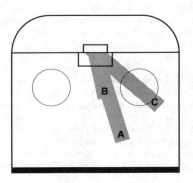

MARKUS NASLUND

Yrs. of NHL service: 0
Born: Härnösand, Sweden; July 30, 1973
Position: left wing
Height: 5-11
Weight: 174
Uniform no.: na
Shoots: left

1992-93 Swedish statistics:

GP	G	A	TP	PIM
28	18	10	28	47

LAST SEASON

Played for MoDo in Swedish League. First-round draft pick (16th overall) of Penguins in 1991.

THE FINESSE GAME

Naslund is a sniper, pure and simple. He has excellent slap and wrist shots, and can score in just about every way imaginable, including the backhand in tight. He has quick, quick hands and is extremely effective in tight around the net.

Naslund is a good skater who can stop and start quickly. He handles the puck in traffic and has outstanding hockey sense. He finds the openings and hits his man, moving the puck quickly.

Scouts have noted that Naslund dedicated last season to becoming more of a complete player. He can kill penalties and is well on his way to becoming a dominant player. The thought of Naslund and Mario Lemieux on the same line might convince some goalies to find another line of work.

THE PHYSICAL GAME

Naslund is not a big hitter, but he will take the body and is capable of playing an in-your-face style that can be very annoying to play against. He received 33 PIM in the World Junior Tournament. He has a reputation for having a temper, and opponents will surely challenge him physically to sucker him into taking bad penalties. Naslund will have to walk that fine line between maintaining discipline and standing up for himself.

THE INTANGIBLES

Naslund led all goal scorers at the World Junior Championships and was named to the all-tournament team, drawing raves from scouts who had turned out to gape at his linemate Peter Forsberg. Naslund could have joined the Penguins last season but fulfilled his commitments to his Swedish team. He should step right in and not look out of place. This could be the Year of the Swede in the Calder Trophy race between Naslund and Forsberg, who were born only 10 days apart and have played on the same line since they were 15 years old.

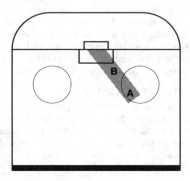

MIKE RAMSEY

Yrs. of NHL service: 14
Born: Minneapolis, Minn.; Dec. 3, 1960
Position: left defense
Height: 6-3
Weight: 195
Uniform no.: 6
Shoots: left

Career statistics:

GP	G	A	TP	PIM
923	74	258	332	932

1991-92 statistics:

GP	G	A	TP	+/-	PIM	PP	SH	GW	GT	S	PCT
66	3	14	17	+8	67	0	0	1	0	55	5.5

1992-93 statistics:

GP	G	A	TP	+/-	PIM	PP	SH	GW	GT	S	PCT
45	3	10	13	+17	28	0	0	0	0	35	8.6

LAST SEASON

Acquired from Buffalo for Bob Errey. Missed 23 games with injuries. Games played lowest total for full NHL season.

THE FINESSE GAME

Ramsey is a stay-at-home defenseman, a throwback in this era of offensive specialists. No run-and-gun for Ramsey, thanks. He'll stay back in his zone and hurl his body fearlessly at shots. He is one of the better "goalies" among the league's defense corps for his shot-blocking abilities.

Ramsey played most of his career in Buffalo, where the building was smaller than regulation and his limited skating range wasn't as much of a factor. With the trade to the more expansive Pittsburgh ice surface, Ramsey's slow-footedness is more glaring. He will probably be even more defensive, if that's possible, with the Penguins.

Ramsey does not get involved in the offense much. He will jump up into the play if it is safe, but his shots will be limited to slaps or long wrists from the left point.

THE PHYSICAL GAME

Ramsey is an aggressive hitter. He has a long reach and can get a piece of faster skaters, which makes it hard to beat him to the outside even though he isn't terribly nimble. Injuries have taken their toll, but he is still a fearless checker and shot-blocker who will make the sacrifice first and think about the consequences later.

THE INTANGIBLES

Never a brisk skater to begin with, Ramsey has continued to show signs of slowing even more (last season he was one of three players — along with Neal Broten and Dave Christian — left in the NHL from the 1980 U.S. Olympic team).

He remains a character player on the ice and a classy athlete off it, and could see another useful season as a No. 5 or 6 defenseman.

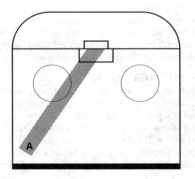

KJELL SAMUELSSON

Yrs. of NHL service: 7
Born: Tyngsryd, Sweden; Oct. 18, 1958
Position: right defense
Height: 6-6
Weight: 235
Uniform no.: 28
Shoots: right

Career statistics:

GP	G	A	TP	PIM
509	34	103	137	859

1991-92 statistics:

GP	G	A	TP	+/-	PIM	PP	SH	GW	GT	S	PCT
74	5	11	16	+1	110	0	0	1	0	91	5.5

1992-93 statistics:

GP	G	A	TP	+/-	PIM	PP	SH	GW	GT	S	PCT
63	3	6	9	+25	106	0	0	1	0	63	4.8

LAST SEASON

Missed 20 games due to injury and illness: broken foot (nine games), broken cheekbone (nine), bruised knee (one), and flu (one). Highest plus/minus rating among all NHL players with 10 points or fewer.

THE FINESSE GAME

Pittsburgh seems to have such an inordinate number of players with long reaches — Mario Lemieux, Mike Ramsey, Kevin Stevens and Kjell Samuelsson — that you have to wonder how opposing skaters ever find any room to move. Samuelsson does his best to make sure they don't. He has the wingspan of a condor and is strong with his long stick, so that he can control the puck dangling out miles away from his body after he has knocked it off the puck carrier's blade.

Samuelsson's enormous stride just eats up the ice. It doesn't look like he's moving fast, because he doesn't have to. He isn't very quick and doesn't get involved in the rush, but instead concentrates on his own zone. He makes the simple play, forcing the attacking player to the boards and taking him out of the play with a solid hit. He doesn't do much with the puck, just banking it off the boards or driving it deep. He won't be caught looking for the perfect play. He doesn't amass many points, or many minuses, with his ultraconservative style.

Samuelsson has a strong point shot but does not get it away very quickly. He won't be found deep, either, so don't expect to see him scrambling to get back into defensive position. He's already there.

THE PHYSICAL GAME

Samuelsson is a strong and nasty hitter for someone who looks so benign. In addition to using his body and powerful leg drive, he will rub his glove or elbow against an opponent's jaw or offer his stick for use as a dental device. He also clutches and grabs, but does it in a smart veteran way, hanging on just long enough to provoke irritation but not long enough to merit a penalty. He will also yap to distraction.

He will pay the physical price to block shots and clear his crease.

THE INTANGIBLES

Samuelsson has great poise for pressure situations. His contributions are overlooked on a team of thoroughbreds, but he is a workhorse night in and night out.

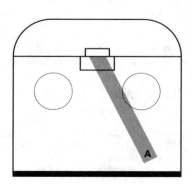

ULF SAMUELSSON

Yrs. of NHL service: 9
Born: Fagersta, Sweden; Mar. 26, 1964
Position: left defense
Height: 6-1
Weight: 195
Uniform no.: 5
Shoots: left

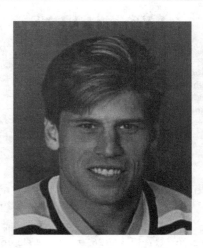

Career statistics:

GP	G	A	TP	PIM
616	36	188	224	1602

1991-92 statistics:

GP	G	A	TP	+/-	PIM	PP	SH	GW	GT	S	PCT
62	1	14	15	+2	206	1	0	1	0	75	1.3

1992-93 statistics:

GP	G	A	TP	+/-	PIM	PP	SH	GW	GT	S	PCT
77	3	26	29	+36	249	0	0	1	0	96	3.1

LAST SEASON

Third on team and fourth in NHL in plus/minus. Second on team in PIM with career high. Assists and points four-season high. Missed seven games due to injuries: shoulder (two games), cheekbone (two), knee (one), and back (two).

THE FINESSE GAME

Samuelsson has wonderful skills that are often overshadowed by the more irritating aspects of his nature. He is a very good skater for his size, with flat-out speed and one-step quickness, agility, mobility and balance. He skates very well backwards. He reads plays well defensively and is always well-positioned. He is tough to beat one-on-one and sometimes even two-on-one because of his anticipation.

Samuelsson is not as effective offensively. He can't carry the puck at high tempo and is better off making the escape pass than trying to rush it up-ice himself. Although he likes trying to handle the puck himself, this is a mistake. He just doesn't read offensive plays well. He does have a nice shot but lacks poise and confidence in the attacking zone.

Samuelsson is an excellent penalty killer. He blocks shots and challenges aggressively.

His biggest drawback remains his lack of mental sharpness. While he has improved over the seasons, Samuelsson is still prone to vapour lock at odd times.

THE PHYSICAL GAME

Samuelsson is a big hitter, sometimes too big. He will try to put someone through the wall when a simple take-out would do. He also needs to hit cleaner, but bringing his stick up on a hit is the most natural move, and he takes many unnecessary penalties because of this tendency.

Players have complained for years about Samuelsson's borderline open-ice hits, dating back to Cam Neely's injury in the 1991 playoffs. He still gets away with most of them, although knee checks are ex-pected to be the next focus of NHL officials after Greg Adams and Gary Roberts suffered similar injuries this season (not as a result of Samuelsson hits).

THE INTANGIBLES

One of the most aggravating players in the NHL, Samuelsson can distract another player — sometimes, an entire opposing team — from the task at hand. Instead of focussing on the game, they cry "Get Ulf!" Samuelsson can just chuckle behind his high sticks. He has more than enough talent to go with the goonery, but sometimes gets so carried away with himself that he forgets that the game is more important than his antics. He still lacks the mental edge that might place him among the league's top defensemen.

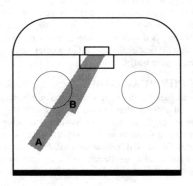

305

KEVIN STEVENS

Yrs. of NHL service: 6
Born: Brockton, Mass.; Apr. 15, 1965
Position: left wing
Height: 6-3
Weight: 217
Uniform no.: 25
Shoots: left

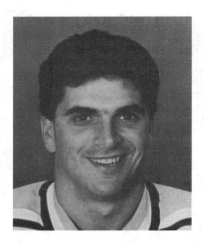

Career statistics:

GP	G	A	TP	PIM
348	195	217	412	760

1991-92 statistics:

GP	G	A	TP	+/-	PIM	PP	SH	GW	GT	S	PCT
80	54	69	123	+8	252	19	0	4	0	325	16.6

1992-93 statistics:

GP	G	A	TP	+/-	PIM	PP	SH	GW	GT	S	PCT
72	55	56	111	+17	177	26	9	5	1	325	16.9

LAST SEASON

Second on team in goals with career high. Second on team in points. Led team and was fourth in NHL in power play goals. Second consecutive season with 50 or more goals and 100 or more points. Led team in shots. Missed nine games with knee injury and two games with bronchitis.

THE FINESSE GAME

Stevens has the size and strength to battle for and win position in front of the net. He has an astonishingly quick release on his shot. His objective is to get rid of the puck as fast as he can, even if he doesn't know where it's going.

Stevens simply drops anchor in the slot on the power play. His huge frame blocks the goalie's view from Mario Lemieux doing God knows what in the left circle or Ron Francis cueing up another clever play from the right point. Stevens has good hand-eye co-ordination for tips and deflections. He also has a devastating one-timer. He does not have to be overly clever with the puck, since he can overpower goalies with his shot. Stevens is a power play specialist.

His play at even strength is not as strong, as he still needs to improve his defensive awareness. Stevens is an average skater at best, and often seems overanxious to get started on the attacking rush to keep up with his fleeter linemates.

Stevens is developing into a better playmaker. Although his first instinct is still to shoot, he can make a smart pass in traffic.

THE PHYSICAL GAME

Stevens had some surprisingly invisible playoff games in 1993. Either something was bugging him personally or physically, or he has forgotten what has made him a success in the NHL. He is now the blueprint for an NHL power forward. Every wannabe from John LeClair to Steven Rice gets compared to Stevens, but some nights even Stevens doesn't measure up.

Stevens has to hit first. He doesn't react well to being knocked down (it's surprising, given his size and strength, that he all too often is). He isn't one of the meanest guys around, although he can throw 'em (punches and devastating hits both). He was stunned in a collision with the Islanders' Rich Pilon in their 1993 playoff tilt. It will bear watching to see if the hit (which broke Stevens's nose) has any lingering effects.

THE INTANGIBLES

Stevens came back from his knee injury to pick up right where he left off scoring-wise. His playoff performance was just one of the puzzlers in Pittsburgh's upset loss. The one question mark on Stevens was whether he would be able to carry his consistent play from one year to the next. He has proven that he can, at least during the regular season.

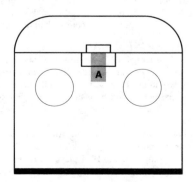

MARTIN STRAKA

Yrs. of NHL service: 1
Born: Pilsen, Czechoslovakia; Sept. 3, 1972
Position: centre
Height: 5-10
Weight: 178
Uniform no.: 82
Shoots: left

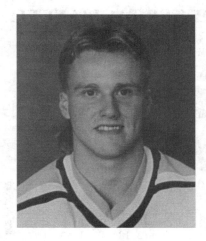

Career statistics:

GP	G	A	TP	PIM
42	3	13	16	29

1992-93 statistics:

GP	G	A	TP	+/-	PIM	PP	SH	GW	GT	S	PCT
42	3	13	16	+2	29	0	0	1	0	28	10.7

LAST SEASON
First NHL season.

THE FINESSE GAME
Straka is a speedy little centre, a waterbug with imagination. He makes clever passes that always land on tape and give the recipient time to do something with the puck. He's more of a playmaker than a shooter and will have to learn to go to the net more to make his game less predictable.

Straka has confidence in his finesse skills. He needs to adjust to smaller ice surfaces. Though he's a speedy skater who is tough to knock off balance, he is not very strong and can get muscled off the puck in close quarters.

THE PHYSICAL GAME
Straka has shown little inclination for the typical North American style of play. He is small and avoids corners and walls, and will have to be teamed with more physical linemates to give him some room.

THE INTANGIBLES
Straka overcame a poor start, despite getting little ice time on the talent-packed Pittsburgh team. He needs at least another season of adjustment to the NHL, but has the raw talent to be an impact player.

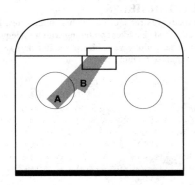

PETER TAGLIANETTI

Yrs. of NHL service: 7
Born: Framingham, Mass.; Aug. 15, 1963
Position: left defense
Height: 6-2
Weight: 200
Uniform no.: 32
Shoots: left

Career statistics:

GP	G	A	TP	PIM
378	16	61	77	952

1991-92 statistics:

GP	G	A	TP	+/-	PIM	PP	SH	GW	GT	S	PCT
44	1	3	4	+7	57	0	0	0	0	23	4.3

1992-93 statistics:

GP	G	A	TP	+/-	PIM	PP	SH	GW	GT	S	PCT
72	2	12	14	+12	184	0	0	0	0	78	2.6

LAST SEASON

Acquired from Tampa Bay for a 1993 third-round draft pick. Missed one game with concussion. Points three-season high.

THE FINESSE GAME

Taglianetti is a solid citizen in his own zone, a stay-at-home defenseman who knows his limitations and doesn't care to wander outside his self-proscribed boundaries.

He has average skills on a good night, relying on his intelligence to compensate for what his legs and hands can't do. Taglianetti never ventures deep inside the other team's zone, with his sole offensive contribution coming from a low point shot.

He makes the smart, safe play with the puck out of his zone. He won't lug it or even look for a pretty play, but just pounds it off the boards. As long as it's over the blue line, he's a happy guy.

THE PHYSICAL GAME

Taglianetti plays a sound physical game. He's a surprisingly solid hitter for someone who doesn't have very good skating balance. He uses his good upper body strength around his net and along the boards.

THE INTANGIBLES

Taglianetti was reacquired for his intangibles, his work ethic and character combining with his adequate skills to make him a valuable competitor. His worth can't be judged by numbers.

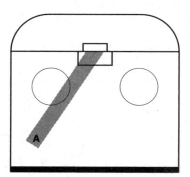

RICK TOCCHET

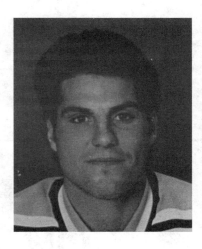

Yrs. of NHL service: 9
Born: Scarborough, Ont.; Apr. 9, 1964
Position: right wing
Height: 6-0
Weight: 205
Uniform no.: 22
Shoots: right

Career statistics:

GP	G	A	TP	PIM
630	277	524	601	1986

1991-92 statistics:

GP	G	A	TP	+/-	PIM	PP	SH	GW	GT	S	PCT
61	27	32	59	+15	151	8	1	2	1	166	16.3

1992-93 statistics:

GP	G	A	TP	+/-	PIM	PP	SH	GW	GT	S	PCT
80	48	61	109	+28	252	20	4	5	0	240	20.0

LAST SEASON

Career highs in goals, assists and points. Third on team in goals and points. Fourth on team in assists. Led team in PIM. Second on team in power play goals. Second on team in shooting percentage. First season with 100 or more points. Missed three games with foot injury and one game with ankle injury.

THE FINESSE GAME

Tocchet has worked hard to make the most of the finesse skills he has, and that makes everything loom larger. His skating is powerful, although he does not have great mobility. He is explosive in short bursts and is at his most effective in small areas. He works extremely well down low and in traffic. Tocchet exceeded all expectations on his power play work this season. He drives to the front of the net and into the corners for the puck.

Tocchet's shooting skills are ahead of his passing skills. He has limited vision of the ice for making a creative play, but he is a master at the bang-bang play. He'll smack in rebounds and deflections and set screens as defenders work to try to budge him or knock him down.

He has a strong, accurate wrist shot and gets most of his goals from close range, although he can also fire a one-timer from the tops of the circles. He'll rarely waste a shot from the blue line. He is a good give-and-go player because his quickness allows him to jump into the holes. He will beat few people one-on-one because he lacks stickhandling prowess.

THE PHYSICAL GAME

Tocchet is a tough hitter and frequently gets his stick and elbows up. He has long had a history of letting his emotions get the better of him, and while he has matured somewhat, he is acutely aware of his position as one of the few tough, physical forwards on a team of finesse players. Tocchet knows he has to play rugged to be effective, and he can do that cleanly, but he will also get everyone's attention by bending the rules.

THE INTANGIBLES

Tocchet's work ethic is inspiring. He is always one of the last players off the ice, usually working on puck-handling drills. Before games, he's one of the first to the rink and is riding the bike; after games, he's lifting weights. He started his career as a goon but has remade himself into a solid NHL player. He is competitive and physical, and was a huge addition to the Penguins line-up.

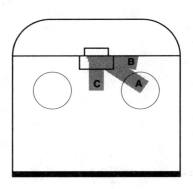

QUEBEC
NORDIQUES

STEVE DUCHESNE

Yrs. of NHL service: 7
Born: Sept-Îles, Que.; June 30, 1965
Position: right defense
Height: 5-11
Weight: 195
Uniform no.: 28
Shoots: left

Career statistics:

GP	G	A	TP	PIM
542	133	297	430	540

1991-92 statistics:

GP	G	A	TP	+/-	PIM	PP	SH	GW	GT	S	PCT
78	18	38	56	-7	86	7	2	3	0	229	7.9

1992-93 statistics:

GP	G	A	TP	+/-	PIM	PP	SH	GW	GT	S	PCT
82	20	62	82	+15	57	8	0	2	1	227	8.8

LAST SEASON

Led team defensemen and tied for fourth in NHL in scoring. Career highs in assists and points. Reached 20-goal mark for fourth time in last five seasons.

THE FINESSE GAME

The trade to the Nordiques made for a match in heaven for Duchesne. He is a fluid, quick, smart skater who loves to join the attack, and with the horde of skilled finesse players up front, run and gun was the name of the game at Le Colisée.

Duchesne often plays like a fourth forward. He is unfraid to gamble down deep, but he is such a good skater that he recovers quickly and is back in position in a flash. He does not waste time with the puck. He has good offensive sense, and when the play is over he is out of there.

Duchesne has an excellent shot from the point, and is a mainstay on the power play. He has good poise and patience, and can either drill a puck or take a little edge off it for his teammates to handle in front.

In the defensive zone, Duchesne uses his lateral mobility and quickness to maintain good position. He is almost impossible to beat one-on-one in open ice. Duchesne helps his team out tremendously by being able to skate the puck out of danger or make a brisk headman pass.

THE PHYSICAL GAME

Not only does Duchesne fail to knock anyone down in front of the net, but most of the time he doesn't even tie him up effectively. Duchesne is not very big or strong, and doesn't play tough. Positioning is the key to Duchesne's defense, and he needs to play with a physical partner.

THE INTANGIBLES

At 28, Duchesne is reaching the peak of his game, and he should be able to maintain it for several seasons. The Nordiques are poised to be one of the dominating teams of the decade, and Duchesne will be quarterbacking the potent attack.

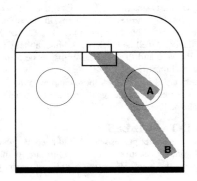

STEVEN FINN

Yrs. of NHL service: 7
Born: Laval, Que.; Aug. 20, 1966
Position: left defense
Height: 6-0
Weight: 198
Uniform no.: 29
Shoots: left

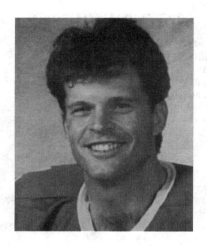

Career statistics:

GP	G	A	TP	PIM
485	25	57	82	1289

1991-92 statistics:

GP	G	A	TP	+/-	PIM	PP	SH	GW	GT	S	PCT
65	4	7	11	-9	192	0	0	0	0	63	6.3

1992-93 statistics:

GP	G	A	TP	+/-	PIM	PP	SH	GW	GT	S	PCT
80	5	9	14	-3	160	0	0	0	0	61	8.2

LAST SEASON

Third on team in PIM. PIM declined for third consecutive year. Games played career high.

THE FINESSE GAME

On a team of high-priced talent, Finn is a glamour-free foot soldier. He has some nice finesse skills, but the weakest of them is his skating. He is slow, with limited lateral movement. He is a smart player and makes good defensive reads, which makes him less of a liability than he could be, but he doesn't have a lot of confidence in his skating ability — when he is trying to outwit an opponent, he often outwits himself.

Finn has to play a simple game to be his most effective: play his position, angle the attacker to the boards and use his good strength to pin the skater while he waits for a teammate to swoop in and gain control of the puck. Finn can handle the puck fairly well and will surprise with a quick breakout pass from behind his goal line.

Finn is not a very creative player. His offensive involvement is limited to shots from the point. There are so many teammates hungry for the puck that he just makes the quick feed and lets them go play.

THE PHYSICAL GAME

Finn has a nasty side to him. He will bring his stick up, chop at ankles, and retaliate for any liberties taken with a teammate, but he's not much of a fighter. He takes the body well and makes solid hits, although he lacks the size and the skating ability to be a more punishing hitter.

Finn has been a bit of a loose cannon in the past. Every so often his temper gets the best of him, and he will take bad penalties.

THE INTANGIBLES

Finn is a character player who should keep his job on the Nordiques because players like him are in short supply on the team. He is tough and hard-working, and will stay home and mind the store while everyone else is driving the opposing goalie crazy down at the other end of the ice. He is a fifth or sixth defenseman now on the team, and after having been a leader through the lean seasons, he might find this a difficult role to handle.

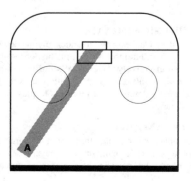

ADAM FOOTE

Yrs. of NHL service: 2
Born: Toronto, Ont.; July 10, 1971
Position: right defense
Height: 6-1
Weight: 200
Uniform no.: 52
Shoots: right

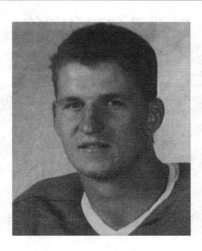

Career statistics:

GP	G	A	TP	PIM
127	6	17	23	212

1991-92 statistics:

GP	G	A	TP	+/-	PIM	PP	SH	GW	GT	S	PCT
46	2	5	7	-4	44	0	0	0	0	55	3.6

1992-93 statistics:

GP	G	A	TP	+/-	PIM	PP	SH	GW	GT	S	PCT
81	4	12	16	+6	168	0	1	0	0	54	7.4

LAST SEASON

Second on team in PIM. All totals career highs in second NHL season.

THE FINESSE GAME

With all of the talent up front on the Nordiques last season, it's easy to understand how this young defenseman got overlooked. Make no mistake: Foote is one of the top quality defensemen in the NHL, and he is only going to get better.

Foote is already being handed the responsibility of working on the penalty unit and getting crunch-time play-protected leads. He is an excellent skater, with good first-step quickness, balance and agility. He is flat-out fast as well, and can't get knocked off the puck. A chase into the corner will result in the opponent down on the ice and Foote wheeling away with the puck.

Foote's hand skills don't match up to his skating. He may never get the attention he merits because he will never get the gaudy numbers. Foote is a reluctant shooter (note his shot total), although he has an accurate slap shot. He does not get any power play time, but he has good vision and is a decent passer, so he could function there in a pinch.

THE PHYSICAL GAME

If it's a skating game, Foote excels. If it's a physical game, Foote excels. Any way you want to play it, Foote can compete. He is a willing hitter, and added about 20 pounds after his rookie season since he realized the need for more strength to compete in front of the net.

THE INTANGIBLES

In only his second NHL season, Foote has developed into a defenseman of great poise, well above that of most 21-year-olds. His tremendous skating gives him the edge that so many other players lack, and in another season or two he will be an All-Star calibre defenseman. We think it's high time he got rid of his training camp number.

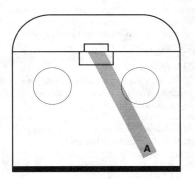

PETER FORSBERG

Yrs. of NHL service: 0
Born: Omskoldsvik, Sweden; July 20, 1973
Position: centre
Height: 5-11
Weight: 190
Uniform no.: na
Shoots: left

1992-93 statistics (in Sweden):

GP	G	A	TP	PIM
26	19	16	35	60

LAST SEASON

Will play first season in NHL. Drafted in first round, sixth overall, by Philadelphia in 1991. Rights acquired by Quebec in Eric Lindros trade.

THE FINESSE GAME

Forsberg dominated the 1993 World Junior Championships for gold medallist Sweden, and became a good prospect who blossomed into an excellent one.

Forsberg is the complete package. He is a smooth skater with explosive speed (think Teemu Selanne) and can accelerate while carrying the puck. He has excellent vision of the ice and is an outstanding playmaker. One of the few knocks on him is that he doesn't shoot enough. Forsberg is best down between the circles with a wrist or backhand shot off the rush.

Forsberg is already one of the top five playmakers in the world — which will make things a little crowded in Quebec, since Joe Sakic is in or close to that elite group right now.

All signs say Forsberg is ready to step into the NHL this season.

THE PHYSICAL GAME

Forsberg is competitive and stands up for himself. He has a cockiness that many great athletes carry about them like an aura, and he can expect to be challenged. His drive to succeed will help him handle the cheap stuff and keep going.

THE INTANGIBLES

In 1992, GM Pierre Page's task was to sign or deal Eric Lindros. He made the best of that situation, virtually restocking his team with the trade with the Flyers. Now he faces the same crossroads with Forsberg, who is considered to be the best player not to have played in the NHL last season.

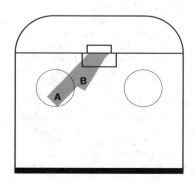

ALEXEI GUSAROV

Yrs. of NHL service: 3
Born: Leningrad, Russia; July 8, 1964
Position: right defense
Height: 6-2
Weight: 170
Uniform no.: 5
Shoots: left

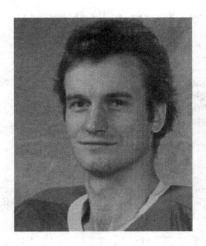

Career statistics:

GP	G	A	TP	PIM
147	16	49	65	52

1991-92 statistics:

GP	G	A	TP	+/-	PIM	PP	SH	GW	GT	S	PCT
68	5	18	23	-9	22	3	0	1	0	66	7.6

1992-93 statistics:

GP	G	A	TP	+/-	PIM	PP	SH	GW	GT	S	PCT
79	8	22	30	+18	18	0	2	1	0	60	13.3

LAST SEASON

Third on team in plus/minus. Games played, goals, assists and points at career highs.

THE FINESSE GAME

Gusarov has very good offensive skills, and sometimes he gets too wrapped up in the offensive frenzy. Someone has to stay calm on the ice while everyone is running around in the attacking zone, and you would like that person to be a controlling defenseman like Gusarov. While Gusarov has improved his positional play, he will often give in and start wandering.

Gusarov is a shifty skater, with a long reach and great range. He can handle the puck on the rush (he scored a penalty shot goal) and likes to gamble deep in front of the net. Unlike his teammate Steve Duchesne, who knows when to time his play low and when to bail out, Gusarov will get trapped.

Gusarov is confident in his skills and is aggressive, but he gets careless in the neutral zone and will get his partner in trouble by overcommitting.

Gusarov is used on the first penalty-killing unit and can also work the point on the power play, although his point shot isn't the greatest.

THE PHYSICAL GAME

Gusarov does not like the physical game. He has a long reach and would rather fish around for the puck when he should be bumping people. He's tall and lean, and he doesn't have the best build for contact work, but he should develop a little upper body strength to go with his leg drive.

THE INTANGIBLES

Gusarov stepped up his play last season and became comfortable both in his role as one of the team's top four defensemen and with life in North America. His game still has some holes — consistency being his major flaw — but he has shown steady improvement.

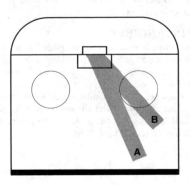

VALERI KAMENSKY

Yrs. of NHL service: 2
Born: Voskresensk, Russia; Apr. 18, 1966
Position: left wing
Height: 6-2
Weight: 198
Uniform no.: 31
Shoots: right

Career statistics:

GP	G	A	TP	PIM
55	22	36	58	28

1991-92 statistics:

GP	G	A	TP	+/-	PIM	PP	SH	GW	GT	S	PCT
23	7	14	21	-1	14	2	0	1	0	42	16.7

1992-93 statistics:

GP	G	A	TP	+/-	PIM	PP	SH	GW	GT	S	PCT
32	15	22	37	+13	14	2	3	0	1	94	16.0

LAST SEASON

Missed 49 games with broken ankle. Missed three games with broken thumb.

THE FINESSE GAME

Kamensky is one of the league's great one-way players. He is a world-class scorer and playmaker with a knack for scoring the big goals at key times.

A gifted skater with speed and quickness, he's as dangerous with the puck as without it because of his sense for the open ice. Kamensky is at his most dangerous on a four-on-four situation, as he is a top transition player. His passes are flat and on the money, with just the right velocity. The recipient does not have to slow down, but can accept the feed in stride.

The Nordiques used Kamensky down low on the power play, but he is equally comfortable on the point should he slide back as the puck is worked around. He likes to work off the left-wing boards. He has quick hands and an accurate wrist shot.

THE PHYSICAL GAME

Kamensky generally avoids scrums in the corners. He will venture there if he believes he can zip in quickly, nab the puck and dance back out, but he is not fond of contact. Other teams make it a point to thump Kamensky early and often.

THE INTANGIBLES

If Kamensky can ever stay in one piece for an entire season (or even 55 games), he could be a superstar. He changed his number (from 17 to a goalie's number, 31) to change his luck. Maybe it will work. He averages a point per game when he is able to get into the line-up, and after only two half-seasons of NHL play, he is still learning the North American game. And let's face it, he should be well rested.

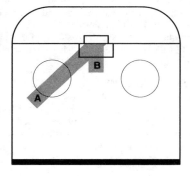

ANDREI KOVALENKO

Yrs. of NHL service: 1
Born: Nizhniy Novgorod, Russia; June 7, 1970
Position: right wing
Height: 5-9
Weight: 161
Uniform no.: 51
Shoots: left

Career statistics:

GP	G	A	TP	PIM
81	27	41	68	57

1992-93 statistics:

GP	G	A	TP	+/-	PIM	PP	SH	GW	GT	S	PCT
81	27	41	68	+13	57	8	1	4	0	153	17.6

LAST SEASON

First NHL season. Fourth among NHL rookies in assists. Fifth among NHL rookies in points. Tied for fourth among NHL rookies in power play goals.

THE FINESSE GAME

Kovalenko has some nice offensive skills, but what sets him apart from the traditional Russian forward is his perky playing style. Kovalenko blows right into traffic areas, and he makes things happen around the net.

Kovalenko is a very smart player. He controls the puck well down low on the power play. He doesn't like to hang on to the puck long, but keeps it moving briskly, and always has his sturdy legs in motion.

Kovalenko is not as energetic defensively, and he needs to be more conscientious about his checks.

THE PHYSICAL GAME

Kovalenko is tough around the net and in the corners in the offensive zone. He works the front of the net on the power play and gets a lot of goals off the rebound. He is stocky and powerful; it's no wonder that his nickname is "The Little Tank."

THE INTANGIBLES

One of the unheralded rookies of the awesome crop of '93, Kovalenko should be a reliable 30-goal scorer who enlivens things with his playing style.

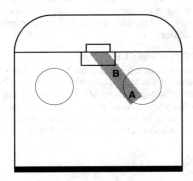

CLAUDE LAPOINTE

Yrs. of NHL service: 2
Born: Lachine, Que.; Oct. 11, 1968
Position: centre
Height: 5-9
Weight: 173
Uniform no.: 47
Shoots: left

Career statistics:

GP	G	A	TP	PIM
165	25	48	73	188

1991-92 statistics:

GP	G	A	TP	+/-	PIM	PP	SH	GW	GT	S	PCT
78	13	20	33	-8	86	0	2	2	0	95	13.7

1992-93 statistics:

GP	G	A	TP	+/-	PIM	PP	SH	GW	GT	S	PCT
74	10	26	36	+5	98	0	0	1	0	91	11.0

LAST SEASON

Assists and points at career highs.

THE FINESSE GAME

Lapointe is impossible to ignore. Many nights he is the smallest player on the ice, but he doesn't play like it. He is smart, heady and aggressive, and plays with spice on every shift. He was the 234th player chosen overall (in 1988) and spent most of two seasons in the minors, and you have to understand and appreciate the dedication it took for him to overcome his small stature and make it to the NHL. Lapointe obviously hasn't forgotten.

Lapointe drives to the front of the net, knowing that's where good things happen. He has good acceleration and quickness with the puck, and the good hand skills to create scoring chances down low. He's very good on face-offs. He gets first call on the penalty-killing unit, and is intelligent and aggressive playing shorthanded.

THE PHYSICAL GAME

Lapointe is small but powerfully built. He uses his low centre of gravity and good balance to bump people that are bigger and will surprise some of them by knocking them off the puck. Lapointe doesn't quit. He keeps going in the corners and in front of the net, and his extra effort has made him an NHL regular despite his small size.

THE INTANGIBLES

Lapointe was an excellent third-line centre for the Nordiques last season. He works hard every shift, providing intelligent defense with a scoring touch. The problem will be finding him ice time with the imminent arrival of yet another talented centre, Peter Forsberg, to join Joe Sakic and Mike Ricci up the middle.

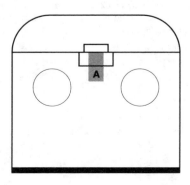

CURTIS LESCHYSHYN

Yrs. of NHL service: 5
Born: Thompson, Man.; Sept. 21, 1969
Position: left defense
Height: 6-1
Weight: 205
Uniform no.: 7
Shoots: left

Career statistics:

GP	G	A	TP	PIM
318	23	57	80	267

1991-92 statistics:

GP	G	A	TP	+/-	PIM	PP	SH	GW	GT	S	PCT
42	5	12	17	-28	42	3	0	1	0	61	8.2

1992-93 statistics:

GP	G	A	TP	+/-	PIM	PP	SH	GW	GT	S	PCT
82	9	23	32	+25	61	4	0	2	0	73	12.3

LAST SEASON

Led team in plus/minus. Goals, assists and points at career highs.

THE FINESSE GAME

Leschyshyn may have become the Nordiques' top all-around defenseman. He has very good skills for a big man, especially his skating, which is strong forwards and backwards. He has very good lateral movement and quickness.

He has very good stick skills. His passes are soft, and he will jump into the rush by skating the puck out of the defensive zone and moving it off his forehand or backhand. Leschyshyn is not as effective with his passes out of the zone, as he tends to get flustered, so he will usually lug it out when he gets the chance.

Leschyshyn has a nice point shot. It's low and accurate, and he gets it away quickly. He will also make a foray into the circle on occasion, and can utilize his quick wrist shot. He knows the importance of getting the shot on target, and would rather take a little velocity off the puck to make sure his aim is true. His shooting percentage is very high for a defenseman.

THE PHYSICAL GAME

Leschyshyn is probably the most physically fit player on the Nordiques. He made a successful comeback from a potentially career-threatening knee injury, and is no doubt one of the team's biggest surprises.

Leschyshyn needs to hit more. He lacks a mean streak to establish a presence, something he has been unable to do and which his team desperately needs. He will move out players and battle along the boards, but not with any authority.

THE INTANGIBLES

Leschyshyn is quietly developing into a solid defenseman. He still seems to lack some confidence, and would really benefit from the addition of a veteran defenseman who is willing to work with the youngster.

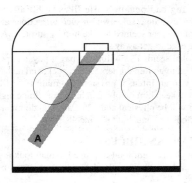

OWEN NOLAN

Yrs. of NHL service: 3
Born: Belfast, N. Ireland; Feb. 12, 1972
Position: right wing
Height: 6-1
Weight: 195
Uniform no.: 11
Shoots: right

Career statistics:

GP	G	A	TP	PIM
207	81	82	173	477

1991-92 statistics:

GP	G	A	TP	+/-	PIM	PP	SH	GW	GT	S	PCT
75	42	31	73	-9	183	17	0	0	1	190	22.1

1992-93 statistics:

GP	G	A	TP	+/-	PIM	PP	SH	GW	GT	S	PCT
73	36	41	77	-1	185	15	0	4	1	241	14.9

LAST SEASON

Led team in PIM with career high. Second on team in PIM. Assists and points at career highs. Missed games with hand injury.

THE FINESSE GAME

Nolan has one of the best shots in the NHL. He rips one-timers from the circle with deadly speed and accuracy. He is a pure shooter because his other hand skills are limited, and his game suffers when he tries to get too fancy and ventures away from a meat-and-potatoes game. When that happens, he holds on to the puck too long and tries to make plays instead of shooting. He saw reduced time on the power play because of this. Two seasons ago he was the top man on their top unit.

Nolan is a strong skater with good balance and fair agility. He is quick straight ahead but won't split the defense when carrying the puck. He's better without the puck, driving into open ice for the pass and quick shot.

Defensively, Nolan remains a liability with little instinct and awareness for positioning.

THE PHYSICAL GAME

Nolan had a poor first half, and much of it was marked by taking bad penalties. He likes to hit after the whistle, and the crackdown on such infractions at the start of the year seemed to take him by surprise. After all, he used to get away with it.

Nolan seems less willing to pay a physical price, reluctant to go into corners for the puck, and he has to play with an intense, physical linemate (like Mike Ricci) to keep him involved in the game. Some nights, Nolan will be physical and feisty and can dominate in the offensive zone, but he is inconsistent.

THE INTANGIBLES

Although his point total improved, Nolan took a step backwards in his overall play. The Nordiques need some forwards to play a physical style, and Nolan has the size and the temperament to do it. His desire remains a question mark.

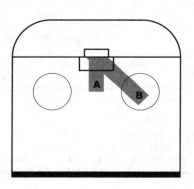

MIKE RICCI

Yrs. of NHL service: 3
Born: Scarborough, Ont.; Oct. 27, 1971
Position: centre
Height: 6-0
Weight: 190
Uniform no.: 9
Shoots: left

Career statistics:

GP	G	A	TP	PIM
223	68	107	175	280

1991-92 statistics:

GP	G	A	TP	+/-	PIM	PP	SH	GW	GT	S	PCT
78	20	36	56	-10	93	11	2	0	0	149	13.4

1992-93 statistics:

GP	G	A	TP	+/-	PIM	PP	SH	GW	GT	S	PCT
77	27	51	78	+8	123	12	1	10	1	142	19.0

LAST SEASON

Led team and tied for third in NHL in game-winning goals. Fourth on team in assists and points. Career highs in goals, assists, points and PIM. Missed seven games with knee and rib injuries.

THE FINESSE GAME

Ricci has terrific hand skills, combined with hockey sense and an outstanding work ethic. He always seems to be in the right place, ready to make the right play. He sees his passing options well, and is a solid performer on the power play because of his patience with the puck. Ricci can rifle it as well. He has a good backhand shot from in deep and scores most of his goals from the slot by picking the top corners. His lone drawback is his speed. He's fast enough to not look out of place, and he has good balance and agility, but his lack of quickness prevents him from being more of an offensive force.

Ricci is very good on face-offs. He has good hand speed and hand-eye coordination for winning draws outright, or he can pick a bouncing puck out of the air. This serves him well in scrambles in front of the net, too, or he can deflect mid-air slapshots.

Ricci is a very good penalty killer with poise and a controlled aggression for forcing the play.

THE PHYSICAL GAME

Ricci is so strong that it's not unusual to see him skate out from behind the net, dragging along or fending off a checker with one arm while he makes a pass or takes a shot with his other arm. He plays a tough game without being overly chippy. He is very strong in the corners and in front of the net.

Ricci will play hurt, and it takes a serious injury to knock him out of the line-up. He pays attention to conditioning and has a great deal of stamina.

THE INTANGIBLES

Ricci has all the makings of being the next Ron Francis. He is talented enough to step into the top centre's role when needed (in the event of injury to Joe Sakic, as happened last season), but he will also kill penalties, take face-offs, get you 80 points, drive the Zamboni, whatever. His quality, character, leadership and dedication to the game and his teammates are impeccable.

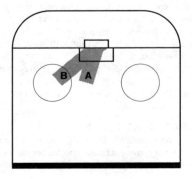

JOE SAKIC

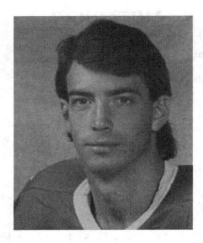

Yrs. of NHL service: 5
Born: Burnaby, B.C.; July 7, 1969
Position: centre
Height: 5-11
Weight: 185
Uniform no.: 19
Shoots: left

Career statistics:
GP	G	A	TP	PIM
377	187	285	472	135

1991-92 statistics:
GP	G	A	TP	+/-	PIM	PP	SH	GW	GT	S	PCT
69	29	65	94	+5	20	6	3	1	1	217	13.4

1992-93 statistics:
GP	G	A	TP	+/-	PIM	PP	SH	GW	GT	S	PCT
78	48	57	105	-3	40	20	2	4	1	264	18.2

LAST SEASON

Led team in goals, matching career high. Second on team in points. Third on team in assists. Led team in power play goals and shots. Third season with 100 or more points. PIM career high. Missed six games with eye injury.

THE FINESSE GAME

The bonus of all the attention being focussed on the Quebec Nordiques last season was that Sakic was finally able to get some of the credit he deserves for being one of the best playmakers in the NHL, if not the world. There is no one — repeat, no one — better in the league than Sakic at one remarkable skill: he will hold on to the puck until the last possible nanosecond before making the perfect pass. That used to be Wayne Gretzky's dominant skill. Now it is Sakic's. No coach can teach it, and it makes Sakic a scoring threat every time he is on the ice, because he can craft a dangerous scoring chance out of a situation that looks innocent.

Sakic has quick hands and can shoot the instant the puck is on his stick. He doesn't have a great deal of speed, but he has enough quickness and mobility to be effective without being flashy. He appears to glide along, disappearing here and then suddenly materializing in an open area of the ice in his quiet manner. He is lethal trailing the rush, because he can take a pass in full stride without slowing, deke and shoot before the goalie can even flinch. His shot isn't hard, but it is accurate and firm.

Sakic works the point on the power play not because of his point shot (although he will rifle the occasional blast in), but because of his awesome vision and patience with the puck.

THE PHYSICAL GAME

Sakic is not a physical player. He's stronger than he looks and will bounce off some checks, but he doesn't initiate contact. He will use his body to protect the puck when he is carrying deep, and you have to go through him to get it away. Sakic will try to keep going through traffic or along the boards with the puck, and often squirts free with it because he is able to maintain control and his balance.

THE INTANGIBLES

Sakic drew considerable criticism for a poor playoff, but remember this was his first taste of postseason play, and neither he nor many of his teammates had much notion of what playing in mid-April means. He will be better for the experience. Signing a new contract (four years at $8.8 million) should prove the Nordiques know just how valuable a player he is, but Peter Forsberg's arrival will be a tense situation when it comes time to divvy up on-ice duties.

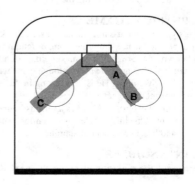

CHRIS SIMON

Yrs. of NHL service: 0
Born: Wawa, Ont.; Jan. 30, 1972
Position: left wing
Height: 6-3
Weight: 230
Uniform no.: 12
Shoots: left

Career statistics:
GP	G	A	TP	PIM
16	1	1	2	67

1992-93 statistics:
GP	G	A	TP	+/-	PIM	PP	SH	GW	GT	S	PCT
16	1	1	2	-2	67	0	0	1	0	15	6.7

LAST SEASON
First NHL season.

THE FINESSE GAME
Simon is a bit of a plodder, but he gets a head of steam once he's in gear. He is very strong, with a powerful stride and good balance and mobility, but lacks quickness.

Simon is a good passer as well as finisher. He sees his options well and makes accurate passes, although he is still adjusting to NHL tempo. He will establish position in the slot and is not easy to budge.

Simon has good hockey sense and is an intense player, although his emotions will sometimes gets the better of him; he needs to develop better focus and concentration.

THE PHYSICAL GAME
Simon reported to training camp in excellent condition after dropping 20 pounds during the off-season, and might have made the team at the start of the season but for some nagging injuries. He likes to hit, and if he uses his size consistently well without taking bad penalties (something that hurt him in the handful of games he had near the end of the season), the Nordiques would happily pencil him in as a power forward. As a team, the Nordiques are not strong along the wall, and Simon could help improve their play in that area.

THE INTANGIBLES
Simon has matured in the past season with improved off-ice habits and is a solid prospect — yet another blue chipper to come from the Eric Lindros deal.

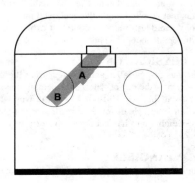

MATS SUNDIN

Yrs. of NHL service: 3
Born: Bromma, Sweden; Feb. 13, 1971
Position: right wing
Height: 6-3
Weight: 215
Uniform no.: 13
Shoots: right

Career statistics:

GP	G	A	TP	PIM
240	103	146	249	259

1991-92 statistics:

GP	G	A	TP	+/-	PIM	PP	SH	GW	GT	S	PCT
80	33	43	76	-19	105	8	2	2	1	231	14.3

1992-93 statistics:

GP	G	A	TP	+/-	PIM	PP	SH	GW	GT	S	PCT
80	47	67	114	+21	96	13	4	9	1	215	21.9

LAST SEASON

Led team in assists and points with career highs. Led team regulars in shooting percentage. Second on team in plus/minus. Second on team in goals.

THE FINESSE GAME

Sundin is a big skater who looks huge since he also uses a loo-o-ng stick that gives him a broad wingspan. For a big man, he is an agile skater, but his balance is only fair, maybe because he sprouted up so quickly as a teenager that he is still getting used to the redistribution of muscle. He has good lower body strength, getting good drive for battles along the boards.

In open ice, Sundin doesn't look fast, but he has ground-eating strides that allow him to cover in two strokes what other skaters do in three or four. Sundin is quick, too, and can get untracked in a heartbeat.

Sundin is somewhat overrated as a playmaker, which is why he will be more effective in the NHL as a winger than a centre. Sundin doesn't have a great knack for holding on to the puck until the last second to make a pass. He is a playmaker through force, using his long reach and strength to power through with the puck rather than doing nifty plays.

His shot is excellent. He can use a slapshot, one-timer, wrister or backhand. The only liability to his reach is that he will dangle the puck well away from his body and doesn't always control it, which makes him vulnerable to a poke check.

THE PHYSICAL GAME

Sundin has grown taller and stronger over the past several years (the out-of-date NHL media guide still lists him at the 6-1, 190-pound boy he was when drafted in 1989). He devoted some off-season time to lifting weights and has become more of a physical presence.

THE INTANGIBLES

Sundin is emerging as a player who can dominate on any given night. He has trouble on smaller ice surfaces (games in Buffalo and Boston tend to hem him in) and often has quiet nights when he is challenged physically. Nonetheless, he has shown constant improvement, and 100-point seasons should be the norm.

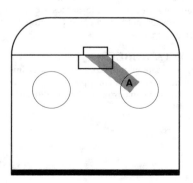

SCOTT YOUNG

Yrs. of NHL service: 4
Born: Clinton, Mass.; Oct. 1, 1967
Position: right wing
Height: 6-0
Weight: 190
Uniform no.: 48
Shoots: right

Career statistics:

GP	G	A	TP	PIM
322	90	135	225	137

1991-92 statistics:
Did not play in NHL

1992-93 statistics:

GP	G	A	TP	+/-	PIM	PP	SH	GW	GT	S	PCT
82	30	30	60	+5	20	9	6	5	0	225	13.3

LAST SEASON

Led team in shorthanded goals. Returned to NHL after playing 1991-92 in Italy and for U.S. Olympic team. Goals career high.

THE FINESSE GAME

Young may have the hardest shot on the team. He loves to fire it off the carry up the wing, or he can one-time the puck low on the face-off, or he will battle for pucks and tips in front of the net. Young simply loves to score, and always goes to the net with his stick down, ready for the puck.

With all of that in mind, his defensive awareness is even more impressive, because Young is basically a checking winger. He reads plays in all zones equally well and has good anticipation.

Young is a very fast skater, which combined with his reads makes him a sound forechecker. He will often outrace defensemen to touch up pucks and avoid icings, and his speed allows him to recover when he gets overzealous in the attacking zone.

THE PHYSICAL GAME

Young's drawback is that he is not a very physical player. He will do what he has to do in battles along the boards in the defensive zone, but he's more of a defensive force with his quickness and hand skills. He should play a little bigger.

THE INTANGIBLES

Role players who can get you 60 points don't skate along every day. Young is a valuable veteran who has the speed to fit in nicely with the Nordiques. In a pinch, he can switch back to playing defense, his college position.

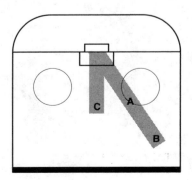

SAN JOSE SHARKS

GAETAN DUCHESNE

Yrs. of NHL service: 12
Born: Les Saulles, Que.; July 11, 1962
Position: left wing
Height: 5-11
Weight: 200
Uniform no.: 10
Shoots: left

Career statistics:

GP	G	A	TP	PIM
900	164	227	391	568

1991-92 statistics:

GP	G	A	TP	+/-	PIM	PP	SH	GW	GT	S	PCT
73	8	15	23	+6	102	0	2	1	0	106	7.5

1992-93 statistics:

GP	G	A	TP	+/-	PIM	PP	SH	GW	GT	S	PCT
84	16	13	29	+6	32	0	2	3	0	134	11.9

LAST SEASON

One of four Stars to play in all 84 games. Goals at five-season high. Acquired from Dallas for a sixth-round draft pick in 1993.

THE FINESSE GAME

Intelligence is the key to Duchesne's game. His defensive reads are excellent, which, coupled with his good skating, makes him very efficient. He knows where to position himself before the attacking player knows what he's going to do with the puck, and that makes him one of the top penalty killers in the league.

Duchesne's scoring chances come from his forechecking and anticipation in picking off passes and forcing turnovers. He radiates confidence when he's checking and takes advantage of the errors made by other teams' top offensive lines, which usually aren't so keen on defense.

Duchesne's scoring skills are average, and he will get most of his goals from close range.

THE PHYSICAL GAME

Duchesne doesn't initiate contact, but he's fearless in that he always puts himself in the middle of the road and doesn't get pushed away from what he has to do. He wore down in the second half, even though he is a well-conditioned athlete. The Stars may have overused him.

THE INTANGIBLES

At 31, Duchesne still has several serviceable years left as an experienced checking forward. If he continues to play with checkers with some offensive ability, as he did with Russ Courtnall and Neal Broten last season, he could chip in another 15 goals while performing his usual yeoman work as a checker. He is a character player and a favourite among his teammates.

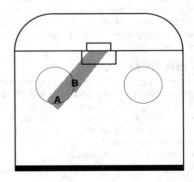

PAT FALLOON

Yrs. of NHL service: 2
Born: Foxwarren, Man.; Sept. 22, 1972
Position: centre
Height: 5-11
Weight: 192
Uniform no.: 17
Shoots: right

Career statistics:

GP	G	A	TP	PIM
93	39	48	87	28

1991-92 statistics:

GP	G	A	TP	+/-	PIM	PP	SH	GW	GT	S	PCT
79	25	34	59	-32	16	5	0	1	2	181	13.8

1992-93 statistics:

GP	G	A	TP	+/-	PIM	PP	SH	GW	GT	S	PCT
41	14	14	28	-25	12	5	1	1	0	131	10.7

LAST SEASON
Missed 43 games with dislocated right shoulder.

THE FINESSE GAME
Falloon is a centre who likes to use all of the ice, and he's equally comfortable bursting down either wing or shimmying through the middle. Puck control is his forte. He has great patience with the puck, and can dish off to either side.

Falloon is not a natural goal-scorer. He is opportunistic around the net, using his quickness to follow up a shot and pounce on a loose rebound. He has soft hands and good instincts for the right play. He will be at his most effective playing at centre with a big winger who will drive to the net. The Sharks don't yet have the perfect linemate for him.

Falloon is a quick skater, with acceleration and balance for agile moves. He employs a smart array of shots, using a wrist shot or slap shot with confidence. He's a good two-on-one player, coming across the blue line with speed and forcing the defenseman to stand up to brace for the slap shot. Falloon then cuts wide or slides a pass across to the player breaking with him.

Like so many players out of junior hockey, Falloon needs to work on his defensive game. He is -57 over one and a half seasons. There is nothing deceptive in those numbers. Before his injury, though, Falloon did appear to be making better choices away from the puck.

THE PHYSICAL GAME
Falloon gets a great deal of checking attention. Though his game can't be characterized as physical, he uses his stocky build and good skating to work free of those checks. He goes willingly into the traffic areas in front of the net and along the boards, but our suspicion is that his serious shoulder injury may hamper his enthusiasm for contact.

THE INTANGIBLES
We've heard of sophomore slumps, but Falloon's second season was a sophomore disaster. Off to a slow start, he didn't seem to get comfortable until he was moved from right wing to centre, and then the injury wiped out the second half of his season. There is not much improvement on the horizon for the Sharks, and Falloon will struggle again this season.

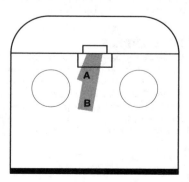

JOHAN GARPENLOV

Yrs. of NHL service: 3
Born: Stockholm, Sweden; Mar. 21, 1968
Position: left wing
Height: 5-11
Weight: 183
Uniform no.: 10
Shoots: left

Career statistics:

GP	G	A	TP	PIM
178	46	73	119	82

1991-92 statistics:

GP	G	A	TP	+/-	PIM	PP	SH	GW	GT	S	PCT
28	6	7	13	+13	8	1	0	1	0	34	17.6

1992-93 statistics:

GP	G	A	TP	+/-	PIM	PP	SH	GW	GT	S	PCT
79	22	44	66	-26	56	14	0	1	0	171	12.9

LAST SEASON

Second on team in assists and points with career highs. Career high in goals. Led team in power play goals.

THE FINESSE GAME

Garpenlov is a better playmaker than finisher. A solid forechecker, he will create turnovers and then look to do something creatively with the puck.

A strong skater with good balance, he will carry the puck through checks. He has a good wrist shot from the off-wing and shoots well in stride, but he doesn't shoot often enough. His quickness gets him into high-quality scoring areas, but he then looks to make a pass.

The story is different on the power play, perhaps because the open ice gives him more time and confidence. He likes to work low and use his one-timer from the left circle. If he were as eager to shoot in five-on-five situations, he could elevate his game another level.

THE PHYSICAL GAME

Garpenlov is not physical. His forechecking pressure comes not from physical contact, but by his skating ability, which simply gets him in on top of a player to force a pass that Garpenlov can intercept.

THE INTANGIBLES

Garpenlov gets first call on the power play and a lot of ice time, and he should be on the first line again this season. He is capable of 30 goals.

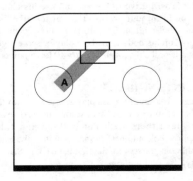

ROB GAUDREAU

Yrs. of NHL service: 1
Born: Lincoln, R.I.; Jan. 20, 1970
Position: right wing
Height: 5-11
Weight: 185
Uniform no.: 37
Shoots: right

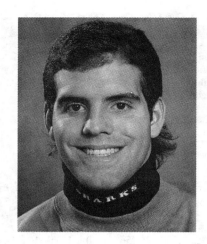

Career statistics:

GP	G	A	TP	PIM
59	23	20	43	18

1992-93 statistics:

GP	G	A	TP	+/-	PIM	PP	SH	GW	GT	S	PCT
59	23	20	43	-18	18	5	2	1	0	191	12.0

LAST SEASON

First NHL season. Third on team in assists and points. Second on team in goals. Led team and fifth among NHL rookies in shots. Had 12-game point-scoring streak, tied for third-longest by an NHL rookie last season. Missed one game with hand injury.

THE FINESSE GAME

Gaudreau has nice scoring instincts and a good shot. He does not have a big slap shot, but most of his goals come from going to the net and getting the shot away quickly. He has some sense around the net. He is short but wide and blockily built and can go into traffic.

Most of his goals are close in to the net, but Gaudreau can also zip down the right side and shoot on the fly. He is quick and gets a step or two on his defenders. He is not a gifted skater. He has to work at it, but he gets there.

Gaudreau works hard defensively and has good awareness. He spends time on both special teams, and plays the point on the power play on the off side, where he one-times a shot well. He played defense in his last year of college, so he has a good foundation for two-way play.

THE PHYSICAL GAME

Gaudreau will drive to the net and use his chunky, small build through traffic. He's gritty, like Tony Granato (but without Granato's emotion). Gaudreau will give up his body to make a play or score a goal, and that is probably worth an extra 10 to 15 points per season.

THE INTANGIBLES

Gaudreau is a smart finesse player who loves to shoot and figures to be on the Sharks' top line next season. If he plays there with Pat Falloon and Johan Garpenlov, he could net 30 goals. He is in the team's record books for scoring the first hat trick in San Jose history.

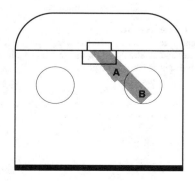

MARTIN GELINAS

Yrs. of NHL service: 4
Born: Shawinigan, Que.; June 5, 1970
Position: left wing
Height: 5-11
Weight: 195
Uniform no.: 7
Shoots: left

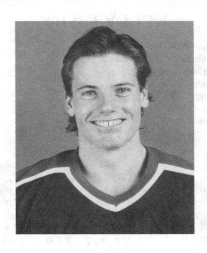

Career statistics:

GP	G	A	TP	PIM
258	60	60	120	156

1991-92 statistics:

GP	G	A	TP	+/-	PIM	PP	SH	GW	GT	S	PCT
68	11	18	29	+14	62	1	0	0	0	94	11.7

1992-93 statistics:

GP	G	A	TP	+/-	PIM	PP	SH	GW	GT	S	PCT
65	11	12	23	+3	30	0	0	1	0	93	11.8

LAST SEASON

Tied for team lead in plus/minus. Acquired by Quebec with a sixth-round draft pick in 1993 for Scott Pearson.

THE FINESSE GAME

Gelinas is a frustrating package. He broke into the league as an all-finesse player, then set himself to the task of learning the defensive game that is much ignored in junior (and especially in the QMJHL, where Gelinas was a scoring star for Hull).

That combination should have made him a better all-around player, but something got lost in the mix: his production. Still, Gelinas seems to have all of the skills to make more of a contribution offensively. He has quickness, and can handle the puck while on the go.

He plays more of a grinding game than his physique and his skills might suggest, and now most of his scoring comes from his forechecking. He is strong along the boards and in front of the net. He doesn't have a lot of offensive sense, but he works hard.

Gelinas is a good penalty killer, but the Oilers didn't use him much in that role last season.

THE PHYSICAL GAME

Gelinas is a small player and seems to get himself into situations where he just gets flattened. He isn't intimidated, but he does get wiped out of the play, and he has to be smarter about jumping in and out of holes, paying the price only when necessary.

THE INTANGIBLES

The best thing for Gelinas could be a change of scenery. He was one of the kid heroes in Edmonton when the team won its last Stanley Cup, but little has gone right for him since. He needs ice time, and confidence. He could have a big bounce-back season.

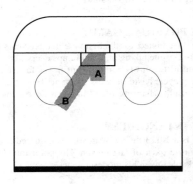

KELLY KISIO

Yrs. of NHL service: 11
Born: Peace River, Alta.; Sept. 18, 1959
Position: centre
Height: 5-9
Weight: 183
Uniform no.: 11
Shoots: right

Career statistics:

GP	G	A	TP	PIM
698	215	402	617	734

1991-92 statistics:

GP	G	A	TP	+/-	PIM	PP	SH	GW	GT	S	PCT
48	11	26	37	-7	54	2	3	2	0	68	16.2

1992-93 statistics:

GP	G	A	TP	+/-	PIM	PP	SH	GW	GT	S	PCT
78	26	52	78	-15	90	9	2	2	0	152	17.1

LAST SEASON

Led team in goals and points, matching career highs. Led team in assists and shooting percentage. Second on team in power play goals.

THE FINESSE GAME

Kisio is a small forward who has always played with the heart of a lion. His NHL skills are adequate at best, but he has always enhanced his natural abilities with his work ethic and intelligence.

Kisio is an effective checker because he seems to know what the puck carrier is going to do with the play before he has even decided. He is always well positioned. Along the boards, he has quick hand skills and determination for mining the rubber out of a tangle of sticks and skates. He will even use his skates to keep the puck alive, and kick it free to a teammate. Even if he is knocked to his knees, Kisio will find a way to move it.

He's very good on draws, especially in the defensive zone. He is built low to the ice and had good hand-eye co-ordination and focus.

Kisio's points come from his buzzsaw work around the net. He will try to stuff in a forehand from behind the cage, then take the rebound around behind the net on his backhand and try a play on the other side.

THE PHYSICAL GAME

Kisio stayed intact for the first time in three years last season. Despite taking physical lumps every night for a dreadful team, his commitment never faltered. A proud player, Kisio delivers the same honest effort every night, shaming many bigger, more talented players.

THE INTANGIBLES

Kisio is a No. 3 defenseman who was forced into a No. 1 role most of last season. His point totals are remarkable, given his modest talents.

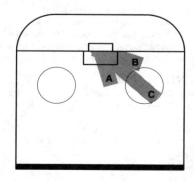

VIKTOR KOZLOV

Yrs. of NHL service: 0
Born: Togliatti, Russia; Feb. 14, 1975
Position: right wing
Height: 6-5
Weight: 219
Uniform no.: NA
Shoots: Right

Career Russian statistics:				
GP	G	A	TP	PIM
35	7	4	11	10

1992-93 Russian statistics:				
GP	G	A	TP	PIM
32	7	4	11	10

LAST SEASON
Played for Moscow Dynamo.

THE FINESSE GAME
Kozlov's finesse skills are world-class. He is an excellent skater for a player of his size, with good quickness. Kozlov has very good hockey sense, and is a good passer possessing timing and accuracy. He can score in a variety of ways, and has an accurate shot with a quick trigger.

What's missing? Intensity. On the nights when Kozlov is on, he dominates the ice. But when he's not — and this has occurred too many times in too many key situations — his perimeter play leads to a glaringly dull effort.

THE PHYSICAL GAME
Kozlov gained 18 pounds over the last season, but it didn't add strength, it only made him sluggish. He had a subpar World Junior tournament in front of just about every scout in creation, and his stock plummeted. With his generous size, Kozlov is expected to by more of a physical force, and he should be. He has a long reach, but doesn't care to play the body defensively, although offensively he will work with the puck to get in front of the net into scoring position. Kozlov needs to develop more lower body strength.

THE INTANGIBLES
The BIG question mark of the 1993 draft is Kozlov. He is a human enigma who can invite comparisons to Mario Lemieux on one night and be invisible the next. A gamble, but one that will pay off huge profits if he clicks.

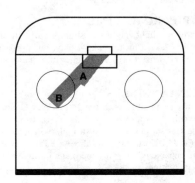

IGOR LARIONOV

Yrs. of NHL service: 3
Born: Voskresensk, Russia; Dec. 3, 1960
Position: centre
Height: 5-9
Weight: 160
Uniform no.: na
Shoots: left

Career statistics:

GP	G	A	TP	PIM
210	51	92	143	88

1991-92 statistics:

GP	G	A	TP	+/-	PIM	PP	SH	GW	GT	S	PCT
72	21	44	65	+7	54	10	3	4	0	97	21.6

1992-93 statistics:

Did not play in NHL

LAST SEASON

Signed as free agent. Played 1992-93 season in Switzerland.

THE FINESSE GAME

Larionov will be 33 in the upcoming season, and there is some question as to how much gas in left in his tank. The Sharks signed him to a three-year contract, so they must be convinced that his great finesse gifts are still NHL calibre.

Larionov is among the best playmakers ever to come out of the old Russian system. He's an agile, elusive skater with marvellous hand skills and a creative mind. He challenges his wingers to get open, and he has an exceptional passing touch for finding the breaking man. But it was apparent in his last NHL season two years ago that Larionov has slowed, and he cannot hang on to the puck forever waiting for his wingers to break free.

Larionov does not shoot much. He cannot overpower a goalie with his shot, but prefers to work in tight, deking a defender, getting a step and using an accurate wrist shot.

Larionov is smart and plays well positionally. He can be used on both special teams and is a shorthanded scoring threat because of his crafty play.

THE PHYSICAL GAME

Larionov is a lightweight and slightly built. He will sometimes take a hit to make a play, but it doesn't make much sense to ask him to get into one-on-one confrontations.

THE INTANGIBLES

A contract squabble with the Vancouver Canucks resulted in Larionov leaving the NHL to play in Europe last season. He may struggle with readjustment (as Jari Kurri did), and there are few San Jose players capable of finishing the plays Larionov is so adept at creating.

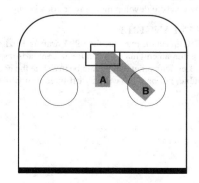

SERGEI MAKAROV

Yrs. of NHL service: 4
Born: Chelyabinsk, Russia; June 19, 1958
Position: right wing
Height: 5-11
Weight: 185
Uniform no.: 42
Shoots: left

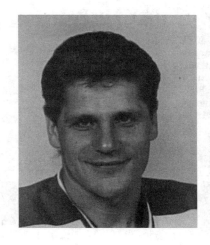

Career statistics:

GP	G	A	TP	PIM
297	94	198	292	199

1991-92 statistics:

GP	G	A	TP	+/-	PIM	PP	SH	GW	GT	S	PCT
68	22	48	70	+14	60	6	0	2	0	83	26.5

1992-93 statistics:

GP	G	A	TP	+/-	PIM	PP	SH	GW	GT	S	PCT
71	18	39	57	0	40	5	0	3	0	105	17.1

LAST SEASON

Goals, assists and points at career lows. Acquired by San Jose from Hartford with second- and third-round draft picks for a switch in first-round picks in 1993.

THE FINESSE GAME

Makarov was once among the world's elite in offensive skills, but at 35 his skating has slowed and, worst of all, his interest has waned. Makarov battled with Flames coach Dave King last season and his ice time was limited, but in a specialized role he could still dazzle.

Makarov has superb hand skills and vision of the ice. He has lost some speed but is still very strong and balanced, especially with the puck. He has little energy for the defensive part of the game, but on the attack he will make brilliant little passes through traffic.

Like most players from the old Soviet system, Makarov doesn't shoot often enough. When he does, it will be a high-quality shot, usually a wrist shot, from the face-off dots in.

THE PHYSICAL GAME

Makarov is strong, and when he has the puck it's almost impossible for a checker to part him from it. But he won't fight to get the puck along the boards or in the corners, and he has to play with a grinder.

THE INTANGIBLES

By signing Igor Larionov and acquiring Makarov, the Sharks have reassembled two-thirds of one of the great lines in Soviet hockey history, the Central Red Army's KLM Line (quick trivia quiz: who was the left wing?). The problem is that these once-great players are well past their prime, and without the finishers in San Jose they may struggle. We would be surprised if Makarov netted more than 20 goals.

Quiz answer: Vladimir Krutov, who played one season with Vancouver.

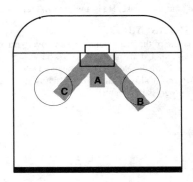

JAY MORE

Yrs. of NHL service: 2
Born: Souris, Man.; Jan. 12, 1969
Position: right defense
Height: 6-1
Weight: 202
Uniform no.: 4
Shoots: right

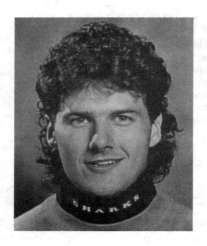

Career statistics:

GP	G	A	TP	PIM
125	9	19	25	280

1991-92 statistics:

GP	G	A	TP	+/-	PIM	PP	SH	GW	GT	S	PCT
46	4	13	17	-32	85	1	0	1	0	60	6.7

1992-93 statistics:

GP	G	A	TP	+/-	PIM	PP	SH	GW	GT	S	PCT
73	5	6	11	-35	179	0	1	0	0	107	4.7

LAST SEASON

Games played and PIM at career highs.

THE FINESSE GAME

In the past, More's mean streak has overshadowed his other talents. More has dedicated himself to being more of a complete player, but there are still a lot of missing parts.

More is an average skater but fairly agile in open ice, although not very fast. He doesn't get enough drive from his legs for power in either hitting or driving through a check, and he needs to improve his overall skating.

He has a low, accurate point shot and is used on the second power play, but he is not very creative. Breaking out of the defensive zone, he makes a nice outlet pass.

More lacks hockey sense and needs to improve his defensive reads. Time and again, he goes for the fake when the rush is coming at him, and he leaves his defense partner outnumbered.

THE PHYSICAL GAME

For a player who is not very strong on his skates, More likes to get involved physically. He makes a lot of late hits, getting his licks in after the fact instead of clearing out the crease. He is a willing fighter.

THE INTANGIBLES

More is one of the many young players overburdened by being No. 1 draft picks (in 1987, he was chosen 10th overall, by the New York Rangers). Defensemen develop more slowly than forwards as it is, and More's progress has been slow.

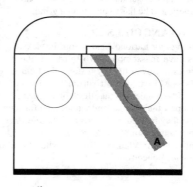

JEFF NORTON

Yrs. of NHL service: 5
Born: Acton, Mass.; Nov. 25, 1965
Position: right defense
Height: 6-2
Weight: 195
Uniform no.: 8
Shoots: left

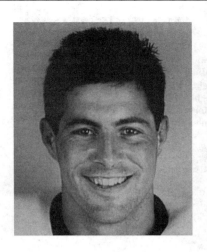

Career statistics:

GP	G	A	TP	PIM
282	22	166	188	232

1991-92 statistics:

GP	G	A	TP	+/-	PIM	PP	SH	GW	GT	S	PCT
28	1	18	19	+2	18	0	1	0	0	34	2.9

1992-93 statistics:

GP	G	A	TP	+/-	PIM	PP	SH	GW	GT	S	PCT
66	12	38	50	-3	45	5	0	0	0	127	9.4

LAST SEASON

Games played most since rookie season. Second among team defensemen in scoring. Points three-season high. Goals career high. Missed eight games with injuries: hip (five), shoulder (one), groin (two). Traded to San Jose for a conditional draft pick.

THE FINESSE GAME

Norton's game is based on his exceptional skating. Among NHL defensemen, perhaps only Paul Coffey is better. Norton has deep edges and seems to make his turns and cuts with his body at a 45-degree angle to the ice.

His hockey sense is good, especially offensively, but he has never been able to combine his skating with the kind of scoring impact he should. He doesn't have a great shot. He will generate a play with his skating and puckhandling and get the puck into the attacking zone, but he never seems to have the finishing touch, either with a shot or the good pass down low. Norton has had problems with injuries throughout his career. If he stays healthy and gets the playing time, he could improve offensively, but that appears to be a pretty big if.

THE PHYSICAL GAME

Norton is not strong in his own end of the ice. On many nights, he will drift up as if he is ready to leave the zone prematurely, and leave his teammates scrambling behind. His mental toughness is a question mark, and his focus and concentration waver.

THE INTANGIBLES

Norton and former coach Al Arbour never hit it off during Norton's four seasons with the New York Islanders. A fresh start could revitalize him in San Jose, where he figures to get prime ice time and a lot of work on the power play. He's a smart man and is aware of the opportunity he's been granted.

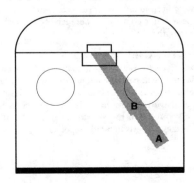

SANDIS OZOLINSH

Yrs. of NHL service: 1
Born: Riga, Latvia; Aug. 3, 1972
Position: left defense
Height: 6-1
Weight: 189
Uniform no.: 6
Shoots: left

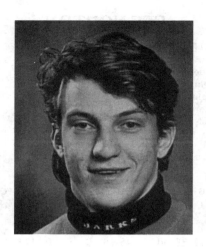

Career statistics:

GP	G	A	TP	PIM
37	7	16	23	40

1992-93 statistics:

GP	G	A	TP	+/-	PIM	PP	SH	GW	GT	S	PCT
37	7	16	23	-9	40	2	0	0	0	83	8.4

LAST SEASON

First NHL season. Led team defensemen in scoring despite missing 47 games with torn knee ligaments.

THE FINESSE GAME

Ozolinsh has good straightaway speed, but he can't make a lot of agile, pretty moves along the Paul Coffey lines. Because he can't weave his way through a number of defenders, he has to power his way into open ice with the puck and drive the defenders back through intimidation.

Ozolinsh has good passing skills, but he sometimes hangs on to the puck too long. He has a variety of shots, with his best a one-timer from the off side on the power play. He does not function as well when he works down low.

He pinches aggressively and likes to make things happen on the attack. He is not as effective defensively. He does not stop and start well, especially when moving backwards, and he tends to get mixed up on checking assignments when the attacking team crisscrosses.

THE PHYSICAL GAME

Ozolinsh lacks strength for the one-on-one battles and needs to develop more power for his work along the boards and in front of the net. He isn't very big, but he could be a better contributor defensively with some added strength.

THE INTANGIBLES

Ozolinsh gives the Sharks an element they desperately need. He is a puck-carrying defenseman who can rush the puck out of the zone and up-ice. He needs a lot of work defensively, but for now his offensive contributions will outweigh his shortcomings. A healthy Ozolinsh could be worth 50 to 60 points.

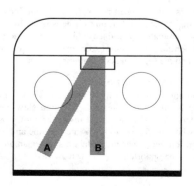

MIKE RATHJE

Yrs. of NHL service: 0
Born: Mannville, Alta.; May 11, 1974
Position: left defense
Height: 6-5
Weight: 203
Uniform no.: na
Shoots: left

1992-93 Junior statistics:

GP	G	A	TP	PIM
57	12	37	49	103

LAST SEASON

Drafted in first round, third overall, in 1992 entry draft. Played for Medicine Hat (WHL) last season.

THE FINESSE GAME

Rathje is a stay-at-home defenseman whose skills may at first seem too subtle to help the Sharks improve right away, but he is a cornerstone for a new and improved defense and will be a welcome addition to the weakest aspect of the team's game.

He has the ability to get involved in the attack but is prized primarily for his defense. He is a good skater for his size and steps up aggressively.

Rathje helps get the puck out of the zone quickly, which is a major need for the Sharks. He can either carry the puck out and make a smart headman pass, then follow the play, or make the safe move and chip the puck out along the wall. He has great poise for a young player.

THE PHYSICAL GAME

Rathje has good size and he is adding more muscle — remember, he's just 19, and we're sure he's not done growing. He will look a bit awkward at times, because as his body changes he has to get accustomed to his new strength and balance. He has a little bit of mean in him, and he likes to hit. He has to avoid the temptation to get too involved and run all over the ice.

THE INTANGIBLES

Rathje played for the gold medal-winning Canadian team at the World Junior Championships and was a second-team all-tournament selection on defense. San Jose's defense was the worst in the NHL last season (4.93 team GAA). The addition of Rathje is a step towards cutting those goals-against down.

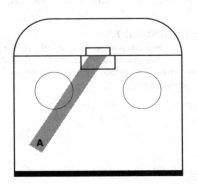

MIKE SULLIVAN

Yrs. of NHL service: 2
Born: Marshfield, Mass.; Feb. 27, 1968
Position: centre
Height: 6-2
Weight: 193
Uniform no.: 47
Shoots: left

Career statistics:

GP	G	A	TP	PIM
145	14	19	23	45

1991-92 statistics:

GP	G	A	TP	+/-	PIM	PP	SH	GW	GT	S	PCT
64	8	11	19	-18	15	1	0	1	0	72	11.1

1992-93 statistics:

GP	G	A	TP	+/-	PIM	PP	SH	GW	GT	S	PCT
81	6	8	14	-42	30	0	2	0	0	95	6.3

LAST SEASON

Goals, assists and points declined from first season.

THE FINESSE GAME

Sullivan's primary asset is his speed. He finished first among Campbell Conference players in the preliminary phase of the fastest-skater contest in the All-Star skills competition. He doesn't have the anticipation or the hand skills to take full advantage of his blazing speed, though; he is much faster without the puck than with it.

Sullivan works hard and forechecks energetically, but his decision-making process is slow and he does not create dangerous plays from his chances. He neither finishes nor makes plays. His point totals are woefully inadequate for someone who skates as fast as he does.

He is effective killing penalties because of his quickness. He is fairly good on face-offs. He is able to bend low (although he is a rather tall player) and tie up the opposing centre's stick.

THE PHYSICAL GAME

Sullivan is a good-sized forward who plays much smaller. If he were willing to get more involved physically, his speed would generate some power in his hitting.

THE INTANGIBLES

Sullivan is a blur when he is skittering all over the ice without the puck, but he will not be an asset until he develops some other quality, either a scoring touch or better defensive play.

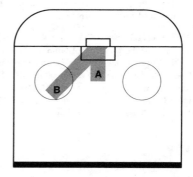

JIMMY WAITE

Yrs. of NHL service: 1
Born: Sherbrooke, Ont.; Apr. 15, 1969
Position: goaltender
Height: 6-1
Weight: 182
Uniform no.: 29
Catches: left

Career statistics:

GP	MINS	GA	SO	GAA	A	PIM
53	2610	162	2	3.72	1	0

1991-92 statistics:

GP	MINS	GAA	W	L	T	SO	GA	S	SAPCT	PIM
17	877	3.69	4	7	4	0	54	347	.844	0

1992-93 statistics:

GP	MINS	GAA	W	L	T	SO	GA	S	SAPCT	PIM
20	996	2.95	6	7	1	2	49	411	.881	0

LAST SEASON

Acquired from Chicago for future considerations.

THE PHYSICAL GAME

Waite is a good-sized goalie who plays his angles well and maximizes his size. He is aggressive and likes to challenge the shooter. He reads the play coming at him well and is a good skater in his net. Waite has fine lateral mobility and slides across with the shooter.

He has very good reflexes and a quick glove hand and recovers well for a second shot.

Waite does not come out of his net to move the puck well. He is adroit with his stick around the net, using it to break up passes. He's also very good at directing rebounds into the corner.

THE MENTAL GAME

Waite has been waiting (pun fully intended) for his shot at being a No. 1 goalie. He will come into training camp with Arturs Irbe as his chief competition, but Irbe is no Ed Belfour, and Waite has to believe he has a chance. He will have to put up with the inevitable pressure of being a goalie for a bad defensive team, but he is a battler who will keep his team in the game as long as he can.

THE INTANGIBLES

Goalies like Felix Potvin are rare. Few 19- or 20-year-olds are ready to step into the NHL cages, and Waite has needed time to develop. He is only 24, yet has parts of five seasons of NHL experience. He has excelled at the minor league level and is ready for the NHL test.

DOUG WILSON

Yrs. of NHL service: 16
Born: Ottawa, Ont.; July 5, 1957
Position: left defense
Height: 6-1
Weight: 187
Uniform no.: 24
Shoots: left

Career statistics:

GP	G	A	TP	PIM
1024	237	590	827	830

1991-92 statistics:

GP	G	A	TP	+/-	PIM	PP	SH	GW	GT	S	PCT
44	9	19	28	-38	26	4	0	0	0	123	7.3

1992-93 statistics:

GP	G	A	TP	+/-	PIM	PP	SH	GW	GT	S	PCT
42	3	17	20	-28	40	1	0	0	0	110	2.7

LAST SEASON

Missed 42 games with knee injuries. Least-productive season of career. Played in 1000th NHL game.

THE FINESSE GAME

Wilson isn't nearly the scoring threat he used to be in his glory days in Chicago. His booming slap shot off the fly is a thing of the past, and he does not dash in deep as often as he once did. He plays a more conservative game, but since his forte is offense, he becomes a less valuable contributor.

Wilson still provides flashes of his former brilliance. He is capable of rushing the puck out of his own zone, which few of the Sharks' defensemen can do well. There is nothing wrong with his vision of the ice, either, and he can hit a breaking teammate at centre ice with a pass right on the tape.

Wilson is still an effective point man. He is poised and confident with the puck and will wheel away from an aggressive forechecker and then slide into the top of the circle for a shot or a pass.

THE PHYSICAL GAME

Wilson's durability is a question mark because of the injuries that have hurt him (he has missed 117 games over the past three seasons). He's strong defensively in open ice, because he is tough to beat with any one-on-one moves, but he has trouble along the boards and in front of the net because he isn't that big. He relies on his offensive skills to bail him out defensively.

THE INTANGIBLES

Wilson is among the league's elder statesmen (one of the few remaining helmetless players). He is probably good for another season, but injuries have been a major stumbling block for him. The Sharks' defense should be improved this season with the addition of rookie Mike Rathje and a healthy Sandis Ozolinsh, and Wilson would be more effective in a specialist's role.

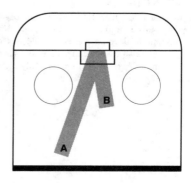

ROB ZETTLER

Yrs. of NHL service: 4
Born: Sept-Îles, Que.; Mar. 8, 1968
Position: right defense
Height: 6-3
Weight: 190
Uniform no.: 2
Shoots: left

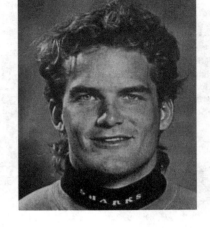

Career statistics:

GP	G	A	TP	PIM
234	2	27	29	407

1991-92 statistics:

GP	G	A	TP	+/-	PIM	PP	SH	GW	GT	S	PCT
74	1	8	9	-23	103	0	0	0	0	72	1.4

1992-93 statistics:

GP	G	A	TP	+/-	PIM	PP	SH	GW	GT	S	PCT
80	0	7	7	-50	150	0	0	0	0	60	0.0

LAST SEASON

Tied with two teammates for worst plus/minus on team and in NHL. PIM at career high.

THE FINESSE GAME

Zettler is a defensive defenseman, but you can't label him as a stay-at-home type. He is a good skater and will step up into the play in the neutral zone. He is aggressive and likes to force the attacker rather than sit back.

He doesn't get involved in the attack, but he has some nice finesse skills. He just applies them to getting the puck out of danger, by either carrying it out of the zone or making a smart outlet pass.

Zettler is an ideal support player who needs to be paired with an offensive defenseman.

THE PHYSICAL GAME

Zettler is tall but needs more upper body strength. He is willing to scrap along the boards and in front of the net, but gets knocked off the puck too easily. He showed more initiative last season and needs to continue along that route to establish more of a presence on the ice.

THE INTANGIBLES

Zettler is quietly developing into a reliable defenseman and a team leader. He has shown the willingness to pay the price to stick in the NHL, and he should be among the Sharks' top four defensemen this season.

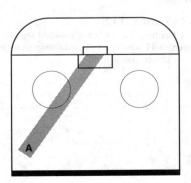

DOUG ZMOLEK

Yrs. of NHL service: 1
Born: Rochester, Minn.; Nov. 3, 1970
Position: right defense
Height: 6-1
Weight: 195
Uniform no.: 19
Shoots: left

Career statistics:

GP	G	A	TP	PIM
84	5	10	15	229

1992-93 statistics:

GP	G	A	TP	+/-	PIM	PP	SH	GW	GT	S	PCT
84	5	10	15	-50	229	2	0	0	0	94	5.3

LAST SEASON

First NHL season. Second on team in PIM. One of two Sharks to play in all 84 games. Tied with two team-mates for worst plus/minus on team and in NHL.

THE FINESSE GAME

Zmolek is a good skater with a strong stride. He has good balance and agility, and moves well laterally. His skating helps him angle attackers to the boards, and he is tough to beat one on one.

Zmolek has some nice offensive instincts. He moves the puck out of the zone well with quick, accurate passes, and he has soft hands for touch passes in tighter quarters.

Zmolek is a very good penalty killer. He is intelligent and alert, and stops and starts well forwards to backwards.

THE PHYSICAL GAME

Zmolek developed in college (University of Minnesota) where the physical element of the game is not as important. He has more to learn, but he will sacrifice his body to make a play. While not a big hitter, he will tie up his man in front of the net. There is a little wild streak in Zmolek, and he needs to cut down on bad penalties.

THE INTANGIBLES

Zmolek has the signs of being a solid two-way defenseman, and his point totals could jump as he gains more confidence and maturity.

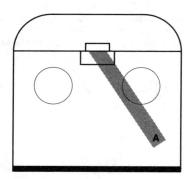

ST. LOUIS BLUES

MURRAY BARON

Yrs. of NHL service: 4
Born: Prince George, B.C., June 1, 1967
Position: left defense
Height: 6-3
Weight: 210
Uniform no.: 34
Shoots: left

Career statistics:

GP	G	A	TP	PIM
203	15	20	35	239

1991-92 statistics:

GP	G	A	TP	+/-	PIM	PP	SH	GW	GT	S	PCT
67	3	8	11	-3	94	0	0	0	0	55	5.5

1992-93 statistics:

GP	G	A	TP	+/-	PIM	PP	SH	GW	GT	S	PCT
53	2	2	4	-5	59	0	0	1	0	42	4.8

LAST SEASON

Missed 31 games with injuries, including a broken foot. Games played three-season low. Goals, assists and points match career low.

THE FINESSE GAME

Baron is the perfect example of how a player with good hockey sense and lesser skills can be more valuable than someone — like Baron — with better skills and lesser sense.

A good skater with some agility, Baron jumps into the play rather than lead a rush, but he doesn't do anything the least bit creative. He doesn't seem to know when a hard or a soft lead pass is required. He can lug the puck at a pretty good clip, but does little more than stop inside the blue line and fire a shot from the point. His shot is merely average. You will rarely find Baron gambling in deep. He seldom works on specialty teams.

Baron has developed more poise defensively and is now less likely to get rid of the puck in a panic; instead, he will make a safe, if unspectacular, play.

THE PHYSICAL GAME

Too many nights go by when you can't recall if Baron was on the ice or not. For a player of his healthy size, this is a huge negative. Baron doesn't clear the front of the net with any authority, and never establishes a physical presence on the ice. Neither aggressive nor mean, he doesn't have the offensive credentials to compensate for his lack of physical play.

THE INTANGIBLES

Baron remains a frustrating package. Injuries last season didn't help his development, of course, but it appears that his contributions are never going to match his potential. He remains a role player and is a reminder of one of GM Ron Caron's worst trades (Baron and Ron Sutter were acquired from Philadelphia for Rod Brind'Amour and Dan Quinn).

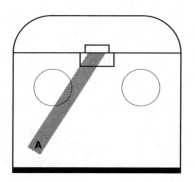

BOB BASSEN

Yrs. of NHL service: 8
Born: Calgary, Alta.; May 6, 1965
Position: centre/left wing
Height: 5-11
Weight: 170
Uniform no.: 28
Shoots: left

Career statistics:

GP	G	A	TP	PIM
450	53	97	150	698

1991-92 statistics:

GP	G	A	TP	+/-	PIM	PP	SH	GW	GT	S	PCT
79	7	25	32	+12	167	0	0	1	0	101	6.9

1992-93 statistics:

GP	G	A	TP	+/-	PIM	PP	SH	GW	GT	S	PCT
53	9	10	19	0	63	0	1	0	0	61	14.8

LAST SEASON

Games played three season low. Points four-season low. Missed 31 games with a broken foot.

THE FINESSE GAME

Bassen has average straightaway speed, and with the playing time missed due to injury he looked even slower last season. But he does have quickness and agility, which he puts to work in close quarters to avoid hits from bigger players. Don't get us wrong: if Bassen has to take a hit, he will, but he's also smart enough to avoid unneccessary punishment.

Bassen doesn't have great hands or a great shot to go with his work ethic. All of his finesse skills are average at best. His few goals come from going for the puck in scrambles around the net.

Bassen is only so-so on face-offs. He's not big enough to tie up most opposing centres, and lacks the hand speed to win draws outright.

THE PHYSICAL GAME

If there had been Sutter triplets instead of twins, Bassen would have been the third member of the trio. Bassen plays much bigger than his size, aware every night that if he isn't scrapping along the boards or in front of the net, he will be on the bench, which is where a Sutter — er, a Bassen — hates to sit. He has a low centre of gravity, which makes it tough to knock him off his feet, and he's closer to the puck than a lot of other skaters. Bassen often wins scrums just by being able to pry the loose puck out from flailing feet.

THE INTANGIBLES

Bassen scores highest in this category. He is a reliable team man, one of those players who don't promise much in the way of skills but always deliver in terms of effort. He matches up night after night against most of the league's bigger, better forwards, and makes them work for what they get. He is a valuable role player.

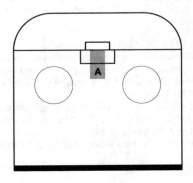

JEFF BROWN

Yrs. of NHL service: 8
Born: Ottawa, Ont.; Apr. 30, 1966
Position: right defense
Height: 6-1
Weight: 204
Uniform no.: 21
Shoots: right

Career statistics:

GP	G	A	TP	PIM
503	123	283	403	338

1991-92 statistics:

GP	G	A	TP	+/-	PIM	PP	SH	GW	GT	S	PCT
80	20	38	58	+8	38	10	0	2	1	214	9.3

1992-93 statistics:

GP	G	A	TP	+/-	PIM	PP	SH	GW	GT	S	PCT
71	25	53	78	-6	58	12	2	3	0	220	11.4

LAST SEASON

Missed 13 games with a broken foot. Led team defensemen in scoring. Goals, assists and points career highs. Second on team in assists, fourth in points.

THE FINESSE GAME

Brown is a natural quarterback on the power play. He moves to the off-wing on the point, opening up his shot for one-timers. Since forward Nelson Emerson usually plays the other point, there is more pressure than usual on Brown to make the smart play at the point and not leave the Blues vulnerable to a two-on-one shorthanded try against a forward (the Blues gave up 15 shorthanded goals last season). This leaves Brown in a dilemma, because he likes to take a chance and work the puck low himself, but won't do it unless it's a safe option.

Brown's game stems from his skating ability. He has very good lateral movement and can handle the puck at tempo. He's a very good playmaker for a defenseman, ready to unleash his strong point shot, or fake the slap and pass, or headman the pass off a break out of the defensive zone. He sees the ice well.

Defensively, Brown took a step back from the development he started to show in 1991-92. There is no reason that this can't be corrected. Brown has too much hockey sense and too much skill not to be a better player.

THE PHYSICAL GAME

Yes, Brown is an offensive defenseman, but that doesn't mean he should be fishing for the puck in front of the net when he should be dropping someone onto the seat of his pants.

Brown doesn't finish his checks consistently, and he lacks the mean streak needed to be a more dominating player. He has been thrust into a leadership role with the Blues, and has to be willing to take it another step.

THE INTANGIBLES

This could have been a breakout season for Brown but for the injury (which forced him to miss the All-Star game, his first). Brown will never be in the top 10 in defenseman scoring, but he should contribute a consistent 80 points a season. If he would elevate his defensive game, he could be a B version of Ray Bourque.

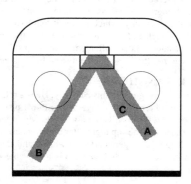

GARTH BUTCHER

Yrs. of NHL service: 9
Born: Regina, Sask.; Jan. 8, 1963
Position: right defense
Height: 6-0
Weight: 200
Uniform no.: 5
Shoots: right

Career statistics:

GP	G	A	TP	PIM
775	43	136	179	2100

1991-92 statistics:

GP	G	A	TP	+/-	PIM	PP	SH	GW	GT	S	PCT
68	5	15	20	+5	189	0	0	0	0	50	10.0

1992-93 statistics:

GP	G	A	TP	+/-	PIM	PP	SH	GW	GT	S	PCT
84	5	10	15	0	211	0	0	2	0	83	6.0

LAST SEASON

Led team in PIM. One of three Blues to play in all 84 games. Points seven-season low.

THE FINESSE GAME

Smart and consistent, Butcher is one of the most quietly effective defensemen in his division. There are a lot of things Butcher can't do. He is not a very good skater — average speed, below-average agility, above-average strength — but he compensates by playing a sound positional game and not taking low-percentage chances.

Butcher doesn't go for the home-run pass up the middle, but makes safe yet creative short plays, off the boards or just after a defender has moved out of position to come to him. He does not panic with the puck and anchors what was the top penalty-killing unit in the NHL last season.

Given some room to skate, Butcher will rush the puck and move it smartly, but he won't venture too deep into the attacking zone. His offensive contributions are limited to shots from the right points.

THE PHYSICAL GAME

Butcher's reputation as a fierce competitor and hitter is well established. He will protect himself and is the first one to step up in defense of a teammate. He is only a decent size for an NHL defenseman (or, for that matter, forward) these days, but Butcher's demeanour adds a few inches and a few pounds to his frame. He is a willing hitter but not a great puncher. He is very good at goading his rivals, and often whips up opposing forwards to the point of fury.

THE INTANGIBLES

Butcher will turn 31 during the season. He still has enough jump and desire to be a strong leader, and, as some of the Blues' young defensemen continue to develop, Butcher will look better and better. Remember that this team's defense was decimated when it lost Scott Stevens to New Jersey as compensation for signing Brendan Shanahan in 1991.

NELSON EMERSON

Yrs. of NHL service: 2
Born: Hamilton, Ont.; Aug. 17, 1967
Position: centre
Height: 5-11
Weight: 165
Uniform no.: 7
Shoots: right

Career statistics:

GP	G	A	TP	PIM
165	45	90	135	130

1991-92 statistics:

GP	G	A	TP	+/-	PIM	PP	SH	GW	GT	S	PCT
79	23	36	59	-5	66	3	0	2	0	143	16.1

1992-93 statistics:

GP	G	A	TP	+/-	PIM	PP	SH	GW	GT	S	PCT
82	22	51	73	+2	62	5	2	4	0	196	11.2

LAST SEASON

Third on team in assists. Career highs in assists and points in second full NHL season.

THE FINESSE GAME

Despite playing in only his second NHL season, Emerson was given top dog status on the Blues' No. 1 line (with Craig Janney and Brendan Shanahan) and as point man (with Jeff Brown) on the power play. Emerson has an excellent point shot. He keeps it low, on target and tippable. The Blues' power play ranked third overall last season. He is very intelligent with the puck, and doesn't always fire from the point, but works the puck to the middle of the blue line and uses screens well.

Emerson works well down low at even strength. He is mature and creative, with a terrific short game. He has quick hands for passing or snapping off a shot. Both he and Janney like to work from behind a net, and the two players will weave in and out of the territory, tempting the defense to chase behind the cage.

Emerson has good quickness and balance, and darts in and out of traffic in front of the net. He's too small to do any physical damage.

THE PHYSICAL GAME

Small players can excel in the NHL, as Theo Fleury, Mark Recchi and Emerson demonstrate night after night. Emerson has good skating balance, and that will give him a little edge to knock a bigger player off-stride once in a while. He will work hard defensively, but has to play a smart, small man's game to avoid getting pasted.

THE INTANGIBLES

Emerson was one of the most quietly successful rookies of 1992, and he continued his development in his sophomore season. Emerson will never be a star, but he proved worthy of playing on the Blues' top line.

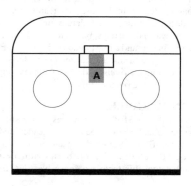

BRETT HULL

Yrs. of NHL service: 6
Born: Belleville, Ont.; Aug. 9, 1964
Position: right wing
Height: 5-10
Weight: 201
Uniform no.: 16
Shoots: right

Career statistics:

GP	G	A	TP	PIM
459	356	247	603	184

1991-92 statistics:

GP	G	A	TP	+/-	PIM	PP	SH	GW	GT	S	PCT
73	70	39	109	-2	48	20	5	9	1	408	17.2

1992-93 statistics:

GP	G	A	TP	+/-	PIM	PP	SH	GW	GT	S	PCT
80	54	47	101	-27	41	29	0	2	1	390	13.8

LAST SEASON
Second in NHL in power play goals. Second in NHL in shots. Led team in goals, power play goals and shots. Second on team in points. Goals four-season low. First time in four seasons Hull failed to score 70 goals. Fourth consecutive season with 100 or more points. Missed four games with wrist injury. Worst plus/minus on team.

THE FINESSE GAME
No one, least of all Hull himself, thought the prolific scorer would play on the second (and sometimes the third) line in St. Louis last season. Such was the fall-out of the Blues' decision to shun Adam Oates's contract demands in 1992 and ship him to Boston for Craig Janney. The Blues found a new top line with Nelson Emerson, Brendan Shanahan and Janney, but lost the Hull touch.

Hull still shoots the puck at a thousand miles an hour, but not enough, and not with the same accuracy that made his one-timers so deadly. His confidence, once so supreme, has been obviously lacking.

When things are going well, Hull is always working to get himself in position for a pass. On the power play, he will be in open ice, constantly moving, and can fire off any kind of shot, accurately. His release may be the quickest in the NHL. Hull usually moves to his off-wing on the power play.

Hull is also an underrated playmaker who can threadneedle a pass through traffic right onto the tape of a teammate. But who pays to watch Hull pass?

In 1991-92, Hull was used to kill penalties and scored 5 shorthanded goals. He saw almost no time on the shorthanded unit last season, and missed the ice time.

THE PHYSICAL GAME
Hull is a power forward with superior finesse skills, but he seemed to abandon the physical part of the game last season. Hull has to go back to bulling his way through checkers when he can't outmanoeuvre them. Last season, he would make his shifty moves and then give up the effort. Driving to the net with his old abandon would wake up his game. He didn't score as many goals last season as he has in the past off his work in front of the net.

THE INTANGIBLES
Fifty goals is far from a mediocre season...unless your name is Brett Hull. The Golden Brett played with almost every forward on the Blues last season, and none of them was Adam Oates. The top priority for St. Louis management is to find a player to recreate that old Hull and Oates magic, or else settle for 50 goals from a player who once looked ready to net 90.

In addition to losing Oates the playmaker, Hull lost Oates the friend. Combined with (or perhaps because of) his scoring drop-off, Hull lost his zest for the game, and on the ice he was often a sad sight, a non-factor.

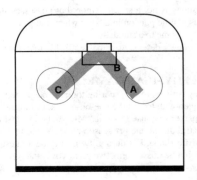

CRAIG JANNEY

Yrs. of NHL service: 6
Born: Hartford, Conn.; Sept. 26, 1967
Position: centre
Height: 6-1
Weight: 190
Uniform no.: 15
Shoots: left

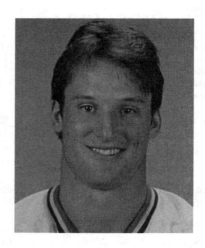

Career statistics:

GP	G	A	TP	PIM
371	115	310	425	58

1991-92 statistics:

GP	G	A	TP	+/-	PIM	PP	SH	GW	GT	S	PCT
78	18	69	87	+6	22	6	0	2	0	127	14.2

1992-93 statistics:

GP	G	A	TP	+/-	PIM	PP	SH	GW	GT	S	PCT
84	24	82	106	-4	12	8	0	6	0	137	17.5

LAST SEASON

Led team in assists and points. One of three Blues to play in all 84 games. Points career high; first season with 100 or more points. Second on team in game-winning goals.

THE FINESSE GAME

Probably one of the top five passers in the NHL, Janney finds his target and finds him in time to allow the shooter enough room to do something with the puck off the pass. He will draw the defender to him to open up ice, but by keeping the puck close to his body (he uses a very short stick), he makes it difficult for anyone fishing for the puck to knock it away. Janney then makes the pretty pass.

He is very creative and sees the ice and all of his options well.

Janney has few flaws, but one of them is his unselfishness. That used to be the knock, oddly enough, on Adam Oates as well, but Oates scored 45 goals for the Bruins last season. Janney should be worth at least 30 with his quick release, but he would rather pass than shoot. He is patient with the puck and will not always make the obvious pass, meaning his teammates have to be exceptionally alert, because Janney can turn a seemingly dead play into a scoring chance.

Janney is not a speed demon, but possesses slick moves that he puts on in a burst when it appears he is about to come to a standstill.

Janney's defensive game is still his major weakness.

THE PHYSICAL GAME

Janney isn't more of a scoring threat because he isn't strong enough to win the one-on-one battles in traffic. The player they used to call "Mr. Michelin" lost his spare tire during the off-season and reported to camp in terrific shape. His durability used to be a question mark, but he missed only two games over the past two seasons.

The opponent's book is to hit Janney early and often. He will keep himself out of the trenches. He has fairly good size, but doesn't have the upper body strength to knock anyone off the puck or prevent the puck being stripped from him. Janney is not a coward and will take a hit to make a play, since he controls the puck until the last moment, waiting for the perfect play. Playing with a physical linemate (Brendan Shanahan) complements Janney well.

THE INTANGIBLES

The pressure was on Janney to produce after St. Louis dealt Adam Oates, and while he never clicked with Brett Hull, he centred the team's new dynamic trio with Nelson Emerson and Shanahan. Janney worked hard and emerged as one of the team's leaders as well as one of its stars. His 100+ point total was no fluke.

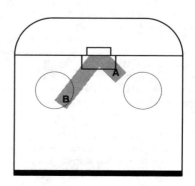

CURTIS JOSEPH

Yrs. of NHL service: 4
Born: Keswick, Ont.; Apr. 29, 1967
Position: goaltender
Height: 5-10
Weight: 182
Uniform no.: 31
Catches: left

Career statistics:

GP	MINS	GA	SO	GAA	A	PIM
173	9946	508	3	3.06	12	20

1991-92 statistics:

GP	MINS	AVG	W	L	T	SO	GA	S	SAPCT	PIM
60	3494	3.01	27	20	10	2	175	1953	.910	12

1992-93 statistics:

GP	MINS	AVG	W	L	T	SO	GA	S	SAPCT	PIM
68	3890	3.02	29	28	9	1	196	2202	.911	8

LAST SEASON

Finalist for 1993 Vezina Trophy. Led NHL in save percentage. Fourth in NHL in GAA. Second in NHL in minutes played. Career high in wins.

THE PHYSICAL GAME

Parents of young aspiring goaltenders should avert their child's eyes from Joseph. Nothing the Blues' star goalie does is by the book. Joseph always looks unorthodox and off-balance, but he is one of those hybrid goalies — like Ed Belfour and Felix Potvin — whose success can't be argued with.

Joseph positions himself well, angling out to challenge the shooter, and is one of the best breakaway goalies in the league. He stopped the only penalty shot he faced last season — by Winnipeg's Phil Housley — and stopped two attempts in 1991-92. Joseph goes to his knees quickly but bounces back to his skates fast for the rebound. He tends to keep rebounds in front of him.

Joseph is a strong, if bizarre, stickhandler. He has to move his hands on the stick, putting the butt-end of the stick into his catching glove and lowering his blocker. His favourite move is a weird backhand whip off the boards. Joseph is a good skater who moves out of his cage confidently and well to handle the puck. He needs to improve his lateral movement. He also uses his stick to harass anyone who dares to camp on his doorstep. He's not Billy Smith, but he's getting more aggressive with his whacks.

THE MENTAL GAME

Since the NHL began tabulating shots against goaltenders in 1982, no goalie has faced more shots in a season than Joseph did last year. All of that pressure mounts up, and while Joseph sometimes gets worn down physically from the effort, mentally he remains sharp through the wildest flurries. There are a few nights when he falls apart under assault, but he always bounces back with a solid game.

His focus and concentration are excellent. Joseph steals games on nights when his team is outshot by a 2:1 ratio. Joseph has gotten smarter about drawing penalties, too, and some players have accused him of feigning injuries to get sympathetic calls from the referee.

THE INTANGIBLES

Joseph is nicknamed "CuJo" from the first two letters of his first and last name, and you would be a mad dog, too, if you were left to your own devices as much as he is.

BASIL MCRAE

Yrs. of NHL service: 9
Born: Beaverton, Ont.; Jan. 5, 1961
Position: left wing
Height: 6-2
Weight: 205
Uniform no.: 17
Shoots: left

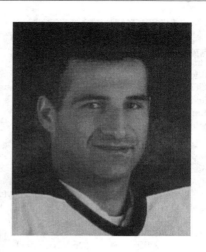

Career statistics:

GP	G	A	TP	PIM
489	51	75	126	2230

1991-92 statistics:

GP	G	A	TP	+/-	PIM	PP	SH	GW	GT	S	PCT
59	5	8	13	-14	245	0	0	0	0	64	7.8

1992-93 statistics:

GP	G	A	TP	+/-	PIM	PP	SH	GW	GT	S	PCT
47	3	6	9	-16	169	2	0	0	0	45	6.7

LAST SEASON

Acquired from Tampa Bay with Doug Crossman and a fourth-round draft pick in 1996 for Jason Ruff, a fourth-round pick in 1994, and a fifth-round pick in 1995. PIM career low. Missed more than 30 games with broken left leg.

THE FINESSE GAME

McRae's already limited finesse skills have continued to deteriorate. Age (he will turn 33 this season) and injuries have slowed him, but McRae is such a smart and heady player that he merits a jersey ahead of some more talented players.

McRae has pretty good hands for someone who has staked his reputation on being a tough dude. He can handle the puck and make a play — not at top speed, true, but he is usually given some extra skating room and he makes good use of it. McRae will score his precious few goals from around the crease.

McRae is a strong forechecker but becomes more and more of a defensive liability as he slows down. He was -13 in just 33 games with the Blues.

THE PHYSICAL GAME

McRae wants to play and will do whatever it takes to stay on the ice — even if it means having to go off the ice to serve yet another penalty. He will protect his team's smaller finesse players. Anyone who wants to mess with a teammate will have to answer to McRae.

THE INTANGIBLES

McRae's value is not always readily apparent on the ice. But every coach he has ever played for speaks glowingly of McRae's value in the dressing room and on the bench. McRae is a character player, and when he is able to keep himself in the line-up he allows his teammates to play a little bigger.

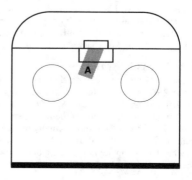

KEVIN MILLER

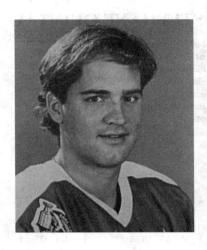

Yrs. of NHL service: 3
Born: Lansing, Mich.; Sept. 9, 1965
Position: right wing
Height: 5-11
Weight: 190
Uniform no.: 14
Shoots: right

Career statistics:

GP	G	A	TP	PIM
276	69	90	159	224

1991-92 statistics:

GP	G	A	TP	+/-	PIM	PP	SH	GW	GT	S	PCT
80	20	26	46	+6	53	3	1	4	0	130	15.4

1992-93 statistics:

GP	G	A	TP	+/-	PIM	PP	SH	GW	GT	S	PCT
82	24	25	49	+2	100	8	3	4	2	163	14.7

LAST SEASON

Acquired from Washington for Paul Cavallini. Career highs in goals and points. Tied for team lead in short-handed goals.

THE FINESSE GAME

Like his older brother, Kelly in Washington, Kevin Miller is a two-way forward with a tremendous work ethic. The role of checker was once limited to players who didn't have scoring skills, but players like the Miller brothers have added to the reputation of two-way players who can create turnovers with their smart, persistent forechecking, then have the finesse skills to produce points as well.

Miller is a better playmaker than finisher. While he's not overly creative, most of his scoring chances come from opportunities from the forecheck. He has fairly quick hands but lacks a soft goal-scorer's touch.

He has always succeeded at every level he has played — college, Olympic and minor league — but it wasn't until last season that he got the playing time to prove himself an NHL regular. The knock is that he's small, but he plays much larger.

THE PHYSICAL GAME

Miller takes the body well, although he doesn't have great size. He is very strong and has a low centre of gravity, which makes it tough to knock him off the puck. He will get overpowered in heavy traffic areas, but that doesn't keep him from trying.

THE INTANGIBLES

Miller had only 3 assists in 10 games before the Caps gave up on him and sent him to St. Louis, where he bloomed on the team's top checking line. Every team in the NHL should be lucky enough to have a Miller or Sutter brother. The Blues have cornered the market with three.

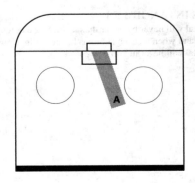

STEPHANE QUINTAL

Yrs. of NHL service: 5
Born: Boucherville, Que.; Oct. 22, 1968
Position: right defense
Height: 6-3
Weight: 215
Uniform no.: 33
Shoots: right

Career statistics:

GP	G	A	TP	PIM
259	9	35	44	349

1991-92 statistics:

GP	G	A	TP	+/-	PIM	PP	SH	GW	GT	S	PCT
75	4	16	20	-11	109	0	0	0	0	71	5.6

1992-93 statistics:

GP	G	A	TP	+/-	PIM	PP	SH	GW	GT	S	PCT
75	1	10	11	-6	100	0	1	0	0	81	1.2

LAST SEASON

Games played match career high. Goals, assists and points two-season lows.

THE FINESSE GAME

Quintal's game is limited by his lumbering skating. He has other nice touches, like a decent point shot and a good head and hands for passing. But all of the rest has to be done at a virtual standstill. Quintal has to be paired with a quick skater, or his shifts will be spent solely in the defensive zone.

Fortunately, Quintal is as aware as anyone else of his flaws. He smartly plays a positional game and doesn't get involved in any low-percentage plays in the offensive zone. He will not step up in the neutral zone to risk an interception, but will fall back into a defensive mode.

While he can exist as an NHL regular in the five-on-five mode, he is a risky proposition for any specialty teams play.

THE PHYSICAL GAME

Quintal is slow but very strong on his skates. He thrives on contact and works hard along the boards and in front of the net. He hits hard without taking penalties, and is a tough and willing fighter.

THE INTANGIBLES

Quintal will never be better than a No. 5 or 6 defenseman, and when a coach shortens his bench in a game, Quintal will be sitting on it.

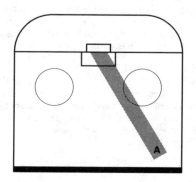

BRENDAN SHANAHAN

Yrs. of NHL service: 6
Born: Mimico, Ont.; Jan. 23, 1969
Position: right wing
Height: 6-3
Weight: 210
Uniform no.: 19
Shoots: right

Career statistics:

GP	G	A	TP	PIM
432	172	205	377	869

1991-92 statistics:

GP	G	A	TP	+/-	PIM	PP	SH	GW	GT	S	PCT
80	33	36	69	-3	171	13	0	2	2	215	15.3

1992-93 statistics:

GP	G	A	TP	+/-	PIM	PP	SH	GW	GT	S	PCT
71	51	43	94	+10	174	18	0	8	8	232	22.0

LAST SEASON

Led team in plus/minus, game-winning goals and shooting percentage. Second on team in goals with career high. Third in team in points with career high. Career high in assists. Second on team in power play goals. Missed 12 games with a groin injury.

THE FINESSE GAME

We predicted in last year's *HSR* that Shanahan would hit the 40-goal mark. He blew by it, and if he hadn't missed 12 games with an injury he would have netted 60. That gives him something to shoot for this season.

Shanahan is a wonderful package of grit, skills and improving smarts. He will battle in front of the net for a puck, but he is also savvy enough to avoid an unnecessary thrashing. On the power play, he is one of the best in the league at staying just off the crease, waiting for a shot to come from the point, then timing his entry to the front of the net for the moving screen, the tip or the rebound.

He has wonderfully soft hands (he was a centre in junior) for nifty goalmouth passes, and he has a hard, accurate snap and slap shot with a quick release. He will take some face-offs, especially in the offensive zone, and succeeds by tying up the opposing centre and using his feet to control the puck. He has become one of the Blues' top go-to guys.

One of Shanahan's few flaws is his skating. He lacks quickness but does have great strength and balance.

THE PHYSICAL GAME

The Shanahan dilemma for rival teams: if you play Shanahan aggressively, it brings out the best in him. If you lay off and give him room, he will kill you with his skills. Shanahan spent his formative NHL years establishing his reputation by dropping his gloves with anybody who challenged him, but he has gotten smarter without losing his tough edge. He had only one fighting major last season, compared with 10 in 1991-92. He has a controlled nasty streak.

Shanahan will take or make a hit to create a play. He is willing to eat glass to make a pass.

THE INTANGIBLES

All the signs of the past few seasons pointed toward Shanahan stamping himself as one of the league's elite power forwards. Now he has joined the ranks of Cam Neely, Kevin Stevens et al, and all he has to do is keep working to stay there. He is a tremendous talent and one of the few NHL stars who deserves his own talk show besides.

Brett Hull wears the captain's "C" for the Blues, but Shanahan is the team's true leader.

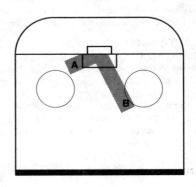

RICH SUTTER

Yrs. of NHL service: 10
Born: Viking, Alta.; Dec. 2, 1963
Position: right wing
Height: 5-11
Weight: 188
Uniform no.: 23
Shoots: right

Career statistics:

GP	G	A	TP	PIM
754	137	149	286	1265

1991-92 statistics:

GP	G	A	TP	+/-	PIM	PP	SH	GW	GT	S	PCT
77	9	16	25	+7	107	0	1	3	0	113	8.0

1992-93 statistics:

GP	G	A	TP	+/-	PIM	PP	SH	GW	GT	S	PCT
84	13	14	27	-4	100	0	2	1	0	148	8.8

LAST SEASON

One of three Blues to appear in all 84 games. Goals two-season high.

THE FINESSE GAME

Only an average NHL talent, Sutter endures on his grit and work ethic. He is alert to game situations, and will be on the ice at crunch time when the team needs a lead protected. In a playoff game against Toronto, Sutter was poised enough in the late stages to hold off touching the puck on a delayed offside, allowing precious seconds to click off the clock. Little plays like that mean fewer Maalox tablets for the coaching staff.

Sutter scores his goals from hard work around the net and by creating turnovers from his strong forechecking. He takes "smart" penalties and creates power play chances for his team by keeping his legs driving as he works to get in scoring position.

You never have to worry about Sutter being ready to play. His intensity is a constant.

THE PHYSICAL GAME

Sutter plays with the arrogance of a skater at least four inches taller and 25 pounds heavier. He is annoying to play against, always in your face and yapping. He'll take whatver piece of a player he can to distract. If knocked down (which he often is by bigger skaters), he will bounce right back up and get into the play.

THE INTANGIBLES

We'll admit when we're wrong (even though we hate to) and say we underrated the youngest Sutter last season. With his coaching brother Brian leaving after 1991-92, we thought Rich would drop right off the Blues' depth chart. Instead, he played even better, becoming a reliable checking winger who brings a spark to his shifts. Our lesson is learned: we'll never again underestimate a Sutter.

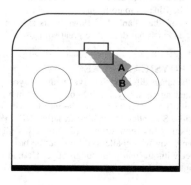

RON SUTTER

Yrs. of NHL service: 11
Born: Viking, Alta.; Dec. 2, 1963
Position: centre
Height: 6-0
Weight: 180
Uniform no.: 22
Shoots: right

Career statistics:

GP	G	A	TP	PIM
623	156	249	405	945

1991-92 statistics:

GP	G	A	TP	+/-	PIM	PP	SH	GW	GT	S	PCT
68	19	27	46	+9	91	5	4	1	1	106	17.9

1992-93 statistics:

GP	G	A	TP	+/-	PIM	PP	SH	GW	GT	S	PCT
59	12	15	27	-11	99	4	0	3	0	90	13.3

LAST SEASON

Goals five-season low. Assists career low. Missed 25 games with injuries, including a separated right shoulder and strained abdominal muscles.

THE FINESSE GAME

Sutter is an ideal checking-line centre, a player with great defensive awareness who can take advantage of the scoring chances generated from his forechecking. But he hasn't been allowed to fill that role for the past two seasons due to the team's lack of depth at the position, and he suffers from trying to be something he's not.

Sutter's skills are all average but loom larger because of his aggressive nature and his reliable intensity. Sutters *hate* to lose. Somehow you get the feeling that their parents always set one dinner plate too few on the table — musical meals instead of musical chairs — and the boys had to battle one another or go hungry.

Sutter has a choppy stride, but he reads plays so well that he's often a jump ahead of faster players because of his intelligence. His anticipation is excellent.

He is also strong on face-offs. The top Blues man on the draws, he can win them outright or scrap with the opposing centre for control.

THE PHYSICAL GAME

Anyone who goes into a corner with a Sutter pays the price. He plays bigger than his size and is fearless regardless of the size of his opponent. He will badger and intimidate with body or stick, and will not back down from any challenge.

THE INTANGIBLES

A healthy Ron Sutter means a solid two-way centre, heavier on defense than offense, who can provide 20 goals and 50 assists a season. He is a better No. 3 centre than No. 2, but right now the Blues don't have anyone else capable of the job.

Incidentally, twins Rich and Ron ended up with an identical number of points (27) last season, and Ron had just one fewer penalty minutes.

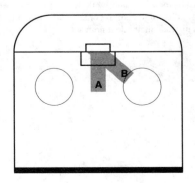

RON WILSON

Yrs. of NHL service: 13
Born: Toronto, Ont.; May 13, 1956
Position: centre
Height: 5-9
Weight: 180
Uniform no.: 18
Shoots: left

Career statistics:

GP	G	A	TP	PIM
784	108	206	314	403

1991-92 statistics:

GP	G	A	TP	+/-	PIM	PP	SH	GW	GT	S	PCT
64	12	17	29	+10	46	5	2	2	0	100	12.0

1992-93 statistics:

GP	G	A	TP	+/-	PIM	PP	SH	GW	GT	S	PCT
78	8	11	19	-8	44	0	3	1	0	75	10.7

LAST SEASON

Most games played since rookie season. Tied for team lead in shorthanded goals. Goals three-season low. Points four-season low. Missed four games with knee injury.

THE FINESSE GAME

Wilson as Brett Hull's linemate? It's a ridiculous notion, but that's what the offense-desperate Blues tried last season. At this stage of his career, Wilson is strictly an earnest fourth-line centre.

Wilson has some skating quickness, which he utilizes in his solid forechecking game. He is a smart, sensible veteran without being gifted in any one area. His hand speed is nil, and Wilson provides scoring chances only off his hard checking work.

He takes a lot of defensive zone draws but is only so-so.

THE PHYSICAL GAME

Wilson is not a banger. He'll absorb a hit to protect the puck but is simply outmuscled in one-on-one confrontations and is not a physical factor.

THE INTANGIBLES

Wilson plays on a team that is simply overloaded with defensive forwards, and while he fills his role well, he'll find ice time hard to come by when (and if) the Blues upgrade their talent up front.

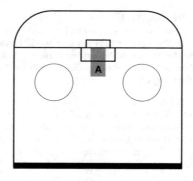

RICK ZOMBO

Yrs. of NHL service: 8
Born: Des Plaines, Ill.; May 8, 1963
Position: right defense
Height: 6-1
Weight: 195
Uniform no.: 4
Shoots: right

Career statistics:

GP	G	A	TP	PIM
488	17	108	125	566

1991-92 statistics:

GP	G	A	TP	+/-	PIM	PP	SH	GW	GT	S	PCT
67	3	15	18	+1	61	0	0	0	0	48	6.3

1992-93 statistics:

GP	G	A	TP	+/-	PIM	PP	SH	GW	GT	S	PCT
71	0	15	15	-2	78	0	0	0	0	43	0.0

LAST SEASON

Goals career low for full season. Points six-season low.

THE FINESSE GAME

Zombo is a good skater (if not a pretty one), so good that it's a bit depressing he never developed into more of a two-way defenseman. He has above average agility and quickness, with a strong stride and very good balance. Zombo has good lateral mobility and fares well in the defensive zone, where he will step up boldly to make a hit. He was one of the unsung heroes of the Blues' top-ranked penalty-killing unit.

However, he doesn't read offensive plays very well, which is why he doesn't get involved in rushes up ice. He can key a breakout with a hard or soft pass as the occasion dictates, but he doesn't jump into the play or lead the rush. His scoring instincts are negligible.

He has focussed himself on becoming a steady, stay-at-home defenseman, and he has just about perfected the role. Once in a great while he will start running around a bit in his own zone, but he settles down quickly.

THE PHYSICAL GAME

Zombo should be a more physical presence than he is. He's big and sturdy, and though he's not huge, he has a skating edge that many bigger skaters lack, and he should be able to do more with his body. Zombo wants to do just enough — just enough to win the puck along the boards, just enough to eliminate the player in front of the net — without really trying to scare anybody.

THE INTANGIBLES

Zombo could take the phrase "Just do it" and turn it around to his own personal slogan, "Just don't overdo it." He has never risen to the level that his skills indicated he could; instead, he has developed into a poised defenseman who will never surprise but seldom disappoints.

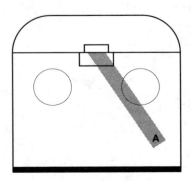

TAMPA BAY LIGHTNING

MIKAEL ANDERSSON

Yrs. of NHL service: 7
Born: Malmo, Sweden; May 10, 1966
Position: centre/left wing
Height: 5-11
Weight: 185
Uniform no.: 34
Shoots: left

Career statistics:

GP	G	A	TP	PIM
341	55	104	159	60

1991-92 statistics:

GP	G	A	TP	+/-	PIM	PP	SH	GW	GT	S	PCT
74	18	29	47	+18	14	1	3	1	0	149	12.1

1992-93 statistics:

GP	G	A	TP	+/-	PIM	PP	SH	GW	GT	S	PCT
77	16	11	27	-14	14	3	2	4	0	169	9.5

LAST SEASON

Second on team in game-winning goals. Missed four games with back spasms.

THE FINESSE GAME

Speed is the name of Andersson's game. He has the speed to bolt past defenders to the outside, and he's an open-ice threat. He is small and quick, with good puck control skills. Andersson doesn't have a lot of moves and doesn't like to shoot, and that makes him one-dimensional.

Andersson is more of a perimeter player who likes the wide open spaces, but he will go through traffic with or for the puck. It seems that just one necessary ingredient is missing in his game, and that is his will-ingness or ability to be a finisher. He is wonderful to watch on breakaways, since he can do so much with the puck at top speed, not unlike Pat LaFontaine (al-though he doesn't have as many opportunities as LaFontaine, and he isn't quite as fast). Andersson doesn't always finish what his speed would allow him to do.

Andersson is responsible defensively.

THE PHYSICAL GAME

He has shown more of a penchant for working through checks around the net. He will never be mistaken for a power forward; however, he has learned to play hard-er.

THE INTANGIBLES

Andersson tailed off considerably from his 1991-92 season, in which he played out his option in Hartford — always a danger signal in terms of motivation. He gets enough ice time in Tampa Bay to be more of a factor.

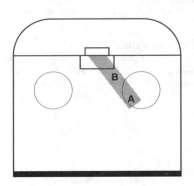

BOB BEERS

Yrs. of NHL service: 2
Born: Pittsburgh, Pa.; May 20, 1967
Position: right defense
Height: 6-2
Weight: 200
Uniform no.: 2
Shoots: right

Career statistics:

GP	G	A	TP	PIM
114	12	31	43	115

1991-92 statistics:

GP	G	A	TP	+/-	PIM	PP	SH	GW	GT	S	PCT
31	0	5	5	-13	29	0	0	0	0	25	0.0

1992-93 statistics:

GP	G	A	TP	+/-	PIM	PP	SH	GW	GT	S	PCT
64	12	24	36	-25	70	7	0	0	0	138	8.7

LAST SEASON

Career highs in games played, goals, assists, points and PIM. Tied for worst plus/minus on team.

THE FINESSE GAME

Beers can do some things with the puck. He ended up on the top power play unit on the right point with a slapshot that was heavy and quick. He is not very creative, but, given the basic tasks, he can perform with some level of competence.

Beers is an average skater at best and can be victimized, especially by outside speed. With experience, he is learning how to compensate and position himself better.

In his own zone, he doesn't try to carry the puck, instead looking for the safe play by banging it off the boards or glass. He does not move the puck quickly, though, and can be careless when faced with a strong forecheck.

THE PHYSICAL GAME

Beers is a big force and tries to play consistently to his size and with some authority. Because 1992-93 was the first season in which he was given a full-time role, he is growing slowly into the notion that he can try to dominate with his size. More enthusiasm about the job, combined with some confidence, will improve his game.

THE INTANGIBLES

Beers is a support player. If he has to do a lot himself, it doesn't add to his game, but he will make a reliable complement to most defensive partners.

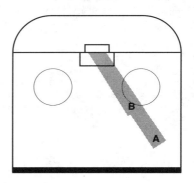

MARC BERGEVIN

Yrs. of NHL service: 7
Born: Montreal, Que.; Aug. 11, 1965
Position: right defense
Height: 6-0
Weight: 185
Uniform no.: 25
Shoots: left

Career statistics:

GP	G	A	TP	PIM
499	23	75	98	509

1991-92 statistics:

GP	G	A	TP	+/-	PIM	PP	SH	GW	GT	S	PCT
75	7	17	24	-13	64	4	1	1	0	96	7.3

1992-93 statistics:

GP	G	A	TP	+/-	PIM	PP	SH	GW	GT	S	PCT
78	2	12	14	-16	66	0	0	0	0	69	2.9

LAST SEASON

Signed as free agent. Goals, assists and point production declined from career highs in 1991-92. Missed one game with bruised foot.

THE FINESSE GAME

Bergevin plays his best when he's straight-ahead and on the attack. His game is beating people to the puck and being able to do something with it, and he has above-average finesse skills for a defenseman.

He's a good skater with a long stride. He doesn't have a great deal of agility, but he can carry the puck with some speed through the neutral zone if he has to. Bergevin can help get his team out of trouble in the defensive zone by either looking for the quick outlet pass or skating it out if his receivers are covered.

Bergevin has a fairly good point shot but does not get it away quickly; because of that, he doesn't get first-unit power play duty.

THE PHYSICAL GAME

Though a fairly strong defenseman, Bergevin doesn't carry a lot of weight and is not a physical presence on the ice.

THE INTANGIBLES

Although it isn't particularly reflected in Bergevin's point totals, he has become more important as an offensive defenseman in the sense of someone who can move the puck out of the zone.

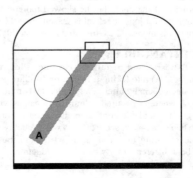

BRIAN BRADLEY

Yrs. of NHL service: 6
Born: Kitchener, Ont.; Jan. 21, 1965
Position: centre
Height: 5-10
Weight: 177
Uniform no.: 19
Shoots: right

Career statistics:

GP	G	A	TP	PIM
403	113	176	289	331

1991-92 statistics:

GP	G	A	TP	+/-	PIM	PP	SH	GW	GT	S	PCT
59	10	21	31	-3	48	4	0	3	0	78	12.8

1992-93 statistics:

GP	G	A	TP	+/-	PIM	PP	SH	GW	GT	S	PCT
80	42	44	86	-24	92	16	0	6	1	205	20.5

LAST SEASON

Led team in goals, assists and points with career highs. Led team in power play goals, game-winning goals, shots and shooting percentage.

THE FINESSE GAME

Bradley is an above-average skater with good speed, and he has a nice shot and passing skills. It doesn't sound like much to get excited about, so how did he manage a 40-goal, 80-point season? Mainly because he was the best the Lightning had. He got the prime ice time, played with the best wingers (the best the expansion team could muster) and saw duty on the first power play unit. Bradley made the most of it.

Bradley used to be reluctant to shoot, but when he arrived in Tampa Bay it was shoot first and ask questions later. He will work low around the net amd likes to shoot from in tight. He has always had a nose for the net. Bradley doesn't have a big cannon. He has the quickness to jump into holes and the good hockey sense to work give-and-gos.

THE PHYSICAL GAME

Bradley is a small centre and doesn't play a physical game. He uses fairly good leg drive and will force people to drag him down and take penalties. He can get pushed off the puck, but he showed more eagerness to battle for loose pucks this season, probably as a result of his increased ice time and responsibility.

THE INTANGIBLES

Tony Esposito had to talk big brother Phil (the Lightning GM) into taking a chance on Bradley, who had flopped dismally after being traded to Toronto in 1991-92 (where he endured a slump of 26 games without a goal). Bradley's confidence has been restored, and he believes he can score 50. His was probably the most astonishing turnaround of last season, but it could be a different story when that production is expected, as it will be this season.

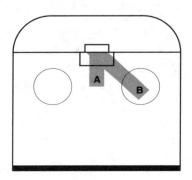

MARC BUREAU

Yrs. of NHL service: 2
Born: Trois-Rivières, Que.; May 19, 1966
Position: centre/left wing
Height: 6-1
Weight: 198
Uniform no.: 28
Shoots: right

Career statistics:

GP	G	A	TP	PIM
128	16	31	47	171

1991-92 statistics:

GP	G	A	TP	+/-	PIM	PP	SH	GW	GT	S	PCT
46	6	4	10	-5	50	0	0	0	0	53	11.3

1992-93 statistics:

GP	G	A	TP	+/-	PIM	PP	SH	GW	GT	S	PCT
63	10	21	31	-12	111	1	2	1	0	132	7.6

LAST SEASON

Acquired on waivers from Minnesota. Led team in PIM. Games played, goals, assists and points at career highs in second NHL season. Missed six games with bruised shoulder.

THE FINESSE GAME

Bureau plays with concentration and intensity, and he has the makings of one of those terrier-forwards who are so annoying to play against. Bureau can play all three forward positions, although his best and natural position is centre.

He has good hands and can shoot the puck well. Pretty smart, he's a solid penalty killer who is a short-handed threat. He will work consistently hard on the forecheck and create chances off the turnover.

Bureau is a chopper when he skates, but he does it with vigour and effort. He has no end-to-end speed, but in the throes of a game he is very effective. He will get there quickly and be able to do something with the puck when he arrives.

THE PHYSICAL GAME

Bureau is an in-your-face agitator. He's very feisty and skilled at getting opponents ticked off enough to take swats or runs at him. He could be a stronger hitter, but he doesn't have very good skating balance, and though he will hit people, he is more often the one who gets dropped. To his credit, he bounces right back up and rejoins the fray.

THE INTANGIBLES

The Stars may be sorry they let this one get away. Bureau is developing into a checking forward who can produce a reliable 15 to 18 goals a season as well as make his presence felt on the other team's bench.

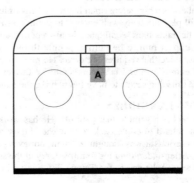

SHAWN CHAMBERS

Yrs. of NHL service: 6
Born: Royal Oaks, Mich.; Oct. 11, 1966
Position: right defense
Height: 6-2
Weight: 200
Uniform no.: 22
Shoots: left

Career statistics:

GP	G	A	TP	PIM
255	25	76	101	244

1991-92 statistics:

GP	G	A	TP	+/-	PIM	PP	SH	GW	GT	S	PCT
2	0	0	0	-3	2	0	0	0	0	1	0.0

1992-93 statistics:

GP	G	A	TP	+/-	PIM	PP	SH	GW	GT	S	PCT
55	10	29	39	-21	36	5	0	1	0	152	6.6

LAST SEASON

Missed 22 games after knee surgery. Goals, assists and points at career highs. Led team defensemen in scoring. Games played at three-season high.

THE FINESSE GAME

Chambers was never asked to play much of an offensive role before he came to Tampa Bay, but he learned on the job and graduated to first team duty on the point on the power play. He has a very awkward-looking shot, but he manages to get it away quickly, low and on net. He has the poise and the hand skills to be able to fake out a checker with a faux slapper, move to the top of the circle and drill it.

His smarts put him a cut above the rest. Though his finesse skills may be average, he has great anticipation. He understands the game well and knows where the puck is going before the play is made. He does the little things well — little wrist shots, little dump-ins, nothing that shouts out.

His skating isn't dazzling, but even though he looks like he's lumbering he usually gets to where he has to go. Chambers finds a way to get things done. He kills penalties well — overall, a stalwart player.

THE PHYSICAL GAME

Chambers is a big defenseman but not a heavy hitter. He will play the body well enough to get in the way. Until he gains more confidence in his repaired knee, don't expect him to be putting people through the boards, since that requires leg drive. He plays with a lot of enthusiasm and is a workhorse. He thrives on the ice time and seems to have fun playing the game.

THE INTANGIBLES

Chambers is a gamble that paid off. He has worked long and hard to come back from a knee injury that was so serious it was thought he might not ever play again. After undergoing his fourth surgery at the start of the season, he was in the Tampa Bay line-up in 32 days. The knee remains fragile, but a healthy Chambers is an impact defenseman, and he's one of the most talented players on the Lightning.

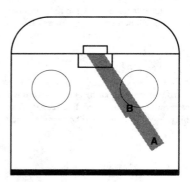

DANTON COLE

Yrs. of NHL service: 3
Born: Pontiac, Mich.; Jan. 10, 1967
Position: right wing
Height: 5-11
Weight: 189
Uniform no.: 24
Shoots: right

Career statistics:

GP	G	A	TP	PIM
187	33	32	65	79

1991-92 statistics:

GP	G	A	TP	+/-	PIM	PP	SH	GW	GT	S	PCT
52	7	5	12	-15	32	1	2	0	0	65	10.8

1992-93 statistics:

GP	G	A	TP	+/-	PIM	PP	SH	GW	GT	S	PCT
67	12	15	27	-2	23	0	1	1	0	100	12.0

LAST SEASON

Missed 14 games with injuries. Acquired from Winnipeg for future considerations. Games played, assists and points at career highs.

THE FINESSE GAME

A scorer at the college and minor league level, Cole has shown no indication of that ability in the NHL. His skills are very, very average. His goals come from his work around the net, picking up rebounds. He does have a decent wrist shot with a fairly quick release.

Cole does not create much offensively. He doesn't have the size or speed to make anyone worry about defending against him.

THE PHYSICAL GAME

Cole is a hard-nosed forward who will bump and grind and work the boards and corners. He isn't very big, and is basically just a blue-collar player who will give his utmost for his team. Unfortunately for him, there isn't that much to give.

THE INTANGIBLES

Cole fits into a team concept for the expansion Lightning, where everyone is asked to do just a little to make the team successful. Cole did his part, but he is not the type to make any impact. Even on an expansion team, he was a fourth-line winger.

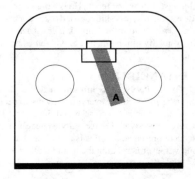

ADAM CREIGHTON

Yrs. of NHL service: 10
Born: Burlington, Ont.; June 2, 1965
Position: centre
Height: 6-5
Weight: 210
Uniform no.: 10
Shoots: left

Career statistics:

GP	G	A	TP	PIM
527	151	174	325	875

1991-92 statistics:

GP	G	A	TP	+/-	PIM	PP	SH	GW	GT	S	PCT
77	21	15	36	-5	118	4	0	2	1	140	15.0

1992-93 statistics:

GP	G	A	TP	+/-	PIM	PP	SH	GW	GT	S	PCT
83	19	20	39	-19	110	7	1	0	0	168	11.3

LAST SEASON

Acquired from N.Y. Islanders in 1992 waiver draft. Fifth on team in points with two-season high. Second on team in PIM.

THE FINESSE GAME

Getting Creighton on a team is like receiving a big present with fancy ribbons that looks impressive until it's opened and reveals a jelly bean. It always seems like there's more there, until he gets on the ice.

Creighton has his moments, but not enough of them. He is not a great skater, so he has to utilize his long reach — which he does, but not intelligently enough. He doesn't have the mastery of his reach that Dave Andreychuk (similarly built at 6-3 and 225 pounds) possesses. Andreychuk is a soft big player too, but his effectiveness with his reach compensates for it, whereas Creighton does not. He doesn't position himself well offensively or use the long wraparound from behind the net that forwards with his wingspan can employ to frustrate goalies.

Creighton is not a very well-balanced skater, either, which leads to him losing battles against smaller competitors.

THE PHYSICAL GAME

Creighton isn't strong or feisty. He is a big player who has always relied on his skill, or tried to, going back to when he was a junior, and his skill level isn't high enough to justify him being as uninvolved as he is on most nights.

THE INTANGIBLES

Creighton inevitably finds himself in the doghouse wherever he plays, since everyone always expects a player as big as he is to be mean and dominant. That isn't Creighton's style or personality. He can't deliver the physical presence, and this is a constant battle for him and whoever is running the team he plays for.

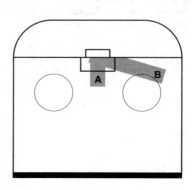

ROB DIMAIO

Yrs. of NHL service: 4
Born: Calgary, Alta.; Feb. 19, 1968
Position: centre
Height: 5-8
Weight: 175
Uniform no.: 18
Shoots: right

Career statistics:

GP	G	A	TP	PIM
128	15	17	32	137

1991-92 statistics:

GP	G	A	TP	+/-	PIM	PP	SH	GW	GT	S	PCT
50	5	2	7	-23	43	0	2	0	0	43	11.6

1992-93 statistics:

GP	G	A	TP	+/-	PIM	PP	SH	GW	GT	S	PCT
54	9	15	24	0	62	2	0	0	0	75	12.0

LAST SEASON

Missed 20 games with injuries. Only forward on team among regulars who was not minus.

THE FINESSE GAME

DiMaio can't do much offensively at the NHL level, so he thrives as a checking forward. When he scores, his goals come from very tight to the net. Put it this way: if he can get in between the goalie and the goal line, then he has a chance to score.

As a forechecker, he has good anticipation, quickness and strength. He is a stocky skater with a low centre of gravity, which gives him good balance and makes it difficult for larger skaters to move him off the puck. DiMaio's small stature also gets him closer to the puck for face-offs, where he is above average.

DiMaio is gaining in experience and confidence and believes he can play as he did in junior; a lot of people took notice this year of what he could do and do well.

THE PHYSICAL GAME

DiMaio stretches himself to play consistently and effectively. He has a big heart and plays tough. He also plays big. He is not afraid to try to bulldoze through to his destination.

THE INTANGIBLES

DiMaio has always been well liked by his coaches wherever he has played, because his effort is never lacking. He is already becoming an identifying part of the heart and soul of the Lightning, and he could have a long career if he stays healthy.

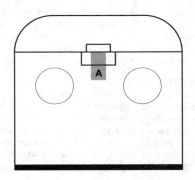

CHRIS GRATTON

Yrs. of NHL service: 0
Born: Brantford, Ont.; July 5, 1975
Position: centre
Height: 6-3
Weight: 202
Uniform no.: na
Shoots: left

Career junior statistics:				
GP	G	A	TP	PIM
120	82	123	175	51

1992-93 junior statistics:				
GP	G	A	TP	PIM
58	55	54	109	16

LAST SEASON

Played for Kingston (OHL). Named to Third OHL All-Star Team. Drafted overall by Tampa Bay in '93.

THE FINESSE GAME

Gratton reminds many scouts of another Kingston alumnus: Montreal's Kirk Muller. Although his idol is power forward Cam Neely, Gratton is a lot like Muller in his work ethic and simple game. There is nothing fancy here. He has a hard shot that he likes to use at close range, and he gets his goals from digging around the net. But there's some Neely in him, too. Gratton has to improve his skating and develop a longer, stronger and more efficient stride to become Neely-deadly around the net.

Gratton is an unselfish playmaker. He's not the prettiest of passers, but he has some poise with the puck and knows when to pass and when to shoot.

Gratton worked both special teams in junior. He is a shorthanded threat because of his strong fore-checking. Once he creates a turnover, he can make something happen with the puck. On the power play, Gratton will battle for a screen or tip in front.

THE PHYSICAL GAME

Gratton is a hard-working sort who doesn't shy away from contact but has to initiate more. Once his skating improves, he will be able to establish a more physical presence. He won't be an NHL impact player until he does, but he's got a lot of skill and character that says he'll take the next step.

THE INTANGIBLES

Gratton has yet to demonstrate a soft touch around the net to go with the straight-ahead power game. He lacks some quickness around the net, and until his NHL defensive play improves, the team that drafts him may shift him to wing to lessen his defensive responsibilities — which, by the way, is how Muller developed.

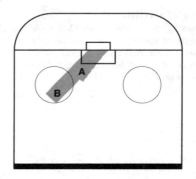

ROMAN HAMRLIK

Yrs. of NHL service: 1
Born: Gottwaldov, Czechoslovakia; Apr. 12, 1974
Position: left defense
Height: 6-2
Weight: 189
Uniform no.: 44
Shoots: left

Career statistics:

GP	G	A	TP	PIM
67	6	15	21	71

1992-93 statistics:

GP	G	A	TP	+/-	PIM	PP	SH	GW	GT	S	PCT
67	6	15	21	-21	71	1	0	1	0	113	5.3

LAST SEASON

First NHL season. Missed games with back injuries.

THE FINESSE GAME

Hamrlik was the first player drafted overall in 1992, and he probably would have benefited from staying with his country's national team another season. He looked lost in the NHL. When he wasn't watching from the sidelines, he was struggling on the ice. Coming into the league as an 18-year-old defenseman is tough enough, but doing it in a strange country and on an expansion team is nearly impossible.

The scouts who have watched him in international competition swear that Hamrlik is the real deal. He is a mobile defenseman with a good shot and good passing skills, but he is not very creative and does not become overly involved in the attack.

THE PHYSICAL GAME

Hamrlik likes to take the body, and his back injuries put a damper on the most aggressive part of his game. If he comes back healthy this season, he should start making more of a physical impact, since he loves the hitting part of the game.

THE INTANGIBLES

Hamrlik's first season made for a very difficult period of adjustment. There were few glimmers of what he is supposed to be able to do well, and in the second half of the season he made more mistakes than good moves. Tampa Bay probably rushed him, and now the coaches have to undo the damage and start rebuilding his game.

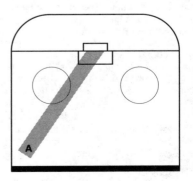

PAT JABLONSKI

Yrs. of NHL service: 1
Born: Toledo, Ohio; June 20, 1967
Position: goaltender
Height: 6-0
Weight: 178
Uniform no.: 35
Catches: right

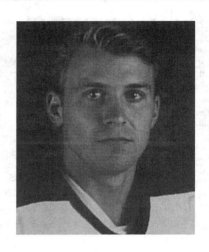

Career statistics:

GP	MINS	GA	SO	GAA	A	PIM
65	3436	230	1	4.02	2	11

1991-92 statistics:

GP	MINS	GAA	W	L	T	SO	GA	S	SAPCT	PIM
10	468	4.87	3	6	0	0	38	259	.853	4

1992-93 statistics:

GP	MINS	GAA	W	L	T	SO	GA	S	SAPCT	PIM
43	2268	3.97	8	24	2	1	150	1194	.874	7

LAST SEASON

Acquired from St. Louis along with Darin Kimble, Rob Robinson and Steve Tuttle for future considerations. First full NHL season.

THE PHYSICAL GAME

Jablonski stands tall, plays a technical, stand-up game and seems to fill the net. He plays his angles fairly well but stays too deep in the net to be successful on technique alone. He is not confident or aggressive in challenging the shooter, and he suffers from the reverse of the problem that afflicts many goalies for poor teams: goalies playing behind weak defenses usually try to do too much; Jablonski doesn't do enough.

Jablonski is very conservative about coming out of his net to handle the puck. He does not stickhandle well and is only an average skater.

His reflexes aren't Lightning-quick (you should pardon the inevitable pun), so his angle play must improve.

THE MENTAL GAME

Backstopping an expansion team can take its toll on a goalie's psyche, not to mention his GAA. The Lightning performed better than expected in their inaugural season, but now expectations will be higher. Jablonski seemed to hold up well under the pressure and bounced back after blowouts.

THE INTANGIBLES

Jablonski paid his dues in the minors for a number of seasons before getting his NHL job with the Lightning. When Wendell Young suffered a dislocated shoulder, the job was Jablonski's, and he was adequate, but he will have to fight for the No. 1 role again unless Tampa Bay secures a goalie in the off-season.

PETR KLIMA

Yrs. of NHL service: 8
Born: Choamutov, Czechoslovakia; Dec. 23, 1964
Position: left wing
Height: 6-0
Weight: 190
Uniform no.: 85
Shoots: right

Career statistics:

GP	G	A	TP	PIM
549	247	178	425	485

1992-93 statistics:

GP	G	A	TP	+/-	PIM	PP	SH	GW	GT	S	PCT
68	32	16	48	-15	100	13	0	2	0	175	18.3

LAST SEASON

Led team in goals, points, and power play goals. All totals improved over career lows in goals, assists, and points last season. Acquired by Tampa Bay for future considerations.

THE FINESSE GAME

There are a lot of things Klima can do. He can score in a variety of ways and in a variety of areas on the ice. He has elite speed with the puck and without it. He is flashy and blesses with great offensive instinct, and on any given night, Klima can be a game-breaker.

He can just as easily be Mr. Perimeter. Since he is a lax player defensively, he hurts his team when he is not in his "on" mode.

Klima is an expert at drawing penalties. He keeps his legs pumping, grasps an opponent's stick, and jumps into the air before falling to the ice. Is it a dive? Sure, but how many times did you see diving penalties called last season? He will also take cheap shots with his stick or an elbow and tends to take these penalties at inopportune moments.

THE PHYSICAL GAME

Klima is erratic in the application of his body. Some nights he will check, and hard, or sneak up from behind a player and hound him until he strips the puck away. He uses his feet well and keeps the puck alive along the boards. But on even more nights, he'll do none of those things.

THE INTANGIBLES

Klima is a disciplinary headache, both on and off the ice. His inconsistency is legendary. In the right place, with the right coach, and in the right mood, he can be a 40-goal scorer again. With his gifts, he should be.

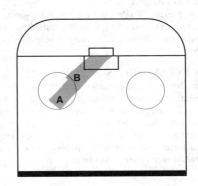

CHRIS KONTOS

Yrs. of NHL service: 5
Born: Toronto, Ont.; Dec. 10, 1963
Position: left wing/centre
Height: 6-1
Weight: 195
Uniform no.: 16
Shoots: left

Career statistics:

GP	G	A	TP	PIM
230	54	69	123	103

1991-92 statistics:
Did not play in the NHL

1992-93 statistics:

GP	G	A	TP	+/-	PIM	PP	SH	GW	GT	S	PCT
66	27	24	51	-7	12	12	1	3	0	136	19.9

LAST SEASON

Signed as free agent after playing with Canadian National Team in 1991-92. Second on team in goals with career high. Third on team in points with career high. Assists career high. Second on team in power play goals and shooting percentage. Missed two weeks with knee injury.

THE FINESSE GAME

Kontos has some great gifts for putting the puck in the net from three or four feet away. He has a knack for positioning himself and tipping or redirecting pucks, and he's very effective on the power play that way. He had streaks where everything he touched seem to end up in the net. He had 22 goals in the team's first 33 games, but only 5 in the remaining 51 (he missed some playing time with a knee injury in the second half). Injuries aside, he has a history of streaks and slumps.

Kontos's skating is good. He doesn't have breakaway speed, but he has good quickness, change of direction and balance.

He does not work as hard defensively, and he lacks intensity and tenacity.

THE PHYSICAL GAME

Kontos does not like the physical part of the game. He is a perimeter player who will go into traffic only with the puck. He will not use his body to help out defensively.

THE INTANGIBLES

Kontos belongs in the streaky Hall of Fame. When things are going well, nobody is hotter. But he does not handle adversity well, and his heart is a question mark. Tampa Bay is his fourth NHL organization; he wore out his welcome at the other three as those teams waited for him to show the consistency to carry his scoring through an entire season.

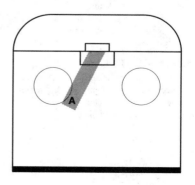

CHRIS LIPUMA

Yrs. of NHL service: 0
Born: Chicago, Ill.; Mar. 23, 1971
Position: left defense
Height: 6-0
Weight: 183
Uniform no.: 40
Shoots: left

Career statistics:

GP	G	A	TP	PIM
15	0	5	5	34

1992-93 statistics:

GP	G	A	TP	+/-	PIM	PP	SH	GW	GT	S	PCT
15	0	5	5	+1	34	0	0	0	0	17	0.0

LAST SEASON

Signed as free agent. Played most of 1992-93 season with Atlanta (IHL).

THE FINESSE GAME

LiPuma could become a Mark Tinordi type of defenseman — or so the Tampa Bay coaches dare to imagine. His fame has come as an enforcer, but LiPuma has been set to work on other skills. Though not a fast skater, he's mobile enough to be a big hitter. His reputation will earn him the extra room and time needed to develop the other components of his game.

To survive in the NHL, LiPuma will have to learn to do other things competently, and the Lightning believe he will develop into an offensive force as well. From all indications, he's willing to work, and the club is willing to wait on him.

THE PHYSICAL GAME

LiPuma racked up 379 PIM in 66 games with Atlanta last season, which tells you just about all you need to know about his toughness. He loves to hit, cleans out the front of his net with authority, is plenty mean and intimidates the heck out of opponents. He will have to develop a longer fuse, and will, once he establishes his NHL reputation and faces the challenges that will be mounted from the other teams' tough guys.

THE INTANGIBLES

LiPuma is one of those rare finds: a late-blooming free agent signing out of Kitchener (OHL) as an overage junior, he made a bruising impact as he played most of last season with the Atlanta Knights, and he may start this season in the minors as well. Tampa Bay does not want to rush him, but he figures very prominently in their future.

STEVE MALTAIS

Yrs. of NHL service: 1
Born: Arvida, Que.; Jan. 25, 1969
Position: left wing
Height: 6-2
Weight: 210
Uniform no.: 37
Shoots: left

Career statistics:

GP	G	A	TP	PIM
90	9	14	23	41

1991-92 statistics:

GP	G	A	TP	+/-	PIM	PP	SH	GW	GT	S	PCT
12	2	1	3	-1	6	0	0	0	0	6	33.3

1992-93 statistics:

GP	G	A	TP	+/-	PIM	PP	SH	GW	GT	S	PCT
63	7	13	20	-20	35	4	0	1	0	96	7.3

LAST SEASON

Games played, goals, assists and points at career highs.

THE FINESSE GAME

Maltais is a big winger who plays an honest game. He is an average skater, smart enough in both zones to use his quickness to good effect as a checker, although he doesn't play the body well enough to be used specifically in that role.

He doesn't create much of a threat. He has a decent shot selection, using either his wrist or slap shot, and gets the shots away quickly, but he doesn't work hard enough for the best scoring chance or see the best play developing. He likes to handle the puck.

THE PHYSICAL GAME

Maltais is not a rugged player, especially for a player with size. He will take a check but won't initiate. He plays a clean physical style and will block shots.

THE INTANGIBLES

Maltais is another one of those average players who are not asked to do much for an average team. He is not much of an impact player, offensively or defensively.

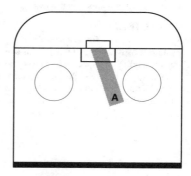

JOHN TUCKER

Yrs. of NHL service: 8
Born: Windsor, Ont.; Sept. 29, 1964
Position: right wing/centre
Height: 6-0
Weight: 200
Uniform no.: 14
Shoots: right

Career statistics:

GP	G	A	TP	PIM
481	145	216	361	225

1991-92 statistics:
Did not play in the NHL

1992-93 statistics:

GP	G	A	TP	+/-	PIM	PP	SH	GW	GT	S	PCT
78	17	39	56	-12	69	5	1	1	0	179	9.5

LAST SEASON

Signed as free agent after playing 1991-92 in Italy. Missed six games with knee injury. Second on team in assists with career high. Second on team in points with second-highest career total.

THE FINESSE GAME

Tucker is an honest, up-and-down winger who fits nicely into coach Terry Crisp's style. Nothing about him is flashy, but he has the anticipation to get himself into the right situations, plus the nifty hand skills to make things happen.

Tucker is a finisher and also worked the corners for centre Brian Bradley. He took advantage of being put into a responsible situation, where he hadn't been for some seasons with other teams (Tampa Bay is his fourth NHL organization). Tucker's hands and his good hockey sense blend well for a dangerous threat down low. He won't stand in front of the net and take needless punishment, but instead will dart in and out of holes.

Tucker is a good penalty killer, showing intelligence and tenacity, and he can be a shorthanded threat.

THE PHYSICAL GAME

Tucker made good use of his size along the boards and is not afraid to work through traffic in the offensive zone.

THE INTANGIBLES

Tucker is an average journeyman player who is making the most of his ice time with the Lightning. With no drastic improvement anticipated in the quality of the team's forwards this season, he should be among Tampa Bay's scoring leaders again.

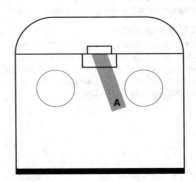

ROB ZAMUNER

Yrs. of NHL service: 1
Born: Oakville, Ont.; Sept. 17, 1969
Position: centre
Height: 6-2
Weight: 202
Uniform no.: 7
Shoots: left

Career statistics:

GP	G	A	TP	PIM
93	16	30	46	76

1991-92 statistics:

GP	G	A	TP	+/-	PIM	PP	SH	GW	GT	S	PCT
9	1	2	3	+2	2	0	0	0	0	11	9.1

1992-93 statistics:

GP	G	A	TP	+/-	PIM	PP	SH	GW	GT	S	PCT
84	15	28	43	-25	74	1	0	0	2	183	8.2

LAST SEASON

First NHL season. Signed as free agent. Only Tampa Bay player to play in all 84 games. Tied for worst plus/minus on team. Fourth on team in points.

THE FINESSE GAME

Zamuner is a complementary player, a grinder who can also handle the puck and has some good hand skills. The problem is finding a niche for him. He is not a good enough player to be a No. 1 or No. 2 centre on most teams, and not good enough defensively to be a No. 3 centre. With a better supporting cast, however, his stock will rise. He needs to be bolstered, because whatever line he plays on won't be dominated by his personality or skills.

Zamuner has a decent touch for scoring or passing. He was a scorer at the minor league level, and he's eager for the puck.

He is fairly alert defensively. He has to be, since he is not a fast enough skater to recover if he is caught napping in the offensive zone.

THE PHYSICAL GAME

Zamuner plays with authority and power. He has good size and uses it effectively. On most nights, he will be the most active forward on the Tampa Bay team, bumping and grinding. He gives an honest effort.

THE INTANGIBLES

Zamuner was regarded as one of the brighter prospects out of the New York Rangers' system before the Lightning signed him away. His skating remains the major drawback in his development, but it's not bad enough to be a liability.

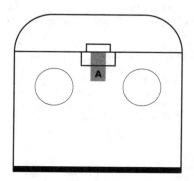

TORONTO
MAPLE LEAFS

GLENN ANDERSON

Yrs. of NHL service: 13
Born: Vancouver, B.C.; Oct. 2, 1960
Position: right wing
Height: 6-1
Weight: 190
Uniform no.: 9
Shoots: left

Career statistics:

GP	G	A	TP	PIM
976	459	559	1018	988

1991-92 statistics:

GP	G	A	TP	+/-	PIM	PP	SH	GW	GT	S	PCT
72	24	33	57	-13	100	5	0	4	1	188	12.8

1992-93 statistics:

GP	G	A	TP	+/-	PIM	PP	SH	GW	GT	S	PCT
76	22	43	65	+19	117	11	0	3	0	161	13.7

LAST SEASON

Fourth on team in points. Goals four-season low. Assists four-season high. Points five-season high. Missed seven games with knee injuries. Suspended for one game. Recorded 1000th NHL point.

THE FINESSE GAME

Anderson's character and charisma were revitalized with the acquisition of Doug Gilmour in the middle of the 1991-92 season. Anderson's skating legs are still there, and it is his speed that keeps him an effective NHL forward, although his finishing touch is diminished, meaning he can no longer dominate with his speed. He's simply not as dangerous as he once was.

Anderson still has the capacity to score big goals, but he doesn't score as often. He can score with his shot off the wing, or from his work in front of the net. He will still be a productive player as long as he is working alongside Gilmour, as both are creative, intelligent players, but should Anderson be bumped down to a second- or third-line role, his numbers will trail off dramatically.

Anderson still has fun playing the game, as corny as that may sound, and it shows.

THE PHYSICAL GAME

Anderson no longer plays with the reckless carelessness he once did. He's not as consistently tenacious, but on the nights when he is up, he is fearless driving to the net. Anderson keeps himself in excellent shape and is durable. He carries his stick high.

THE INTANGIBLES

Anderson's numbers are starting to decline. He no longer gets the top power play ice time, and he is not a sure bet in front of the net.

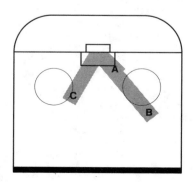

DAVE ANDREYCHUK

Yrs. of NHL service: 11
Born: Hamilton, Ont.; Sept. 29, 1963
Position: left wing
Height: 6-3
Weight: 220
Uniform no.: 14
Shoots: right

Career statistics:

GP	G	A	TP	PIM
794	373	436	809	572

1991-92 statistics:

GP	G	A	TP	+/-	PIM	PP	SH	GW	GT	S	PCT
80	41	50	91	-9	71	28	0	2	2	337	12.2

1992-93 statistics:

GP	G	A	TP	+/-	PIM	PP	SH	GW	GT	S	PCT
83	54	45	99	+4	56	32	0	4	1	310	17.4

LAST SEASON

Led NHL in power play goals for second consecutive season. Led team in goals, power play goals, shots and shooting percentage. Goals at career high; first season with 50 or more goals. Points at career high. Acquired from Buffalo with Daren Puppa for Grant Fuhr. Fourth player in NHL history to record 30 or more power play goals in a season.

THE FINESSE GAME

Andreychuk has slow feet but a cherry-picker reach, which he uses with strength and intelligence. He is a lumbering skater, but since he works in tight areas, he only needs a big stride or two to plant himself where he wants. He has marvellous hand skills in traffic. He can pick pucks out of midair, slap at rebounds or use his stick for wraparounds. He has quick and accurate wrist and snap shots.

Andreychuk is in his glory from the tops of the circles to the net. On the other four-fifths of the ice, he is a liability. He doesn't finish his checks; he doesn't skate well; he understands the game well enough to position himself but won't battle anywhere other than right in front of the net. When Gilmour takes an offensive-zone draw, Andreychuk curls in behind him, using the centre as a screen or pick.

At even strength, Andreychuk can still be a threat. He has a clever head and has to play with people, like Doug Gilmour, who can get him the puck in the right area of the ice. He also needs to play with people who can skate, to cover up for his deficiency there.

Andreychuk's hands are so quick, he is proficient on face-offs and often takes draws.

THE PHYSICAL GAME

If you're seeking someone to protect his smaller teammates, or inspire his team with his hitting, then Andreychuk is not the man for you.

He's tough in his own way, in front of the opponent's net, at least. He is huge and impossible to budge, and with his long arms can control pucks, so he forces defenders to play his stick instead of his body. He plants his feet wide and puts his stick on the ice, like a huge tripod. He isn't dominating, but he is physically prominent with five feet of the crease. He pays the price and knows how to use his talent.

THE INTANGIBLES

Andreychuk was the perfect fit for Toronto and needed to get out of Buffalo, the site of so many playoff failures. The trade helped him immensely, and the defense-first philosophy of the Leafs' system will tolerate Andreychuk's weak five-on-five play as long as he keeps producing on the power play.

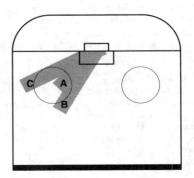

BILL BERG

Yrs. of NHL service: 3
Born: St. Catharines, Ont.; Oct. 21, 1967
Position: left wing
Height: 6-1
Weight: 190
Uniform no.: 10
Shoots: left

Career statistics:

GP	G	A	TP	PIM
212	28	36	64	208

1991-92 statistics:

GP	G	A	TP	+/-	PIM	PP	SH	GW	GT	S	PCT
47	5	9	14	-18	28	1	0	1	0	60	8.3

1992-93 statistics:

GP	G	A	TP	+/-	PIM	PP	SH	GW	GT	S	PCT
80	13	11	24	+3	103	0	3	2	0	113	11.5

LAST SEASON

Games played, goals, points and PIM career highs. Tied for team lead in shorthanded goals. Acquired on waivers from New York Islanders.

THE FINESSE GAME

A converted defenseman, Berg has developed into a solid checking forward who is starting to produce some points as he gains more ice time and confidence. He can finish a play, shoot the puck and make or receive a pass, and he has the skill to make something happen if the checking line creates an offensive chance with its pressure, as so often happens.

Berg skates well, although he doesn't have a lot of shifty speed. He is very strong and effective with his skating and angles well.

Berg took a big bite into his new role and has a future as a Gaetan Duchesne-type defensive forward. He is a character player with quiet leadership and is very honest with his efforts. The team comes first, and Berg will do whatever is asked.

THE PHYSICAL GAME

Berg added an element to his game that hadn't been seen before when he started getting under people's skins. Maybe it came from playing with an agitator like Peter Zezel, but whatever the reason, it worked to Berg's benefit. People knew when he was on the ice.

He finishes his checks consistently and solidly. He will take a poke in the nose to get his team a power play.

THE INTANGIBLES

Berg is a reliable checking winger who can be counted on to make his presence felt and chip in 15 goals a season or so as well. After playing most of his NHL career on the bubble, or just struggling to make the majors, Berg has finally won a job. He will work hard to keep it.

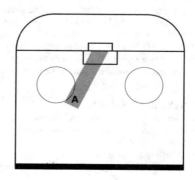

NIKOLAI BORCHEVSKY

Yrs. of NHL service: 1
Born: Tomsk, Russia; Jan. 12, 1965
Position: right wing
Height: 5-9
Weight: 180
Uniform no.: 16
Shoots: left

Career statistics:

GP	G	A	TP	PIM
78	34	40	74	28

1992-93 statistics:

GP	G	A	TP	+/-	PIM	PP	SH	GW	GT	S	PCT
78	34	40	74	+33	28	12	0	4	2	204	16.7

LAST SEASON

First NHL season. Led team in plus/minus. Third on team in points. Missed three games with neck injuries.

THE FINESSE GAME

An older Russian "rookie," Borchevsky started slowly in his first NHL season but got up to speed quickly. He's a great skater in tight spaces. If the game were played in a phone booth, he would be a superstar, because he can do so much with the puck so quickly and in so little space.

Borchevsky likes to position himself down low along the goal line on the power play, and he dances out at the right moment to take a pass. He has very quick hands and uses a wrist shot accurately.

Borchevsky is quick but doesn't have dynamic, breakaway speed. He is very patient with the puck, understands the team concept and uses his teammates well.

THE PHYSICAL GAME

The question mark concerning European and Russian players is whether they will stand up to the extra punishment in the NHL. Borchevsky is willing to play the extra price. He looks too small to survive for long, but plays bigger than he is, especially offensively.

THE INTANGIBLES

Will Borchevsky continue to improve off his solid performance of last season, or go the other way and soften up? For now he seems like a good fit, but he can't afford to become a perimeter player.

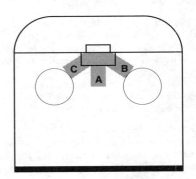

WENDEL CLARK

Yrs. of NHL service: 8
Born: Kelvington, Sask.; Oct. 25, 1966
Position: left wing
Height: 5-11
Weight: 195
Uniform no.: 17
Shoots: left

Career statistics:

GP	G	A	TP	PIM
399	162	116	432	1228

1991-92 statistics:

GP	G	A	TP	+/-	PIM	PP	SH	GW	GT	S	PCT
43	19	21	40	-14	123	7	0	4	0	158	12.0

1992-93 statistics:

GP	G	A	TP	+/-	PIM	PP	SH	GW	GT	S	PCT
66	17	22	39	+2	193	2	0	5	1	146	11.6

LAST SEASON

Missed 13 games with rib injury. Missed four games with groin injury. Led team in game-winning goals. Goals at four-season low. Assists second highest of career. Second on team in PIM.

THE FINESSE GAME

Clark doesn't complement his linemates well. He plays in his own tunnel, and his vision is narrow. If he gets rolling and gets the emotion going, it's like a freight train. He is one of the rare players who can overpower a goalie from the blue line, even with his wrist shot, which has tremendous power.

Clark is not a clever player. He doesn't pass the puck. His effectiveness depends on him charging down the ice, wreaking havoc and letting his teammates trail in his wake, picking through the debris to make a play. It would be a waste to play him with someone like Doug Gilmour, for example.

Clark plays as a straight-ahead player on a second line and makes things happen by bulldozing. He is not a smart player positionally. Though a strong skater, he's not very agile, fast or mobile. When he's playing well, he uses his leg-drive like a linebacker in football to hit hard.

Defensive work is not his forte.

THE PHYSICAL GAME

In his younger days, Clark played like a raging bull. Injuries have taken some of that away. He had to undergo acupuncture treatments on his back in order to keep going in the playoffs (you would have needed a tranquillizer gun to keep him away). He has a short fuse, and he hits to hurt, but more often than not it's Clark who ends up the damaged party.

THE INTANGIBLES

Clark doesn't bring a lot to the table when he doesn't play with zeal. The catch is that his body may no longer be able to sustain the punishment it must for him to be effective. You may question Clark's ability or health, but not his hockey courage.

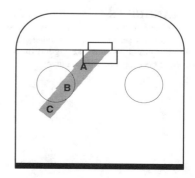

JOHN CULLEN

Yrs. of NHL service: 5
Born: Puslinch, Ont.; Aug. 2, 1964
Position: centre
Height: 5-10
Weight: 185
Uniform no.: 19
Shoots: right

Career statistics:

GP	G	A	TP	PIM
372	127	251	378	612

1991-92 statistics:

GP	G	A	TP	+/-	PIM	PP	SH	GW	GT	S	PCT
77	26	51	77	-28	141	10	0	4	0	172	15.1

1992-93 statistics:

GP	G	A	TP	+/-	PIM	PP	SH	GW	GT	S	PCT
66	18	32	50	-23	111	13	0	1	0	124	14.5

LAST SEASON

Acquired from Hartford for a second-round draft choice. Missed 16 games with neck injury. Goals fewest since rookie season. Assists career low. Worst plus/minus on team (-15 in nine games with Hartford; -23 in 47 games with Toronto).

THE FINESSE GAME

Cullen was once one of the league's top playmakers, but little of the brilliance he flashed while with Pittsburgh has revealed itself over the past two seasons in Hartford and Toronto.

Cullen is not a very fast skater, but he uses his quickness well in small areas of the ice. He is especially effective down low on the power play, popping in and out of holes.

He uses a small stick and keeps the puck in tight to his feet. That makes it very difficult for a defender to get the puck away without fouling him in some way. He has good vision of the ice and patience with the puck, and he can finish plays as well, although he doesn't shoot enough.

Cullen is an effective performer on the power play, but he became somewhat superfluous after the acquisition of Dave Andreychuk (not that both played the same kind of role, but only so many skaters can be on the ice at one time).

THE PHYSICAL GAME

Cullen is a small, feisty, hard-working centre, but injuries are taking their toll on a body that wasn't that strong to begin with. He will take a hit to make a play but won't try to go through anyone to get the puck. He could be a solid No. 2 centre but for his lack of defensive play. He needs to score or he's a zero.

THE INTANGIBLES

Cullen had a miserable start to the season, rebounded when he received some playing time on the power play, then saw his career come to its near conclusion with a neck injury. His future as a regular performer is very iffy.

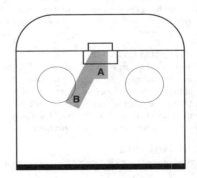

DAVE ELLETT

Yrs. of NHL service: 9
Born: Cleveland, Ohio; Mar. 30, 1964
Position: left defense
Height: 6-1
Weight: 200
Uniform no.: 4
Shoots: left

Career statistics:

GP	G	A	TP	PIM
684	127	301	428	714

1991-92 statistics:

GP	G	A	TP	+/-	PIM	PP	SH	GW	GT	S	PCT
79	18	33	51	-13	95	9	1	4	0	225	8.0

1992-93 statistics:

GP	G	A	TP	+/-	PIM	PP	SH	GW	GT	S	PCT
70	6	34	40	+19	46	4	0	1	0	186	3.2

LAST SEASON

Missed 14 games with separated shoulder. Goals at career low. Assists at five-season high.

THE FINESSE GAME

A conservative role was new for Ellett last season, but it suited him well. The offensive part of his game was once stronger than his defense, but now both aspects have come into a pleasing balance.

His game has always been powered by his exceptional skating. He is a graceful mover who possesses agility, quickness and mobility, but not blinding or flashy speed — although his strides are so effortless he is often moving faster than it appears.

Ellett's hand skills are fine too, but instead of using his skills to jump into the offense at every opportunity, he conserves his energy for the defensive part of the ice. He understands the game and his new role, shoring up his defensive game while adding to the offense. He is not expected to go end to end, but instead to be steady and able to move the puck. He is a good passer with a soft touch, and he can use his skills to get to the puck, get turned, make the first pass and watch the forwards go.

Ellett can still get involved in the attack as a quarterback on the power play. His release isn't lightning fast, but he keeps his shot low and gets it through to the front of the net, where it can sneak through a screen or be tipped.

THE PHYSICAL GAME

Ellett uses his skills to keep himself out of physical situations. By getting to the puck and moving it briskly out of the corner, he can avoid getting crunched. He doesn't have a physical presence and doesn't clear out the front of his net as well as he should for a player of his size. He will tie up players with his long reach.

THE INTANGIBLES

The arrival of new coach Pat Burns last season created

a new Dave Ellett. Instead of automatically thinking offense, he turned his considerable finesse skills to defense first, and became a much better all-around defenseman. The 32-point swing in his plus/minus is indicative of that, and he will continue to net 55 to 60 points a season when healthy.

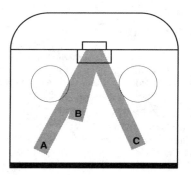

TODD GILL

Yrs. of NHL service: 7
Born: Brockville, Ont.; Nov. 19, 1965
Position: right defense
Height: 6-0
Weight: 180
Uniform no.: 23
Shoots: left

Career statistics:

GP	G	A	TP	PIM
473	41	142	183	698

1991-92 statistics:

GP	G	A	TP	+/-	PIM	PP	SH	GW	GT	S	PCT
74	2	15	17	-22	91	1	0	0	0	82	2.4

1992-93 statistics:

GP	G	A	TP	+/-	PIM	PP	SH	GW	GT	S	PCT
69	11	32	43	+4	66	5	0	2	0	113	9.7

LAST SEASON

Led team defensemen in scoring. Assists and points at career highs. Goals matched career high. Missed 11 games with foot contusion. Missed two games with back injury.

THE FINESSE GAME

Gill has a flair for offense that was seen last season for the first time. He has good hockey sense and can do some things with the puck. His passing touch will never make people forget Brian Leetch, and his shot won't impress Al MacInnis, but Gill has above-average finesse skills in all departments.

He isn't afraid to venture deep and use a wrist or snap shot from the left circle, and once in a while will brave the front of the net (although he has to be darned sure when he tries it). He is smart and talented enough to work the point on the power play on the second unit, and he filled in ably on the top unit when Dave Ellett was sidelined by injury.

Gill thrived under the team's new philosophy. He moves the puck briskly and competently without overhandling it and doesn't try to do too much. He uses his teammates well.

THE PHYSICAL GAME

Gill is a tough, snotty-nosed defenseman with a ton of heart and spunk. He's on the slight side for an NHL defenseman, and through his career he will have to be mindful of conditioning and nutrition to keep up with the grind. And he himself has to grind to be effective. He will drop the gloves and go if he has to, and he stands up for his teammates.

THE INTANGIBLES

Under any other coach, Gill might have been only a journeyman defenseman. The effect Pat Burns had on him might be comparable to the change we saw in Dave Manson under Mike Keenan in Chicago a few seasons ago. Gill has taken his game to a new level.

He had a career year last season, and now he only has to maintain that consistency to become a respected defenseman.

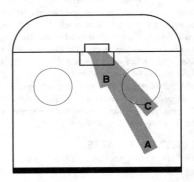

DOUG GILMOUR

Yrs. of NHL service: 9
Born: Kingston, Ont.; June 25, 1963
Position: centre
Height: 5-11
Weight: 185
Uniform no.: 93
Shoots: left

Career statistics:

GP	G	A	TP	PIM
773	277	548	825	682

1991-92 statistics:

GP	G	A	TP	+/-	PIM	PP	SH	GW	GT	S	PCT
78	26	61	87	+25	78	10	1	4	1	168	15.5

1992-93 statistics:

GP	G	A	TP	+/-	PIM	PP	SH	GW	GT	S	PCT
83	32	95	127	+32	100	15	3	2	2	211	15.2

LAST SEASON

Finalist for 1993 Hart and Selke Trophies. Tied for second in NHL in assists. Led team in assists and points, both at career highs. Goals six-season high. Tied for team lead in shorthanded goals. Second on team in power play goals.

THE FINESSE GAME

Gilmour was the Leafs' best offensive *and* defensive player, its heart, its soul, its emblem. He anchored both special teams and was probably the MVP of the playoffs, even though Toronto did not reach the final. He is a complete package. "Killer" was this season's revelation.

The mark of a great player is that he takes his team upwards with him. Wayne Gretzky has done it, Mario Lemieux has done it, and now Gilmour has.

Gilmour is a creative playmaker. He is one of those rare NHL players who has eschewed the banana blade for a nearly straight blade, so he can handle the puck equally well on his forehand or backhand. He will bring people right in on top of him before he slides a little pass to a teammate, creating time and space. He is very intelligent and has great anticipation. He loves to set up from behind the net and intimidates because he plays with such supreme confidence.

Gilmour is a set-up man who needs finishers around him and doesn't shoot much. When he does, he won't use a big slap, but instead scores from close range either as the trailer or after losing a defender with his subtle dekes and moves. He's not a smooth, gifted skater, but he is nimble and quick.

Gilmour is one of the best face-off men in the NHL, possibly in the top three with Ron Francis and Adam Oates. His intelligence and hockey sense make him the best two-way forward in the NHL.

THE PHYSICAL GAME

Gilmour plays with passion and intelligence, challenging bigger opponents regardless of where or when he plays. He puts life into the Leafs with his relentless work ethic. Though he's listed at 185 pounds, he plays at around 165 during the season and has lost up to seven pounds in a single playoff game.

The only drawback to all of Gilmour's intensity is that he can become so fierce and intense that he loses his focus. He does not turn the other cheek. He goes into the trenches because that's where the puck is, and that's what he hungers for.

THE INTANGIBLES

You have to wonder where Gilmour gets the energy. He gets at least 30 minutes of ice time a game. He has established himself as a major presence in the league, and if his body can take another season like that last one, the Leafs will be among the dominant teams of the upcoming season. It would be no surprise if Gilmour racked up 100 assists.

Gilmour provides never-say-die leadership. He will come out with a big shift after his team has been scored upon, and will ignite the Leafs and the crowd with an inspirational bump or goal. He will do everything he has to do to win a game.

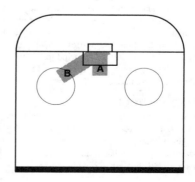

SYLVAIN LEFEBVRE

Yrs. of NHL service: 4
Born: Richmond, Que.; Oct. 14, 1967
Position: defense
Height: 6-2
Weight: 204
Uniform no.: 2
Shoots: left

Career statistics:

GP	G	A	TP	PIM
281	13	54	67	272

1991-92 statistics:

GP	G	A	TP	+/-	PIM	PP	SH	GW	GT	S	PCT
69	3	14	17	+9	91	0	0	0	0	85	3.5

1992-93 statistics:

GP	G	A	TP	+/-	PIM	PP	SH	GW	GT	S	PCT
81	2	12	14	+8	90	0	0	0	0	81	2.5

LAST SEASON

Acquired from Montreal for a 1994 third-round draft choice. Goals career low. Assists and points three-season lows.

THE FINESSE GAME

Lefebvre makes the first pass and then forgets about the puck. He couldn't be any less interested in the attack. If he has the puck at the offensive blue line and doesn't have a lane, he just throws it into the corner. His game is defense first, and he is very basic and consistent in his limited role.

Lefebvre actually has below-average skills with regard to speed and puckhandling, yet he became one of the Leafs' most reliable defensemen by playing within his boundaries and within the system.

THE PHYSICAL GAME

Lefebvre plays tough and physical. He patrols and controls the front of his net and plays a hard-nosed style.

THE INTANGIBLES

Lefebvre could have been lost in another system, but Pat Burns knew him from Montreal and it became a matter of Lefebvre being in the right place at the right time. He was usually put on the ice against the opposition's best forwards, and he didn't betray the confidence Burns placed in him.

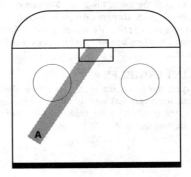

JAMIE MACOUN

Yrs. of NHL service: 10
Born: Newmarket, Ont.; Aug. 17, 1961
Position: left defense
Height: 6-2
Weight: 197
Uniform no.: 34
Shoots: left

Career statistics:

GP	G	A	TP	PIM
702	69	212	281	737

1991-92 statistics:

GP	G	A	TP	+/-	PIM	PP	SH	GW	GT	S	PCT
76	5	25	30	+10	71	3	0	0	0	129	3.9

1992-93 statistics:

GP	G	A	TP	+/-	PIM	PP	SH	GW	GT	S	PCT
77	4	15	19	+3	55	2	0	1	0	114	3.5

LAST SEASON

Goals, assists and points at two-season lows. Missed four games with groin injury.

THE FINESSE GAME

The surprising thing about Macoun — and after 10 years in the league, it shouldn't be a surprise — is how effective he can be when he steps up into the attack. Even his own team doesn't think of him as an offensive threat, as he gets little power play time. He can do unexpected things. He is a strong skater and is also deceptively fast. Macoun will go to the net and finish. Sometimes he will just get it into his head and go, and jaws drop.

For the most part, though, Macoun plays a solid game on defense. He moves the puck ahead well and quickly out of his own zone. He plays a good positional game and doesn't get suckered into chasing people behind the net. He is a solid penalty-killer and isn't fooled by weaving patterns coming at him. Macoun is an intelligent defenseman.

Macoun can still be turned to the outside and burned by outside speed, so he is careful to maintain his angle play.

THE PHYSICAL GAME

When he is at the top of his game, Macoun can be a force. He plays the man, not the puck, and anyone in his territory pays a price. He will play with a little bit of meanness in him and will get his stick up and tick people off.

THE INTANGIBLES

The bigger the game, the more you notice Macoun blocking shots and making big hits. His experience has a calming effect on his team's no-star defense corps. He's an on-ice leader.

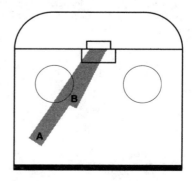

DIMITRI MIRONOV

Yrs. of NHL service: 1
Born: Moscow, Russia; Dec. 25, 1965
Position: left defense
Height: 6-2
Weight: 191
Uniform no.: 15
Shoots: right

Career statistics:

GP	G	A	TP	PIM
66	8	24	32	40

1991-92 statistics:

GP	G	A	TP	+/-	PIM	PP	SH	GW	GT	S	PCT
7	1	0	1	-4	0	0	0	1	0	7	14.3

1992-93 statistics:

GP	G	A	TP	+/-	PIM	PP	SH	GW	GT	S	PCT
59	7	24	31	-1	40	4	0	1	1	105	6.7

LAST SEASON
Missed 10 games with complications from dental operation. First NHL season.

THE FINESSE GAME
Mironov can shoot the puck, given the time and the room, but he was rattled by the pressure and the pace of NHL play and didn't unleash his shot often or effectively enough to have much of a presence last season.

Mironov is a good skater and good passer, but he often looks to make the one extra pass, or holds on to the puck too long. His ice time was limited, and a lack of confidence probably played a major part in his uncertainty on the ice.

THE PHYSICAL GAME
Mironov has a long reach and is big, but he plays very soft and doesn't use either to his best advantage. He didn't have the numbers last season to compensate for his lack of involvement.

THE INTANGIBLES
Mironov was brought in specifically to become a power play specialist on the point. He didn't fire the way the Leafs had hoped. This will be his watershed season, and he will be pushed by younger defensemen like Drake Berehowsky.

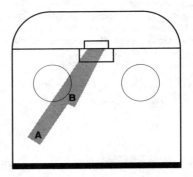

MARK OSBORNE

Yrs. of NHL service: 12
Born: Toronto, Ont.; Aug. 13, 1961
Position: right wing
Height: 6-2
Weight: 205
Uniform no.: 21
Shoots: left

Career statistics:

GP	G	A	TP	PIM
809	202	299	501	988

1991-92 statistics:

GP	G	A	TP	+/-	PIM	PP	SH	GW	GT	S	PCT
54	7	13	20	-10	73	0	2	0	0	66	10.6

1992-93 statistics:

GP	G	A	TP	+/-	PIM	PP	SH	GW	GT	S	PCT
76	12	14	26	-7	89	0	2	2	0	110	10.9

LAST SEASON

Goals three-season high. Missed seven games with knee injury.

THE FINESSE GAME

Osborne used all of his experience last season to have an effective season as a checking winger. He is a strong skater with some jump, with the anticipation and the hand skills to make something out of forced turnovers.

When asked to function in an offensive role, Osborne can create some havoc in front of the net. He will go to the net, or through it, and is consistent with his efforts. A left-handed shooter, he played right wing most of the season.

Osborne has fair hockey sense and can work nifty little give-and-gos deep. He is a sound penalty killer.

THE PHYSICAL GAME

Osborne gets nasty and can be effective that way, but it doesn't come naturally for him. He will work the boards and corners, bump and hack. He doesn't fight much. He seemed to thrive on the Leafs' new style last season.

THE INTANGIBLES

Osborne seems settled in his role of checking and scoring 10 to 15 goals a season. There are a few nights when he is more involved, but those nights don't occur consistently enough. He is near the end of his usefulness as a everyday player.

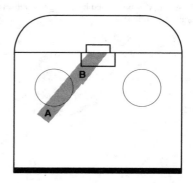

ROB PEARSON

Yrs. of NHL service: 2
Born: Oshawa, Ont.; Aug. 3, 1971
Position: right wing
Height: 6-1
Weight: 180
Uniform no.: 12
Shoots: right

Career statistics:

GP	G	A	TP	PIM
125	37	24	61	269

1991-92 statistics:

GP	G	A	TP	+/-	PIM	PP	SH	GW	GT	S	PCT
47	14	10	24	-16	58	6	0	0	1	79	17.7

1992-93 statistics:

GP	G	A	TP	+/-	PIM	PP	SH	GW	GT	S	PCT
78	23	14	37	-2	211	8	0	3	0	164	14.0

LAST SEASON

Led team in PIM. Goals, assists and points at career highs in second NHL season. Fourth on team in goals. Served one-game suspension.

THE FINESSE GAME

Pearson's timing is off. He made the jump in 1991-92 from the AHL but still hasn't found the way to get himself open enough to unleash his good shot. His skating is merely adequate, and he may need to do a great deal of work in that area to get himself open. (Brendan Shanahan is a prime example of a player who had that flaw early in his career and fought to overcome.)

Pearson will succeed with his power, and not finesse. He has to bull his way to the net and force players to back off to give him room. He has a strong snap shot and has been a proficient scorer at every level.

Defensively his game needs work, but he's hooked up with the right coach for that.

THE PHYSICAL GAME

Pearson works in the corners with great enthusiasm but isn't always effective. He is utterly obnoxious along the wall and in front of the net, and he knows he has to play that way to be effective. We wouldn't call him tough, necessarily, since he will cling to his stick rather than drop his gloves, but he sure is annoying.

THE INTANGIBLES

Pearson will make his way in the NHL as a power forward, if he makes it at all. He appears to have a good work ethic and wants to pay the price to be an NHL regular. Still, stardom appears a long way off.

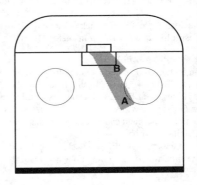

FELIX POTVIN

Yrs. of NHL service: 1
Born: Anjou, Que.; June 23, 1971
Position: goaltender
Height: 6-1
Weight: 183
Uniform no.: 29
Catches: left

Career statistics:

GP	MINS	GA	SO	GAA	A	PIM
52	2991	124	2	2.49	1	4

1991-92 statistics:

GP	MINS	GAA	W	L	T	SO	GA	S	SAPCT	PIM
4	210	2.29	0	2	1	0	8	120	.933	0

1992-93 statistics:

GP	MINS	GAA	W	L	T	SO	GA	S	SAPCT	PIM
48	2781	2.50	25	25	7	2	116	1286	.910	4

LAST SEASON

First NHL season. Finalist for Calder Trophy. Led NHL in GAA. Second in NHL in save percentage.

THE PHYSICAL GAME

How does Felix Potvin stop pucks? A butterfly goalie, he leaves a five-hole the size of the Grand Canyon, then denies the shooter by snapping his pads closed at the last minute.

Everything about Potvin's stance looks wrong. He plants his skates so far apart and is so anchored along the goal line that he has almost no lateral mobility and doesn't take away much of the shooter's angle. He is excellent down low, so the book is to shoot high, yet the top corners are the most difficult spots for a shooter to hit, and Potvin just dares anyone to beat him there. He is almost impossible to beat on the first shot.

Potvin controls his rebounds well for a butterfly goalie. He can also be comfortable hanging on to the puck for a face-off, since his teammates include two of the best face-off men in the league — Doug Gilmour and Peter Zezel.

He has excellent anticipation and just seems to get the puck stopped. To beat Potvin, shooters must force him to move side to side, and also must be able to lift the puck. Potvin will take his chances against those odds.

He does not handle the puck or move it much, and he doesn't like to come out of his net.

THE MENTAL GAME

Potvin is so confident and mentally tough that to him the puck must look like it's sailing in at only about 36 mph. He was sent down to the minors at midseason (when Grant Fuhr was still a Maple Leaf), but he took the demotion well and came back better than ever. He had a stellar playoff.

The Leafs brought him along slowly before deciding the time was right to deal Fuhr and hand the top job to the rookie. It's hard to believe now, but Potvin wasn't drafted when he was eligible for the first three rounds in 1989, generally considered a weak draft year.

THE INTANGIBLES

Potvin is a likely candidate for a sophomore slump. A goalie who relies on his reflexes as much as he does is bound to hit the wall now and again. Fortunately for him, he plays behind a strong defense, so his lapses may be less noticeable than if he played for another team.

BOB ROUSE

Yrs. of NHL service: 9
Born: Surrey, B.C.; Apr. 18, 1964
Position: right defense
Height: 6-2
Weight: 210
Uniform no.: 3
Shoots: right

Career statistics:

GP	G	A	TP	PIM
655	26	125	151	1196

1991-92 statistics:

GP	G	A	TP	+/-	PIM	PP	SH	GW	GT	S	PCT
79	3	19	22	-20	97	1	0	0	0	115	2.6

1992-93 statistics:

GP	G	A	TP	+/-	PIM	PP	SH	GW	GT	S	PCT
82	3	11	14	+7	130	0	1	1	0	78	3.8

LAST SEASON
PIM four-season high.

THE FINESSE GAME
Rouse is another one of the stay-at-home defensemen, well suited to Toronto's conservative style.

His mobility is effective only in his own zone. He won't dance through the neutral zone. He will use his agility to get the puck, take a step and make a pass. He pivots well and has good first-step quickness, but will not join the rush. His occasional contribution to offense consists of a shot from the blue line.

Rouse works well paired with an offensive defenseman, but the Leafs really don't have one capable of making the most of his steady play. He could really set a rover free.

THE PHYSICAL GAME
Rouse plays a solid checking game. He can scrap when challenged, although he is more concerned with taking the body and keeping his area of the ice free from invaders.

THE INTANGIBLES
Rouse will pay any price in his own zone to make the defensive play. He will sacrifice his body, block shots, make or take a hit to protect the puck. He is an honest, basic player.

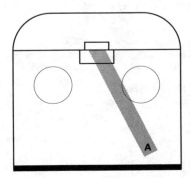

PETER ZEZEL

Yrs. of NHL service: 9
Born: Toronto, Ont.; Apr. 22, 1965
Position: centre
Height: 5-9
Weight: 200
Uniform no.: 25
Shoots: left

Career statistics:

GP	G	A	TP	PIM
563	182	328	510	351

1991-92 statistics:

GP	G	A	TP	+/-	PIM	PP	SH	GW	GT	S	PCT
64	16	33	49	-22	26	4	0	1	0	125	12.8

1992-93 statistics:

GP	G	A	TP	+/-	PIM	PP	SH	GW	GT	S	PCT
70	12	23	35	0	24	0	0	4	0	102	11.8

LAST SEASON

Goals declined for third consecutive season. Missed five games with bruised knee, five with bruised shoulder.

THE FINESSE GAME

Zezel is a checking forward who can pick up his offensive chances. While his major duty these days is to shut down the other team's top scoring lines, he can also provide some offensive dazzle of his own by polishing off a two-on-one or scoring with his powerful shot off a breakaway. The bonus to playing against other teams' scoring lines is that they are prone to a weak defensive game, and Zezel has the hand skills, quickness and anticipation to cash in on his offensive chances. He has a knack for big, timely goals.

Zezel is dominant on face-offs (giving Toronto two of the league's quickest draws, along with Doug Gilmour). This skill makes him an excellent penalty killer, since winning a draw can quickly eat seconds off the clock.

Zezel is a choppy skater, but he is tenacious and gets where he has to go.

THE PHYSICAL GAME

Zezel is not merely intense: he's wired. If anything, he gets too intense and will sometimes overdo things and take bad penalties. He is a compact, solid player who does not gets pushed around.

Zezel has become a bit injury prone in recent years, which makes him reluctant to initiate physical play as often as the coaches wish he would.

THE INTANGIBLES

Zezel has evolved into an excellent checking forward. He has always worked hard, but now he is working much smarter than he did in the past. He is a strong force and a major part of Toronto's resurgent season.

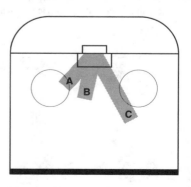

VANCOUVER CANUCKS

GREG ADAMS

Yrs. of NHL service: 9
Born: Nelson, B.C.; Aug. 1, 1963
Position: left wing
Height: 6-3
Weight: 185
Uniform no.: 8
Shoots: left

Career statistics:

GP	G	A	TP	PIM
576	228	234	462	185

1991-92 statistics:

GP	G	A	TP	+/-	PIM	PP	SH	GW	GT	S	PCT
76	30	27	57	+8	26	13	1	5	0	184	16.3

1992-93 statistics:

GP	G	A	TP	+/-	PIM	PP	SH	GW	GT	S	PCT
53	25	31	56	+31	14	6	1	3	0	124	20.2

LAST SEASON

Missed 31 games with charleyhorse in right leg. Goals and points at two-season lows. Assists five-season high. Second-best shooting percentage on team.

THE FINESSE GAME

The Canucks missed Adams grievously when he was sidelined twice during the season with injuries. Pavel Bure missed him most of all, since Adams was the lone Vancouver winger who could keep pace with the Russian Rocket. Adams has terrific speed, deceptive because he is such an efficient skater that his skating looks effortless.

He can shoot a hard slap shot on the fly off the wing, but most of his goals come from within five feet of the net. He drives fearlessly to the goal, and he likes to arrive by the most expedient route possible. If that means crashing through defensemen, then so be it. Adams has good shifty moves in deep and is an unselfish player. He played a lot of centre early in his career and is nearly as good a playmaker as finisher. One of the few knocks on him is that he should shoot more, but playing with Bure, he doesn't get as many opportunities. Pavel loves to shoot, and Adams's job is to get to the net for rebounds.

His plus/minus is no accident. He has worked hard at improving his defensive awareness and has become a complete hockey player.

THE PHYSICAL GAME

Adams's crease-crashing style exacts a price, and he is nearly always wearing an ice pack or getting medical attention for a nick or bruise somewhere on his person. Yet he always comes right back for more. He is physical and tough without being an aggressor. Adams does not fight and, considering the checking attention he gets, he remains remarkably calm and determined, seldom taking bad retaliatory penalties. He just gets the job done.

THE INTANGIBLES

Adams is one of the more underrated players on a Canucks squad that has enjoyed some success (at least during the regular season) over the past two seasons. He always shows up for the opening face-off and is battling through the final buzzer.

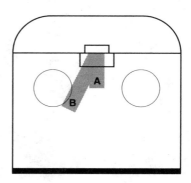

PAVEL BURE

Yrs. of NHL service: 2
Born: Moscow, Russia; Mar. 31, 1971
Position: left wing
Height: 5-11
Weight: 176
Uniform no.: 10
Shoots: left

Career statistics:

GP	G	A	TP	PIM
148	94	76	170	99

1991-92 statistics:

GP	G	A	TP	+/-	PIM	PP	SH	GW	GT	S	PCT
65	34	26	60	0	30	7	3	6	0	268	12.7

1992-93 statistics:

GP	G	A	TP	+/-	PIM	PP	SH	GW	GT	S	PCT
83	60	50	110	+35	69	13	7	9	0	407	14.7

LAST SEASON

Led NHL in shots. Tied for NHL lead in shorthanded goals. Fifth in NHL in goals. Tied for fifth in NHL in plus/minus. Led team in goals, points, plus/minus, power play goals, shorthanded goals and shots. Second on team in game-winning goals. All totals at career highs in second NHL season.

THE FINESSE GAME

Every time Bure touches the puck, fans in his home rink at Pacific Coliseum move to the edge of their collective seats. The Russian Rocket's quickness — and his control of the puck at supersonic speed — means anything is possible. He intimidates with his skating, driving back defenders who must play off him or risk being deked out of their skates at the blue line. He opens up tremendous ice for his teammates and will leave a drop pass or, more often, try to do it himself.

Bure's major weakness is his failure to use his teammates better. He will try to go through a team one-on-five rather than use his support. Of course, once in a while he can actually do it. That's the scary part. Bure has great balance and agility, and he seems to move equally well with the puck or without it. The puck doesn't slow him down a fraction.

He took some heat from the Canucks' management for floating, especially late in the season, when fatigue seemed to catch up with him. Bure had 44-33-77 in 53 games before the All-Star break (1.45 points per game average) and 16-17-33 in 30 games after the break (1.1 PPG). He doesn't do much defensively. He prefers to hang out at centre ice, and when he is going through a slump he doesn't do the other little things that can make a player useful until the scoring starts to click again. Bure is a shorthanded threat because of his breakaway speed and anticipation. There are few better breakaway scorers in the league.

THE PHYSICAL GAME

Bure is fairly physical for a smallish player, especially in the offensive zone. He was in his first altercation last season, with San Jose's Rob Zettler (although it wasn't an official fight, as the players were given double roughing minors).

THE INTANGIBLES

What sophomore slump? All that Bure, the 1992 Calder Trophy winner, did was eclipse all of the staggering expectations that were heaped on him after his sensational rookie season.

Yet he took some heat for his playoff performance, despite scoring 5-7-12 in 12 games. That is an indication of the pressure on him to produce. He is one of the NHL's most exciting players, well worth the price of admission as a solo act. The big challenge for the Canucks will be to find yet another centre to complement him, after losing Anatoli Semenov in the expansion draft.

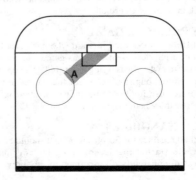

GEOFF COURTNALL

Yrs. of NHL service: 9
Born: Victoria, B.C.; Aug. 18, 1962
Position: left wing
Height: 6-1
Weight: 190
Uniform no.: 14
Shoots: left

Career statistics:

GP	G	A	TP	PIM
661	246	274	520	948

1991-92 statistics:

GP	G	A	TP	+/-	PIM	PP	SH	GW	GT	S	PCT
70	23	34	57	-6	118	12	0	3	0	281	8.2

1992-93 statistics:

GP	G	A	TP	+/-	PIM	PP	SH	GW	GT	S	PCT
84	31	46	77	+27	167	9	0	11	0	214	14.5

LAST SEASON

Tied for NHL lead in game-winning goals. One of four Canucks to appear in all 84 games. Third on team in assists and points. Goals at three-season high; assists career high.

THE FINESSE GAME

Courtnall is a streaky scorer, and when he's hot he uses a variety of shots to pepper the net. He can score off the backhand, muscle a close-range shot top shelf, use a snap shot off the wing on the fly or wrist in a rebound.

He finds the holes and is a textbook give-and-go player. Courtnall makes the first pass, burns for the opening, then rips a one-timer from the circle to complete the play.

Courtnall has good hands for passing, making especially nice touch passes to breaking teammates. He has good hand-eye co-ordination to play up front on the power play. He doesn't stand in front of the net to take punishment, but instead times his moves in for deflections with his stick.

Courtnall made one of the headier and stranger plays of last season, when he reached in from the front of the net to free a loose puck off the back of the goal netting. The puck popped loose to a teammate who fed it back in front for Courtnall.

THE PHYSICAL GAME

Courtnall is a good-sized forward who has never had much of a physical element to his game. He goes to his stick first when he is trying to intimidate an opponent or battle along the boards for the puck. He will sometimes use his body, but not consistently, although he did a better job of it last year.

THE INTANGIBLES

Courtnall regained the 30-plus form that should be his norm. He started the season hungrier and more motivated, apparently disappointed by his previous season and eager to atone. He has to maintain that edge.

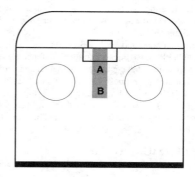

MURRAY CRAVEN

Yrs. of NHL service: 11
Born: Medicine Hat, Alta.; July 20, 1964
Position: left wing/centre
Height: 6-2
Weight: 185
Uniform no.: 32
Shoots: left

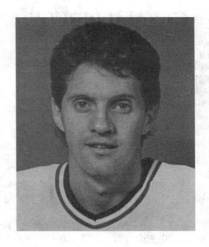

Career statistics:

GP	G	A	TP	PIM
707	205	365	570	397

1991-92 statistics:

GP	G	A	TP	+/-	PIM	PP	SH	GW	GT	S	PCT
73	27	33	60	-2	46	9	4	1	1	152	17.8

1992-93 statistics:

GP	G	A	TP	+/-	PIM	PP	SH	GW	GT	S	PCT
77	25	52	77	-1	32	6	3	2	0	151	16.6

LAST SEASON

Acquired from Hartford with fifth-round pick for Robert Kron, a third-round pick and future considerations (Jim Sandlak). Second on team in assists with career high. Sixth season with 20 or more goals. Points at career high.

THE FINESSE GAME

Craven is a chameleon. He will check. He will score. He will play first unit on the power play or penalty-killing. He will take draws. He will play right wing, left wing, or centre. He's the ultimate fill-in forward.

He has never attained star status because, while he does a lot of things well, he isn't great at any one thing. He's a good skater but doesn't have the hockey sense to use it as well he should. He isn't a natural scorer. He has to work hard for his 25 to 30 goals a season and scores most of his goals from close range. He does have a good slap shot and can be used on the point on the power play.

Craven is unselfish, and poised down low. He will confidently slide a backhand pass across the goal mouth to a teammate. He goes to the net with determination and has good hands for picking up loose pucks. He has a long reach and can beat a defender one on one by using his speed and dangling the puck away from his body but under control.

THE PHYSICAL GAME

Craven is wiry but not very big. He will lose some one-on-one battles in tight, but he will use his body well in the defensive as well as the offensive zone.

THE INTANGIBLES

Craven has become a very good defensive role player who can also produce upwards of 25 goals a season — a pretty formidable combination. He is a complete hockey player, one who fits nicely into a role as a No. 2 or No. 3 centre.

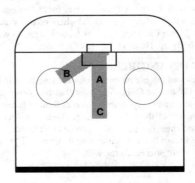

GERALD DIDUCK

Yrs. of NHL service: 8
Born: Edmonton, Alta.; Apr. 6, 1965
Position: right defense
Height: 6-2
Weight: 207
Uniform no.: 4
Shoots: right

Career statistics:

GP	G	A	TP	PIM
534	42	107	149	1080

1991-92 statistics:

GP	G	A	TP	+/-	PIM	PP	SH	GW	GT	S	PCT
77	6	21	27	-3	224	2	0	1	0	128	4.7

1992-93 statistics:

GP	G	A	TP	+/-	PIM	PP	SH	GW	GT	S	PCT
80	6	14	20	+32	171	0	1	0	0	92	6.5

LAST SEASON

Goals and points at two-season lows.

THE FINESSE GAME

Diduck is one of the better skaters among defensemen in the league. He gets a great deal of drive and power from his lower body. He has good balance, is mobile and likes to jump into the play to support the rush. Diduck often gets too caught up in the excitement of the attack, when it would be wiser for him to be more conservative and not pinch.

Diduck makes a strong first pass out of the zone. He doesn't try to carry the puck himself but makes good use of his teammates. The puck travels much faster without him, and he's aware of that.

Diduck has a powerful slap shot but needs a range-finder to get it on net. If he could master the strong, accurate wrist shot from the point, he wouldn't have to listen so often to the discouraging sound of the puck banging off the glass.

He kills penalties well. He doesn't overhandle the puck, and he positions his body intelligently.

THE PHYSICAL GAME

The Canucks rely on Diduck as their most consistently tough defenseman. He cleans out the front of his crease well, but he fell into several funks last season (along with his defense partners) where no one wanted to hit. When that happens, it is Diduck's job to wake everybody up. He can be more of a leader.

THE INTANGIBLES

Diduck had trouble handling pressure situations in the past. Coach Pat Quinn rectified that by giving him more and more responsibility and defining his role as the anchor of the team's defense. Diduck answered the challenge, but there is one more level he needs to attain: that of being a dominating defenseman. He has the skill but also needs the will.

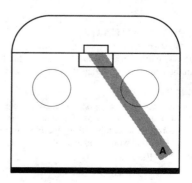

ROBERT DIRK

Yrs. of NHL service: 4
Born: Regina, Sask.; Aug. 20, 1966
Position: left defense
Height: 6-4
Weight: 218
Uniform no.: 22
Shoots: left

Career statistics:

GP	G	A	TP	PIM
246	9	21	30	551

1991-92 statistics:

GP	G	A	TP	+/-	PIM	PP	SH	GW	GT	S	PCT
72	2	7	9	+6	126	0	0	0	1	44	4.5

1992-93 statistics:

GP	G	A	TP	+/-	PIM	PP	SH	GW	GT	S	PCT
69	4	8	12	+25	150	0	0	2	0	41	9.8

LAST SEASON

Goals double previous season high. Points and PIM at career highs.

THE FINESSE GAME

Dirk is a stay-at-home defenseman who rarely ventures beyond the blue line into the attacking zone. When he did once last season — a foray that resulted in a game-winning goal — the play was so shocking it rated headlines in the Vancouver papers.

He doesn't skate well, nor does he handle the puck very cleverly. His job is to patrol the boards, corners and front of his net. He bangs the puck out as quickly and efficiently as possible, not looking to make a play. He plays a positional game. He's vulnerable to outside speed, so he tries to angle his attacker to the boards.

He needs to be paired with a mobile partner, because he just doesn't cover enough ice on his own.

THE PHYSICAL GAME

Dirk finishes every check, hits everything he can reach and is strong on one-on-one battles along the wall. He blocks shots and dives headlong for pucks. He is a willing hitter limited only by his skating.

THE INTANGIBLES

Dirk can't be used in a lot of specialty situations because of his lack of skating ability, but he will give an honest and consistent effort to the best of his ability at even strength.

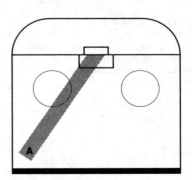

DOUG LIDSTER

Yrs. of NHL service: 9
Born: Kamloops, B.C.; Oct. 18, 1960
Position: right defense
Height: 6-1
Weight: 200
Uniform no.: 3
Shoots: right

Career statistics:

GP	G	A	TP	PIM
666	65	242	307	526

1991-92 statistics:

GP	G	A	TP	+/-	PIM	PP	SH	GW	GT	S	PCT
66	6	23	29	+9	39	3	0	2	0	89	6.7

1992-93 statistics:

GP	G	A	TP	+/-	PIM	PP	SH	GW	GT	S	PCT
71	6	19	25	+9	36	3	0	0	0	76	7.9

LAST SEASON

PIM career low. Points four-season low. Acquired by New York Rangers for John Vanbiesbrouck.

THE FINESSE GAME

Lidster is a finesse defenseman who uses his skills e-qually well in the offensive and defensive zones.

On the attack, he can lead or join a rush, and he works the point on the power play. He is patient and poised with the puck, and can do a lot of things while skating. Lidster has a decent slap shot from the point, and also has the moves to fake a defender, then burst past for a shot from the circle.

Defensively, he's tough to beat one on one. He is agile and can stop and start skating backwards. Lidster holds his position and forces the attacker to make the first move.

When it is crunch time and his team is holding a lead, he will make the safe plays.

THE PHYSICAL GAME

Lidster has good size but does not use it well. He is not very strong in one-on-one battles along the boards or in front of the net. He's erratic about finishing his checks. Sometimes he will really deck an opponent, while other times he will only give him a push.

THE INTANGIBLES

Because of Brian Leetch's uncertain health, Lidster's offensive ability is important insurance for the Rangers. Lidster should benefit from the change in scenery. He will also have to convince a lot of people he's not Jerry Seinfeld.

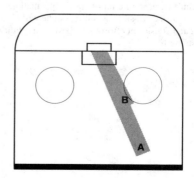

TREVOR LINDEN

Yrs. of NHL service: 5
Born: Medicine Hat, Alta.; Apr. 11, 1970
Position: right wing
Height: 6-4
Weight: 205
Uniform no.: 16
Shoots: right

Career statistics:

GP	G	A	TP	PIM
397	148	178	326	338

1991-92 statistics:

GP	G	A	TP	+/-	PIM	PP	SH	GW	GT	S	PCT
80	31	44	75	+3	99	6	1	6	1	201	15.4

1992-93 statistics:

GP	G	A	TP	+/-	PIM	PP	SH	GW	GT	S	PCT
84	33	39	72	+19	64	8	0	3	0	209	15.8

LAST SEASON

One of four Canucks to play in all 84 games. Goals and points matched career highs. Assists at career high. PIM at three-season low. Fifth on team in scoring after leading Canucks in scoring previous two seasons.

THE FINESSE GAME

Not a graceful skater, at times Linden looks very awkward, and he's not as strong on his skates as a player of his size should be. Despite his heavy feet, his agility is satisfactory, but he lacks first-step quickness and doesn't have the all-out speed to pull away from a checker.

Linden has a slow release on his shot. He has a long reach but unlike, say, Dave Andreychuk (who is built along similar lines), his short game is not as effective as it should be. He uses a slap shot off the wing that is released more quickly than his wrist shot.

Linden is unselfish and makes quick passing decisions that help his team break smartly up-ice, often creating odd-man rushes. He seems to lack confidence in his shooting, and when he is the open man on the outnumbered rush he passes to a covered teammate rather than take the shot himself.

He has improved tremendously in his defensive coverage. He often plays with teammates who are smaller and somewhat lax in that department, so he takes it upon himself to get back in time.

THE PHYSICAL GAME

Playing a physical game does not come naturally to Linden. Because of his size, he knows he is most effective playing that way, but he has to push himself to do it. It's an easy style to back away from. It requires effort and energy, and a lot of nights it hurts, but if he doesn't play that gritty style, his finesse game alone does not compensate.

When Linden is throwing his weight around, he drives to the net and drags a defender or two with him, opening up a lot of ice for his teammates. He creates havoc in front of the net on the power play, planting himself for screens and deflections. When the puck is at the side boards, he's smart enough to move up higher, between the circles, and force the penalty killers to make a decision. If the defenseman on that side steps up to cover Linden, space will open behind the defenseman; if a forward collapses to cover him, a point shot will open up.

THE INTANGIBLES

Linden has matured so quickly and is so big that it's easy to forget he just turned 23 at the end of last season. He is good for 30 to 35 goals and 75 points a season, yet it always seems like he should be delivering more. As captain of the Canucks, he feels the pressure, too.

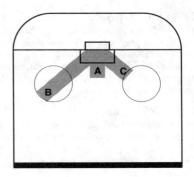

JYRKI LUMME

Yrs. of NHL service: 5
Born: Tampere, Finland; July 16, 1966
Position: right defense
Height: 6-1
Weight: 207
Uniform no.: 21
Shoots: left

Career statistics:

GP	G	A	TP	PIM
315	30	124	154	238

1991-92 statistics:

GP	G	A	TP	+/-	PIM	PP	SH	GW	GT	S	PCT
75	12	32	44	+25	65	3	1	1	0	106	11.3

1992-93 statistics:

GP	G	A	TP	+/-	PIM	PP	SH	GW	GT	S	PCT
74	8	36	44	+30	55	3	2	1	0	123	6.5

LAST SEASON

Led team defensemen in scoring for second consecutive season. Career high in assists. Matched career high in points. Missed games with a sprained left knee.

THE FINESSE GAME

Lumme is one of the Canucks' more mobile defenseman, a good puck-carrier who can rush the puck out of danger and make a smart first pass to start the attack. He likes to gamble a bit offensively, but he has the good skating ability to be able to wheel back into a defensive mode.

He plays the right point on the power play. His shot isn't overpowering, but he keeps it low and on net, and he times it well. He has very good hands and is adept at keeping the puck in. He also uses his lateral mobility to slide along the blue line into the centre to quarterback the power play from there.

Defensively, Lumme uses his hand skills for sweep and poke checks. He will challenge at the blue line to try to knock the puck free, but he doesn't always follow through with his body if the poke check fails.

Lumme is a strong penalty killer because of his range and anticipation.

THE PHYSICAL GAME

Lumme is all finesse. He will take a hit to protect the puck or make a play, but won't throw himself at anybody. Other teams like to key on Lumme, because if he gets hit often and hard enough, he can be taken out of a game early, depriving the Canucks of a valuable component of their offense.

THE INTANGIBLES

Lumme has improved defensively, but his key value remains his open-ice play and involvement in the attack.

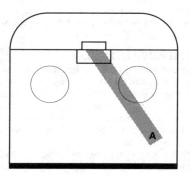

KIRK MCLEAN

Yrs. of NHL service: 6
Born: Willowdale, Ont.; June 26, 1966
Position: goaltender
Height: 6-0
Weight: 177
Uniform no.: 1
Catches: left

Career statistics:

GP	MINS	GA	SO	GAA	A	PIM
312	17,949	1002	13	3.35	11	40

1991-92 statistics:

GP	MINS	GAA	W	L	T	SO	GA	S	SAPCT	PIM
65	3852	2.74	38	17	9	5	176	1780	.901	0

1992-93 statistics:

GP	MINS	GAA	W	L	T	SO	GA	S	SAPCT	PIM
54	3261	3.39	28	21	5	3	184	1615	.886	16

LAST SEASON

Victories down by 10 and GAA up by more than a half-goal over last season, in which he posted his career bests.

THE PHYSICAL GAME

McLean stays on his feet more than any goalie in the NHL. He has great lateral movement. Maybe because of his soccer training, his movement and balance are advanced.

From the Jacques Plante and Bernie Parent school of making a little work go a long way, McLean is into energy conservation. His style is effortless. Even when he's bombarded with shots, the barrage seems to take little out of him. If he does drop down for a save, he is back up quickly for a rebound. He is down but seldom out of the play.

He makes himself look big in the net because of his positioning and stand-up play. He is very solid technically, and has good reflexes besides. His solid foundation means very few bad stretches of play. He will blow the occasional angle, especially on the stick side, but he has a great deal of confidence in his game and does not rattle easily.

He's good up high, with a quick glove hand. He is strong on his stick and uses it well around the net for jabbing at puckhandlers or breaking up passes. He also moves well out of his net to stop hard-arounds or make strong passes.

THE MENTAL GAME

McLean did not have a great season, but that reflected the play of the team in front of him more than it did any serious cracks in this netminder's composure. McLean tends to need some time to get into a game. He can be beaten early, then get better as the game moves along.

THE INTANGIBLES

Playoff success still eludes McLean — and, unlike forwards and defensemen, goalies are never judged to be elite players until their playoff performances are strong.

It will be worth keeping an eye on the Kay Whitmore situation this season. McLean has been the team's No. 1 goalie for several seasons. A strong threat from Whitmore will mean either a more competitive, better-rested McLean, or a goalie who is surly about losing his ice time.

SERGIO MOMESSO

Yrs. of NHL service: 9
Born: Montreal, Que.; Sept. 4, 1965
Position: left wing
Height: 6-3
Weight: 215
Uniform no.: 27
Shoots: left

Career statistics:

GP	G	A	TP	PIM
481	116	150	266	1153

1991-92 statistics:

GP	G	A	TP	+/-	PIM	PP	SH	GW	GT	S	PCT
58	20	23	43	+16	198	2	0	3	0	153	13.1

1992-93 statistics:

GP	G	A	TP	+/-	PIM	PP	SH	GW	GT	S	PCT
84	18	20	38	+11	200	4	0	1	0	146	12.3

LAST SEASON

One of four Canucks to play in all 84 games. Career high in PIM, which was second on team.

THE FINESSE GAME

Momesso is a power forward, but one without the hand skills to do too much damage in the scoring column. He is big and strong and has enough speed to drive defenders back.

He knows his game is to go to the net. He can also use a big, heavy slap shot from the wing, but it is not very accurate. When he does get it on target, he just about knocks the goalie into the cage. Momesso uses his power and balance well in front of the net to create traffic and scrap for loose pucks.

He does a respectable job defensively. He's turned into an ideal third-line winger (where he played much of the season on a physically imposing line with Petr Nedved and Jim Sandlak). Expectations will always be there for Momesso to deliver more, but he seems to have levelled off at the 15- to 20-goal range.

THE PHYSICAL GAME

Momesso's great balance and size make him tough to knock off the puck — and also make it difficult for anyone to withstand one of his punishing hits. He is unpredictable, which gets him plenty of room most nights. Momesso could go ballistic at any moment, and it's not a pretty sight. Two inconsistencies: the intensity isn't there every night, and occasionally he tends to take bad penalties.

THE INTANGIBLES

Momesso's season got off to a low start when he reported out of shape. He has worn out his welcome in the past because of his lack of dedication and self-motivation, and that pattern could be repeated if he starts off slowly again this season.

DANA MURZYN

Yrs. of NHL service: 8
Born: Regina, Sask.; Dec. 9, 1966
Position: left defense
Height: 6-3
Weight: 205
Uniform no.: 5
Shoots: left

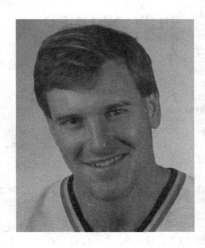

Career statistics:

GP	G	A	TP	PIM
545	38	110	148	1020

1991-92 statistics:

GP	G	A	TP	+/-	PIM	PP	SH	GW	GT	S	PCT
70	3	12	15	+15	145	0	1	0	0	99	3.0

1992-93 statistics:

GP	G	A	TP	+/-	PIM	PP	SH	GW	GT	S	PCT
79	5	11	16	+34	196	0	0	2	0	82	6.1

LAST SEASON

Led team defensemen in plus/minus. Tied for second on team in plus/minus. Goals and points at three-season highs.

THE FINESSE GAME

Murzyn's skating has long been the bane of his game. He has heavy feet, or else insufficient lower-body strength, and has no power in his skating. He can't skate the puck out of the zone and must rely on his above-average passing skills to move the puck.

He has a big shot that he gets away quickly, accurately and reluctantly. Murzyn seems to have lost interest in the attacking zone. Perhaps his skating weighs so heavily on his mind that he concentrates first and foremost on staying back. For much of the season, he was paired with the fleet Jyrki Lumme, who helped cover much of the ground that Murzyn couldn't, and Murzyn was content to stay back.

He has learned to play a smarter positional game to cover up for his skating. He is a poised penalty killer.

THE PHYSICAL GAME

Murzyn has to play a more physical game to be a better player. He is slow and can't hit what he can't catch, but when he is in close quarters, he can knock people down and doesn't always do it. He lacks the mean streak that big hitters need to be punishing ones, to make attackers leery of skating into his territory. Murzyn doesn't scare people, but he could. And should.

He blocks shots and uses his reach effectively.

THE INTANGIBLES

Murzyn was given a great deal of responsibility last season, probably for the first time in his career. He was one of the defensemen usually sent out against the opposing team's top forward line. Although he has good finesse skills, he has apparently decided to apply them more to defense than offense.

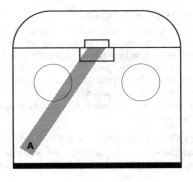

PETR NEDVED

Yrs. of NHL service: 3
Born: Liberec, Czechoslovakia; Dec. 9, 1971
Position: centre
Height: 6-3
Weight: 178
Uniform no.: 19
Shoots: left

Career statistics:

GP	G	A	TP	PIM
222	63	61	124	152

1991-92 statistics:

GP	G	A	TP	+/-	PIM	PP	SH	GW	GT	S	PCT
77	15	22	37	-3	36	5	0	1	1	99	15.2

1992-93 statistics:

GP	G	A	TP	+/-	PIM	PP	SH	GW	GT	S	PCT
84	38	33	71	+20	96	2	1	3	0	149	25.5

LAST SEASON

Second in NHL in shooting percentage. One of four Canucks to play in all 84 games. Second on team in goals. Career highs in goals, assists, points and PIM.

THE FINESSE GAME

Much of the season went the way it should for a first-round draft pick (second overall in 1990): Nedved was confident, he played with a great attitude, and his scoring touch was golden.

The biggest improvement is in Nedved's skating. He's traded his choppiness for a more fluid stride with better balance and power. Tall but slightly built, he can handle the puck well in traffic or in open ice at tempo. He uses his forehand and backhand equally well for a pass or a shot. He sees the ice very well and has a creative mind. Nedved has a sense of where his teammates are, and a feathery touch for getting the puck to a blade.

He still doesn't shoot enough. He gets his best chances down low, using a wrist shot in tight, and is an incredibly accurate shooter when he does pull the trigger. He needs to drive to the net more and take advantage of the space that that will get him.

Although he lacks a big slap shot, Nedved can run a power play from the point.

THE PHYSICAL GAME

Nedved is strong on face-offs. He has good hand quickness and cheats well. On offensive-zone draws, he turns his body so he is almost facing the boards.

Nedved protects the puck well with his body, and he is not afraid of taking the hit if it means holding on to the puck until the last second to dish off a pass.

He doesn't initiate much. It would help to see more competitive fire.

THE INTANGIBLES

Nedved wanted to get out of Vancouver, so he started playing better to enhance his trade value. He played so well that the Canucks couldn't trade him. Now the question will be whether he steps up to the No. 1 role — meaning he gets to play with Pavel Bure and Greg Adams — and succeed in Vancouver, or start sulking again and demand another trade. He was a playoff dud (2-3-5 in 12 games), so he makes a risky pick for either a pool or a team looking for a No. 1 centre.

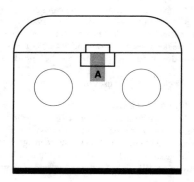

GINO ODJICK

Yrs. of NHL service: 3
Born: Maniwaki, Que.; Sept. 7, 1970
Position: left wing
Height: 6-2
Weight: 205
Uniform no.: 29
Shoots: left

Career statistics:

GP	G	A	TP	PIM
185	15	20	35	1014

1991-92 statistics:

GP	G	A	TP	+/-	PIM	PP	SH	GW	GT	S	PCT
65	4	6	10	-1	348	0	0	0	0	68	5.9

1992-93 statistics:

GP	G	A	TP	+/-	PIM	PP	SH	GW	GT	S	PCT
75	4	13	17	+3	370	0	0	1	0	79	5.1

LAST SEASON

Second in NHL in PIM with career high. Career high in points and assists. Underwent arthroscopic knee surgery.

THE FINESSE GAME

Odjick is a goon who knows that goons are facing extinction in the NHL. To preserve his job, he has added important elements to become more than a one-dimensional player. For openers, he reported to training camp almost 20 pounds lighter. Not only did he retain all of his strength and toughness, but he moved better on the ice. Never a great skater, Odjick was quicker and better able to sustain momentum once he did get going. He'll never threaten Eric Heiden, but his dedication to improving his overall game is significant.

Odjick's scoring chances come from in tight. He works tirelessly around the net for loose pucks, just slamming and jamming. He could use a little more patience, since he gets a lot of room for his first move, but his theory seems to be that three whacks at the puck (which he can get easily) are worth one finesse move (which he might not be able to make anyway).

THE PHYSICAL GAME

Odjick takes cheap penalties. He aggravates, hits late, hits from behind, yet is a legitimate tough guy when the gloves come off. He protects his teammates. He is also strong enough to simply run over people en route to the net.

THE INTANGIBLES

Odjick is a huge favourite with the fans in Vancouver, and the coaches can't help but love the effort he puts into his game and his career. If he continues to work at the little parts of his game, he will be making a big impact for seasons to come. It's the Bob Probert blueprint.

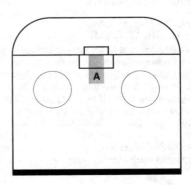

CLIFF RONNING

Yrs. of NHL service: 6
Born: Vancouver, B.C.; Oct. 1, 1965
Position: centre
Height: 5-8
Weight: 175
Uniform no.: 7
Shoots: left

Career statistics:

GP	G	A	TP	PIM
350	113	180	293	118

1991-92 statistics:

GP	G	A	TP	+/-	PIM	PP	SH	GW	GT	S	PCT
80	24	47	71	+18	42	6	0	2	1	216	11.1

1992-93 statistics:

GP	G	A	TP	+/-	PIM	PP	SH	GW	GT	S	PCT
79	29	56	85	+19	30	10	0	2	0	209	13.9

LAST SEASON

Led team in assists with career high. Second on team in points with career high. Career high in goals. Second on team in power play goals.

THE FINESSE GAME

Ronning's forte is not scoring goals, but creating chances for his wingers. He lets bigger linemates like Trevor Linden attract defenders, so that Ronning attracts the puck. He's quick, shifty and smart. He likes to work from behind the net, using the cage as a shield and daring defenders to chase him. Much of his game is a dare. He is a tempting target, and even smaller-sized defensemen fantasize about smashing Ronning to the ice, but he keeps himself out of the trouble spots by dancing in and out of openings and finding free teammates.

Ronning is a quick thinker and is unpredictable. He can curl off the wall into the slot, pass to the corners or the point and jump to the net, or beat a defender wide to the top of the circle and feed a trailing teammate coming into the play late.

He puts a lot of little dekes into a compact area. He opens up the ice with his bursts of speed and his fakes. Unless the defense can force him along the wall and contain him, he's all over the ice trying to make things happen.

THE PHYSICAL GAME

No one asks jockeys to tackle running backs. Ronning is built for speed and deception. He is smart enough to avoid getting crunched, and talented enough to compensate for his lack of strength.

He gets involved with his stick, hooking at a puck-carrier's arm and worrying at the puck in a player's skates. He keeps the puck in his skates when he protects it, so that a checker will often have to pull Ronning down to get at the puck, which creates a power play for the Canucks.

THE INTANGIBLES

Tough in his way, Ronning has excelled at a game that everyone told him he was too small to play. Of course, it helps that he plays on a team that has a lot of large kitchen appliances disguised as forwards.

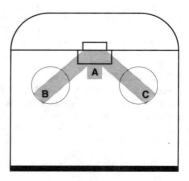

JIRI SLEGR

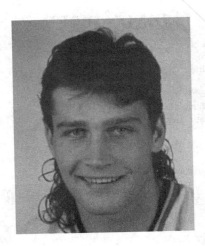

Yrs. of NHL service: 1
Born: Litvinov, Czechoslovakia; May 30, 1971
Position: left defense
Height: 5-11
Weight: 190
Uniform no.: 24
Shoots: left

Career statistics:

GP	G	A	TP	PIM
41	4	22	26	109

1992-93 statistics:

GP	G	A	TP	+/-	PIM	PP	SH	GW	GT	S	PCT
41	4	22	26	+16	109	2	0	0	0	89	4.5

LAST SEASON
First NHL season.

THE FINESSE GAME
Slegr's offensive gifts were sufficient to get him in to the Canucks' line-up for half the season, since they were so desperate for rushing defensemen. He is an excellent skater, fluid and mobile, with excellent balance. His forte is puck control, and he rushes the puck well. From the offensive part of the red line in, Slegr's season could be rated a success.

He plays the left point on the first power play, often with Pavel Bure, and sees the offensive play well.

His troubles emerge in his own end of the ice. He does not read defensive plays well and needs a great deal of improvement in handling the rush until he can emerge as an everyday player.

THE PHYSICAL GAME
Slegr is very strong, and when so inclined, he can tie up opponents in front of the net. He isn't big enough to bulldoze people out of the slot, so he usually resorts to his finesse skills, trying to pick off passes or playing the attacker's stick. He tends to carry his stick high.

THE INTANGIBLES
Slegr's overall game needs work. At present, he is strictly a one-way offensive defenseman.

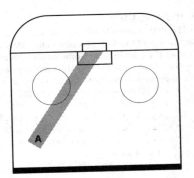

DIXON WARD

Yrs. of NHL service: 1
Born: Leduc, Alta.; Sept. 23, 1968
Position: right wing
Height: 6-0
Weight: 195
Uniform no.: 17
Shoots: right

Career statistics:

GP	G	A	TP	PIM
70	22	30	52	82

1992-93 statistics:

GP	G	A	TP	+/-	PIM	PP	SH	GW	GT	S	PCT
70	22	30	52	+34	82	4	1	0	1	111	19.8

LAST SEASON

First NHL season. Tied for second on team in plus/minus. Led NHL rookies in plus/minus. Third among NHL rookies in shooting percentage.

THE FINESSE GAME

Ward is a powerful skater with good anticipation and quickness. His work along the boards and in front of the net is consistent and effective. He has good hands to take advantage of whatever opportunities are created from his hard work. He has a good shot from the top of the slot and also drives to the net to follow up his shot.

Ward could improve his skating a bit more, but he applied himself to becoming a better skater in his final year of college and the work has paid off.

He is alert defensively and is a good penalty killer. He saw limited time on the power play, but he could have a future there as well on the second unit. He was a scorer at the college level and knows what to do with the puck. He has very good hockey sense.

THE PHYSICAL GAME

Ward has above-average size and uses it willingly. The college game is not overly physical, but Ward has taken to it with enthusiasm, and he finishes his checks.

THE INTANGIBLES

Older (24 at the start of last season) and more mature than most rookies (he didn't break into the NHL until completing his four years at North Dakota), Ward is already a fairly polished two-way forward. He was the biggest pleasant surprise for the Canucks last season.

WASHINGTON CAPITALS

DON BEAUPRE

Yrs. of NHL service: 13
Born: Kitchener, Ont.; Sept. 19, 1961
Position: goaltender
Height: 5-9
Weight: 165
Uniform no.: 33
Catches: left

Career statistics:

GP	MINS	GA	SO	GAA	A	PIM
532	30,166	1749	13	3.48	5	226

1991-92 statistics:

GP	MINS	GAA	W	L	T	SO	GA	S	SAPCT	PIM
54	3108	3.20	29	17	6	1	166	1435	.884	30

1992-93 statistics:

GP	MINS	GAA	W	L	T	SO	GA	S	SAPCT	PIM
58	3282	3.31	27	23	5	1	181	1530	.882	20

LAST SEASON

Fourth season with 20 or more wins. Victories two fewer than career high established last season. Missed three games with groin injury.

THE PHYSICAL GAME

The game has changed to make hockey more of an east-west game than a north-south game, and that makes Beaupre's style more valuable today than it was a few seasons ago. He is a butterfly goalie and reads plays well.

In Washington, the team scores a fair amount of goals but always seems to play close games, and that puts a lot of pressure on the goaltender every night. Until the team gets a game-breaker, it's going to stay that way, and there will always be the heat on the goalie not to allow a bad goal. The power play helped the Caps out in this area last season, but who knows if it will be as successful again.

Beaupre's lack of size hurts, but he has very quick feet to take away the low shots. He will stack the pads and go down on his side, and that takes him out of the play. He doesn't have to do this, since he moves well laterally with the shooter; it's one of his weaknesses.

Beaupre is not very active in moving the puck. Much of that is by design, since the Washington defense corps features so many excellent skaters and puckhandlers on defense. If pressure is on, though, Beaupre can be relied upon to bang the puck out of the zone.

THE MENTAL GAME

Beaupre was more insulted than challenged by the acquisition of Rick Tabaracci and the coy games played as to who was the No. 1 goalie. Beaupre has had to battle year after year either for a job or in a salary dispute, and while he normally loves a challenge, he seems to be wearying of the process. Beaupre is focussed within the game. The Caps are usually slow starters, and Beaupre keeps them in it early.

THE INTANGIBLES

Another season, another playoff collapse for the Capitals. Rightly or wrongly, Beaupre gets fingered for much of the blame. He has certainly never come through with the kind of playoffs that stamp a goalie's reputation, not since his 1983-84 season with Minnesota, and he is due for a change of scenery.

CRAIG BERUBE

Yrs. of NHL service: 5
Born: Calahoo, Alta.; Dec. 17, 1965
Position: left wing
Height: 6-1
Weight: 205
Uniform no.: 16
Shoots: left

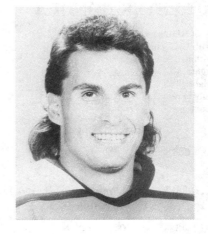

Career statistics:

GP	G	A	TP	PIM
388	26	45	71	1321

1991-92 statistics:

GP	G	A	TP	+/-	PIM	PP	SH	GW	GT	S	PCT
76	6	11	17	-5	264	1	0	1	0	69	8.7

1992-93 statistics:

GP	G	A	TP	+/-	PIM	PP	SH	GW	GT	S	PCT
77	4	8	12	-6	209	0	0	2	0	58	6.9

LAST SEASON

Led team in PIM. Games played career high. PIM four-season low. Missed one game with suspension.

THE FINESSE GAME

Berube has limited skills but is proficient enough in all areas not to embarrass himself on the ice. He is a strong and powerful but slow skater. He is at his best in tight in front of the net, where he can plant himself and force others to try to move him. He does not have the quickness to do much else.

His hand skills are average. He has the intelligence to do something with the puck, and when he drives to the net and slides a backpass to a trailer, he adds the element of surprise as he sets up a screen.

Most of Berube's goals are generated from his hard work around the net. He is an eager player, but he isn't quick enough to convert most of the chances his big size creates around the net.

THE PHYSICAL GAME

Berube is one of the top five fighters in the league, but that is no longer enough to sustain a player's NHL career. He is a bit of a loose cannon, which makes other players on the ice wary, but he has to be more judicious in his use of muscle or his ice time will become more limited — and it's scarce enough as it is.

THE INTANGIBLES

Berube has been working to make himself a more complete player but is not doing enough to merit a full-time role. He could become a useful fourth-line winger who chips in 10 goals or so a season, but he has to stay out of the penalty box in order to do so. He can play tough without leaving the ice.

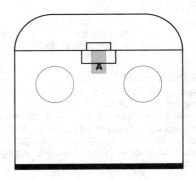

PETER BONDRA

Yrs. of NHL service: 3
Born: Lutsk, Ukraine; Feb. 7, 1968
Position: right wing
Height: 5-11
Weight: 180
Uniform no.: 12
Shoots: left

Career statistics:

GP	G	A	TP	PIM
208	77	92	169	159

1991-92 statistics:

GP	G	A	TP	+/-	PIM	PP	SH	GW	GT	S	PCT
71	28	28	56	+16	42	4	0	3	0	158	17.7

1992-93 statistics:

GP	G	A	TP	+/-	PIM	PP	SH	GW	GT	S	PCT
83	37	48	85	+8	70	10	0	7	0	239	15.5

LAST SEASON

Career-high point total one more than previous two seasons combined. Led team in goals, points and game-winning goals. Tied for third on team in power play goals. Goals, assists and PIM career highs.

THE FINESSE GAME

Bondra's speed is exceptional and he is intelligent on the ice offensively. He accelerates quickly and smoothly and drives defenders back because they have to play off his speed. He doesn't drive to the net as well as he should. He is not a big skater, but he shouldn't spend all of his time on the perimeter, either.

Bondra cuts in on the off-swing and shoots in stride. He has a very good backhand shot and likes to cut out from behind the net and make things happen in tight. He has very good balance and quickness.

Bondra is either very good or invisible. He has to develop consistency or add other parts to his game to make himself a contributor when the goals aren't going in.

Bondra can't be trusted defensively. He will make some nice steals because of his anticipation and reach, but his overall defensive game is lax.

THE PHYSICAL GAME

Bondra tries to avoid congested areas unless he has the puck. Then he will scurry through holes and try to get the defenders mixed up in their checking assignments.

THE INTANGIBLES

We hate to get into the Don Cherry vein of Euro-bashing, but in the case of Bondra, it fits. The focus is on Bondra because he can score goals in bunches, but he is nowhere to be found in the big games. With Dale Hunter out of the line-up for the first quarter of the season, some of the Caps' forwards may be playing even smaller.

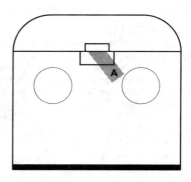

SYLVAIN COTE

Yrs. of NHL service: 8
Born: Quebec City, Que.; Jan. 19, 1966
Position: left defense
Height: 5-11
Weight: 185
Uniform no.: 3
Shoots: right

Career statistics:

GP	G	A	TP	PIM
537	63	119	182	212

1991-92 statistics:

GP	G	A	TP	+/-	PIM	PP	SH	GW	GT	S	PCT
78	11	29	40	+7	31	6	0	2	0	151	7.3

1992-93 statistics:

GP	G	A	TP	+/-	PIM	PP	SH	GW	GT	S	PCT
77	21	29	50	+28	34	8	2	3	0	206	10.2

LAST SEASON

One of three Capitals defensemen with 20 or more goals, establishing an NHL record. Second on team in plus/minus, leading team defensemen. Career highs in goals and points. Tied career high in assists.

THE FINESSE GAME

Cote has matured into a solid two-way defenseman. He has very good puckhandling skills, and can make a pass to his forehand or backhand side with confidence.

He can do everything in stride. Carrying the puck does not slow him down, and he is gifted in all of the skating areas — fine agility, good balance, quick stops and starts.

His hockey sense has improved. He can lead a rush or come into the play as a trailer, but he knows enough not to force and to play more conservatively when the situation dictates.

Cote still needs to improve his defensive reads, but he is working hard at it and his skating helps cover up for most of his lapses. His instincts lag well behind his skill level.

THE PHYSICAL GAME

Cote is the strength of the Washington defense. He doesn't have great size, but he is more willing than most of his blueline mates to mix it up. He finishes his checks and is an effective hitter, but not a mean one.

THE INTANGIBLES

The Caps' system is conducive to the development of a defenseman with good offensive skills, and Cote has the added advantage of not having to be the No. 1 or 2 defenseman, because he is ideal on the second unit. Opposing teams usually pit their top defensive units against the Kevin Hatcher-Calle Johansson unit, and Cote took advantage of the slack.

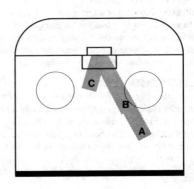

PAT ELYNUIK

Yrs. of NHL service: 4
Born: Foam Lake, Sask.; Oct. 30, 1967
Position: right wing
Height: 6-0
Weight: 185
Uniform no.: 19
Shoots: right

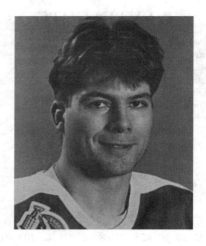

Career statistics:

GP	G	A	TP	PIM
369	137	164	301	328

1991-92 statistics:

GP	G	A	TP	+/-	PIM	PP	SH	GW	GT	S	PCT
60	25	25	50	-2	65	9	0	1	0	127	19.7

1992-93 statistics:

GP	G	A	TP	+/-	PIM	PP	SH	GW	GT	S	PCT
80	22	35	57	+3	66	8	0	1	0	121	18.2

LAST SEASON

Acquired from Winnipeg for John Druce. Goals career low. Assists three-season high. Points two-season low.

THE FINESSE GAME

Elynuik is a scorer. Period. That is his bread and butter, his way of making his living. He is a pretty heady player in the offensive zone, and he's good on the off wing on the power play, but his skating, which is just average, limits his ability to do much creatively.

Elynuik is sometimes indecisive. Someone who expects to score goals to earn his keep should have more than 121 shots in a season. His shooting percentage is always good, which usually means a player is getting himself into the high-quality shooting areas. He does that, but then looks to make a play instead of just firing his shot. He is unselfish and often looks for a teammate in a better position, and while Elynuik is a good playmaker, he should dedicate himself more to finishing.

Elynuik plays on the second power play unit. Again, his skating prevents him from being more of a factor. He is quite sluggish.

THE PHYSICAL GAME

Elynuik is not physical at all. If the rule changes continue to give an edge to smaller, skilled players, then he will be at the forefront of the players taking advantage. He seems willing to battle for some loose pucks but doesn't win many one-on-one battles.

THE INTANGIBLES

A player who is traded for the first time doesn't always handle the situation well, and that seemed to be the case for Elynuik, who struggled when he first came to the Capitals. This is a very important year for him if he wants to prove himself as an NHL scorer.

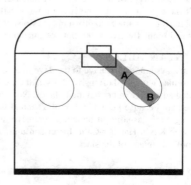

KEVIN HATCHER

Yrs. of NHL service: 8
Born: Detroit, Mich.; Sept. 9, 1966
Position: right defense
Height: 6-4
Weight: 225
Uniform no.: 4
Shoots: right

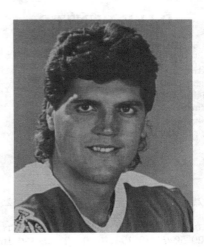

Career statistics:

GP	G	A	TP	PIM
613	133	253	386	893

1991-92 statistics:

GP	G	A	TP	+/-	PIM	PP	SH	GW	GT	S	PCT
79	17	37	54	+18	105	8	1	2	1	246	6.9

1992-93 statistics:

GP	G	A	TP	+/-	PIM	PP	SH	GW	GT	S	PCT
83	34	45	79	-7	114	13	1	6	0	329	10.3

LAST SEASON

One of three Capitals defensemen to score 20 or more goals, establishing an NHL record. Sixth in NHL in shots. Led NHL defensemen in power play goals. Led team in power play goals and shots. Career highs in goals, assists and points. Worst plus/minus among regular team defensemen.

THE FINESSE GAME

Hatcher has wonderful anticipation in his own zone for picking off passes, which he then carries up the middle to start a counterattack. He has the speed and strength to elude checkers in the neutral zone, and he's solid enough on his skates that he seldom goes off-course or loses the puck if bumped.

Hatcher makes decisions quickly in all zones. If the heat is on him in his own zone, he is aware of his teammates' positions on the ice and makes the smart outlet pass or bangs the puck off the glass. He is constantly looking to see which attackers might be bearing in on him, but he is poised under pressure.

Hatcher is sometimes slow with his first step, but he achieves top speed rather quickly for a big skater. He is not afraid to charge in to the front of the net and try to create some confusion down low. He has good hands and fine offensive instincts. He also has a powerful low shot from the right point.

THE PHYSICAL GAME

There are a lot of demands now on Hatcher. When you battle for a bigger salary *and* for more ice time, you have to provide the leadership that is expected. One change in Hatcher is the danger of getting away from the physical part of his game. He has to have that element in his game. When he is in the mood to hit, he can hurt.

THE INTANGIBLES

Hatcher can have an off night, but he should never have a very bad game or a very bad stretch, because he has too many talents. It's a lot more fun (and less painful) to play the offensive game, but when that is not forthcoming Hatcher must go back to playing the defensive game at which he also shines.

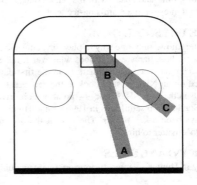

DALE HUNTER

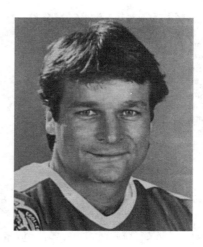

Yrs. of NHL service: 13
Born: Petrolia, Ont.; July 31, 1960
Position: centre
Height: 5-10
Weight: 198
Uniform no.: 32
Shoots: left

Career statistics:

GP	G	A	TP	PIM
1002	269	570	849	2874

1991-92 statistics:

GP	G	A	TP	+/-	PIM	PP	SH	GW	GT	S	PCT
80	28	50	78	-2	205	13	0	4	1	110	25.5

1992-93 statistics:

GP	G	A	TP	+/-	PIM	PP	SH	GW	GT	S	PCT
84	20	59	79	+3	198	10	0	2	0	120	16.7

LAST SEASON

One of two Caps to play in all 84 games. Led team in assists with career high. Matched career high in points. Played in 1000th NHL game. Will open 1993-94 season with 21-game suspension from 1993 playoffs. Career PIM leader among active players; third all-time.

THE FINESSE GAME

Hunter is a complete player. At this stage of his career, he should have settled into a nice role-playing position. Instead, the Caps need him just about full time to wake up their moribund forwards and add zest to the team.

Hunter is canny. He is a crafty player, especially down low. He doesn't skate well enough to be very effective in open ice, but when the Caps have control of the offensive zone, Hunter is digging in down deep, setting screens and picks, and driving to the net. He is not a very big player, but he forces teams to pay attention to him with his effort.

Hunter is skilled on face-offs. He gets very low to the ice, then moves forward and drives back the opposing centre. He never fails to bump his opposite number. He works at buying time for his linemates by creating time and space with his puck control. He is without question the team's on-ice leader.

THE PHYSICAL GAME

Hunter knows only one way to play the game. He gets shots in, hits, harasses and does whatever it takes to win. That has been his hallmark from the first day he pulled on an NHL jersey. Look at the few great moments in the Capitals' history — notably their drive to the Stanley Cup semifinals in 1990 — and Hunter has always been a key player. The size of the opponent doesn't matter to him.

THE INTANGIBLES

Early in Hunter's career, furious opponents would always mutter that someday someone would "get" Hunter. Well, 13 seasons later, someone finally did, but it wasn't an irate recipient of a high stick, but NHL commissioner Gary Bettman. Bettman slammed Hunter with a 21-game suspension — Hunter is also barred from training camp — for his cheap shot in the 1993 playoffs that separated the shoulder of Islanders' star Pierre Turgeon. The layoff will hurt Hunter physically, but we have no doubt the intensity, and the annoying tactics, will return when Hunter does.

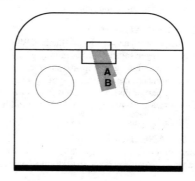

AL IAFRATE

Yrs. of NHL service: 9
Born: Dearborn, Mich.; Mar. 21, 1966
Position: left defense
Height: 6-3
Weight: 220
Uniform no.: 34
Shoots: left

Career statistics:

GP	G	A	TP	PIM
661	129	252	381	1019

1991-92 statistics:

GP	G	A	TP	+/-	PIM	PP	SH	GW	GT	S	PCT
78	17	34	51	+1	180	6	0	1	1	151	11.3

1992-93 statistics:

GP	G	A	TP	+/-	PIM	PP	SH	GW	GT	S	PCT
81	25	41	66	+15	169	11	1	4	0	289	8.7

LAST SEASON

One of three Capitals defensemen to score 20 or more goals, establishing NHL record. Second on team in power play goals and shots. Career highs in goals and points. Assists second-highest season total of career. Passed 1000 PIM.

THE FINESSE GAME

Iafrate won the NHL All-Star skills competition with a shot clocked at 101.4 mph, and he was second to Mike Gartner as fastest skater. That devastating combination of power and speed explains Iafrate's success.

Iafrate is not only fast but agile, and very quick on his feet. He is capable of rushing end to end, but is better at jumping up into the play. He moves the puck quickly out of his own zone, often taking it himself. He can stickhandle and uses all of the ice.

Iafrate can play either point on the power play. He has a deadly one-timer. His point shot is intimidating, and he will fake the shot, freeze the defense, then move around for a snap shot or slide the puck in deep. There isn't much he can't do as far as finesse skills are concerned.

Iafrate can recover defensively because he has great legs, but it's hard to say how good he could be there, since he enjoys the offensive part so much.

THE PHYSICAL GAME

For a big guy, Iafrate does not hit with much intensity. He can, but he is more intent on playing the offensive game. He does not enjoy the one-on-one battles. He will be a booming open-ice hitter when the spirit moves him, but just as often he will be wiped out along the boards.

THE INTANGIBLES

Iafrate is a fragile commodity mentally. A free sprit, he has to be allowed to do his own thing, yet keep his game focussed. He was probably the league's best de-fenseman in the first half of the season, but he had a poor second half and didn't even end up as a Norris Trophy nominee.

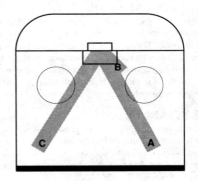

CALLE JOHANSSON

Yrs. of NHL service: 6
Born: Göteborg, Sweden; Feb. 14, 1967
Position: left defense
Height: 5-11
Weight: 205
Uniform no.: 6
Shoots: left

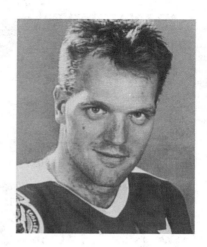

Career statistics:

GP	G	A	TP	PIM
437	47	208	255	227

1991-92 statistics:

GP	G	A	TP	+/-	PIM	PP	SH	GW	GT	S	PCT
80	14	42	56	+2	49	5	2	2	0	119	11.8

1992-93 statistics:

GP	G	A	TP	+/-	PIM	PP	SH	GW	GT	S	PCT
77	7	38	45	+3	56	6	0	0	1	133	5.3

LAST SEASON

Goals four-season low. Points and assists three-season lows. Missed games with rib injury.

THE FINESSE GAME

Johansson has tremendous legs, big, strong thighs that generate the power for his shot and his explosive skating. He makes every move look easy. He is agile, mobile and great at moving up-ice with the play. Speed, balance and strength allow him to chase a puck behind the net, pick it up without stopping and make an accurate pass. He is confident, even on the backhand, and likes to have the puck in key spots.

Johansson is smart offensively. He moves the puck with a good first pass, then has enough speed and instinct to jump up and be ready for a return pass. He keeps the gap tight as the play enters the attacking zone, which opens up more options: he is available to the forwards if they need him for offense, and closer to the puck if it turns over.

Johansson has a low accurate shot that can be tipped. He is unselfish to a fault, often looking to pass when he should use his good shot.

He has good defensive instincts and reads plays well.

THE PHYSICAL GAME

Johansson is not an aggressive player, but he is strong and knows what he has to do with his body in the defensive zone. This part of the game has not come naturally, but Johansson has worked at it. He is still not an impact player defensively, although he wins his share of the one-on-one battles because he gets so much power from his legs.

THE INTANGIBLES

Johansson has quietly been very good for the Caps. He went through a slump when he had no goals in 45 games. Without bringing up the other elements of his game, especially the physical part, "quiet" will remain the operative word to describe this otherwise talented skater.

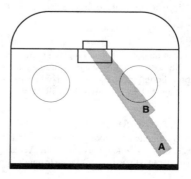

KEITH JONES

Yrs. of NHL service: 1
Born: Brantford, Ont.; Nov. 8, 1968
Position: right wing
Height: 6-2
Weight: 190
Uniform no.: 26
Shoots: right

Career statistics:

GP	G	A	TP	PIM
71	12	14	26	124

1992-93 statistics:

GP	G	A	TP	+/-	PIM	PP	SH	GW	GT	S	PCT
71	12	14	26	+18	124	0	0	3	0	73	16.4

LAST SEASON
First NHL season.

THE FINESSE GAME
Jones saw limited ice time as a role player on the fourth line. Considering his minutes played, his point production was actually pretty impressive.

Jones is a sparkplug. He likes to make things happen by driving to the front of the net and taking a defenseman with him. His skating is adequate, and he uses quick bursts of speed to power himself to and through the traffic areas.

He has decent hands, is an eager finisher and plays well at both ends of the ice.

THE PHYSICAL GAME
The Caps threw Jones on the ice whenever the team or the crowd needed a lift. He is energetic and uses his size well. He needs more experience, of course, but is tough and willing to pay a physical price. The Caps could use another couple of players like him.

THE INTANGIBLES
Jones was a scorer at Western Michigan and plays with grit and determination. He has a few rough edges to his game yet, but the Caps are in desperate need of his sandpaper qualities.

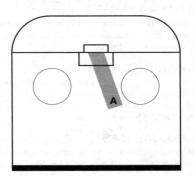

DIMITRI KHRISTICH

Yrs. of NHL service: 3
Born: Kiev, Ukraine; July 23, 1969
Position: centre/left wing
Height: 6-2
Weight: 190
Uniform no.: 8
Shoots: right

Career statistics:

GP	G	A	TP	PIM
184	80	87	167	84

1991-92 statistics:

GP	G	A	TP	+/-	PIM	PP	SH	GW	GT	S	PCT
80	36	37	73	+24	35	14	1	7	0	188	19.1

1992-93 statistics:

GP	G	A	TP	+/-	PIM	PP	SH	GW	GT	S	PCT
64	31	36	67	+29	28	9	1	1	1	127	24.4

LAST SEASON

Led team in shooting percentage for second consecutive season. Led team in plus/minus. Missed 20 games with broken right foot. Scored 30 goals for second consecutive season.

THE FINESSE GAME

Khristich is an immensely talented forward. He is a key component on the power play, because while the defensemen rocket the puck back and forth at the point, Khristich is ready and waiting down low, just off to the goalie's right, with his forehand open and ready for the pass. When the puck reaches his blade, he slams it in in one motion. When a penalty killer concentrates on Khristich, it then opens the ice for another forward. Either way, Kristich gets the job done.

Khristich has good hand-eye co-ordination for deflections and for winning face-offs. He is not a very fast skater, but he has a long, strong stride and very good balance. His hockey sense is very good, and he is responsible defensively as well as creative offensively.

One weakness is that he puts himself into a position where he gets hit — and hurt. Perhaps he is holding on to the puck too long, or else he isn't smart enough to know when to go into the corners or the front of the net and when to back off. In Europe, the game is different because of the wider ice surface there, and Khristich has not mastered the timing of the North American-sized rinks.

THE PHYSICAL GAME

Khristich is a very strong skater and is willing to go into the trenches. He is tough to knock off the puck and protects it well with his body. If he can avoid getting hurt, he will be more of a factor.

THE INTANGIBLES

Khristich has the best size of the Caps' "Euroforwards" and the most tenacity. His skill level is there, too, but so far he has been unable to take his game out of the 30-goal range. We think he could get closer to 50 if he stays in one piece. A little more muscle on his line wouldn't hurt.

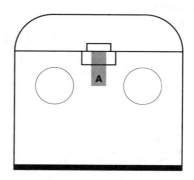

TODD KRYGIER

Yrs. of NHL service: 4
Born: Northville, Mich.; Oct. 12, 1965
Position: left wing
Height: 5-11
Weight: 180
Uniform no.: 21
Shoots: left

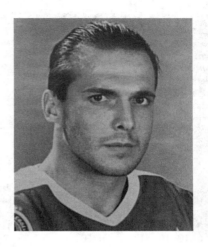

Career statistics:

GP	G	A	TP	PIM
274	55	58	113	314

1991-92 statistics:

GP	G	A	TP	+/-	PIM	PP	SH	GW	GT	S	PCT
67	13	17	30	-1	107	1	0	1	0	127	10.2

1992-93 statistics:

GP	G	A	TP	+/-	PIM	PP	SH	GW	GT	S	PCT
77	11	12	23	-13	60	0	2	0	1	133	8.3

LAST SEASON

Goals and points career lows. Assists match career low.

THE FINESSE GAME

Krygier may be too fast for his own good. He has blazing speed and anticipation, which gets him his share of breakaways and odd-man rushes. But when it comes time to shoot or move the puck to a teammate, he can't do it. He has to slow down in order to do something with the puck, but he doesn't have very good hand skills.

Krygier uses his outside speed to get around a defender, but then doesn't have an outside move. Most of his successful shots come with his hard wrist shot, but he doesn't beat many goalies cleanly. He usually needs someone screening in front, but he doesn't know how to time his plays to use the opposing defenseman in that manner.

Krygier is a smart hockey player and can be used to kill penalties. He is, of course, a very good man on the penalty-killing unit. His speed allows him to backcheck and badger the puck carrier from behind, lifting his stick and poking at the puck.

Krygier is a useful member of the team, but he just can't be counted on for scoring.

THE PHYSICAL GAME

Krygier is not strong on the puck. He intimidates with speed, but unless he is racing for a puck in open ice, he is not likely to get into a fight for it. He won't drive through anyone along the boards.

THE INTANGIBLES

Krygier played Division II hockey on an outdoor rink at the University of Connecticut. He has paid his dues to get to the NHL and hasn't forgotten the work ethic it took to get this far. But unless a scoring touch suddenly develops, he is a victim of the Randy Wood syndrome: all speed, all effort, 20 goals tops.

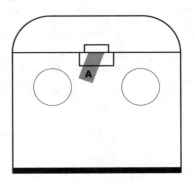

ALAN MAY

Yrs. of NHL service: 4
Born: Swan Hills, Alta.; Jan. 14, 1965
Position: left wing
Height: 6-1
Weight: 200
Uniform no.: 16
Shoots: right

Career statistics:

GP	G	A	TP	PIM
308	24	35	59	1014

1991-92 statistics:

GP	G	A	TP	+/-	PIM	PP	SH	GW	GT	S	PCT
75	6	9	15	-7	221	0	0	1	0	43	14.0

1992-93 statistics:

GP	G	A	TP	+/-	PIM	PP	SH	GW	GT	S	PCT
83	6	10	16	+1	268	0	0	1	0	75	8.0

LAST SEASON

Led team in PIM for fourth consecutive season. Fourth straight season with 200 or more PIM; reached 1000-PIM mark for career.

THE FINESSE GAME

May is noted as a strong and tough presence, but he has elevated other parts of his game to go from being a fourth-line forward to a third-line player.

He is skating better than ever. He has good quickness and balance, and he drives to the front of the net with some intelligence. May doesn't have great hands to finish a play, but he can nudge in a puck off a scramble or tie up a defender while a teammate uses the open ice to create a scoring opportunity.

He fires a shot off the wing now and then, but he has a very long reaction time and is not very accurate.

THE PHYSICAL GAME

May is a middleweight against heavyweights. When the going gets tough, May answers the bell, but he is not really a fighter. He has been shoehorned into that role and does it because he knows the team needs that element from him. He does have the guts to try.

May will also initiate to try to get his team jazzed up. He is a strong forechecker, because of his skating and his willingness to pay a physical price. He eagerly goes after the league's bigger defensemen. If he can make them eat glass, he has done his job.

THE INTANGIBLES

May was one of the most improved players in the league last season. He tries to do a lot of things for the team. He is a bright player on the ice, but the lone ranger on the team as far as enforcing goes.

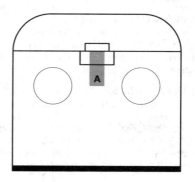

KELLY MILLER

Yrs. of NHL service: 8
Born: Lansing, Mich.; Mar. 3, 1963
Position: left wing
Height: 5-11
Weight: 196
Uniform no.: 10
Shoots: left

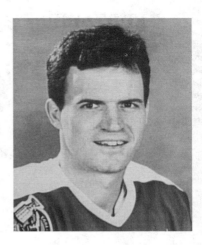

Career statistics:

GP	G	A	TP	PIM
636	131	205	336	341

1991-92 statistics:

GP	G	A	TP	+/-	PIM	PP	SH	GW	GT	S	PCT
78	14	38	52	+20	49	0	1	3	0	144	9.7

1992-93 statistics:

GP	G	A	TP	+/-	PIM	PP	SH	GW	GT	S	PCT
84	18	27	45	-2	32	3	0	3	0	144	12.5

LAST SEASON

One of three Capitals to play in all 84 games. In six full seasons with Caps, has missed only four of 484 games.

THE FINESSE GAME

Think of Kelly Miller and a host of adjectives spring quickly to mind. Smart. Consistent. Fast. Dedicated. Defensive.

Scorer? No, because Miller has always thought defense first, but he is at the stage of his career when he might well be moved out of that checking role and given a little more freedom. It wouldn't surprise us to see him hit the 30-goal mark, because he has the skating ability, hockey sense and hands to do it, but first he has to be turned loose.

There is no weak part to Miller's game. A complete player, he is always in motion. He is a strong forechecker and creates a lot of scoring chances off of turnovers. He reads plays when he forechecks, and either goes to the net or finds a teammate in front with a good short pass. He is one of the best penalty killers in the game.

Miller's shooting skills are unexceptional, but he works with great determination and doesn't give up until the puck is in the net or in the goalie's glove.

Miller has great work habits, every night. His commitment to the game is remarkable.

THE PHYSICAL GAME

Miller is not very big but he is strong and durable. His stamina allows him to forecheck hard all night, and he drives opponents batty because he is always on them. There is never a moment's peace when Miller is on the ice.

THE INTANGIBLES

With better P.R., Miller would have been a Selke Trophy finalist for the second straight season. His reputation as a two-way player is such that, despite his less-than-gaudy offensive numbers, he was one of the most attractive free agents (Group III) of the summer.

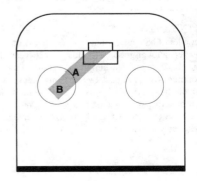

PAT PEAKE

Yrs. of NHL service: 0
Born: Rochester, Mich.; May 28, 1973
Position: centre
Height: 6-0
Weight: 195
Uniform no.: na
Shoots: right

1992-93 Junior statistics:

GP	G	A	TP	PIM
33	50	48	98	50

LAST SEASON

Played with Detroit (OHL). First-round draft pick (14th overall) in 1991. Missed 20 games with broken ankle.

THE FINESSE GAME

Peake is among the Class of '91. One of the best drafts in ages, it has already produced NHLers Eric Lindros, Pat Falloon, Scott Niedermayer, Scott Lachance and Patrick Poulin, with future stars Peter Forsberg and Markus Naslund ready to burst onto the scene.

Peake won't be one of the luminaries of the group, but he is maturing into a decent prospect. He is a very good skater with agility and good lateral movement. Something Peake flashed this year was the talent to dominate games. He has good playmaking skills and can pass equally well to either side.

Peake has a hard shot and loves to score. He has good hockey vision and creativity.

THE PHYSICAL GAME

Peake is a finesse player who is competitive but will have to learn to pay the physical price necessary in the NHL. That is one of the toughest adjustments for any player coming out of junior. He won't have as much time or room to shoot, and he will have to fight for what he wants.

THE INTANGIBLES

Expect a lot of bad puns about "Peake" performance. Also expect a lot of good buzz about this 20-year-old, who has encouraged Washington personnel with his development over the past two seasons. Peake was one of the best U.S. forwards at the World Junior Championships, with 4-13-17 in seven games. He may be one of the players ready to take advantage of Dale Hunter's suspension.

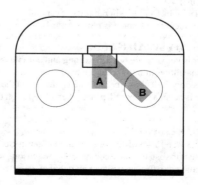

MICHAL PIVONKA

Yrs. of NHL service: 7
Born: Kladno, Czechoslovakia; Jan. 28, 1966
Position: centre/left wing
Height: 6-1
Weight: 198
Uniform no.: 20
Shoots: left

Career statistics:

GP	G	A	TP	PIM
501	146	266	412	300

1991-92 statistics:

GP	G	A	TP	+/-	PIM	PP	SH	GW	GT	S	PCT
80	23	57	80	+10	47	7	4	2	1	177	13.0

1992-93 statistics:

GP	G	A	TP	+/-	PIM	PP	SH	GW	GT	S	PCT
69	21	53	74	+14	66	6	1	5	0	147	14.3

LAST SEASON

Missed 15 games with groin injury. Fifth on team in points, third in assists. Fourth consecutive season with 20 or more goals.

THE FINESSE GAME

Pivonka is far too streaky a player for someone with his talents. He gets into funks and gets down on himself, and when that happens he is useless because he doesn't even do the little things well. A reliable player will contribute in any way he can when his scoring touch temporarily deserts him; Pivonka just chucks it.

Pivonka has marvellous skills. On the power play and in four-on-four situations, he takes full advantage of the extra ice. He skates well, with quickness and breakaway speed. He moves the puck quickly and jumps into the play for a give-and-go.

He shoots well in stride (a trait of many Europeans), but he is too shy about shooting, usually looking to make the pass first. His stick is always on the ice. It's a small detail, but it allows him to pick up pucks that bounce off other players' sticks or skates.

Pivonka makes a lot of little dekes in tight, forcing a goalie to move his feet, and then he finds the opening.

THE PHYSICAL GAME

On any given night, he can play a forceful game, hitting and taking hits. Other nights he will be AWOL. It is frustrating to see because Pivonka has the size and strength to be an on-ice leader, yet he has no consistency.

THE INTANGIBLES

The Caps may have grown tired of waiting for Pivonka to be their No. 1 centre. He has the job by default, because it does not appear that he will ever join the elite class of NHL centremen. Scoring 25 goals a season just doesn't cut it, and frankly we don't see Pivonka taking the next step.

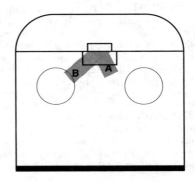

MIKE RIDLEY

Yrs. of NHL service: 8
Born: Winnipeg, Man.; July 8, 1963
Position: centre
Height: 6-1
Weight: 200
Uniform no.: 17
Shoots: left

Career statistics:

GP	G	A	TP	PIM
625	230	348	578	315

1991-92 statistics:

GP	G	A	TP	+/-	PIM	PP	SH	GW	GT	S	PCT
80	29	40	69	+3	38	5	5	3	0	123	23.6

1992-93 statistics:

GP	G	A	TP	+/-	PIM	PP	SH	GW	GT	S	PCT
84	26	56	82	+5	44	6	2	3	0	148	17.6

LAST SEASON

One of three Capitals to play in all 84 games. Has missed only one game in last three seasons. Second on team in scoring with highest point total in four seasons. Second on team in assists with career high. Sixth consecutive season with 20 or more goals.

THE FINESSE GAME

The Caps may lead the league in complete players who aren't quite star calibre. Ridley can certainly be counted among their number.

Ridley is a solid two-way centre, smart and strong, and has good offensive instincts to combine with his defensive awareness. He concentrates on defense first. If the opponent has a big centre, then Ridley gets the assignment.

He is a strong skater who can win one-on-one battles against all but the biggest defensemen. He grinds in the corners and in front of the net. A sneaky passer down low, he scores most of his goals from wrist shots in tight as well.

Ridley doesn't shoot enough. He is very accurate, but often holds on to the puck too long, and opponents will always play the pass until he is more willing to fire away.

THE PHYSICAL GAME

Ridley is a crunch-time player. He will protect the puck with his body or work like crazy to get the puck free. He pays the toll in the traffic areas, and plays every inch of the ice. He is an excellent penalty killer and a very disciplined player. For someone as involved as Ridley is, he takes only a tiny number of bad penalties.

THE INTANGIBLES

Nothing Ridley has accomplished in his career — from making the Rangers as a free agent tryout from the University of Manitoba (!) in 1985 — has been done without hard work. That ethic hasn't deserted him for a single shift. He is supposed to be a solid No. 2 centre, but no one ever emerges as No. 1 and Ridley keeps inheriting the role. Ridley is a gamer.

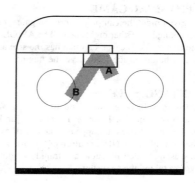

RICK TABARACCI

Yrs. of NHL service: 3
Born: Toronto, Ont.; Jan. 2, 1969
Position: goaltender
Height: 5-10
Weight: 185
Uniform no.: 31
Catches: right

Career statistics:

GP	MINS	GA	SO	GAA	A	PIM
68	3394	207	3	3.66	2	26

1991-92 statistics:

GP	MINS	GAA	W	L	T	SO	GA	S	SAPCT	PIM
18	996	3.23	6	7	3	0	52	470	.889	4

1992-93 statistics:

GP	MINS	GAA	W	L	T	SO	GA	S	SAPCT	PIM
25	1302	3.69	8	12	0	2	80	658	.878	14

LAST SEASON
Acquired from Winnipeg for Jim Hrivnak and future considerations. Games, minutes played and wins at career highs.

THE PHYSICAL GAME
Tabaracci is an acrobatic and aggressive netminder. He has learned better technique in recent seasons, and he doesn't flop all over the ice and expend his energy foolishly. If a scramble develops, Tabaracci will be there with his great reflexes, but he prefers to keep his feet.

He doesn't give up many five-hole goals. He is out at the top of his crease well on the initial shot, and covers well low. Shooters are forced to go top shelf, stick side, although Tabaracci will dare them to go glove side, where he has a quick glove hand. He's small, and that works against him, but when he is out well on his angles he takes away a lot of net.

He loves coming out of the net to handle the puck, which is odd because he came up with a team (Winnipeg) that has mobile defensemen and he has been traded to a team with the same characteristics. He is a very good skater. Maybe he grew up wanting to play defense.

THE MENTAL GAME
Tabaracci is likely to be the No. 1 goalie at the start of the season, or at least the job will be his to lose. He is an intelligent goalie with a great attitude. Tabaracci's confident — almost cocky — demeanour can have a positive effect on his teammates.

THE INTANGIBLES
For a player who has been a backup goalie, as Tabaracci has for three seasons, the move up to No. 1 is a challenge. Sometimes he will play well over the short haul, but can't sustain his play over the long haul. Tabaracci may get 50 or 60 starts this season alone, and he has only played in 68 through his entire career.

WINNIPEG JETS

SERGEI BAUTIN

Yrs. of NHL service: 1
Born: Murmansk, Russia; Mar. 11, 1967
Position: right defense
Height: 6-3
Weight: 185
Uniform no.: 3
Shoots: left

Career statistics:

GP	G	A	TP	PIM
71	5	18	23	96

1992-93 statistics:

GP	G	A	TP	+/-	PIM	PP	SH	GW	GT	S	PCT
71	5	18	23	-2	96	0	0	0	0	82	6.1

LAST SEASON

First NHL season. Missed 13 games with a broken right foot.

THE FINESSE GAME

Bautin is not a finished product, but there are some raw materials to work with. He is big and lanky but not strong. He has a long, fluid stride, once he gets moving, and can rush the puck out of danger or make a long pass, soft or hard, up the middle to break his teammates.

Bautin's skating is limited because he does not have great balance. He looks awkward back-skating, and any movement requiring a quick change of direction will find his skates in a tangle. His hockey sense is good enough that he is usually positioned well and doesn't have to chase people around. He kills penalties on the first unit.

Bautin has a nice, quick slap shot that is usually on target, but he will succeed better as a complement to a more skilled offensive player.

THE PHYSICAL GAME

Bautin is tall and can fill a lot of space vertically and horizontally, but he is also a little on the light side for an NHL defensemen today. He doesn't clear the front of the net, but basically stick checks or hangs on to an attacker's arms. He does not get great leg drive to budge anyone off his goalie's porch, and needs to develop more lower and upper body strength. There isn't much mean in Bautin.

THE INTANGIBLES

Bautin's poise will go a long way in covering up some of his physical shortcomings, but the Jets are a team overloaded with finesse players, and a defenseman of his size simply has to add a more physical element. He worked well paired most of the season with Teppo Numminen.

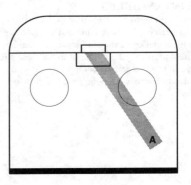

LUCIANO BORSATO

Yrs. of NHL service: 2
Born: Richmond Hill, Ont.; Jan. 7, 1966
Position: centre
Height: 5-10
Weight: 180
Uniform no.: 38
Shoots: right

Career statistics:

GP	G	A	TP	PIM
124	30	42	72	85

1991-92 statistics:

GP	G	A	TP	+/-	PIM	PP	SH	GW	GT	S	PCT
56	15	21	36	-6	45	5	0	1	0	81	18.5

1992-93 statistics:

GP	G	A	TP	+/-	PIM	PP	SH	GW	GT	S	PCT
67	15	20	35	-1	38	1	1	3	0	101	14.9

LAST SEASON

Goals matched rookie total.

THE FINESSE GAME

Borsato's skills are unimpressive. He is an average skater, with average hand skills and shots. What sets Borsato apart is his determination. He will outwork bigger players to get to the front of the net, and is a very dogged forechecker.

Borsato can play alongside finesse players and get the dirty work done, and he provides inspiration with his nonstop hustle. He has good hockey sense and will find the openings for a pass.

He often kills penalties on the second unit but has been prone to mistakes under pressure. Instead of just eating the puck or ragging it until he could make a safe play, he simply fired a blind pass that was vulnerable to being picked off by the attack.

THE PHYSICAL GAME

Borsato is a little guy who is willing to use his body to bump, but he won't knock anyone down. His lower centre of gravity gives him some good balance, but he will still get outmuscled in man-to-man combat along the boards and in front of the net.

THE INTANGIBLES

Borsato's grit earned him ice time on the Jets' second line last season. His work ethic and effort move him up on the depth chart ahead of more talented but less consistent players — he is similar to San Jose's Kelly Kisio, and that is a serious compliment. Still, Borsato will have to improve his point production to merit the ice time.

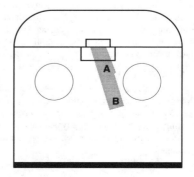

EVGENY DAVYDOV

Yrs. of NHL service: 1
Born: Chelyabinsk, Russia; May 27, 1967
Position: right wing
Height: 6-0
Weight: 183
Uniform no.: 11
Shoots: right

Career statistics:

GP	G	A	TP	PIM
91	32	24	56	74

1991-92 statistics:

GP	G	A	TP	+/-	PIM	PP	SH	GW	GT	S	PCT
12	4	3	7	+7	8	2	0	0	0	32	12.5

1992-93 statistics:

GP	G	A	TP	+/-	PIM	PP	SH	GW	GT	S	PCT
79	28	21	49	-2	66	7	0	2	0	176	15.9

LAST SEASON

First NHL season.

THE FINESSE GAME

Davydov is fast. Too fast. He was frequently ahead of the play, and the Jets spent most of the season trying to get him to slow down (instead of finding faster forwards to go with him). No doubt he would have wanted the left wing slot on the Alexei Zhamnov-Teemu Selanne line, but the Jets needed a more physical winger (Keith Tkachuk or Darrin Shannon) to provide some insurance for their two gifted rookies, and Davydov had a hard time getting shifts.

Davydov is a marvellous skater, with balance, speed and agility. A right shot playing the left side, he has the hand skills to accept passes on the backhand or position himself for a one-timer. He has an excellent release and strong wrists for accurate snap or wrist shots. Most of his goals are generated by his speed driving into the left circle.

In his first full season in the NHL (he joined the Jets after winning a gold medal with the Unified Team in 1992), Davydov proved to be a typical rookie: he still has a lot of learning to do.

THE PHYSICAL GAME

Davydov is still adjusting to the North American style of play. He will not initiate any contact, but will take a hit to make a play in the offensive zone. He's more of a liability in the defensive zone and, like the stereotypical Russian player, prefers to hook and hold with his stick rather than use his body to check.

THE INTANGIBLES

Davydov was a disappointment this season after the 12-game preview the Jets had after the '92 Olympics. But a coach can teach a player defensive responsibility. He can't teach the kind of skills that Davydov is blessed with.

After being a fourth-liner most of the season,

Davydov should be ready to step up with a strong sophomore season in 1993-94.

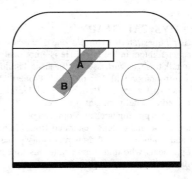

TIE DOMI

Yrs. of NHL service: 3
Born: Windsor, Ont.; Nov. 1, 1969
Position: right wing
Height: 5-10
Weight: 195
Uniform no.: 20
Shoots: right

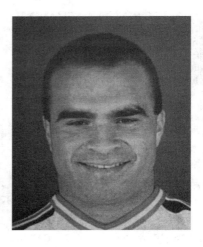

Career statistics:

GP	G	A	TP	PIM
133	8	14	22	817

1991-92 statistics:

GP	G	A	TP	+/-	PIM	PP	SH	GW	GT	S	PCT
42	2	4	6	-4	246	0	0	1	0	20	10.0

1992-93 statistics:

GP	G	A	TP	+/-	PIM	PP	SH	GW	GT	S	PCT
61	5	10	15	+1	344	0	0	0	0	40	12.5

LAST SEASON

Third in NHL in PIM with career high. Led team in PIM. Games played, goals, assists and points career highs. Acquired with Kris King from New York Rangers for Ed Olczyk.

THE FINESSE GAME

Finesse? Should that even be discussed in analyzing this rock-hard (some would add rock-headed) right winger?

Yes, indeed, because Domi has skills surpassing those of the average goon. He is a pretty nifty skater, and in his role as a checking winger will often be in quickly on the opposing goalie behind the net, trying to force a bad pass or a turnover by the netminder. If he gets the puck, he is poised enough to work a nice short pass out front. He's no Gretzky, but he has sufficient confidence to try something ambitious and surprise the defense.

Domi has a good short-range shot. He will wade into traffic and dig for loose pucks. He has more trouble with high-tempo plays off the rush, where he lacks the great hands and hockey sense to make the high percentage plays. He is surprisingly good with his feet, and if his stick is tied up or dropped, he'll work along the boards and kick a puck free to a teammate.

THE PHYSICAL GAME

There is no question that Domi is one of the best and most eager fighters in the NHL. He is emotional and loves to talk trash, as witnessed by the absurd build-up to the confrontation with Detroit's Bob Probert while Domi was still with the Rangers (give Domi and Probert credit for delivering as promised).

When he is playing hockey, Domi can play a clean and hard game, his checks generated from his good power and balance. He will draw retaliatory penalties from opponents who don't appreciate this aspect of his game.

THE INTANGIBLES

It wasn't until Domi (and Kris King) arrived in Winnipeg from the Rangers that the Jets started putting things together for a playoff run. Domi makes others braver. He will stick up for his teammates — even the Europeans and Russians that other North Americans are often loath to sacrifice themselves for. Domi is starting to play smarter, and if his ice time continues to increase, he will improve and be more valuable to the Jets.

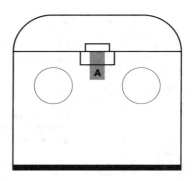

MIKE EAGLES

Yrs. of NHL service: 7
Born: Sussex, N.B.; Mar. 7, 1963
Position: centre
Height: 5-10
Weight: 180
Uniform no.: 36
Shoots: left

Career statistics:

GP	G	A	TP	PIM
487	55	91	146	586

1991-92 statistics:

GP	G	A	TP	+/-	PIM	PP	SH	GW	GT	S	PCT
65	7	10	17	-17	118	0	1	0	0	60	11.7

1992-93 statistics:

GP	G	A	TP	+/-	PIM	PP	SH	GW	GT	S	PCT
84	8	18	26	-1	131	1	0	1	0	67	11.9

LAST SEASON

Goals five-season high. Assists six-season high. PIM career high. One of three Jets to play in all 84 games.

THE FINESSE GAME

Eagles is the prototypical checking centre. He is in the puck in a hurry when forechecking, creating turnovers and blind passes. His stock would be a lot higher if he had the offensive instincts and hands to convert those chances into points, but the touch is simply not there.

The effort, though, always is. Eagles hustles and hits, and if the points come, they are a bonus. He usually concentrates simply on shutting down the opposing centre. He serves as the first unit penalty killer, takes defensive zone draws (he is very good on draws) and blocks shots.

Eagles has paid his dues in the minors and for three different organizations, and he can't take his sweater for granted. He has to earn it every game with his work habits.

THE PHYSICAL GAME

Eagles can drive other players to distraction with his dogged pursuit. He is easily knocked down by bigger opponents, but he's always back up on his skates in a hurry, ready for another bump. He is frustrating to play against.

THE INTANGIBLES

What a relief it must be for a coach to be able to look down his bench and see a steady veteran performer like Eagles sitting there. You know exactly what you'll get from Eagles, shift after shift and night after night. No surprises here, just the same even job every time.

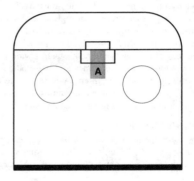

BOB ESSENSA

Yrs. of NHL service: 5
Born: Toronto, Ont.; Jan. 14, 1965
Position: goaltender
Height: 6-0
Weight: 170
Uniform no.: 35
Catches: left

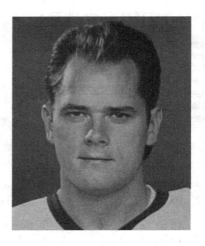

Career statistics:

GP	MINS	GA	SO	GAA	A	PIM
225	12,535	681	13	3.26	12	12

1991-92 statistics:

GP	MINS	GAA	W	L	T	SO	GA	S	SAPCT	PIM
47	2627	2.88	21	17	6	5	126	1407	.910	2

1992-93 statistics:

GP	MINS	GAA	W	L	T	SO	GA	S	SAPCT	PIM
67	3855	3.53	33	26	6	2	227	2119	.893	2

LAST SEASON

Third in NHL in minutes played with career high. Fifth in NHL in wins with career high. GAA second-highest of career.

THE PHYSICAL GAME

Essensa doesn't like to waste energy. You will seldom catch him scrambling to his feet or back into the net after playing a puck. He plays a V-style and is a good skater with lateral movement. He is often on his knees and is sometimes slow to get back to his feet once he's down, and doesn't recover well for second shots. His glove is fairly quick, but he is better low than high. He uses his size well to cover as much net as possible and just lets the puck hit him. Essensa used to be much more of a reflex goalie, but he has added a better technique to his natural quickness, and this has made him more consistent.

Essensa needs to improve his stickhandling, which has become so important for NHL goalies. He prefers to just stop the puck and leave it for his defense; fortunately for him, this fits in nicely with the mobile blueliners that populate the Jets' roster.

THE MENTAL GAME

Essensa doesn't show any emotions on the ice. His approach to the game is mature and businesslike. He maintains his concentration through scrambles and screens, and bumping him to get him off his game won't work. He worries only about the puck.

He sees a lot of shots behind his team's wide-open style and sloughs off bad games and bad goals with little sulking. He has the intensity to make the big saves and is capable of winning games on his own when the totals start mounting up on the shot clock.

THE INTANGIBLES

Essensa won the highest salary arbitration hearing in NHL history ($1.125 million CDN annually), and players who get huge contract bumps have a history of struggling the next season. He will have enough trouble stopping the puck behind a Jets team that showed considerable lack of defensive attention, but he'll have to maintain his focus to regain his status among the NHL's top goalies.

PHIL HOUSLEY

Yrs. of NHL service: 11
Born: St. Paul, Minn.; Mar. 9, 1964
Position: right defense
Height: 5-10
Weight: 185
Uniform no.: 6
Shoots: left

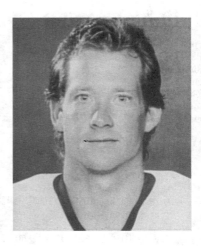

Career statistics:

GP	G	A	TP	PIM
840	242	575	817	554

1991-92 statistics:

GP	G	A	TP	+/-	PIM	PP	SH	GW	GT	S	PCT
74	23	63	86	-5	92	11	0	4	1	234	9.8

1992-93 statistics:

GP	G	A	TP	+/-	PIM	PP	SH	GW	GT	S	PCT
80	18	79	97	-14	52	6	0	2	0	249	7.2

LAST SEASON

Led NHL defensemen in scoring with career high in points. Led team and tied for seventh in NHL in assists with career high. Second on team in scoring and shots. Worst plus/minus on team. Missed two games with wrist injury.

THE FINESSE GAME

Housley is one of the three best skating defensemen in the NHL, along with Al Iafrate and Paul Coffey (and we'll throw in a healthy Brian Leetch). Like Coffey, Housley takes a lot of heat for his defensive shortcomings, but his offensive skills are extraordinary.

Housley's skating fuels his game. He can accelerate in a heartbeat, and his edges are deep and secure, giving him the ability to avoid checks with gravity-defying moves. Everything Housley does is at high tempo. He intimidates with his speed and skills, forcing defenders back on their heels and opening up more ice for himself and his teammates.

He has an excellent grasp of the ice. On the power play he is a huge threat. He and Fredrik Olausson work the off-points on the first power play unit, and they will set one another up for one-time shots. Housley's shots are low and heavy, either beating the goalie outright or setting up a rebound for the forwards down deep. Housley will also set up low on the power play, and doesn't mind shooting from an "impossible" angle that can catch a goalie napping on the short side.

Housley has great anticipation, and can break up a rush by picking off a pass and turning the play into a counterattack. He is an excellent passer for a long headman or a short cup-and-saucer pass over a defender's stick.

THE PHYSICAL GAME

Housley is not the least bit physical. Who wants a player as gifted as Housley risking life and limb in routine plays along the boards when there are a dozen less gifted players who could do it for him? He is not strong enough to shove anyone out of the zone, so his defensive play is based on his pursuit of the puck.

Housley is at his best defending against a rush. Even a two-on-one against him is no guarantee, since he is so good a skater that he will position himself well and try to break up the play with his stick. He'll block shots at crunch time.

THE INTANGIBLES

Despite leading NHL defensemen in scoring, Housley wasn't even a finalist for the Norris Trophy, an award that in recent years has become little more than the Art Ross Trophy for blueliners. No doubt the Jets' team play hurt him there.

Another factor to consider: Housley played out his option last season and spent much of the season wondering just what he was worth to the Jets. Our answer: he's invaluable.

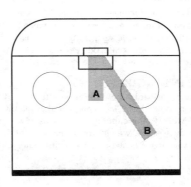

DEAN KENNEDY

Yrs. of NHL service: 9
Born: Redvers, Sask.; Jan. 18, 1963
Position: right defense
Height: 6-2
Weight: 205
Uniform no.: 26
Shoots: right

Career statistics:

GP	G	A	TP	PIM
601	22	94	116	929

1991-92 statistics:

GP	G	A	TP	+/-	PIM	PP	SH	GW	GT	S	PCT
18	2	4	6	+2	21	0	0	1	0	20	10.0

1992-93 statistics:

GP	G	A	TP	+/-	PIM	PP	SH	GW	GT	S	PCT
78	1	7	8	-3	105	0	0	1	0	50	2.0

LAST SEASON

Games played three-season high.

THE FINESSE GAME

Kennedy is a perfect fit on the team of skating, rushing, shooting, scoring defensemen. He does none of those things. Let the others carry the mail; he'll stay home to take delivery.

Skill-wise, Kennedy is Mr. Average. Thanks to his more skilled teammates, Kennedy — who was usually paired with the gifted Fredrik Olausson — doesn't get many calls to rush the puck. When he does get involved offensively, he uses a nice, heavy shot. But he has settled more and more into the role of the hard-hitting, stay-at-home defenseman, and it is a role that suits him.

Kennedy doesn't panic under pressure, and will make a tidy outlet pass to start a rush.

THE PHYSICAL GAME

Kennedy is strong along the boards, and anyone who tries to move the puck past him pays the price. He bumps, hacks, checks, pushes and batters. He will use his body, his stick or his fists to establish control in the defensive zone, and his effort is consistent no matter what the score.

Kennedy is a mainstay on the penalty-killing unit and is one of the more aggressive Jets when the team is shorthanded. The Jets generally play a passive box, but Kennedy will take the odd chance and step out to force the play.

THE INTANGIBLES

Kennedy probably drew the least attention of any member of the flashy Jets team, but after the trade of Troy Murray, the captain's "C" was sewn onto Kennedy's jersey, which proved that somebody has been watching. Kennedy is a solid citizen and a team leader.

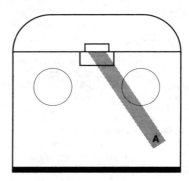

KRIS KING

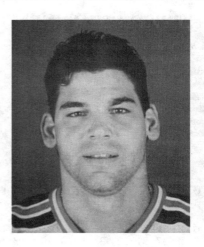

Yrs. of NHL service: 5
Born: Bracebridge, Ont.; Feb. 18, 1966
Position: left wing
Height: 5-11
Weight: 210
Uniform no.: 17
Shoots: left

Career statistics:

GP	G	A	TP	PIM
355	38	44	82	1039

1991-92 statistics:

GP	G	A	TP	+/-	PIM	PP	SH	GW	GT	S	PCT
79	10	9	19	+13	224	0	0	2	0	97	10.3

1992-93 statistics:

GP	G	A	TP	+/-	PIM	PP	SH	GW	GT	S	PCT
78	8	11	19	+4	203	0	0	1	0	74	10.8

LAST SEASON

Acquired from New York Rangers with Tie Domi for Ed Olczyk. Third season with 200 or more PIM. Surpassed 1000 PIM career total.

THE FINESSE GAME

King is a checking winger, a role that can wear on a player night after night, but he brings enthusiasm and hustle to every shift. He has to play that way to stay in the NHL, because he doesn't have much in the way of skills. He will generate some scoring chances with his speed, but can't do much with the puck at tempo. He's more intent on chasing the puck carrier. He will create turnovers but doesn't do much with the puck when he gets it. Most of his scoring chances will be garbage goals off the scrums in front from his hard work.

King is a superb crunch time player. Whether protecting a lead or needing a big play in overtime, he'll do his utmost to deliver.

THE PHYSICAL GAME

King is strictly peasant stock on a team of aristocrats. But somebody's got to do the grunt work, and he's willing and able. He's relentless along the boards and in the corners, and anyone who has his back to King or his head down will pay the physical price. King takes no prisoners. He will fight if needed, but his reputation as a clean, hard checker is no secret.

THE INTANGIBLES

Shortly after coming to the Jets, King was named one of the team's alternate captains. King brings sandpaper to the finesse-dominated team, along with his former Ranger teammate, Domi. For some reason, King fell out of favour in New York. He's getting a second chance in Winnipeg and will be one of the team's leaders by example.

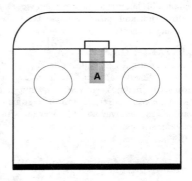

TEPPO NUMMINEN

Yrs. of NHL service: 5
Born: Tampere, Finland; July 3, 1968
Position: left defense
Height: 6-1
Weight: 190
Uniform no.: 27
Shoots: right

Career statistics:

GP	G	A	TP	PIM
374	32	135	167	149

1991-92 statistics:

GP	G	A	TP	+/-	PIM	PP	SH	GW	GT	S	PCT
80	5	34	39	+15	32	4	0	1	0	143	3.5

1992-93 statistics:

GP	G	A	TP	+/-	PIM	PP	SH	GW	GT	S	PCT
66	7	30	37	+4	33	3	1	0	0	103	6.8

LAST SEASON

Missed 18 games with broken foot.

THE FINESSE GAME

Numminen's agility and anticipation make him look much faster than he is. He is very graceful, with a smooth change of direction, and never telegraphs what he is about to do. His skating makes him valuable on the first penalty-killing unit. He will not get caught out of position and is seldom bested one-on-one.

He's not afraid to give up the puck on a dump and chase rather than force a neutral zone play if he is under pressure. He would rather dish off that rush with the puck, and he is a savvy passer, moving the puck briskly and seldom overhandling it. He is not a finisher. He will join the play but not lead it. Most of his offense is generated from point shots.

Numminen is uncannily adept at keeping the puck in at the point when the defense tries time and again to clear the puck out around the boards.

THE PHYSICAL GAME

Numminen plays an acceptable physical game. He can be intimidated, which makes him a target of other teams who want to neutralize his smart passing game. He'll employ his body as a last resort, but would rather use his stick and gain the puck. He is even-tempered and not at all nasty.

THE INTANGIBLES

Numminen continues to improve, and if he stays healthy he could have a career year this season as his supporting cast matures. He was frequently paired with Russian rookie Sergei Bautin, a somewhat awkward skater, and was able to cover up with his own superior skating.

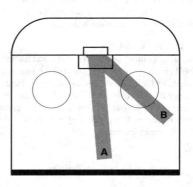

FREDRIK OLAUSSON

Yrs. of NHL service: 7
Born: Vazsjo, Sweden; Oct. 5, 1966
Position: left defense
Height: 6-2
Weight: 200
Uniform no.: 4
Shoots: right

Career statistics:

GP	G	A	TP	PIM
478	84	244	328	186

1991-92 statistics:

GP	G	A	TP	+/-	PIM	PP	SH	GW	GT	S	PCT
77	20	42	62	-31	34	13	1	2	0	227	8.8

1992-93 statistics:

GP	G	A	TP	+/-	PIM	PP	SH	GW	GT	S	PCT
68	16	41	57	-4	22	11	0	3	0	165	9.7

LAST SEASON

Missed 16 games with knee injury. Fifth consecutive season with 40 or more points. Second among team defensemen in scoring.

THE FINESSE GAME

One of the great treats of watching the Jets' power play is seeing Olausson and Phil Housley dancing inside the blue line, switching points and setting one another up for one-time blasts. These are two gifted finesse defensemen, with a similar flaw in their defensive shortcomings. Olausson has improved his defensive awareness (no doubt a credit to the Jets' coaching staff's tenacity). His speed helps him cover up for errors. He has real jets but is more determined on the attack than backchecking.

Olausson has the hand skills to cradle the puck when he is gliding up-ice, and he sees the ice well. The Jets moved Olausson to left defense this year, and he's skilled enough to rush down the left side, beat the defender, show the puck on his backhand and pull it quickly to his forehand for a shot. To his credit, though, he gambles low only on rare occasions and usually stays at the point to prevent breakouts.

Still, Olausson's work ethic is far more evident in the attacking zone than back in his own.

THE PHYSICAL GAME

Olausson is a big player who plays small. He uses his stick instead of his 200-pound body, loses one-on-one battles and doesn't use his body and skating skill as well as he could. With more intensity in the defensive zone, he could become a real physical force, but he has shown no inclination to do so, and the Jets have probably long given up on the idea.

THE INTANGIBLES

Having Olausson and Housley on one team seems like too much of a good thing, which is why all the Housley trade rumours keep cropping up. But we would rather take Housley and his minuses than Olausson, who has yet to show the leadership and command of the ice that Housley had. Olausson has the physical tools, but the mental edge is missing.

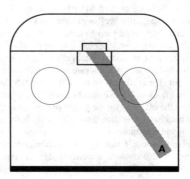

TEEMU SELANNE

Yrs. of NHL service: 1
Born: Helsinki, Finland; July 3, 1970
Position: right wing
Height: 6-0
Weight: 181
Uniform no.: 13
Shoots: right

Career statistics:
GP	G	A	TP	PIM
84	76	56	132	45

1992-93 statistics:
GP	G	A	TP	+/-	PIM	PP	SH	GW	GT	S	PCT
84	76	56	132	+8	45	24	0	7	0	387	19.6

LAST SEASON

First NHL season. Won Calder Trophy. Tied for NHL lead in goals. First first-year player in NHL history to lead or tie for lead in goals scored. Set NHL record for goals and points by a rookie. Led team in almost every major category: goals, points, power play goals, game-winning goals, shots, plus/minus and shooting percentage. Second among NHL rookies in assists. Ended season on 17-game point-scoring streak, longest of season by a rookie and a tie for third-longest in the NHL. Tied for fifth in NHL scoring. Tied for fifth in NHL in power play goals. Third in NHL in shots. One of three Jets to play all 84 games.

THE FINESSE GAME

Selanne's success stunned even the scouts who had seen his remarkable development in Finland. He came to the NHL a polished, 22-year-old rookie and was a devastating force. His skating is exceptional. He has turbo speed, Porsche speed. He gets down low and then simply explodes past defensemen, even when he starts from a standstill. He gets tremendous thrust from his legs and has quick feet. Acceleration, balance, it's all there.

Everything you could ask for in a shot is there as well. Once teamed with another rookie, Alexei Zhamnov, Selanne worked all varieties of attacks. The two work especially well weaving back and forth, with Zhamnov setting up Selanne with a one-time from the low right circle. Selanne is constantly in motion. If his first attempt is stopped, he'll pursue the puck behind the net, make a pass and circle out again for a shot. He is almost impossible to catch and is tough to knock down because of his balance. He will set up on the off-wing on the power play and can score on the backhand. His shot is not especially hard, but it is quick and accurate.

Selanne doesn't just try to overpower with his skating, he also outwits opponents. He has tremen-dous hockey instincts and vision, and is as good a playmaker as a finisher.

THE PHYSICAL GAME

Selanne was tested early and often. Nobody scores 76 goals and gets ignored by other team's checkers, and Selanne took his share of abuse. He proved remarkably durable, fighting his way through slashes and hooks. When the referees are slow on the whistle, he takes matters into his own hands, usually with his stick. He is one of the toughest young players in the league, European or otherwise.

THE INTANGIBLES

Unlike Alexander Mogilny, with whom he tied for the NHL goal lead, Selanne did not sweat at all under the spotlight. He was calm and collected, and not only welcomed the attention but seemed to regard it as his due. Repeating or even coming close to his success of last season is a long shot, but because of his attitude, the sophomore Selanne is a better bet than Mogilny. Selanne is going to be one of the dynamic stars of the '90s for the NHL. Sure, it was an expansion year and all scoring totals were up, but Selanne's rookie numbers were out of this galaxy.

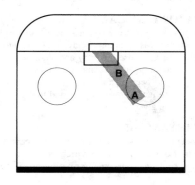

DARRIN SHANNON

Yrs. of NHL service: 4
Born: Barrie, Ont.; Dec. 8, 1969
Position: left wing
Height: 6-2
Weight: 200
Uniform no.: 34
Shoots: left

Career statistics:

GP	G	A	TP	PIM
207	43	80	123	148

1991-92 statistics:

GP	G	A	TP	+/-	PIM	PP	SH	GW	GT	S	PCT
69	13	27	40	+6	41	3	0	3	1	93	14.0

1992-93 statistics:

GP	G	A	TP	+/-	PIM	PP	SH	GW	GT	S	PCT
84	20	40	60	-4	91	12	0	2	0	116	17.2

LAST SEASON

One of three Jets to play all 84 games. Second on team in power play goals. Fifth on team in scoring with career high. Career highs in goals and assists.

THE FINESSE GAME

Shannon was often the trailer on the left side with speedy teammates Alexei Zhamnov and Teemu Selanne. Shannon, who doesn't have much speed, does have agility and power. He drives to the net while his linemates do all the fast and fancy work. His scoring chances all come from close range. He will screen the goalie for a shot or scrap for rebounds. Garbage goals aren't so bad when you're digging in Selanne's trash.

Shannon works down low on the power play. He will stand just off the crease, take a pass and wheel for a shot, or reach in with his stick for a tip. He shows excellent instincts on the power play.

The Jets would like to see even more of a power forward. Shannon has good size and strength for the job, and he has the good sense not to get too fancy. He's got a strong support crew for that.

THE PHYSICAL GAME

Shannon's PIM total is lower than you might expect for someone being asked to act as a policeman for fancy linemates. Shannon doesn't really fit that role. He is a solid physical player, strong in front of the net and along the boards, but isn't mean or even assertive. A little more aggressiveness, without loss of focus, would move his game up a notch.

THE INTANGIBLES

Shannon has continued to grow every season, and with almost every NHL team in the market for a strong left wing, he is a valuable commodity. If he remains on the Jets' top line, he should gain even more confidence.

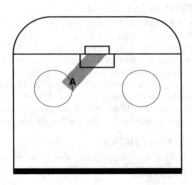

THOMAS STEEN

Yrs. of NHL service: 12
Born: Grums, Sweden; June 8, 1960
Position: centre
Height: 5-10
Weight: 195
Uniform no.: 25
Shoots: left

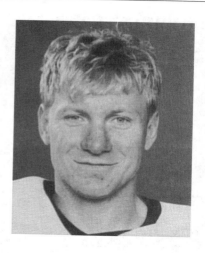

Career statistics:

GP	G	A	TP	PIM
843	240	511	751	707

1991-92 statistics:

GP	G	A	TP	+/-	PIM	PP	SH	GW	GT	S	PCT
38	13	25	38	+5	29	10	0	0	0	75	17.3

1992-93 statistics:

GP	G	A	TP	+/-	PIM	PP	SH	GW	GT	S	PCT
80	22	50	72	-8	75	6	0	6	0	150	14.7

LAST SEASON

First healthy season in four years resulted in four-season highs in goals, assists and points. Tied for third on team in scoring. Third on team in assists. Missed four games with back injuries.

THE FINESSE GAME

The development of rookie Alexei Zhamnov dropped Steen into the No. 2 centre's role and could have added two or three seasons to his NHL career. With less ice time, Steen was not as worn down or susceptible to injury. Yet when the other team's checking attention was focussed on the top line, Steen had the zip to make up for their missing production.

Steen is one of the league's top two-way centres. He works on the Jets' top penalty-killing unit, although he does not take draws (which were never his strong suit).

He is on the second power play unit now. His quickness and vision make him a threat down low. He will keep moving to set up at the low edges of either circle, and he needs little room or time to change direction and shake a defender. Steen has always kept himself in good physical condition and doesn't run out of steam at the end of a shift.

THE PHYSICAL GAME

So much for Europeans playing soft. Steen is an average-sized player who plays big. He is a willing hitter who will also take a hit to make the play. Part of what has distinguished Steen's passing is that he will hang on to the puck, draw a defender's check, than slide the puck to a teammate in the just-vacated ice. He draws penalties by driving to the net. Nothing attracts a referee's attention like a player churning along the boards or in front of the goal and being dragged down.

THE INTANGIBLES

Steen's unexpected resurgence was a huge bonus for the Jets, who would like to keep the veteran centre around while their younger players mature. Steen doesn't get much attention, but is one of the most respected players in the league for his class and competitiveness.

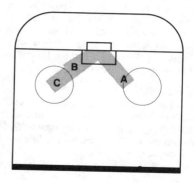

KEITH TKACHUK

Yrs. of NHL service: 1
Born: Melrose, Mass.; Mar. 28, 1972
Position: left wing
Height: 6-3
Weight: 218
Uniform no.: 7
Shoots: left

Career statistics:

GP	G	A	TP	PIM
100	31	28	59	229

1991-92 statistics:

GP	G	A	TP	+/-	PIM	PP	SH	GW	GT	S	PCT
17	3	5	8	0	28	2	0	0	0	22	13.6

1992-93 statistics:

GP	G	A	TP	+/-	PIM	PP	SH	GW	GT	S	PCT
83	28	23	51	-13	201	12	0	2	1	199	14.1

LAST SEASON

First NHL season. Tied for fourth among NHL rookies in goals. Second on team and among NHL rookies in power play goals. Third among NHL rookies in shots.

THE FINESSE GAME

Tkachuk is at his best when he is banging and playing with the tenacity and grit that made him such a sensation when he joined the Jets right after the 1992 Olympics. The problem for the youngster is that, just as physical play is contagious on a team, so is finesse play. Dazzled by the likes of Phil Housley and Teemu Selanne, Tkachuk tries to emulate them. But though he has some nice finesse skills, he can't match them. Fancy dress doesn't suit a construction worker, and Tkachuk has to pick his times for using his power or using a soft touch.

Tkachuk is by build and talent a power forward. His skating is above average but still needs improvement. He is powerful and balanced, but he lacks one-step quickness and lateral movement.

In front of the net, Tkachuk will bang and crash, but he also has very nice hands for picking pucks out of skates and flicking strong wrist shots. He can also kick at the puck with his skates without going down.

THE PHYSICAL GAME

Tkachuk is a rugged scrapper who will pay the price, as his PIM total — third on the team — illustrates. On nights when his game is on, Tkachuk can dictate the physical tempo of a game with his work in the corners and along the boards, a rare gift for so inexperienced a player. He has to play that way every night.

THE INTANGIBLES

Tkachuk's 28 goals in a rookie season only paled by comparison in the 1992-93 rookie crop, which may prove to be the best in NHL history. Tkachuk was by no means a disappointment. Only consistency eludes him, but that is hardly insurmountable for a 21-year-old.

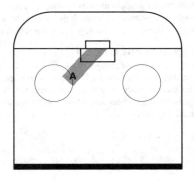

IGOR ULANOV

Yrs. of NHL service: 2
Born: Perm, Russia; Oct. 1, 1969
Position: left defense
Height: 6-1
Weight: 198
Uniform no.: 5
Shoots: right

Career statistics:

GP	G	A	TP	PIM
83	4	23	27	191

1991-92 statistics:

GP	G	A	TP	+/-	PIM	PP	SH	GW	GT	S	PCT
27	2	9	11	+5	67	0	0	0	0	23	8.7

1992-93 statistics:

GP	G	A	TP	+/-	PIM	PP	SH	GW	GT	S	PCT
56	2	14	16	+6	124	0	0	0	0	26	7.7

LAST SEASON

Career highs in assists and goals in first full NHL season. Missed games with back spasms.

THE FINESSE GAME

Ulanov's skills are all magnified by the kind of tough physical game he is capable of playing. A player who can skate and handle the puck as well as Ulanov, or level you with a hit, is going to command a lot of space. And Ulanov knows what to do with that space when he gets it. He loves to join the attack. He has good first-step quickness, with agility and balance.

He goes eagerly to the net, something he did not do often in his rookie year. He has quick hands and sees his scoring options.

Ulanov has good anticipation. He will break up a rush at his own blue line and start a quick counter-attack.

THE PHYSICAL GAME

Ulanov is inconsistent in his physical play. He is a punishing open-ice hitter with nasty intent and will unload bone-jarring checks right in front of the opponent's bench. But in the same game he'll lose an attacker by failing to make a take-out hit and consequently leaving his defense partner outmanned. He raises the temperature of the opposition by raising his stick, too.

Ulanov frequently panics with the puck in his own zone and is vulnerable to an aggressive forechecker.

THE INTANGIBLES

Ulanov was a major, major disappointment. The Russian defenseman struggled to put two good games together back-to-back. The skills are there; the desire seemed to be there a year ago. Now Ulanov has to put it all back together.

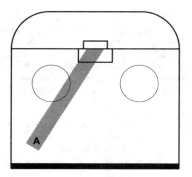

PAUL YSEBAERT

Yrs. of NHL service: 3
Born: Sarnia, Ont.; May 15, 1966
Position: left wing
Height: 6-1
Weight: 190
Uniform no.: 21
Shoots: left

Career statistics:

GP	G	A	TP	PIM
231	89	95	184	119

1991-92 statistics:

GP	G	A	TP	+/-	PIM	PP	SH	GW	GT	S	PCT
79	35	40	75	+44	55	3	4	3	1	211	16.6

1992-93 statistics:

GP	G	A	TP	+/-	PIM	PP	SH	GW	GT	S	PCT
80	34	28	62	+19	42	3	3	8	1	186	18.3

LAST SEASON

Tied for team lead in game-winning goals. Assists down 12 and points down 13 from career-best season last year. Plus/minus down 25 from league-leading +44 last season. Missed one game with flu. Acquired from Detroit for Aaron Ward.

THE FINESSE GAME

Ysebaert has very good quickness, which served him well on a fleet Wings team. He accelerates in a heartbeat and has the speed and balance to beat defenders wide. He has a wide scoring stance, which makes him tough to knock off the puck even though he's not overly strong.

Ysebaert has an excellent array of shots and will work hard for his scoring opportunities around the net. He goes to the net hard with the puck, and is among the most accurate shooters on the team. He has a quick release, and his shot is heavy.

Playing with the crafty, creative Fedorov opened a lot of ice for Ysebaert, who knew what to do with it. Ysebaert jumped into the holes while Fedorov drew two defenders with his puck control, or he trailed when Fedorov burst up the middle with his great speed. He teamed well with Fedorov on the penalty-killing unit and was a shorthanded scoring threat.

THE PHYSICAL GAME

Ysebaert has worked on his upper body strength and has increased confidence in his ability to win battles along the wall. He might still get outmuscled by bigger defenders, but he'll scrap for the puck with great enthusiasm. He isn't much of a fighter, but he won't be intimidated, either.

THE INTANGIBLES

Ysebaert broke into the league as a one-way centre who couldn't play defense. The Wings moved him to the wing, and while he's still not a Selke Trophy winner (he can credit former linemates Sergei Fedorov and Shawn Burr with his fluffy plus/minus ranking), Ysebaert has at least become a responsible citizen on defense while losing none of his scoring touch. On the Jets, he could continue as a consistent 35-goal, 65-point producer.

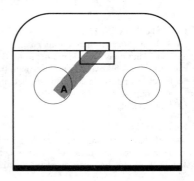

ALEXEI ZHAMNOV

Yrs. of NHL service: 1
Born: Moscow, Russia; Oct. 1, 1970
Position: centre
Height: 6-1
Weight: 187
Uniform no.: 10
Shoots: left

Career statistics:

GP	G	A	TP	PIM
68	25	47	72	58

1992-93 statistics:

GP	G	A	TP	+/-	PIM	PP	SH	GW	GT	S	PCT
68	25	47	72	+7	58	6	1	4	1	163	15.3

LAST SEASON

First NHL season. Missed 16 games with back spasms. Fourth among NHL rookies in points. Third among rookies in assists. Had 10-game assist streak, longest of season by rookie. Tied for third on team in scoring. Fourth on team in assists.

THE FINESSE GAME

Zhamnov's game is puck control. He can carry it at top speed or work give-and-gos with his favourite linemate, Calder Trophy winner Teemu Selanne. The two rookies showed flair and poise well beyond their (lack of) NHL experience.

Zhamnov is a crafty playmaker and is not too unselfish. While he will look first to set up Selanne's one-timer or to spring his right winger on a breakaway, he also has an accurate if not overpowering shot. As well, he can blast off the pass, or manoeuvre until he has a screen and then wrist it. On the power play, he can dart in and out in front of the goalie, using his soft hands for a tip.

Zhamnov also kills penalties on the second unit, a credit to his quickness and overall hockey sense.

Defensively, he is well ahead of most rookies. He is a sound backchecker and never leaves the zone too quickly — an asset when playing with the Finnish Flash.

THE PHYSICAL GAME

Zhamnov will bump to prevent a scoring chance or go for a loose puck, but body work is not his forte. He is very strong and fights his way through traffic in front of the net to get to a puck. He needs to do a better job of tying up the opposing centre on face-offs, since he wins few draws cleanly.

THE INTANGIBLES

The Jets should have a dynamic duo for the rest of the decade. Zhamnov meshed wonderfully with Selanne. Their skating skills matched their offensive creativity and anticipation. Selanne got all the attention, but Zhamnov was a major part of that success. The best part about Zhamnov was that he continued to improve throughout the season.

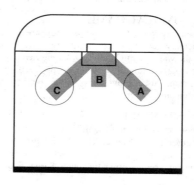

PLAYER INDEX

Player Index

Player Index